THE BEAUTIES OF BOSTON

Thomas Boston

THE BEAUTIES OF THOMAS BOSTON

A selection of his writings

Edited by
SAMUEL M'MILLAN

CHRISTIAN FOCUS PUBLICATIONS

The Beauties of Thomas Boston
first published 1831

This edition reprinted by
CHRISTIAN FOCUS PUBLICATIONS
Henderson Road, Inverness IV1 1SP

©*Copyright 1979*

ISBN 0 906731 01 1

Printed by offset Litho
by Bookmag, Henderson Road, Inverness IV1 1SP

Contents

THE PUBLIC ORDINANCES

GOD'S DECREES

GOD THE CREATOR

CHRIST'S PRIESTHOOD

BELIEVING IN CHRIST

GOD'S PROVIDENCE

ELECTION

THE COVENANT OF WORKS

THE FALL OF MAN

Foreword

Of the many great divines who have adorned the ecclesiastical and theological scene in Scotland, Thomas Boston must be reckoned as among the greatest. Dr. Andrew Thomson who wrote *Thomas Boston: his life and times*, asserts that 'if Scotland had been searched during the earlier part of the eighteenth century there was not a minister of Christ within its bounds who, alike in personal character and in the discharge of his pastoral functions, approached nearer the apostolic model than did this man of God'.

Thomas Boston was born at Duns in Berwickshire, in the year 1676. In his *Memoirs*, he informs us that, at about the age of seven, he 'began to conceive a remarkable pleasure' in reading the Bible. Some four years later, under a sermon by Henry Erskine, he was 'awakened to a deep concern about the eternal state' of his soul. After receiving the elements of education at the local grammar school, he proceeded to the University of Edinburgh. At the end of the usual three years' course, he commenced the systematic study of divinity. In 1697, he was licensed to preach by the Presbytery of Duns and Chirnside. It was during the period of his probationership that Boston penned his little classic — *A Soliloquy on The Art of Man-fishing*. While reading the Scriptures in private, the words of Matthew 4.19, 'Follow me and I will make you fishers of men', deeply impressed him, and his heart 'cried out' for their accomplishment.

In 1699, Boston was ordained and inducted to the small pastoral charge of Simprin, a village within a few miles of his home town. While he was understandably discouraged by the fewness of his hearers, such were his self-effacing views that he felt Simprin, or any other place, good enough for him, and 'rather superior' to his 'small talents'. Under his anointed ministry, however, the wilderness was to blossom as the rose. Boston remained at Simprin until 1707 when he was translated to Ettrick. It was here he died in 1732, in the fifty-seventh year of his life. His biographer remarks that even before Boston's death, young and old had come to pronounce his name with reverence. It has become 'a synonym for holy living'.

It was while Boston was at Simprin that a copy of Edward Fisher's *Marrow of Modern Divinity* came into his hands. The book was to have a profound effect upon him. He writes: 'I rejoiced in it as a light which the Lord had seasonably struck up to me in my darkness'. Up to this time, Boston had felt a certain inhibition in proclaiming the free and universal offer of Christ to men. This inhibition arose from the supposed antinomy between the decree of election and the indiscriminate offer of salvation to all men. But once he had grasped the formula, according to the theology of the *Marrow*, that 'Jesus Christ is the Father's deed of gift and grant unto all mankind lost', his inhibition faded away, and he began to preach with a fulness and freeness he had hitherto not known. His parishioners could not fail to recognise the deep transformation in their pastor and his ministrations.

One of Boston's acquaintances, the worthy Rev. Thomas Davidson of Bruntee, affirmed that he looked upon the frequent opportunities he had of hearing him preach as one of the most exquisite privileges with which he was favoured. There was, he wrote, a 'majestic energy' about Boston's preaching, and while there were few (if any) who courted popularity less than Boston did, yet, 'like his shadow, it followed him wherever he went'.

Boston's popularity still persists among those who relish the truth as it is in Jesus. He invariably studied with pen in hand, and his sermons were written out in full before he delivered them. These facts, under the divine providence, contributed to the perpetuation of his productions. Due to his self-diffidence, however, Boston was very reluctant to publish, but he was prevailed on by those who recognised his genius as a preacher and theologian. The book for which he is most remembered is, of course, his *Human Nature in Its Fourfold State* — a book which was designed by God to lead thousands to Christ. But apart from the *Fourfold State*, a *Collection of Sermons*, and an edition of the *Marrow* which he annotated, no other book by Boston issued from the press in his life-time. Among those published posthumously are his *View of The Covenant of Works* and *of Grace*, *The Christian Life*, *A Body of Divinity*, and *The Crook in The Lot*, to mention but a few. Between 1720 and 1776, sixteen different works by Boston were published.

Very few today are so fortunate as to possess the whole of Boston's works. The *Beauties*, originally published in 1831, was compiled by the Rev. Samuel M'Millan with the worthy object of presenting the public with a compend of Bostonian theology, which he hoped would effect much spiritual good, and countervail 'the leaven of the Arminian scheme'. In his preface, M'Millan wrote: 'Boston was eminently blessed with a happy talent for using his great learning just as every godly minister should use it; not in flights of oratory, calculated to dazzle and astonish, but in bringing down the high mysteries of the gospel to the common capacity and in making them quite intelligible to the meanest understanding'. It was the editor's prayer that this volume would be greatly blessed by God in turning sinners from darkness to light and from the power of Satan unto God. This, we may add, is the prayer of the present publishers.

In the last letter he wrote, Boston left his MSS. to the Lord and the management of his friends as the Lord would direct them. It gives us much pleasure to be the instruments in taking up his writings again, under God's direction we trust, and in furthering Ralph Erskine's prediction of their illustrious author:

> *Whose golden pen to future times will bear*
> *His fame, till in the clouds his Lord appear.*

Ian R. Tallach
Perth, February, 1979.

BEAUTIES

OF THE

REV. THOMAS BOSTON.

The Nature of that Faith and Obedience which the Holy Scriptures teach.

FIRST, As to faith. Divine faith is a believing of what God has revealed, because God has said it, or revealed it. People may believe scripture truths, but not with a divine faith, unless they believe it on that very ground, the authority of God speaking in his word. And this divine faith is the product of the Spirit of God in the heart of a sinner, implanting the habit or principle of faith there, and exciting it to a hearty reception and firm belief of whatever God reveals in his word. And the faith which the scripture teaches is what a man is to believe concerning God. This may be reduced to four heads : What God is ; the persons in the Godhead ; the decrees of God relating to every thing that comes to pass ; and the execution of them in his works of creation and providence. Now, though the works of creation and providence show that there is a God, yet that fundamental truth, that God is, and the doctrines relating to the Trinity of Persons in the Unity of the Divine Essence, God's acts and purposes, the creation of all things, the state of man at his creation, his fall, and his recovery by the mediation and satisfaction of

B

Christ, are only to be learned from the holy scriptures. Hence we may infer,

1. That there can be no right knowledge of God acquired in an ordinary way without the scriptures, Matt. xxii. 29. 'Ye do err,' said Christ to the Sadducees, 'not knowing the scriptures.' As there must be a dark night where the light is gone, so those places of the earth must needs be dark, and without the saving knowledge of God, that want the scriptures. Thus the Apostle tells the Ephesians, that, before they were visited with the light of the gospel, they were 'without Christ, being aliens from the commonwealth of Israel, and strangers from the covenants of promise, having no hope, and without God in the world.' Eph. ii. 12.

2. That where the scriptures are not known, there can be no saving faith. For, says the Apostle, Rom. x. 14, 15. 17. 'How shall they call on him in whom they have not believed? and how shall they believe in him of whom they have not heard? and how shall they hear without a preacher? and how shall they preach, except they be sent? as it is written, How beautiful are the feet of them that preach the gospel of peace, and bring glad tidings of good things! So then faith cometh by hearing, and hearing by the word of God.'

3. That there is nothing we are bound to believe as a part of faith but what the scripture teaches, be who they will that propose it, and whatever they may pretend for their warrant. 'To the law and to the testimony: if they speak not according to this word, it is because there is no light in them,' Isa. viii. 20. No man must be our master in these things: 'For one is our master even Christ,' Matt. xxiii. 10. He is Lord of our faith, and we are bound to believe whatever he has revealed in his word.

Secondly, As to obedience, it is that duty which God requires of man. It is that duty and obedience which man owes to God, to his will and laws, in respect of God's universal supremacy and sovereign authority over man; and which he should render to him out of love and gratitude. The scriptures are the holy oracle from whence we are to learn our duty, Psal. xix. 11. 'By them is thy servant warned,' says David. The bible is the light we are to take heed to, that we may know how to steer our course, and order the several steps of our life. 'Thy word is a lamp unto my feet, and a light to my path,' says the Psalmist, Psal. cxix. 105. From whence we may infer,

1. That there can be no sufficient knowledge of the duty which we owe to God without the scriptures. Though the light of nature does in some measure show our duty to God, yet it is too dim to take up the will of God sufficiently in order to salvation.

2. That there can be no right obedience yielded to God without them. Men that walk in the dark must needs stumble; and the works that are wrought in the dark will never abide the light; for there is no working rightly by guess in this matter. All proper obedience to God must be learned from the scriptures.

3. That there is no point of duty that we are called to, but what the scripture teaches, Isa. viii. 20, forecited. Men must neither make duties to themselves or others, but what God has made duty. The law of God is exceeding broad, and reaches the whole conversation of man, outward and inward, Psal xix. ; and man is bound to conform himself to it alone as the rule of his duty.

Thirdly, As to the connexion of these two : faith and obedience are joined together, because there is no true faith but what is followed with obedience, and no true obedience but what flows from faith. Faith is the loadstone of obedience, and obedience the touchstone of faith, as appears from Jam. ii. They that want faith cannot be holy; and they that have true faith, their faith will work by love. Hence we may see,

1. That faith is the foundation of duty or obedience, and not obedience or duty the foundation of faith, Tit. iii. 8. 'This is a faithful saying, and these things I will that thou affirm constantly, that they which have believed in God might be careful to maintain good works. These things are good and profitable unto men ;' and that the things to be believed are placed before the things to be practised, in order to distinguish between the order of the things in the covenant of grace, and what they were under the covenant of works. Under the latter, doing, or perfect obedience to the law, was the foundation of the promised privilege of life ; but under the former, the promise is to be believed, and the promised life is to be freely received : and thereupon follows the believer's obedience to the law, out of gratitude and love for the mercy received. This appears from the order laid down by God himself in delivering the moral law from mount Sinai. He lays the foundation of faith, first of all, in these words, 'I am the Lord thy God,' &c. which is the sum and substance of the covenant of grace ; and then follows the law of the ten commandments, which is as it were grafted upon this declaration of sovereign grace and love, Exod. xx. 2—18. And let it be remembered, that the Apostle Paul calls gospel-obedience the obedience of faith, as springing from and founded upon faith. And if we examine the order of doctrine laid down in all his epistles, we shall find, that he first propounds the doctrine of faith, or what man is to believe, and upon that foundation inculcates the duties that are to be practised.

2. That all works without faith are dead, and so cannot please God. For whatsoever is not of faith is sin ; and without or separate from Christ we can do nothing. Faith is the principle of all holy and acceptable obedience.

3. That those who inculcate moral duties without discovering the necessity of regeneration, and union with Christ, as the source of all true obedience, are

foolish builders ; they lay their foundation on the sand, and the superstructure they raise will soon be over-turned ; and they pervert the gospel of Christ. Such would do well to consider what the Apostle says, Gal. i. 9. 'If any man preach any other gospel un-to you than that ye have received, let him be accur-sed.' *

The manner of discovering the true sense of Holy Scripture.

1. THE sense of the scripture is but one, and not manifold. There may be several parts of that one sense subordinate one to another ; as some proph ecies have a respect to the deliverance from Babylon, the spiritual by Christ, and the eternal in heaven ; and some passages have one thing that is typical of an-other : yet these are but one full sense, only that may be of two sorts ; one is simple, and another compound.

* The usual method of gospel doctrine, as it is delivered to us in the holy scriptures, is first to comfort our hearts, and thereby to establish us in every good word and work, Phil. iv. 7. 'And the peace of God, which passeth all understanding, shall keep your hearts and minds through Christ Jesus.' And it appears how clearly this method is adjusted and several epistles written by the apostles, wherein they first acquaint the churches with the rich grace of God towards them in Christ Jesus, and the spiritual blessings which they are made partakers of, for their strong con-solation ; and then they exhort them to a holy conversation, an-swerable to such privileges. And it is not only the method of whole epistles, but of many particular exhortations to duty, wherein the comfortable benefits of the grace of God in Christ are made use of as arguments and motives to stir up the saints to a holy practice ; which comfortable benefits must first be believed, and the comfort of them applied to our own souls, or else they will not be forcible to engage us to the practice for which they are intended. For example, in proof of this, read Rom. vi. 11, 14, and viii. 9, 11 ; 1 Cor. vi. 15, 19 ; 2 Cor. v. 21.

Marshall on Sanct., Direct. 9.

Some scriptures have only a simple sense, containing a declaration of one thing only; and that is either proper or figurative. A proper sense is that which arises from the words taken properly, and the figurative from the words taken figuratively. Some have a simple proper sense, as, 'God is a Spirit, God created the heavens and the earth;' which are to be understood according to the propriety of the words. Some have a simple figurative sense, as, 'I am the true vine, and my Father is the husbandman. Every branch in me that beareth not fruit, he taketh away,' &c. These have but one simple sense; but then it is the figurative, and is not to be understood according to the propriety of the words, as if Christ were a tree, &c. Thus you see what the simple sense is. The compound or mixed sense is found wherein one thing is held forth as a type of the other; and so it consists of two parts, the one respecting the type, the other the antitype; which are not two senses, but two parts of that one and entire sense intended by the Holy Ghost: e. g. Moses lifted up the serpent in the wilderness, that those who were stung by the fiery serpents might look to it and be healed. The full sense of which is, 'As Moses lifted up the serpent in the wilderness, that, &c. even so must the Son of Man be lifted up; that whosoever believeth in him should not perish, but have eternal life.' Here is a literal and mystical sense, which make up one full sense betwixt them. Those scriptures that have this compound sense, are sometimes fulfilled properly (or literally, as it is taken in opposition to figuratively) in the type and antitype both; as Hos. xi. 1. 'I have called my Son out of Egypt,' which was literally true both of Israel and Christ. Sometimes figuratively in the type, and properly in the antitype, as Psal. lxix. 21. 'They gave me vinegar to drink.' Sometimes properly in the type, and figuratively in the antitype, as Psal. ii. 9. 'Thou shalt break them with a rod of iron.' Compare 2 Sam. xii. 31. Sometimes figuratively in both, as Psal. xli.

9. 'Yea, mine own familiar friend—hath lifted up his heel against me; which is meant of Ahithophel and Judas. Now the sense of the scripture must be but one, and not manifold, that is, quite different and nowise subordinate one to another, because of the unity of truth, and because of the perspicuity of the scripture.

2. Where there is a question about the true sense of scripture, it must be found out what it is by searching other places that speak more clearly, the scripture itself being the infallible rule of interpreting of scripture. Now that it is so, appears from the following arguments.

(1.) The Holy Spirit gives this as a rule, 2 Pet. i. 20, 21. After the apostle had called the Christians to take heed to the scripture, he gives them this rule for understanding it, 'Knowing this first, that no prophecy of the scripture is of any private interpretation of our own exposition. For the prophecy came not in old time by the will of man; but holy men of God spake as they were moved by the Holy Ghost.' As it came, so is it to be expounded: but it came not by the will of man; therefore we are not to rest on men for the sense of it, but holy men speaking as they were moved by the Holy Ghost, and so never erring; therefore we are to look to the dictates of the same Spirit in other places.

(2.) There are several approved examples of this, comparing one scripture with another, to find out the meaning of the Holy Ghost, as Acts xv. 15. 'And to this agree the words of the prophet,' &c. The Bereans are commended for this, Acts xvii. 11. Yea, Christ himself makes use of this to show the true sense of the scripture against the devil, Matt. iv. 6. 'Cast thyself down,' said that wicked spirit; 'for it is written, He shall give his angels charge concerning thee,' &c. ver. 7. 'It is written again,' says Christ, 'Thou shalt not tempt the Lord thy God.' And thus our Lord makes out the true sense of that scripture,

that it is to be understood only with respect to them
who do not cast themselves on a tempting of God.*

Reason not the Supreme Judge of Controversies in Religion.

1. REASON in an unregenerate man is blind in the
matters of God, 1 Cor. ii. 14. 'The natural man receiveth not the things of the Spirit of God; for they
are foolishness unto him : neither can he know them,
because they are spiritually discerned;' Eph. iv. 17,
18; Eph. v. 8. *Except.* This only respects reason
not illustrated by divine revelation. *Ans.* By that illustration of reason by divine revelation, they understand either subjective or objective illustration. If
they understand it of subjective illustration, they quit
that article of their religion, wherein they believe that
the mind of man is capable of itself, without the illumination of the Spirit, to attain sufficient knowledge
of the mind of God revealed in the scripture. If of
objective illustration, by the mere revelation of these
truths, then it is false that they assert: For the
apostle opposes here the natural man to the spiritual
man ; and therefore by the natural man is understood
every unregenerate man, even that has these truths
revealed to him ; for, says the apostle, 'they are foolishness unto him.' Now, how can he judge them
foolishness if they be not revealed?

2. Reason is not infallible, and therefore cannot be
admitted judge in matters concerning our souls. Rea-

---

* The infallible rule of interpretation of scripture is the scripture itself; and, therefore, when there is a question about the
true and full sense of any scripture which is not manifold but
one, it must be searched and known by other places that speak
more clearly. 2 Pet. i. 20, 21 ; Acts xv. 16.
Confession of Faith, ch. 1.

son may be deceived, Rom. iii. 4, and is not this to shake the foundations of religion, and to pave a way to scepticism and atheism? *Except.* That is not to be feared where sound reason is admitted judge. But what talk they of sound reason? The adversaries themselves will yield, that reason is unsound in the most part of men. We say, that it is not fully sound in the world; for even the best know but in part; darkness remains in some measure on the minds of all men.

3. Reason must be subject to the scripture, and submit itself to be judged by God speaking there, 2 Cor. x. 4, 5. 'The weapons of our warfare are—mighty—to the pulling down of strong holds, casting down imaginations,—and bringing into captivity every thought to the obedience of Christ.' Matters of faith are above the sphere of reason; and therefore as sense is not admitted judge in those things that are above it, so neither reason in those things that are above it, 1. Tim. iii. 16. 'And without controversy, great is the mystery of Godliness : God was manifest in the flesh, justified in the Spirit, seen of angels, preached unto the Gentiles, believed on in the world, received up into glory.'

4. If reason were the supreme judge of controversies, then our faith should be built on ourselves, and the great reason why we believe any principle of religion would be, because it appears so and so to us, which is most absurd. The scripture teaches otherwise, 1 Thess. ii. 13. 'Ye received it not as the word of men, but as it is in truth the word of God.' Most plainly does our Lord teach this, John v. 34. 'I receive not testimony from men;' chap. v. 39. 'Search the scriptures.'

The orthodox assert the supreme judge of controversies in religion to be the Holy Spirit speaking in the scriptures. This is proved by the following arguments.

1. In the Old and New Testament, the Lord still

c

sends us to this judge. So that we may neither
turn to the right hand nor left from what he there
speaks, Deut. v. 32. and xvii. 11. 'According
to the sentence of the law which they shall teach
thee;' Is. viii. 20. 'To the law and to the testimony,' &c.; Luke xvi. 29. 'They have Moses and the
prophets; let them hear them;' John v. 39. 'Search
the scriptures.' Some hereto refer that passage,
Matt. xix. 28. 'Verily I say unto you, that ye
which have followed me in the regeneration, when
the Son of Man shall sit in the throne of his glory, ye
also shall sit upon twelve thrones judging the twelve
tribes of Israel.' In this sense it must be meant of
the doctrine they taught, as dictated to them by the
Holy Ghost.

2. It was the practice of Christ and his apostles to
appeal to the Spirit speaking in the scriptures, Matt.
iv. where Christ still answers Satan with that, 'It is
written.' And so while discoursing with the Sadducees about the resurrection, Matt. xxii. 31, 32. So
also in John, chap. v. and x. and Luke xxiv. 44.
And so did others, Acts xvii. 11, and xxvi. 22, 23.;
2 Pet. i. 19.; Acts xv. 15, 16. A careful examina-
tion of which passages I recommend to you for your
establishment in the truth.

3. To the Spirit of God speaking in the scriptures,
and to him only, agree those things that are requisite
to constitute one the supreme judge. (1.) We may
certainly know that the sentence which he pronounces is true, for he is infallible, being God. (2.) We
cannot appeal from him, for he is one above whom
there is none. (3.) He is no respecter of persons,
nor can be biassed in favour of one in preference to
another.

To search and study the Scriptures is the duty of all classes of Men.

If ye ask, by whom this is to be done? it is by all into whose hands, by the mercy of God, it comes. Some never had it, and so they will not be condemned for slighting of it, Rom. ii. 12. Magistrates are called to look to it, and be much conversant in it, Josh. i. 8. 'This book of the law shall not depart out of thy mouth, but thou shalt meditate therein day and night, that thou mayest observe to do according to all that is written therein.' Deut. xvii. 18, 19. 'And it shall be, when he sitteth upon the throne of his kingdom, that he shall write him a copy of this law in a book, out of that which is before the priests the Levites. And it shall be with him, and he shall read therein all the days of his life; that he may learn to fear the Lord his God, to keep all the words of this law, and these statutes, to do them.' Ministers are in a special manner called to the study of it. 1 Tim. iv. 13. 'Give attendance to reading.' 2 Tim. iii. 16, 17. 'All scripture is given by inspiration of God, and is profitable for doctrine, for reproof, for correction, for instruction in righteousness.' But not they only are so commanded, but all others within the church, John v. 39. 'Search the scriptures.' Deut. vi. 6, 7. 'These words which I command thee this day, shall be in thine heart. And thou shalt teach them diligently unto thy children, and shalt talk of them when thou sittest in thine house, and when thou walkest by the way, and when thou liest down, and when thou risest up.'

Several things of great importance pre-supposed in these words, Isaiah xxxiv. 16. ' *Seek ye out of the book of the Lord, and read,'* &c.

1. That man has lost his way, and needs direction to find it, Psal. cxix. 176. 'I have gone astray like a lost sheep; seek thy servant.' Miserable man is bemisted in a vain world, which is a dark place, and has as much need of the scriptures to direct him, as one has of a light in darkness, 2 Pet. i. 19. What a miserable case is that part of the world in that wants the Bible? They are vain in their imaginations, and grope in the dark, but cannot find the way of salvation. In no better case are those to whom it has not come in power.

2. That man is in hazard of being led farther and farther wrong. This made the spouse say, ' Tell me, O thou whom my soul loveth, where thou feedest, where thou makest thy flock to rest at noon: for why should I be as one that turneth aside by the flocks of thy companions?' There is a subtile devil, a wicked world, corrupt lusts within one's own breast, to lead him out of the right way, that we had need to give over, and take this guide. There are many false lights in the world, which, if followed, will lead the traveller into a mire, and leave him there.

3. That men are slow of heart to understand the mind of God in his word. It will cost searching diligently ere we can take it up, John v. 39. ' Search the scriptures; for in them ye think ye have eternal life: and they are they which testify of me.' Our eyes are dim to the things of God, our apprehensions dull, and our judgment is weak. And therefore, because the iron is blunt, we must put too the more strength. We lost the sharpness of our sight in spi-

ritual things in Adam; and our corrupt wills and carnal affections, that favour not the things of God, do more blind our judgments: and therefore it is a labour to us to find out what is necessary for our salvation.

4. That the book of the Lord has its difficulties, which are not to be easily solved. Therefore the Psalmist prays, 'Open thou mine eyes, that I may see wondrous things out of thy law,' Psal. cxix. 18. Philip asked the eunuch, 'Understandest thou what thou readest? And he said, How can I, except some man should guide me?' There are depths there wherein an elephant may swim, and will exercise the largest capacities, with all the advantages they may be possessed of. God in his holy providence has so ordered it, to stain the pride of all glory; to make his word the liker himself, whom none can search out to perfection, and to sharpen the diligence of his people in their inquiries into it.

5. That yet we need highly to understand it, otherwise we would not be bidden search into it. 'Of the times and seasons,' says the apostle, 'ye have no need that I write unto you;' and therefore he wrote not of them. There is a treasure in this field; we are called to dig for it; for though it be hid, yet we must have it, or we will pine away in our spiritual poverty.

6. That we may gain from it by diligent inquiry. The holy humble heart will not be always sent empty away from these wells of salvation, when it plies itself to draw. There are shallow places in these waters of the sanctuary, where lambs may wade.

---

*Weighty reasons for diligently reading and search-
ing the Book of God.*

1. Because the way of salvation is to be found only therein, John v. 39. 'Search the scriptures; for
in them ye think ye have eternal life : and they are
they which testify of me.' This is the star risen in
a dark world, to guide us where Christ is. All the
researches of the wise men of the world, all the inventions of men, can never guide us to Emmanuel's
land, John i. 18. 'No man has seen God at any
time, the only begotten Son, which is in the bosom
of the Father, he hath declared him.' Here, and here
only, the counsels of God touching man's salvation
are discovered. And so, as salvation is the most necessary thing, the study of the scriptures, is the most
necessary exercise. To slight it, is to judge ourselves
unworthy of eternal life.

2. It is the only rule of our faith and lives, Isa.
viii. 20. 'To the law and to the testimony : if they
speak not according to this word, it is because there
is no light in them,' Eph. ii. 20. 'Ye are built upon the foundation of the prophets and apostles, Jesus
Christ himself being the chief corner-stone,' Rev. xxii.
18, 19. 'I testify unto every man that heareth the
words of the prophecy of this book, If any man shall
add unto these things, God shall add unto him the
plagues that are written in this book : and if any
man shall take away from the words of the book of
this prophecy, God shall take away his part out of
the book of life, and out of the holy city, and from
the things which are written in this book.' The
Bible is the pattern shown on the mount, to which
our faith and lives must be conformed, if we would
please God. The Lord says to us, as Deut. xxviii.

14. 'Thou shalt not go aside from any of the words which I command thee this day, to the right hand or to the left.' None can walk regularly unless they observe the rule; but how can one observe it unless he know it? Matt. xxii. 29. 'Jesus answered and said unto them, Ye do err, not knowing the scriptures, nor the power of God.' God has given each of us our post in the world : the Bible is the book of our instructions; and shall we not study it? The lawyer studies his law-books, the physician his medical books, and shall not a Christian study the book of the Lord?

3. The Lord himself dictated it, and gave it us for that very end, 2 Tim. iii. 16, 17. 'All scripture is given by inspiration of God, and is profitable for doctrine, for reproof, for correction, for instruction in righteousness; that the man of God may be perfect, throughly furnished unto all good works.' Rom. v. 4. 'Whatsoever things were written aforetime were written for our learning.' And has the Spirit of the Lord written it, and will not we read it? Has he given it us to be studied by us, and will we slight it? This must be horrid contempt of God, and ingratitude to him, with a witness. Whose image and superscription is this on the scriptures? Is it not the Lord's? Then take it up and read.

4. We must be judged by the scriptures at the great day, John xii. 48. 'He that rejecteth me, and receiveth not my words, hath one that judgeth him : the word that I have spoken, the same shall judge him in the last day.' That is one of the books opened, Rev. xx. 12. This is the book of the Lord's laws and ordinances, by which he will proceed in absolving or condemning us. I own God will go another way to work with those who never had the Bible. Rom. ii. 12. But know thou, that seeing it is in the country where thou livest, though thou never readest a letter of it, thou must be judged by it. Is there not good reason then for reading the scriptures?

-----

*Earnest exhortations and powerful motives to read
and search the Book of God.*

1. Let such as cannot read, learn to read. Ye
that have children, as ye tender their immortal souls,
cause them learn to read the Bible. Remember
therefore the vows taken upon you at their baptism,
and the duty laid upon you by the Lord himself,
Eph. vi. 4. 'Fathers, bring up your children in the
nurture and admonition of the Lord,' 2 Tim. iii. 15.
Timothy from a child knew the holy scriptures. Ye
who got no learning when ye were young, labour to
get it now. Alas! some parents, or others that have
had some when young with them, have been cruel to
their souls, as the ostrich to her young. They have
learned them to work, but have been at no pains to
learn them to read : so have sent them out into the
world a prey to the devourer's teeth, without the ordinary means of the knowledge of God. Thus they
are destroyed with bloody ignorance.

But will ye pity your own souls, though others did
not that brought you up? And do not enter yourselves heirs to their sins, by being as negligent of
yourselves as they were. Though perhaps they left
you nothing to live upon, yet for a livelihood ye have
done for yourselves. And will you do nothing for
your souls.

Think not it will excuse thee at the hand of God,
that thou art a servant; for thy soul is in as great
danger as thy master's, and ignorance of religion will
destroy it, Isa. xxvii. 11. There are few but know
how to improve the scarcity of servants to the raising
of the fee; but will you improve it by getting it in
your condition to learn to read, and seek out such
families where you may have that advantage, for

some such there are, like Abraham's, Gen. xviii.
10. Nay, rather than not do it, give over service for
a time, and learn.

Neither will it excuse you that now you have a family; for you have an immortal soul still, which
gross ignorance of the mind of God in the scriptures
will ruin eternally, 2 Thess. i. 8. 'In flaming fire,
taking vengeance on them that know not God, and
that obey not the gospel of our Lord Jesus Christ.'
And the more need you have to read the scriptures,
that you have a family, that you may know the
Lord's mind yourself, and teach it your family. Such
an excuse will no more screen you from everlasting
destruction, than covering yourself with leaves will
save you from the flames of a devouring fire.

Say not you are too old now to learn. It is never
out of time to learn to do well for your eternal salvation. If your eyes can serve you to learn, you ought
to do it, whatever your age be. But if your sight be
so far gone, that you cannot, though you were ever so
willing, then tremble at the thoughts of the awful
judgment of God that has taken away sight from you,
that when you had it, would not use it for his glory,
and the good of your own soul; and humble thyself,
and apply to the blood of Christ, for this thy neglect,
lest it prove ruining to thee for ever. And cause
others read to you, and beg the teaching of the Spirit, if so be such an old careless slighter of salvation
may find mercy.

2. Let such as can read procure bibles. I dare
say one that has a love to the bible (and that all who
love the Lord have) will make many shifts ere they
want one. But they must be lawful shifts: for stealing of bibles, or keeping them up from the owners,
is like a thief stealing a rope to hang himself in. But
spare it off your bellies or your backs, and procure
one rather than want.

3. Let such as have bibles read them frequently,
and acquaint themselves with the book of the Lord.

D

Read them in your families morning and evening; and read them in secret by yourselves; it should be a piece of your duties in secret. Make the bible your companion abroad and at home, in the house and in the field. It is lamentable to think how unacquainted with the bible many are, and how little heart they have to it. Ballads and song-books get the place of the bible with many; and many have no use for it but once in the week, on the sabbath-day, as if it were more for a show with them than the necessity of their souls.

4. Not only read it, but search into it, and study it, to know the mind of God therein, and that ye may do it. Be not superficial in your reading of the scriptures, but do it with application, painfulness, and diligence; using all means to read it with understanding; breaking through the surface that ye may come at the hid treasure therein. Reading as well as praying by rote is to little purpose; for a parcel of bare words will neither please God, nor edify your own souls.

I shall now give some motives to enforce this important duty of reading the scriptures.

Mot. 1. God requires it of us; he commands us to do it, John v. 39. 'Search the scriptures.' The Jews had once the scriptures committed to them; but did God design they should only have them in the temple? nay, in their houses also: Only laid up in the ark? nay, he designed another chest for them, even their hearts, Deut. vi. 6, 7, formerly cited. Let the authority of God sway you, then, and as you have any regard to it, study the scriptures.

Mot. 2. Nay, the very being of the bible among us is enough to move us to study it, seeing it is that by which we must stand or fall for ever. The proclaiming of the law publicly is sufficient to oblige the subjects; and they cannot plead ignorance, though they get not every one a copy of it. For every one ought to know the rule of his duty. And sinners will be condemned by it, if they conform not to it, whether they knew it or not, John iii. 19. 'And this is the condemnation, that light is come into the world, and men loved darkness rather than light, because their deeds were evil.'

Mot. 3. It is an exercise very pleasing to God, so that it be done in a right manner, namely, in faith. For thereby God speaks to us, and we hear and receive his words at his mouth; and obedient ears are his delight.

1. The Spirit of God commends it. It was the commendation of the Bereans, Acts xvii. 11. 'These were more noble than those in Thessalonica, in that they received the word with all readiness of mind, and searched the scriptures daily, whether those things were so;' of Apollos, chap. xviii. 24; of Timothy, 2 Tim. iii. 15. 'And that from a child thou hast known the holy scriptures, which are able to make thee wise unto salvation through faith which is in Christ Jesus' And why does the Spirit of God commend others for this, but to recommend the scriptures to us?

2. There is a particular blessing annexed to this exercise, Rev. i. 3. 'Blessed is he that readeth.' And the children of God in all ages have sucked the sap of it, while they have had sweet fellowship with God in his word, and the influences of the Spirit, to the quickening, enlightening, fructifying, and comforting their souls.

Mot. 4. Consider what a great privilege it is, that we have the scriptures to read and study at this day. If Christ had not died for our salvation, the world had never been blessed with this glorious light, but had been in darkness here, as a pledge of eternal darkness. Let us compare our case with that of others, and see our privilege.

1. Look back to the case of the church in its first age before the flood, or the time of Moses, while they had not the written word. The will of God was re-

vealed to some of them by visions, voices, dreams, &c.; but we may say, as 2 Pet. i. 19. 'We have a more sure word of prophecy.' But that was not the lot of all, but of a few among them; the rest behoved to learn by tradition. Now every one has alike access to the word of divine revelation.

2. Look to the case of the church under the Old Testament. In David's time there was little more than the five books of Moses written; yet how does that holy soul swell in commendation of his little bible, when little more than the ground-work of this glorious structure was laid! Psal. cxix. Take that church at her best in this respect, when the canon of the Old Testament was completed, they saw not the light of the New. Now the whole canon of the scripture is in our hands, this glorious image of God has got the finishing stroke; no more is to be added thereto for ever. The New Testament casts a light upon the types, shadows, and dark prophecies of the Old. And shall we not be sensible of our mercy?

3. But look abroad into the Pagan world at this day, in comparison of which all that know any part of the scriptures are but few, and the bible is not heard of among them. That precious treasure is not opened to them to this day, and they can know no more of God but what they can learn from the dark glimmerings of nature's light. O may we not in some sort say, as Psal. cxlvii. 19, 20. 'He showeth his word unto Jacob, his statutes and his judgments unto Israel. He hath not dealt so with any nation: and as for his judgments, they have not known them. Praise ye the Lord.'

4. Look back but a few years hence, when no bibles were but such as were manuscript, namely, before the art of printing was found out, which was but a little before the reformation from popery. How rare behoved they then to be! and how dear, ye may easily perceive. But now how common and easy are they to be had?

5. Look to the case of those that lived, or yet live, under Popish tyranny, where it is a crime to have or read the bible without a special licence. What a struggle had our reformers in this church, ere they could get allowance by the laws of the land to read the bible in English? And how is the bible kept out of the people's hands to this day in Popish countries? Whereas now ye are pressed to read and study it. A New Testament was very precious in those days of Popish persecution, when one gave a cart-load of hay for a leaf of the bible. But, alas! as one says of the French Protestants, When they burned us for reading of the scriptures, we burned in zeal to be reading them; now with our liberty is bred also negligence and disesteem of God's word.

6. Consider the many helps there are to understand the scriptures beyond what there were formerly. Many have run to and fro, and knowledge that way has been increased, both by preaching and writing. And that useful exercise of lecturing, which our church has commanded to be of a large portion of scripture, is no small help. What will we be able to answer to the Lord, if this great privilege be slighted?

Mot. 5. Consider it has been the way of the people of God, to be much addicted to and conversant in the scripture. So true is it that wisdom is justified of her children. O take heed ye go forth by the footsteps of the flock, and ye will not find them in the way of slighting, but prizing of the word of God. Consider,

1. Ye shall find the saints highly prizing the word, Psal. xix. and cxix. what large commendations of the word are there! How sweet was it to Jeremiah! chap. xv. 16. 'Thy words were found and I did eat them; and thy word was unto me the joy and rejoicing of my heart.' Peter, who heard the voice on the mount, yet prefers the scriptures to voices from heaven, 2 Pet. i. 19. Paul speaks highly of it, 2 Tim. iii. 16.

' All scripture is given by inspiration of God, and is profitable for doctrine, for reproof, for correction, for instruction in righteousness.' The martyrs highly prized it, and ventured their lives for it. One cast away at sea, and swimming for his life on a mast, having five pounds, which was all his stock, in the one hand, and a bible in the other, and being obliged to let go one of them, kept the bible, and let the five pounds go.

2. Ye shall find them much addicted to the study of the word. It was David's companion and bosom oracle, Psal. cxix. 97. Daniel at Babylon searches the scriptures of the prophets, Dan. ix. 2. So did the noble Bereans, Apollos, and Timothy.

3. Yea, the Spirit of God makes it the character of a godly man, Psal. i. 2. ' His delight is in the law of the Lord ; and in his law doth he meditate day and night.' O how rational is that! The man that is born of God has a natural desire after the word, as the child after the mother's breast, 1 Pet. ii. 2. The new nature tends to communion with God ; it is by the word the soul has communion with him, for thereby God speaks to us. And therefore it is a sad sign, that there are few true Christians, while there are so few that diligently ply the word.

Mot. 6. Consider the excellency of the scriptures. There is a transcendent glory in them, which whoso discern cannot miss to hug and embrace them. To commend the bible to you, I shall say these eight things of it.

1. It is the best of books. They may know much, ye think, that have many good books ; but have ye the bible, and ye have the best book in the world. It is the book of the Lord, dictated by unerring, infinite wisdom. There is no dross here with the gold, no chaff with the corn. Every word of God is pure. There is nothing for our salvation to be had in other books, but what is learned from this. They are but the rivulets that run from this fountain, and all shine

with light borrowed from hence. And it has a blessing annexed to it, a glory and a majesty in it, an efficacy with it, that no other book has the like. Therefore Luther professed he would burn his books he had writ, rather than they should divert people from reading the scriptures.

2. It is the greatest and most excellent of the works of God to be seen in the world, Psal. cxxxviii. 2. ' I will worship toward thy holy temple, and praise thy name for thy loving-kindness and for thy truth : for thou hast magnified thy word above all thy name.' If the world beautified with sun, moon, and stars, be as a precious ring, the bible is the diamond in the ring. The sparkling stars, and that glorious globe of light the sun, yet leave but a dark world, where there is no bible. Were it put to the choice of the saints either to quit the sun out of the firmament, or the bible out of the world, they would choose the former, but never the latter ; for that they cannot want till they go there where they shall read all in the face of Jesus. For that must needs be most excellent that has most of God in it.

3. It is the oracles of God, Rom. iii. 2. This was the chief of the Jewish privileges, without which their temple, altar, &c. would have been but dumb signs. The Pagan world did highly reverence and prize the devil's oracles : but we have God's oracles, while we have the scriptures that manifest to us the secrets of heaven. And if we discern aright who speaks in them, we must say, The voice of God, and not of man. Here is what you may consult safely in all your doubts and darknesses ; here is what will lead you into all truth.

4. It is the laws of heaven, Psal xix. 7. ' The law of the Lord is perfect, converting the soul : the testimony of the Lord is sure, making wise the simple.' The Lord and King of heaven, is our great Lawgiver, and the laws are written in this book. It concerns us to study it. Hence we must prove our title

to heaven, the blessed inheritance, or we will never obtain it. From hence the sentence of our justification must be drawn, else we are still in a state of wrath. Here is the rule we must follow, that we may please God here; and from this book shall the sentence of our absolution or condemnation be drawn at the great day.

5. It is Christ's testament and latter-will, 1 Cor. xi. 25. Our Lord has died, and he has left us this bible as his testament; and that makes his children have such an affection to it. Herein he has left them his legacy, not only moveables, but the eternal inheritance; and his last will is now confirmed, that shall stand for ever without alteration. So all the believer's hopes are in this bible, and this is the security he has for all the privileges he can lay claim to. This is his charter for heaven, the disposition by which he lays claim to the kingdom. And therefore, if ye have any interest in the testament, ye must needs not be slighters of it.

6. It is the sceptre of his kingdom, Psal. cx. 2. and it is a sceptre of righteousness. It is by this word he rules his church, and guides all his children in their way to the land that is far off. Wherever he hath a kingdom, he wields it; and the nations subjecting themselves to him, receive it. And where he rules in one's heart, it has place there too, Col. iii. 16. It is a golden sceptre of peace, stretched forth to rebels to win them by offering them peace: to fainting believers to give them peace. And whosoever will not subject themselves to it, shall be broken with his rod of iron.

7. It is the channel of influences, by which the communications of grace are made, and the waters of the sanctuary flow into the soul, Isa. lix. The apostle appeals for this to the experience of the Galations, chap. iii. 2. 'Received ye the Spirit by the law, or by the hearing of faith? Is the elect soul regenerated? the word is the incorruptible seed, where-

of the new creature is formed, 1 Pet. i. 23. Is faith
begotten in the heart? it is by the word, Rom. x. 17.
'Faith cometh by hearing, and hearing by the word
of God.' Is the new creature to be nourished,
strengthened, quickened, actuated, &c. ? Christ is
the fountain, faith the mouth of the soul, the word
the pipes of conveyance, whereat faith must suck, as
the child at the nipples.

8. It is the price of blood even the blood of Christ,
1 Cor. xi. 25. Had not the personal Word become
flesh, and therein died to purchase redemption for us,
we had never seen this written word among us. For
it is the book of the covenant which is founded on
the blood of the Mediator. It is the grant and conveyance of the right to the favour of God, and all saving benefits to believers ; for which there could have
been no place had not Christ died. And they that
slight it, will be found to tread under foot the blood
of the covenant.

Mot. 7. Consider the usefulness of the word. If
we consider the Author, we may be sure of the usefulness of the word. The apostle tells us, that it
alone is sufficient to make the man of God perfect,
throughly furnished unto all good works, 2 Tim. iii.
16, 17. ' All scripture is given by inspiration of God,
and is profitable for doctrine, for reproof, for correction, for instruction in righteousness ; that the man
of God may be perfect, throughly furnished unto all
good works.' There is no case a soul can be in, but
it is suitable to their case, that desire to make use of
it. To commend it to you from its usefulness, I will
say these eight things.

1. It is a treasure to the poor, and such are we all
by nature, Rev. iii. 17. 'Because thou sayest, I am
rich, and increased with goods, and have need of nothing ; and knowest not that thou art wretched and
miserable, and poor, and blind, and naked.' 2 Cor.
iv. 7. 'But we have this treasure in earthen vessels,
that the excellency of the power may be of God, and

E

not of us.' Therefore the Lord bids us search the scriptures, in allusion to those that search in mines for silver and gold. If the poor soul search here, receiving the word by faith, he is made up. He shall find there the discharge of his debt, a new right and title to the mortgaged inheritance. This word of the Lord is a treasure,

(1.) For worth. People make not treasures of any but valuable things. There is nothing in the scriptures but what is highly valuable. There are the eternal counsels of God touching our salvation; life and immortality brought to light; there are the purest precepts, the most awful threatenings, and the most precious promises, 2 Pet. i. 4, &c.

(2.) For variety. In the scriptures shines the manifold wisdom of God. They that nauseate this book of the Lord, because they find not new things in it after some time perusing it, discover their senses not to be exercised to discern. For should we come to it ever so often, bringing fresh affections with us, we would find fresh entertainment there; as is evident by the glorious refreshment sometimes found in a word, that has been often gone over before without any thing remarkable. And truly the saints shall never exhaust it while here; but as new discoveries are made in it in several ages, so it will be to the end.

(3.) For abundance. There is in it not only for the present, but for the time to come, Isa. xlii. 23. There is abundance of light, instruction, comfort, &c. and what is needful for the saints travelling heavenward, Psal. cxix. 162. And indeed it is the spoil to be gathered by us. Our Lord having fought the battle against death and devils, here the spoil lies to be gathered by us that remained at home when the fight was.

(4.) For closeness. This word contains the wisdom of God in a mystery. It is a hid book to most of the world, and indeed a sealed book to those that remain in their natural blindness. Nor can we get

into the treasure without the illumination of the same
Spirit which dictated it, 1 Cor. ii. 10. There is a
path here which the vulture's eye hath not seen,
which the carnal eye cannot take up, ver. 14.
Therefore have we need to seek diligently, and pray,
as Psal. cxix. 18. 'Open thou mine eyes, that I may
see wondrous things out of thy law.'

2. It is life to the dead : 'The words that I speak
unto you,' says Christ, 'they are spirit, and they are
life,' John vi. 63. We are naturally dead in sins ;
but the word is the means of spiritual life. It is the
ordinary means of conversion, Psal. xix. 7. 'The
law of the Lord—converteth the soul ;' and of regeneration, 1 Pet. i. 23. 'Being born again of incorruptible seed by the word of God.' By it the soul is
persuaded into the covenant, and brought to embrace
Jesus Christ. For thereby the Spirit is communicated to the elect of God. Thus it is of use to bring
sinners home to God, from under the power of darkness to the kingdom of his dear Son.

3. It is light to the blind, Psal. xix. 8. 'The commandment of the Lord is pure, enlightening the eyes.'
It is a convincing light, to discover one's state to
him, and so to rouse up the soul from its natural security. It pierces the heart as an arrow, and makes
the careless sinner stand and consider his way : for
it freely tells every one his faults, Jam. i. 25. And
while the child of God travels through a dark world,
it serves to light him the way, 2 Pet. i. 19.—'A light
shining in a dark place ;' and lets him see how to set
down every step. Hence David says, ' Thy word is
a lamp unto my feet, and a light unto my path,' Psal.
cxix. 105.

4. It is awakening to those that are asleep, Cant.
vii. 9. It is the voice of God which is full of majesty, to awaken the sleepy christian to the exercise of
grace. For as it is the means of begetting grace in
the heart, so it is also the means of actuating and
quickening thereof, Psal. cxix. 50. ' Thy word hath

quickened me.' Here the Christian may hear the
alarm sound to rise up and be doing. Here are the
precious promises as cords of love to draw, and the
awful threatenings to set idlers to work.

5. It is a sword to the Christian soldier, Eph. vi. 17.
'The sword of the Spirit, which is the word of God.'
Whoever has a mind for heaven must fight his way
to it; for none get the crown but the conquerors,
Rev. iii. 21. They must go through many temptations, from the devil, the world, and the flesh; and
the word is the sword for resisting of them. It is an
offensive and defensive weapon. We see how our
Lord Jesus wielded it, Matt. iv. 4, 7. 'It is written,
Man shall not live by bread alone, but by every word
that proceedeth out of the mouth of God.—It is written again, Thou shalt not tempt the Lord thy God.'
And whatever be our temptations, if we be well
versed in the word, we may from thence bring answers to them all.

6. It is a counsellor to those who are in straits,
doubts, and difficulties, Psal. cxix. 24. 'Thy testimonies are—my counsellors.' Many a time the children of God, when tossed with doubts and fears, have
found a quiet harbour there; and have got their way
cleared to them there, when they knew not what to
do. And no doubt, if we were more exercised unto
godliness, and looking to the Lord in our straits, we
would make more use of the bible, as the oracles of
Heaven.

7. It is a comforter to those that are cast down,
Psal. cxix. 49, 50. 'Remember the word unto thy
servant, upon which thou hast caused me to hope.
This is my comfort in my affliction: for thy word
hath quickened me.' The way to heaven lies through
many tribulations, and afflictions are the trodden path
to glory. But the Lord has left his people the bible
as a cordial to support them under all their pressures
from within and without. And indeed the sap of the
word, and the sweetness of the promises, are never

more lively relished, than when the people of God are exercised under afflictions. Then does that heavenly fountain flow most plentifully, when, created streams being dried up, the soul goes for all to the Lord. To sum up all in one word,

8. It is a cure for all diseases of the soul, Prov. iv. 22. 'My words are—health to all their flesh.' There is no malady that a soul is under, but there is a suitable remedy for it in the word, 2 Tim. iii. 16, 17. frequently quoted above, being adapted by infinite wisdom to the case of poor sinners. By it the simple may be made wise, the weak strengthened, the staggering confirmed, the hard heart melted, the shut heart opened, &c. it being the means the Spirit makes use of for these and all other such purposes.

Mot. 8. Consider the honourable epithets given to the scriptures. Amongst which I name only three.

1. The scriptures of truth, Dan. x. 21. Men may wrest the scriptures to patronise their errors but the whole word of God is most pure truth. Here are no mistakes, no weaknesses that adhere to all human composures. Here we may receive all that is taught us without hesitation. The hearers of men, or readers of their works, are divided into four sorts: Some like spunges, that suck up all, both good and bad : Some like sand glasses, who, what they receive at the one ear let go at the other : Some like a strainer, that lets all the good pass through, but keeps the dregs : Some like the sieve, that keeps the good grain, and lets through what is not worth. These last are only to be approved ; but in the reading of the word we must be as the first sort.

2. Holy scriptures, 2 Tim. iii. 15. They are the word of a holy God, from whom nothing can come but what is holy. It consists of holy commands, holy promises, holy threatenings, instructions, directions, &c. And holy hearts will love and reverence them for that very reason.

3. The book of the Lord. What can be said

more to commend it to us, if we have any regard to the Lord himself? If I could tell you of a book that fell down from heaven, and were to be had by any means, who would not be curious to have such a book and study it? This is the book that contains the counsels of heaven, and is given from heaven to the church, to let men see the way to it.

Mot. last. Consider the danger of slighting the word. It exposes to sin, and consequently to the greatest danger. How can they keep the way of the Lord that do not study to acquaint themselves with it? They must needs walk in darkness that do not make use of the light; and this leads to everlasting darkness, John iii. 19. If by this word we must be judged, how can they think to stand that neglect it?

Useful directions for reading and searching the Scriptures.

1. Keep an ordinary in reading of them, that ye may be acquainted with the whole; and make this reading a part of your secret duties. Not that ye should bind up yourselves to an ordinary, so as never to read by choice, but that ordinarily this tends most to edification. Some places are more difficult, some may seem very bare for an ordinary reader; but if you would look on it all as God's word, not to be slighted, and read it with faith and reverence, no doubt ye would find advantage.

2. Set a special mark, one way or other, on those passages you read, which you find most suitable to your case, condition, or temptations; or such as ye have found to move your hearts more than other passages. And it will be profitable often to review these.

3. Compare one scripture with another, the more obscure with that which is more plain, 2 Pet. i. 20.

This is an excellent means to find out the sense of
the scriptures; and to this good use serve the mar-
ginal notes on bibles. And keep Christ in your eye,
for to him the scriptures of the Old Testament (in its
genealogies, types, and sacrifices) look, as well as
those of the New.

4. Read with a holy attention, arising from the
consideration of the majesty of God, and the reverence due to him. This must be done with attention, 1st, to the words; 2d, to the sense; and, 3d,
to the divine authority of the scripture, and the bond
it lays on the conscience for obedience, 1 Thess. ii. 13.
'For this cause also thank we God without ceasing,
because, when ye received the word of God which ye
heard of us, ye received it not as the word of men,
but (as it is in truth) the word of God, which effectually worketh also in you that believe.'

5. Let your main end in reading the scriptures be
practice, and not bare knowledge, Jam. i. 22. 'But
be ye doers of the word, and not hearers only, de-
ceiving your own selves.' Read that you may learn
and do, and that without any limitation or distinction, but that whatever you see God requires, you
may study to practice.

6. Beg of God and look to him for his Spirit. For
it is the Spirit that dictated it, that it must be savingly understood by, 1 Cor. ii. 11. 'For what man knoweth the things of a man, save the spirit of man which
is in him? even so the things of God knoweth no
man, but the Spirit of God.' And therefore before
you read, it is highly reasonable you beg a blessing
on what you are to read.

7. Beware of a worldly fleshly mind : for fleshly
sins blind the mind from the things of God ; and the
worldly heart cannot favour them. In an eclipse of
the moon, the earth comes between the sun and the
moon, and so keeps the light of the sun from it. So
the world, in the heart, coming betwixt you and the
light of the word, keeps its divine light from you.

8. Labour to be exercised unto godliness, and to observe your case. For an exercised frame helps mightily to understand the scriptures. Such a Christian will find his case in the word, and the word will give light to his case, and his case light into the word.

9. Whatever you learn from the word, labour to put it in practice. For to him that hath shall be given. No wonder they get little insight into the bible, who make no conscience of practising what they know. But while the stream runs into a holy life, the fountain will be the freer.

Explanation of what it is to pray in the name of Christ.

1. Negatively. It is not a bare faithless mentioning of his name in our prayers, nor concluding our prayers therewith, Matt. vii. 21. The saints use the words, 'through Jesus Christ our Lord,' 1 Cor. xv. 57. but often is that scabbard produced, while the sword of the Spirit is not in it. The words are said, but the faith is not exercised.

2. Positively. To pray in the name of Christ is to pray,

1st, At his command, to go to God by his order, John xvi. 24. 'Hitherto have ye asked nothing in my name,' says he, ' ask, and ye shall receive.' Christ as God commands all men to pray, to offer that piece of natural duty to God; but that is not the command meant. But Christ as Mediator sends his own to his Father to ask supply of their wants, and allows them to tell that he sent them, as one recommends a poor body to a friend, John xvi. 24. just cited. So to pray in the name of Christ is to go to God as sent by the poor man's friend. So it imports,

(1.) The souls being come to Christ in the first place, John xv. 7. ' If ye abide in me, and my words abide in you, ye shall ask what ye will, and it shall be done unto you.' He that would pray aright, must do as those who made Blastus the king's chamberlain their friend first, and then made their suit to their king, Acts xii. 20.

(2.) The soul's taking its encouragement to pray from Jesus Christ, Heb. iv. 14—16. ' Seeing then that we have a great High Priest, that is passed into the heavens, Jesus the Son of God, let us hold fast our profession. For we have not an High Priest which cannot be touched with the feeling of our infirmities : but was in all points tempted, like as we are, yet without sin. Let us therefore come boldly unto the throne of grace, that we may obtain mercy, and find grace to help in time of need.' The way to the throne in heaven is blocked up by our sins. And sinners have no confidence to seek the Lord. Jesus Christ came down from heaven, died for the criminals, and gathers them to himself by effectual calling. He, as having all interest with his Father, bids them go to his Father in his name, and ask what they need, assuring them of acceptance. And from thence they take their encouragement, viz. from his promises in the word. And he gives them his token with them, which the Father will own, and that is his own Spirit, Rom. viii. 26, 27. ' Likewise the Spirit also helpeth our infirmities : for we know not what we should pray for as we ought : but the Spirit itself maketh intercession for us with groanings which cannot be uttered. And he that searcheth the hearts, knoweth what is the mind of the Spirit, because he maketh intercession for the saints according to the will of God.'

2dly, It is to direct our prayers to God through Jesus Christ, Heb. vii. 25. ' Wherefore he is able also to save them to the uttermost, that come unto God by him, seeing he ever liveth to make interces-

F

sion for them,' chap. xiii. 15. ' By him therefore let us offer the sacrifice of praise to God continually, that is, the fruit of our lips, giving thanks to his name ;' depending wholly on Christ's merit and intercession for access, acceptance, and a gracious return.

(1.) Depending on Christ for access to God, Eph. iii. 12. ' In whom we have boldness, and access with confidence by the faith of him.' There is no access to God but through him, John xiv. 6. ' No man cometh unto the Father but by me.' They that attempt otherwise to come unto God, will get the door thrown in their face. But we must take hold of the Mediator, and come in at his back, who is the Secretary of heaven.

(2.) Depending on him for acceptance of our prayers, Eph. i. 6. ' He hath made us accepted in the Beloved.' Our Lord Christ is the only altar that can sanctify our gift. If one lay the stress of the acceptance of his prayers on his frame, enlargement, tenderness, &c. the prayer will not be accepted. A crucified Christ only can bear the weight of the acceptance of either our persons or performances.

(3.) Depending on him for a gracious return, 1 John v. 14, ' and this is the confidence that we have in him, that if we ask any thing according to his will, he heareth us.' No prayers are heard and answered but for the Mediator's sake ; and whatever petitions agreeable to God's will are put up to God, in this dependence, are heard.

But why must we pray in the name of Christ ? The reason of this may be taken up in these two things.

1. There is no access for a sinful creature to God without a Mediator, Isa. lix. 2. ' But your iniquities have separated between you and your God, and your sins have hid his face from you, that he will not hear.' John xiv. 6. ' Jesus saith unto him, I am the way, and the truth, and the life : no man cometh unto the Fa-

ther, but by me.' Sin has set us at a distance from God, and has bolted the door of our access to him, that it is beyond our power, or that of any creature, to open it for us. His justice staves off the criminal, his holiness the unclean creature, without there be an acceptable person to go betwixt him and us. Our God is a consuming fire : and so there is no immediate access for a sinner to him.

2. And there is none appointed nor fit for that work but Christ, 1 Tim. ii. 5. It is he alone who is our great High Priest. None but he has satisfied justice for our sins. And as he is the only Mediator of redemption, so he is the only Mediator of intercession, 1 John ii. 1. ' If any man sin, we have an Advocate with the Father, Jesus Christ the Righteous.' The sweet savour of his merit only is capable to procure acceptance to our prayers, in themselves unsavoury, Rev. viii. 3, 4.

By what means Believers pray in a manner acceptable to God.

By the help of the Holy Spirit, Gal. iv. 6. ' And because ye are sons, God hath sent forth the Spirit of his Son into your hearts, crying, Abba, Father.' Rom. viii. 26. ' Likewise the Spirit also helpeth our infirmities : for we know not what we should pray for as we ought ; but the Spirit itself maketh intercession for us with groanings which cannot be uttered.' There are two sorts of prayers. 1*st*, A prayer wrought out by virtue of a gift of knowledge and utterance. This is bestowed on many reprobates, and that gift may be useful to others, and to the church. But as it is merely of that sort, it is not accepted, nor does Christ put it in before the Father for acceptance. For, 2*d*, There is a prayer wrought in

men by virtue of the Holy Spirit, Zech. xii. 10. ' I
will pour upon the house of David, and upon the inhabitants of Jerusalem, the Spirit of grace and of
supplications :' and that is the only acceptable prayer to God, Jam. v. 16. ' Confess your faults one to
another, and pray one for another, that ye may be
healed. The effectual fervent prayer of a righteous
man availeth much,' *effectual*, Gr. *inwrought*. The
right praying is praying in the Spirit. It is a gale
blowing from heaven, the breathing of the Spirit in
the saints, that carries them out in the prayer, which
comes the length of the throne. Now, the Spirit
helps to pray,

1. As a teaching and instructing Spirit, affording
proper matter of prayer, causing us to know what we
pray for, Rom. viii. 26. forecited ; enlightening the
mind in the knowledge of our needs, and those of
others ; bringing into our remembrance these things,
suggesting them to us according to the word, together with the promises of God, on which prayer is
grounded, John xiv. 26. ' The Comforter, which is
the Holy Ghost,—shall teach you all things, and
bring all things to your remembrance whatsoever I
have said unto you.' Hence it is that the saints are
sometimes carried out in prayer for things which they
had no view of before, and carried by some things
they had.

2. As a quickening, exciting Spirit, Rom. viii. 26. ;
the Spirit qualifying the soul with praying graces
and affections, working in the praying person sense
of needs, faith, fervency, humility, &c. Psal. x. 17.
' Thou wilt prepare their heart.' The man may go
to his knees in a very unprepared frame for prayer,
yet the Spirit blowing, he is helped. It is for this
reason the Spirit is said to *make intercession* for us,
namely, in so far as he teaches and quickens, puts
us in a praying frame, and draws our petitions, as it
were, which the Mediator presents.

This praying with the help of the Spirit is pecu-

liar to the saints, Jam. v. 16. ; yet they have not
that help at all times, nor always in the same measure ; for sometimes the Spirit, being provoked, departs, and they are left in a withered condition. So
there is great need to look for a breathing, and pant
for it, when we are to go to duty : for if there be not
a gale, we will tug at the oars but heartlessly.

Let no man think that a readiness and volubility
of expression in prayer, is always the effect of the
Spirit's assistance. For that may be the product of
a gift, and of the common operations of the Spirit,
removing the impediment of the exercise of it. And
it is evident one may be scarce of words, and have
groans instead of them, while the Spirit helps him to
pray, Rom. viii. 26. Neither is every flood of affections in prayer, the effect of the Spirit of prayer.
There are of those which puff up a man, but make him
never a whit more holy, tender in his walk, &c. But
the influences of the Spirit never miss to be humbling
but sanctifying. Hence, says David, ' Who am I,
and what is my people, that we should be able to offer so willingly after this sort ? for all things come of
thee, and of thine own have we given thee,' 1 Chron.
xxix. 14. ; and, says the apostle, ' We have no confidence in the flesh,' Phil. iii. 3.

What classes of Men we are to pray for.

Not for the dead. David ceased praying for his
child when once dead, 2 Sam. xii. 21—23. It is vain
and useless ; for as the tree falls, it must lie. We
have neither precept nor promise about it ; and it
was raised upon the false opinion of purgatory. But
the dead are in an unalterable state, Heb. ix. 27. ' It
is appointed unto men once to die, but after this the
judgment.'

Nor for those who are known to have sinned the sin against the Holy Ghost, 1 John v. 16. for God has declared that sin to be unpardonable. This is very rare, and therefore one would beware of rashness in this matter. But,

1. In general, we are to pray for all sorts of men living, ' for kings, and all that are in authority,' 1 Tim. ii. 1, 2. ' I exhort, therefore, that, first of all, supplications, prayers, intercessions, and giving of thanks, be made for all men ; for kings, and for all that are in authority ; that we may lead a quiet and peaceable life in all godliness and honesty :' for Christians, Jews, Mahometans, Pagans, noble and ignoble, &c. They are capable of God's grace and favour, and we are to desire it for them. But we are not to pray for every particular person whatsoever, 1 John v. 16. ' There is a sin unto death : I do not say that ye shall pray for it.' So that it is an unwarrantable petition, that God would have mercy on, and save all mankind, for the contrary of that is revealed. Yea, we should pray for all sorts of men who shall live hereafter, as our Lord did, John xvii. 20. ' Neither pray I for these alone, but for them also which shall believe on me through their word.' But,

2. In particular, we are to pray, not only for ourselves, as Jacob did for deliverance from the hand of his brother Esau, Gen. xxxii. 11. but for,

(1.) The whole church of Christ upon earth. Hence says the text, *Praying always with all prayer,—and supplication for all saints.* To no party must we confine the communion of prayers, to whom God has not confined his grace. All the members of the mystical body must share particularly in our prayers, because they are the members of Christ, whatever difference be betwixt us and them in lesser things. The sympathy betwixt the members of the same body of our Lord requires this. And it is a

sad sign not to be so affected, Amos vi. 6. ' They are
not grieved for the affliction of Joseph.'

(2.) Magistrates : ' Kings, and all that are in authority,' 1 Tim. ii. 2. It was about three hundred
years after Christ ere the magistrates were Christians,
nevertheless the apostle bids pray for them ; because
the quiet and peace of the commonwealth and kingdom depends much on their management; and infidelity, or indifference in religion, does not make void
the magistrate's just and legal authority, nor free
the people from their due obedience to him. Their
hearts are in the Lord's hand, Prov. xxi. 1. Their
influence is great, so is their work, and so are their
temptations ; and if they be evil men, there is the
more need to be earnest with God on their behalf.
Let us bless God that we have a Protestant King on
the throne, remembering how seasonably the Lord
sent him, and how much depends on his safety, and
the safety of his royal family.

(3.) Ministers, Col. iv. 3. ' Withal praying also for
us, that God would open unto us a door of utterance,
to speak the mystery of Christ, for which I am also
in bonds.' Psal. cxxxii. 9. ' Let thy priests be
clothed with righteousness ; and let thy saints shout
for joy.' There is a near relation betwixt the people
of God and their ministers. They have a weighty
work in their hands, which, if it misgive, will not
only be their own loss, but the people's. People
may have a minister so straitened, as to do them
no good, Col. iv. 3. Though he be not so, yet he
may be useless to them ; therefore, says the apostle,
1 Thess. v. 25. ' Brethren, pray for us.' I leave it
with that, Rom. xv. 30. ' Now I beseech you, brethren, for the Lord Jesus Christ's sake, and for the love
of the Spirit, that ye strive together with me in your
prayers to God for me.'

(4.) Our Christian acquaintance, Jam. v. 16.
' Pray one for another.' Communion of prayers is
a special benefit of Christian friendship and acquain-

tance. And it is no small mercy and encouragement to have interest in their prayers, who have interest at the throne of grace.

(5.) The place and congregation we live in, and are members of. The captives of Babylon were to pray for the place they lived in, Jer. xxix. 7. how much more should we pray for a Christian congregation whereof we are members ? The better it be with them, it will be the better with you ; and so contrariwise.

(6.) Our families and relations. The nearer any stand related to us, we have the more need to be concerned for them at the throne of grace. We find Job sacrificing for his family, Job i. 5 ; a master praying for his servant, 2 Kings vi. 17 ; and a servant for his master, Gen. xxiv. 12.

(7.) We must pray for enemies, Matth. v. 44. This is hardest to bring men to. But we have the express command of Christ for it, and his example, Luke xxiii. 34. followed by the martyr Stephen, Acts vii. 60. Nay, forgiving them is necessary to our forgiveness : ' Forgive us our debts, as we forgive our debtors.' There may be much selfishness in praying for those that love us ; but that kindly concern for our enemies makes us liker God, Matth. v. 45.

For what, and how we are to pray.

We are to pray for things agreeable to God's revealed will, and for such things only, 1 John v. 14. ' And this is the confidence that we have in him, that if we ask any thing according to his will, he heareth us.' We may not present unto God unlawful desires, nor petitions, in favour of our lust, Jam. iv. 3. These must needs be an abomination, and a daring

affront to a holy God. And indeed wicked things
are so much the more wicked, as they are brought
into our addresses to a holy God.

The matter of our prayers must be regulated by
the word of God, wherein he has shown what is
pleasing to him, and what is not so. The signification of God's will and good pleasure as to the good
to be bestowed on men, and our prayers, are to be of
equal extent. Wherefore, let us see that whatever
we pray for be within the compass of the command
or the promise.

Such are all things tending to the glory of God,
Matt. vi. 9. ' After this manner therefore pray ye :
Our Father which art in heaven, hallowed be thy
name ;' or to the welfare of the church, Psal. cxxii.
6. ' Pray for the peace of Jerusalem : they shall
prosper that love thee ;' to our own good, temporal,
spiritual, or eternal, Matt. vii. 11. ' If ye, then, being evil, know how to give good gifts unto your children, how much more shall your Father which is in
heaven give good things to them that ask him ? ' or
that of others, Psal. cxxv. 4, ' Do good, O Lord, unto
those that be good, and to them that are upright in
their hearts.'

But how are we to pray, if we would pray rightly
and acceptably ?

1. Understandingly ; understanding what we say,
1 Cor. xiv. 15. Therefore they must be in a known
tongue. And to repeat words before God, while we
know not what they mean, can never be prayer indeed.

2. Reverently, Eccl. v. 1. ' Keep thy foot when
thou goest to the house of God, and be more ready
to hear than to give the sacrifice of fools : for they
consider not that they do evil.' We must maintain
an outward reverence in expression, voice, and gesture ; since in prayer we are before the great God :
an inward reference especially, having an awful apprehension of the majesty of God before whom we

appear, Psal. lxxxix. 7. ' God is greatly to be feared
in the assembly of the saints, and to be had in reverence of all them that are about him.'   Heb. xii. 28.
' Wherefore, we receiving a kingdom which cannot
be moved, let us have grace, whereby we may serve
God acceptably with reverence and godly fear.'   Fear
and trembling become a creature, much more a
guilty creature, before a holy God.   And fearless
presumptuous addresses to God are the produce of a
hard heart.

3. Humbly, Psal. x. 17. ' Lord, thou hast heard
the desire of the humble : thou wilt prepare their
heart, thou wilt cause thine ear to hear ;' with a deep
sense of our own unworthiness and sinfulness on our
spirits.   In prayer we come to beg, not to buy or
demand our right, and therefore should be sensible
of unworthiness, Gen. xxxii. 10. ' I am not worthy
of the least of all the mercies, and of all the truth,
which thou hast showed unto thy servant ; for with
my staff I passed over this Jordan, and now I am
become two bands ;' and the more grace, the more
unworthy will we be in our own eyes, Gen. xviii. 27.
' And Abraham answered and said, Behold, now, I
have taken upon me to speak unto the Lord, which
am but dust and ashes.'   And going to God, we must
turn our eyes inward, with the Publican, Luke
xviii. 14. ; on our own evils of heart and life.

4. Feelingly ; being deeply affected with a sense of
our needs, like the prodigal, Luke xv. 17, 18, 19.
' And when he came to himself, he said, How many
hired servants of my father's have bread enough, and
to spare, and I perish with hunger ! I will arise, and
go to my father, and will say unto him, Father, I
have sinned against heaven, and before thee, and am
no more worthy to be called thy son ; make me as
one of thy hired servants.'   Alas ! what does it avail
to go to God with an insensible heart ; to sit down
at his table without spiritual hunger ; to come to his
door rich and increased with goods, in our own con-

ceit! Such are sent empty away. Therefore it is a piece of very necessary preparation for prayer, to look over our wants, ere we go to prayer.

5. Believingly, Matt. xxi. 22. ' All things whatsoever ye shall ask in prayer, believing, ye shall receive.' He who prays acceptably must be endued with saving faith, Heb. xi. 6. An unbeliever cannot pray acceptably, Rom. x. 14. ' How then shall they call on him in whom they have not believed? and how shall they believe in him of whom they have not heard? and how shall they hear without a preacher?' Hence the prayers of the unrenewed man are all lost in respect of gracious acceptance. Moreover, the believer must be in the exercise of faith in prayer, which must be mixed with faith.

One must have a faith of particular confidence in prayer, as to the things prayed for, Mark xi. 24. ' What things soever ye desire when ye pray, believe that ye receive them, and ye shall receive them.' For where that is altogether wanting, the prayer can never be accepted, Jam. i. 6. ' Let him ask in faith, nothing wavering.' Since it must needs be highly dishonouring to God, to come to him to ask, without any expectation from, or trust in him, as to what is asked.

Quest. How may one have that faith? *Ans.* By applying the promises, and believing them. If the things be absolutely necessary, the promise makes these very things sure to them who come to God through Christ for them, as peace, pardon, &c. If they be not, then the promise secures God's doing the best, that either he will give the very thing desired, or what is as good. And we are to believe accordingly.

6. Sincerely, Psal. cxlv. 18. ' The Lord is nigh unto all them that call upon him, to all that call upon him in truth.' Hypocrisy and dissimulation in prayer, when the heart goes not along with the lips, mars the acceptance of prayers. There are feigned lips,

Psal. xvii. 1. when the affections do not keep pace
with the words in prayer: when sin is confessed,
but the heart not humbled under it; petitions are
put up, but no serious desire of the things asked,
Jer. xxix. 13. ' And ye shall seek me, and find me,
when ye shall search for me with all your heart.'

7. Fervently, Jam. v. 16. ' Confess your faults one
to another, and pray one for another, that ye may be
healed. The effectual fervent prayer of a righteous
man availeth much.' Cold, lifeless, and formal prayers, are not of the right stamp. We should, as in a
most weighty matter, be boiling hot, Rom. xii. 11.
Importunity in prayer is most pleasing to God. It
consists not in a multitude of words, Matt. vi. 7;
but in a holy earnestness of heart to be heard, Psal.
cxliii. 7; and pleading with the Lord, by allowable
arguments, as one who is in deep earnest, Job xxiii. 4.
A heart warmed by a live-coal from God's altar will
produce this.

8. Watchfully; *watching unto prayer*, as in the
text; taking heed to our spirits, that they do not
wander. Wandering thoughts in prayer mar many
prayers. They come on like the fowls on the carcase, and will devour it, if not driven away. A carnal frame of heart is the mother of them, and rash
indeliberate approaches to God help them forward.

In that case one should be like the builders of the
wall, having the trowel in the one hand, and the
sword in the other, resolutely to resist vain thoughts,
and refuse to harbour them. Nay, turn the cannon
on the enemy, consider them as affording new matter of humiliation, and a clamant occasion of plying
the throne of grace more closely. If they be striven
against, they will not mar your acceptance; but if
not they will.

9. Perseveringly; *watching thereunto with all
perseverance*, as in the text. When we have tabled
our suit before the throne, we must not let it fall, but
insist upon it, Luke xviii. 1. Hold on, with one pe-

tition, one prayer, on the back of another, till it be granted, Isa. lxii. 1. ' In due time ye shall reap, if ye faint not.'

Lastly, Dependingly ; waiting upon the Lord with humble submission to his holy will, and looking for an answer, Micah vii. 7. ' Therefore I will look unto the Lord ; I will wait for the God of my salvation : my God will hear me.' We must come away in a waiting depending frame. No wonder those prayers be not regarded which we never look after, and are not concerned for the answer of.

But are all such prayers accepted, heard, and answered ?

1. An unrenewed man cannot thus pray, neither are such a one's prayers at any time accepted, Prov. xv. 8. ' The sacrifice of the wicked is an abomination to the Lord,' John ix. 31. ' God heareth not sinners.'

2. God's own people do not always thus pray, neither are all their prayers accepted. For, says the Psalmist, Psal. lxvi. 18. ' If I regard iniquity in my heart, the Lord will not hear me.'

3. But all such prayers, being the produce of God's Spirit in the saints, are presented by the Mediator ; and are accepted, heard, and answered by the Father, though not presently answered, Psal. xxii. 2. yet they shall be answered in due time, either by granting the very thing desired, 1 John v. 15. ' And if we know that he hear us, whatsoever we ask, we know that we have the petitions that we desired of him ;' or something as good, Gen. xvii. 18, 19. ' And Abraham said unto God, O that Ishmael might live before thee ! And God said, Sarah thy wife shall bear thee a son indeed ; and thou shalt call his name Isaac : and I will establish my covenant with him for an everlasting covenant, and with his seed after him ;' 2 Cor. xii. 8, 9. ' For this thing I besought the Lord thrice, that it might depart from me. And he said unto me, My grace is sufficient for thee ; for

my strength is made perfect in weakness. Most
gladly therefore will I rather glory in my infirmities,
that the power of Christ may rest upon me.' *

The necessity of Secret Prayer.

It is not necessary in regard of merit, as if we
could procure heaven by it. The only ground of
eternal life in the mansions of bliss is the righteousness of a crucified Redeemer. Beggars pay no
debts, but confess insufficiency, saying with the prophet, Dan. ix. 5. ' We have sinned, and have committed iniquity, and have done wickedly, and have
rebelled, even by departing from thy precepts, and
from thy judgments.' But it is necessary,
    1. In regard of the command of God. He, by a
plain and express command, requires it ; and that
command binds it as a necessary duty upon us. To
neglect it, therefore, is a direct violation of the command of the great God and Lawgiver ; and to make

---

* Consider the many excellencies and privileges of prayer.
    1. This is our greatest honour. To have leave to approach
the throne of grace, to come with freedom and boldness into
God's presence, and disclose all our thoughts and desires before
him, is a singular privilege. That weak and sinful creatures
may be admitted to hold intercourse with the heavenly majesty,
is an unspeakable dignity vouchsafed to them. Prayer is a great
preferment, because it brings us nigh to God.
    2. Prayer is a great comfort. That we may go to our Father
and open our hearts and unburden before him, is a solace of no
mean nature, of no low degree. For by laying open our wound,
we partly heal it : By discovering our grievances, we in some
measure redress them ; by complaining of our burden, we make
it lighter ; by communicating our wants, we find relief and ease.
    3. By prayer, we receive all manner of benefits and favours
from God. To supplicate God is the way to partake of all those.
To beg of God is the way to become rich. An apostle certifies
that every thing is sanctified by prayer.
                    Edwards on the Lord's Prayer.

conscience of it is a necessary and proper act of obedience to the divine will.

2. To give God the glory of his omniscience and omnipresence. When we pray to *our Father which is in secret*, we plainly declare, that we believe he knows and sees all things, that the darkness and the light are alike unto him ; and that he is the witness and inspector of all our actions, and will call us to an account for all our thoughts, words, and actions, which are well known to him.

3. To evidence our sincerity, that it is not to be seen of men that we pray ; that we are not actuated from motives of ostentation and vain-glory, but from regard to the divine command, and a sincere desire to serve God ; though indeed it will not hold that all such as pray in secret are sincere ; for, alas ! men may be very assiduous in this duty, and yet be far from being sincere Christians, or accepted of God therein.

4. In regard that none know our case so well as ourselves : and therefore, though the master of the family pray in the family, yet we ought to pray by ourselves, in order to make known our particular case and wants unto God, which none other can know, and to ask such blessings and mercies of him as we stand in need of, and are suitable to our circumstances.

5. In regard that, if we know our own hearts, we cannot but have somewhat to say unto the Lord, that we cannot, nor would it be at all proper to say before others, respecting both confession of sins and supplication for mercies. Hence the spouse says, Cant. vii. 11, 12. ' Come, my Beloved, let us go forth unto the fields : let us lodge in the villages. Let us get up early to the vineyards, let us see if the vine flourish, whether the tender grape appear, and the pomegranates bud forth : there will I give thee my loves.'

6. In regard of our wants continually recurring on

our hands, and daily and hourly temptations, that may call for this exercise, when family-prayer cannot be had. What man is so well supplied, both as to temporal and spiritual blessings, as to have no occasion for asking supplies from above ? Man is a needy and indigent creature in all respects ; as a creature he lives on the bounties of providence, and as a Christian on the grace which is in Christ Jesus ; and therefore he must daily apply to the throne of grace for necessary supplies in both. And as we are daily surrounded with temptations, and have no strength to resist or repel them, we must fetch in strength from God in Christ by prayer, lest we fall and be overcome by the temptations in our way.

Thus it appears from these considerations, that prayer is a necessary duty incumbent on all. And surely all who have tasted that the Lord is gracious will make conscience of this important and useful exercise.

Important Questions concerning Secret Prayer stated and answered.

Quest. 1. What is the proper season of this duty of secret prayer ? or when are we called to this exercise ?

Ans. 1. We are doubtless to be very frequent in this duty. Thus we are called to ' pray always,' Eph. vi. 18, and ' without ceasing,' 1 Thess. v. 17, that is, at all proper times, and to be continually in a praying frame, or to pray inwardly, though we utter not a word with our lips.

2. Whenever God calls us to it, putting an opportunity in our hands, and moving and inciting us to it, then we are to go about it. Thus, when the Lord Jesus says, ' Seek ye my face ;' our hearts

should say unto him, ' Thy face, Lord, will we seek,' Psal. xxvii. 8. And thus we have daily calls and invitations to this duty, which we should carefully regard, and conscientiously embrace, lest we quench the Spirit, and provoke the Lord to harden our hearts from his fear.

3. The saints in scripture have sometimes been more, sometimes less frequent in this exercise. Thus David was sometimes employed thrice, sometimes seven times a-day in prayer, Psal. lv. 17. and cxix. 164, and Daniel three times, even at a very perilous juncture, Dan. vi. 10. From whose practice the frequency of performing this duty evidently appears.

4. Morning and evening at least we should pray, and not neglect this duty. This appears from our Lord's practice, Mark i. 35. ' And in the morning, rising up a great while before day, he went out, and departed into a solitary place, and there prayed ;' Matt. xiv. 23. ' And when he had sent the multitudes away, he went up into a mountain apart to pray ; and when the evening was come, he was there alone ;' from the practice of the saints in scripture, Psal. lv. 2. ' Attend unto me, and hear me : I mourn in my complaint, and make a noise ;' and chap. v. 2. ' Hearken unto the voice of my cry, my King, and my God : for unto thee will I pray ;' and from the morning and evening sacrifice under the legal dispensation, which were daily offered, and should excite us to offer up unto God daily the morning and evening sacrifice of prayer and praise. And the very light of nature teaches us so much ; that when we are preserved through the silent watches of the dark night, and from the perils we may be exposed unto in that gloomy season, we should acknowledge the goodness and kindness of God therein ; and that when we are preserved through the day, from the many snares and temptations we are liable to amidst the cares and distractions of our business, we should bless God for his preserving and protecting mercy, and commit our-

H

selves, and all our concerns, into the hand of God,
when we are going to take necessary rest, that we
may fall asleep under a sense of his love, and may
rise again to resume the business of our callings with
his blessing and favour.

Quest. 2. What is the proper place for secret
prayer ?

Ans. A secret place is the most proper place for
this exercise ; and though every body has not a
closet, or retired apartment, into which he may go
in and shut the door, yet any place where we may
be retired from the view and observation of others,
answers the purpose ; though in other respects it be a
public place, yet if it be dark, and the voice kept low,
it is justly a secret place. And to a place of that
sort did our Lord retire for secret prayer, Matt. xiv.
23. perhaps not having proper conveniency in the
place where he lodged all night. And indeed there
is not a person but may meet with such a secret
place every day, if he have a disposition for this exercise.

Quest. 3. What gesture are we to use in secret
prayer ?

Ans. 1. Holy scripture does not bind us to any
gesture particularly ; but we find these four gestures
of the body in prayer spoken of there, viz. standing,
Mark xi. 25 ; lying along on the face, Matt. xxvi.
39 ; kneeling, Dan. vi. 10. Eph. iii. 14 ; and sitting,
2 Sam. vii. 18.

2. Whatever the gesture be, let it be a reverent
one, that may express a humble and reverent frame
of spirit. Hence we are commanded to ' glorify God
in our bodies,' 1 Cor. vi. 20.

3. I shall say these two things for the further de-
termination of this question. 1*st*, Let it be such a
gesture as is conformable unto, or flows natively from,
the present disposition of the heart. Thus in extraordinary cases we find the saints were wont to fall
on their faces, 2 Sam. xii. 16. And so likewise did

the Lord Jesus in the garden, on the eve of his sufferings, Matt. xxvi. 39. 2d, Yet let it be always to edification ; and let that gesture be chosen which is most conducive to devotion, and occasions least distraction in the duty : As if kneeling be dangerous for the body, and so may tend to disturb the mind, let another gesture be chosen that is not attended with these inconveniences ; though kneeling is certainly the most eligible gesture, and expressive of that humility which must ever accompany this exercise. And the same thing we may say of closing the eyes, or keeping them open ; though praying with the eyes shut is certainly to be preferred.

Quest. 4. What are we to say of the voice in secret prayer ?

Ans. 1. The duty may be performed without using the voice, as was done by Moses in the strait the children of Israel were reduced to, after their escape from Egypt, when high and inaccessible mountains were on each side of them, the Red Sea before them, and the Egyptian host at their heels ready to cut them off. In this dilemma we find that great man crying to the Lord, though not with an audible voice, Exod. xiv. 15. Thus the voice is not to be used when people cannot do so without being heard, or when through weakness of body, or disquiet of mind, they are unfit for speaking with the tongue.

2. Yet where the voice may be used, and that with convenience and propriety, it should be made use of ; and that, 1*st*, because we are to glorify God with our bodies ; and particularly our tongue is given to be an instrument of glorifying God ; ' Awake, my glory,' says David, Psal. lvii. 8. 2*d*, Because the voice is of good use in secret prayer, to stir up the affections, and to stay the mind from wandering. Yet an affected loudness of the voice, whereby the secret prayer is made public, is a sad sign of great hypocrisy, which every serious Christian will guard against.

Quest. 5. Is secret prayer a sure mark of sincerity?
or can one pray in secret, and yet be an hypocrite?

Ans. This is not out of the reach of the hypocrite?
A hypocrite may come this length, and much farther.
Judas was among the rest whom our Lord taught to
pray in secret, and ye all know what was his fate.
But though a hypocrite may continue a long time,
nay, many years, in the practice of secret prayer;
yet it is scarcely to be thought that he will always
do so, if he live a long life : For, says Job, ' Will he
[the hypocrite] always call upon God?' chap. xxvii.
10. It is not to be thought that he will, as he has
no communion with God in the duty. And therefore
adds the same holy man, ' Will he always delight
himself in the Almighty?' It is communion with God
that is to be enjoyed in secret prayer, and the delight
the soul has in it, that inclines a person to persevere
in that exercise.

Inst. But if one pray not to be seen of men, can he
be a hypocrite?

Ans. Yes, he may. For the terrors of God scald-
ing the conscience, and a desire to lay the ferment
thereby brought into the mind, may excite one to the
duty, and put the applause of men entirely out of the
mind. But secret prayer, conscientiously practised,
and attended with manifestations of the Lord's love
and favour, smiles of his face, returns of what was
asked, and continued faith and fervency, are undoubt-
ed signs of sincerity.

*Motives to Secret Prayer, with Answers to Objections
commonly made to the performance of this Duty.*

1. It is a piece of worship expressly commanded
of God, and it is directly required by him, Eph. vi. 18.
' Praying always with all prayer and supplication in

the Spirit, and watching thereunto with all perseverance and supplication for all saints.' Will ye then
counteract God's express command ? If ye do, it will
be at your peril.

2. Are you not engaged to this duty ? Are not the
vows of God upon you for the performance of it ?
Were ye not baptised in the name of the Father,
Son, and Holy Ghost, to worship them, and that in
all parts of worship, of which prayer is a principal
one ? Have not some of you been admitted to the
Lord's table, when ye professed to renew your bap-
tismal engagements ? And perhaps some of you have
sick-bed vows on you to that purpose.

3. Have ye not secret sins, secret wants, and secret temptations ? and shall ye not have secret prayers adapted to each, requesting of the Lord the pardon of your secret sins, the supply of your secret
wants, and grace to resist and overcome your secret
temptations ?

4. This is your known duty ; and therefore remember, that ' the servant that knew his master's will,
but did it not, shall be beaten with double stripes.'
Wherefore, I charge you, as you will answer to God
at death and at judgment, and as you love your own
souls, and would not eternally perish, to set about
this necessary and important duty.

But some are ready to muster up a variety of objections against this duty ; the chief of which I shall
endeavour to obviate.

Object. 1. I have no time for secret prayer, for my
work and business. *Ans.* 1. This is thy greatest
work, even the salvation of thy soul, in comparison
of which all thy other work is a mere trifle : and wilt
thou take time for thy other work, and not for this
work, that challenges thy utmost care and attention ?
2. Fool's haste is no speed. To rise out of the bed,
and to go immediately to secular work, is foolish
cursed haste. How canst thou look for a blessing
on thy work without prayer ? 3. Rise the sooner

every morning, that you may not be scrimped as to
time for this exercise, as our blessed Lord did, Mark
i. 35. ' And in the morning, rising up a great while
before day, he went out, and departed into a solitary
place, and there prayed.' How wilt thou answer to
God at the great day, for spending that time in sleep,
which thou shouldst have spent in secret prayer?
Daniel would not omit this exercise, though at the
hazard of his life.

Object. 2. We are so wearied with our work
through the day, that we are not able to pray in the
evening. *Ans.* 1. What difference is there betwixt
you and the beasts that take their ease when their
work is done, without any more ado? 2. You will
take your meat for your bodies, though ever so weary;
and why will ye not think of and provide meat for
your perishing souls? John iv. 6. 32. ' Now Jacob's
well was there. Jesus, therefore, being wearied with
his journey, sat thus on the well : and it was about the
sixth hour. But he said unto them, I have meat to
eat that ye know not of.' 3. Notwithstanding ye may
be tired, do what ye are able. We are not commanded to tell you to make your prayers short or long;
but by no means to neglect secret prayer altogether,
which is very dangerous. But I suppose, that when
you say your body is not able to subsist with secret
prayer, that yet if ye could gain a sixpence at that
very time, you would spend twice much more time for
that paltry gain ; and yet slight the concerns of your
souls, under this frivolous pretence.

Object. 3. We have no convenient place for secret
prayer. *Ans.* Find out once a willing heart for this
exercise, and I shall engage for it you shall find a
place.

Object. 4. But there are prayers in our family, and
I join therein ; what needs more! *Ans.* Poor soul!
hast thou no more to say of thyself to God, but what
the master of the family says? Alas! thou knowest
not thyself, and the dreadful case thou art in by na-

ture; which if thou didst, thou wouldst not think of joining in prayer with others enough. Thou thinkest it sufficient that the master of the family pray for thee, and the other members of his family, and thou liest by without concerning thyself about duty for thyself; wilt thou think it enough, that he go to heaven for thee, and thou be shut out for ever?

Object. 5. But (says the master of the family) I pray with my family, and I hope that is enough for me. *Ans.* In this command in the text, Christ has not excepted thee, neither dare I. Again, dost thou so well discharge family prayer, that thou hast no escapes or failures to be matter of secret prayer? I tell you plainly, that God will not have his worship halved: he will have either the whole or nothing. Being conscientious in family-prayer is good, but can never excuse the neglect of secret prayer, which is as much thy duty. Yea, the more thou art helped to discharge family-duty, the more wilt thou be inclined to the practice of secret duty. The false mother was for dividing the child, not the true one.

Object. 6. Some women that have children to nurse and wait on, think that frees them from this duty. *Ans.* It is a sad observation of many women, who, while they are unmarried, and are not involved in the cares and troubles of a family, have some profession and practice of religion; but as soon as they get a house to manage, and have the care of young children especially, they cast off all religion, as if they had no more concern therein. But surely the very sight of the child whom thou hast conceived in sin, and brought forth in iniquity, should remind thee of thy original guilt and corruption, and incite thee to apply to the blood and Spirit of Christ for pardon and cleansing, and be a powerful spur to thee to set about this great duty of secret prayer. And remember, that the welfare of thy own soul, and that of the child, is more than that of the child's bodily welfare, which deserves but the second care in comparison of

the other. I would not have you by any means to
cast off the care of the young one's temporal welfare ;
but thou mayst so observe times and seasons, as thou
mayst take time for this duty morning and evening,
though it be not immediately after thou risest, or
before thou liest down. Thou mayst even do it
when thou art rocking the cradle, or suckling the
child. Alas ! it had been telling many, that they had
the womb that never bare, and the paps that never
gave suck.

Object. 7. God knows the heart, and what needs
so much ado about praying in secret, as if God knew
not what we wanted, or what we would be at, till we
sit down on our knees, and tell him ? *Ans.* God knows
the heart of such an objector to be a graceless heart,
and his end to be destruction, Matt. vii. 15. 20 ; and
his heart to be a foolish atheistical heart, that will
not call upon God, Psal. xiv. 1. ' The fool hath said
in his heart, there is no God. They are corrupt ;
they have done abominable works ; there is none that
doeth good.' Again, what is this but to argue God's
command to be foolish ? He bids you pray, and you
say it is needless. O daring presumption ! Though
the Lord not only knows your heart, but has a mind
to give blessings to poor sinners, he will have you
seek them by prayer : ' For these things,' says he,
' will I be inquired of by the house of Israel, that I
may do it for them,' Ezek. xxxvi. 37. God never
confers signal mercies on his people, without first
pouring out on them the Spirit of faith and prayer,
and determines them to seek ardently the very thing
he has a mind to grant them. And this method is
for the glory of his name, and for our real benefit.

Object. 8. Age and infirmity will not suffer me to
go about that duty. *Ans.* Will it suffer you to do
your business in the world, and will it not suffer you
to manage your soul's business, which is of infinitely
greater importance ? It would seem, that the nearer
we draw to the grave, the more active we should be

in preparing for it. It were good that old people would mind heaven more, and the world less, as they have so short a time to stay here. The concerns of the other world should mainly engross their care and attention, and they should then redouble their diligence in improving their span of time, and doing that which perhaps they too much neglected in the days of health and vigour. 'The hoary head is a crown of glory, if it be found in the way of righteousness,' Prov. xvi. 31 ; 'But the sinner being an hundred years old shall be accursed,' Isa. lxv. 20. Let this sound an alarm to all the old sinners among you, that ye may yet apply to the merciful Redeemer, who sets even some to work in the vineyard at the eleventh hour. It is sad to be tottering under the miseries and infirmities of old age, and yet to have no prospect of a happy landing. Fly then to Christ, thou old decrepit sinner, while his call reaches thee, lest thou speedily perish without remedy.

Object. 9. I am too young to mind secret prayer. *Ans.* You are too old never to have entered on God's service. Remember that Josiah, when he was but eight years old, began to seek the Lord God of his father David. Obadiah, Ahab's steward, feared the Lord greatly from his youth. John Baptist was sanctified from the womb ; and so was the prophet Jeremiah. Timothy knew the holy scriptures from a child. You can never begin to be religious too soon. None ever repented that they sought the Lord ; but all have repented that they did not begin to seek him sooner. You are as liable to death as the oldest person here, have a soul as precious as theirs, and as much need to mind your best and eternal interests as they. Up then and be doing, without putting off a moment longer.

Object. 10. I cannot pray. *Ans.* The truth is thou wilt not pray, Psal. x. 4. If thou hadst a will to the duty, thou wouldst soon learn. But if thou wouldst learn to pray, go to God that he may teach thee, as

Christ taught the disciples ; and consider the absolute need thou hast of divine instruction in this matter. Use the one talent, and God will increase it.
Wherefore set about this weighty duty, and neglect
it not. Think seriously with yourselves, whether
those who are now in hell, and when they lived neglected secret prayer like you, would do so still if
they were in the world again. I scarce think they
would. Pray now, therefore, lest ye repent your neglect, when it will be too late, and ye are tormented
in the lake of fire and brimstone. Again, think with
yourselves how you will get this criminal neglect digested on a death-bed, when ye are ready to leap into
eternity, without having once prayed for God's mercy
through Christ to your souls ; and how you will get
it digested before the awful tribunal of God, when
he will drive you from his blessed presence for ever.
Think with yourselves how precious time is, and
what a sad business it is to spend it in pursuing the
world and lying vanities, and neglecting communion
with God, wherein lies the life of the soul. What!
will ye delay it yet awhile ? O do it not! for delays
are dangerous. Will ye be so foolish as to venture
all on two or three words on a sick-bed or death-bed ?
Perhaps you will not get one, but may be hurried
away in a moment. Consider the awful passage,
Prov. i. 24—28. ' Because I have called and ye refused, I have stretched out my hand, and no man regarded ; but ye have set at nought all my counsel,
and would none of my reproof : I also will laugh at
your calamity, I will mock when your fear cometh ;
when your fear cometh as desolation, and your destruction cometh as a whirlwind ; when distress and
anguish cometh upon you. Then shall they call upon me, but I will not answer ; they shall seek me
early, but they shall not find me.'

Exhort. 2. Be frequent in this duty, morning and
evening at least, and at other times when your con-

veniency will allow, and go not only to it now and
then. Consider,

1. God's express command, which ties you to *pray
always continually*, and *without ceasing*. This does
not mean, that you should do nothing but pray, or
spend your whole time in this exercise. No ; but
denotes frequency, and embracing every opportunity
that offers for so delightful and profitable a duty. It
says you should be always in a praying frame, never
having your minds so much engrossed in worldly
concerns, as to be indisposed to call upon God in
prayer.

2. Frequency in this duty is a good sign of a good
frame and an excellent mean to maintain and preserve it. They who are not frequent in this exercise, do thereby show that their frame and disposition is not spiritual, but carnal, much under the conduct of sense, and attachment to sensible things.
Whereas, if a person were frequent in this duty, it
would be a token of a heart weaned from the world,
and much conversant in the things of God.

3. It is dangerous to grow slack and remiss in this
duty, as mournful experience has testified in the case
of many. They who having been for years frequently employed in this heavenly exercise do at last turn
careless, restrain prayer before the Lord, or but now
and then bow a knee before him, do thereby declare
they have lost the life and relish of the power of religion, and are in the high road to apostacy. There
are not wanting instances of such having returned
with the dog to his vomit, and with the sow that was
washed to her wallowing in the mire. Others have
been made signal monuments of judgment, and set
up as beacons to backsliders. And some who have
had the root of the matter in them, have had such a
storm raised in their consciences, as has made them
a terror to themselves, and all around them ; and it
has cost them much and sore wrestling with God ere
they recovered the light of his countenance. For the

Lord's sake, then, and your own soul's sake, be frequent in this exercise, and grow not remiss therein, lest ye feel the vengeance of God's temple.

Exhort. 3. To parents and masters of families. I beseech and entreat you, by the mercies of God, by the love ye bear to the Lord Jesus, and the regard ye have to the souls of your children and servants, not only to pray in secret yourselves, but by all the means that are competent to you, by command, advice, exhortation, &c. to stir them up to this duty of secret prayer. For motives consider,

1. It was the practice of John the Baptist, yea, and of Christ himself, the great Prophet of the church, Luke xi. 1. Thus this duty comes recommended by the best authority, and the most excellent approved patterns. Christ taught and urged his disciples to pray, and for that end gave them an excellent directory, suited to their then state ; and which ye would do well to make your rule in instructing your children and servants.

2. God expressly commands it, Deut. vi. 7. ' Thou shalt teach them diligently unto thy children, and shalt talk of them when thou sittest in thine house, and when thou walkest by the way, and when thou liest down, and when thou risest up.' Thus they were to be daily employed in this duty, not only to let their children know what they were bound to do, but to press them to the performance of it. And this command being of moral obligation, is equally incumbent upon you that are Christian parents and masters of families ; and ye have far superior advantages for this exercise than the Israelites had, a small part of the bible having been then written ; whereas ye have the whole of it among your hands.

3. God commends the practice in Abraham, Gen. xviii. 19. ' I know him,' says Jehovah, ' that he will command his children, and his household after him, and they shall keep the way of the Lord, to do justice and judgment.' Thus, if thou make conscience

of this duty, thou wilt tread in the steps of the father of the faithful, and receive tokens of the divine approbation, by the Lord's blessing thy family, and prospering thy outward concerns, and be an example to others to excite them to their duty. This will be the ready way to have dutiful and affectionate children, and obedient and careful servants.

4. Consider the engagements which thou tookest on thee at the baptism of thy children, to train them up in the good and holy ways of the Lord ; to inform them of their natural depravity, impotency, and aversion to what is good, of the method of salvation by the obedience and death of Christ ; and to press them to yield themselves to the Lord, by taking hold of his covenant by faith. Thou became then engaged to instruct them in the principles of our holy religion, to show them their duty to God and man, and to observe his ordinances and commandments. And canst thou fulfil these thy engagements, unless thou be at pains to instruct them, and especially to stir them up to the practice of secret prayer.

5. Their souls are committed to thy charge ; and if they perish through thy neglect, their blood will be required at thy hand. Ah ! my friends, Papists and others will rise up in judgment against you, who take more pains on their children, to breed them up in their false and corrupt doctrines, and their idolatrous and superstitious courses, than ye to instruct them in the pure doctrines and precepts of religion. If thou now neglect their religious education and instruction, thy lost children and servants shall curse the day that ever they saw thy face, who tookest no more care of them than of thy beasts. Oh ! let this melancholy consideration excite and stir thee up to thy duty now, lest thy children and servants rise up in judgment against thee, and be a dreadful addition to thy condemnation.

What shall we do then ? may ye say.

1. As soon as they can speak perfectly, give them

a few words to speak to God upon their knees every morning and evening, and see that they do so. Let these words consist of a short confession of sin, an acknowledgment of God's goodness in preservation, and an application for pardon through the blood of Jesus.

2. When they advance farther in years, give them the help of a form, composed chiefly in scripture words, and particularly that which Christ taught his disciples. And be sure to vary and enlarge any form you give them, from time to time ; and in a little time, by reading the bible, and duly considering their own case and wants, they will be able to pray without a set form ; for it is often observed, that where young ones make conscience of practising the helps that are given them, and take pleasure in the duty, the Holy Spirit strikes in with his assistance, and lays suitable matter of prayer before them ; so that even some very young persons have been found to pray with great fluency and fervour, to the admiration of those who happened to overhear them.

3. Pray frequently with your children ; which will be an excellent means to instruct them both as to the matter and manner of the duty, and have a powerful influence upon them to induce them to pray for themselves. And indeed I must say, if parents made more conscience of this practice, in praying with their children, the young ones would not discover such aversion to the duty as many do ; nor would there be such a numerous fry of young prayerless sinners among us, who, though they have not learned to pray, yet are great proficients in speaking vain and idle words, and in cursing and swearing.

4. Furnish them daily with proper materials of prayer, which ye can extract from the Lord's word, your own observation of the state and temper of your souls, the disposition and inclination of your children, the sins and vanities they are most addicted to, your knowledge of their peculiar wants and desires, and

what appears to be suitable to their circumstances
and situation.

5. Carefully observe, whether they perform this
duty or not ; that you may encourage them when
they do well, and check and rebuke them when they
neglect it. Show them that you are influenced by a
regard to the command and authority of God, and
are actuated with a hearty zeal and concern for the
salvation of their souls, in all you do in this matter,
whether respecting the encouragements and advices
you give them, or the rebukes and chastisements you
administer to them, in case of non-compliance, neglect, or careless performance of the duty enjoined.
This will have no small influence upon them to comply with your instructions and directions, and by degrees conquer their aversion to the exercise ; and
you may come, through the divine blessing, to see
the happy fruit of your labours and endeavours.

The only Rule which God hath given to direct his People in their Prayers to him.

First, There is a general rule given us for that
end ; and that is the whole word of God, the scriptures of the Old and New Testament, in which God's
will is revealed, as to all things to be believed or done
by us, 1 John v. 14. ' And this is the confidence that
we have in him, that if we ask any thing according
to his will, he heareth us.' By our bible we may
learn to pray ; for there we are furnished with all
sorts of helps and directions for this duty, as to matter, manner, and words ; and therefore it is a complete directory for prayer.

1. It furnishes us abundantly with matter of prayer, in all the parts of it, petition, confession, &c.
Psal. li. 4, 5. ' Against thee, thee only, have I sinned,

and done this evil in thy sight ; that thou mightest
be justified when thou speakest, and be clear when
thou judgest.   Behold, I was shapen in iniquity ;
and in sin did my mother conceive me ;' Phil. iv. 6.
' Be careful for nothing : but in every thing by prayer and supplication, with thanksgiving, let your requests be made known unto God.'   And whoso has
the word of God dwelling richly in him, will not want
of matter for prayer, for himself or for others.   There
is a storehouse of it there, of great variety ; and we are
welcome to the use of it, agreeable to our own case.
   2. It fully directs us as to the manner of prayer : as,
for instance, that we must pray with sincerity, Heb.
x. 22. ' Let us draw near with a true heart, in full
assurance of faith, having our hearts sprinkled from
an evil conscience, and our bodies washed with pure
water ;' with humility, Psal. x. 17. ' Lord, thou hast
heard the desire of the humble : thou wilt prepare
their heart, thou wilt cause thine ear to hear ;' in
faith, Jam. i. 6 ; and with fervency, Jam. v. 16.
' Confess your faults one to another, and pray one
for another, that ye may be healed.   The effectual
fervent prayer of the righteous man availeth much.'
And there is no qualification necessary in prayer,
but what we may learn from the holy word.
   3. It furnishes us with the most fit words to be
used in prayer.   Do ye want words to express your
desires before the Lord ? He has given us his own
words in the bible, that we may use them according
to our needs, Hos. xiv. 2. ' Take with you words,
and turn to the Lord : say unto him, Take away all
iniquity, and receive us graciously ; so will we render the calves of our lips.'
   Secondly, There is a special rule given us by Jesus
Christ for that end, namely, that form of words which
Christ taught his disciples, commonly called ' The
Lord's prayer ;' that excellent pattern and example
of prayer, composed by Jesus Christ himself for our
direction, which every Christian is obliged to receive

with the utmost reverence, as the Lord's own word.
But it was never imposed by Jesus Christ, or his
apostles, as a set form to which his church is bound
to pray in *these very* words, and no other. It is true,
in the year 618, the Council of Toledo imposed it on
the clergy, under the pain of deposition; but then
Antichrist had mounted the throne, and the Papists
since have superstitiously abused it to this day. I
would all Protestants could plead, Not guilty.

To clear this matter,

1. The Lord's prayer is given us as a directory for
prayer, a pattern and an example, by which we are
to regulate our petitions, and make other prayers by.
This is clear from the text, *After this manner pray
ye,* &c. And it is a most ample directory in few
words, to be eyed by all praying persons, if studied
and understood. There we are taught to pray in a
known tongue, and without vain repetitions, to God
only, and for things allowed; to have chief respect
to the glory of God and our own advantage.

2. It may also be used as a prayer, so that it be
done with understanding, faith, reverence, and other
praying graces. So we own the very words may
lawfully be used, Matt. vi. 9. compared with Luke
xi. 2. See Larger Catechism, quest. 187. and the
Directory for Public Worship, under the title, *Of
prayer after Sermon,* para. 5. Who can refuse this,
since it is a piece of holy scripture, of the Lord's own
word? And they who are so weak, as that they cannot conceive prayer, do well to use this holy form;
though they should endeavour to make further progress in prayer. And sometimes knowing Christians,
under great desertions, not able to conceive prayer,
have used it with good success. But,

3. Our Lord hath not tied us to this very form of
words when we pray to God. This is evident,

(1.) Because the prayers afterwards recorded in the
scripture, were neither this form of words, nor yet
concluded with it. Christ himself used it not in his

prayer at Lazarus's grave, John xi. 41 ; nor in his
last prayer, John xvii. Nor did his apostles, Acts
i. 24 ; nor the Church, Acts iv. 24. &c.

(2.) This prayer is diversely set down by Matthew
and Luke, the only two evangelists that make mention of it. And though it is obvious, that there is an
entire harmony between them, as to the matter and
sense of the words ; yet it is equally obvious to all
who compare them together, that there is some difference as to mode or manner of expression, particularly as to the fourth and fifth petitions ; which certainly there would not have been, had it been designed
for a form of prayer. In Luke, the fourth petition
runs thus, ' Give us day by day our daily bread ;'
but in Matthew, it is thus expressed, ' Give us this
day our daily bread.' The latter contains a petition
for the supply of present wants ; and the former for
the supply of wants as they daily recur upon us :
so that both accounts being compared together, we
are directed to pray for those temporal blessings
which we want at present, and for a supply of those
we stand in need of as they daily recur : which shows
a considerable difference in the expressions. In
Luke, the fifth petition is, ' Forgive us our sins ;
for we also forgive every one that is indebted to us ;'
whereas, in Matthew the expression is very different,
viz. ' Forgive us our debts as we forgive our debtors.' Again, Luke leaves out the doxology, ' For
thine is the kingdom, and the power, and the glory,
for ever. Amen ;' which Matthew adds. From
whence it may be justly inferred, that our Lord's design in furnishing his disciples with this prayer, was
not that they should confine themselves solely to the
manner of expression used therein, without the least
variation ; for then undoubtedly the two evangelists
would have recorded it in the very same words ; but
he rather intended it as a directory respecting the
matter of prayer. So that it is impossible to keep
by the form of words precisely, since it is not one.

It is said, Luke xi. 2. 'When ye pray, say, &c. Here we are tied to the form of words, say our adversaries. *Ans.* By this phrase is to be understood the manner, viz. Say this on the matter, pray after this manner. Compare Matt. vi. 9. If it is to be understood otherwise, then, (1.) According to Matt. x. 7. ' Go, preach, saying, The kingdom of heaven is at hand ;' the disciples preaching was confined to these very words, which we are sure it was not. (2.) It would be unlawful to pray in any other words, which no Christian dare assert. (3.) Neither Papists nor Episcopalians stick to these words in Luke, but use the words in Matthew ; by which they give up the cause.

Further, it may be observed, that our Saviour chiefly intended this prayer as a directory, respecting the matter of our petitions, rather than a form ; because it does not explicitly contain all the parts of prayer, particularly confession of sin, and thankful acknowledgment of mercies. Again, there is no explicit or direct mention of the Mediator, in whose name we are to pray ; nor of his obedience, sufferings, and intercession, on which the efficacy of our prayers is founded, and their success depends : which things are to be supplied from other parts of scripture ; all which, taken together, give us a complete directory for prayer.

From the whole, I think it is evident, that a prayer formed upon the model of this excellent pattern, having the substance of the several petitions interspersed through it, though expressed in other words, is a true scriptural prayer ; and that there is no necessity to conclude with the Lord's prayer. And therefore, I cannot but think, that Papists, and many Protestants, who conclude their prayers with the very words of the Lord's prayer, make a very superstitious use of it ; causing people imagine, that the bare recital of the words of the Lord's prayer sanctifies their other prayers ; and that no prayer can be accepted of God where this, I cannot but call it vain, repetition is omitted. *

....

Directions to aid us in forming right notions of God as a Spirit, infinitely pure and perfect.

1. That God has no body nor bodily parts. *Object.* How then are eyes, ears, hands, face, and the like, attributed in scripture to God ? *Ans.* They are attributed to him not properly, but figuratively ; they are spoken of him after the manner of men, in condescension to our weakness ; but we are to understand them after a sort becoming the Divine Majesty. We are to consider what such bodily parts serve us for, as our eyes for discerning and knowing, our arms for strength, our hands for action, &c. and we are to conceive these things to be in God infinitely, which these parts serve for in us. Thus, when eyes and ears are ascribed to God they signify

* There is a use of words in prayer, to excite and convey, and give vent to affection, Hos. xiv. 2. ' Take with you words and turn to the Lord, and say, take away all iniquity and receive us graciously.' Now these may be considered either when we are alone, or in company.

1. When we are alone. Here take the advice of the Holy Ghost, Eccl. v. 2. ' God is in heaven, and thou art upon earth, therefore let thy words be few.' Few in weight, affecting rather to speak matter than words. Few in conscience. Pray neither too short nor too long ; do it not merely to lengthen out the prayer, or as counting the better for being long. Few with reverence, and managed with that gravity, awfulness, and seriousness, as would become an address to God.

2. In company. There our words must be apt and orderly, moving as much as may be not to God but to the hearers ; managed with such reverence and seriousness as may suit with the gravity of the duty ; conceiving aright of God, particularly that He is, and that He is a Spirit, and they who worship him must worship him in spirit and in truth.

Dr. Manton on the Lord's Prayer.

his omniscience; his hands denote his power, and his face the manifestation of his love and favour.

2. That God is invisible, and cannot be seen with the eyes of the body, no not in heaven; for the glorified body is still a body, and God a Spirit, which is no object of the eyes, more than sound, taste, smell, &c. 1 Tim. i. 17. ' Now, unto the King eternal, immortal, invisible, the only wise God, be honour and glory for ever and ever. Amen.'

3. That God is the most suitable good to the nature of our souls, which are spirits; and can communicate himself, and apply those things to them, which only can render them happy, as he is the God and Father of our spirits.

4. That it is sinful and dishonourable to God, either to make images or pictures of him without us, or to have any image of him in our minds, which our unruly imagination is apt to frame to itself, especially in prayer. For God is the object of our understanding, not of our imagination. God expressly prohibited Israel to frame any similitude or resemblance of him, and tells them, that they had not the least pretence for so doing, inasmuch as they ' saw no similitude of him, when he spake to them in Horeb,' Deut. iv. 12. 15, 16. And, says the prophet, ' To whom will ye liken God? or what likeness will ye compare unto him?' Isa. xl. 18. We cannot form an imaginary idea of our own souls or spirits, which are absolutely invisible to us, and far less of him who is the invisible God, whom no man hath seen or can see. Therefore to frame a picture or an idea of what is invisible, is highly absurd and impracticable; nay, it is gross idolatry, prohibited in the second commandment.

5. That externals in worship are of little value with God, who is a spirit, and requires the heart. They who would be accepted of God must worship him in spirit and in truth, that is, from an apprehension and saving knowledge of what he is in Christ to

poor sinners. And this saving knowledge of God in Christ is attainable in this life : for it is the matter of the divine promise, ' I will give them an heart to know me, that I am the Lord,' Jer. xxiv. 7. ' It is written in the prophets, They shall be all taught of God, John vi. 45. And therefore it should be most earnestly and assiduously sought after by us, as unless we attain to it, we must perish for ever.

That we may know what sort of a spirit God is, we must consider his attributes, which we gather from his word and works, and that two ways : 1. By denying of, and removing from God, in our minds, all imperfection which is in the creatures, Acts xvii. 29. ' Forasmuch then as we are the offspring of God, we ought not to think that the Godhead is like unto gold, or silver, or stone, graven by art and man's device.' And thus we come to the knowledge of his incommunicable attributes, so called because there is no shadow or vestige of them in the creatures, such as infinity, eternity, unchangeableness. 2. By attributing unto him, by way of eminency, whatever is excellent in the creatures, seeing he is the fountain of all perfection in them, Psal. xciv. 9. ' He that planted the ear, shall he not hear ? he that formed the eye, shall he not see ? ' And thus we have his communicable attributes, whereof there are some vestiges and small scantlings in the creature, as being, wisdom, power, &c. amongst which his spirituality is to be reckoned.

Now, both these sorts of attributes in God are not qualities in him distinct from himself, but they are God himself. God's infinity is God himself ; his wisdom is himself ; he is wisdom, goodness, 1 John i. 5. ' This then is the message which we have heard of him, and declare unto you, that God is light, and in him is no darkness at all.' Neither are these attributes so many different things in God ; but they are each of them God himself : for God swears by him-

self, Heb. vi. 13. ' For when God made promise to
Abraham, because he could swear by no greater, he
sware by himself ;' yet he swears by his holiness,
Amos iv. 2. ' The Lord God hath sworn by his holiness, that, lo, the days shall come upon you, that he
will take you away with hooks, and your posterity
with fish-hooks.' He creates by himself, Isa. xliv. 24.
' Thus saith the Lord, thy Redeemer, and he that
formed thee from the womb, I am the Lord that maketh all things ; that stretcheth forth the heavens
alone ; that spreadeth abroad the earth by myself ;'
yet he creates by his power, Rom. i. 20. Therefore
God's attributes are God himself. Neither are these
attributes separable from one another ; for though
we, through weakness, must think and speak of them
separately, yet they are all truly but the one infinite
perfection of the divine nature, which cannot be separated therefrom, without denying that he is an infinitely perfect Being.

*In what God's Attribute of Wisdom is gloriously
displayed.*

1. In the works of creation. The universe is a
bright mirror, wherein the wisdom of God may be
clearly seen. ' The Lord by wisdom made the heavens,' Psal. cxxxvi. 5. ' The Lord by wisdom
hath founded the earth ; by understanding hath he
established the heavens,' Prov. iii. 19. ' He hath established the world by his wisdom, and hath stretched out the heavens by his discretion.' More particularly, the wisdom of God appears, (1.) In the vast
variety of creatures which he hath made. Hence
the Psalmist cries out, ' How manifold are thy works,
O Lord ! in wisdom hast thou made them all,' Psal.
civ. 24. (2.) In the admirable and beautiful order

and situation of the creatures. God hath marshalled every thing in its proper place and sphere. For instance, the sun, by its position displays the infinite wisdom of its Creator. It is placed in the midst of the planets, to enlighten them with its brightness, and inflame them with its heat, and thereby derive to them such benign qualities as make them beneficial to all mixed bodies. If it were raised as high as the stars, the earth would lose its prolific virtue, and remain a dead carcase for want of its quickening heat ; and if it were placed as low as the moon, the air would be inflamed with its excessive heat, the waters would be dried up, and every plant scorched. But at the due distance at which it is placed, it purifies the air, abates the superfluities of the waters, temperately warms the earth, and so serves all the purposes of life and vegetation. It could not be in another position without the disorder and hurt of universal nature. Again, the expansion of the air from the ethereal heavens to the earth is another testimony of divine wisdom : for it is transparent and of a subtile nature, and so a fit medium to convey light and celestial influences to this lower world. Moreover, the situation of the earth doth also trumpet forth the infinite wisdom of its Divine Maker : for it is as it were the pavement of the world, and placed lowermost, as being the heaviest body, and fit to receive the weightiest matter. (3.) In fitting every thing for its proper end and use, so that nothing is unprofitable and useless. After the most diligent and accurate inquiry into the works of God, there is nothing to be found superfluous, and there is nothing defective. (4.) In the subordination of all its parts, to one common end. Though they are of different natures, as lines vastly distant in themselves, yet they all meet in one common centre, namely, the good and preservation of the whole, Hos. ii. 21, 22. ' I will hear, saith the Lord, I will hear the heavens, and they shall hear the earth, and the earth shall

hear the corn and the wine, and the oil, and they
shall hear Jezreel.'

2. In the government of the world. God sits in
his secret place, surrounded with clouds and darkness, holding the rudder of the world in his hand,
and steering its course through all the floatings and
tossings of casualty and contingency to his own appointed ends. There he grasps and turns the great
engine of nature, fastening one pin and loosing another, moving and removing the several wheels of it,
and framing the whole according to the eternal idea
of his own understanding. By his governing providence he directs all the actions of his creatures ; and,
by the secret and efficacious penetration of the divine influence, he powerfully sways and determines
them which way he pleases.

3. In the work of redemption. This is the very
masterpiece of Divine wisdom ; and here shines the
manifold or diversified wisdom of God, Eph. iii. 10.
It appears, (1.) In the contrivance thereof. When
man had ruined himself by sin, all the wisdom of
men and angels could never have devised a method
for his recovery. Heaven seemed to be divided upon
this awful event. Mercy inclined to save man, but
Justice interposed for satisfaction. Justice pleaded
the law and the curse, by which the souls of sinners
are forfeited to vengeance. Mercy, on the other
hand, urged, Shall the Almighty build a glorious
work, and suffer it to lie in eternal ruins ? Shall the
most excellent creature in the inferior world perish
through the subtilty of a malicious and rebellious
spirit ? Shall that arch-rebel triumph for ever, and
raise his trophies from the final ruin of the works of
the Most High ? Shall the reasonable creature lose
the fruition of God, and God lose the subjection and
service of his creature ? And, shall all mankind be
made in vain ? Mercy further pleaded, That if the
rigorous demands of Justice be heard, it must lie an
obscure and unregarded attribute in the divine essence

L

for ever ; that it alone must be excluded, while all
the rest of the attributes had their share of honour.
Thus the case was infinitely difficult, and not to be
unravelled by the united wit of all the celestial spirits.
A bench of angels was incapable to contrive a method of reconciling infinite mercy with inflexible justice, of satisfying the demands of the one, and granting the requests of the other.   In this hard exigence
the wisdom of God interposed, and in the vast treasure of its incomprehensible light, found out an admirable expedient to save man without prejudice to
the other divine perfections.   The pleas of Justice,
said the wisdom of God, shall be satisfied in punishing, and the requests of Mercy shall be granted in
pardoning.   Justice shall not complain for want of
punishment, nor Mercy for want of compassion ; I
will have an infinite sacrifice to content Justice, and
the virtue and fruit of that sacrifice shall delight
Mercy.   Here Justice shall have punishment to accept, and Mercy shall have pardon to bestow.   My
Son shall die, and satisfy Justice by his death ; and
by the virtue and merit of that sacrifice sinners shall
be received into favour, and herein Mercy shall triumph and be glorified.   Here was the most glorious
display of wisdom.   (2.) In the ordination of a Mediator every way fitly qualified to reconcile men unto
God.   A Mediator must be capable of the sentiments
and affections of both the parties he is to reconcile,
and a just esteemer of the rights and injuries of the
one and the other, and have a common interest in
both.   The Son of God, by his incarnation, perfectly
possesses all these qualities.   He hath a nature to
please God, and a nature to please sinners.   He had
both the perfections of the Deity, and all the qualities
and sinless infirmities of the humanity.   The one
fitted him for things pertaining to God, and the
other furnished him with a sense of the infirmities of
man.   This union of the divine and human nature in
the person of Christ was necessary to fit and qualify

him for the discharge of his threefold office of Prophet, Priest, and King.—As a Prophet, it was requisite he should be God, that so he might acquaint us with his Father's will, and reveal the secret purposes and hidden counsels of heaven concerning our salvation, which were locked up in the bosom of God from all eternity. And it was needful he should be man, that he might converse with poor sinners in a familiar manner, and convey the mind and counsels of God to them, in such a way as they could receive them. —As a Priest, he behoved to be a man, that so he might be capable to suffer, and to bear the wrath which the sins of the elect had justly deserved. And it behoved him to be God, to render his temporary sufferings satisfactory. The great dignity and excellency of the divine Mediator's person made his sufferings of infinite value in God's account. Though he only suffered as a man, yet he satisfied as God.—As a King, he must be God, to conquer Satan, convert an elect world, and effectually subdue the lusts and corruptions of men. And he must be man, that by the excellency of his example, he might lead us in the way of life. (3.) In the manner whereby this redemption is accomplished, namely, by the humiliation of the Son of God. By this he counteracted the sin of angels and men. Pride is the poison of every sin : for in every transgression the creature prefers his pleasure to and sets up his own will above God's. This was the special sin of Adam. The devil would have levelled heaven by an unpardonable usurpation. He said in his heart, *I will be like the Most High ;* and man, infected with his breath (when he said, *Ye shall be like gods*), became sick of the same disease. Now the Divine Redeemer, that he might cure our disease in its source and cause by the quality of the remedy, applied to our pride an unspeakable humility. Man was guilty of the highest robbery in affecting to be equal with God ; and the Son, who was in the bosom of God, and equal to him in majesty and authority, emptied himself by assuming the human nature in its servile state, Phil. ii. 6, 7, 8. It is said, John i. 14. 'The word was made flesh.' The meanest part of our nature is specified to signify the greatness of his abasement. There is such an infinite distance between God and flesh, that the condescension is as admirable as the contrivance. So great was the malignity of human pride, that such a profound humility was requisite for the cure of it. And by this Christ destroyed the works of the devil. (4.) In appointing such contemptible, and in appearance opposite means, to bring about such glorious effects. The way is as admirable as the work. Christ ruined the devil's empire by the very same nature that he had vanquished, and by the very means which he had made use of to establish and confirm it. He took not upon him the nature of angels, which is equal to Satan in strength and power ; but he took part of flesh and blood, that he might the more signally triumph over that proud spirit in the human nature, which was inferior to his, and had been vanquished by him in paradise. For this end he did not immediately exercise omnipotent power to destroy him, but managed our weakness to foil the roaring lion. He did not enter the lists with Satan in the glory of his Deity, but disguised under the human nature which was subject to mortality. And thus the devil was overcome in the same nature over which he first got the victory. For as the whole race of mankind was captivated by him in Adam the representative, so believers are made victorious over him by the conquest which their representative obtained in the whole course of his sufferings. As our ruin was effected by the subtilty of Satan, so our recovery is wrought by the wisdom of God, who takes the wise in their own craftiness. Thus eternal life springs from death, glory from ignominy, and blessedness from a curse. We are healed by stripes, quickened by death, purchased by blood, crowned by a cross, advanced to the highest honour by the lowest humility, comforted by sorrows, glorified by disgrace, absolved by condemnation, and made rich by poverty. Thus the wisdom of God shines with a radiant brightness in the work of redemption.

In what God's Attribute of Power is gloriously displayed.

1. In the creation of the world, Rom. i. 20. ' For the invisible things of him from the creation of the world are clearly seen, being understood by the things that are made, even his eternal power and Godhead.' O how great must that power be, which produced the beautiful fabric of the universe, without the concurrence of any material cause! This proclaims it to be truly infinite : for nothing less could make such distant extremes as nothing and being to meet together. All this was done by a word, one simple act of his will ; for ' he spake, and it was done ; he commanded, and it stood fast,' Psal. xxxiii. 9.

2. In the preservation of the world, and all things therein. He ' upholdeth all things by the word of his power,' Heb. i. 3. He preserves all the creatures in their proper place, for their proper use and end. It is by the Divine Power that the heavenly bodies have constantly rolled about in their spheres for so many ages, without wearing or moving out of their proper course ; and that the tumultuous elements have persisted in their order to this very day. He preserves the confederacies of nature, sets bounds to the raging sea, and keeps it within its limits by a girdle of sand. He is the powerful Preserver of man and beast. He preserves them in their kind and species, by the constant succession of them one after another ; so that, though the individuals perish yet

the species continues. O what a mighty power must that be that sustains so many creatures, sets bounds to the raging sea, holds the wind in his fists, and preserves a comely order and sweet harmony among all the creatures!

3. In the government of the world. He is the supreme Rector of the universe, and manages all things, so that they contribute to the advancement of his own glory, and the advantage of his people. By his governing providence he directs all the actions and motions of his creatures, and powerfully determines them which way soever he pleases. All the creatures are called his host, because he marshals them as an army to serve his important purposes. The whole system of nature is ready to favour and act for men when he commands it, and it is ready to punish them when he gives it a commission. Thus he checked the Red Sea, and it obeyed his voice, Psal. cvi. 9. Its rapid motion quickly ceased, and the fluid waters were immediately ranged as defensive walls to secure the march of his people. At the command of God, the sea again recovered its wonted violence, and the watery walls came tumbling down upon the heads of the proud Egyptian oppressor and his host. The sea so exactly obeyed its orders, that not one Israelite was drowned, and not one Egyptian was saved alive. More particularly, the power of God appears in the moral government of the world.

(1.) In governing and ordering the hearts of men, so that they are not masters of their own affections, but often act quite contrary to what they had firmly resolved and purposed. Of which we have eminent instances in Esau and Balaam. He hath the hearts of all men in his hands, and can turn them what way he pleases. Thus he bent the hearts of the Egyptians to favour the Israelites, by sending them away with great riches given them by way of loan. He turned Jehoshaphat's enemies from him when they came with a purpose to destroy him, 2 Chron. xviii.

31. ' And it came to pass, when the captains of the chariots saw Jehoshaphat, that they said, It is the king of Israel ; therefore they compassed about him to fight : but Jehoshaphat cried out, and the Lord helped him : and God moved them to depart from him.'

(2.) In governing and managing the most stubborn creatures, as devils and wicked men. 1st. In his governing devils. They have great power, and are full of malice. The devil is always going about as a roaring lion, seeking whom he may devour. We could have no quiet nor safety in the world, if his power were not restrained, and his malice curbed by one that is mightier than the infernal fiend. He would turn all things topsy-turvy, plague the world, burn cities and houses, and plunder us of all the supports of life, if he were not held in a chain by the Omnipotent Governor of the world. But God overmasters his strength, so that he cannot move one hair's breadth beyond his tether. God has all the devils chained, and he governs all their motions. The devil could not touch Job in his person and goods without the divine permission ; nor could he enter into the Gadarene swine without a special licence. If we consider the great malice of these invisible enemies, and the vast extent of their power, we will easily see that there could be no safety or security for men, if they were not curbed and restrained by a superior power. 2d. In governing wicked men. All the imaginations of their hearts are evil, and only evil continually. They are fully bent upon mischief, and drink iniquity like water. What unbridled licentiousness and headstrong fury would triumph in the world, and run with a rapid violence, if the Divine Power did not interpose to bear down the flood gates of it ? Human society would be rooted up, the whole world drenched in blood, and all things would run into a sea of confusion, if God did not bridle and restrain the lusts and corruptions of men. The king

of Assyria triumphed much in his design against
Jerusalem; but how did God govern and manage
that wild ass! Isa. xxxvii. 29. ' I will put my hook
into thy nose, (says Jehovah), and my bridle in thy
lips, and I will turn thee back by the way by which
thou camest.' And we are told, Psal. lxxvi. 10. that
' the very wrath of man shall praise him, and that he
will restrain the remainder of wrath.'

(3.) In raising up a church to himself in spite of
all his enemies. This is specially seen in founding
the New Testament church, and propagating the
gospel through the world. The power of God appears admirable in planting the gospel, and converting the world to Christianity. For there were many
and great difficulties in the way, as gross and exe-
crable idolatry; and the nations were strongly confirmed and rooted in their idolatry, being trained up
and inured to it from their infant state. It was as
hard to make the Gentiles forsake the religion which
they received from their birth, as to make the Afri-
cans change their skin, and the leopard his spots.
The Pagan religion was derived from their progeni-
tors through a long succession of ages. Hence the
heathens accused the Christian religion of novelty,
and urged nothing more plausibly than the argument of immemorial prescription for their superstition. They would not consider whether it was just
and reasonable, but with a blind deference yielded up
themselves to the authority of the ancients. The
pomp of the Pagan worship was very pleasing to the
flesh; the magnificence of their temples, adorned
with the trophies of superstition, their mysterious
ceremonies, their music, their processions, their
images and altars, their sacrifices and purifications,
and the rest of the equipage of a carnal religion,
drew their respects and strongly affected their minds
through their senses. Whereas the religion of the
gospel is spiritual and serious, holy and pure, and
hath nothing to move the carnal part. There was

then an universal depravation of manners among men ; the whole earth was covered with abominations : the most unnatural lusts had lost the fear and shame that naturally attends them. We may see a melancholy picture of their most abandoned conversation, Rom. i. The powers of the world were bent against the gospel. The heathen philosophers strongly opposed it. When Paul preached at Athens, the Epicureans and Stoics entertained him with scorn and derision ; ' What will this babbler say ?' said they. The heathen priests conspired to obstruct it. The princes of the world thought themselves obliged to prevent the introduction of a new religion, lest their empire should be in hazard, or the greatness and majesty of it impaired thereby. If we consider the means by which the gospel was propagated, the Divine power will evidently appear. The persons employed in this great work were a few illiterate fishermen, with a publican and a tentmaker, without authority and power to force men to obedience, and without the charms of eloquence to enforce the belief of the doctrines which they taught. Yet this doctrine prevailed, and the gospel had wonderful success through all the parts of the then known world, and that against all the power and policy of men and devils. Now, how could this possibly be, without a mighty operation of the power of God upon the hearts of men ?

(4.) In preserving, defending, and supporting his church under the most terrible tempests of trouble and persecution which were raised against her. This is promised by our blessed Saviour, Matt. xvi. 18. ' The gates of hell shall not prevail against it.' The most flourishing monarchies have decayed and wasted, and the strongest kingdoms have been broken in pieces ; yet the church hath been preserved to this very day, notwithstanding all the subtle and potent enemies which in all ages have been pushing at her. Yea, God has preserved and delivered his church in

M

the greatest extremities, when the danger in all human appearance was unavoidable ; as in Egypt, at the Red Sea, and in Esther's days, when a bloody decree was issued to slay all the Jews.   Yea, God hath sometimes delivered his church by very weak and contemptible-like instruments, such as Moses, a fugitive from Egypt, and Aaron, a poor captive in it ; and sometimes by very unlikely means, as when he smote Egypt with armies of locusts and lice.   In all ages of the world God has gloriously displayed his power in the preservation of his church and people, notwithstanding all the rage, power, and malice of their enemies.

(5.) In the conversion of the elect.   Hence the gospel, which is the means and instrument of conversion, is called *the power of God*, and *the rod of his strength ;* and the day of the success of the gospel in turning sinners to Christ, is called *the day of his power*, Psal. cx. 2.   O what a mighty power must that be that stills the waves of a tempestuous sea, quells the lusts and stubbornness of the heart, demolishes the strong holds of sin in the soul, routs all the armies of corrupt nature, and makes the obstinate rebellious will strike sail to Christ ! The power of God that is exerted here makes a man to think on other objects, and speak in another strain, than he did before.   O how admirable is it, that carnal reason should be thus silenced ; that legions of devils should be thus driven out ; and that men should part with those sins which before they esteemed their chiefest ornaments, and stand at defiance with all the charming allurements and bitter discouragements of the world? The same power that raised Christ from the grave is exerted in the conversion of a sinner, Eph. i. 19, 20.   There is greater power exerted in this case than there was in the creation of the world.   For when God made the world, he met with no opposition : he spake the word, and it was done : but when he comes to convert a sinner, he meets with all the opposition which the devil and a corrupt heart can make against him. God wrought but one miracle in the creation : he spake the word and it was done ; but there are many miracles wrought in conversion. The blind is made to see, the dead raised, and the deaf hears the voice of the Son of God. O the infinite power of Jehovah! In this work the mighty arm of the Lord is revealed.

(6.) In preserving the souls of believers amidst the many dangers to which they are exposed, and bringing them safely to glory at last. They have many enemies without, a legion of subtle and powerful devils, and a wicked and ensnaring world, with all its allurements and temptations ; and they have many strong lusts and corruptions within ; and their graces are but weak, and in their infancy and minority, while they are here : So that it may justly be matter of wonder how they are preserved. But the apostle tells us, that they ' are kept by the power of God through faith unto salvation,' 1 Pet. i. 5. Indwelling corruption would soon quench grace in their hearts, if it were not kept alive by a Divine power. But Christ hath pledged his faithfulness for it, that they shall be kept secure, John x. 28. It is his power that moderates the violence of temptations, supports his people under them, defeats the power of Satan, and bruises him under their feet.

4. *Lastly*, The power of God appears gloriously in the redemption of sinners by Jesus Christ. Hence in scripture Christ is called *the power* as well as *the wisdom of God*. This is the most admirable work that ever God brought forth in the world. More particularly,

(1.) The power of God shines in Christ's miraculous conception in the womb of a virgin. The power of the Highest did overshadow her, Luke i. 35. and by a creative act framed the humanity of Christ of the substance of the virgin's body, and united it to the Divinity. This was foretold many ages before as the effect of the divine power. When Judah was oppressed by two potent kings, and despaired of any escape and deliverance to raise their drooping spirits, the prophet tells them, that he would give them a sign ; and a wonderful one it was. Therefore it is said 'Behold a virgin shall conceive, and bear a son, and shall call his name Emmanuel,' Isa. vii. 14. The argument is from the greater to the less : For if God will accomplish that stupendous and unheard-of wonder, much more will he rescue his people from the fury of their adversaries.

(2.) In uniting the divine and human nature in the person of Christ, and that without any confusion of the two natures, or changing the one into the other. The two natures of Christ are not mixed together, as liquors that incorporate with one another, when poured into the same vessel. The divine nature is not turned into the human, nor the human into the divine. One nature doth not swallow up another, and make a third distinct from both. But they are distinct, and yet united : conjoined, and yet unmixed : the properties of each nature are preserved entire. O what a wonder of power was here ! that two natures, a divine and a human, infinitely distant in themselves, should meet together in a personal conjunction ! Here one equal with God is found in the form of a servant ; here God and man are united in one ; the Creator and the creature are miraculously allied in the same subsistence. Here a God of unmixed blessedness is linked personally with a man of perpetual sorrows. That is an admirable expression, 'The Word was made flesh,' John i. 14. What can be more miraculous than for God to become man, and man to become God ? that a person possessed of all the perfections and excellencies of the Deity should inherit all the infirmities and imperfections of humanity, sin only excepted ? Was there not need of infinite power, to bring together terms which were so far asunder ? Nothing less than an omnipotent power could effect and bring about what an infinite and incomprehensible wisdom did project in this matter.

(3.) In supporting the human nature of Christ, and keeping it from sinking under the terrible weight of divine wrath that came upon him for our sins, and making him victorious over the devil and all the powers of darkness. His human nature could not possibly have borne up under the wrath of God and the curse of the law, nor held out under such fearful contests with the powers of hell and the world, if it had not been upheld by infinite power. Hence his Father says concerning him, Isa. xlii. 1. ' Behold my Servant whom I uphold.'

(4.) The Divine power did evidently appear in raising Christ from the dead. The apostle tells us, that God exerted his mighty power in Christ when he raised him from the dead, Eph. i. 19. The unlocking the belly of the whale for the deliverance of Jonah, the rescue of Daniel from the den of lions, and restraining the fire from burning the three children, were signal declarations of the Divine power, and types of the resurrection of our Redeemer. But all these are nothing to what is represented by them : for that was a power over natural causes, and curbing of beasts and restraining of elements ; but in the resurrection of Christ, God exercised a power over himself, and quenched the flames of his own wrath, that was hotter than millions of Nebuchadnezzar's furnaces : he unlocked the prison doors wherein the curses of the law had lodged our Saviour, stronger than the belly and ribs of a leviathan. How admirable was it, that he should be raised from under the curse of the law, and the infinite weight of our sins, and brought forth with success and glory after his sharp encounter with the powers of hell! In this the power of God was gloriously manifested. Hence he is said to be raised from the dead ' by the glory of the Father,' *i. e.* by his glorious power ; and ' de-

clared to be the Son of God with power, by the resurrection from the dead,' Rom. i. 4. All the miraculous proofs by which God acknowledged him
for his Son during his life, had been ineffectual without this. If he had remained in the grave, it had
been reasonable to believe him only an ordinary person, and that his death had been the just punishment of his presumption in calling himself the Son
of God. But his resurrection from the dead was the
most illustrious and convincing evidence, that really
he was what he declared himself to be.

In what God's glorious Attribute of Holiness is manifested.

1. In his word ; and that both in the precepts and
promises thereof, God manifested his hatred and detestation of sin, even in a variety of sacrifices under
the ceremonial law ; and the occasional washings
and sprinklings upon ceremonial defilements, which
polluted only the body, were a clear proof that every
thing that had a resemblance to evil was loathsome
to God. All the legal sacrifices, washings, and purifications, were designed to express what an evil sin
is, and how hateful and abominable it is to him.
But the holiness of God is most remarkably expressed in the moral law. Hence *the law* is said to be
holy, Rom. vii. 12. It is a true transcript of the holiness of God. And it is holy in its precepts. It requires an exact, perfect, and complete holiness in the
whole man, in every faculty of the soul, and in every
member of the body. It is holy in its prohibitions. It
forbids and condemns all impurity and filthiness
whatsoever It discharges not only sinful words
and actions, gross and atrocious crimes, and profane, blasphemous, and unprofitable speeches, but all

sinful thoughts and irregular motions of the heart.
Hence is that exhortation, Jer. iv. 14. 'O Jerusalem,
wash thine heart from wickedness, that thou mayest
be saved : how long shall thy vain thoughts lodge
within thee ?' It is holy in its threatenings. All
these have their fundamental root in the holiness of
God, and are a branch of this essential perfection.
All the terrible threatenings annexed to the law are
declarations of the holiness and purity of God, and of
his infinite hatred and detestation of sin.

Again, the holiness of God appears in the promises
of the word. They are called *holy promises*, Psal.
cv. 42. and they are designed to promote and encourage true holiness. Hence, says the apostle, 2 Cor.
vii. 1. 'Having these promises, let us cleanse ourselves from all filthiness of the flesh and spirit, perfecting holiness in the fear of the Lord.' By them
we are 'made partakers of a divine nature,' 2 Pet.
i. 4.

2. The holiness of God is manifested in his works.
Hence the Psalmist saith, ' The Lord is holy in all
his works,' Psal. cxlv. 17. More particularly,

(1.) The divine holiness appears in the creation of
man. Solomon tells us, Eccl. vii. 29. that ' God
made man upright ;' and Moses says, that he was
' made after the image of God,' Gen. i. 27. Now,
the image of God in man consists chiefly in holiness.
Therefore the *new man* is said to be ' created after
God in righteousness and true holiness,' Eph. iv 24.
Adam was made with a perfection of grace. There
was an entire and universal rectitude in all its faculties, disposing them to their proper operations. There
was no disorder among his affections, but a perfect
agreement between the flesh and the spirit ; and they
both joined in the service of God. He fully obeyed
the first and great command, of loving the Lord
with all his soul and strength, and his love to other
things was regulated by his love to God. When
Adam dropt from the creating finger of God, he had

knowledge in his understanding, sanctity in his will, and rectitude in his affections. There was such a harmony among all his faculties, that his members yielded to his affections, his affections to his will, his will obeyed his reason, and his reason was subject to the law of God. Here then was a display of the Divine purity.

(2.) In the works of Providence : particularly in his judicial proceedings against sinners for the violation of his holy and righteous laws. All the fearful judgments which have been poured down upon sinners, spring from God's holiness and hatred of sin. All the dreadful storms and tempests in the world are blown up by it. All diseases and sicknesses, wars, pestilence, plagues, and famines, are designed to vindicate God's holiness and hatred of sin. And therefore, when God had smitten the two sons of Aaron for offering strange fire, he says, ' I will be sanctified in them that draw nigh me, and before all the congregation I will be glorified,' Lev. x. 3. He glorified himself in declaring by that act, before all the people, that he is a holy God, that cannot endure sin and disobedience. More particularly,

[1.] God's holiness and hatred of sin is clearly manifested in his punishing the angels that sinned. It is said, 2 Pet. ii. 4. ' God spared not the angels that sinned, but cast them down to hell, and delivered them into chains of darkness, to be reserved unto judgment.' Neither their mighty numbers, nor the nobility of their natures, could incline their offended Sovereign to spare them ; they were immediately turned out of heaven, and expelled from the Divine presence. Their case is hopeless and helpless ; no mercy will ever be shown to one of them, being under the blackness of darkness for ever.

[2.] In the punishment threatened and inflicted on man for his first apostacy from God. Man in his first state was the friend and favourite of heaven ; by his extraction and descent he was the Son of God, a little lower than the angels ; consecrated and crowned for the service of his Maker, and appointed as king over the inferior world; he was placed in paradise, the garden of God, and admitted to fellowship and communion with him. But sin hath divested him of all his dignity and glory. By his rebellion against his Creator, he made a forfeiture of his dominion, and so lost the obedience of the sensible creatures, and the service of the insensible. He was thrust out of paradise, banished from the presence of God, and debarred from fellowship and communion with him. God immediately sentenced him and all his posterity to misery, death, and ruin. This is a clear demonstration of the infinite purity and holiness of God. But blessed be God, for Jesus Christ, the second Adam, who hath restored that which the first Adam took away.

[3.] In executing terrible and strange judgments upon sinners. It was for sin that God drowned the old world with a deluge of water, rained hell out of heaven upon Sodom and Gomorrah, and made the earth open her mouth, and swallow up Korah, Dathan, and Abiram. It was for sin that God brought terrible destroying judgments upon Jerusalem. All calamities and judgments spring from this bitter root, as sword, pestilence, distempers of body, perplexities of mind, poverty, reproach, and disgrace, and whatever is grievous and afflictive to men. All this shows how hateful sin is to God.

[4.] In punishing sins seemingly small with great and heavy judgments. A multitude of angels were sent down to hell for an aspiring thought, as some think. Uzzah, a good man, was struck dead in a moment for touching the ark ; yea, fifty thousand Bethshemites were smitten dead for looking into it. We are apt to entertain slight thoughts of many sins : but God hath set forth some as examples of his hatred and abhorrence of sins seemingly small, for a warning to others, and a testimony and demonstration of his exact holiness.

[5.] In bringing heavy afflictions on his own people for sin. Even the sins of believers in Christ do sometimes cost them very dear. He will not suffer them to pass without correction for their transgressions. Though they are exempted from everlasting torments in hell, yet they are not spared from the furnace of affliction here on earth. We have instances of this in David, Solomon, Jonah, and other saints. Yea, sometimes God in this life, punishes sin more severely in his own people than in other men. Moses was excluded from the land of Canaan but for speaking unadvisedly with his lips, though many greater sinners were suffered to enter in. Such severity towards his own people is a plain demonstration that God hates sin as sin, and not because the worst men commit it.

[6.] In sentencing so many of Adam's posterity to everlasting torments for sin. That an infinitely good God, who is goodness itself, and delights in mercy, should adjudge so many of his own creatures to the everlasting pains and torments of hell, must proceed from his infinite holiness, on account of something infinitely detested and abhorred by him.

3. The holiness of God appears in our redemption by Jesus Christ. Here his love to holiness and his hatred of sin is most conspicuous. All the demonstrations that ever God gave of his hatred of sin were nothing in comparison of this. Neither all the vials of wrath and judgment which God hath poured out since the world began, nor the flaming furnace of a sinner's conscience, nor the groans and roarings of the damned in hell, nor that irreversible sentence pronounced against the fallen angels, do afford such a demonstration of the Divine holiness, and hatred of sin, as the death and sufferings of the blessed Redeemer. This will appear, if ye consider,

(1.) The great dignity and excellency of his person.

He was the eternal and only begotten Son of God, the brightness of his Father's glory, and the express image of his person. Yet he must descend from the throne of his majesty, divest himself of his robes of insupportable light, take upon him the form of a servant, become a curse, and bleed to death for sin. Did ever sin appear so hateful to God as here? To demonstrate God's infinite holiness, and hatred of sin, he would have the most glorious and most excellent person in heaven and earth to suffer for it. He would have his own Son to die on a disgraceful cross, and be exposed to the terrible flames of Divine wrath, rather than sin should live, and his holiness remain for ever disparaged by the violations of his law.

(2.) How dear he was to his Father. He was his only begotten Son, he had not another ; the only darling and the chief delight of his soul, who had lain in his bosom from all eternity. Yet as dear as he was to God, he would not and could not spare him, when he stood charged with his people's sins. For saith the apostle, Rom. viii. 32. 'God spared not his own Son, but delivered him up for us all.' As he spared him not in a way of free bounty, giving him freely as a ransom for their souls ! so he spared him not in a way of vindictive justice, but exacted the utmost mite of satisfaction from him for their sins.

(3.) The greatness of his sufferings. Indeed the extremity of his sufferings cannot be expressed. Insensible nature, as if it had been capable of understanding and affection, was disordered in its whole frame at his death. The sun forsook his shining, and clothed the whole heavens in black ; so that the air was dark at noon-day, as if it had been midnight. The earth shook and trembled, the rocks were rent asunder, and universal nature shrank. Christ suffered all that wrath which was due to the elect for their sins. His sufferings were equivalent to those of the damned. He suffered a punishment of loss : for all the comforting influences of the Spirit were suspended for a time. The Divine nature kept back all its joys from the human nature of Christ, in the time of his greatest sufferings. We deserved to have been separated from God for ever ; and therefore our Redeemer was deserted for a time. There was a suspension of all joy and comfort from his soul, when he needed it most. This was most afflicting and cutting to him, who had never seen a frown in his Father's face before. It made him cry out with a lamentable accent, ' My God, my God, why hast thou forsaken me ?' Again, he suffered a punishment of sense, and that with respect to both his body and soul. The elect had forfeited both soul and body to Divine vengeance; and therefore Christ suffered in both. The sufferings of his body were indeed terrible. It was filled with exquisite torture and pain. His hands and his feet, the most sensible parts were pierced with nails. His body was distended with such pains and torments as when all the parts are out of joint. Hence it is said of him, Psal. xxii. 14, 15. ' I am poured out like water, and all my bones are out of joint : my heart is like wax, it is melted in the midst of my bowels, my strength is dried up like a potsherd ; and my tongue cleaveth to my jaws ; and thou hast brought me unto the dust of death.' Now, thus did the Son of God suffer. His pure and blessed hands, which were never stretched out but to do good, were pierced and rent asunder ; and those feet which bore the Redeemer of the world, and for which the very waters had a reverence, were nailed to a tree. His body, which was the precious workmanship of the Holy Ghost, and the temple of the Deity, was destroyed. But his bodily sufferings were but the body of his sufferings. It was the sufferings of his soul that was the soul of his sufferings. No tongue can tell you what he endured here. When all the comforting influences of the Spirit were suspended, then an impetuous torrent of unmixed sorrows broke into his soul. O what agonies and conflicts, what sharp encounters, and distresses did he meet with from the wrath of God that was poured out upon him! He bore the wrath of an angry God, pure wrath without any allay or mixture, and all that wrath which was due to the elect through all eternity for their innumerable sins. Sin was so hateful to God, that nothing could expiate it, or satisfy for it, but the death and bitter agonies of his dear Son.

(4.) Consider the cause of his sufferings. It was not for any sin of his own, for he had none, being holy, harmless, undefiled, and separate from sinners. They were made his only by a voluntary susception, by taking his people's sins upon him. And though they were only imputed to him, yet God would not spare him. So that there is nothing wherein the Divine holiness and hatred of sin is so manifest as in the sufferings of his own dear Son. This was a greater demonstration thereof than if all men and angels had suffered for it eternally in hell-fire.

....

In what God's awful Attribute of Justice is manifested.

1. In the temporal judgments which he brings upon sinners even in this life. The saints own this, Neh. ix. 33. 'Thou art just in all that is brought upon us.' The end and design of all God's judgments is to witness to the world, that he is a just and righteous God. All the fearful plagues and terrible judgments which God has brought upon the world proclaim and manifest his justice.

2. In sentencing so many of Adam's posterity to everlasting pains and torments for sin, according to that dreadful sentence which shall be pronounced at the last day, Matt. xxv. 41. 'Depart from me, ye cur-

sed, into everlasting fire, prepared for the devil and
his angels.' If you could descend into the bottomless
pit, and view the pains and torments of hell, and hear
the terrible shrieks and roarings of the damned wallowing in these sulphureous flames, you could not shun
to cry out, O the severity of divine justice ! Though
they are the works of God's own hands, and roar
and cry under their torments, yet they cannot obtain
any mitigation of their pains, nay, not so much as one
drop of water to cool their tongues. That an infinitely good and gracious God, that delights in mercy,
should thus torment so many of his own creatures,
O how incorruptible must his justice be !

3. In the death and sufferings of Christ. God gave
his beloved Son to the death for this end, that it might
be known what a just and righteous God he is. So
the apostle shows us, Rom. iii. 25. ' Whom God hath
set forth to be a propitiation, through faith in his
blood, to declare his righteousness,' &c. He set him
forth in garments rolled in blood, to declare his justice and righteousness to the world. After man
turned rebel, and apostatised from God, there was no
way to keep up the credit and honour of Divine justice, but either a strict execution of the law's sentence,
or a full satisfaction. The execution would have
destroyed the whole race of Adam. Therefore Christ
stepped in, and made a sufficient satisfaction by his
death and sufferings, that so God might exercise his
mercy without prejudice to his justice. Thus the
blood of the Son of God must be shed for sin, to let
the world see that he is a just and righteous God.
The justice of God could and would be satisfied with
no less. Hence it is said, Romans viii. 32. ' God
spared not his own Son, but delivered him up to the
death for us all.' If forbearance might have been
expected from any, surely it might from God, who is
full of pity and tender mercy : yet God in this case
spared him not. If one might have expected sparing
mercy and abatement from any, surely Christ might

most of all expect it from his own Father; yet God spared not his own Son. Sparing mercy is the lowest degree of mercy; yet it was denied to Christ, when he stood in the room of the elect. God abated him not a minute of the time appointed for his sufferings, nor one degree of the wrath which he was to bear. Nay, though in the garden, when Christ fell on the ground, and put up that lamentable and pitiful cry, ' Father, if it be possible, let this cup pass from me;' yet no abatement was granted to him. The Father of mercies saw his dear Son humbled in his presence, and yet dealt with him in extreme severity. The sword of justice was in a manner asleep before, in all the terrible judgments which had been executed on the world, but now it must be awakened and roused up to pierce the heart of the blessed Redeemer. Hence it is said, Zech. xiii. 7. ' Awake, O sword, against my shepherd, and against the man that is my fellow, saith the Lord of hosts : smite the shepherd.' If divine justice had descended from heaven in a visible form, and hanged up millions of sinners in chains of wrath, it had not been such a demonstration of the wrath of God, and his hatred of sin, as the death and sufferings of his own Son. When we hear that God exposed his own Son to the utmost severity of wrath and vengeance, may we not justly cry out, O the infinite evil of sin! O the inflexible severity of Divine justice! It is a fearful thing to fall into the hands of the living God!

4. The justice of God will be clearly manifested at the great day. God hath reared up many trophies already to the honour of his power and justice out of the ruins of his most insolent enemies ; but then will be the most solemn triumph of Divine justice. The apostle tells us, Acts xvii. 31. that ' he hath appointed a day in the which he will judge the world in righteousness, by that man whom he hath ordained : whereof he hath given assurance unto all men, in that he hath raised him from the dead. On that

awful day the justice and righteousness of God shall
be clearly revealed, therefore it is called ' the day of
the revelation of the righteous judgment of God,'
Rom. ii. 5. The equity of God's dealings and dispensations is not now so fully seen : but all will be
open and manifest on that day. Then he will liberally reward the righteous, and severely punish the
wicked.

5. God's justice will shine for ever in the torments
of the damned in hell. The smoke of their furnace,
their yellings and roarings, will proclaim through eternity the inexorable justice and severity of God. It
is not enough for the satisfaction of his justice to deprive them of heaven and happiness ; but he will inflict the most tormenting punishment upon sense and
conscience in hell For as both soul and body were
guilty in this life, the one as the guide, the other as
the instrument of sin, so it is but just and equal that
they should both feel the penal effects of it hereafter.
Sinners shall then be tormented in that wherein they
most delighted ; they shall then be invested with
those objects which will cause the most dolorous per-
ceptions in their sensitive faculties. The lake of
fire and brimstone, the blackness of darkness, for
ever, are words of a terrible signification. But no
words can fully express the terrible ingredients of
their misery. Their punishment will be in proportion to the glory of God's majesty that is provoked,
and the extent of his power. And as the soul was
the principal, and the body but an accessary in the
works of sin ; so its capacious faculties shall be far
more tormented than the limited faculties of the outward senses. The fiery attributes of God shall be
transmitted through the glass of conscience, and con-
centred upon damned spirits. The fire without will
not be so tormenting as the fire within them. Then
all the tormenting passions will be inflamed. What
rancour, reluctance, and rage, will there be against
the just power that sentenced them to hell ! what

impatience and indignation against themselves for
their wilful and inexcusable sins, the just cause of it !
How will they curse their creation, and wish their
utter extinction as the final remedy of their misery !
But all their ardent wishes will be in vain. For the
guilt of sin will never be expiated, nor God so far reconciled as to annihilate them. As long as there is
justice in heaven, or fire in hell, as long as God and
eternity shall continue, they must suffer those torments which the strength and patience of an angel
cannot bear one hour. The justice of God will
blaze forth for ever in the agonies and torments of
the damned.

....

*Plausible Objections to the Justice of God stated
and answered.*

Object. 1. If God be infinitely just and righteous,
how stands it with his justice that insolent contem-
ners of his majesty and laws should prosper in the
world ? This was observed by the saints long ago;
see Psal. lxxiii. 5, 6, 7. 12. ; and has proved a stumbling-block to some of God's own children, and has
been apt to make them question his justice ; see Job
xxi. 7—14. ' Wherefore do the wicked live, become
old, yea, are mighty in power ? Their seed is established in their sight with them, and their offspring
before their eyes. Their houses are safe from fear,
neither is the rod of God upon them. Their bull
gendereth, and faileth not ; their cow calveth, and
casteth not her calf. They send forth their little
ones like a flock, and their children dance. They
take the timbrel and harp, and rejoice at the sound
of the organ. They spend their days in wealth, and
in a moment go down to the grave.' Jer. xii. 1. 2.
' Righteous art thou, O Lord, when I plead with

o

thee ; yet let me talk with thee of thy judgments :
Wherefore doth the way of the wicked prosper ?
wherefore are all they happy that deal very treacherously ?   Thou hast planted them ; yea they have
taken root : they grow ; yea, they bring forth fruit :
thou art near in their mouth, and far from their
reins.'   But in answer, consider,

1. That the wicked may be sometimes instruments
to do God's work.   Though they do not design and
intend his glory, yet they may be instrumental in promoting it.   Thus Cyrus was instrumental for the
building of God's temple at Jerusalem.   Now there
is some kind of justice in it that such persons should
have a temporal reward.   God is pleased to suffer
those to prosper under whose wings his own people
are sheltered.   He will not be in any man's debt.
Nebuchadnezzar did some service for God, and the
Lord rewarded him for it, by granting him an enlargement of greatness, Ezek. xxix. 18, 19, 20. ' Son
of man, Nebuchadnezzar king of Babylon caused his
army to serve a great service against Tyrus : every
head was made bald, and every shoulder was peeled ;
yet had he no wages, nor his army, for Tyrus, for
the service that he had served against it : Therefore
thus saith the Lord God, Behold, I will give the land
of Egypt unto Nebuchadnezzar king of Babylon ; and
he shall take her multitude, and take her spoil, and
take her prey ; and it shall be the wages for his
army. I have given him the land of Egypt for his
labour wherewith he served against it, because they
wrought for me, saith the Lord God.'

2. God doth not always let the wicked prosper in
their sin.   There are some whom he punisheth openly, that his justice may be observed by all.   Hence
the Psalmist saith, ' The wicked is snared in the
work of his own hands,' Psal. ix. 16.   Sometimes
their prosperity is but short-lived, and they are suddenly cast down, as the Psalmist remarks, Psal.
lxxiii 18, 19, 20. ' Surely thou didst set them in slip-

pery places : thou castedst them down into destruction. How are they brought into desolation, as in a
moment! they are utterly consumed with terrors.
As a dream when one awaketh ; so, O Lord, when
thou awakest, thou shalt despise their image.' His
justice is seen striking men dead sometimes in the
very act of sin ; as in the case of Zimri and Cozbi,
Pharaoh, Sennacherib, &c.

3. God suffers men to go on in sin and prosper,
that he may render them the more inexcusable.
This goodness and forbearance should lead them to
repentance ; and when it does not, it aggravates
their sin, and makes them the more inexcusable,
when he comes to reckon with them. Hence it is
said of Jezebel, ' I gave her space to repent of her
fornication, and she repented not,' Rev. ii. 21. God
spins out his mercies towards sinners ; and if they
do not repent and amend, his patience will be a witness against them, and his justice will be more
cleared in their condemnation.

4. If God let the wicked prosper for a while,
the vial of his wrath is all that while filling up, his
sword is whetting, and though he forbear them for a
time, yet long-suffering is not forgiveness. The longer it be ere he give the blow, it will be the heavier
when it comes. The last scene of justice is coming,
when the wicked shall be turned into hell, and all
the nations that forget God. There is a day of wrath
approaching, and revelation of the righteous judgment of God. Then he will glorify his justice in taking vengeance on them for all their sins. God hath
an eternity in which he will punish the wicked. Divine justice may be as a lion asleep for a time ; but
at last this lion will awake, and roar upon the sinner. Their long continued prosperity will heighten
their eternal condemnation. There are many sinners
in hell who lived in great pomp and prosperity in the
world, and are now roaring under the terrible lashes
of inexorable justice. Thus ye may see that the pros-

perity of the wicked is consistent enough with the
justice of God.

Object. 2. God's own people oft-times suffer great
afflictions in the world ; they are persecuted and oppressed, and meet with a variety of troubles, Psal.
lxxiii. 14. ' For all the day long have I been plagued,
and chastened every morning.' How stands this
with the justice of God ?

Ans. 1. The ways of God's judgments, though
they are sometimes secret, yet they are never unjust.
God doth not afflict willingly, nor grieve the children
of men. There are culpable causes in them from
which their afflictions spring. They have their spots
and blemishes as well as others. Though they may
be free from gross and atrocious crimes, yet they are
guilty of much pride and passion, censoriousness,
wordliness, &c. And the sins of God's people are
more provoking in his sight than the sins of other
men. And God will not suffer them to pass without
correction, Amos iii. 2. ' You only have I known of
all the families of the earth ; therefore I will punish
you for your iniquities.' This justifies God in all the
evils that befal them.

2. All the trials and sufferings of the godly are designed to refine and purify them, to promote their spiritual and eternal good, Heb. xii. 10. ' For they verily for a few days chastened us after their own pleasure ; but he for *our* profit, that we might be partakers of his holiness.' Nothing proclaims God's faithfulness more than his taking such a course with them
as may make them better. Hence says David, Psal.
cxix. 75. ' I know, O Lord, that thy judgments are
right, and that thou in faithfulness hast afflicted me.'
Though they are sometimes pinched with wants, and
meet with various outward troubles, yet even these
are the accomplishments of a gracious promise, and
are ordered for their good. It is to chastise them
for their sin, and quicken them to repentance and
mortification, to try and exercise their faith and pa-

tience, their sincerity and love to God, to wean their hearts from the world, and to promote their growth in grace.

3. It is no injustice in God to inflict a lesser punishment to prevent a greater. The best of God's children have that in them which is meritorious of hell ; and doth God any wrong to them when he useth only the rod, when they deserved the scorpion ? An earthly parent will not be reckoned cruel or unjust, if he only correct his children who deserved to be disinherited. When God corrects his children, he only puts wormwood into their cup, whereas he might fill it up with fire and brimstone. Under the greatest pressure, they have just cause rather to admire his mercy, than to complain of his justice. So did the afflicted church, ' It is of the Lord's mercies that we are not consumed.'

Object. 3. If God be infinitely just, how could he transfer the punishment from the guilty ? This is the objection of the Socinians against Christ's sufferings for the sins of the elect. It is a violation of justice, say they, to transfer the punishment from one to another. How then could the righteous God punish his innocent Son for our sins ?

I answer to this in general, That in some cases it is not unjust to punish the innocent for the guilty. For though an innocent person cannot suffer as innocent without injustice, yet he may voluntarily contract an obligation which will expose him to deserved sufferings. The innocent may suffer for the guilty, when he has power to dispose of his own life, and puts himself freely and voluntarily under an obligation to suffer, and is admitted to suffer by him who has power to punish, and when no detriment, but rather an advantage, accrues to the public thereby. In these circumstances, justice hath nothing to say against the punishing of an innocent person in the room of the guilty. Now there is a concurrence of all these in the case in hand. For,

1. Christ had absolute power to dispose of himself. One reason why a man is not allowed to lay down his life for another is, because his life is not at his own disposal. But Christ was absolute lord of his own life, and had power to keep it or lay it down as he pleased. So he declares, John x. 18. ' No man taketh it from me, but I lay it down of myself : I have power to lay it down, and I have power to take it again. This commandment have I received of my Father.'

2. He freely consented to suffer for his people, and to undergo the punishment that they deserved. To compel an innocent person to suffer for the offences of another, may be an injury. But in this case there was no constraint : for Christ most willingly offered himself : yea, he was not only willing, but most earnest and desirous to suffer and die in our room, Luke xii. 50. ' I have a baptism to be baptized with ; and how am I straitened till it be accomplished ?'

3. The Father admitted him as our Surety, and was well content that his sufferings should stand for ours, and that we thereupon should be absolved and discharged. It was the Father's will that Christ should undertake this work. Hence it is said, Psal. xl. 8. ' I delight to do thy will, O my God.' And the Father loved Christ, because he so cheerfully consented to it, John x. 17. ' Therefore doth my Father love me, because I lay down my life, that I might take it again.'

4. There was no detriment to the public by Christ's death ; but, on the contrary, many advantages redounded to it thereby. One reason why an innocent man cannot suffer for a malefactor, is, because the community would lose a good man, and might suffer by the sparing of an ill member, and the innocent sufferer cannot have his life restored again, being once lost. But in this case all things are quite otherwise : for Christ laid down his life, but so as

to take it up again.   He rose again on the third day,
and death was swallowed up of victory.   And those
for whom he suffered were reclaimed, effectually
changed, and made serviceable to God and man.
So that here there was no injury done to any party
by Christ's sufferings, though an innocent person.
Not to them for whom he died ; for they have inexpressible benefit thereby : he is made to them wisdom, righteousness, sanctification, and redemption.
Not to the person suffering : for he was perfectly
willing, and suffered nothing without his own consent.   Not to God : for he himself found out the ransom, and admitted Christ as our Surety.   Not to
any thing concerned in the government of God : for
by the death of Christ all the ends of God's government were secured.   His honour was hereby vindicated, the authority of his law preserved, and his
subjects, by such an instance of severity on his own
Son, were deterred from violating it.   So that there
is no injustice to any in God's punishing Christ in
his people's stead.

Object. 4. How is it consistent with the justice of
God to punish temporary sins with eternal torments
in hell ?   Some think it hard, and scarce consistent
with infinite justice, to inflict eternal punishment for
sins committed in a little time.   But to clear the justice of God in this, consider,

1. That eternal punishment is agreeable to the
sanction of the law.   The wisdom of God required
that the penalty threatened upon the transgressor
should be in its own nature so dreadful and terrible,
that the fear of it might conquer and over-rule all
the allurements and temptations to sin.   If it had
not been so, it would have reflected upon the wisdom
of the Lawgiver, as if he had been defective, in not
binding his subjects firmly enough to their duty, and
the ends of government would not have been obtained.
And therefore the first and second death was threatened to Adam in case of disobedience.   And fear, as

a watchful sentinel, was placed in his breast, that no
guilty thought or irregular desire should enter in, to
break the tables of the law deposited there.   So that
eternal death is due to sinners by the sanction of the
law.

2. The righteousness of God in punishing the
wicked for ever in hell, will appear, if ye consider
that God by his infallible promise assures us, that
all who sincerely serve and obey him shall be rewarded with everlasting happiness.   They shall receive a blessedness most worthy of God to bestow, a
blessedness that far surmounts our most comprehen-
sive thoughts and imaginations.   For eye hath not
seen, ear hath not heard, nor hath it entered into the
heart of man to conceive, what God hath prepared
for them that love him.   Now, if everlasting felicity
be despised and rejected, nothing remains but endless misery to be the sinner's portion.   The consequence is infallible : For, if sin, with an eternal hell
in its retinue be chosen and embraced, it is most just
and equal that the rational creature should inherit
the fruit of its own choice.   What can be more just
and reasonable, than that those who are the slaves
of the devil, and maintain his party here in the world,
should have their recompence with him for ever hereafter ?   Nothing can be more just, than that those
who now say to the Almighty, *Depart from us, we
desire not the knowledge of thy ways*, should receive
that dreadful sentence at last, *Depart from me, ye
cursed into everlasting fire*.

3. The punishment of the damned must be eternal,
because of the immense guilt and infinite evil of sin.
It is owned by common reason, that there ought to
be a proportion between the quality of the offence
and the degree of the punishment.   Justice takes
the scales into its hand before it takes the sword.
It is a rule in all sorts of judicature, that the degrees
of an offence arise according to the degrees of dignity in the person offended.   Now, the majesty of

God is truly infinite, against whom sin is committed ; and consequently the guilt of sin exceeds our boundless thoughts. One act of sin is rebellion against God, and includes in it the contempt of his majesty, the contradiction of his holiness, which is his peculiar glory, the denial of his omniscience and omnipresence, as if he were confined to the heavens, and busied in regulating the harmonious order of the stars, and did not observe what is done here below. And there is in it a defiance of his eternal power, and a provoking him to jealousy, as if we were stronger than he. O what a dishonour is it to the God of glory, that proud dust should flee in his face, and control his authority ! What a horrid provocation is it to the Most High, that the reasonable creature, that is naturally and necessarily a subject, should despise the Divine law and Lawgiver ! From this it appears that sin is an infinite evil. There is in it a concurrence of impiety, ingratitude, perfidiousness, and whatever may enhance a crime to an excess of wickedness. Now, sin being an infinite evil, the punishment of it must also be infinite ; and because a creature is not able to bear a punishment infinite in degree, by reason of its finite and limited nature, therefore it must be infinite in its duration. And for this cause the punishment of the damned shall never have an end. The almighty power of God will continue them in their being, but they will curse and blaspheme that support, which shall be given them only to perpetuate their torments ; and ten thousand times wish that God would destroy them once for all, and that they might for ever shrink away into nothing. But that will never be granted to them. No ; they shall not have so much as the comfort of dying, nor shall they escape the vengeance of God by annihilation.

4. Their punishment must be eternal : for they will remain for ever unqualified for the least favour. The damned are not changed in hell, but continue

P

their hatred and blasphemies against God. The seeds of this are in obstinate sinners here in the world, who are styled *haters of God :* but in the damned this hatred is direct and explicit ; the fever is heightened into a phrenzy. The glorious and ever-blessed God is the object of their curses and eternal aversion. Our Lord tells us, that in hell ' there is weeping and gnashing of teeth,' *i. e.* extreme sorrow and extreme fury. Despair and rage are the proper passions of lost souls. For when the guilty sufferers are so weak, that they cannot by patience endure their torments, nor by strength resist the power that inflicts them, and withal are wicked and stubborn, they are enraged and irritated by their misery, and foam out blasphemies against the righteous Judge. We may apply to this purpose what is said of the worshippers of the beast, Rev. xvi. 10, 11. 'They gnawed their tongues for pain, and blasphemed the God of heaven, because of their pains and their sores, and repented not of their deeds.' The torment and blasphemies of these impenitent idolaters are a true representation of the state of the damned. Now, as they will always sin ; so they must always suffer. On these accounts, then, it is agreeable to the wisdom and justice of God that their pains and torments be eternal.

Important Lessons from the Justice of God.

1. Is God infinitely just ? Then there is a judgment to come. The justice of God requires that men should reap according to what they have sown ; that it should be well with the righteous, and ill with the wicked. But it is not apparently so now in this present world. Here things are out of course ; sin is rampant, and runs with a rapid violence. Many

times the most guilty sinners are not punished in the present life ; they not only escape the justice of men, but are under no conspicuous marks of the justice of God.   As sinners prosper and flourish, so saints are wronged and oppressed.   They are often cast in a right cause, and can meet with no justice on the earth ; yea, the best men are often in the worst condition, and merely upon account of their goodness. They are borne down and oppressed, because they do not make resistance ; and are loaded with sufferings many times, because they bear them with patience. And the reason of these dispensations is, because now is the time of God's patience and of our trial. Therefore there must be a day wherein the justice of God shall be made manifest.   Then he will set all things right.   He will crown the righteous, and condemn the wicked.   Then God shall have the glory of his justice, and his righteousness shall be openly vindicated.   At the last day God's sword shall be drawn against offenders, and his justice shall be revealed before all the world.   At that day all mouths shall be stopped, and God's justice shall be fully vindicated from all the cavils and clamours of unjust men.

2.   This lets us see how unlike to God many men are.   Some have no justice at all.   Though their place and office oblige them to it, they neither fear God nor regard man.   Many times they pervert justice, they decree unrighteous decrees, Isa. x. 1. ' Woe unto them that decree unrighteous decrees, and that write grievousness which they have prescribed.' Many are unjust in their dealings ; they trick, cheat, and defraud their neighbours ; sometimes in using false weights, the balances of deceit are in their hands, Hos. xii. 7.   Some hold the Bible in one hand, and false weights in the other ; they cozen, defraud, and cheat, under a specious profession of religion.   Some adulterate their commodities ; their wine is mixed with water, Isa. i. 22. ; they mix bad grain with good, and yet sell it for pure grain.   There are many ways

by which men deceive and impose upon their neighbours. All which show what a rare commodity justice is among them. But remember this is very unlike God. For he is the just and right one; he is righteous in all his ways. That man cannot possibly be godly who is not just. We are commanded to imitate him in all his imitable perfections. Though he doth not bid you be omnipotent, yet you ought to be just.

3. Is God infinitely just? Then we must not expostulate with or demand a reason of his actions. He hath not only authority on his side, but justice and equity. In all his dispensations towards men, however afflictive they be, he is just and righteous. He layeth judgment to the line, and righteousness to the plummet, Isa. xxviii. 17. It is below him to give an account to us of any of his proceedings. The plumb-line of our reason is too short to fathom the great depths of God's justice: for his judgments are unsearchable, and his ways past finding out, Rom. xi. 33. We are to adore his justice, where we cannot see the reason of it. God's justice hath often been wronged, but never did wrong to any. How unreasonable, then, is it for men to expostulate with and dispute against God?

4. Is God infinitely just? Then the salvation of sinners who have believed in Christ is most secure, and they need not doubt of pardon and acceptance. ' God is faithful and just to forgive them their sins,' 1 John i. 9. God hath promised it, and he will not break his word; yea, he stands bound in justice to do it; for Christ hath satisfied his justice for all your sins who are believers, so that it hath nothing to crave of you. It doth not stand with the justice of God to exact the same debt from you. Your Redeemer did not only satisfy justice, but also merited the exercise of it on your behalf. Hence it is that God is bound in justice to justify believers in Jesus; for he is just, and the justifier of him that believeth in Jesus, Rom. iii. 26. So that the thoughts even

of Divine justice, which are terrible to others, may
be comfortable to believers.

5. Is God infinitely just? Then the destruction of
wicked and impenitent sinners is infallibly certain.
For the just God will by no means acquit the guilty.
His justice, which is essential to him, cannot but
take vengeance on you.

Lastly, However severely the Lord deals with us,
he neither doth nor can do us any wrong ; and therefore we should lay our hand on our mouth, Lam. iii.
39. ' Why doth a living man complain, a man for
the punishment of his sins ?'

In what the wondrous Goodness of God is manifested.

1. In creation. There is no other perfection of
the Divine nature so eminently visible in the whole
book of the creatures as this is. His goodness was
the cause that he made any thing, and his wisdom
was the cause that he made every thing in order and
harmony. Here the goodness of God shines with a
glorious lustre. All the varieties of the creatures
which he hath made are so many beams and appari-
tions of his goodness. It was great goodness to communicate being to some things without himself, and
to extract such a multitude of things from the depths
of nothing, and to give life and breath to some of
these creatures. Divine goodness formed their natures, beautified and adorned them with their several ornaments and perfections, whereby every thing
was enabled to act for the good of the common world.
Every creature hath a character of Divine goodness
upon it. The whole world is a map to represent,
and a herald to proclaim, this amiable perfection of

God. But the goodness of God is manifested especially in the creation of man. He raised him from the dust by his almighty power, and placed him in a more sublime condition, and endued him with nobler prerogatives, than the rest of the creatures. What is man's soul and body but like a cabinet curiously carved, with a rich and precious gem inclosed in it! God hath made him an abridgment of the whole creation : the links of the two worlds, heaven and earth, are united in him. He communicates with the earth in the dust of his body, and he participates with the heavens in the crystal of his soul. He has the life of angels in his reason, and that of animals in his sense. Further, the divine goodness is manifested in making man after his image, in furnishing the world with so many creatures for his use, in giving him dominion over the works of his hands, and making him lord of this lower world.

2. In our redemption by Jesus Christ. O what astonishing goodness was it for the great and glorious God to give his only begotten Son to the death for such vile rebels and enemies as we all are by nature! The goodness of God, under the name of his love, is rendered as the only cause of our redemption by Christ, John iii. 16. ' God so loved the world, that he gave his only begotten Son, that whosoever believeth in him should not perish but have everlasting life.' This is an inexpressible *so*, a so that all the angels of heaven cannot analyse. None can conceive or understand the boundless extent and dimensions of it. God gave Christ for us to commend his love, and set it off with an admirable lustre. ' God commended his love towards us (saith the apostle), in that while we were yet enemies, Christ died for us.' O what an expensive goodness and love was this! Our redemption cost God more than what was laid out on the whole creation. ' The redemption of the soul is precious,' says the Psalmist. ' We are not redeemed with corruptible things, such

as silver and gold, but with the precious blood of
Christ.' Here God parted with his richest jewel,
and with the eternal delight of his soul. This cost
Christ dear. The Sun of righteousness behoved to
be eclipsed, and must vail the beams of his Divine
glory. He made himself of no reputation, took upon
him the form of a servant, and was found in the likeness of sinful flesh. He did not appear in worldly
pomp and magnificence, attended with a splendid retinue, and faring deliciously, but in a mean and low
condition, without a settled dwelling-place, and was
exposed to poverty and reproach. He was a man
of sorrows, and acquainted with grief. The last
scene of his life was most painful. Upon the very
apprehension of his last sufferings it is said, ' he began to be sorrowful,' as if he had been a stranger to
grief till then. He endured with unparalleled patience all that wrath and misery that his people deserved to have suffered for ever in hell. O what a
dreadful deluge of wrath and fiery indignation fell
from heaven upon our Ark, of which that of Noah
was only but a type! He was bruised and ground
to powder as it were in his agony in the garden. O
how did his innocent soul boil under the fire of Divine wrath! His blood brake through every pore of
the vessel, by the extremity of that flame. God
spared not his own Son, but dealt with him in extreme severity. He paid the utmost mite of satisfaction for his people's sins that justice could demand.
O what admirable love and goodness is manifested
here!

3. In his providential conduct and government.
Here we must distinguish a twofold goodness of God,
common and special.

(1.) There is God's common goodness, which is
common to all the creatures. ' God is good to all,'
says the Psalmist. All the creatures taste of his
goodness. He preserves them in their beings, continues the species of all things, concurs with them

in their distinct offices, and quickens the womb of
nature. ' O Lord, thou preservest man and beast,'
says David. He visits us every day, and makes us
feel the effects of his goodness, in giving us rain and
fruitful seasons,' and filling our hearts with food and
gladness. He waters the ground with his showers,
and every day shines with new beams of his goodness.

(2.) There is a special goodness of God to his own
people, whom he privileges with spiritual and saving blessings. His goodness to them is truly wonderful, in pardoning their iniquities, healing their
spiritual diseases, sanctifying their natures, hearing
and answering their prayers, bearing with their infirmities, accepting their imperfect services, supporting them under and delivering them from temptations,
solving their doubts, directing and guiding them in
their difficulties.

4. The goodness of God will be most signally
manifested at the last day. It is laid up in heaven,
Psal. xxxi. 19. ' Oh how great is thy goodness,
which thou hast laid up for them that fear thee ;
which thou hast wrought for them that trust in thee
before the sons of men !' O who can tell how great
goodness is laid up there ? In heaven they shall have
full draughts of his goodness, even as much as they
can hold. There, God will be all in all to them, and
communicate himself to them immediately, without
the intervention of ordinances.

*In what God's glorious Attribute of Truth is
manifested.*

1. In his works both of creation and providence ;
and that both in his common and more ordinary
works of providence, in preserving and governing

the creatures ; and extraordinary ones, such as the
glorious work of redemption, his great and miraculous operations, and the wonderful preservations of
and deliverances granted to his church and people
when exposed to the greatest dangers.   God is true
in all these ; as Psal. cxi. 7, 8. ' The works of his
hands are verity and judgment ; all his commandments are sure.   They stand fast for ever and ever,
and are done in truth and uprightness.'   Psal. xxv.
10. ' All the paths of the Lord are mercy and truth.'
It is a part of the church's song, Rev. xv. 3. ' Great
and marvellous are thy works, Lord God Almighty ;
just and true are thy ways, thou King of saints. Rev.
xvi. 7. ' Even so, Lord God Almighty, true and
righteous are thy judgments.'   All God's works are
true and real things, not chimeras or appearances.
He executes true judgments, grants true deliverances, works true miracles ; his mercies are true mercies, and his comforts are true comforts.   He does
not deceive or delude his people with vain shows
and appearances.

4. In his word. His word is most pure truth.
' Thy word is truth,' says our Saviour, John xvii. 17.
And,

(1.) God is true in all the doctrines which he hath
revealed.   There is no flaw nor corruption in any of
them.   They are all the true form of sound words.
And especially he is true in the doctrines of the gospel.   Hence we read of the ' truth of the gospel,'
Gal. ii. 5. ; and the gospel is called ' the word of
truth,' Eph. i. 13.   Some of the doctrines revealed
there are above the reach of human reason, as the
doctrines of the glorious and adorable Trinity, the
union of the two natures in the person of Christ, and
the mystical union between him and believers.   But
though they cannot be comprehended by reason,
they are not contrary to it.

(2.) In the historical narratives which he hath recorded in his word, as those of the creation, the fall

Q

of man, the drowning of the old world with the deluge, the incarnation of Christ, the many miracles
which he wrought, his life and bloody death, &c.
In these and other historical relations which we have
in the word of God, there is no lie nor mistake at
all. Hence Luke says, in his preface to his history,
chap. i. 3, 4. ' It seemed good to me also, having
had perfect understanding of all things from the
very first, to write unto thee in order, most excellent
Theophilus, that thou mightest know the certainty of
those things wherein thou hast been instructed.'

(3.) In his prophetical predictions. None of them
fail or come short of their accomplishment, but they
are all fulfilled in their season. A man may foretell
such things as depend on natural causes, as rain
and snow, heat and cold, the eclipses of the sun and
moon, &c. But things are foretold in the scriptures
which are merely contingent, depending upon the
free grace of God, or the free will of man, as the rejecting of the Jews, the calling of the Gentiles, &c.
None of its predictions have fallen to the ground.
Heaven and earth shall pass away, but his words
shall not pass away. The Lord tells the prophet,
' The vision is for an appointed time, but at the end
it shall speak, and not lie,' Hab. ii. 3. And after divers prophetical predictions, it is said, Rev. xxii. 6.
' These sayings are faithful and true.'

(4.) In his commands. All his commands are faithful, and his law is truth. All his precepts which he
has given us are counterparts of his own heart, real
copies of his approving will. The matter of them is
exactly consonant to his holiness, and most acceptable and well-pleasing in his sight. God approves of
all that he commands : so that his precepts are a
true and perfect rule of holiness, without any flaw
or defect.

(5.) In his threatenings. They are always accomplished in their season ; not one of them shall
fail. Says the Lord to the Jews, by the prophet,

Zech. i. 6. ' Did not my word take hold of your fathers ?' And the apostle Paul tells us, Rom. ii. 2.
' We are sure that the judgment of God is according to truth against them which commit such things.'
It is true, indeed, some threatenings are conditional,
and to be understood with the exception of repentance ; so that unfeigned repentance and reformation
prevents the execution of them ; as is clear in the
case of Nineveh, and from Jer. xviii. 7, 8. ' At what
instant I shall speak concerning a nation, and concerning a kingdom, to pluck up, and to pull down,
and to destroy it : if that nation against whom I
have pronounced, turn from their evil, I will repent
of the evil that I thought to do unto them.' But
Divine threatenings will surely be executed upon impenitent and incorrigible sinners.

(6.) In his promises. All the promises are *yea*
and *amen, i. e.* there shall be an infallible accomplishment of them. Therefore promised blessings
are called *sure mercies,* Is. lv. 3. ' Incline your ear,
and come unto me ; hear, and your soul shall live ;
and I will make an everlasting covenant with you,
even the sure mercies of David.' And the gospel,
which is the compend of all the promises, is often
called *the word of truth.* God's people have found
the truth of the promises many times in their comfortable experience. Says Joshua to the Israelites,
Joshua xxiii. 14. ' Ye know in all your hearts and
in all your souls, that not one thing hath failed of all
the good things which the Lord your God spake
concerning you ; all are come to pass unto you, and
not one thing hath failed thereof.' Joshua was now
about to die, and therefore could not be supposed to
feign and dissemble ; and he appeals to their own
consciences, ' Ye know,' &c. And Solomon speaks
to the same purpose, 1 Kings, viii. 56. ' Blessed be
the Lord, that hath given rest unto his people Israel,
according to all that he promised : there hath not
failed one word of all his good promise, which he

promised by the hand of Moses his servant.   All
the promises which he hath made to his people shall
have their accomplishment in due time.   Now, the
truth of God is most frequently taken in this sense
in scripture, and in this his faithfulness doth peculiarly consist.   And,

(1.) This truth and faithfulness of God shines
with peculiar lustre in accomplishing the many promises recorded in the holy scriptures ; such as that
made to Abraham concerning his seed, that, after
their sojourning in a strange land four hundred and
thirty years, they should come out again with great
substance ; which was punctually fulfilled, as Moses
tells us, Exod. xii. 41. ' And it came to pass, at the
end of the four hundred and thirty years, even the
self-same day it came to pass, that all the hosts of
the Lord went out from the land of Egypt.'   Such
also was the accomplishment of the promise relating
to the return of the Israelites from the Babylonish
captivity after seventy years.   No length of time nor
distance of place can wear the remembrance of his
promise from the Divine mind.   ' He remembered
his holy promise,' says the Psalmist, ' and Abraham
his servant,' Psal. cv. 42.

(2.) In accomplishing the promises concerning
the Messiah.   So it is said, *Grace and truth came
by Jesus Christ ;* grace in regard of our pardon, and
truth in regard of the promise of God,   This appears in performing the promise of Christ's incarnation after so many revolutions of time, and many expectations of his coming, and many contrary appearances, and long stay of four thousand years after the
first promise.   After all this, God made good his
word, by sending his Son into the world.—It appears
in performing the promise of his death and sufferings.
God passed his word to the church, that his Son
should suffer death and the wrath of God for elect
sinners.   And having once passed his word for this,
he would not spare him.   Rather than God should

break his word, his own dear Son must suffer a painful, shameful, and cursed death in his body, and the wrath of God in his innocent soul.—It appears in performing the promise of his resurrection from the dead. God had said, *he would not leave his soul in hell*, [the state of the dead], *nor suffer his holy One to see corruption.* This prophecy and promise was accordingly fulfilled : for he was raised from the dead in solemn triumph. Angels attended his resurrection, and the earth trembled and shook, as a sign of triumph and a token of victory ; by which Christ intimated to the whole world, that he had overcome death in his own dominions, and lifted up his head as a glorious conqueror over all his enemies. It was promised that he should rise from the dead on the third day : and this was made good to a tittle

(3.) In fulfilling his promises, when great difficulties and seeming improbabilities lay in the way of their accomplishment. Thus God promised to give Abraham a son, and he made it good, though Sarah was barren, and both Abraham and she were past age. Again, he brought back the captives from Babylon, though the thing seemed most improbable, and many great difficulties lay in the way. Difficulties are for men not for God. ' Is any thing too hard for Jehovah ?' Gen. xviii. 14. See Zech. viii. 6. He is not tied to the rod of human probabilities. He will turn nature upside-down, rather than not be as good as his word.

(4.) In fulfilling promises to his people, when their hopes and expectations have been given up. See instances, Ezek. xxxvii. 11. ' Then he said unto me, Son of man, these bones are the whole house of Israel : behold they say, Our bones are dried, and our hope is lost : we are cut off for our parts.' Isa. xlix. 14. ' But Zion said, The Lord hath forsaken me, and my Lord hath forgotten me,' There may be much unbelief in good men, their faith may be sorely staggered. Yet God is faithful and true. Men may question his promise, but God cannot deny himself, 2 Tim. ii. 13. ' If we believe not, yet he abideth faithful ; he cannot deny himself.'

(5.) God's truth and faithfulness in keeping promise is confirmed by testimonies given to it by the saints in all ages. They have all set to their seal that God is true. They have all borne witness for God, and attested his unspotted faithfulness to the generations that were to come. See instances, Deut. vii. 9. Josh. xxiii. 14. 1 Kings, viii. 56. Psal. cxlvi. 6. All learned men are for experiments : now, the saints in all ages have made experiments upon God's word of promise, and have always found him to be true and faithful. ' The word of the Lord is tried,' says the Psalmist. None that relied on his promise were ever disappointed.

We may here also take a short view of the grounds of God's faithfulness. There are divers glorious attributes and perfections of the Divine nature, upon which his truth and faithfulness in keeping promise is built, as so many strong and unshaken pillars. As,

1. His perfect knowledge of all things past. His knowledge is called ' a book of remembrance,' Mal. iii. 16. to signify the continual presence of all things past before him. Men do often break their word, because they forget their promise ; but forgetfulness cannot befal a God of infinite knowledge. He will ever be mindful of his covenant, and remember his holy covenant and promises, as the Psalmist speaks.

2. His immutability. Though men in making promises may have a real purpose to perform them, yet they may afterwards change their mind. But God is always firm to his purpose, and cannot change his mind, because of his unchangeable nature. Mal. iii. 6. ' For I am the Lord, I change not ; therefore ye sons of Jacob are not consumed ;' Jam. i. 17. ' Every good gift and every perfect gift is from above, and cometh down from the Father of lights, with

whom is no variableness, neither shadow of turning.' Again, men are often inconsiderate in making promises, and do often meet with what they did not foresee. But all events are eternally foreseen by God. So all his promises are made with infinite wisdom and judgment. To this purpose is that promise, Hos. ii. 19. ' I will betroth thee unto me for ever, yea, I will betroth thee unto me in righteousness, and in judgment, and in loving-kindness, and in mercies.'

3. His power. Whatsoever he hath promised to his people, he is able to perform it. Sometimes men falsify their promise, and cannot make good their word through a defect of power. But God never out-promised himself. He can do whatsoever he pleased to do. It is said, Psal. cxxxv. 6. ' Whatsoever the Lord pleased, that did he in heaven and in earth,' &c. Yea, all things are possible with God. This was the foundation of Abraham's faith, which kept it from staggering at the thoughts of the improbabilities which lay in the way of the accomplishment of the promises, Rom. iv. 21. ' And being fully persuaded that what he had promised he was able also to perform.' In the case of civil debts, many a man cannot keep his promise, because others break to him. But though the whole creation should break, God is as able as ever. Hence the prophet says, Hab. iii. 17, 18. ' Although the fig-tree shall not blossom, neither shall fruit be in the vines, the labour of the olive shall fail, and the fields shall yield no meat, the flock shall be cut off from the fold, and there shall be no herd in the stalls : Yet I will rejoice in the Lord, I will joy in the God of my salvation.' Believers in Christ can never be undone, though the whole creation should disband and go into ruin.

4. His holiness. Some men are so wicked and malicious, that though they can, yet they will not keep their word. But it is not so with God. He cannot be charged with any wickedness ; for there

is no unrighteousness in him, Psal. xcii. 15. by reason of the perfect holiness of his nature. It is impossible for him to lie. The deceitfulness and trea-
chery that is to be found in men, flows from the corruption that is lodged in their hearts : but the Divine
nature is infinitely pure and holy. ' God is not a
man, that he should lie, neither the son of man that
he should repent ; hath he said, and shall he not do
it ? or hath he spoken, and shall he not make it
good ?' Numb. xxiii. 19.

5. His justice and righteousness. A man by virtue of a promise hath a right to the thing promised ;
so that it is his due ; and justice requires to give
every one their due. So God by his promise makes
himself a debtor, and his justice obliges him to pay.
Hence it is said, 1 John i. 9. ' God is faithful and
just to forgive us our sins.' He is faithful to pardon,
as he hath promised it ; and faithful in keeping promise, because he is just. Though it was his goodness and mercy to make the promise, yet his justice
binds him to make it good. It is true, when God
makes himself a debtor by his promise, it is indeed
a debt of grace ; yet it is a debt which it is just for
God to pay. Therefore his word of promise is called
' the word of his righteousness,' Psal. cxix. 123.

6. The glory and honour of his name may give
us full assurance of his faithfulness in making good
his promises. He doth all things for his own glory ;
and therefore, wherever you find a promise, the honour of God is given as security for the performance
of it. Hence his people plead this as a mighty argument to work for them. So Joshua, chap. vii. 9.
' What wilt thou do unto thy great name ? *q. d.* ' O
Lord, thy honour is a thousand times more valuable
than our lives. It is not much matter what become
of us. But, O ! it is of infinite importance that the
glory of thy name be secured, and thy faithfulness
kept pure and unspotted in the world. We find Moses pleading to the same purpose, Ex. xxxii. 11, 12.

' Lord, why doth thy wrath wax hot against thy people, which thou hast brought forth out of the land of Egypt, with great power, and with a mighty hand ? Wherefore should the Egyptians speak and say, For mischief did he bring them out, to slay them in the mountains, and to consume them from the face of the earth ? Turn from thy fierce wrath, and repent of this evil against thy people ;' *q. d.* ' It will be sad enough for the hands of the Egyptians to fall upon thy people ; but infinitely worse for the tongues of the Egyptians to fall upon thy name.' In a word, the glory of all God's attributes is engaged for the performance of his promises, especially his faithfulness and power. Now, these are strong pillars upon which God's truth and faithfulness in keeping promise is built. He can as soon cease to be omniscient, unchangeable, omnipotent, infinitely just and holy, as he can cease to be true and faithful. He can as soon divest himself of his glory, and draw an eternal veil over all the shining perfections and excellencies of his nature, as cease to be faithful and true.

There is, and can be but ONE *God.*

1. The scripture is very express and pointed on this head : Deut. vi. 4. ' Hear, O Israel, the Lord our God is one Lord.' Isa. xliv. 6. ' I am the first, and the last, and besides me there is no God. Mark xii. 32. ' There is one God, and there is none other but he.' Consult also the following passages, which clearly establish this article, viz. 1 Sam. ii. 2. ' There is none holy as the Lord : for there is none besides thee ; neither is there any rock like our God.' Psal. xviii. 31. ' For who is God save the Lord ? or who is a rock save our God ?' Isa. xlvi. 9. ' Remember the former things of old ; for I am God, and there

is none else ; I am God, and there is none like me ;'
1 Cor. viii. 4. 6. ' As concerning therefore the eating
of those things that are offered in sacrifice unto idols,
we know that an idol is nothing in the world, and
that there is none other God but one.   But to us
there is but one God, the Father, of whom are all
things, and we in him ; and one Lord Jesus Christ,
by whom are all things, and we by him.'

2. This truth is clear from reason.

(1.) There can be but one First Cause, which hath
its being of itself, and gave being to all other things,
and on which all other things depend, and that is
God : for one such is sufficient for the production,
preservation, and government of all things : and therefore more are superfluous, for there is no need of them
at all.   Certainly he that made the world can preserve, govern, and guide it, without the assistance
of any other God.   For if he needed any assistance,
he were not God himself, an infinitely perfect and
all-sufficient Being.   And whatever power, wisdom,
or other requisite perfections can be imagined to be
in many gods, for making, preserving, and governing
the world, all these are in one infinitely-perfect Being.
Therefore it is useless to feign many, seeing one is
sufficient.

(2.) There can be but one Infinite Being, and therefore there is but one God.   Two infinites imply a
contradiction.   Seeing God fills heaven and earth
with his presence, and is infinite in all the perfections
and excellencies of his nature, there can be no place
for another infinite to subsist.

(3.) There can be but one Independent Being,
and therefore but one God.   1st, There can be but
one independent in being : for if there were more
gods, either one of them would be the cause and author of being to the rest, and then that one would
be the only God : or none of them would be the cause
and author of being to the rest, and so none of them
would be God ; because none of them would be in-

dependent, or the fountain of being to all.   2*d*,
There can be but one independent in working.   For
if there were more independent beings, then in those
things wherein they will and act freely, they might
will and act contrary things, and so oppose and hinder one another : so that being equal in power, nothing would be done by either of them.   Yea, though
we should suppose a plurality of gods agreeing in all
things, yet seeing their mutual consent and agreement would be necessary to every action, it plainly
appears, that each of them would necessarily depend
on the rest in his operations ; and so none of them
would be God, because not absolutely independent.

(4.) There can be but one Omnipotent.   For if
there were two omnipotent beings, then the one is
able to do whatsoever he will, and yet the other is
able to resist and hinder him.   And if the one cannot hinder the other, then that other is not omnipotent.   Again, we must conceive two such beings, either as agreeing, and so the one would be superfluous ; or as disagreeing, and so all would be brought
to confusion, or nothing would be done at all ; for
that which the one would do, the other would oppose
and hinder ; just like a ship with two pilots of equal
power, where the one would be ever cross to the
other ? when the one would sail, the other would
cast anchor.   Here would be a continual confusion,
and the ship must needs perish.   The order and harmony of the world, the constant and uniform government of all things, is a plain argument, that there is
but one only Omnipotent Being that rules all.

(5.) The supposition of a plurality of gods is destructive to all true religion.   For if there were more
than one God, we would be obliged to worship and
serve more than one.   But this it is impossible for
us to do ; as will plainly appear, if ye consider what
divine worship and service is.   Religious worship
and adoration must be performed with the whole
man.   This is what the divine eminence and excel-

lency requires, that we love him with all our heart, soul, and strength, and serve him with all the powers and faculties of our souls, and members of our bodies ; and that our whole man, time, strength, and all we have, be entirely devoted to him alone. But this cannot be done to a plurality of gods. For in serving and worshipping a plurality, our hearts and strength, our time and talents, would be divided among them. To this purpose our Lord argues, Matt. vi. 24. ' No man can serve two masters : for either he will hate the one, and love the other ; or else he will hold to the one, and despise the other. Ye cannot serve God and mammon.' Mammon is thought to be an idol, which the heathens reckoned to be the god of money and riches. Now, says Christ, you cannot serve them both ; if you would have the Lord for your God, and serve him, you must renounce mammon. We cannot serve two gods or masters : if but one require our whole time and strength, we cannot serve the other.

6. If there might be more gods than one, nothing would hinder why there might not be one, or two, or three millions of them. No argument can be brought for a plurality of gods, suppose two or three, but what a man might, by parity of reason, make use of for ever so many. Hence it is, that when men have once begun to fancy a plurality of gods, they have been endless in such fancies and imaginations. To this purpose is that charge against the Jews, who in this conformed themselves very much to the nations round about them, ' According to the number of thy cities are thy gods, O Judah,' Jer. ii. 28. Varro reckons up three hundred gods whom the heathens worshipped, and Hesiod reckons about three thousand of them. Indeed, if we once begin to fancy more gods than one, where shall we make an end ? So that the opinion or conception of a plurality of gods is most ridiculous and irrational.

And this should be observed against those who

pretend, that the Father is the Most High God, and
that there is no Most High God but one, yet that
there is another true God, viz. Christ, who in very
deed, as to them, is but a mere man ; yet they pretend he is the true God. Christ is God, and the
True and Most High God. But, in opposition to
them, consider that to be a man, and to be a God
are opposite, and cannot be said of one in respect of
one nature, Jer. xxxi. 3. ; Acts xiv. 15. ; Jer. x. 11.

****

The awful and destructive nature of Atheism.

1. Wo to atheists, then, whether they be such in
heart or life ; for their case is dreadful and desperate :
and they shall sooner or later feel the heaviest strokes
of the vengeance of that God whom they impiously
deny, whether in opinion or by works. To dissuade
from this fearful wickedness, consider,

(1.) That atheism is most irrational. It is great
folly ; and therefore the Psalmist saith, Psal. xiv. 1.
' The fool hath said in his heart, There is no God.'
It is contrary to the stream of universal reason ; contrary to the natural dictates of the atheist's own soul ;
and contrary to the testimony of every creature.
The atheist hath as many arguments against him as
there are creatures in heaven and earth. Besides, it
is most unreasonable for any man to hazard himself
on this bottom in the denial of a God. May he not
reason thus with himself, what if there be a God, for
any thing that I know ? then what a dreadful case
will I be in when I find it so ? If there be a God,
and I fear and serve him, I gain a blessed and glorious eternity ; but if there be no God, I lose nothing
but my sordid lusts, by believing that there is one.
Now, ought not reasonable creatures to argue thus

with themselves ? What a doleful meeting will there be between the God who is denied, and the atheist that denies him ! He will meet with fearful reproaches on God's part, and with dreadful terrors on his own : all that he gains is but a liberty to sin here, and a certainty to suffer for it hereafter, if he be in an error, as undoubtedly he is.

(2.) Atheism is most impious. What horrid impiety is it for men to deny their Creator a being, without whose goodness they could have had none themselves ? Nay, every atheist is a Deicide, a killer of God as much as in him lies. He aims at the destruction of his very being. The atheist says upon the matter, that God is unworthy of a being, and that it were well if the world were rid of him.

(3.) Atheism is of pernicious consequence both to others and to the atheist himself. To others : for 1*st*, It would root out the foundation of government, and demolish all order among men. The being of God is the great guard of the world : for it is the sense of a Deity, upon which all civil order in cities and kingdoms is founded. Without this, there is no tie upon the consciences of men to restrain them from the most atrocious impieties and villanies. A city of atheists would be a heap of confusion. There could be no traffic nor commerce, if all the sacred bonds of it in the consciences of men were thus snapt asunder by denying the existence of God. 2*d*, It is introductive of all evil into the world. If you take away God, you take away conscience, and thereby all rules of good and evil. And how could any laws be made, when the measure and standard of them is removed ? for all good laws are founded upon the dictates of conscience and reason, and upon common sentiments in human nature, which spring from a sense of God. So that if the foundation be destroyed, the whole superstructure must needs tumble down. A man might be a thief, a murderer, and an adulterer, and yet in a strict sense not be an offender. The

worst of actions could not be evil, if a man were a
god to himself.   Where there is no sense of God, the
bars are removed, and the flood-gates of all impiety
rush in upon mankind.   The whole earth would be
filled with violence, and all flesh would corrupt their
way.

Again, atheism is pernicious to the atheist himself,
who denies the being of God, or endeavours to erase
all notions of the Deity out of his mind.   What can
he gain by this but a sordid pleasure, unworthy of a
reasonable nature ?   And suppose there were no God,
what can he lose but his fleshly lusts, by believing
there is one?   By believing and confessing a God, a
man ventures no loss ; but by denying him, he runs
the most desperate hazard if there be one.   For this
exposes him to the most dreadful wrath and vengeance of God.   If there be a hotter receptacle in
hell than another, it will be reserved for the atheist,
who strikes and fights against God's very being.

(4.) Atheists are worse than heathens : for they
worshipped many gods, but these worship none at
all.   They preserved some notion of God in the
world, but these would banish him from heaven and
earth.   They degraded him, but these would destroy
him.   Yea, they are worse than the very devils : for
the devils are under the dread of this truth, That
God is.   It is said they ' believe and tremble,' Jam.
ii. 19.   It is impossible for them to be atheists in opinion ; for they feel there is a God by that sense of
his wrath that torments them.   There may be atheists in the church, but there are none in hell.   Thus
atheism is a most dreadful evil, most carefully to be
guarded against.

****

Directions how to guard against Atheism.

1. Beware of such opinions as tend to atheism, and aim at the undermining of this supreme truth, that God is. There are many opinions which have a woful tendency this way. Such is that of denying the immortality of the soul. This is a stroke at a distance at the very being of God, who is the Supreme Spirit. There is an order among spirits ; first the souls of men, then angels, and then God. Now, these degrees of spirits are, as it were, a rail and fence about the sense we have of the being and majesty of God. And such as deny the immortality of the soul, strike at a distance at the eternity and existence of the Deity.

Another opinion is, that men of all religions shall be saved ; so that it is no matter what religion a man be of, if he walk according to the principles of it, and be of a sober moral life. In these latter times some are grown weary of the Christian religion, and by an excess of charity betray their faith, and plead for the salvation of heathens, Turks, and infidels. But ye should remember, that, as there is but one God, and one heavenly Jerusalem, so there is but one faith, and one way by which men can come to the enjoyment of God there. Such libertine principles have a manifest tendency to shake people loose of all religion. To make many doors to heaven, as one says, is to widen the gates of hell.

Another opinion tending to atheism is, the denying of God's providence in the government of the world. Some make him an idle spectator of what is done here below, asserting that he is contented with his own blessedness and glory, and that whatever is without him is neither in his thoughts nor care.

Many think that this world is but as a great clock or machine, which was set a-going at first by God, and afterwards left to its own motion.   But if ye exempt any thing from the dominion of providence, then you will soon run into all manner of libertinism. If Satan and wicked men may do what they will, and God be only a looker-on, and not concerned with human affairs, then ye may worship the devil, lest he hurt you, and fear men, though God be propitious to you.

2. Beware of indulging sin.   When ye take a liberty to sin, and gratify your vile and sordid lusts, you will hate the law that forbids it; and this will lead you to a hatred of the Lawgiver ; and hatred of God strikes against his very being.   When once you allow yourselves an indulgence to sin, you will be apt to think, O that there were no God to punish me for my crimes! and would gladly persuade yourselves that there is none ; and will think it your only game to do what he can to root out the notions of God in your own minds, for your own quiet, that so ye may wallow in sin without remorse.

3. Prize and study the holy scriptures, for they show clearly that there is a God.   There are more clear marks and characters of a Deity stamped upon the holy scriptures than upon all the works of nature. Therefore converse much with them.   By this means was Junius converted from atheism.   His father perceiving him to be so atheistical, caused lay a Bible in every room, so that into whatsoever room he entered, a Bible haunted him ; and he fancied it upbraided him thus : ' Wilt thou not read me, atheist? wilt thou not read me ? '   Whereupon he read it, and was thereby converted.   I say then, study the holy scriptures, and in doing so, learn to submit your reason to divine revelation.   For some men, neglecting the scriptures, and going forth in the pride of their own understandings, have at last disputed themselves into flat atheism.

s

4. Study God in the creatures as well as in the scriptures. The creatures were all made to be heralds of the divine glory, and his glorious being and perfections appear evidently in them. Hence saith the Psalmist, Psal. xix. 1—4. ' The heavens declare the glory of God ; and the firmament showeth his handy-work, day unto day uttereth speech, and night unto night showeth knowledge. There is no speech nor language, where their voice is not heard. Their line is gone out through all the earth, and their words to the end of the world : in them hath he set a tabernacle for the sun.' The world is sometimes compared to a book, and sometimes to a preacher. The universe is like a great printed book, wherein God sets forth himself to our view ; and the great diversity of creatures which are in it, are as so many letters, out of which we may spell his name. And they all preach loudly unto us the glorious being and excellencies of God. And therefore the apostle tells us, Rom. i. 20. ' The invisible things of him from the creation of the world are clearly seen, being understood by the things that are made, even his eternal power and Godhead ; so that they are without excuse.' In the book of the creatures God hath written a part of the excellency of his name ; and you should learn to read God wherever he hath made himself legible to you.

5. Ye who are yet sinners, lying in your natural state of sin and misery, come unto God in Christ, and receive him as your God by faith, and so ye will be preserved from atheism. And ye who are believers in Christ, be often viewing God in your own experiences of him. Have you not often found God in the strengthening, reviving, and refreshing influences of his grace upon your souls ? Have ye not had sweet manifestations of his love ? Have you not had frequent refreshing tastes of his goodness, in pardoning your iniquities, hearing and answering your prayers, supplying your wants, and feasting

your souls? The reviewing of such experiences will be a mighty preservative against atheism. Can you doubt of his being, when you have been so often revived, refreshed, and supported by him? The secret touches of God upon your hearts, and your inward converses with him, are to you a clearer evidence of the being of God, than all the works of nature.

Clear evidence of the Godhead subsisting in three persons.

1. The Old Testament plainly holds forth a plurality of persons in the Godhead, Gen. i. 26. ' God said, let us make man in our own image, after our likeness ;' chap. iii. 22. ' And the Lord God said, Behold the man is become as one of us, to know good and evil.' This cannot be understood of angels : for man is said to be created after the image of God, but never after the image of angels ; and the temptation was, ' Ye shall be as gods,' not as angels. Nor must it be conceived, that God speaks so after the manner of kings ; for that way of speaking is used rather to note modesty than royalty. But when God speaks so as to discover most of his royalty, he speaks in the singular number, as in the giving of the law, ' I am the Lord thy God.' This trinity of persons is also not obscurely mentioned in Psal. xxxiii. 6. ' By the word of the Lord, or JEHOVAH, were the heavens made ; and all the host of them, by the breath, or spirit, of his mouth.' Here is mention made of *Jehovah the Word and the Spirit*, as jointly acting in the work of creation. Accordingly we find, that ' all things were made by the Word,' John i. 3. and that ' the Spirit garnished the heavens,' Job xxvi. 13. Nay, a Trinity of persons is mentioned, Isa. lxiii. where, besides that the Lord,

or Jehovah, is three times spoken of, ver. **7.** we read of ' the angel of his presence,' which denotes two persons and ' his Spirit,' ver. **9, 10.** So that it evidently appears, that the doctrine of the Trinity was revealed under the Old Testament.

2. The New Testament most plainly teaches this doctrine.

(1.) I begin with the text, where it is expressly asserted, *There are three that bear record,* &c. Here are three witnesses, and therefore three persons. Not three names of one person : for if a person have ever so many names, he is still but one witness. Not three Gods, but one.

(2.) In the baptism of Christ, Matt. iii. **16, 17.** mention is made of the Father speaking with an audible voice, the Son in the human nature baptized by John, and the Holy Ghost appearing in the shape of a dove ; plainly importing three Divine persons.

(3.) This appears from our baptism, Matt. xxviii. **8. 19.** ' Go ye and teach all nations baptizing them in the name of the Father, the Son, and the Holy Ghost.' Observe the words, *in the name,* not *names ;* which denotes, that these three are one God : and yet they are distinctly reckoned three in number, and so are three distinct persons.

(4.) It appears from the apostolical benediction, where all blessings are sought from the three persons distinctly mentioned, 2 Cor. xiii. **14.** ' The grace of the Lord Jesus Christ, and the love of God, and the communion of the Holy Ghost, be with you all.'

How the three persons of the Godhead are distinguished.

The Son is distinct from the Father ' being the express image of his person,' Heb. i. **2.** ; and in John

viii. **17, 18.** he reckons his Father one witness and himself another. And that the Holy Ghost is distinct from both, appears from John xiv. **16, 17.** ' I will pray the Father, and he shall give you another Comforter, that he may abide with you for ever : even the Spirit of truth.' And the text is plain for the distinction of all the three. Now, they are distinguished by their order of subsisting, and their incommunicable personal properties. In respect of the order of subsistence, the Father is the first person, as the fountain of the Deity, having the foundation of personal subsistence in himself ; the Son is the second person, and hath the foundation of personal subsistence from the Father ; and the Holy Ghost is the third person, as having the foundation of personal subsistence from the Father and the Son. And so for their personal properties,

1. It is the personal property of the Father to beget the Son, Heb. i. 5, 6. 8. ' Unto which of the angels said he at any time, Thou art my Son, this day have I begotten thee ? And again, I will be to him a Father, and he shall be to me a Son. And again, when he bringeth in the first-begotten into the world, he saith, And let all the angels of God worship him. —But unto the Son he saith, Thy throne, O God, is for ever and ever ; a sceptre of righteousness is the sceptre of thy kingdom.' This cannot be ascribed either to the Son or Holy Ghost.

2. It is the property of the Son to be begotten of the Father, John i. 14. 18. ' We beheld his glory, the glory as of the only-begotten of the Father. No man hath seen God at any time : the only-begotten Son, which is in the bosom of the Father, he hath declared him.'

3. The property of the Holy Ghost is to proceed from the Father and the Son, John xv. 26. ' When the comforter is come, whom I will send unto you from the Father, even the Spirit of truth, which proceedeth from the Father, he shall testify of me,' in

Gal. iv. 6. he is called ' the Spirit of the Son ;' and in Rom. viii. 9. ' the Spirit of Christ,' He is said to ' receive all things from Christ,' John xiv. 14, 15. ; to be ' sent by him,' John xv. 26. ; and to be ' sent by the Father in Christ's name,' John xiv. 26. All this plainly implies, that the Holy Spirit proceedeth both from the Father and the Son. This generation of the Son and Holy Ghost was from all eternity. For as God is from everlasting to everlasting, so must this generation and procession be : and to deny it, would be to deny the supreme and eternal Godhead of all the three glorious persons.

Clear evidence of the three persons of the Godhead being one God.

1. How express is that text, *These three are one.* When the apostle speaks of the unity of the earthly witnesses, ver. 8. he says, they ' agree in one,' acting in unity of consent or agreement only. But the heavenly witnesses are *one*, viz. in nature or essence. They are not only of a like nature or substance, but one and the same substance ; and if so, they are and must be equal in all essential perfections, as power and glory.

2. There is but one true God, as was before proved, and there can be but one true God. Now, the Father, Son, and Holy Ghost, are each of them the true God ; and therefore they are one God, the same in substance, equal in power and glory. And this I shall prove by scripture testimony.

First, That the Father is true God, none that acknowledge a God do deny. Divine worship and attributes are ascribed to him. But,

Secondly, That the Son is true God, appears if ye consider,

THE REV. THOMAS BOSTON. 135

1. The scripture expressly calls him *God,* Rom.
ix. 5.; John i. 1.; Acts xx. 28.; ' the true God,' 1 John
v. 20. ; ' the great God,' Tit. ii. 13. ; the ' mighty
God,' Isa. ix. 6. ' Jehovah or Lord,' Mal. iii. 1. which
is a name proper to the true God only, Psal. lxxxiii.
ult.

2. The attributes of God, which are one and the
same with God himself, are ascribed to him ; as eternity, Micah v. 2. ' Whose goings forth have been
from of old, from everlasting ; independency and
omnipotence, Rev. i. 8.—' The almighty ;' omnipresence, John iii. 13. where he is said to be ' in heaven,'
when bodily on earth ; and Matt. xxviii. 20. ' Lo, I
am with you alway, even unto the end of the world :'
omniscience, John xxi. 17. ' Lord thou knowest all
things,' says Peter to him ; and unchangeableness,
Heb. i. 11, 12. ' They shall perish, but thou remain-
est : and they all shall wax old as doth a garment ;
and as a vesture shalt thou fold them up, and they
shall be changed : but thou art the same, and thy
years shall not fail.'

3. The works proper and peculiar to God are ascribed to him ; as creation, John i. 3. ' All things
were made by him ; and without him was not any
thing made that was made.' Conservation of all
things, Heb. i. 3.—' upholding all things by the
word of his power.' Raising the dead by his own
power, and at his own pleasure, John v. 21. 26.
' The Son quickeneth whom he will.' The Father
' hath given to the Son to have life in himself.' The
saving of sinners, Hos. i. 7.—I will save them by
the Lord their God.' Compare chap. xiii. 4. ' in me
is thine help.' Yea, whatsoever the Father doth,
the Son doth likewise.

4. Divine worship is due to him, and therefore he
is true God, Matt. iv. 10. The angels are commanded to ' worship him,' Heb. i. 8. All must give the
same honour to him as to the Father, John v. 23.
We must have faith in him, and they are blessed

that believe in him, Psal. ii. 12. compare Jer. xvii. 5.
We are to pray to him, Acts vii. 58. ;   and we are
baptized in his name, Matt. xxviii. 19.   Nay, he is
expressly said to be ' equal with the Father,' Phil.
ii. 6. and ' one with him.' John x. 30.   Now, seeing
God ' will not give his glory to another,' Isa. xlviii. 11.
because he is true and cannot lie, and he is just, it
follows, that though Christ be a distinct person, yet
he is not a distinct God from his Father, but one
God with him, the same in substance equal in power
and glory.   And it is no contradiction to this doctrine, when Christ says, ' My Father is greater than
I,' John xiv. 28. ; for he is not speaking there of his
nature as God, but of his mediatory office ; and
hence he is called the Father's ' servant,' Is. xlii. 1.

   Thirdly, That the Holy Ghost is true God, or a
Divine person, appears, if ye consider,

   1. The scripture expressly calls him God, Acts v.
3, 4.; 1 Cor. iii. 16.; Isa. vi. 9. compared with Acts
xxviii. 25, 26.; 2 Samuel xxii. 2, 3.   He is called
' Jehovah, or the Lord,' Num. xii. 6. compare 2 Pet.
i. 21.

   2. Divine attributes are ascribed to him ; as omnipotence, he ' worketh all in all,' 1 Cor. xii. 6. 9, 10,
11. ; omnipresence, Psalm, cxxxix. 7. ; and omniscience, 1 Cor. ii. 10.

   3. Works peculiar to God are ascribed to him ; as
creation, Psal. xxxiii. 6 ; conservation, Psal. civ. 30. ;
working miracles, Matt. xii. 28. ; raising the dead,
Rom. viii. 11. ; inspiring the prophets, 2 Tim. iii. 16.
compare 2 Pet. i. 21.

   4. Divine worship is due to him.   We are baptized in his name, Matt. xxviii. 19. ; we are to pray
to him, 2 Cor. xiii. 14.; Acts iv. 23. 25. compare 2
Sam. xxiii. 2, 3.

   Hence it appears,

   1. That the Godhead is not divided, but that each
of the three persons hath the one whole Godhead, or
divine nature.

2. That it is sinful to imagine any inequality amongst the three Divine persons, or to think one of them more honourable than another, seeing they are all one God.

....

The great importance of the doctrine of the Holy Trinity.

It is a fundamental article, the belief whereof is necessary to salvation. For those that are ' without God,' Eph. ii. 12. and ' have not the Father,' cannot be saved; but ' whoso denieth the son, the same hath not the Father,' 1 John ii. 23. Those that are none of Christ's cannot be saved : but ' he that hath not the Spirit, is none of his,' Rom. viii. 9. None receive the Spirit but those that know him. John xiv. 17. This mystery of the Trinity is so interwoven with the whole of religion, that there can neither be any true faith, right worship, or obedience without it. For take away this doctrine, and the object of faith, worship, and obedience is changed ; seeing the object of these declared in the scripture, is the three persons in the Godhead ; and the scriptures know no other God. Where is faith, if this be taken away? John xvii. 3. ' This is life eternal, that they might know thee the only true God, and Jesus Christ whom thou hast sent.' Here it is to be observed, that our Lord does not call the *Father only* the true God, exclusive of the other persons of the Trinity ; but that he (including the other persons who all subsist in the same one undivided essence) is the *only true God*, in opposition to idols, falsely called gods. 1 John ii. 23. ' Whosoever denieth the Son, the same hath not the Father.' There is no more true worship or fellowship with God in it : ' For through him we both have access by one Spirit unto

T

the Father,' Eph. ii. 18.   And there is no more obedience without it, John xv. 23.   ' He that hateth
me,' says Christ, ' hateth my Father also,' John
v. 23.   ' He that honoureth not the Son, honoureth
not the Father which hath sent him.'   We are debtors to the Spirit, to live after the Spirit, and are
bound by baptism to the obedience of the Father,
the Son, and the Spirit. *

Interesting explanation of Acts x. 33.

' Immediately therefore I sent to thee ; and thou hast well
   done that thou art come.   Now therefore are we all
   here present before God, to hear all things that are
   commanded thee of God.'

Here we have,
1. A call to Peter related.   The person calling is
Cornelius, a soldier.   A Gentile he was, yet a prose-
lyte ; a good man, but one who as yet knew not the
doctrine of Christ crucified.   The person called was

* The unity and distinction of the divine three, is a mystery
which infinitely transcends all our limited powers to comprehend.
If the works and ways of God are inscrutable to us, how much
more must this be the case with regard to the manner in which
he himself exists.   Under a consciousness, therefore, of our own
ignorance, it becomes us to contemplate this subject, not only
with modesty and humility, but with most profound reverence
and godly fear, it being revealed as a matter of faith, not of curious investigation.   When the glory of the Lord appeared on
mount Sinai, the people were strictly charged, lest they break
through unto the Lord to gaze, and many of them perish, Exod.
xix. 21.   And though we cannot now, like them, transgress with
our bodily sight, yet by unhallowed speculation, we are in danger of rashly intruding into those things respecting the diety,
which he has not thought proper to reveal, and which it is neither possible nor profitable for us to know, at least in our present
state.

Jones's Biblical Cyclopædia.

Peter ; him God honoured to break the ice for the
calling of the Gentiles, and to take down the first
stone in the partition-wall betwixt Jews and Gentiles. The call itself is in these words, *I sent*. He
had sent three men to invite Peter to his house, ver. 7.
The reason of the call is thus expressed, *Therefore*,
because he had the command of God for that effect.
He made quick dispatch in the call ; it was done immediately after the mind of God was discovered to
him.

2. Peter's compliance with the call commended,
Thou hast well done that thou art come. It is acceptable to God and to us. Peter had no great inclination to this work ; he had his scruples about
the lawfulness of it : but God condescends to solve
his doubts, and clear his way. It was very offensive
to the Christian Jews, which necessitated him to
make an apology for his practice, Acts xi. yet after
all it was well done to come, because he came in obedience to the call of God.

3. An address made to Peter when he was come,
by Cornelius the caller, in name of himself and those
who were with him. In which take notice, 1*st*, Of
a congregation, though small, yet well convened.
What the congregation was, see ver. 24. ' his kins-
men and near friends.' These, with his family, and
those that came with Peter, made up the assembly.
The good man made it his business to get not only
his own family, but his friends, to wait on the ordinances. 2*d*, An acknowledgment of God's presence
in a special manner in religous assemblies, *We are
all here present before God*. 3*d*, The great end of
their meeting was their souls' edification, *to hear*,
that is, to hear and obey. And here is what the
minister is to preach and the people to receive ; it is
what is commanded of God. The minister has a
commission from God, and he must preach, not what
men would have him to preach, but what God commands ; and the people are to receive nothing that is

beyond his commission. The extent of both is *all
things ;* the minister is to preach, and the people to
receive, *all things commanded of God.*

Obs. 1. When God discovers his mind in any particular to a person or people, it is their duty presently to comply with it without delay. There should
be no disputing after the discovery of the Lord's
mind, Gal. i. 15—17. ' But when it pleased God,
who separated me from my mother's womb, and called me by his grace, to reveal his Son in me, that I
might preach him among the heathen ; immediately
I conferred not with flesh and blood : Neither went
I up to Jerusalem to them which were apostles before me ; but I went into Arabia, and returned again
unto Damascus.' The contrary was the fault of Balaam, and of the Jews in Egypt, Jer. xliv.

2. It is a blessed thing for a people to call that
minister to whom God himself directs and inclines
them. It is like Cornelius, who did not so much as
know Peter by name, Acts x. 5. ; but he goes to God,
and God directs him.

3. It is a commendable thing in a minister of Christ
to comply with the call of God and his people,
though it should be offensive to some, and not very
agreeable to his own inclinations. Ministers are to
go, not where they will and others would wish them,
but where God wills. It was Levi's commendation,
' who said unto his father and to his mother, I have
not seen him, neither did he acknowledge his brethren,
nor knew his own children : for they have observed thy
word, and kept thy covenant.' Deut. xxxiii. 9.

THE REV THOMAS BOSTON.

****

Reasons why we should be careful to attend the Public Ordinances of God.

1. Because God has commanded it, Heb. x. 25. ' Not forsaking the assembling of ourselves together, as the manner of some is ; but exhorting one another : and so much the more, as ye see the day approaching.' The Lord calls his people to be present there, where-ever it is. Thus there was the tabernacle of the congregation in the wilderness, thither the people resorted to the public worship ; and afterwards the temple. And for ordinary the synagogues under the Old Testament were the places of public worship, the ruins of which the church complains of, Psal. lxxiv. 8. It was the practice of Christ himself to attend these places, as we find, Luke iv. 16. He sends ministers to preach, and therefore commands people to hear.

2. Because the public assemblies are for the honour of Christ in the world. They are that place where his honour dwells, where his people meet together to profess their subjection to his laws, to receive his orders, to seek his help, to pay him the tribute of praise, the calves of their lips. And forasmuch as all are obliged to these things, all are obliged to be present and attend, and to cast in their mite into this treasury. And therefore the people of God look on Christ's standard in the world as fallen, when these assemblies are gone, as Elijah did, 1 Kings xix. 10.

3. Because these assemblies are the ordinary place where Christ makes his conquest of souls, Rom. x. 14. ' How then shall they call on him in whom they have not believed ? And how shall they believe in him of whom they have not heard ? And how shall they hear without a preacher ?' The gospel is Christ's net wherein souls are catched. And it is

always good to be in Christ's way. Who knows
when that good word may come that may take hold
of the man's heart, and make him Christ's prisoner,
bound with the cords of love ? A great number were
catched at the first sermon preached after Christ's
ascension, and cried out ' What shall we do ? ' Acts
ii. 37.   So Lydia hearing the apostle Paul, her heart
was opened, Acts xvi. 14.   The gospel is the power
of God unto salvation.   Happy are they that get the
deepest wounds in this field, ' For the weapons of
this warfare are not carnal, but mighty through God
to the pulling down of strong holds, casting down
imaginations, and every high thing that exalteth itself against the knowledge of God, and bringeth into captivity every thought to the obedience of Christ,'
2 Cor. x. 4, 5.

4. They are Christ's trysting-place with his people,
the galleries wherein our Lord walks, Exod. xx. 24. ;
the mountains of myrrh, where he will be till the
day break.   Those that mind for communion with
God, should seek him there, and wait on him where
he has promised to be found.   What a disadvantage
had Thomas by his absence from one meeting where
Christ met with the rest of the disciples !

5. The delights of Christ and his people meet
there ; for ordinances are the heaven on earth.
Christ delights to be there with his people, Psal.
lxxxvii. 2. ' The Lord loveth the gates of Zion, more
than all the dwellings of Jacob,' Luke xxii. 15. ' With
desire,' said our Lord, I have desired to eat this passover with you before I suffer.'   And they delight to
be there with him, and for him.   How passionately
does David desire the ordinances ! Psal. lxxxiv. 1, 2.
' How amiable are thy tabernacles, O Lord of Hosts !
My soul longeth, yea, even fainteth for the courts of
the Lord : my heart and my flesh crieth out for the
living God.'   He prefers a day in God's courts to a
thousand : ' I had rather,' says he, ' be a door-keep-
er in the house of my God, than to dwell in the tents

of wickedness.' And again, ' One thing,' says he,
' have I desired of the Lord, that will I seek after,
that I may dwell in the house of the Lord all the days
of my life, to behold the beauty of the Lord, and to
inquire in his temple,' Psal. xxvii. 4. What good
news was it to him to hear of an opportunity of waiting on God there! Psal. cxxii. 1. ' I was glad,' says
he, ' when they said unto me, Let us go up into the
house of the Lord.'

Lastly, The necessities of all that mind for heaven
require it. Had the ordinances not been necessary,
God would never have appointed them. And sure
they are not more necessary for any than those that
least see their need of them. These are the blind
souls that have need to come to the market of free
grace, for that eye-salve that opens the eyes of those
that see not. Have not Christ's soldiers need of them
to clear their rusty armour? Do not dead souls need
them to quicken them? Sleepy souls, to awaken
them? They are the pools in the way to Zion, which
the travellers to Zion have much need of to quench
their thirst in their weary journey.

Surely the due consideration of these things may
engage us all to make conscience of being all there
present, as God gives opportunity.

In what respects we are before the Lord at Public Ordinances.

The Lord is every where present; we can be no
where but he is there, Psal. cxxxix. 7. ' Whither
shall I go from thy Spirit? or whither shall I flee
from thy presence?' But we are before him in a
special manner in the public assemblies. He holds
the stars in his right hand, and walks in the midst
of the golden candlesticks. Our Lord has a special

concern there ; the main part of his business on
earth lies there ; and must he not be about his Father's business ! This consideration should engage
us to be there. Satan will not miss to be there :
where Christ has a church, the devil will endeavour
to have a chapel. The fowls will be where there is
seed sowing. So some understand that, 1 Cor. xi. 10.
' For this cause ought the woman to have power on
her head, because of the angels.' Now Christ is in
the assemblies of his people,

1. Representatively. He has his agents there, his
ministers, who are the Lord's proxies to court a wife
for their Master's Son, 2 Cor. xi. 2. his ambassadors
to negotiate a peace betwixt God and sinners, 2 Cor.
v. 20. ; Matt. x. 40. Christ's ministers are but as
John was, ' the voice of one crying in the wilderness.'
The Speaker is in heaven. Hence the Lord is said
to speak in or by the prophets. It is the Lord's
goodness that the treasure is lodged in earthen, not
in heavenly vessels, lest their splendour should dark-
en his glory in men's eyes, and so dazzle their eyes.
And for the now glorified, God ' holdeth back the
face of his throne, and spreadeth his cloud upon it,'
Job xxvi. 9.

2. Efficaciously. His power is there, he works
there, Psal. lxxv. 1. ' For that thy name is near,'
says the Psalmist, ' thy wondrous works declare.'
The word of the Lord is a powerful word. The
ministers of Christ drive not an empty chariot, Psal.
xlv. 4. ' In thy majesty ride prosperously.' Christ
is there giving life to some, strength to others, and
death's wounds to others, Mic. ii. 7. ; Psal. xlv. 5. ;
Hos. vi. 5. The Lord's word returns not empty ; it
does always something. Every preaching will either
harden or soften you ; it will drive you a step nearer
heaven or hell. Now, are we before him in his ordinances,

1. As our witness. They had need to carry wa-
rily that have many eyes on them. While we are

at ordinances, men's eyes and the devil's eyes are upon us ; but what should affect us most is, that God's
eye is on us in a special manner, noticing how we
behave, with what tenderness we handle holy things :
and though our outward carriage be never so promising, God is witness to the heart-wanderings,
Ezek. xxxiii. 31.

2. As our judge. God has a tribunal as well as
a throne in the public ordinances, to reward or punish his worshippers according to their works. This
has made the blood of some to be mingled with their
sacrifices, as in the case of Nadab and Abihu, Lev.
x. 3. God is jealous of his honour. A curious look
into the ark cost the Bethshemites dear ; and a wrong
touch of it cost Uzziah his life. And we would make
the same use of that that David did, 1 Chron. xv. 12,
13, ' Sanctify yourselves, both ye and your brethren,
that you may bring up the ark of the Lord God of
Israel, unto the place that I have appointed for it.
For because ye did it not at first, the Lord our God
made a breach upon us, for that we sought him not
after the due order.' It is true, the gospel-dispensa-
tion is more spiritual ; and therefore spiritual plagues
are more usual now ; but these ordinances cure the
worst of plagues.

3. As our lawgiver, Isa. xxxiii. 22. ' For the Lord
is our judge, the Lord is our lawgiver, the Lord is
our king ; he will save us.' We are his creatures,
and therefore his will must be our law. We are his
upon many accounts ; we know not our duty. He
has set up the ministry in his church, to declare to
people what is their duty, Mal. ii. 7. But, alas !
many, by their despising the messengers of the Lord
and their message, say, as Psal. xii. 4. ' Who is lord
over us ?' But God will lord it over such in spite of
their hearts, Hos. xiii. 10. ' I will be thy King.' But
the heralds must proclaim the subjects' duty, whether they will hear, or whether they will forbear.

4. As the Lord and master of the family, who has

provided liberally for all of his house. Ministers are
the stewards of the house ; but he is the Master, that
has made the provision in the gospel, Isa. xxv. 6.
He sends out his servants, saying, ' Come, eat of my
bread, and drink of the wine which I have mingled,'
Prov. ix. 5. Look then how obedient children will
stand and wait for supply of their necessities from an
affectionate parent ; so ought we to stand and wait
on in ordinances for the supply of our spiritual wants
from our heavenly Father.

5. As our God, which should strike us with reverence, Psal. lxxxix. 7. ' God is greatly to be feared in
the assembly of the saints ; and to be had in reverence of all them that are about him.' Psal. xcv. 6.
' O come, let us worship and bow down ; let us kneel
before the Lord our Maker.' And this challenges the
most serious disposition of our hearts to worship him.

The chief end of God's decrees explained.

And this is no other than his own glory. Every rational agent acts for an end ; and God being the
most perfect agent, and his glory the highest end,
there can be no doubt but all his decrees are directed to that end. ' For—to him are all things,' Rom.
xi. 36. ' That we should be to the praise of his glory,' Eph. i. 12. In all, he aims at his glory ; and
seeing he aims at it, he gets it even from the most
sinful actions he has decreed to permit. Either the
glory of his mercy or of his justice he draws therefrom. Infinite wisdom directs all to the end intended. More particularly,

1. This was God's end in the creation of the
world. The divine perfections are admirably glorified here, not only in regard of the greatness of the
effect, which comprehends the heavens and the earth,

and all things therein ; but in regard of the marvellous way of its production. For he made the vast
universe without the concurrence of any material
cause ; he brought it forth from the womb of nothing
by an act of his efficacious will. And as he began
the creation by proceeding from nothing to real existence, so in forming the other parts he drew them
from infirm and indisposed matter, as from a second
nothing, that all his creatures might bear the signa-
tures of infinite power. Thus he commanded light
to arise out of darkness, and sensible creatures from
an insensible element. The lustre of the divine glory appears eminently here. Hence says David, Psal.
xix. 1. ' The heavens declare the glory of God.'
They declare and manifest to the world the attributes and perfections of their great Creator, even in
his infinite wisdom, goodness, and power. All the
creatures have some prints of God stamped upon
them, whereby they loudly proclaim and show to the
world his wisdom and goodness in framing them.
Hence says Paul, Rom. i. 20. ' The invisible things
of him from the creation of the world are clearly
seen, being understood by the things that are made,
even his eternal power and Godhead.'

2. The glory of God was his chief end and design
in making men and angels. The rest of the creatures glorified God in an objective way, as they are
evidences and manifestations of his infinite wisdom,
goodness, and power. But this higher rank of beings
are endued with rational faculties, and so are capable to glorify God actively. Hence it is said, Prov.
xvi. 4. ' The Lord hath made all things for himself.'
If all things were made for him, then man and angels especially, who are the master-pieces .of the
whole creation. We have our rise and being from
the pure fountain of God's infinite power and goodness ; and therefore we ought to run towards that
again, till we empty all our faculties and excellencies
into that same ocean of divine goodness.

3. This is likewise the end of election and predestination. For ' he hath predestinated us unto the adoption of children, to the praise of the glory of his grace.' That some are ordained to eternal life, and others passed by, and suffered to perish eternally in their sin, is for the manifestation of the infinite perfections and excellencies of God. The glory and beauty of the divine attributes is displayed here with a shining lustre ; as his sovereign authority and dominion over all his creatures to dispose of them to what ends and purposes he pleaseth ; his knowledge and omniscience, in beholding all things past, present, and to come ; his vindictive justice, in ordaining punishments to men, as a just retribution for sin ; and his omnipotence, in making good his word, and putting all his threatenings in execution. The glory of his goodness shines likewise here, in making choice of any, when all most justly deserved to be rejected. And his mercy shines here with an amiable lustre, in receiving and admitting all who believe in Jesus into his favour.

4. This was the end that God proposed in that great and astonishing work of redemption. In our redemption by Christ, we have the fullest, clearest, and most delightful manifestation of the glory of God that ever was or shall be in this life. All the declarations and manifestations that we have of his glory in the works of creation and common providence, are but dim and obscure in comparison with what is here. Indeed the glory of his wisdom, power, and goodness, is clearly manifested in the works of creation. But the glory of his mercy and love had lain under an eternal eclipse without a Redeemer. God had in several ages of the world pitched upon particular seasons to manifest and discover one or other particular property of his nature. Thus his justice was declared in his drowning the old world with a deluge of water, and burning Sodom with fire from heaven. His truth and power were clearly manifest-

ed in freeing the Israelites from the Egyptian chains, and bringing them out from that miserable bondage. His truth was there illustriously displayed in performing a promise which had lain dormant for the space of 430 years, and his power in quelling his implacable enemies by the meanest of his creatures. Again, the glory of one attribute is more seen in one work than in another : in some things there is more of his goodness, in other things more of his wisdom is seen, and in others more of his power. But in the work of redemption all his perfections and excellencies shine forth in their greatest glory. And this is the end that God proposed in their conversion and regeneration. Hence it is said, Isa. xliii. 21. ' This people have I formed for myself, they shall show forth my praise.' Sinners are adopted into God's family, and made a royal priesthood on this very design,' 1 Pet. ii. 9. ' But ye are a chosen generation, a royal priesthood, an holy nation, a peculiar people ; that ye should show forth the praises of him who hath called you out of darkness into his marvellous light.'

****

The properties of God's decrees explained.

1. They are eternal. God makes no decrees in time, but they were all from eternity. So the decree of election is said to have been ' before the foundation of the world,' Eph. i. 4. ' According as he hath chosen us in him before the foundation of the world, that we should be holy and without blame before him in love.' Yea, whatever he doth in time, was decreed by him, seeing it was known to him before time, Acts xv. 18. ' Known unto God are all his works from the beginning.' And this foreknowledge is founded on the decree. If the divine decrees were not eternal, God would not be most perfect and un-

changeable, but, like weak man, should take new counsels, and would be unable to tell every thing that were to come to pass.

2. They are most wise, ' according to the counsel of his will.' God cannot properly deliberate or take counsel, as men do ; for he sees all things together and at once. And thus his decrees are made with perfect judgment, and laid in the depth of wisdom, Rom. xi. 33. ' O the depth of the riches both of the wisdom and knowledge of God! how unsearchable are his judgments, and his ways past finding out!' So that nothing is determined that could have been better determined.

3. They are most free, *according to the counsel of his own will ;* depending on no other, but all flowing from the mere pleasure of his own will, Rom. xi. 34. ' For who hath known the mind of the Lord, or who hath been his counsellor?' Whatsoever he decreeth to work without himself, is from his free choice. So his decrees are all absolute, and there are none of them conditional. He has made no decrees suspended on any condition without himself. Neither has he decreed any thing because he saw it would come to pass, or as that which would come to pass on such or such conditions; for then they should be no more according to the counsel of his will, but the creature's will. For God's decrees being eternal, cannot depend upon a condition which is temporal. They are the determinate counsels of God, but a conditional decree determines nothing. Such conditional decrees are inconsistent with the infinite wisdom of God, and are in men only the effects of weakness; and they are inconsistent with the independency of God, making them depend on the creature.

4. They are unchangeable. They are the unalterable laws of heaven. God's decrees are constant ; and he by no means alters his purpose, as men do, Psal. xxxiii. 11. ' The counsel of the Lord standeth

for ever, the thoughts of his heart to all generations.'
Hence they are compared to mountains of brass,
Zech. vi. 1.   As nothing can escape his first view,
so nothing can be added to his knowledge.   Hence
Balaam said, ' God is not a man that he should lie,
neither the son of man, that he should repent : hath
he said, and shall he not do it ? or hath he spoken,
and shall he not make it good ?' Numb. xxiii. 19.
The decree of election is irreversible : ' The foundation of God, (says the apostle), standeth sure, having this seal, The Lord knoweth them that are his,'
2 Tim. ii. 19.

5. They are most holy and pure.   For as the sun
darts its beams upon a dunghill, and yet is no way
defiled by it ; so God decrees the permission of sin,
yet is not the author of sin : 1 John i. 5. ' God is
light, and in him is no darkness at all,' Jam. i. 13.
17. ' God cannot be tempted with evil, neither tempteth he any man.   With him is no variableness, neither shadow of turning.'

6. They are effectual ; that is, whatsoever God
decrees, comes to pass infallibly, Isa. xlvi. 10. ' My
counsel shall stand, and I will do all my pleasure.'
He cannot fall short of what he has determined.
Yet the liberty of second causes is not hereby taken
away ; for the decree of God offers no violence to the
creature's will ; as appears from the free and un-
forced actings of Joseph's brethren, Pharaoh, the
Jews that crucified Christ, &c.   Nor does it take
away the contingency of second causes, either in
themselves or as to us, as appears by the lot cast into the lap.   Nay, they are thereby established, because he hath efficaciously foreordained that such
effects shall follow on such causes.

Objections to God's decrees stated and answered.

Object. 1. It is objected by some, that if all things that come to pass in time be appointed of God by an irreversible decree, then this seems to make God the author of sin, as if he had ordained that horrid and hateful evil to come into the world, which is so dishonourable to himself, and so destructive to the children of men. In answer to this, you would know,

1. That all sinful actions fall under the divine decree. Though sin itself flows from transgressing the law, yet the futurition of it is from the decree of God. No such thing could ever have been in the world, if it had not been determined by the eternal counsel of Heaven for a holy and just end. This is plainly asserted by the apostle Peter, with respect to the greatest villany that was ever committed on the earth, namely, the death and sufferings of the Lord Jesus Christ, at the hands of sinful men, Acts ii. 23. forecited. And the church gives this account of it, Acts iv. 27, 28. ' For of a truth against thy holy child Jesus, whom thou hast anointed, both Herod and Pontius Pilate, with the Gentiles, and the people of Israel, were gathered together, for to do whatsoever thy hand, and thy counsel determined before to be done.' There was never such an atrocious crime or higher act of wickedness committed, than the murdering of the Lord of glory. And yet it appears from these texts of scripture, that, in this bloody and horrid scene, wicked men did no more than God's hand and counsel determined before to be done.

2. That the decree of God is properly distinguished into that which is effective, and that which is permissive.

(1.) His effective decree respects all the good that

comes to pass, whether it be moral or natural goodness. All the actions and motions of the creatures
have a natural goodness in them; and even sinful
actions considered abstractly from any irregularity,
obliquity, or deformity cleaving to them, have a natural goodness in them, so far as they are actions:
they have a goodness of being considered purely
and simply as actions. Now, God has decreed to
effect all these, yea even sinful actions considered
purely as natural. For he is the first and universal
cause of all things, the fountain and original of all
good. And it is said with respect to the oppressions of the church by wicked men, Psal. cxv. 3.
' Our God is in the heavens; he hath done whatsoever he pleased.'

(2.) His permissive decree doth only respect the
irregularity and pravity that is in sinful actions.
God decreed to permit the same, or he determined it
to be, himself permitting it. Hence it is said, Acts
xiv. 16. ' In times past he suffered all nations to
walk in their own ways.' And God doth nothing in
time, but what he did from eternity decree to do.
So that the futurition of sin is from the decree of
God. God determined that it should be. He did
not decree to have any efficiency in sin, considered
as such; but he willed that it should be done, himself permitting it. The counsel of God did not determine to do it, but that it should be done.

3. God decreed the permission of sin for great and
glorious ends. It is true, sin in its own nature has
no tendency to any good. If it end in any good, it
is from the overruling providence of God, and that
infinite divine skill that can bring good out of evil,
as well as light out of darkness. Now, the great and
glorious end for which God decreed the after-being
of sin, is his own glory: and the ends subordinate
thereunto are not a few. Particularly, God decreed
the futurition of sin, 1st, That he might have occasion of glorifying his infinite wisdom, love, and grace

x

in the redemption and salvation of a company of lost
sinners through the death and sufferings of his own
dear Son.   2d, That his patience and long-suffering
in bearing with and forbearing sinners, might be
magnified, admired, and adored.   3d, That he might
be honoured and glorified by the faith and repentance of his people, and their walking humbly with
him.   4th, That his justice might be illustriously displayed and glorified in the eternal damnation of reprobate sinners for their own sins and abominations,
sin being the cause of their damnation, though not
of their reprobation.   Thus God decreed the futurition of sin for these holy and wise ends, that he might
glorify his wisdom in bringing good out of so great
an evil, and a greater good than the evil he decreed
to permit.

4. The decree of God about the permission of sin
does not infringe the liberty of man's will.   For sin
doth not follow the decree by a necessity of co-action
or compulsion, which indeed would destroy human
liberty ; but by a necessity of infallibility, which is
very consistent with it.   It is sufficient unto human
liberty, or the freedom of man's will, that a man act
without all constraint, and out of choice.   Now, this
is not taken away by the decree.   Men sin as freely
as if there were no decree, and yet as infallibly as if
there were no liberty.   And men sin, not to fulfil
God's decree, which is hid from them, but to serve
and gratify their vile lusts and corrupt affections.

Object. 2. If God hath determined the precise
number of every man's days by an unalterable decree, then the use of means for the preservation of
our health and lives is altogether unnecessary ; for
nothing can frustrate the divine decree.   We will
certainly live as long as God hath appointed us, whether we use any means or not.   And therefore when
we are hungry, we need not eat and drink ; and
when we are sick, we need not take physic, or use
any medicines.

In answer to this, you would know, that as God
hath decreed the end, so he hath decreed the means
that are proper for attaining that end ; so that these
two must not be separated. Though God hath decreed how long we shall live, yet seeing it is his ordinary way to work by means, and he hath commanded and enjoined the use of them to men, therefore it
is still our duty to use lawful means for preserving
our life and health, and to wait on God in the due
use of them, referring the event to his wise determi-
nation. In Paul's dangerous voyage to Rome, an
angel of the Lord assured him, that God had given
him all that sailed with him in the ship ; and Paul
assured them from the Lord, that there should be no
loss of any of their lives : yet when some were about
to flee out of the ship, he says to the centurion who
had the command, ' Except these abide in the ship,
you cannot be saved,' Acts xxvii. 31. And he exhorted them to take some meat after their long ab-
stinence, telling them, that it was for their health.
From which it plainly appears, that as God had decreed to save their lives, so he had decreed to save
them in the due use of ordinary means ; so that they
were to use means for the preservation of their life
and health. And when Hezekiah was recovered
from a mortal disease, and received a promise from
God that he should have fifteen years added to his
days, and the promise was confirmed by a sign, the
miraculous going back of the sun, he did not neglect
or cast off the use of means ; but, as was prescribed
by the prophet, he applied a bunch of dry figs to his
sore, and used still his ordinary diet. Therefore it
is gross ignorance and madness in men to reason so
against God's decrees. The Lord, by an unchangeable counsel and purpose, hath decreed and set down
all things, and how they shall come to pass ; and
therefore it is a wrong way of arguing for people to
say, If God hath determined how long I shall live,

then I shall not die sooner, though I never eat or drink.

Object. 3. If God hath determined the eternal state and condition of men, whether they shall be happy or miserable for ever, then it is in vain to repent and believe, or use any means for their own safety. For if God hath elected them to salvation, they shall certainly be saved, whether they use any means or not ; and if they are not elected to everlasting life, all that they càn possibly do will be to no purpose at all, for they shall never be saved by it.

For answer to this, you would know,

1. That God's degree of election is a great secret, which we ought not to pry into. It is simply impossible for men to know whether they are elected or not, before they believe. Indeed, if a man were certain that he is not elected to eternal life, it would be another case : but as it is not certain that thou art elected, so it is not certain that thou art not elected. You have no means to know either the one or the other certainly, till you get saving faith. Till then the Lord reserves it in his own breast, as a secret which we are not to pry into. For it is said, Deut. xxix. 29. ' Secret things belong unto the Lord our God ; but those things which are revealed belong unto us and to our children, that we may do all the things of his law.' Here the Lord shows what belongs to him and what belongs to us, and that we should mind our duty, and not busy and perplex ourselves about impertinencies. Whether men be elected or not elected, is a secret that God never discloses to an unbeliever ; but that we should believe on Christ is no secret. This is a duty clearly revealed and enjoined by the gospel.

2. It is our duty to look to God's commands, and not to his decrees ; to our own duty, and not to his purposes. The decrees of God are a vast ocean, into which many possibly have curiously pried to their own horror and despair ; but few or none have ever

pried into them to their own profit and satisfaction.
Our election is not written in particular in the word
of God ; but our duty is plainly set down thère. If
men conscientiously perform their duty, this is the
way to come to the knowledge of their election.
Men therefore should not question whether they be
elected or not, but first believe on Christ, and endeavour diligently to work out their own salvation ; and
if their works be good, and their obedience true, thereby they will come to a certain knowledge that they
were elected and set apart to everlasting life.

3. As God elects to the end, so he elects also to
the means. Now, faith and obedience are the means
and way to salvation ; and therefore, if you be elected to salvation, you are also elected to faith and obedience. See what is said to this purpose, 2 Thess.
ii. 13. ' God hath chosen you to salvation,' there is
the end ; ' through sanctification of the Spirit and
belief of the truth,' there is the means which lead to
that end. Both are decreed by God. If therefore
you heartily and sincerely believe and obey, then
your election to salvation stands firm and sure.
Nay, further, the scriptures make election to be terminated as well in obedience as salvation. So 1 Pet.
i. 2. ' Elect', says the apostle, ' unto obedience,
through sanctification of the Spirit.' In the former
place it was, ' elect to salvation through sanctification ;' but here it is, ' elect to obedience through
sanctification ;' to denote unto us, that none are elected unto salvation but those that are elected unto obedience. And therefore it is unreasonable, yea, it is
contradictory to say, if I am elected, I shall be saved,
whether I believe and obey or not ; for none are elected to salvation but through faith and obedience.

4. Men do not pry into the decrees of God in other
things, but do what they know to be incumbent upon
them as their duty. And certainly it is as unreasonable here. When you are dangerously sick, and the
physician tells you, that unless you take such and

such medicines, your case is desperate ; you do not use to reason thus, Then if God hath decreed my recovery, I will certainly be restored to my health, whether I take that course of physic or not ; but you presently fall in with the advice given you, and make use of the means prescribed for your health. And will you not do so here ? You are dangerously sick and mortally wounded with sin, and God commands you to flee to Christ the only physician that can cure you, and cast yourselves upon him, and you shall certainly be saved. But O, says the sinner, if I knew that God had decreed my salvation, I would venture on Christ ; but till once I know this, I must not believe : O how unreasonable is unbelief! The devil's suggestions make poor creatures act as if they were entirely distracted and out of their wits. This is just as if an Israelite stung with the fiery serpents should have said, If I knew that the Lord had decreed my cure, I would look upon the brazen serpent, and if he hath decreed it, I will certainly recover whether I look to it or not. If all the stung Israelites had been thus resolved, it is likely they had all perished. Or this is as if one pursued by the avenger of blood, should have set himself down in the way to the city of refuge, where he should have been flying for his life, and said, If God has decreed my escape, then I will be safe, whether I run to the city of refuge or not ; but if he hath not decreed it, then it is in vain for me to go thither. Now, would not men count this a wilful casting away of his life, with a careless neglect of that provision which God had made to save it ? Was it not sufficient that a way was made for his escape, and a way feasible enough, the city of refuge being always open ? Thus the arms of Christ are always open to receive and embrace poor humbled perishing sinners fleeing to him for help. And will men destroy themselves by suffering Satan to entangle them with a needless, impertinent, and unreasonable scruple ? In

other cases, if there be no way but one, and any encouraging probability to draw men into it, they run
into it without delay, not perplexing and discourag-
ing themselves with the decrees of God.   Now, this
is thy case, O sinner ; Christ is the way, the truth,
and the life ; there is no other by whom you can
be saved ; flee to him then as for ·thy life ; and
let not Satan hinder thee, by diverting thee to im-
possibilities and impertinencies.   Comply with the
call and offer of the gospel.   This is present and
pertinent duty, and trouble not thyself about the secrets of God.

Important lessons drawn from the decrees of God

1. Has God decreed all things that come to pass ?
Then there is nothing that falls out by chance, nor
are we to ascribe what we meet with either to good
or ill luck and fortune.   There are many events in
the world which men look upon as mere accidents,
yet all these come by the counsel and appointment
of Heaven.   Solomon tells us, Prov. xvi. 33. that
' the lot is cast into the lap, but the whole disposing
thereof is from the Lord.'   However casual and fortuitous things may be with respect to us, yet they
are all determined and directed by the Lord.   When
that man drew a bow at a venture, 1 Kings xxii. 34.
it was merely accidental with respect to him, yet it
was God that guided the motion of the arrow so as
to smite the king of Israel rather than any other
man.   Nothing then comes to pass, however casual
and uncertain it may seem to be, but what was decreed by God.

2. Hence we see God's certain knowledge of all
things that happen in the world, seeing his knowledge is founded on his decree.   As he sees all

things possible in the glass of his own power, so he
sees all things to come in the glass of his own will ;
of his effecting will, if he hath decreed to produce
them ; and of his permitting will, if he hath decreed
to suffer them.   Hence his declaration of things to
come is founded on his appointing them, Isa. xliv. 7.
' Who, as I, shall call, and shall declare it, and set
it in order for me, since I appointed the ancient
people ? and the things that are coming and shall
come ? let them show unto them,'   He foreknows
the most necessary things according to the course of
nature, because he decreed that such effects should
proceed from and necessarily follow such and such
causes :   and   he   knows   all   future   contingents,
all things which shall fall out by chance, and the
most free actions of rational creatures, because he
decreed that such things should come to pass con-
tingently or freely, according to the nature of second
causes.   So that what is casual or contingent with
respect to us, is certain and necessary in regard of
God.

3. Whoever be the instruments of any good to us,
of whatever sort, we must look above them, and eye
the hand and counsel of God in it, which is the first
spring, and be duly thankful to God for it.   And
whatever evil of crosses or afflictions befal us, we
must look above the instruments of it to God.   Affliction doth not rise out of the dust, or come to men by
chance ; but it is the Lord that sends it, and we
should own and reverence his hand in it.   So did
David in the day of his extreme distress ; 2 Sam.
xvi. 11. ' Let him alone, and let him curse ; for the
Lord hath bidden him.'   We should be patient under whatever distress befals us, considering that
God is our party, Job ii. 10. ' Shall we receive good
at the hand of God, and shall we not receive evil ? '
This would be a happy means to still our quarrel-
ings at adverse dispensations.   Hence David says,

' I was dumb, I opened not my mouth, because thou didst it,' Psal. xxxix. 9.

4. See here the evil of murmuring and complaining at our lot in the world.   How apt are ye to quarrel with God, as if he were in the wrong to you, when his dealings with you are not according to your own desires and wishes? You demand a reason, and call God to an account, Why am I thus? Why so much afflicted and distressed? Why so long afflicted? And why such an affliction rather than another? Why am I so poor and another so rich? Thus your hearts rise up against God. But you should remember, that this is to defame the counsels of infinite wisdom, as if God had not ordered your affairs wisely enough in his eternal counsel. We find the Lord reproving Job for this, chap. xl. 2. ' Shall he that contendeth with the Lord instruct him?' When ye murmur and repine under cross and afflictive dispensations, this is a presuming to instruct God how to deal with you, and to reprove him as if he were in the wrong. Yea, there is a kind of implicit blasphemy in it, as if you had more wisdom and justice to dispose of your lot, and to carve out your own portion in the world. This is upon the matter the language of such a disposition, Had I been on God's counsel, I had ordered this matter better; things had not been with me as now they are. O presume not to correct the infinite wisdom of God, seeing he has decreed all things most wisely and judiciously.

5. There is no reason for people to excuse their sins and falls, from the doctrine of the divine decrees. Wicked men, when they commit some villany or atrocious crime, are apt to plead thus for their excuse, Who can help it? God would have it so; it was appointed for me before I was born, so that I could not avoid it. This is a horrid abuse of the divine decrees, as if they did constrain men to sin: Whereas the decree is an immanent act of God, and so can have no

Y

influence, physical or moral, upon the wills of men, but leaves them to the liberty and free choice of their own hearts ; and what sinners do, they do most freely and of choice. It is a horrid and detestable wickedness to cast the blame of your sin upon God's decree. This is to charge your villany upon him, as if he were the author of it. It is great folly to cast your sins upon Satan who tempted you, or upon your neighbour who provoked you : but it is a far greater sin, nay, horrid blasphemy, to cast it upon God himself. A greater affront than this cannot be offered to the infinite holiness of God.

6. Let the people of God comfort themselves in all cases by this doctrine of the divine decrees ; and, amidst whatever befals them, rest quietly and submissively in the bosom of God, considering that whatever comes or can come to pass, proceeds from the decree of their gracious friend and reconciled Father, who knows what is best for them, and will make all things work together for their good. O what a sweet and pleasant life would ye have under the heaviest pressures of affliction, and what heavenly serenity and tranquillity of mind would you enjoy, would you cheerfully acquiesce in the good will and pleasure of God, and embrace every dispensation, how sharp soever it may be, because it is determined and appointed for you by the eternal counsel of his will !

God alone created the World.

This will be evident from the following particulars :

1. The world could not make itself ; for this would imply a horrid contradiction, namely, that the world was before it was ; for the cause must always be be-

fore its effect. That which is not in being, can have no production ; for nothing can act before it exists. As nothing hath no existence, so it hath no operation. There must therefore be something of real existence, to give a being to those things that are ; and every second cause must be an effect of some other before it be a cause. To be and not to be at the same time, is a manifest contradiction, which would infallibly take place if any thing made itself. That which makes is always before that which is made, as is obvious to the most illiterate peasant. If the world were a creator, it must be before itself as a creature.

2. The production of the world could not be by chance. It was indeed the extravagant fancy of some ancient philosophers, that the original of the world was from a fortuitous concourse of atoms, which were in perpetual motion in an immense space, till at last a sufficient number of them met in such a happy conjunction as formed the universe in the beautiful order in which we now behold it. But it is amazingly strange how such a wild opinion, which can never be reconciled with reason, could ever find any entertainment in a human mind. Can any man rationally conceive, that a confused rout of atoms, of diverse natures and forms, and some so far distant from others, should ever meet in such a fortunate manner, as to form an entire world, so vast in the bigness, so distinct in the order, so united in the diversities of natures, so regular in the variety of changes, and so beautiful in the whole composure ? Such an extravagant fancy as this can only possess the thoughts of a disordered brain.

3. God created all things, the world, and all the creatures that belong to it. He attributes this work to himself, as one of the peculiar glories of his Deity, exclusive of all the creatures. So we read, Isa. xliv. 24. ' I am the Lord that maketh all things ; that stretcheth forth the heavens alone ; that spreadeth

abroad the earth by myself.' Chap. xlv. **12**. ' I have
made the earth, and created man upon it ; I, even
my hands, have stretched out the heavens, and all
their host have I commanded. Chap. xl. **12, 13.**
' Who hath measured the waters in the hollow of his
hand ? and meted out heaven with the span, and
comprehended the dust of the earth in a measure,
and weighed the mountains in scales, and the hills
in a balance ? Who hath directed the Spirit of the
Lord, or being his counsellor hath taught him ? Job
ix. 8. ' Which alone spreadeth out the heavens, and
treadeth upon the waves of the sea. These are mag-
nificent descriptions of the creating power of God,
and exceed every thing of the kind that hath been
attempted by the pens of the greatest sages of anti-
quity. By this operation God is distinguished from
all the false gods and fictitious deities which the
blinded nations adored, and shows himself to be the
true God. Jer. x. 11, 12. ' The gods that have not
made the heavens and the earth, even they shall perish from the earth, and from under these heavens.
He hath made the earth by his power, he hath established the world by his wisdom, and hath stretched
out the heavens by his discretion.' Psal. xcvi. 5.
' All the gods of the nations are idols : but the Lord
made the heavens.' Isa. xxxvii. 19. ' Thou art the
God, even thou alone, of all the kingdoms of the
earth : thou hast made heaven and earth.' None
could make the world but God, because creation is
a work of infinite power, and could not be produced
by any finite cause : For the distance between being
and not being is truly infinite, which could not be
removed by any finite agent, or the activity of all finite agents united.

This work of creation is common to all the three
persons in the adorable Trinity. The Father is described in scripture as the Creator, 1 Cor. viii. 6.
—' The Father, of whom are all things.' The same
prerogative belongs to the Son, John i. 3. ' All things

were made by him' the Word, the Son ; ' and without him was not any thing made that was made.'
The same honour belongs to the Holy Ghost, as Job
xxvi. 13. ' By his Spirit he hath garnished the heavens.' Chap. xxxiii. 4. ' The Spirit of God hath
made me, says Elihu, and the breath of the Almighty
hath given me life.' All the three persons are one
God ; God is the Creator ; and therefore all the external works and acts of the one God must be common to the three persons. Hence, when the work
of creation is ascribed to the Father, neither the Son
nor the Holy Spirit are excluded ; but because, as
the Father is the fountain of the Deity, so he is the
fountain of divine works. The Father created from
himself by the Son and the Spirit ; the Son from the
Father by the Spirit ; and the Spirit from the Father
and the Son ; the manner or order of their working
being according to the order of their subsisting. The
matter may be conceived thus : All the three persons being one God, possessed of the same infinite
perfections ; the Father, the first in subsistence, willed the work of creation to be done by his authority :
' He spake, and it was done ; he commanded, and it
stood fast.'—In respect of immediate operation, it peculiarly belonged to the Son. For ' the Father created all things by Jesus Christ,' Eph. iii. 9. And
we are told, that ' all things were made by him,'
John iii. 3. This work in regard of disposition and
ornament, doth peculiarly belong to the Holy Ghost.
So it is said, Gen. i. 2. ' The Spirit of God moved
upon the face of the waters,' to garnish and adorn
the world, after the matter of it was formed. Thus
it is also said, Job xxvi. 13. above cited, ' By his Spirit he hath garnished the heavens.'

****

*Important lessons from the doctrine of God's
creation of the world.*

1. God is a most glorious being, infinitely lovely
and desirable, possessed of every perfection and excellency. He made all things, and bestowed upon
them all the perfections and amiable qualities with
which they are invested. So that there is no perfection in any of the creatures which is not in him in an
eminent way, Psal. xciv. 9. ' He that planted the ear,
shall he not hear ? he that formed the eye, shall he
not see ?' Whatever excellency and beauty is in the
creatures, is all from him ; and sure it must be most
excellent in the fountain.

2. God's glory should be our chief end.   And seeing whatever we have is from him, it should be used
and employed for him : For ' all things were created
by him and for him,' Col. i. 16.   Have we a tongue ?
it should be employed for him, to show forth his
praise ;—hands ? they should do and work for him ;—
life ? it should be employed in his service ;—talents
and abilities ? they should be laid out for promoting
his interest and honour ; and, upon a proper call, we
should be ready to suffer for him.

3. God is our Sovereign Lord Proprietary, and
may do in us, on us, and by us, what he will : Rom.
ix. 20, 21. ' Shall the thing formed say to him that
formed it, Why hast thou made me thus ? Hath not
the potter power over the clay, of the same lump to
make one vessel unto honour, and another unto dishonour ?' There is no reason to murmur and fret under the cross, or any afflicting dispensations, that he
exercises us with.   Should he destroy that being that
he gave us, to whom would he do wrong ? As he gave
it us freely, he may take it away, without any im-

peachment of his goodness and justice. May not God do with his own what he will ?

4. We should use all the creatures we make use of with an eye to God, and due thankfulness to him, the giver ; employing them for our use, and in our service, soberly and wisely, with hearts full of gratitude to our Divine Benefactor ; considering they stand related to God as their Creator, and are the workmanship of his own hands. For every creature of God is good, and nothing to be refused, if it be received with thanksgiving, 1 Tim. iv. 4. They are not to be used to his dishonour, or the feeding of our base lusts and irregular appetites, but to fit us for and strengthen us in the performance of our duty to him.

5. There is no case so desperate, but faith may get sure footing with respect to it in the power and word of God. Let the people of God be ever so low, they can never be lower than when they were not at all. Hence the Lord says, Isa. lxv. 18. ' But be ye glad and rejoice for ever in that which I create : for, behold, I create Jerusalem a rejoicing, and her people a joy.' He spoke a word and so the creature was made at first ; and it will cost him but a word to make it over again. Hence Christ is called ' the beginning of the creation of God,' Rev. iii. 14. O seek to be new-made by him ; that old things may pass away, and all things become new.

6. Give away yourselves to God through Jesus Christ, making an hearty, a cheerful, and an entire dedication and surrender of your souls and bodies, and all that ye are and have, to him as your God and Father, resolving to serve and obey him all the days of your life ; that as he made you for his glory, you may in some measure answer the end of your creation, which is to show forth his praise. Serve not sin or Satan any longer. God made you upright and holy ; but Satan unmade you, stripping you of your highest glory and ornament. Relinquish his service, which

is the basest drudgery and slavery, and will land all
that are employed in it in hell at last ; and engage
in the service of God in Christ, which is truly honourable and glorious, and will be crowned with an everlasting reward in the other world : for where he is,
there shall his servants also be.

7. This doctrine affords a ground of love, peace,
justice and mercy betwixt men, which should be carefully cultivated by all that would desire to be with
God for ever. For, says the prophet, Mal. ii. 10.
' Have we not all one Father ? Hath not one God created us ? Why do we deal treacherously every man
against his brother, by profaning the covenant of our
fathers?' The consideration of being created by God,
should be a powerful inducement to us to practise all
the duties we owe to one another as men and Christians.

In what the image of God, in which man was created, consisted.

1. The image of God after which man was created,
consisted in knowledge, Col. i. 10. ' That ye might
walk worthy of the Lord unto all pleasing, being
fruitful in every good work, and increasing in the
knowledge of God.' He was created wise : not that
he knew all things, for that is proper to the Omniscient Being alone ; but he was ignorant of nothing
that he was obliged to know ; he had all the knowledge that was necessary for life and godliness. He
had clear and distinct apprehensions of God, his nature and perfections, far superior to any knowledge
of that kind that can now be acquired by the most
diligent and the most laboured researches of human
industry. And we can hardly suppose that he was
ignorant of the great mystery of the Trinity, consider-

ed abstractly ; as it was most certainly the second person who appeared to and conversed with him. This knowledge or wisdom of man appeared in his knowledge of the miraculous formation of Eve, whose nature and duty, as well as his own towards her, he declares ; which he could not know but by a prophetical spirit. The primitive pair had God's law written on their hearts, Rom. ii. 15. even that same law which was afterwards written on tables of stone, and promulgated from Mount Sinai. It was concreated with them ; so that no sooner were they man and woman, than they were knowing and intelligent creatures, endowed with all the knowledge necessary for their upright state. Adam's giving names to the beasts, and those such as were expressive of their natures, Gen. ii. 19. was a great evidence of his knowledge of nature. Thus his knowledge reached from the sun, that glorious fountain of light, to the meanest glow-worm that shines in the hedge. And that God gave them dominion over the earth and all the inferior creatures, is an evidence that they were endued with the knowledge of managing civil affairs, which a wise man will manage with discretion.

2. The image of God consisted in righteousness, Eph. iv. 24. ' And that ye put on the new man, which after God is created in righteousness and true holiness.' There was a perfect conformity in his will to the will of God. He was endued with a disposition to every good thing, Eccl. vii. 29. ' God made man upright.' His will was straight with God's will, not bending to the right or left hand, without any irregular bias or inclination. And he had full power and ability to fulfil the whole law of God. As, in respect of knowledge, he perfectly knew the whole extent of his duty, so he was created with sufficient powers for the due performance thereof.

3. It consisted in holiness, Eph. iv. 24. ' And that ye put on the new man, which after God is created in righteousness and true holiness.' Man's affections

z

were pure and holy, without being tinctured with any vicious appetite. They were regular and orderly, free from all disorder and distemper. They were set on lawful objects, and that in a right manner, loving what God loved, and hating what he hated ; loving and delighting in God with all his heart, strength, soul, and mind. Yet all this happy disposition was mutable, he was not confirmed therein, nor set beyond the reach of falling therefrom, as the event has mournfully showed.

This is that image of God wherein man was created, consisting in original righteousness, where his reason was naturally subject to God, his will to his reason, and his affections to his will, and consequently all duly subordinated to God, and directed to him, without any propensity or inclination to evil. A signal of this was, that both our first parents were naked, and yet were not ashamed, nor susceptive of shame.

That man was created in this condition, wise, altogether righteous, and holy, is not only clear from the above cited scriptures, but is also agreeable to reason ; which suggests, that nothing impure or imperfect, nothing having any vicious tendency or inclination, could proceed out of the hands of an holy God, who cannot be the author of evil. Man was created after the image of God ; and in knowledge, righteousness, and true holiness, the scripture shows us, the image of God consists. Moreover, God made all very good, Gen. i. 31. Man's goodness consists in these excellent qualities ; and without these he would not have been fit for the end of his creation. How was it possible for him to have exercised the dominion he was invested with over the creatures, or served his Creator in the manner that became him, without such endowments ?

****

*Important Lessons deduced from the consideration
of Man's state of innocence.*

1. How are we fallen from heaven! What a lamentable change has sin brought on man! It has defaced
the moral image of God, with which man's soul was
beautifully decorated in his primitive state, and rent
in pieces that pleasant picture of himself which God
set up in this lower world. This stately fabric lies
now in ruins, and calls us to lament over its ruins
with weeping eyes and grieved hearts. Now there
is ignorance in the mind, instead of that knowledge
of God and divine things, with which it was richly
furnished in its primitive state. The understanding,
that as a lamp or candle shone brightly, is now en-
veloped with darkness. The will, that was exactly
conformable to the will of God, and naturally disposed
to comply with every intimation thereof, is now filled
with irregularity, enmity, and rebellion against God
and his law. The affections that were all regular,
holy, and pure, are now disordered and distempered,
placed upon and eagerly bent towards improper and
sinful objects, loving and doating upon what men
should hate, hating what they should love, joying in
what they ought to mourn for, glorying in what is
shameful, abhorring the chief good, and desiring what
is ruinous to them. All the members of the body
that were subordinated to the upright mind, and entirely at its command, are now in rebellion, and mis-
lead and enslave the mind and superior faculties.
And the creatures that were man's humble servants,
ready to execute his commands, are now risen up
against him, and the least of them having a commission, would prove more than a match for him. Nay,
it is with difficulty and much pains that any of them

are brought to engage in his service. Ah! how dismal is man's case! The crown is fallen from our head : wo unto us that we have sinned. Let us weep and mourn over our ruined state, and never rest till we get it repaired by faith in the Lord Jesus, the great Repairer of this spiritual breach.

2. How lovely are knowledge, righteousness, and holiness, wherein the image of God consists! They shine with a dazzling brightness, and should charm and captivate our minds. But, alas! by nature we are blind, and see not their beauty and excellency. O! let us endeavour, through grace, to put off the old man, which is corrupt according to the deceitful lusts, and to be renewed in the spirit of our minds, putting on the new man, which after God is created in righteousness and true holiness. Try if this blessed change has passed upon you, if ye be now light in the Lord, be disposed to do his will, and are holy in heart and life. Study righteousness and holiness if ye would be like God. And beware of ignorance, unrighteousness, and impurity, which proceed from Satan, and make you so unlike a righteous and holy God.

3. Come to the Lord Christ, who is the image of the invisible God, and the beginning of the creation of God, who at first made man after the divine image, and can make him so over again, and will do so to those who come to him by faith, with this addition, that the image of God which he will impress on the soul anew, shall never be lost any more. O! come to him now, that ye may become God's workmanship, created in Christ Jesus unto good works.

The evidence of Christ's true Priesthood.

That Christ is truly and properly a Priest, is evident, if we consider, 1. That the scripture holds him forth as such, Psalm cx. 4. and Heb. v. and other places of that epistle. 2. Because he exercises the acts of the priestly office, in offering sacrifice, and praying for his people. 3. Because he was typified by such as were really priests, as all the Levitical priests, and Melchizedec.

Quest. Wherein did Christ's priestly office differ from the priestly office under the ceremonial law?

1. The priests under the law were priests after the order of Aaron : but Christ is a priest after the order of Melchizedec. Who this Melchizedec was, it is in vain to enquire, and cannot possibly be known ; the Holy Ghost designedly concealing his genealogy, beginning, and ending, and descent, that so he might be a fitter type of Christ and his everlasting priesthood. He was like a man dropt from the clouds, and at last caught up again, and none knew how. It is said of him, Heb. vii. 3. ' that he was without father, without mother, without descent, having neither beginning of days, nor end of life ; but made like unto the Son of God, abideth a Priest continually.' Now, Christ was a priest after the order of this Melchizedec, not by a corporeal unction, legal ceremony, or the intervening act of a human ordination, but by a divine and heavenly institution, and immediate unction of the Spirit of life, in that extraordinary manner, whereby he was to be both King and Priest unto God, as Melchizedec was, Heb. vii. 16. He was not a Priest after the order of Aaron, because the law made nothing perfect, but was weak and unprofitable ; and therefore was to be abolished, and to give place to another priesthood. Men were not to rest in it, but to be led by it to him who was to abolish it, Heb. vii. 11, 12. The ministry and promises of Christ were better than those of the law : and therefore his priesthood, which was the office of dispensing them, was to be more excellent too, Heb. viii. 6. For when the law and covenant were to be

abolished, the priesthood, in which they were established, was likewise to die.

2. The priests under the law were sinful men, and
therefore offered sacrifices for their own sins, as well
as for the sins of the people, Heb. v. 3. But Christ
was ' holy, harmless, undefiled, separate from sinners,
and made higher than the heavens ; who needeth
not daily, as those high priests, to offer up sacrifice,
first for his own sins, and then for the people's ; for
this he did once when he offered up himself,' Heb.
vii. 26, 27. He was perfectly pure and holy, and
could stand before God even in the eye of his strict
justice, ' as a lamb without blemish and without
spot.' Though he ' made his soul an offering for
sin,' yet he ' had done no iniquity, neither was there
any guile found in his mouth.' And indeed his sacrifice had done us no good, had he been tainted with
the least sin.

3. The priests under the law were many, because
they were mortal ; death as an universal deluge was
continually sweeping them off the stage. But Christ
as a Priest for ever, Psal. cx. 4. Heb. vii. 23. ' This
man continueth ever.'

4. The priesthood under the law was changeable ;
but Christ's priesthood is unchangeable. The legal
dispensation was to continue only for a time. It was
but like the morning-star to usher in the rising sun,
which so soon as he appears in our horizon, it eva-
nishes and shrinks away, Heb. vii. 12. God confirmed this priesthood with an oath, Psal. cx. 4. Heb.
vii. 21. as well as a King. Those offices which were
divided before between two families, were both united and vested in Christ ; this being absolutely necessary for the discharge of his Mediatory undertaking, and for the establishment of his kingdom, which
being of another kind than the kingdoms of this
world, even spiritual and heavenly, therefore needed
such a King as was also a minister of holy things.
And the apostle tells us, Heb. vii. 24. that ' this

man, because he continueth ever, hath an unchangeable priesthood.'

5. The priests under the law offered many sacrifices, and of various kinds, as lambs and rams, calves and bullocks, and the blood of many beasts : but Christ offered but once, and that but one sacrifice, even the sacrifice of himself. So it is said, Heb. ix. 25, 26. ' Nor yet that he should offer himself often, as the high priest entereth into the holy place, every year with the blood of others ; (for then must he often have suffered since the foundation of the world) : but now once in the end of the world, hath he appeared to put away sin by the sacrifice of himself.' And herein he excelled and far transcended all other priests, in this that he had something of his own to offer. He had a body given him to be at his own disposal for this very end and purpose. It is said, Heb. x. 5. 7. 10. ' Wherefore when he cometh into the world, he saith, Sacrifice and offering thou wouldst not, but a body hast thou prepared me. Then said I, Lo, I come (in the volume of the book it is written of me) to do thy will, O God. By the which will we are sanctified, through the offering of the body of Jesus Christ once for all.' He offered up his body, and not only his body, but his soul also was made an offering for sin, Isa. liii. 10. We had made a forfeiture both of our souls and bodies by sin. It was therefore necessary that the sacrifice of Christ should be answerable to the debt which we owed to God. And when Christ came to offer up his sacrifice he stood not only in the capacity of a Priest, but also in that of a Surety ; and so his soul stood in the stead of ours, and his body in the stead of our bodies.

6. All those sacrifices that the priests offered under the law were types of the sacrifice of Christ, which he was to offer in the fulness of time, they not being sufficient in themselves to purge away sin, nor acceptable to God any further than Christ was eyed in them. But Christ's sacrifice was the thing typi-

fied by all these oblations, and is efficacious in itself for the satisfaction of justice, and the expiation of sin, Heb. x. 1. 4. 14. ' For the law having a shadow of good things to come, and not the very image of the things, can never with those sacrifices which they offered year by year continually, make the comers thereunto perfect. For it is not possible that the blood of bulls and of goats should take away sins. For by one offering he hath perfected for ever them that are sanctified.' His sacrifice was invaluably precious, and of infinite efficacy and virtue. And such it behoved to be : for it being offered as an expiatory sacrifice, it ought to be proportioned and equivalent, in its own intrinsic value, to all the souls and bodies that were to be redeemed by it. So that as one rich diamond is more in worth than ten thousand pebbles, or one piece of gold than many counters, so the sacrifice of Christ's soul and body is far more valuable than all the souls and bodies in the world.

7. The priests under the law appeared before God in behalf of the people, in the temple made with hands ; but Christ appeareth in heaven itself. The Levitical priests offered sacrifices and made prayers for the people in the temple ; and the high priest, who was an eminent type of Christ, entered into the holy of holies, the figure of heaven, once a year, and that not without blood. This was typical of Christ's entering into heaven itself in his people's name, to appear for them before the throne of God. Hence it is said, Heb. ix. 24. ' For Christ is not entered into the holy places made with hands, which are the figures of the true ; but into heaven itself, now to appear in the presence of God for us.' 1 John ii. 1. If any man sin, we have an Advocate with the Father, Jesus Christ the righteous.'

8. The priests under the law had only the office of priesthood ; but Christ is Prophet, Priest, and King.

The import of Christ's offering himself a Sacrifice.

It signifies the voluntariness of Christ's sufferings,
Eph. v. 2. ' Christ hath given himself for us, an offering, and a sacrifice to God for a sweet-smelling
savour. He laid down his life of himself, that he
might take it again. He was led as a lamb to the
slaughter, and as a sheep before her shearers is
dumb, so he opened not his mouth.' For,

1. Though he well knew his sufferings before-
hand, and that dreadful storm of the divine wrath and
indignation that was to fall upon him, and all the
abuse, indignities, and torments, he was to meet
with from wicked men and on the cross, yet he did
not withdraw from that dreadful apparatus of a violent death when his time was come ; he would not
suffer his disciples, could they have done it, to rescue
him from the impending danger : nay, his delivering
himself up to his blood-thirsty pursuers, after he had
exhibited a remarkable instance of his divine power,
in making them fall to the ground with a word, John
xviii. 28. was an evidence, that he was nowise con-
strained, but a hearty volunteer in his then intended
offering. The cup of his sufferings was continually
before his eyes ; he never declined to drink of it :
nay, he was pained and straitened till he drank it to
the bottom.

2. The strong cry he uttered immediately before
his yielding up his soul on the cross, was an evidence
there was more than a natural power attending him
in that important crisis. He was no criminal in the
eye of God and scripture, and could not have been
put to death unless he had pleased, being the Most
High God, and Sovereign of men and angels, and
therefore having the whole creation at his command.

A a

The strong cry he then uttered was not the effect of weakness or reluctance to part with his life, such as a criminal may be supposed to give, but rather a shout of triumph, proceeding from one who had spontaneously offered himself to such a dreadful death, testifying before God, angels, and men, his joy and exultation in having performed the arduous work he had of his own proper motion engaged to achieve.

What the Sacrifice was which Christ offered.

To explain this, observe, that sacrifices were of two sorts.

1. Some were eucharistical, or thank-offerings in testimony of homage, subjection, duty, and service ; as the dedication of the first fruits, the meat and drink offerings. By these the sacrificer acknowledged the bounty and goodness of God, and his own unworthiness to receive the least of his favours, rendered praise for mercies received, and desired the divine blessing. But Christ's sacrifice was not of this kind.

2. Some sacrifices were expiatory, for the satisfaction of justice, and the purging away of sin. The institution of this kind of sacrifices was upon a double account. 1*st*. That man is a sinner, and therefore obnoxious to the just indignation and extreme displeasure of the holy and righteous God, and laid fairly open to all the fierceness of wrath and vengeance. 2*d*. That God was to be propitiated, that so he might pardon man. These truths are rooted and deeply engraven in the natural consciences of men, as appears by the pretended expiations of sin among the heathens. But they are more clearly revealed in sacred writ. Under the law, without the effusion of blood there was no remission, to intimate

unto us, that God would not forgive sin without the atonement of justice, which required the death of the offender : but it being tempered with mercy, accepted of a sacrifice in his stead.

Of this last kind was the sacrifice of Christ, which he offered for us, even a sacrifice of expiation.   All that was requisite to a real and proper sacrifice, concurred in his sacrifice.   As,

1. The person offering was to be a priest.   It was the peculiar office of a priest under the law to offer sacrifices.   So says the apostle, Heb. v. 1. ' Every high priest taken from among men, is ordained for men in things pertaining to God, that he may offer both gifts and sacrifices for sins.'   In like manner Christ, that he might offer this sacrifice, was called to that office, and made an High Priest in the house of God ; as appears from Heb. v. 4, 5, 6. & 10.   He is called ' the Apostle and High Priest of our profession ;' and it is said, ' Such an High Priest became us, who is holy, harmless, undefiled, and separate from sinners.'

2. There was something to be offered, and that was himself.   He was the sacrifice that he offered up unto God.   Our great High Priest behoved to have a sacrifice answerable to the debt that we owed to God ; and the debt was the forfeiture of both soul and body to the wrath of God, and the curse of the law : and therefore our High Priest was to have a soul and body to suffer in as our Surety.   ' He made his soul an offering for sin,' Isa. liii. 10. ' My soul,' says he, ' is exceeding sorrowful even unto death. A body hast thou prepared me,' Heb. x. 5.   And it is said, Heb. x. 10. ' We are sanctified through the offering of the body of Jesus Christ once.   He himself bare our sins in his own body on the tree,' 1 Pet. ii. 24.   He took upon him our nature, that he might have a proper sacrifice to offer.   Christ was a sacrifice in his human nature.   He suffered in his soul and body.   It is to be observed, that doing or suffer-

ing belongs to the whole person. Hence the church
is said to be redeemed with ' the blood of God,' Acts
xx. 28. Yet the notion of a sacrifice importing suffering, and the divine nature not being capable of it,
he himself was the sacrifice indeed, but not in the
divine but in the human nature. Even as a murderer is said to kill a man, though he kill not the soul.
Now, that he suffered in his body, appears from the
history of his passion in the evangelists. And his
soul-sufferings also are evident from the same history.
His sufferings in his soul he himself testifies, when
he says, ' My soul is exceeding sorrowful even unto
death.' These were the soul of his sufferings, and
far greater than those of his body. They consisted,
1st. In his being deserted of God, whereby all comfort was eclipsed from his holy soul, Psal. xxii. 1.
' My God, my God, why hast thou forsaken me?'
2d. In the impressions of God's wrath on it, which
produced that bloody sweat in the garden, by which
blood transpired from his sacred body. God knew
how to let him feel his wrath as our Surety ; and yet
was pleased with him as a Son. 3d. In the assaults
of the powers of darkness and spiritual wickedness-
es, who assailed him with redoubled fury in that
hour of darkness. The prince of this world attacked
him more fiercely then than ever before.

3. There was an altar on which this sacrifice was
offered : for it is the altar that sanctifieth the offering, and renders it acceptable to God, and useful to
man ; and that was his divine nature. ' Through
the Eternal Spirit,' says the apostle, ' he offered himself without spot unto God,' Heb. ix. 14. and so by
his blood purgeth our consciences from dead works.
For Christ as God sanctified himself as man, that
so, through the virtue and merit of his sacrifice, his
people might be sanctified also, John xvii. 19. There
behoved to be something to add an infinite value and
efficacy to the sufferings of his humanity ; which
could be nothing else but the divine nature. The

human nature suffered, and the divine nature sanctified the humanity ; and, by reason of this admirable
union, and the reflection of the Divinity upon the humanity, what was done to the human nature upon
the cross is ascribed to the whole person. They
' crucified the Lord of glory,' says the apostle ; and,
' God purchased the church with his own blood.' It
was this that made his sufferings acceptable and highly pleasing to God, whose justice was to be appeased
and satisfied ; and it was this that made them efficacious for man, whose happiness and commerce with
God were to be restored, and his guilt removed. So
that he had a human nature that served for a sacrifice, and a divine nature wherein he subsisted, from
whence that sacrifice derived an infinite dignity and
value. Thus Christ was a priest in his person, a sacrifice in his humanity, and the altar in his Divinity.

4. In a sacrifice, the things offered were to be of
God's appointment, or else it had not been an acceptable sacrifice, but will worship ; and no more a sacrifice on God's account, than the cutting off a dog's
neck, or offering swine's blood, as appears by the law
given by Moses concerning free-will offerings, Lev.
5. So that what Christ offered was appointed and
prepared by God. He prepared him a body, that he
might offer it for a sacrifice. It was a living body,
a body animated with a rational soul, which soul was
separated from his body in the offering ; and therefore he is said to ' have made his soul an offering for
sin ;' and that soul and body constituted his human
nature. This was the sacrifice that was appointed
of God for the expiation of the elect's sin. Hence
says the apostle, 1 Pet. i. 18, 19. ' Ye were not redeemed with corruptible things, as silver and gold ;
—but with the precious blood of Christ, as of a lamb
without blemish and without spot.'

5. The thing offered in sacrifice was to be destroyed. This is essential to a sacrifice. Those things
that were endued with life were killed, that so they

might be offered to God in sacrifice, and their blood
was poured out, and the other parts of them, besides
the blood, were burned with fire, either wholly or in
part. And thus was Christ sacrificed. His dying
and bleeding on the cross, answered the killing and
shedding of the blood of the Levitical sacrifices : and
his sufferings (expressed by the pains of hell) were
correspondent to the burning of these sacrifices. It
is said, Heb. xiii. 12, 13. ' Jesus also, that he might
sanctify the people with his own blood, suffered without the gate. Let us go forth therefore unto him
without the camp, bearing his reproach.' His sufferings without the gate are held forth here, as answering the burning of the sacrifices without the camp.

6. The person to whom the sacrifices were offered,
was God, and he only. It was gross idolatry to offer
them to any other. Hence they are called ' things
pertaining to God,' Heb. v. 1. and Christ's sacrifice
was thus offered up to God, Heb. ii. 17. He performed the office of a merciful and faithful High Priest
in offering up himself a sacrifice to God. God was
the party offended by man's sin, and whose justice
behoved to be satisfied, Eph. v. 2. Here is a mystery of wonders, where one party is the party offended,
the priest, and the sacrifice.

For whom Christ offered himself a Sacrifice.

1. It was not for his own sins, for he had none ;
but for the sins and transgressions of others, Dan.
ix. 26. ' The Messiah shall be cut off, but not for
himself.' He could not suffer for any sin of his own ;
for he was ' holy, harmless, undefiled, and separate
from sinners.' Though he made his soul an offering
for sin, yet he had done no iniquity, neither was
guile found in his mouth. As the legal lambs were

without blemish, so Christ was a Lamb without spot. His extraordinary and miraculous conception in the womb of a virgin was an effectual bar against original sin, and he had no actual sin in the course of his life. He was infinitely holy as God, and habitually holy as man. Every power and faculty of his soul, and every member of his body, was elevated and raised to the highest pitch of holiness. And he fulfilled all righteousness in his life, and gave complete satisfaction to all the demands of the law ; so that he needed not, as the Levitical priests, first to offer sacrifice for his own sin, and then for the sins of the people.

2. Christ did not offer up this sacrifice for the sins of fallen angels ; for there was no sacrifice appointed for them. Whenever they rebelled against their Sovereign Lord and Creator, they were immediately expelled from the divine presence, and are kept in everlasting chains under darkness to the judgment of the great day. Christ took not upon him the nature of angels, but the seed of Abraham, He offered up the sacrifice of himself to make an atonement for the sins of men.

3. Christ did not die a sacrifice for every man and woman in the world. It is true, there was virtue and efficacy enough in his oblation to satisfy offended justice for the sins of the whole world, yea, and of millions of worlds more ; for his blood hath infinite value, because of the infinite dignity and excellency of his person. And in this sense some divines understand those places of scripture where he is called the Saviour of the whole world. Yet the efficacy and saving virtue of his sacrifice extendeth not unto all. For,

1*st*. It is restricted in scripture to a certain number, called sometimes the church of God, as Acts xx. 28. ' Feed the church of God which he hath purchased with his own blood,' Eph. v. 25. ' Christ loved the church, and gave himself for it.' Sometimes they

are called his sheep, as John x. 15. ' I lay down my
life for my sheep.' They are also called those that
were given to him by the Father, John xvii. 2. ' Thou
hast given him power over all flesh, that he should give
eternal life to as many as thou hast given him.' See
also John x. 26—29. In these places of scripture,
and others that might be named, you see that Christ's
death is restricted to a certain number of persons,
exclusive of all others,

2*dly*, If Christ would not pray for every one in
the world, then certainly he did not die for every one
in particular. But so it is that he excludes the reprobate world from the benefit of his prayer, John
xvii. 9. ' I pray not for the world, but for them whom
thou hast given me.' Both the parts of Christ's
priesthood, his offering sacrifice and his intercession,
are of the same latitude and extent. We find them
joined together in the scripture by an inseparable
connexion, Rom. viii. 34. ' It is Christ that died,
yea rather, that is risen again, who is even at the
right hand of God, who also maketh intercession for
us, 1 John ii. 1, 2. ' If any man sin, we have an Advocate with the Father, Jesus Christ the righteous :
and he is the propitiation for our sins.' So that
Christ intercedes for all those for whom he satisfied
offended justice : but he intercedes not for the whole
world, but only for those whom God hath given him ;
and therefore he did not satisfy offended justice for
all men.

3*dly*, Christ's death is an act of the highest love
that ever was or can be manifested to the world.
' Greater love,' says he, ' hath no man than this, that
a man lay down his life for his friends.' And, says
the apostle, Rom. v. 8. ' God commendeth his love
towards us, in that while we were yet sinners, Christ
died for us.' Now, it is plain, and cannot be denied,
that every one of Adam's posterity is not the object
of Christ's dearest love : and therefore he did not lay
down his life for every one of them.

4thly, To affirm that Christ offered up himself a sacrifice with a design and intention to save all mankind, great absurdities would follow.   As,

(1.) That Christ died for many, yea for innumerable multitudes, who never heard of his blessed name, nor of the blessings and benefits which were purchased by his death.—But this runs cross to the strain and current of the scripture, which tells us plainly, that there can be no salvation but by faith in Christ; and that without hearing of him there can be no faith, Rom. x. 14, 15, 16.

(2.) If Christ died for all, then this absurdity would follow, that he died for those whom he knew to be children of wrath and sons of perdition, whom God had passed by, and left to perish eternally in that miserable condition into which they had plunged themselves by sin.

(3.) If Christ died for all men, then he died for those who are now roaring in hell, and scorched and tormented with unquenchable fire, without any hope of redemption; and so he bare the punishment of their sins, and they are also now bearing and shall bear it for ever themselves.

(4.) If Christ died with an intention to save all men, then he is an imperfect and incomplete Saviour, who hath satisfied offended justice for their sins, and purchased redemption by his blood, but cannot apply it.   He is only a true Saviour of those who are actually saved, and obtain salvation by him.

(5.) If Christ died for all men, then he died in vain for the most part, and his death and sacrifice had little effect; for the generality of men and women will perish eternally.   There are many nations in the world that never heard of Christ; and even where the gospel is preached, our Saviour tells us, that ' wide is the gate, and broad is the way that leadeth to destruction, and many go in thereat; but that strait is the gate, and narrow is the way that leadeth unto life, and few there be that find it,' Matt. vii.

12, 13. ' Many are called, but few are chosen.'
So that Christ did not offer up the sacrifice of himself for every one in particular.

4. Christ died for the elect, and for all the elect,
and none else. God designed to save some of the
lost posterity of Adam, for the manifestation of the
glory of the exceeding riches of his grace ; and Christ
died for all these, Eph. i. 4, 5, 6. ' According as he
hath chosen us in him before the foundation of the
world, that we should be holy and without blame before him in love : Having predestinated us unto the
adoption of children by Jesus Christ to himself, according to the good pleasure of his will, to the praise
of the glory of his grace, wherein he hath made us
accepted in the Beloved.' Compare the following
scriptures, Acts xiii. 48. ' And when the Gentiles
heard this, they were glad, and glorified the word of
the Lord : and as many as were ordained to eternal
life believed.' Rom. iv. 25. ' Who was delivered for
our offences, and was raised again for our justification ;' and v. 8. ' But God commendeth his love toward us, in that, while we were yet sinners, Christ
died for us.' 1 Cor. xv. 3, 4. ' For I delivered unto
you first of all that which I also received, how that
Christ died for our sins according to the scriptures ;
and that he was buried, and that he rose again the
third day according to the scriptures.' 1 Pet. ii. 21.
24. For even hereunto were ye called, because Christ
also suffered for us, leaving us an example that ye
should follow his steps ; who his own self bare our
sins in his own body on the tree, that we, being dead
to sins should live unto righteousness, by whose
stripes ye were healed.' &c. From which we may
be fully convinced that Christ died only for the elect.*

* The Arminians maintain, that Christ died equally for every
individual of the human race, and paid the same price of redemption equally for all men, yet they allow that many shall perish,
i. e. that many shall suffer eternally in hell for their own sins,
even though Christ suffered for them also to the full. The mere

****

Christ gave full satisfaction to the Justice of God.

This is evident,

1. From many texts of scripture, as Eph. v. 2.
' And walk in love, as Christ also hath loved us,
and hath given himself for us an offering and a sacrifice to God for a sweet-smelling savour.' Heb.
vii. 26, 27. ' For such an high priest became us, who
is holy, harmless, undefiled, separate from sinners,
and made higher than the heavens ; who needeth
not daily as those high priests, to offer up sacrifice,
first for his own sins, and then for the people's : for
this he did once, when he offered up himself.' Heb.
x. 14. ' For by one offering he hath perfected for
ever them that are sanctified.' Heb. ix. 13, 14.
' For if the blood of bulls and of goats, and the ashes
of an heifer sprinkling the unclean, sanctifieth to the
purifying of the flesh ; how much more shall the
blood of Christ, who, through the eternal Spirit, offered himself without spot to God, purge your conscience
from dead works, to serve the living God ? '

2. Christ's resurrection from the dead proves the
validity and completeness of his satisfaction. As
the elect's Surety, he satisfied the law in his death ;
and having thereby paid all their debt, he received
an acquittance, and the discharge was solemnly published to the world in his resurrection. He was released from the grave, as from prison, by a public

statement of such a doctrine is enough to prove it both false and
absurd. It may be observed, also, that all who preach the doctrine of Christ's dying equally for all men, must, of necessity, and
for the sake of consistency, preach also the doctrine of free will,
or of conditional salvation ; or, in other words, the doctrine of
Salvation by the deeds of the law.

Ed.

sentence ; which is an undeniable argument of the validity of the payment made by him in our name. For being under such strong bands as the justice and power of God, God could never have loosed the pains of death, if his sufferings had not been fully satisfactory to God, and received and accepted by him for our discharge. And it is observable to this purpose, that the raising of Christ is ascribed to God as reconciled, Heb. xiii. 20. The divine power was not put forth in loosing the bands of death till God was pacified. Justice incensed exposed him to death, and justice appeased raised him from the dead. If he had not paid all his people's debt by sacrifice, he had been detained a prisoner for ever in the grave. But God having received full satisfaction, set him free.

3. His ascension into heaven proves the completeness and all-sufficiency of his sacrifice. If he had been excluded from the divine presence, there had been just cause to suspect, that anger had been still resting in the breast of God ; but his admission into heaven is an infallible testimony that God is reconciled. Our Saviour produces this as the convincing argument by which the Holy Ghost will effectually overcome the guilty fears of men, John xvi. 10. ' He will convince the world of righteousness, because I go to my Father.' Christ in his sufferings was numbered among transgressors ; he died as a guilty person ; but having overcome death, and returned to his Father again, he made the innocency of his person manifest and apparent, and showed that a complete righteousness is acquired by his sufferings, sufficient to justify all those who shall truly accept of it.

4. The many excellent benefits which God reconciled bestows upon his people, proves the completeness of Christ's satisfaction.

(1.) Justification is a fruit of Christ's death ; for the obligation of the law is made void by it, whereby the sinner was bound over to eternal wrath and pun-

ishment ; Col. ii. 14. ' Blotting out the hand-writing
of ordinances that was against us, which was contrary to us, and took it out of the way, nailing it to
his cross.' The terms are here used which are proper to the cancelling of a civil bond. The killing
letter of the law is abolished by the blood of the cross ;
the nails and the spear, which pierced his sacred body, have rent it in pieces, to intimate that its condemning power is taken away. The forgiveness of sin
is the chief part of our redemption, and it is ascribed
to Christ's blood as the procuring cause of it, Eph.
i. 7. ' In whom we have redemption through his blood,
the forgiveness of sins.' The payment made by the
Surety is a discharge of the principal debtor from
the pursuit of the creditor. As Christ took away
the curse from his people, being made a curse for
them ; so he takes away sin from his people, being
made sin for them.

(2.) The death of Christ procured grace and holiness for men. We made a forfeiture of our original righteousness and sanctity, and were justly deprived of it ; and till once divine justice was appeased, all influences of grace were suspended. Now,
the sacrifice of Christ opened heaven, and brought
down the Spirit, who is the principle and efficient
cause of sanctification in men. The whole world
lay in wickedness, as a dead carcase in the grave,
entirely insensible of its horror and corruption. But
the Holy Spirit inspired it with new life, and by a
marvellous change hath caused purity to succeed
corruption. It had been a great favour indeed to
be delivered from the guilt of sin, that bound us
over to everlasting wrath and punishment ; but it
had not been a perfect and complete favour, without our being delivered from the venom and filth of
sin, which had infected and corrupted our whole
nature. If our guilt were only removed, we had been
freed from punishment ; but without the restoration
of the divine image we had not been qualified for

heaven, and fitted for converse with God. It was
necessary that our souls should be washed, and our
faculties renewed, to put us in a capacity to serve
God, and enjoy communion with him, And this is
only obtained by Christ's death, Tit. ii. 14.

3. The receiving believers into heaven is a convincing proof of the all-sufficiency of Christ's sacrifice. The gates of the New Jerusalem were fast
shut against sinful man, when he fell from his primitive holiness and felicity. God banished him from
his presence, and drove him out of paradise, his native seat, fencing it with cherubims to prevent his
re-entry. But Christ hath set open these everlasting
doors, that believers may enter freely in, Heb. x.
19, 20. ' Having therefore, brethren, boldness to enter into the holiest by the blood of Jesus, by a new
and living way, which he hath consecrated for us
through the vail, that is to say, his flesh.' This
shows the validity of his satisfaction. For divine
justice will not permit that glory and immortality,
which are the privileges of innocency and righteousness, should be given to guilty and polluted criminals ; and therefore it was Christ's first and greatest work to remove the bar that excluded men from
the sanctuary of felicity. Now, what stronger argument can there be, that God is infinitely pleased with
what Christ has done and suffered for his people,
than the taking of them into his presence to behold
his glory ? The apostle sets down this order in the
work of our redemption, Heb. v. 9. that ' Christ being made perfect through sufferings, became the author of eternal salvation to all them that obey him.'
In short, it is observable, that the scripture attributes
to the death of Christ, not only justification, whereby we are redeemed from wrath and misery, that
dreadful punishment which we deserved for sin, but
such an abundant merit also, which purchases adoption for us, and all the glorious privileges of the sons
of God.

From all which it is evident, that the sacrifice of Christ answered all the ends for which it was designed. It gave full satisfaction to the justice of God, and made up an everlasting peace between God and sinners.

⸺⸺⸺⸺

What rendered Christ's Sacrifice so acceptable to God, and so efficacious for men.

1. The quality of his person derived an infinite value to his obedience and sufferings. He was equally God, and as truly infinite in his perfections as the Father who was provoked by our sins. He was the eternal Son of God, equal with the Father in all things. The fulness of the Godhead dwells bodily in him; and he is the brightness of the Father's glory, and the express image of his person. His person was of as great dignity and honour as the Father's was, to whom he was offered. Though there be a distinction of order among the persons of the Godhead, yet there is no priority, nor distinction of dignity. This made his sufferings of infinite and eternal value. For though his Deity was impassible, yet he that was a divine person suffered. And it is especially to be observed, that the efficacy of his blood is ascribed to the divine nature. So the apostle declareth, Col. i. 14. ' In whom we have redemption through his blood, even the forgiveness of sins.' The efficacy of the Deity mingled itself with every groan in his agony, and with every pang and cry upon the cross. And as his blood was the blood of God, as it is called, Acts xx. 28. so his groans were the groans of God, and his cries the cries of God, and therefore of infinite value. What he acted and suffered as man, was dignified and rendered efficacious by his divine nature From this arises the in-

finite difference between the sacrifices of the law,
and the sacrifice of Christ, both in virtue and value.
This is set down by the apostle with admirable em-
phasis, Heb. ix. 13, 14. ' For if the blood of bulls,
and of goats, and the ashes of an heifer sprinkling
the unclean, sanctifieth to the purifying of the flesh ;
how much more shall the blood of Christ, who,
through the eternal Spirit, offered himself without
spot to God, purge your conscience from dead works
to serve the living God ?' By the personal union
with the Deity, great dignity was conferred upon the
sufferings of the human nature.

2. The virtue and efficacy of Christ's sacrifice
flowed from the infinite holiness and purity of his
person. He was holy, harmless, &c. He was as
free from blemish, as he was full of the Spirit. The
spotlessness of his human nature was necessary to
his being a sacrifice, and the union of the divine nature was necessary to his being a valuable sacrifice.
He had no sin naturally imputed, and he had no sin
personally inherent. He had no sin naturally imputed, because he was not descended from Adam by
ordinary generation, who introduced sin into the
world, and derived it down to all his progeny. He
was holy in all his offices, harmless as a priest, faithful as a prophet, holy in his life and death ; no guile
was found in his mouth, nor any inordinate motions
and desires in his heart. His sacrifice could not
have availed us, if he had been tainted with the
least sin.

3. The graces exercised in his sufferings rendered
his sacrifice fragrant and acceptable to God, Phil.
ii. 8. ' He became obedient unto death.' His obedience ran with a cheerful and prevalent strain
through the whole course of his life. He submitted
to a body, fitted to receive all those strokes of wrath
that we should have endured for ever ; a body made
under the law, subject to the obedience and malediction of it. He delighted to do the will of God in

human nature, Psal. xl. 6, 7. He came not to do
his own will, but that of him who sent him. Whatever was ordered him by his Father, that he spake,
did, and suffered. He cheerfully laid down his life
when the hour appointed by the Father was come.
It was not a simple, but an affectionate obedience :
' As the father gave me commandment, (says he,) so
I do,' John xiv. 31. His offering himself a sacrifice
according to the will of God for our sanctification,
was the most significant part of his obedience. This
rendered his sacrifice highly acceptable. Again, his
admirable humility is joined with his obedience, as
the cause of his exaltation, which was an evidence
of its fragrancy, Phil. ii. 8. That the Lord of glory should stoop so low, as to put himself in the room
of sinners, eclipsing the bright lustre and splendour
of his glory, and shrouding under the disguise of our
infirm flesh, submitting himself to a harder piece of
service, and to deeper degrees of humiliation, than
ever any creature in heaven or earth was capable
of ; to descend from the throne of his inaccessible
light, and to expose himself to the rage and fury of
devils and men, without murmuring or impatience,
to submit himself to an infamous death, endure the
wrath of an offended God and Father, whom he infinitely loved, shed his precious blood, and descend
into the grave ; this was an inexpressible and inimi-
table act of humility, lower than which he could not
stoop. Now, since humility renders men so pleasing to God, that he heaps upon them the greatest
testimonies of his favours, and richly dispensed to
them the doles of his grace, it must needs render
the Son most acceptable to the Father in these his
sufferings, and draw from him the greatest testimonies and distributions of his favours, because it was
the greatest act of humility, as well as of obedience,
that could possibly be performed. Further, the high
exercise of his faith, rendered his sacrifice most acceptable to God. He had not one spark of infidelity,

nor any the least grain of distrust in the goodness of
God, in the midst of his deepest sorrows. He suffered the torments of hell for a time, without that
killing despair that preys upon the inhabitants of
that dismal place. He had a working of faith under
the sense of his Father's greatest displeasure and
confidence in his love, while he felt the outward and
inward force of his frowns. He had a faith of the
acceptableness of his death for all his people, and
gave clear evidence of his confidence in the promise,
for a happy and glorious success, in his acting like a
king, while he was hanging as a malefactor upon
the cross, distributing his largesses to the poor thief,
assuring him that on that very day he should be with
him in paradise. Both his obedience to God in
not turning his back, and his trust in God for his
help and assistance, are joined together as the ground
of his justification, Isa. l. 5. 7, 8. ' The Lord God
hath opened mine ear, and I was not rebellious, neither turned away back. For the Lord God will help
me ; therefore shall I not be confounded : therefore
have I set my face like a flint, and I know that I
shall not be ashamed. He is near that justifieth
me ; who will contend with me ? let us stand together : who is mine adversary ? let him come near to
me.' The light of his faith was to be discovered in
opposition to Adam's unbelief, and his great humility
in opposition to Adam's pride. By his active and
passive obedience, he glorified the holiness and justice of God ; by his humility, the power and sovereignty of God ; and by his trust and confidence, the
divine faithfulness and veracity. All which must
needs render his sacrifice a sweet smelling savour to
God, and efficacious for men.

4. The completeness of Christ's satisfaction is
grounded on the degrees of his sufferings. There
was no defect in that payment which he made. We
owed a debt of blood to the law of God, and his life
was offered up as a sacrifice, otherwise the law had

remained in its full force and vigour, and justice had continued unsatisfied. That a divine person hath suffered the punishment that we deserved, is properly the reason of our redemption ; as it is not the quality of the surety that releases the debtor out of prison, but the payment which he makes in his name. The blood of Christ shed, and offered up to God, ratifies the New Testament. In short, our Saviour, in his death, suffered the malediction of the law, even all those degrees of divine wrath and vengeance which the elect should have suffered for ever in hell ; and his divine nature gave a full value, and put a high price upon the sufferings of his human nature ; so that the satisfaction proceeding from them had an intrinsic worth and value ; and God, who was infinitely provoked, is thereby infinitely pleased.

5. The sacrifice of Christ was fragrant and efficacious, because of the great glory and honour which he thereby brought unto God. The glory of his Father was what he had in view, as his main scope and aim in all his actions and sufferings, and that which he also actually perfected. The glory of all the divine attributes appeared in him in its highest lustre, 2 Cor. iv. 6. They all centered in him, and shone forth in their greatest splendour, not only in his incarnation, but also and chiefly in his sacrifice. The mercy and justice of God appear in combination here, and set off one another's lustre. Mercy could not be glorified, unless justice had been satisfied ; and justice had not been evidently discovered, if the tokens of divine wrath had not been seen upon Christ. Grace had never sailed to us, but in the streams of the Mediator's blood. ' Without the shedding of blood,' says the apostle, ' there is no remission.' Divine justice had not been so fully known in the eternal groans and shrieks of a world of guilty creatures, nor could sin have appeared so odious to the holiness of God by eternal scars upon devils and men, as by a deluge of blood from the heart of

this sacrifice. Without the sufferings of Christ, the glory of the divine perfections had lain in the cabinet of the divine nature without the discovery of their full beams. And though they were active in the designing of it, yet they had not been declared to men or angels, without the bringing of Christ to the altar. By the stroke upon his soul, all the glories of God flashed out to the view of the creature. All the divine perfections were glorified in the sufferings of Christ ; his mercy, justice, power, and wisdom. Here the unsearchable depths of manifold wisdom were unfolded. Such a wisdom of God shined in the cross, as the angels never beheld in his face upon his throne ; wisdom to cure a desperate disease, by the death of the physician ; to turn the greatest evil to the greatest good ; to bring forth mercy by the execution of justice, and the shedding of blood : how surprising and astonishing is this ! The ultimate end and design of Christ's sacrifice was the honour of God in our redemption. Christ sought not his own glory, but the glory of him that sent him, John viii. 50. He sought the glory of his Father in the salvation of men. Now, that must needs be fragrant and acceptable to God, which accomplished the triumph of all his attributes.

Objections to the Sufferings of Christ for the sins of his People, stated and answered.

Object. 1. If Christ suffered for the sins of his people, then he that was holy, harmless, undefiled, and separate from sinners, must be accounted a guilty person, yea, even the most guilty of all others, as having charged upon him all the sins of an elect world.

Ans. There is a twofold guilt to be considered,

namely, a culpable, and a penal guilt. He that commits the offence is under culpable guilt ; and he who is obliged to suffer for the offence is under penal guilt, though he did not actually commit it. Now, Christ as our sacrifice was under this penal guilt ; the offences committed by us were charged upon him ; and by his voluntary undertaking to be a sacrifice for us, he came under an obligation to suffer for us, as if he had really sinned, though we only were the transgressors. This is plain in the case of those legal sacrifices, which were shadows of Christ. It appears from them, that these two sorts of guilt may be separated, so that he who is not culpably guilty may be penally guilty, and may justly suffer though he did not personally sin : for the sins of the people being laid upon these sacrifices, they were under penal guilt, and did justly suffer as if they had sinned ; and yet they were not culpably guilty : for they neither had sinned, nor were they capable of sinning.

Quest. 2. Seeing Christ offered up his sacrifice to satisfy divine justice, and he himself is God, how could he die and make satisfaction to himself ?

Ans. 1. God cannot be said properly to satisfy himself ; for that would be the same thing as to pardon sin simply, without any satisfaction.

2. There is a twofold consideration of Christ, one in respect of his divine nature or essence, in which sense he is both the object against which the offence is committed, and to whom for it the satisfaction is made : and there is another consideration of Christ in respect of his person, and economy or office ; in which sense he properly satisfied God, seeing he was, in respect of his manhood, another and inferior to God. So he says, John xiv. 28. ' My Father is greater than I.' The blood of the man Christ Jesus is the matter of the satisfaction ; the divine nature dignifies it, and makes it of infinite value.

3. It is not inconsistent with reason, that the Son

of God, clothed in our nature, should by his death, make satisfaction to the Deity, and consequently to himself. For in the according of two different parties, a person that belongs to one of them may interpose for reconciliation, provided that he divests his own interest, and leaves it with the party from which he comes. As for instance, let us suppose two persons, a father and a son, both possessed of the supreme power, and offended by rebellious subjects : It is not inconsistent that the Son interpose as a Mediator to restore them to the favour of the prince his father. And by this he also reconciles them to himself, and procures pardon for that offence, by which his own majesty was lesed. Now, this is a fit illustration of the great work of our redemption, so far as human things can represent divine. For all the persons of the Holy Trinity were equally provoked by our sin ; and to obtain our pardon, the Son, with the consent of the Father, deposits his interests in his hands, and as a Mediator, intervenes between us and his Father, who in this transaction is considered as the guardian of the rights of heaven ;. and having performed what divine justice required, he reconciled the world to God, *i. e.* to the Father, himself, and the eternal Spirit. In this case his person is the same, but his quality is different. He made satisfaction as a Mediator, and received it as God ; which is no way inconsistent.

Quest. 3. Seeing Christ really suffered for the sins of his people, whether did he suffer the same punishment that they deserved, and which the law threatened, or only something equivalent to it ? It would seem that Christ did not suffer the same thing that the law threatened, and which we justly deserved for sin : for then he must have suffered eternal death. It was not only the first, but the second death that the law threatened. Therefore Christ's temporal death did not satisfy the law and justice of God for us.

There are very learned and pious writers on both sides of this question. Yet I humbly think, that, without any inconvenience, both may be affirmed in different respects. To clear this, you would know, that the punishment which Christ endured in our stead may be considered either as to its substance or essence, or with respect to the accidental circumstances which attend it when inflicted on the damned. Now, if we consider it as to substance or essence, it was the very same which the sinner should have undergone. Man by his fall was liable to death, and to the curse and wrath of God, and Christ hath borne this in the elect's room. But if we consider it with respect to the accidental circumstances which attend it when it is inflicted on the damned, then it was not the very same, but a punishment equivalent to it. The accidental circumstances of this punishment as inflicted on the damned, are, blasphemy, rage, and an impotent fierceness of mind, which are not appointed by the law, but are only accidentals, arising from the wickedness and perverseness of their spirits. Now, our blessed Saviour was not, nor possibly could be, liable to these. The great holiness and sanctity of his person effectually secured him against all these. Besides, the punishment that is inflicted upon the damned is eternal, and attended with final despair, and the intolerable anguish of a guilty stinging conscience. This is the never-dying worm that gnaws upon their vitals. But Christ the Redeemer having no real guilt, was not liable to the worm of conscience ; and his temporary sufferings were equivalent to the eternal punishment of the damned, and fully satisfactory to divine justice, on account of the infinite dignity and excellency of his person ; so that he was not capable of despair.

Thus it evidently appears, that Christ offered himself a sacrifice to satisfy the justice of God offended by sin. And in order to confirm your faith in this important article, one of the fundamental doctrines of our holy religion, let me call your attention to the following particulars, which I shall but barely mention.

1. Consider the necessity of this satisfaction. Without shedding of blood there is no remission, the justice of God, the nature of sin, and the sanction of the law, necessarily required it. And the event manifests it; for it is not conceivable, how, if sin could have been taken away, with a bare word, the Lord would have fetched a compass by the blood of his own Son.

2. Consider the truth of it. Christ did really and truly, by the sacrifice of himself, satisfy the justice of God for us. For he bare the punishment due to our sins, Isa. liii. 5. He died for us, in our room and stead, Rom. v. 6, 7.; and not for our good only, which may be said of all the martyrs. Compare 1 Cor. i. 13. He bought us with his blood, and gave himself a ransom for our souls, and so has taken away our sins in the guilt thereof. His sufferings were the sufferings of a divine person; and so, though not infinite in duration, yet infinite in value. He was Lord of his own life.

3. Consider the perfection of it. He satisfied completely for the sins of his people. His satisfaction fully answered the demands of the justice and law of God. This is plain from the excellency of the person suffering, Col. i. 19. ' For it pleased the Father that in him should all fulness dwell;' this the apostle testifies, Heb. x. 14. ' For by one offering he hath perfected for ever them that are sanctified;' and from the discharge he got in his resurrection, and exaltation to the Father's right hand. Whatever is left to his people to suffer, it is not to satisfy the justice of God, but for their correction, that they be made partakers of his holiness.

Reconciliation by the death of Christ explained and proved.

First, As to the nature of reconciliation, several things are implied in it. As,

1. A former friendship and favour. God and man were once in good terms. There was a time wherein they met and lovingly conversed together. When Adam dropt from the fingers of his Creator, he was the friend and favourite of heaven. He had the law of God written on his heart, and a strong bent and inclination in his will to obey it. In that state there was no place for reconciliation : for then there was no breach between God and his creature.

2. It implies an enmity between God and man. Man fell from his primitive state of favour and friendship with heaven, and joined issue with the devil, God's greatest enemy. Whereupon the Lord took the forfeiture of his possession, turned him out of paradise, and hindered his re-entrance by a flaming sword. There is now a dreadful war betwixt earth and heaven. Men daily rebel against God's laws, labouring to beat down his interest in the world, and employing all their powers and faculties, mercies and comforts, as weapons of unrighteousness to fight against him. And he is an enemy to them ; for he hates all the workers of iniquity, and the foolish cannot stand in his sight. His wisdom, holiness, justice, and power, stand ready charged against them, and they are liable to his eternal vengeance. This is the state wherein man stands with God on the account of sin.

3. Reconciliation with God lies in his receiving rebels into favour, and issuing forth a gracious act of indemnity for all their sins, and cancelling all

those bands of guilt whereby they were bound over
to eternal wrath and misery. This great blessing
formally consists in his ' not imputing their trespasses unto them ;' 2 Cor. v. 19. The forfeiture is taken
off, and they are admitted into his former friendship and favour. Now, this is twofold ; fundamental
and actual.—There was a foundation laid for this
reconciliation in the death of Christ. This is the
mean by which it was purchased, and the chief and
only ground why God lays aside his anger. ' He
made peace,' says the apostle, ' by the blood of his
cross.' And it is actual, when the offer of reconciliation is complied with by faith. He sends forth his
ambassadors, clothed with his authority, to pray them
in Christ's stead to be reconciled to God, declaring
his great willingness to receive them into favour ;
and when men embrace the offer of reconciliation,
then God actually lays aside his anger, and imputes
sin no more to them.

Secondly, I proceed to prove that it is only through
Christ that sinners can obtain reconciliation with
God. This is clear,

1. From the holy scriptures, where this great truth
is expressly declared. So it is said, Acts iv. 12.
' Neither is there salvation in any other : for there
is none other name under heaven given among men
whereby we must be saved.' And we are elsewhere
told, that ' there is but one God, and one Mediator
between God and men, the man Christ Jesus.' And
he is called the Saviour of the world, not only by way
of excellency, in respect of the great danger he saves
us from, but by way of exclusion also, in regard of
the sole designation of his person to this office, exclusive of all others. ' If ye believe not that I am
he,' says he, ' ye shall die in your sins,' John viii. 24.
He is the only person that was designed in all the
prophecies, promises, and types. He is the only
Lamb of God that takes away the sin of the world.
He is the promised seed of the woman, that was to

break the serpent's head. The heart of God is fixed upon him alone, and his resolution concerning the
duration of his office is immutable and unalterable.
He hath summed up all the dispensations of former
ages in him, Eph. i. 10. All other things were pre-
parations to and shadows of him ; God, who had various ways of communicating himself to men, hath
summed up his whole will in his Son, and manifested and declared that all his transactions with men
did terminate in him.

2. The truth of this doctrine will appear, that none
else was ever fitted for the management of this work.
God and men were to be reconciled, and none but he
that was God and man in one person could be a fit
day's-man to lay his hand upon both. Had he been
only man, he had been incapable to satisfy offended
justice ; and had he been only God, he had been incapable of suffering. But being God and man, he
is fitted for both. Infinite satisfaction was requisite
to appease the anger of God ; for without this, guilt
would have remained : and none else was capable to
give it but Christ, in regard of the infinite dignity
and excellency of his person. It was upon no other
person that the Spirit descended like a dove to furnish his human nature with all needful abilities for
the discharge of his trust.

3. If we consider that none else ever did that for
us which was necessary for our reconciliation with
God. It was he that answered the demands of the
law, and silenced the roarings of vindictive justice.
He only filled up the gap that was between God and
sinners. It was only Christ that interposed himself
as a shelter between the wrath of God and the souls
of men. The prophet Isaiah tells us, that ' he bare
our griefs, and carried our sorrows, and that the chastisement of our peace was upon him.' He received
into his own bowels the sword of justice that was
sharpened and pointed for us. He trod the wine-
press alone, and none of the people were with him.

He endured the bruises of God, the darts of the devil, and the reproaches of men ; and would not de-
sist till he had laid the foundation of an everlasting
peace between God and sinners.

4. If ye consider that none else was ever accepted
of God but this Mediator.   The legal sacrifices were
not able to make the comers thereunto perfect, Heb.
x. 1. ' For the law having a shadow of good things
to come, and not the very image of the things, can
never with those sacrifices, which they offered year
by year continually, make the comers thereunto perfect.' They were only shadows of good things to
come ; Christ was the substance and complement of
them all ; and they were no farther regarded of God
but as they were types and representations of his Son.
The daily repetition of them was an undeniable evidence of their inability to effect the reconciliation of
man ; but the blood of Christ typified by the blood
sprinkled by Moses upon the people, does it effectually.   This was a sacrifice wherein God smelt a sweet
savour and was highly accepted of him.

Thirdly, It remains to show you what Christ did
in bringing about this reconciliation.

1. He undertook this work in the eternal transaction that was between the Father and him.

2. He purchased reconciliation by his death, and
thereby procured the egress of the divine favour to
man.   This was the prime article in the covenant of
grace, ' When thou shalt make his soul an offering for
sin, he shall see his seed,' Isa. liii. 10.   God required this sacrifice exclusive of all others, which were
entirely useless for the satisfaction of justice, though
fit to prefigure the grand sacrifice that God intended.
It was by the death of Christ alone that reconciliation was purchased to men, Rom. v. 10. ' For if,
when we were enemies, we were reconciled to God
by the death of his Son ; much more, being reconciled, we shall be saved by his life ;' Eph. ii. 13. ' But
now, in Christ Jesus, ye who sometimes were far off

are made nigh by the blood of Christ;' and Col.
i. 21. ' And you, that were sometime alienated, and
enemies in your mind by wicked works, yet now
hath he reconciled.' And when he was upon the
cross, he cried, ' It is finished;' that is, the work of
redemption is accomplished, reconciliation is purchased, I have done all that was appointed for me to
do, the articles on my part are now fulfilled, there remain no more deaths for me to suffer.

3. He brings about an actual reconciliation between God and sinners by virtue of his efficacious
intercession, Heb. vii. 25. His advocacy in heaven
is the gracious spring of all divine communications.
It is by this that he deals with God in the behalf of
men ; he leads every believer by the hand as it were
unto the gracious presence of God, bespeaking acceptance for them after this manner : ' Father, here
is a poor creature that was born in sin, and hath
lived in rebellion all his days ; he hath broken all
thy laws, and deserves all thy wrath ; yet he is one
of that number that thou gavest me before the world
began ; and I have made full payment to thy justice
by my blood for all his debt ; and now I have opened
his eyes to see the sinfulness and misery of his condition : I have broken his heart for his rebellions
against thee, and bowed his will into obedience to
the offer of thy grace : I have united him to me by
faith, as a living member of my mystical body : and
now, since he is mine by regeneration, let him also
become thine by a special acceptation : since thy
justice is satified for his sins, let thine anger also be
turned away, and receive him graciously into favour.'
In a word, the reconciliation of every elect person
with God, is actually brought about by Christ : He
opens their eyes, and lets them see their sin and danger ; he beats down the stubbornness and obstinacy
of their wills, and brings up their hearts to a full
compliance with the offers of peace made in the gospel ; and he leads them to God, and makes their per-

sons and duties acceptable to him. Hence it is said, Eph. i. 6. ' He hath made us accepted in the Beloved.' *

•••••••••••••••••

Important instructions from the Doctrine of Reconciliation, by the Death of Christ.

1. Here we may see the horrid and hateful evil of sin, which no other sacrifice could expiate but the blood of the Son of God. As the strength of a disease is known and seen by the quality and force of the medicine that is made use of to cure it, and the virtue of a commodity by the greatness of the price that is laid down to buy it, so is the matter here. The sufferings and death of Christ express the evil of sin far above the severest judgments that ever were inflicted upon any creature. The dying groans of our blessed Redeemer set forth the horrid nature of sin, and loudly proclaim how hateful it is in the eye of an infinitely pure and holy God. How much evil must there be in sin that made Christ to groan and bleed to death to take it away! It is strange to imagine how rational agents should dare to commit such an evil, so freely and openly, and that for trifles and perishing vanities, which are of no continuance and du-

* ' Glorious propitiation ! and altogether as complete as glorious ! What now shall terrify the true believer ? What shall stand between him and his eternal hopes ? Shall satan muster up his accusations, and set them in frightful array ? Yet though there may be much guilt, there is no condemnation to them that are in Jesus Christ. Does the law take the guilty mortal by the throat, and, with its rigorous severity, say, pay me that thou owest ? It is paid, fully paid, by the intervention and suretiship, not of a mean man, but of the mighty God made flesh. Does divine justice demand satisfaction for the wrongs received from sinners ? It is not only satisfied, but awfully glorified by this wonderful oblation.'

Harvey's Ser. on 2 Cor. v. 18.

ration. Can they escape, or can they possibly endure, the wrath and vengeance of an incensed Deity? If God spared not his own Son, when he came in the likeness of sinful flesh, how shall sinners escape, who are deeply and universally defiled? Can they encounter with the fury of the Almighty, the very apprehensions of which made Christ's soul exceeding sorrowful even unto death? Have they patience to endure and bear that for ever, which was intolerable for Christ to bear but for a few hours, who had all the strength of the Deity to support him? If it was so with the green tree, what shall become of the dry, when exposed to the fiery trial? O what prodigious madness is it for men to drink iniquity like water, as a harmless thing, when it is a poison so dangerous and deadly, that the least drop of it brings certain ruin? What desperate and monstrous folly is it to have slight apprehensions of that which is attended with the first and second death; even with all the terrors and torments of hell, where the worm dieth not, and the fire is not quenched; where misery will continue in its full extremity, while eternity runs its endless course? Nothing but unreasonable infidelity and want of thought can make men venturous to provoke the living God, who is infinitely sensible of their sins, and who both can and will most terribly punish them for ever.

2. This lets us see the strictness and inexorable severity of divine justice, that required satisfaction equivalent to the desert of sin. All the other demonstrations of it which God hath given to the world, are nothing to this. God spared not his own Son. The fountain of divine mercy stopt its course, and would not let out one drop to Christ in the day of his extreme sorrow and sufferings. The Father of mercies saw his dear Son sweating great drops of blood in a cold night, and crying out with a mournful accent, ' O Father, if it be possible, let this cup pass from me ;' and yet he would not grant the request.

O the inflexible severity of divine justice! What will
ye do, sinners, when it falls upon you in hell? If the
blessed Son of God cried so out, what will become of
you! How will impenitent sinners roar and yell for
ever under the dreadful strokes of incensed justice!
O what a dreadful thing must it be to fall into the
hands of the living God!

3. See here the wonderful love of Christ to poor
miserable sinners, and his great desire for the salvation of their souls. His love here passeth knowledge.
It infinitely transcends the reach of the most illumi-
nated understanding. What Christ suffered from
his birth to his death on the accursed tree, affords
the most striking instance of his great love to poor
sinners. No example of such love can be found
among men. This matchless love of Christ should
inflame our hearts to sing, as Rev. i. 5, 6. ' Unto him
that loved us and washed us from our sins in his own
blood ; and hath made us kings and priests unto God
and his Father ; to him be glory and dominion for
ever and ever. Amen.'

4. This doctrine affords us the strongest assurance
that can be, that God is willing to pardon our sins,
and to be reconciled to us. There is in the natural
conscience of man, when opened by a piercing conviction, such a quick sense of guilt, and of God's
avenging justice, that it can never have an entire confidence in his mercy till justice be atoned. From
hence the convinced sinner is restlessly inquisitive
how to find out the way of reconciliation with a holy
and righteous God. Thus he is represented inqui-
ring by the prophet, ' Wherewith shall I come before the Lord, and bow myself before the high God?
Shall I come before him with burnt-offerings, with
calves of a year old? Will the Lord be pleased with
thousands of rams, or with ten thousands of rivers of
oil? Shall I give my first-born for my transgression,
the fruit of my body for the sin of my soul?' The
scripture tells us, that some consumed their children

in the fire, to render their idols propitious to them :
but all these means were ineffectual, their most costly sacrifices were only food for the fire ; nay, instead
of expiating their old sins, they committed new ones
by them, and were so far from appeasing, that they
inflamed the wrath of God by their cruel oblations.
But in the gospel there is the most rational and easy
way propounded for the satisfaction of divine justice,
and the justification of man. Hence, says the apostle, Rom. x. 6, 7. 9. ' The righteousness which is of
faith speaketh on this wise, Say not in thine heart,
Who shall ascend into heaven? (that is, to bring
Christ down from above) ; or, Who shall descend into the deep ? (that is, to bring up Christ again from
the dead). If thou shalt confess with thy mouth the
Lord Jesus, and shalt believe in thine heart, that
God hath raised him from the dead, thou shalt be
saved.' The apostle here sets forth the care and anxiety of an awakened conscience. He is at a loss to
find out a way to escape deserved judgment : for
such things as are on the surface of the earth or float-
ing on the waters are within our view, and may easily be obtained ; but those which are above our understandings to discover, or our power to obtain, are
proverbially said to be in the heavens above, or in
the depths beneath ; and it is applied here to the different ways of justification by the law and by the gospel. The law propounds life upon an impossible
condition. But the gospel clearly reveals to us, that
Christ hath performed all that was necessary to our
justification, and that by a true faith we shall have
an interest in it. Christ's ascension into heaven is
a convincing proof, that the propitiation for our sins
is perfect ; for otherwise he had not been received
into God's sanctuary, and admitted into the sacred
place. Therefore to be under anxious and perplexing inquiries how we may be justified, is to deny the
value of Christ's righteousness, and the truth of his
ascension. By virtue of the sacrifice and righteous-

ness of Christ, the soul is not only freed from the fear of God's wrath, but hath a lively hope of his favour and love. This is expressed by the apostle, Heb. xii. 23. when he reckons among the privileges of believers, that they are *come to God*, &c. The apprehensions of God as the righteous Judge of the world, strike the guilty creature with dread and terror ; but is sweetened by Christ the Mediator, we may approach unto him with a humble and holy confidence.

5. We must lay hold on this sacrifice, if we would be saved. This is the only sacrifice that satisfied offended justice, and no other could do it. Therefore we must have recourse to this if we would have peace with God. Under the law, the people were to be sprinkled with the blood of the sacrifice ; and so must we be with the blood of Christ. It is said, Exod. xxiv. 8. that ' Moses took the blood of the covenant and sprinkled it on the people.' This signified the sprinkling of their consciences with the blood of Christ, and their obtaining redemption, justification, and access to God, through it alone. Hence our Saviour is described by this part of his office, Isa. lii. 15. ' He shall sprinkle many nations.' Our guilt cannot look upon God as a consuming fire, without a propitiatory sacrifice. All our services are lame and defective, impure and imperfect, so that they will rather provoke God's justice, than merit his mercy. We must therefore have something to put a stop to a just fury, expiate an infinite guilt, and perfume our unsavoury services, and render them acceptable to a holy and righteous God ; and that is only the sacrifice of Christ. This is full of all necessary virtue to save us : but the blood of it must be sprinkled upon our souls by faith. Without this we shall remain in our sins, under the wrath of God, and exposed to the sword of divine justice ; and our misery will be heightened by our having the offers of Christ and his grace. O ! it is a fearful thing for men to have this sacrifice pleading against them, and this

precious blood crying for vengeance from heaven upon them ; as innocent Abel's blood cried to heaven for vengeance against the unnatural cruelty of his wicked and inhuman brother.

6. Hence see that God will never seek satisfaction for sin from those that are in Christ Jesus. He gave full and complete satisfaction to the law and justice of God for all the wrongs and injuries done thereto by the sins of men, the sufferer being God, and his divine nature stamping an infinite value upon the sufferings he endured. Now, if the creditor receives full satisfaction for an offence done, or complete payment of a debt due, by a debtor, from the hands of a surety, neither law nor justice will permit him to ask any further satisfaction or payment from the principal debtor. He can raise no suit or action against the debtor, in regard he has fully satisfied him by the action and deed of his surety. Law and justice are fully satisfied by the obedience and satisfaction of Christ substituting himself in the room of sinners, and making his soul an offering for them, so as they can crave no more : therefore there can be no condemnation to those that are in him, and have taken the benefit of his satisfaction, and present it to God, as theirs, performed in their room and stead. Hence the apostle says, ' There is therefore now no condemnation to them which are in Christ Jesus.' O seek to have your station in Christ, and so you shall be placed beyond the reach of condemnation. You may indeed, though in Christ, suffer chastisements and corrections ; yet these are the corrections and chastisements of a Father, not of a Judge ; and intended for your good, to cause you forsake sin, and enhance the value of the sacrifice of Christ, and not for satisfaction to justice, whose highest demands have been fully satisfied by the Surety in your room.

7. Hence see the the certainty of salvation to, and that God will bestow all the benefits purchased by Christ, on those who believe. Christ has fully satis-

fied justice for all those whom he represented as a
Mediator ; so that it has nothing to demand of the
Surety, nor of those whose persons he sustained in
that undertaking.   Hence their salvation is infallibly
secured ; and justice is bound to accomplish it.
Mercy pleads for it ; justice fully satisfied cannot
dispute the validity of the claim, and cheerfully con-
sents to their acquittal from guilt and condemnation.
Thus righteousness and peace kiss each other in the
absolution of the guilty sinner that believeth in Jesus.

8. Bless God for the gospel, that discovers unto
us this infallible way of being delivered from condemnation and wrath, this sure way to peace and reconciliation with God, this precious balm for a troubled
conscience, and this effectual remedy for appeasing
an angry God.   O prize the gospel, and the precious
discoveries thereof, in which all blessings are contained ; and accept of a slain Saviour as your only
Redeemer from sin and wrath, from hell and condemnation ; and glory in his cross, and what he hath
done for your redemption and deliverance.

The efficacious Intercession of Christ illustrated.

First, We may consider the periods of our Lord's
intercession.   And this may be taken up in a threefold period of time wherein it was made, viz. before
his incarnation, during the state of his humiliation,
and now in his exalted state.

1. Christ interceded for his church and people before his manifestation in the flesh.   Though this office be most eminently performed since the union of
the divine and human natures in the person of Christ,
yet it was also effectually performed by him before
his assumption of our flesh.   He interposed then by
virtue of his engagement to make his soul an offer-

ing for sin; and he intercedes now by virtue of his actual performance of that engagement. 'As he was a Lamb slain from the foundation of the world,' so by that same reason he was an advocate pleading from the foundation of the world. It was through the merciful interposition of the Son of God, in consequence of the covenant betwixt the Father and him, that deserved vengeance came not upon the world for sin at the first commission of it. We find him in the Old Testament pleading for the church long before he assumed the human nature, Zech. i. 12. 'Then the angel of the Lord answered and said, O Lord of hosts, how long wilt thou not have mercy on Jerusalem, and on the cities of Judah, against which thou hast had indignation these threescore and ten years?' and the saints making use of Christ's name in their prayers to God long before he was born, Dan. ix. 17. 'Now therefore, O our God, hear the prayer of thy servant, and his supplications, and cause thy face to shine upon thy sanctuary, that is desolate, for the Lord's sake.' Thus his intercession began in heaven thousands of years before his abode on earth.

2. He interceded for his people in his state of abasement and humiliation, Heb. i. 7. 'In the days of his flesh he offered up prayers and supplications to God with strong cries and tears.' This manner of intercession was suitable and congruous to his abased state. Though he was despised and rejected of men, a man of sorrows and acquainted with grief; yet his intercession was not less prevalent with God, for 'he was heard in that he feared.' Ye may see with what majesty and authority he prayed on the behalf of all the elect, John xvii. 24. 'Father, I will that they also whom thou hast given me, be with me where I am; that they may behold my glory which thou hast given me: for thou lovedst me before the foundation of the world.' Yea, even when he was under the sharpest agonies, when he was bruised by

God, and broken by men, groaning under the wrath of the one, and the wrongs of the other, he forgets not to put up petitions for his crucifiers, Luke xxiii. 34. ' Father, forgive them ; for they know not what they do.' And many of those who imbrued their hands in his innocent blood, obtained a gracious pardon through his prevalent intercession.

3. He is pleading now for his people in heaven, in his exalted state. When he had offered up himself a sacrifice on the cross, he ascended into heaven, and entered into the most holy place, and there prosecutes the same suit that he had commenced on the earth. Hence, says the apostle, Rom. viii. 34. ' It is Christ that died, yea rather, that is risen again, who is even at the right hand of God, who also maketh intercession for us.'

Secondly, I am to show wherein Christ's intercession consists.

1. He does not plead for his people in heaven, in such a supplicatory and humble manner as he prayed for them when he was on the earth. He falls not down upon his knees with a deep prostration of soul, lifting up his eyes with tears and strong cries. Such humble prayers and supplications were suited only to the days of his flesh, when he appeared in the form of a servant, and was found in the likeness of man ; but they do not become him now in his state of glory, when he is stript of all those natural infirmities and marks of indigence wherewith he was clothed in the world. But, positively,

2. His intercession lies in the following things :

1st, In his appearing in heaven in his people's nature, and on their account. After he had shed his precious blood on the earth for the expiation of their sin, he rose again from the dead, and ascended into heaven as their Advocate and Intercessor, that, by the virtue of his meritorious sacrifice, he might answer all the charges brought in against them, and sue out all the good things that belonged to them,

Heb. ix. 24. ' Christ is entered into heaven itself, now to appear in the presence of God for us.'

2*dly*, In presenting the memorials of his death and passion as a moving plea on their account. This was typified and prefigured by the high priest's carrying the blood of the sacrifice into the most holy place, and presenting it before the Lord. He was not to go in before the mercy-seat without it ; and there was no interceding but by virtue of it. So the whole power and efficacy of Christ's intercession is founded upon his meritorious sufferings. His soul that was bruised and made an offering for sin, and his body that was wounded and broken upon the cross, are daily presented before God, and will remain in the divine presence for ever, as an eternal memorial of his bloody sufferings. This has a powerful efficacy in prevailing with God. Hence, by an usual figure, an interceding voice is attributed to his blood, Heb. xii. 24. ' It speaketh better things than that of Abel.' Christ's blood speaks, though not vocally and with oral expressions, yet powerfully and efficaciously. It speaks in the same manner that Abel's blood did, though not for the same end ; this cried for vengeance upon wicked Cain that shed it ; but that pleads for mercy and favour to all believing sinners. We have a rare illustration of the efficacious intercession of Christ in heaven, in the famous story of Amyntas, who appeared as an advocate for his brother Æschylus, who was strongly accused, and in danger of being condemned to die. This Amyntas having performed great services for the state, and merited highly of the commonwealth, in whose service one of his hands was cut off in battle, comes into the court on his brother's behalf, and said nothing, but only lifted up his arm, and showed them an arm without a hand ; which so moved them, that immediately they acquitted his brother. And thus you have Christ represented visionally, Rev. v. 6. as standing between God and us, ' And I beheld, and lo, in the midst of the throne, and of the four beasts, and in the midst of the elders stood a lamb as it had been slain, having seven horns, and seven eyes, which are the seven spirits of God, sent forth into all the earth.' That is, he was represented as bearing in his glorified body the marks of his death and sacrifice; the wounds which he received for his people's sins on the earth, are as it were still visible and fresh in heaven, as a prevailing argument with the Father to give forth the mercies that he pleads for to them.

3dly, In presenting his will and desire to the Father on their behalf, not in a humble and supplicatory manner, in the way of charity, but by a claim in the way of justice. He now pleads that his people may be put in full possession of all the blessings which were purchased for them by his bloody death. We find him pleading to this purpose immediately before his passion, John xvii. 24. ' Father, I will that they also whom thou hast given me be with me where I am ; that they may behold my glory, which thou hast given me : for thou lovedst me before the foundation of the world.' He minds the Father as it were of the covenant that was between them both, of his performing the condition required on his part, and so claims the performance of God's promise as a debt due to his meritorious obedience even unto death. He hath ' made his soul an offering for sin ;' and therefore pleads that he may ' see his seed, prolong his days,' and that ' the pleasure of the Lord may prosper in his hands,' Isa. liii. 10, 11.

4thly, In his presenting his people's prayers and petitions unto God, and pleading that they may be accepted and granted for his sake. Their prayers and religious performances are both impure and imperfect; but his precious merit, applied by his powerful intercession, purifies and perfects them. This skilful Advocate puts them into form and language suited to the methods of the court of heaven, and by his great interest there procures them a speedy hearing. This was excellently typified by the high priest's going in before the Lord with the blood of the sacrifice, and his hands full of incense. After he had offered the sacrifice, without, he was to take his hands full of those aromatic drugs of which the incense was composed, without the vail, and put them in a censer of gold full of fire, and cover the mercy-seat with the fume of it. This was a figure of Christ's intercession and offering up his people's services to God. He is the alone altar upon which our sacrifices must ascend before the Lord with a grateful fume : the incense of his merit must be added to our prayers, to make them ascend before the mercy-seat as a sacrifice of a sweet-smelling savour. Hence he is represented, Rev. viii. 3. as an angel standing at the golden altar which was before the throne, with a golden censer in his hand, offering up the prayers of all the saints, perfuming them with the incense that was given him. By the *much incense* mentioned here, we are to understand the mighty quantity of merit and the great power of his intercession, which was a sweet savour to all his people's sacrifices, and renders them acceptable to God.

5*thly*, In his answering all the bills of indictment which are brought in against them. Many times a believer is brought in as an arraigned criminal before the divine tribunal, where Satan appears as the accuser, brings in the charge of sin, pleads the righteousness of the law, solicits for judgment upon his accusations, and for the execution of the curse due to the crime. The justice of God calls for vengeance, and conscience thunders out nothing but hell and wrath. Now, while the believer is in these dismal circumstances, Christ steps in and answers the charge. He pleads the efficacy of his merit against the greatness of the believing sinner's crimes, and his satisfaction to justice by the death of the cross against all the demands and challenges of the law.

F f

And thus the sentence of condemnation due unto the sinner for his sin is averted, and a sentence of absolution is pronounced, upon the merit and plea of this powerful Intercessor. Hence we find the apostle glorying in this, Rom. viii. 33, 34. ' Who shall lay any thing to the charge of God's elect? It is God that justifieth : who is he that condemneth ? It is Christ that died, yea rather, that is risen again, who is even at the right hand of God, who also maketh intercession for us.' Satan may accuse believers ; but Christ can soon silence him. Thus, when Joshua the high priest stood before the Lord in filthy garments, Satan stood at his right hand to accuse him ; but the angel, namely, the angel of the covenant, Jesus Christ, interposed, saying, ' The Lord rebuke thee, O Satan,' Zech. iii. 1, 2. Though their garments be filthy, yet Christ can take them away, and clothe them with change of raiment. Though Satan be always ready to resist them, yet Christ stands always at the right hand of God in heaven, to plead for them, and silence Satan.

Thirdly, I shall show some of the grounds or reasons of our High Priest's intercession.

1. Christ intercedes for his people, because he had a commission, a call, and command from the Father, for this purpose, Isa. xlii. 6. ' I the Lord have called thee in righteousness.' So far was our mighty Intercessor from engaging in this service as an intruder or usurper, that he entered upon it under the warrant of heaven's commission. The Lord called him to be a priest. For verily ' he glorified not himself, to be made an High priest ; but he that said unto him. Thou art my Son, to-day have I begotten thee,' Heb. v. 5. And as the Lord called him to be a priest, so to all the acts of the priestly office. He called him to make his soul an offering for sin, to pour his life unto death, and to shed his blood for the satisfaction of offended justice. In a word, he called him to make intercession for transgressors. For, says the Lord,

' I will cause him to draw near, and he shall approach unto me.'

2. He intercedes for his people, because they were given him for this end, John xvii. 6. ' Thine they were, and thou gavest them me.' The elect that the Father gave to Christ were his own three ways. They were creatures, and therefore their life and being were derived from him. They were criminals, and therefore their life and being were forfeited to him. They were chosen, and therefore their living and being were designed for him. They were given to Christ that the election of grace might not be frustrated, that none of the little ones might perish. Yea, they were given him, that the undertaking of Christ might not be fruitless ; for they were given him as his seed, in whom he should see of the travail of his soul, and be satisfied, and consequently might not spend his strength and shed his blood in vain. Now, because the elect were thus given to Christ, therefore he intercedes for them, John xvii. 9. ' I pray for them : I pray not for the world but for them which thou hast given me, for they are thine.'

3. He intercedes for his people, because it is a special part of his priestly office to do so. As the high priest under the law was not only to slay and offer the sacrifice in the outer part of the tabernacle, on the anniversary day of expiation, but to enter with the fresh blood into the sanctuary, and sprinkle it seven times ; and not only so, but was to bring a censer full of burning coals off the altar, with incense in his hands, to be put upon the fire before the Lord within the vail, that so the cloud in the incense might cover the mercy-seat : in like manner, after our great High Priest had offered himself a sacrifice to God in his bloody death, he entered into heaven, not only with his blood, but with the incense of his prayers, as a cloud about the mercy-seat, to preserve by his life the salvation which he had purchased by his death. Hence the apostle assures us, that our sal-

vation depends upon his intercession, and his intercession upon his priesthood, Heb. vii. 24, 25. ' This man, because he continueth ever, hath an unchangeable priesthood. Wherefore he is able also to save them to the uttermost, that come unto God by him, seeing he ever liveth to make intercession for them.'

4. He intercedes for his people, because he was their propitiation ; for the efficacy of his plea depends upon the value and virtue of his sacrifice. As the high priest under the law could not enter into the holy of holies, till by the slaying of the sacrifice he had blood to carry with him : so no more could our Priest be admitted to solicit at the throne of grace, till by his death he had satisfied the tribunal of justice. Thus, because he paid the debt as our Surety, he is fit to plead the payment as our Attorney. What he finished on earth, he continually presents in heaven. By shedding his blood he made expiation, and by presenting it he makes intercession. In the one he prepared the remedy, and in the other he applies it.

5. He intercedes for his people, because his doing so is one of the greatest ends of his ascension and session at the right hand of God. In his incarnation, he came down from the Father to acquaint us with his gracious purposes, and how far he had agreed with God in our behalf ; and at his ascension he went from us to the Father, to sue out the benefits which he had so dearly purchased. He drew up an answer upon the cross to the bill that sin, by virtue of the law, had drawn against us, and ascended to heaven as an Advocate to plead that answer upon his throne, and to rejoin to all the replies against it. And therefore the apostle tells us, that he is ' entered into heaven, to appear in the presence of God for us,' Heb. ix. 24.

6. He intercedes for his people, because of that matchless and amazing love which he bears to them. He loves them with a love infinitely transcending the reach of human or angelic conception ; he loves them

with a love that knows neither height nor depth, breadth nor length, but is absolutely incomprehensible. His love to them brought him down from heaven, and made him willingly undergo all those sorrows and sufferings, which, like impetuous torrents, poured in upon him. And certainly, seeing in his love and in his pity he purchased eternal redemption for them, he will never cease to plead for the application of it to them. Seeing in such plentiful streams he shed his precious blood to save them, it is not to be imagined that he will spare his prayers for them.

7. He intercedes for his people, because this service of love is that wherein he takes the greatest delight and pleasure. Before time existed, his delights were with the sons of men ; and when the fulness of time did dawn, he said, ' Lo, I come,' &c. He had a delight to live with the sons of men, and to die for them. And no sooner does he enter heaven after his death and resurrection, but there he delights to act on their account, to plead their cause, and to intercede for all the blessings of his purchase to them. This is the will of the Father, and he delights to do it.

Privileges of those espoused to Christ.

1. That they may call God Father, and that is of more value than a thousand worlds. The most profane wretch may call him Lord, the hypocrite may call him master ; but Father is a kindly name, which only believers may call him. They may at all times cry unto him, *Abba, Father*. Abba is the same, read it backward or forward ; and in all the changes of dispensation, God is still the espoused soul's Father. Hypocrites will call him so, but God disowns the relation, and says to them, ' Ye are of your father the

devil, and the deeds of your father ye will do.' But
he encourages his people to do it, saying, ' Wilt thou
not from this time, cry unto me, my Father, thou art
the guide of my youth.'

2. Access to God. They come much nearer to
him than others. They may come forward, when
others must stand back. ' In Christ they have boldness, and access to God with confidence, by the faith
of him.' God allows them a holy boldness and confidence with him as children, to pour their complaints
in his bosom, to tell him all their wants ; and never
did a father take so much delight in the talking
of his children to him, as God doth in hearing his
people.

3. Special immunities and freedom. Kings' children have great immunities. They are free of tribute.
But God's children have the greatest. They are
free from the law as a covenant of works, which is a
yoke wreathed about the necks of all others. Free
from the curse, which lies hard and fast on all others.
Free from all condemnation, thundered out against
others every day. Nay, from the hurt of every thing.
' Nothing,' says their husband, ' shall by any means
hurt you.' Death itself, that kills others, shall not
hurt them, Rom. viii. 35—39. ' Who shall separate
us from the love of Christ ? shall tribulation, or distress, or persecution, or famine, or nakedness, or
peril, or sword ? (As it is written, For thy sake we
are killed all the day long ; we are accounted as
sheep for the slaughter.) Nay, in all these things
we are more than conquerors, through him that loved us. For I am persuaded, that neither death, nor
life, nor angels, nor principalities, nor powers, nor
things present, nor things to come, nor height, nor
depth, nor any other creature, shall be able to separate us from the love of God, which is in Christ
Jesus our Lord.'

4. Pity, provision, and protection. The severe
avenger of sin pities their infirmities, as a father pi-

tieth his children. He that fights against the wicked as an enemy, will protect them. ' In the fear of the Lord is strong confidence, and his children shall have a place of refuge.' Come what will, they shall be provided for. Though the Lord make not provision for their lusts, he will see to provide for their necessities, Matt. vi. 30—32. ' Wherefore, if God so clothe the grass of the field, which to-day is, and to-morrow is cast into the oven, shall he not much more clothe you, O ye of little faith? Therefore take no thought, saying, What shall we eat? or, What shall we drink? or, Wherewithal shall we be clothed? (For after all these things do the Gentiles seek ;) for your heavenly Father knoweth that ye have need of all these things.'

5. Seasonable correction. ' For whom the Lord loveth he chasteneth, and scourgeth every son whom he receiveth.' This is a benefit of the covenant, Psal. lxxxix. 30—32. ' If his children forsake my law, and walk not in my judgments ; if they break my statutes, and keep not my commandments ; then will I visit their transgression with the rod, and their iniquity with stripes.' Some smart more severely for a lustful look, than others for taking their full swing that way ; some, more for deadness in prayer, than others for neglecting it altogether. What is the reason? A small fault in a child will be checked, when a greater in another will be overlooked.

6. Perseverance. ' The servant abideth not in the house for ever, but the son abideth ever.' The term-day is coming, when God and such as are not espoused shall part, but they that are, never. If a child wander from his father's house, he must be sought, and brought back again. A servant of the house, may be turned out of doors, as Hagar was ; nay, a son of God by nature, may be turned off, as Adam and the fallen angels were ; but they that are God's children, by being espoused to his Son, can never, Psal. lxxxix. 30—34.

Lastly, They have a portion according to their Father's quality. ' They are heirs, heirs of God, and joint heirs with Christ.' So all is theirs. Grace is theirs, glory is theirs. Their portion will tell out through all eternity. Their Father gives them of his moveables as he sees meet, and these may be removed, but their portion is not of these ; they shall receive a kingdom which cannot be moved.

What is imported in the exhortation, ' Hearken, O daughter, and consider, and incline thine ear,' Psal. xlv. 10.

These words import,

1. That Christ's spouse is not left to walk at random. She is to notice every step of her carriage. ' See then that ye walk circumspectly, not as fools, but as wise.' The careless walking at all adventures, is walking contrary to the Lord, and is opposed to hearkening, Lev. xxvi. 21. The espoused are not under the law as a covenant of works, but they are not lawless, but under the law to Christ. The iron yoke of the first covenant is off, but the soft yoke of the second is on them.

2. That those that are espoused to Christ, must renounce their own will, and not seek to please themselves. ' If any man,' saith Jesus ' will come after me, let him deny himself, and take up his cross and follow me.' Our corrupt self will seek this, and that, to please itself, as it was wont to get in our Christless condition ; but we must deny its cravings now, forasmuch as by our espousals with Christ, we have put our desires in the hand of another, to grant them or not, as he thinks fit, according to the law, Gen. iii. 16. In our espousals we made this renunciation of our own will, let us not draw back when it comes

to the point of practice, lest we show we are but mocking, not in earnest.

3. That our great aim in all things, must be to please our Lord and husband, this is the law of marriage. ' She that is married, careth for the things of the world, that she may please her husband.' This is the law of Christ to his spouse, ' That we walk worthy of the Lord, unto all pleasing, being fruitful in every good work, and increasing in the knowledge of God.' Displease whom we will, we must please him. Be they the greatest on earth, and be the danger of displeasing them ever so great, we must not run the risk of our Lord's displeasure for them all ; even as a dutiful wife will never lay the pleasing of her husband and his servants in a balance. So Daniel and his fellows, would not please the king, by worshipping the golden image which he set up.

4. That we must trample upon our own inclinations when contrary to his, and suit ourselves to his will, as Abraham did with respect to offering up his son. Is our inclination to the world, it is not his will, therefore we must subdue this carnal inclination. Is it our desire to be rich and honourable, perhaps this is not his will, but that we should be poor and under a cloud : we must suit ourselves to his pleasure, and ' learn in whatsoever state we are, therewith to be content.'

5. That when Christ's will and pleasure and our own go together, our main end must not be to please ourselves, but to please him. ' Whether we eat or drink, or whatsoever we do, do all to the glory of God.' Otherwise, we do not hearken to our husband, but to ourselves ; as those who will please their husband in those things in which they please themselves, and which they would do, whether they pleased their husband or not. Do we profess to hear and obey him ? Let us then do these things, that we may give contentment to the heart of our Lord. Do we eat and drink ? Let it be because Christ says, ' thou

shalt not kill.' Do we marry ? Let it be because he
says, ' do not commit adultery.' Do we work ? Let
it be because he says, ' do not steal.'

6. That we must not think to please him with our
own devices. Christ's spouse hearkens and considers what her Lord says, that she may do it.

Lastly, That our ear must be to himself, our eye
on him, that we may know his will to do it, Psalm
cxxiii. 2., quoted above. This implies these things,
that we must be content to know sin and duty.
Many sit with much ease under the covert of ignorance. What the ear hears not, the heart receives
not. By their conduct, they say unto God, ' depart
from us, for we desire not the knowledge of thy ways.'
They entertain their lusts, as some did intercom-
muned persons in time of persecution ; they are content they be in the house, but they do not desire to
know it. That not hearkening, they think they have
not to obey. Again, we must learn what is sin and
what is duty from himself. The apostle tells ' wives,
that if they would know any thing, let them ask their
husbands at home.' Our husband is in heaven, we
on earth, yet we may learn of him. His word is in
our hands. His Spirit is in our hearts, if we be
espoused to him. We want not the holy oracle to consult, if willing to learn. Farther, we must apply ourselves diligently, to learn of him our duty. We
must incline our ear. We are so dull and slow at
taking up our duty, there is so much din about us
by our unruly hearts, while our Lord puts our lesson
in our hands, that if we do not take very great care,
we may mistake. Finally, we must hearken with a
readiness to obey, as the servant hears his orders to
do them, and a dutiful wife hears her husband's pleasure to suit herself to it. Hearing that is not for
obeying, our Lord regardeth not.

How Christ speaks to his Spouse, and what it is for his Spouse to hear Christ.

1. By his works. All the works of God are speaking works. He speaks by the works of creation, these silent preachers of his will, Psalm xix. 2—4. See how the Psalmist heard and answered this voice of his : ' When I consider,' said he, ' the heavens the work of thy fingers, the moon and the stars which thou hast ordained : What is man, that thou art mindful of him ? and the son of man, that thou visitest him ?' The very heathens are rendered inexcusable, by this voice of the Lord, how much more Christ's spouse, if she hear it not. The work of redemption is a speaking work : and what is the language of it ? ' It is we are bought with a price, therefore glorify God in your body, and in your spirit, which are God's.' Nay, all the ten commandments come to Christ's spouse, in the language of the Redeemer's blood : I am the Lord thy God, which brought thee out of the land of Egypt, out of the house of bondage. He speaks to his spouse by the works of providence. There is not a mercy but it hath a voice, nor a rod thou meetest with, but it speaks. ' Hear then, O daughter, the rod, and who hath appointed it.'

2. By our own consciences. That is the bosom preacher, or Lord's deputy-governor, whom he hath placed in every man's breast ; and every deaf ear turned to it speaking from the word, is a refusing of him that speaketh from heaven. ' The spirit of man is the candle of the Lord, searching all the inward parts of the belly.'

3. He speaks to us by the word. He speaks to us in the word read. The bible is the book of instructions, which Christ puts in the hands of the espoused, to show them how they are to please him, till the marriage of the Lamb. ' For whatsoever things were written aforetime, were written for our learning, that we, through patience, and comfort of the scriptures, might have hope.' Therefore, they who intend to perform their vows of espousals, will be conversant with the bible. He speaks also by the word preached. ' He that heareth you,' said Jesus of his disciples, ' heareth me.' Taking Christ, you took him for a prophet, and by the ministers of the word, he exerciseth the office. So they that wish to know how to please Christ, will wait on the ordinances for that end.

4. By his Spirit, whereby we have the mind of Christ. ' The Comforter,' saith Jesus, ' which is the Holy Ghost, whom the Father will send in my name, he shall teach you all things, and bring all things to your remembrance, whatsoever I have said unto you.' And you not hearing him, thus grieves the Spirit, and provokes him to depart. Now our duty, with respect to these, consists in these two :

1st, We must discern Christ's voice in one and all of these, saying with the spouse, ' It is the voice of my beloved that knocketh.' Samuel heard the voice of God, but thought it had been Eli's. So alas ! when we hear our duty, ofttimes we do not take up God as the party speaking to us, hence we are nothing bettered.

2d, We must comply with his voice. ' This,' saith God, ' is my beloved Son, hear ye him.' To hear and not obey, is but to expose yourselves to double stripes. He is our Lord and King, and must have our obedience to his will, which, in the day of espousals, we take for our law. This is the hearing which the text requires. And so we must hear him only, whoever speak. Satan, the world, and our lusts, will each of them have their word, and their will is always contrary to Christ's will. But whatever you

did before, being now espoused to Christ, you are to
hear him only, giving a deaf ear to all other.

Again, We must hear him without disputing.
Christ's subjects are not to dispute his will, but to
obey. Any intimation of his will, is sufficient to determine us to a compliance. ' As soon as they hear
of me, they shall obey me.' So did Abraham obey ;
at the call of God he ' went out, not knowing whither
he went.' They to whom Christ's bare will and command, is not a sufficient reason for compliance, give
no evidence of their being espoused to him. Finally,
we must hear and obey, because it is his will. To
do his will, but not because it is his will, is not to
hear him ; for Christ's will must be the reason, as
well as the rule of our obedience. ' Thou hast commanded us to keep thy precepts diligently.'

****

How we are to view Christ, that we may please him in all things.

1. We must eye him as our Lord and Master,
whose will must be our law. ' Behold, as the eyes
of servants look unto the hand of their masters ; and
as the eyes of a maiden unto the hand of her mis-
tress, so our eyes wait upon the Lord our God, until that he have mercy upon us.' Have we given
our ears to be bored, that we might be his servants
for ever, then let us look to him as our master, and
never more say in word or deed, who is Lord over
us. Let us never refuse any work which he puts in
our hand, whether doing work or suffering work.

2. Eye him as our teacher. Christians are Christ's
disciples. Scholars among the Jews, sat at the feet
of their masters, as Paul at the feet of Gamaliel ; so
must we sit at our Lord's feet meekly, and humbly
to learn of him. It is little we know of God or our

duty, and for that end, we profess to have taken
Christ for our teacher. We must then learn of him
what we are to do, and what to forbear.

3. Eye him as our guide and leader. We are in a
wilderness, where we are apt to mistake our way.
We will never get our way to heaven without a guide.
God hath given Christ for that purpose, even a leader
and commander to the people, and we have been professing to receive him as such ; let us then keep our
eye on our leader, to follow him whithersoever he
goes. ' For this God is our God for ever and ever ;
he will be our guide even unto death.'

4. Eye him as our last and chief end, to whose
honour we may direct the whole course of our life.
I have set the Lord always before me : because he
is at my right hand, I shall not be moved. Self must
no more be the mark we aim at, but God must have
the room of self, endeavouring to please him in all
things. Thus the apostle made Christ the end of
his life. ' For me to live is Christ, and to die is gain.'

5. Eye him as our witness in all things. Where-
ever we are, he is present with us. Let us walk as
under the view of his purest eyes. He sees what is
within us, as well as without us. Let us take heed
to our spirits, as under the inspection of the heart-
searching God.

6. Eye him as our Judge, for to him we must give
an account. Did the thief see the eye of the judge
upon him, while his eyes go out after his covetousness, it would oblige him to hold up his hands.

Lastly, Eye him as our husband. That is a name
of love and authority, which as it binds us to obedience, so it should kindly draw us to it. And here
should we observe what pleaseth, and what displeaseth him, that we may carefully follow the one, and
avoid the other. This we may know both by the
word and by experience. An observant Christian
might have a well-confirmed rule hereby, how to
walk ; and this should be the glass by which Christ's

spouse should dress herself, taking up what pleaseth,
and laying aside what displeaseth her husband.

We should also diligently observe his countenance
towards us, whether it be with us, or turned from
us ; that if with us, we may be careful to keep it ;
if turned from us, that we may recover it. Two
things in which the spouse of Christ often shows her
neglect of her husband.

We should also observe his dispensations, and way
of his dealing with us. ' Whoso is wise, and will
observe these things, even they shall understand the
loving-kindness of the Lord.' Some courses deprive
us of the communications of his love and Spirit.
Some others make us a prosperous time while we follow them. Let us eye these, to follow the one and
avoid the other.

Motives to hear Christ, and to suit ourselves to his pleasure.

1. Consider what he did for us, suiting himself to
our case. What Zipporah said to Moses, he may
say to his spouse : A bloody spouse hast thou been
to me. If cords of love will bind us to our duty, in
this we need not want them. He left the bosom of
his Father, the hallelujahs of angels, took upon him
our nature, and died for us ; and shall we not behave
dutifully to him, who did all this for us. Consider
Christ pleased not himself, that he might save us.
His Father put a cup of unmingled wrath into his
hand, and bade him drink it, otherwise his designed
spouse should drink it for ever. His holy human
nature shivered at it, saying, ' O Father ! if it be possible, let this cup pass from me ;' but he suited himself to his Father's will, for our sake. Besides, has
he not bought the satisfaction of our dutifulness to

him, at a dear enough rate? We had never stood
espoused to him, had he not by his death, removed
the impediments which lay in the way of it. And
on every part of the spouse's duty to him, may be
written, *The price of blood!*

2. The angels in heaven suit themselves to his
pleasure in all things. His will is done in heaven.
They run at his command. They stand and wait
his orders, and the least piece of service put in their
hand, they refuse not. They are more excellent
creatures than we; and shall we not be ashamed to
be refractory to him, whom all the angels obey. He
is their head indeed, as well as ours, but he is not
their husband, that is the peculiar privilege of the
saints.

3. His pleasure is that which is best for us. He
bids us do nothing but what is for our good; yea,
for our best. That which seems heaviest in his pleasure concerning us, is really for our advantage. ' He
even chastens us for our profit, that we might be partakers of his holiness.' He hath so linked together
our duty and interest, that it is impossible to separate
them. We cannot consult our own happiness, but
by suiting ourselves to his pleasure. We cannot be
miserable, but by slighting his directions. Consider
we need but our own will to ruin us. It is a fearful
thing for a man to be given up to himself, Hosea
iv. 17. ' Ephraim is joined to idols : let him alone.'
Let us carve for ourselves, and certainly we will be
like the child that cuts his own fingers. O! what a
work do we make to get our own will, and yet a more
fearful plague we cannot meet with out of hell. A
man left to himself, will be his own ruin. Whereas,
on the contrary, we need but suit ourselves to his
pleasure, and we are happy. We have then a sure
hold of our true interest. Whatever is his will concerning his spouse, is really best for her. For why,
it is the product of infinite wisdom, mixed with infinite love. Could we but believe this, how easy would

it be. If it be his pleasure thou be poor and afflicted, it is best.

4. It will be a great satisfaction to thy Lord and husband, if thou suit thyself to his pleasure ; and would you not desire to give contentment to the heart of Christ, ' that he may see of the travail of his soul and be satisfied ?' Would you be lovely in his eyes, and have communion with him, this is the way to attain it, ' for so shall the King greatly desire thy beauty.' O! the many sweet hours of fellowship with heaven, the ravishing sweetness, the blessed communications of the love of the Lord, of which Christ's spouse robs herself, by neglecting her husband.

5. Your neglect and refractoriness will be grieving to his Spirit. The wicked world despise his will, and will have their own, if it should ruin them. But shall he be grieved also with your wilfulness ? The nearer the relation is in which you stand to him, the more piercing is your neglect of him, Psal. lv. 12. And the grieving of his Spirit will, sooner or later, bring a fearful confusion to your case.

6. There is a necessity for suiting yourselves to his pleasure. The rejecting of his commandments doth but lay up matter of repentance for you, and it will be bitterness in the end, go as it will, here or hereafter. Your struggle with the will of his providence is a vain struggle, ' for his counsel shall stand,' and what he will have crooked, thou shalt not make straight. It makes it more heavy than it would be. For, fight against God who will, he will always be the conqueror.

7. The honour of your Lord and husband requires it, so shall you be a crown to him, but otherwise a dishonour to him. O! how is the name of God blasphemed by the undutiful conduct of those espoused to Christ.

8. While you suit not yourself to his will, you suit yourself to the will of his enemies. There is no

midst. And what can you expect but the fire of his
jealousy to burn against you.

Advice.—Put that will of yours in the Lord's
hand, that he may mould it into a conformity to his
own. And believe that he will do it, and in the
faith of the promise use the means. Endeavour to
get the firm faith of this, that what is his will is best
for you, and apply that to particulars, and your own
spirit.

Advice 1. Put that will of yours in the Lord's own
hand, that he may mould it into a conformity to his
own. ' Thy people shall be willing in the day of
thy power.' The will of man is a refractory piece,
which we can no more master of ourselves, than a
child can master a giant. There is no forcing of it,
and we cannot bow it of ourselves. Lay it then before the Lord often, with that, ' Thou hast chastised
me, and I was chastised, as a bullock unaccustomed
to the yoke : turn thou me, and I shall be turned :
for thou art the Lord my God. He is a husband
that can cure the wilfulness of his spouse, can give
her heart a set that it shall be according to his own.
He is the only physician for the stone of the heart ;
and though you cannot break it, put it in his hand
that he may do it. You may tell him where you are
pained, as the child cried to his mother, *my head,*
you may cry to him, *my heart.* You may tell him it
is your burden, and you would fain be freed of it, but
you cannot. You may lay it over on him, that he
may do that for you, which you cannot do for yourselves.

Advice 2. Believe, in order to the getting of your
will suited to your Lord's will. Would you have
this mountain removed, it must be done in the way
of believing. There are three things I would have
you to believe, 1. That you are not fit to be your own
choosers. All the saints, in one voice, have given
this verdict of themselves. ' He shall choose our
inheritance for us, the excellency of Jacob, whom he

loved.' God from heaven has witnessed it, in his
giving of Christ to be a leader, a head and husband
to them ; thereby not trusting them, but him, with
bringing the children to glory.   Christ himself has
put this lesson in our hands, teaching us to deny ourselves, and to be jealous of ourselves.   The event
has proved it often, in that people getting their own
will, has been their ruin, Psalm lxxviii. 29. ; and the
best of the saints getting the reins in their own
hand, have set all on fire.

Again, Believe that whatever is the Lord's will is
always best for you.   All our wilfulness proceeds on
a mistake.   We think sinful liberty best for us, ease,
plenty, and the like.   God knows it is otherwise, and
therefore he will have us hear him for our good.   To
help you to believe this,

1. Consider God's will is the product of infinite
wisdom, and may we not trust that infinite wisdom
that contrived the world, with the guiding of it ? Will
we hold up our taper to the sun shining in its brightness, or shall our weakness pretend to tell him what
is best for his creatures ? Why do we not then sink
down into our seats and say, *Good is the will of the
Lord*, and let him do what seemeth him good.

2. Christ loves his spouse more dearly, and cares
more for their good than they do themselves, and so
whatever is his will for them is best for them.   He
loved them so as to lay down his life for them, and
may not that evidence his will to be best for them.
' As the Father,' saith he, ' hath loved me, so have
I loved you.'   Why doth the father hedge up his unruly child, why does he refuse him his will, but because he loves him ?

3. By virtue of the covenant of grace, God's glory
and his people's good are both in one bottom, and
cannot be separated.   Is his will then always most
for his own glory, consequently it is most for his
people's good.

4. His will is ever right ; it is seldom but our will

is wrong, and never right when opposite to his, Deut.
xxxii. 4.   There is no flaw in the way and will of
God ; and whatever hardships those espoused to
Christ may now seem to see in it, when they come
to the other world, they will make their recantation,
and say, *He has done all things well.*

Lastly, Consider your experience.   Have you not
seen many times, how God has done you good against
your wills, good which you would never have got, had
he given you your will.

Moreover, consider that God will make out his
promise of suiting your will to his, who have put it
in his hands, Ezek. xxxvi. 26, 27.   How shall we get
the good of the promises, but by believing them.
Have you given up your will to him, to be rectified
by him, believe that he will do it, and it shall be
done.

....

Who are our own People mentioned, Psal. xlv. 10.
*we must forget ; in what respects, and why we
must forget them.*

I. To show who are our own people, whom we
must forget.—In a word, it is the wicked world, ' the
children of disobedience, among whom, in time past,
we had our conversation.'   When the soul comes to
Christ, it must say as Ruth to Naomi, ' thy people
shall be my people, and thy God my God.'   When
Christ calls a soul to himself, he calls it out of the
world.   The church is a congregation gathered out
of, and separated from, the world ; though not in
place, yet in respect of affection, which is the greatest separation.   But to be more particular, a saint
may know who are his own people, by taking a look
of himself, as corrupt and carnal.

1. Then they are our own people, who are yet

living in darkness, unacquainted with the corruption
of their nature, and misery of it; strangers to the
spirituality of the law of God; strangers to the majesty and holiness of God, their absolute need of
Christ, and his preciousness and excellency. The
saints may remember the day in which they lived in
that same region of darkness, and knew not more of
these things than they, and may hence conclude these
are their own people. ' Be not ye, therefore, partakers with them. For ye were sometimes darkness,
but now are ye light in the Lord : walk as children
of the light.'

2. They who are living in the same way and manner that the spouse of Christ did before her espousals ;
they are their own people walking on in the way
which they have left, Ephes. ii. **2, 3**. Are they following the course of the world ? Do they venture
frankly over the hedge of God's laws ? You may
know, then, by your former conversation, that they
are your own people, from among whom Christ plucked you as brands out of the burning.

3. They who are going the same way your carnal
hearts would go, if they were left to their own corrupt choice. These are your own people ; for, as in
water, face answers to face, so do your hearts, as
corrupt, answer to theirs. It is grace only that
makes the difference, for the same nature is in both,
only the power of that corrupt nature is broken in
those that are espoused to Christ, but it is entire in
others. There is another principle beside it in the
godly, but it is alone, and sways all, in others.

4. They who are living in the same barren region,
in which the saints lived, before their espousals to
Christ. The state of nature is that barren region ;
that is a far country, far from God and his covenant,
and therefore there is no communication betwixt God
and them, no influences for making them fruitful in the
works of holiness ; but a fulness of the sour grapes
of wickedness. These are our own people : ' For

we ourselves also, were sometimes foolish, disobedient, deceived, serving divers lusts and pleasures,
living in malice and envy ; hateful, and hating one
another.' We now proceed,

II. In what respects we must forget them.

1. We must forsake their company ; it is evil company, unbecoming Christ's spouse ' Forsake the
foolish and live, and go in the way of understanding.'
While we are in the world, indeed, there is no shun-
ning of evil men altogether ; but you must not make
wicked men your familiar friends, you must not chuse
their company ; and if necessity lead you into their
company, you must take heed to yourselves in it,
and haste out of it as a plague-house. They that
are espoused to Christ, and yet keep wicked company as before, give no great evidence of their sincerity. Birds of a feather flock together, and you may
know what a man is, by the company which he loves
best.

2. We must not conform ourselves to them, nor be
like them in their way. The command is, *be not
conformed unto this world.* If we pretend a difference in our state from theirs, let there be a visible
difference betwixt our way and theirs. Do Satan's
drudges bear the devil's mark, let us hate to take it
on, or learn of them their ways. All that have a mind
for heaven, must be nonformists to the world, because
the way of the world is against God and his law.

3. We must forget them in affection, saying, *Depart from me, ye bloody men.* Though we are to
wish well to the persons of all men, we must hate
their evil ways, saying with David, ' I hate the work
of them that turn aside, it shall not cleave unto me.'
We must no more esteem their way as we were wont
nor desire to return into it. Have we been coming
out of Sodom, we must not look back with a rueful
look, otherwise we are not fit for the kingdom of
God.

III. Why we must forget them.

1. Because they are not going our way. All men are on a journey to heaven, or to hell. There is a strait and narrow way that leads to heaven, a broad way to hell. If we are espoused to Christ, then we are on the narrow way ; and how can we but forsake them that are going the quite opposite way Nothing is more opposite than the way of holiness, and the way of the world ; therefore we must either give up pretences to Christ, or give up with the way of the world, ' wherein in time past, we walked according to the course of this world.'

2. Because the godly and the wicked world, are on two different sides, under two opposite heads, Christ and the devil. All the world is divided betwixt these two, the Saviour of the world, and the god of the world. Christ's party are his spouse, brethren, members of his body. The devil's are his captives, prisoners, slaves. And though these of Satan's party may come over, yet the truly godly will never mix with them in their ways. ' Thou shalt keep them, O Lord, thou shalt preserve them from this generation for ever.'

3. Because, in consenting to Christ, we gave up with them. If you take me, let these go their way. Their company is infectious. ' Evil communications corrupt good manners.' Their way is destructive, therefore let not your hearts go after them and their ways. When you engaged with Christ, you engaged against both, and said, ' thy people shall be my people, and where thou goest I will go.'

4. Because the world's friendship is enmity with God, James iv. 4. What is wicked company but a combination against God, to trample on his laws, dishonour his Son, and grieve his Spirit. What are the ways of the world, but a direct opposition to God. So far, then, as we go with them, so far we go away from God. So much as they and their ways get of our affections, so much we lose of affection to Christ.

Lastly, Because there will be a total separation at

last, of the godly and wicked, Matt. xxv. Grace begins it here. Grace gives a new nature, new principles, new designs, and new motives, all which make a new conversation, opposite to the way of the world. Therefore, if we would not lodge with them in eternity, we must give up with them in time.

Motives to forsake evil company.

1. Consider how unaccountable it is, that Christ's sheep should be found among the devil's goats ; and Christ's servants joining issue with the devil's slaves. 2 Cor. vi. 14—16. If you have given up your name to Christ, why are you found on the devil's ground ? Let the swine of the world feed together on the husks of sin, lie down together on the dunghill of their filthy lusts ; but what has any to do among them, that pretends to be a child of God.

2. The closer you are linked with them, the farther are you from God. Mix with the world and their way, and God will not know you as his. He commands a separation from these, if you would have a reception from him. ' Wherefore,' says he ' come out from among them, and be ye separate, saith the Lord ; and touch not the unclean thing, and I will receive you.' Men must go to the one side or the other ; there is no keeping up with both God and ungodly company. Will men be swearing a covenant with God one day, and swearing with profane swearers another ; drinking at the Lord's table, and at the table of drunkards, 1 Cor. x. 21. God will never own such vagrants for members of his household. See their doom, Jude 13.

3. It hardens the wicked in their way. It is Solomon's observation, ' they that forsake the law, praise the wicked ; but such as keep the law contend

with them.' The sins of professors, going the way
of evil men, is a practical testimony to the way of
sin, emboldening the wicked to go on in their way
Whereas a testimony is to be kept up for God in the
world, by a walk contrary to the way of the world.
Thus Noah contended against the security and wickedness of the world, by a holy life, ' by which he
condemned the world, and became heir of the righteousness which is by faith.'

4. Evil company is an infecting plague. *Evil
communications corrupt good manners.* How many
fair blossoms of religion, have been killed in the bud,
by the poisonous breath of evil company ? How
many have been dragged over the belly of good principles, vows, and resolutions, by the violence of it ?
There is a mighty efficacy in it to advance the devil's
kingdom, and men being once drawn in, it is a thousand to one, if they go not far beyond these bounds
which they had prescribed to themselves. For the
devil's agents have that off their master, let them
once get in a finger, and they will endeavour to get
the whole hand to follow.

Lastly, If you do not be separated, you will share
with them. Weighty is that word, *a companion of
fools shall be destroyed.* How many have cursed
the day that ever they saw the face of those, by
whom they have been first led into sin, and next to
ruin. It will be no comfort to suffer God's wrath
with company, whatever may be in sinning together.
If we go in the way with the wicked, we must go to
the same place with them. And though mercy
should rescue you, it will be so as by fire, as we see
in Lot's case.

What they must part with, who forget their Father's house, as commanded, Psal. xlv. 10. and reasons why they must obey this command.

This father is the devil, who keeps house in a wicked world, and in every unregenerate heart. Here we shall,

I. Show with what of our father's house we must give up. And,

1. You must part with the master of the house, Satan, and renounce your relation to the house. Though you have no express compact with him, you have need to do this. There is a twofold relation all natural men have to the house. They are servants of the house, hence it is said, *ye were the servants of sin ;* their work is sin, and their wages is death. It is sad work, miserable wages ; for he is the worst of masters, and they are the meanest sort of servants. Sinners have no term when they may leave their master, for they are slaves to Satan, and wholly in their master's power, taken captive by him at his will. He has a threefold title to them as his slaves. They are his slaves taken in war, ' for of whom a man is overcome, of the same he is brought in bondage.' The devil having proclaimed war against heaven, attacked man as heaven's ally and confederate, and gained the victory over him. He is pursuing this war still against mankind, and driving the unrenewed world before him as prisoners of war, and so at his will, Isaiah xlix. 24, 25. They are also his bought slaves. Men, in general, like the Israelites, ' have sold themselves to do evil in the sight of the Lord, to provoke him to anger.' Where there is such a sale, Satan must needs be the buyer. It is a very low price, indeed, even for nought. The foolish sin-

ner thinks not so, while he makes the bargain ; but
when the latter end comes, he will see it is all naught
he has gained, in comparison of the soul that is lost.
Rome drives this trade, Rev. xviii. 13. Where have
they learned it, but from the devil, who early set it
up, buying our first parents for a parcel of forbidden
fruit, and had the impudence to order the second
Adam to fall down and worship him. He is daily
buying a drunkard for some strong drink, a covetous
worldling for a little pelf, a hypocrite for a name, unjust persons and liars for a very little thing. They
are also his born slaves, born in his house. Eph. ii. 3.
Many are born of parents, slaves to the devil, themselves, all their days ; even those who themselves
are free, yet their children are not therefore free too,
for ' they were shapen in iniquity, and in sin did
their mothers conceive them.' It is not the first
birth, but the second, that will make us free men
Now we must give up that relation to the house.
We must renounce our service, and break away from
our old master, and betake ourselves to Christ, as a
new master, who makes all his servants free men.

They are sons of the house. ' Ye are of your father, the devil,' said our Lord to the Jews. A sad
sonship, for it is an ill house ; it is to be a son of
hell, a prison house, a dark house, a dreadful house.
Never was a child liker a father, than unregenerate
persons are like the devil. His nature is enmity
against God and his law, so is theirs. He is fallen,
and so are they ; lying in wickedness, and so are
they.

Now, we must give up that relation to the house.
We must be born again, we must be new creatures,
or we will be ashamed of our pretended espousals to
Christ. ' For if any man be in Christ he is a new
creature ; old things are passed away ; behold all
things are become new.' The image of Satan must
be defaced, the image of God restored in sanctifica-

tion, and that work advanced in daily mortification
to sin, and living to righteousness.

2. You must quit the work of the house. We
must cast off the works of darkness. There is never
an idle person about our father's house. Satan keeps
all his children and servants busy at their task, that
so they may not think of ways to escape, or of leaving him, as Pharaoh did with the Israelites. And
what are they always about, that keeps them busy.
They are always at one of two things, they are either
weaving the spider's web, or hatching the cockatrice
egg. *They are weaving the spider's web.* They
are very busy doing nothing. Nothing for God,
their souls, or eternity. Their webs will not become
garments, neither shall they cover themselves with
their works. All that they are busy about, will do
no more to help their souls in the day of wrath, than
a cob-web will clothe a man to defend him against
the cold. The besom of death will sweep them and
it away together ; and about this, heads and hands
are employed. Or, *they are hatching the cockatrice
eggs.* ' He that eateth of their eggs dieth ; and
that which is crushed, breaketh out into a viper.
They weary themselves to commit iniquity. They
draw iniquity with cords of vanity, and treasure up
wrath against the day of wrath.' This is work. It
is hard, toilsome, and dark work, soul-ruining work.
Yet it is the work of the house, in which each strives
to outdo another, and undo themselves. But, as in
other houses, some are employed in coarser work,
and others in finer, so it is in this house. The master of the house puts his coarser work in the hands
of the profane ignorant earth-worm, that has not so
much as a form of godliness ; and their task is *to fulfil the lusts of the flesh.* He employs their tongues
in swearing and lying, their bellies in gluttony and
drunkenness, their bodies in uncleanness, their hands
in picking and stealing ; and their heads, hearts,
hands, continually about the world ; so that on their

belly they must go, and can never get up their head
above the world, and their eye must never be satisfied with seeing, nor their ear with hearing, but like
the grave, cry give, give ; and loading themselves
with thick clay, which they will never let go, till
death separate them.

He puts his finer work in the hands of the hypo-
critical professors, who work such a coat to themselves, as they shine in it like angels of light, and
their task is *to fulfil the desires of the mind.* He
employs them to deceive the world with their hypo-
critical pretences to piety, and to deceive themselves
also. Their business is to oppose themselves to the
very heart and life of the gospel, by their unbelief,
self-righteousness, pride, and self-conceit ; and to
keep in the life of some lusts by their form of religion, and shelter them under a cover of religious duties. To do much mischief to the church of God,
and stumble and bring to ruin many poor souls.

Now you must quit the work of the house, of whatever sort it be. You must not be like those that
will give over their master, engage with another, and
yet come back, and fall to their work again. You
must take other work in hand : I do not say more
work, for as the watch that goes wrong, goes as fast
as that which goes right, you will have as much
work in your father's house as in your husband's.

3. You must part with the provision and entertainment of the house. People use to get their meat
where they work their work, and Satan's slaves get
their meat also, in their father's house. And what is
their entertainment ? He sets them down *to eat dust
with the serpent,* Isaiah lxv. 25. He feeds them on
filthy lusts, which may nourish their corruptions, but
is poisonous to their souls. Satan did once eat angel's food in the enjoyment of God, but now dust is
his meat with the serpent, that is, as it was the meat
and drink of Christ to do the will of his Father, so
it is Satan's to sin against God and to do mischief,

all the pleasure he hath lies there. So it is with Christless sinners, the sweetest milk which they suck is out of the breasts of their lusts ; the enjoyment of God was never so sweet to those whose God is their belly, as meat and drink ; the dishonest person hath not so much pleasure in the gospel treasure, as in some thing that he can catch to please the covetous heart.

He sets them also *to eat husks with the swine.* Luke xv. 16. He feeds them with the empty dry things of the world, and they are dressed up according as every one likes best. Some get the pleasures, others the profits, others the honours of it set before them, and on these they feed So the voluptuous man has more delight in carnal pleasures, than in communion with God ; ' for they are lovers of pleasure more than lovers of God.' The worldling hath more pleasure in his goods and chattels, than in all the spiritual gains of true godliness. These things are to him but shadows, but what he can hold is substance. ' I am become rich,' says he, ' I have found me out substance.' The ambitious man hath more delight in a name and honour among men, than in the honour of God's approbation. ' How can ye believe, which receive honour one of another, and seek not the honour that cometh from God only.'

Now you must quit the entertainment of the house, and betake yourself to the entertainment and provision of the house of heaven. ' Wherefore do ye spend money for that which is not bread, and your labour for that which satisfieth not ? hearken diligently unto me, and eat ye that which is good, and let your soul delight itself in fatness.' You ask bread in your father's house, and he gives you a stone, for what he gives is not bread, and satisfies not the soul. The dust of lusts is not good, change your dust then, and ' eat that which is good.' God, grace, communion with God, and all the benefits of the covenant are good. They are good for the soul and the body,

for time and eternity. The husks of the world have
no fatness in them, change them therefore, and ' let
your souls delight themselves in fatness.' Spiritual
things are full of sap, and will make your souls prosper.

4. You must quit the fashions of the house. Every
house hath its own fashions, and so hath your father's ; but that must not keep them up. ' Be not
conformed unto this world.' They are evil fashions,
you are not to bring them along with you to your
husband's house. The fashion of the house in natural actions, is to follow these actions in a mere self-
ish way, to gratify a carnal appetite, without any eye
to God in them, or fitting us thereby for his service.
You must quit it, and must not be like your father's
house in them. Modesty and sobriety, and referring
all to the honour of God, is the fashion you must fall
in with, as the fashion of your husband's house.
' Whether, therefore, ye eat or drink, or whatsoever
ye do, do all to the glory of God.' The fashion of
your father's house in civil actions, is to be sunk and
swallowed up in these things, to be minding them
more *than the one thing needful*, and to have no respect to the command nor honour of God in them ;
and so to make these things either jostle out duty to
God altogether, or to take such a lift of them, that
no vigour of spirit, and sometimes even no strength
of body, is left for duty to God. To be untender in
these things, and even to give conscience a stretch,
if a person can gain any profit or ease by it. To
count truth in words, and exact uprightness in dealing, and to do no other way to others, than we would
they should do to us, but needless nicety. If you
quit not these fashions you will never see the house
of heaven, Luke x. 41, 42. ' And Jesus answered
and said unto her, Martha, Martha, thou art careful
and troubled about many things ; but one thing is
needful : and Mary hath chosen that good part, which
shall not be taken away from her.' 1 Cor. vi. 8, 9.

' Nay, ye do wrong, and defraud, and that your brethren. Know ye not that the unrighteous shall not
inherit the kingdom of God? Be not deceived : neither fornicators, nor idolaters, nor adulterers, nor ef-
feminate, nor abusers of themselves with mankind.'
1 Thess. iv. 6. ' That no man go beyond and defraud
his brother in any matter ; because that the Lord is
the avenger of all such, as we also have forwarned
you, and testified.' If ever men get more religion,
they will get more moral honesty.

The fashion of your father's house in religious actions, (for there is some religion even in that house,
but it is of the fashion of the house,) that it is to hold
with the one half, and that too the worst half, the
outer half, the mere form of godliness. To hold with
bodily exercise, but endeavour not to worship God
in spirit. So that men in that house shut the eyes
of their bodies, yet their hearts are going after their
covetousness ; they bow their knees, but their hearts
remain inflexible. It is their custom to seek to please
themselves more than God, Matth. vi. 2. To go
about these duties that they may sin the more freely,
and so make a covering of them to some lust, Prov.
vii. 14, 15. They put them in Christ's room, *going
about to establish a righteousness of their own.* If
you quit not these fashions, you are not God's people, ' for God is a spirit, and they that worship him,
must worship him in spirit and in truth.' His people are the circumcision, who worship him in spirit,
rejoice in Christ Jesus, and have no confidence in
the flesh.' Hypocrisy is a mask which God will
pluck off.

5. You must quit the garb of the house. Under
the Old Testament, when people were to make any
solemn appearance before God, they were called to
change their garments, Gen. xxxiv. 2. And if you
would show yourselves Christ's spouse, you must
part with the garb of the house, off which you are
come. You must part with the inner garment of the

house, *that is the old man with his deeds*, Eph. iv. 22.
Colos. iii. 9. The old man is the corrupt evil nature;
his deeds are the corrupt workings of that nature in
heart and life. These cleave close to us, as a girdle
to the loins of a man, but we must be putting them
off by daily mortification. In vain do we pretend to
be espoused to Christ, if we still retain our former
lusts. Christ has another garment for his spouse,
which we must put on, if ever we see heaven, that
is *the new man*, the new nature, with a new life, Eph.
iv. 24. It is made up of two pieces : righteousness, the whole of our duty to man ; and holiness,
the whole of our duty to God. For true religion is
universal, and therefore it is called a man ; not a
member or two of a man, but a whole man.

You must also part with the upper garment of the
house, that is the filthy rags of your own righteousness, Isaiah lxiv. 6. ' But we are all as an unclean
thing, and all our righteousnesses are as filthy rags ;
and we all do fade as a leaf ; and our iniquities, like
the wind, have taken us away.' Zech. iii. 4. ' And
he answered and spake unto those that stood before
him, saying, Take away the filthy garments from him.
And unto him he said, Behold, I have caused thine
iniquity to pass from thee, and I will clothe thee
with change of raiment.' The way in our father's
house, is to cover their unrighteousness with their
own righteousness, their evil with their good, their
sins with their duties. But alas! all this is but a
covering of rags, that will not hide thy shame before
the Lord ; a covering of filthy rags, that will make
thee more vile. Christ hath provided the white raiment of his own righteousness for thee, that must be
put on by faith ; and all thou doest, must be washed
in the blood of the lamb, or thou wilt be ruined with
it. You must learn that lesson in your husband's
house, that never one could yet learn in their father's
house, even to work in religion, as if you were to

K k

win heaven by working, and then to overlook all, as if you had done nothing.

Lastly, You must quit the interest of the house. People readily are concerned for the interest of the house of which they are menbers, and none more than the members of our father's, that do their utmost to support it.   Now, if you mind for heaven, you must quit this interest, and pursue the interest of the house of heaven.   You must not interest yourselves in the quarrels of that house.   That house hath a quarrel against the image of God, the power of godliness, and the people of God, Gen. iii. 15. ; and all the members of the house, interest themselves in the quarrel, one way or another, to bear down the exercise of godliness.   Persecutors strike it down ; mockers jest upon, and laugh at it; the worldly man gravely pronounces it to be folly ; the hypocrite's heart rises bitterly against it, and bears it down and smothers it with contention and strife about outward things.   All join together in the quarrel, though they go different ways to work.   But you must stand upon the side of godliness.

You must not support the interest of your father's house.   Christ was sent to pull it down, *to destroy the works of the devil ;* do not you put to your hand to hold it up.   The members of the house are very much concerned to hold it up.   They will not give their help to curb sin, but, on the contrary, they encourage one another by example and otherwise, like Babel-builders, to go on with the work.   Let none that mind for heaven, support the interest of Satan in the family, or in any place where they are.   We now proceed,

II. To give reasons, why these that are espoused to Christ, must forget their father's house.

1. Because our father's house, and husband's house, are quite contrary the one to the other, as heaven and hell, light and darkness, and there is no reconciling them, 2 Cor. vi. 14, 15.   Therefore we

must renounce our part in, and relation to the one, if
we mind to plead a part in, and relation to the other.
They never shall mix. ' God will preserve his people from this generation for ever.' They never can
mix. ' You cannot serve God and mammon.' The
heads of these houses are opposite, the work, the entertainment, the fashions, and interests ; therefore,
as you would not renounce your part in Christ, forget your father's house.

2. Because, as our husband's house is most honourable, so our father's house is most base. These
that are espoused to Christ, as Christ is their husband, they are God's children ; they are of the same
family with the angels ; nay, the very angels are
ministering spirits, to take care of them who are
joint heirs with Christ. They are honourable in
their relations, and rich in their title to heaven and
glory. But our father's house has nothing in it but
baseness, for it is a fallen house, fallen from honour
to the deepest disgrace, from happiness to extreme
poverty and misery. For us to follow the ways of it,
is as if one brought into a noble family could not forget, but bring along with her, the way of the beg-
garly family from which she came.

3. Because we will never apply ourselves to the
way of our husband's house, if we forget not our father's house. While the hearts of the Israelites were
set on the flesh pots of Egypt, they could make no
progress in their journey to Canaan. Laban knew
that Jacob could not enjoy his service, when he
much longed after his father's house. The affectionate remembrance of the work and provision of our
father's house, will be a dead weight on those that
have begun to run the race set before them ; and always, the more we give way to our corruptions, the
more tenderly we handle our lusts, religion will be
the more difficult.

4. Because it is the worst of houses. No wonder,
for the devil, the worst of masters, is the master of

the house.   No slavery like the service of that house.
It is soul slavery.   No entertainment like it, for it
can never satisfy; nay, it is destructive to the soul.
The work thereof is sin, the wages death, eternal
death.   The fashions of the house are the very reverse
of all that is good.   The interests of the house are
the dishonour of God, the ruin of mankind.   The
garb of the house is filthy rags, and the shame of
their nakedness will at length appear before the
world.

*Who they are that will not leave their father's house,
as exhorted and commanded of God,* Psal. xlv. 10.

1. Those, that in the midst of gospel light, yet continue in the darkness of the house; even all grossly
ignorant persons.   They that are brought out of
their father's house to Christ, are brought out of darkness to light, though they know not a letter. ' They
were sometimes darkness, but now are they light in
the Lord.'   If people remain ignorant under gospel means, we know what is the cause, their father
has put out their eyes, 2 Cor. iv. 3, 4.   This will
end in eternal darkness.   ' It is a people of no understanding, therefore he that made them will not have
mercy on them; and he that formed them, will show
them no favour.'
2. Those that retain the language of the house.
When Peter spoke, the damsel knew what country-
man he was,   *Thou art a Gallilean, for thy speech
bewrayeth thee.*   And what shall we say of thee, that
art a curser, a swearer, a liar, a filthy speaker, but
thou art a Hellilean.   I appeal to your own consciences, what sort of language that is, whether it
sounds like heaven or hell.   To hear a man speak
as if hell were opening; breathing out lies, as if in-

spired by the father of them ; speaking, as if an unclean devil were speaking out of him ; what can one
think in such a case, but that the person speaks like
the house to which he belongs.   But if you will not
forbear that language, it will turn to blaspheming at
length through a long eternity.   For the former is
the language of the house in time, the other in eternity.

3. Those that wear the badge of the house on their
breasts, the master of the house's mark on their foreheads, so that those who go by, may easily know
whose they are.   Profane people.   You that will
not bow a knee to God.   ' The wicked through the
pride of his countenance, will not seek after God.'
You that take room to yourselves in all licentiousness, that have nothing to do with religion, but to
show aversion to all that is good ; if not to mock
and reproach others that seem to be religious.   Will
you pretend to any portion in Christ ? No, no, you
know not Christ, and he will disown you.   A dumb
devil possesseth you now, that you cannot, will not
pray to God now ; the day will come, that you will
cry to the hills to fall upon you, and hide you from
the face of the judge.   You will have a merry life of
it now, but you shall weep ; you will make a jest of
religion now, but that will make you roar at length.
Your heart is averse to all that is good now, the
cope stone will be put on it in hell.   You care not
for prayers, godly discourse, examinations, or sermons ; but some of you will go to the hill with the
beasts, sabbath after sabbath, and desire no person
to take that task off your hand.   Well were it for
you, if as you live with the beasts, you were to die
with them also.

4. Those that give up themselves to the trade of
the house, minding nothing but the world, earthly
things.   They have no trade with heaven.   They
know not what communion with God means.   They
will have their work on earth as far advanced as their

neighbours, but their work for eternity is yet to begin.   They are so busy they cannot get time for it.
They have so much to do otherwise, they cannot get
any thing done to purpose for their perishing souls.
That is folly, for the world will be consumed in flames,
when that soul of yours shall continue to exist, to be
either eternally happy or miserable, as it is now seen
to be in time.

Lastly, Those that are the hidden servants of the
house.   It has been said of some, that they have
stealed away to heaven, without being observed ; but
there are others that steal away to hell, and the world
never hears the sound of their feet ; even deep veiled
hypocrites, whited sepulchres.   ' They are disobedient, deceived, serving divers lusts and pleasures.'
They wear Christ's livery, but yet are satan's drudges.
There are always some lusts, that have such persons
absolutely under their power.   The broad way is
wide enough, so that they can easily get a bye path
in it, to go by themselves to destruction, without
mixing with the profane rabble that keep the highway.   However, all come to one lodging at length.
' As for such as turn aside to their crooked ways,
the Lord shall lead them forth with the workers of
iniquity.'

Matt. xi. 28. *explained.*   " *Come unto me, all ye that
labour, and are heavy-laden, and I will give you
rest.*"

The great and main object of gospel-preaching
and gospel-practice, is a coming to Christ.   It is
the first article in Christianity, according to John,
v. 40.   ' Ye will not come to me, that ye might
have life.'   It is the connecting chain, 1 Pet.
ii. 4.   ' To whom coming as unto a living stone, ye

also as lively stones are built up,' &c. And it is
the last exercise of the Christian; for when finishing
his warfare, the invitation is, Matt. xxv. 34. ' Come,
ye blessed of my Father, inherit the kingdom prepared for you.' It is virtually the all which God requir-
eth of us, John vi. 29. ' This is the work of God,
that ye believe on him whom he hath sent.' The
words of the text are a most solemn and ample invitation which Christ gives to sinners. In them I shall
consider,

1. The connexion. For which look to verses 25.
and 26. compare Luke x. 21. ' Jesus rejoiced in spirit.' It was a joyful time to him when he made this
invitation. He rejoiced in the account of the good
news, the success with which the message of the disciples was attended; and in the wise and sovereign
dispensation of grace by the Father, which he here
celebrates, as also upon the view of his own power,
where he shows, that all power was lodged in him.
The keys of the Father's treasures of grace were in
his hand, yea, and whatsoever is the Father's, He
also shows that none could know the Father, but
by him, for that is given to him only. He, as it
were, opens the treasure-door to sinners in the text.
From the connexion of this verse, as just now stated,
I would observe, that the solemnity of this invitation is most observable. There seems something
to be about it more than ordinary. As,

1. It was given in the day of Christ's gladness.
He was a man of sorrows, all made up of sorrows.
Sorrow, sighing, weeping, groaning, were his ordinary fare. Once indeed we read of his being glad,
John xi. 15.; and once of his rejoicing, Luke x. 21.
And, again, on this occasion here that thread of sorrow was interrupted, the sun of joy broke out for a
little from under the cloud. His heart was touched,
and, as it were, leaped for joy, as the word signifies;
compare Matt. v. 12. with Luke vi. 23. In the
Greek, ' he was exceeding joyful.' At this extraordi-

nary time and frame, he gives the invitation in the text. Hence infer,

1*st*, That Christ invites sinners with an enlarged heart. Joy enlarges it. His heart is open to you, his arms are stretched wide. You often see him with sorrow and anger in his face, and this works with you that you will not come. Behold him smiling and inviting you now to himself, sending love-looks to lost sinners, from a joyful heart within! Infer,

2*dly*, May I say, the Mediator's joy is not complete, till you come and take a share? The scriptures will warrant the expression, Isa. liii. 11. ' He shall see of the travail of his soul, and shall be satisfied.' He rejoiceth, but resteth not; but invites sinners to a share, as if all could not satisfy while he goes childless, as to some he has yet an eye upon. Infer,

3*dly*, That nothing can make Christ forget poor sinners, or be unconcerned for them. Sorrow could not do it, joy could not do it; either of these will drive a narrow-spirited man so into himself, as to forget all others. But never was his heart so filled either with sorrow or joy, but there was always room for poor sinners there. When he was entering the ocean of wrath, he remembered them, John xvii.; and as our forerunner, he went into the ocean of joy. Heb. vi. 20. Like Aaron, he carried our names on his heart, when he went in to appear before the Lord in heaven, Exod. xxviii. 29.

2. The invitation was given at a time when there was a great breach made in the devil's kingdom, compare Luke x. 17, 18. Christ was now beginning to set up a new kingdom, and he sends out seventy disciples, which was the number of the Sanhedrim at first. He was to bring his people out of the spiritual Egypt, compare Gen. xlvi. 27. The success of the disciples was a fair pledge of the devil's kingdom coming down, and the delivery of sin-

ners. And when the news of it comes, his heart re-
joices, and his tongue breaks out in this invitation
to the devil's captives, to come away upon this glorious signal. As he had begun to perform this part
of the covenant, the Father had begun to perform
his, which made his heart leap for joy, and sets him
on to cry, that they would all come away, as disciples,
vigorously to pursue the advantage which was got,
Psal. cx. 7. ' He shall drink of the brook in the way,
therefore shall he lift up the head.' Hence infer,

1*st*, That Christ's heart is set upon the work of
sinners' salvation. Ye see no undue haste, but he
would have no delays. He holds hands to the work
calling, *Come unto me.* He preferred it to the eating of his bread ; and what else is the meaning of
all the ordinances and providences ye meet with ?
Infer,

2*dly*, That Christ would have you to come, taking
encouragment from the example of others that have
come before you. There is a gap made in the devil's
prison ; some have made their escape by it already,
O ! will ye not follow ? The Lord has set examples
for us, both of judgment and of mercy. In the be-
ginnings of the Jewish church, there was an example
of God's sovereignty, in the destruction of Nadab
and Abihu, Lev. x. 1, 2. ; and of the Christian church,
in the death of Ananias and Sapphira, Acts, v. ; of
mercy, in the Jewish church, Rahab the harlot, besides Abraham, the father of them all, an idolater,
Josh. xxix. 15. compare Isa. li. 2. Then in the
Christian church, Paul, the blasphemous persecutor,
1 Tim. i. 16. Infer,

3*dly*, That however full Christ's house be, there
is always room for more ; he wearies not of welcom-
ing sinners ; the more that come the better. Christ's
harvest is not all cut down at once, nor his house
built in a day ; if the last stone were laid in the building, the scaffolding of ordinances would be taken
down, and the world be at an end. But none of

these has hitherto taken place ; therefore yet there is room, Joel iii. 21. ' For I will cleanse their blood that I have not yet cleansed, for the Lord dwelleth in Zion.'

3. This invitation is given on a solemn review of that fulness, of that *all* which the Father hath lodged in the hand of the Mediator, and that solely. The Father, as it were, no sooner leads him into these treasures, but he says, ' This and this is for you, sinners ; here is a treasure of mercies and blessings for you ; pardon, life, peace, &c. all is for you. Come, therefore, unto me, the Father has delivered them into my hand, I long to deliver them over to you. Come, therefore, to me, and hence I shall draw my fulness out to you.' Christ had got a kingdom from the Father ; it was as yet thinly peopled, and so he calls you to come to him, that ye may be happy in him. He has no will to enjoy these things alone, but because he has them, he would have you to take a share.

Reasons why Christ is so kind and liberal as to invite sinners of mankind to come to him, that they may share of his special goodness.

1. Because the Father hath given him for that end : Isa. lv. 4. ' Behold, I have given him for a Witness unto the people, a Leader and Commander unto the people.' The Father had thoughts of love to man ; his love designed to distribute a treasure of mercy, pardon, and grace, to lost sinners ; but justice would not allow his giving them immediately out of his own hand ; therefore he gives them to the Mediator to distribute. An absolute God being a consuming fire, guilty creatures, as stubble, could not endure his heat, but they would have been burnt up by it ; there-

fore he sets his own Son in man's nature, as a crystal-wall betwixt him and them; he gives him the Spirit without measure, not only a fulness of sufficiency, but abundance of blessings, is laid up in him; for it hath pleased the Father, that in him should all fulness dwell.—He is so,

2. Because he received a fulness of treasure for that very end. John, xvii. 19. ' For their sakes I sanctify myself, that they also might be sanctified through the truth.' The first Adam got mankind's stock; he soon lost all. Christ takes the elect's stock in his hand for their security, and so he is given for a covenant of the people; he takes the burden upon him for them, and takes the administration of the second covenant, that it might, with them, be a better covenant than the first.—He is so,

3. Because he bought these treasures at the price of his blood for their behoof. Phil. ii. 8. 9. ' He humbled himself, and became obedient unto death, even the death of the cross. Wherefore God also hath highly exalted him, and given him a name, which is above every name.' The Son of God, who is Lord of all, needed no exaltation in the court of heaven, being equal with his Father, but his design was, to exalt man's nature, to make these that were the children of the devil—friends to heaven, and prepare for them room there. ' I go,' said he, ' to prepare a place for you,' John xiv. 2. No wonder, then, that he should long to see the purchase of his blood, the fruit of the travail of his soul, come to him. —He is kind and liberal,

4. Because of his love to them. Where true love is, there is an aptness to communicate; the lover cannot see the beloved want what he has. God's love is giving love : ' he so loved the world, that he gave his only-begotten Son,' John iii. 16. Christ's love is also such ; he loves indeed : ' he loved us, and gave himself for us,' Gal. ii. 20.—For the improvement of this doctrine, I only add an use of exhortation.

Come to Christ, then, O sinners, upon this his invitation, and sit not his blessed call.—To enforce this, I urge these motives.

1. There is a fulness in him, all power is given him ; want what you will, he has a power to give it to you ; the Son of Man had power, even on earth, to forgive sins. Grace without you, or grace within you, he is the dispenser of all. John i. 16. ' And of his fulness have all we received, and grace for grace.' He is the great Secretary of heaven, the keys hang at his girdle ; he shuts, and none can open ; he opens, and none can shut.—Consider,

2. You are welcome to it. He has it not to keep up, but to give out, and to whom but to needy sinners ? Even the worst of you are welcome, if you will take it out of his own hand : ' If any man thirst,' says he, ' let him come to me, and drink,' John vii. 37.

3. Would you do Christ a pleasure ? then come to him, Isa. liii. 11. ' He shall see of the travail of his soul, and shall be satisfied.' Would you content and ease his heart ? then come. It is a great ease to full breasts to be sucked. The breasts of his consolations are full, hear how pressingly he calls you to suck. ' Eat, O friends ! drink, yea, drink abundantly, O beloved !

Lastly, Would you fall in with the designs of the Father's and the Son's love, in the mystery of salvation ? then come to him, Why is a fountain opened, but that ye may run to it, and wash ? Seal not, shut not that to yourselves, which God and Christ have opened.

The character of the persons whom Christ invites to come to him, Matt. xi. 28.

These are they that *labour,* and are *heavy-laden.* The word *labour,* signifies not every labouring, but a labouring to weariness, and so some read it *weary.* Heavy-laden are they that have a heavy burden on their back, which they are not able to bear.

Who are meant by these? I cannot agree with those that restrain these expressions to those that are sensible of their sins and misery, without Christ, and are longing to be rid of the same ; but I think it includes all that are out of Christ, sensible or insensible ; that is, these that have not had, and these that have had, a law-work upon their consciences. And, to fix this interpretation, consider,

1. The words agree to all that are out of Christ, and none have any right to restrain them. None more properly labour, in the sense of the text, than those that are out of Christ, seeking their satisfaction in the creatures, Eccl. i. 8. ' All things are full of labour, man cannot utter it : the eye is not satisfied with seeing, nor the ear filled with hearing.' And who have such a burden of sin and wrath upon their back as they have? The word properly signifies a ship's lading, which, though insensible of it, may yet sink under the weight. Consider,

2. ' The whole world lieth in wickedness,' 1 John v. 19. as men in a deep mire, still sinking. Christ came to deliver men out of that case ; having taken upon him our nature, Heb. ii. 16. he caught hold (Greek) as one doth of a drowning man, even as he did of Peter when sinking, Matt. xiv. 31. And what are the invitations of the gospel, but Christ

putting out his hands to sinking souls, sinking with
their own weight. Consider,

3. That the words, in other scriptures, are without controversy applied to the most insensible sinners. See what labour and weariness! Hab. ii. 13.
' Behold, is it not of the Lord of hosts, that the people still labour in the very fire, and the people shall
weary themselves for very vanity?' In the most solemn invitation to Christ in all the Old Testament,
the word *labouring* is so used, Isa. lv. 2. ' Wherefore do you spend money for that which is not bread,
and your labour for that which satisfieth not?' Luke
xi. 46. ' Ye lade men with burdens grievous to be
borne.' *Lade* is the same Greek word used in the
text. Isa. i. 4. ' Ah! sinful nation, a people laden
with iniquity.' Were they sensible? far from it;
for, ver. 3. ' Israel doth not know, my people doth
not consider.' And, 2 Tim. iii. 6. it is said, ' Silly
women, laden with sins, led away with divers lusts.'

4. Consider the parallel text, Isa. lv. 1. ' Ho, every
one that thirsteth;' where by the thirsty is not so
much understood those that are thirsting after Christ,
as those that are thirsting after happiness and satisfaction, seeking to squeeze it out of the creature;
for the thirsty invited are the same that are spending their labour for that which satisfieth not. But
these that are thirsting after Christ are not such.

5. If the words be a restriction of the call to sensible sinners, then the most part of sinners are excluded. If they are not included, sure they are excluded; and if the words are restrictive, sure they are
not included; and then, so far from being the truth
of the text, that it is no gospel-truth at all; for all,
without exception, that hear the gospel, are called
to come to Christ, Rev. iii. 20. ' Behold, I stand at
the door, and knock; if *any* man hear my voice, and
open the door, I will come in to him, and will sup
with him, and he with me.' And if any *one* be not
called, they have no warrant to come; and if so, un-

belief is not their sin, as in the case of the **Pagans** ; which is absurd.

Lastly, This is a most solemn invitation to come to Christ ; and if I say the most solemn, there is some ground for it by what is said before. And shall that be judged restrained, that so expressly and solemnly comes from that fulness of power lodged in Christ, more than that just quoted ? Rev. iii. 20. where there is no shadow of restriction. Besides, this restriction may well be a snare to an exercised soul, which ordinarily, by a legal disposition in all, will not allow that they may come to Christ, because sin is not heavy enough to them. But although sinners will never come to Christ till they see their need of him, yet this I will ever preach, that all, under pain of damnation, are obliged to come to him, and that they shall be welcome on their coming, be their case what it will ; that such as are willing to come ought not to stop on a defect of their sensibleness, but come to him, that they may get a true sense of sin unto repentance ; for he is ' exalted a **Prince** and a Saviour, to give repentance unto Israel, and remission of sins,' Acts v. 31. He is to give, not to stand and wait, till ' folly bring repentance with it.' *

* The doctrine of the Gospel is preached not for mere amusement to the understandings of those who hear it. It is preached as the word of salvation sent unto them ; as the Gospel of their salvation, as the salvation of God, sent unto the Gentiles. And in this public dispensation of the Gospel, there is made to all the hearers of it, immediately and equally, a most gracious offer of Christ and all his salvation ; with a most gracious call unto them, for their receiving and resting upon him accordingly.

Gibb's Sacred Contemplations.

' Mis-spend not your time, as many do, in poring upon your hearts, to find whether you be good enough to trust on Christ for your salvation, or to find whether you have any faith, before you dare be so bold, as to act faith in Christ. But know, that though you cannot find that you have any faith or holiness, yet, if you will now believe on him that justifieth the ungodly, it shall be accounted to you for righteousness,' Rom. iv. 5.

Marshall on Sanct.

****

*Consideration of what it is that sinners out of
Christ are labouring for.*

No man engageth in a labour, but for some end he
proposeth to himself. Though the devil is oversman
of these labourers, yet he does not make them go
like clocks, without a design. Every one that labours proposes some profit to himself by his work,
and so do these ; there is always something, either
really or seemingly good, that men seek in all their
labours. So, in a word, it is happiness and satisfaction that they are labouring for, as well as the godly.
For, consider,

1. The desire of happiness and satisfaction is natural to man ; all men wish to see good. It is not
the desire of good that may satisfy, that makes the
difference between the godly and the wicked, but the
different ways they take, Psal. iv. 6, 7. ' There be
many that say, Who will show us any good ? Lord,
lift thou up the light of thy countenance upon us.
Thou hast put gladness in my heart, more than in
the time that their corn and their wine increased.'
In whatever case a man is on earth, in heaven or
hell this is still his desire ; and he must cease to be
a man, ere he can cease to desire to be a happy man.
When that desire, mentioned Eccles. xii. 5. shall fail,
this desire is still fresh and green ; and it is good in
itself. Our Lord supposeth this in the text, and
therefore he promises to them what they are seeking, rest, if they will come to him.

2. This desire is the chief of all ; all other things
are desired for it. All men's desires, however different, meet here, as all the rivers meet in the sea,
though their courses may be quite contrary. Therefore this is what they labour for. The devil has

some labourers at his coarse work, others at the more fine, but they all meet in their end.

3. Defects and wants are interwoven with the very nature of the creature ; and the rational creature finds that it cannot be, nor is self-sufficient. Hence it seeks its happiness without itself, and must do it, to satisfy these natural desires.

Lastly, Seeing, then, man's happiness is without himself, it must be brought in, which cannot be done without labour. It is proper to God to be happy in himself; but every creature must needs go out of itself to find its happiness ; so that action is the true way to it, that is, rest cannot be found but in the way of action and labour, and because they are not in the right way, it is wearisome labour.

How it is, that men out of Christ labour for happiness.

Here, it is impossible to reckon up particulars, and that in regard,

1. Of the different dispositions of men, and the various, as well as contrary opinions, concerning what may make a man happy. Varro says, there were two hundred and eighty opinions touching the chief good in his time. It is true, Christianity, in the profession of it, hath fixed this point in principle ; but nothing less than overcoming grace can fix it in point of practice. The whole body of Christless sinners are like the Sodomites at Lot's door ; all were for the door, but one grasps one part of the wall for it, another another part, not one of them found it. The world is, as the air in a summer-day, full of insects ; and natural men, like a company of children, one running to catch one, another another, while none of them is worth the pains. One runs to the

bowels of the earth, another to the ale-house, &c.
—It is impossible to determine here,

2. In regard of men's still altering their opinions
about it, as they meet with new disappointments.
Like a man in a mist, seeking a house in a wilderness, when every bush, tree, &c. deceives, till, by
coming near, he is undeceived. ' O ! thinks the
man, if I had such a thing, I would be well.' Then
he falls to labour for it ; may be he never gets it,
but he ever pursues it. If he gets it, he finds it will
not do, for as big as it was afar off, yet it will not fill
his hand when he grips it : but it must be filled, or
no rest, hence new labour to bring forth just a new
disappointment, Isa. xxvi. 18. ' We have been with
child, we have been in pain, we have as it were
brought forth wind.'—It is difficult also,

3. Because they cannot tell themselves what they
would be at. Their starving souls are like the hungry infant, that gapes, weeps, cries, and sucks every
thing that comes near its mouth, but cannot tell
what it would have, but is still restless till the mother set it to the breast. It is regenerating grace
that does that to the soul. The Hebrew word for
believing, comes from a root that signifies to nurse,
as if faith were nothing but a laying of the soul on
the breasts of Christ, in whom dwelleth all the fulness of the Godhead. The scripture holds him out
as the mother that bare them ; hence his people are
called, Isa. liii. 11. ' The fruit of the travail of his
soul.' He also is their nourisher ; hence he says,
Isa. i. 2. ' I have nourished and brought up children.'
The breasts of the church, Isa. lxvi. 11. at which
they are to suck and be satisfied, are no other than
Christ. But, in the general, to see from whence it
is that men out of Christ go about to squeeze out
their happiness, see Psal. iv. 6, 7. ' There be many
that say, Who will show us any good ? Lord, lift
thou up the light of thy countenance upon us. Thou
hast put gladness in my heart, more than in the

time that their corn and their wine increased.' From
which observe two things.

(1.) That it is not God, for these two are set in opposition ; go to as many doors as they will, they never go to the right door ; hence it follows, that it is
the creatures out of which they labour to draw their
satisfaction : ' Having forsaken the fountain of living waters, they hew out to themselves cisterns, broken cisterns, that can hold no water.'

(2.) That it is good they are seeking out of them :
and indeed men can seek nothing but under that notion, though for the most part they call evil good,
and good evil. All good is either profitable, plea-
surable, or honest ; these, then, are all that they are
seeking, not from God, but from themselves, or other
creatures. The two former have respect to the cravings of men's desires, the latter to the cravings of
the law. And seeing it is not in God that they seek
their happiness and satisfaction, I infer hence, That
all out of Christ are labouring for their happiness
and satisfaction in one or both of these ways, either
from their lusts, or from the law ; and this I take to
be the very labour intended in the text. For which
consider these three things :

1st, That all natural men have two principles in
them, 1st, Corruption ; 2d, Conscience. Both crave
of them, Rom. ii. 15. ' Which show the work of the
law, written in their heart, their conscience also bearing witness, and their thoughts the mean while accusing or else excusing one another.' Hence, because
they do not mortify the lusts, they must be fed, or
no rest ; and therefore they labour for their lusts to
satisfy them. Then, because they fly not to Christ
for the satisfaction of their conscience, they go to
the law.

2dly, The bulk of natural men in the world have
still been of two sorts ; 1st, The profane party ; 2d,
The formal party. These have still been among

Jews, Pagans, and Christians ; the former labouring most in lusts, the latter in the law.

3dly, Adam left us with two yokes on our necks ;
1st, Of lusts ; 2d, Of the law. The last was of
God's putting, but he gave strength with it to bear
it. Adam took away the strength, but left the yoke,
and put on a yoke of lusts beside ; and in opposition
to both these, Christ bids us come and take on his
' yoke which is easy, and his burden, which is light,'
Matt. xi. 29.

As to the labour they have in their lusts, they call
them, and they run after them. These infernal devils in the heart drive the swine of this world into
the sea of perdition ; nay, turn the soul itself into
a very sea, that cannot rest. Isa. lvii. 20. ' The
wicked are like the troubled sea, when it cannot rest,
whose waters cast up mire and dirt.' They labour
like madmen for satisfaction to them, and no calm,
no rest, till the soul come to Christ.

1. They labour hard in the lusts of profit. 1 John
ii. 16. ' For all that is in the world, the lust of the
flesh, the lust of the eyes, and the pride of life, is not
of the Father, but is of the world.' The profits of
the world are the cisterns they squeeze for satisfaction ; they bewitch the hearts of them that have
them, and of them that want them ; they fly after
them with that pains and labour the ravenous bird
doth after its prey. Prov. xxiii. 5. ' Wilt thou set
thine eyes upon that which is not ? for riches take
to themselves wings, they fly away, as an eagle towards heaven.' The strength of men's desires, and
the cream of their affections, are spent on them ;
their happiness depends upon its smiles, their misery
upon its frowns ; if gone, their god is gone. Hence
is that verified, Hab. ii. 13. ' They labour in the
very fire, and weary themselves for very vanity,' like
a poor fool running to catch a shadow. They have
hard labour in lawful profits, how to get them, and
how to keep them, but hardest of all, how to squeeze

satisfaction out of them ; there they labour in the very fire ; they labour also in unlawful profits. The soul is an empty thing ; lusts are ill to guide ; conscience must make a stretch now and then, for the satisfaction of lusts ; and the man will leap over the hedge, though the serpent will bite him. 1 Tim. vi. 9, 10. ' But they that will be rich, fall into temptation and a snare, and into many foolish and hurtful lusts, which drown 'men in destruction and perdition. For the love of money is the root of all evil.' Hence the carnal man, I may say, never gets up his back, but on his belly doth he go, and labours, as if he were a slave condemned to the mines, to dig in the bowels of the earth ; like the blind moles, his constant labour is in the earth, and he never opens his eyes till he is dying. He has his lade of thick clay upon his back, Hab. ii. 6. as the fruit of his labouring in the fire. There is thus a labouring and heavy-laden party. Others take the world in their hand as a staff, nay, tread on it as the dirt, and they get it as a burden on their back, while guilt, many times contracted in the getting of it, whether by oppression, cheatery, or neglecting of the soul for it, is like a sore back under the load, that makes them ready in despair to throw it away, but they know not how to subsist without it.

2. They labour in lusts of pleasure ; they go about as the bee, extracting the sweet out of the creatures for their own satisfaction ; this and the former usually go together. Profits and pleasures are the world's two great baits, at which all natural men are constantly leaping, till they are caught by the hook, and flung out into the fire of wrath. Prov. ix. 17, 18. ' Stolen waters are sweet, and bread eaten in secret is pleasant. But he knoweth not that the dead are there, and that her guests are in the depths of hell.' Pleasure is a necessary ingredient in happiness, and man cannot but seek it ; hence God proposeth it to men in himself, who is the fountain of all sweetness.

Psal. xvi. 11. ' Thou wilt show me the path of life,
in thy presence there is fulness of joy, at thy right
hand there are pleasures for evermore.' But blind
man makes the creature-sweetness his idol, and puts
it in the room of God ; for ' they are lovers of pleasures, (in this sense,) more than lovers of God,' 2 Tim.
iii. 4. It is no fault to seek our profit ; for, Heb.
xi. 26. ' We are to have respect unto the recompence
of the reward.' Nor to seek what may be sweet to
the soul ; for we may wish our souls to be ' satisfied
with marrow and fatness,' Psal. lxiii. 5. But the
natural man's misery and sin both is, he forsakes
God, and fastens on the breasts of the creatures for
these things.

Now, there are two breasts of the creatures at
which men may be sucking.

(1.) The breast of lawful comforts. Natural men
fall on these, instead of the breasts of God's consolations, and labour, though in vain, to squeeze happiness and satisfaction out of them, and that with the
greatest eagerness. They are lawful in themselves,
but they often press so hard, that they draw out
blood instead of milk from them ; and are like men
working at a flinty rock, to bring out water, instead
of which they get fire flashing in their face, as in
that case, Judges, ix. 15. when ' fire came out of
the bramble to devour the cedars of Lebanon.'—
There is,

(2.) The breast of unlawful comforts, Prov. ix. 17.
' Stolen waters are sweet.' Many seek their satisfaction in those things which they ought not so much
as to desire, and fill themselves with what God forbids them so much as to taste. O ! the misery of
Christless sinners, to whom both lawful and unlawful comforts are effectual snares for ruin. Like mad
beasts, if they abide within the hedge, they tear up
all to the red earth, which doth not yet satisfy. But
they most usually break over all hedges ; and they
do so, because the creature can never fully answer

the craving desires and hungry appetite, and yet,
after all, they will not come to Christ, that they may
have rest.

These breasts of the creatures have many springs,
divers lusts and pleasures, Titus, iii. 3. and these are
served ; men must labour in them as a servant at
his master's work. I shall reduce them to these two
heads, mentioned, Eph. ii. 3. the desires of the flesh
and of the mind.

1st, They labour for satisfaction and happiness in
the pleasures of the flesh. And, 1. In sensuality.
This was the door man first went to, after he had
left God. And since the world was turned upside
down by that means, the soul has lain downmost,
and the flesh uppermost, so that they are all sensual,
as Jude says, ver. 19. that have not the Spirit ; and
the soul is made drudge of the body. The belly is a
god, and the pleasures of the flesh are squeezed, for
satisfaction ; all the senses are set a-working for it,
and yet can never do enough. Eccles. vi. 7. ' All the
labour of man is for his mouth, and yet the appetite
is not filled.' Many arts and trades are found out to
bring this to perfection, though all in vain, and there
is no end of these things, which are of no use but to
please the flesh, which, like the grave, never says it
has enough. 2. Ease, sloth, and quiet, which is a
negative kind of sensuality. Luke, xii. 19. ' The
rich man said, Thou hast goods laid up for many
years, soul, take thine ease.' All to please the flesh.
This costs hard labour many times to the soul, many
a throw conscience gets for the sake of this idol,
what by neglect of duties, what by going over the
belly of light to shun what is grieving to the flesh, as
if men's happiness consisted in the quiet enjoyment
of themselves.—They labour for satisfaction,

2dly, In the desires of the mind, and pleasures
thereof. These, if they terminated on right objects,
and were sought in a right manner, it would be well,
for our true happiness consists in the soul's enjoy-

ment of God ; but in the natural man all is in confusion. And, 1. There is much labour in seeking
happiness in the pleasures of the judgment. This
is the snare of thinking graceless men ; this was
among the first doors men went to when they turned
from God. Gen. iii. 5. ' Ye shall be as gods, knowing good and evil.' And there is hard labour without a figure, for the punishment of that. Eccles. i. 13.
' And I gave my heart to seek and search out by wisdom concerning all things that are done under heaven ; this sore travail God hath given to the sons of
men to be exercised therewith.' And what comes it
to at length ? to no rest ; for, ver. 18. ' In much wisdom there is much grief ; and he that increaseth
knowledge, increaseth sorrow.' Here is fulfilled,
Eccles. x. 15. ' The labour of the foolish wearieth
every one of them, because he knoweth not how to
go to the city.' Whereas, would they go to Christ,
they would be in a fair way to get what they are
seeking ; for, John xvii. 3. ' This is life eternal, that
they might know thee the only true God, and Jesus
Christ, whom thou hast sent.' ' In whom are hid,
all the treasures of wisdom and knowledge,' Col. ii. 3.
There is labour, 2. In pleasures of the fancy. What
else are all the lusts of the eye ? all the abundance
of the riches for which men labour so much ? Eccles.
v. 11. ' When goods increase, they are increased
that eat them ; and what good is there to the owners
thereof, saving the beholding of them with their
eyes ?' All they can think or say is, These are mine.
What is honour, credit, and the like, but a tickling
of our fancy, with the fancies of others about us, ad-
ding nothing to real worth ? And how busy is the
soul oftentimes in that. Eccles. vi. 9. ' Better is the
sight of the eyes, than the wandering of the desire,
Heb. *walking of the soul.* This is also vanity and
vexation of spirit.' What satisfaction is sought in
imagination sins, lust, revenge, and the like ? what
restlessness there. 2 Pet. ii. 14. ' Having eyes full

of adultery, that cannot cease from sin.' How busy
is the soul oftentimes in imagination, of wealth, and
the like, as if, when it had tried all other means in
vain, it would try, while awake, to dream itself happy! ' The thoughts of my heart,' says Job, chap.
xvii. 11. Heb. *the passions of my heart,* ' are broken
off.'

3. The other thing in which natural men labour
for rest, is the *law ;* compare the text, Matt. xi. 28.
with ver. 29. and 30. Emphatically is that labour
described, Rom. x. 3. ' For they being ignorant of
God's righteousness, and going about to establish
their own righteousness.' *Go about ;* the word signifies, a seeking, like a disputer in the schools, or a
tormentor of one upon the rack ; to establish, to
make it stand itself alone. They seek to make it
stand, as men that will have a stone to stand on end,
which, at the same time, is ever coming down on
them again. Why all this ? because it is their own :
' Have not submitted.' Christ offers a righteousness ; but to take it, is to them a point of submission, against which they labour, as the untoward
bullock against the yoke. They will never let it on
till God break the iron sinew of the neck, Isa. xlviii. 4.

To confirm this, consider,

1. All men desire to be happy, and no man can
get his conscience quite silenced, more than he can
get the notion of a God quite erased from his mind.
Rom. ii. 14, 15. ' They are a law unto themselves,
their conscience also bearing witness, and their
thoughts the mean while accusing or excusing one
another.' Peace of mind is a natural desire, which
none can divest himself of. Hence it follows, men
cannot but seek inward peace : and though they
may set themselves to murder conscience for that
end, yet seeing it will not do for them totally, they
do of necessity take some other way. There never
was but two ways, either Christ, or the law. The
former they reject, therefore it follows, they follow

N n

the latter.   Let us view this in three sorts of natural
men.

(1.) In the profane person, who has not so much
as a form of godliness ; it is hardest to be found in
them.   But none so profane, but it will readily be
found they have some one good thing or another
about them, and sometimes they will compliment
their consciences with a denial of satisfaction to their
lusts, which is a labour so much the harder to them,
as they are under the greater power of lusts.   This
sure they do not with an eye to make themselves miserable, but happy, that their consciences may excuse them, Rom. ii. 15.   Excusing, even those that
are most at the devil's will, are taken captive, as
hunters who take their prey alive, 2 Tim. ii. 26.   Importing still, a conscience labouring in the law,
though lusts, as being stronger, do for the most part
prevail.—Let us view this,

(2.) In the formal natural man : some of whom labour in the duties of morality ; others in those of religion ; who are at no small travail in the law, if we
consider it all for nought.   Like the Pharisee, Luke
xviii. 11. they take not the gospel-way, yet they labour in the law.   Sure lusts remain in them in their
life and vigour.   It surely costs labour so far to restrain them.—Let us view this,

(3.) In the awakened sinner.   I am not for ex-
cluding these out of the text, but only that it be not
restrained to them.   Acts, ii. 37. ' Now, when they
heard this, they were pricked to the heart, and said
unto Peter, and the rest of the apostles, What shall
we do ?'   These mend their hands at this hard labour, and oft-times labour so to keep the law, that
they are both by themselves, and others taken for
saints of the first magnitude, and yet it is but still in
the law, till converting grace come, and sned them
off the old root.

2. It is natural for men to labour in the law for
happiness, and therefore, till nature be overcome by

grace, men will not be put off it. The law was
Adam's covenant, who, with his children, were to
work and win heaven by their works ; though they
have lost their father's strength, yet they will keep
their father's trade ; though their stock be small, yet
they will keep the merchandising for heaven, and
give God good works for good wages. See nature
speaking out of him, Matt. xix. 16. ' Good Master,
what good thing shall I do that I may have eternal
life ?' And it often happens, that they who have
fewest of good works lay the greater stress upon
them.

3. Consider how this practice has been formed into principles, in the face of the sun of the gospel.
Never was an error yet vented in principle, but in
compliance with some corruption of the heart ; therefore is that made the characteristic of true doctrine,
that it is according to godliness, 1 Tim. vi. 3. No
sooner was the gospel preached, than Cain sets up
for works in opposition to faith. Gen. iv. 4, 5. ' And
the Lord had respect to Abel, and to his offering ;
but unto Cain and his offering he had no respect.'
Paul gives the reason. Heb. xi. 4, ' By faith Abel
offered unto God a more excellent sacrifice than Cain.'
In Abraham's family, to whom the promise of righteousness was more clearly made, Hagar bears her
son ; compare Gal. iv. 24. When the people were
in Egypt, the generality of them knew nothing else.
They had curtailed the law so very short, as all that
labour in it do, that they thought they kept all very
well. Rom. v. 13. ' For until the law, sin was in
the world ; but sin is not imputed, when there is no
law.' For that cause God gave them the law, as in
Exod. xx. Gal. iii. 29. ' The law was added because
of transgressions ;' it prevailed in the days of the
prophets, in Christ's days, and from the beginning of
the Christian church to this day ; hence our swarms
of Papists, &c.—Consider,

4. They turn the very gospel into law, as unclean

vessels sour the sweetest liquor that is put in them.
What a real gospel was the ceremonial law to the
Jews, holding up blood, death, and translation of
guilt, from them to the substitute, every day before
their eyes in their sacrifices! But, Rom. ix. 11.
' Their very table (that is, their altar, so called, Mal.
i. 12.) became a snare ;' and they went about these
things, as if by them they would have made up what
was wanting in their observation of the moral law.
Just so was it turned in Popery ; yea, and, alas!
among Protestants it is found thus soured, to whom
the gospel is the law, and faith, repentance, and new
obedience, the fulfilling of the law.   But would to
God it stood in principles only ; but as sure as every
unrenewed man is out of Christ, as sure even these
natural men, whose heads are set right in this point,
in their hearts and practice the very gospel is turned into law, and their obedience, their very faith and
repentance, such as it is, is put in the room of Christ.
For practice, when fairly traced, will show the principles from which it proceeds.

   Lastly, Consider, though all would be saved, yet
natural men are enemies to the gospel-way of salvation. 1 Cor. i. 23. ' It is to the Jews a stumbling-
block, and unto the Greeks foolishness.'   They must
then be in love with the law, for there is no mids ;
yea, so cleave they to it, that nothing but death can
part Adam's sons and it, and this even a violent
death in a day of God's power, Psal. cx. 3.   Rom.
vii. 4. ' Ye also are become dead to the law ;' Greek,
deadened, killed, or put to death.   As long as a soul
sees how to shift without Christ, it will never come
to him ; add to this, that the godly find the remains
of this principle in them to struggle against.   Self-
denial is the first lesson Christ gives, but they are
a-learning it all their days.   If it is thus in the green
tree, what shall it be in the dry ?

The nature of the labour of sinners out of Christ,
considered, 1st, As it respects their lusts ; 2d. As
it respects the law.

We are,

1*st*, To consider this labour of sinners, as it respects their lusts, their going up and down among
the creatures, extracting from them a comfort and
pleasures, which they take for happiness. I shall
here show the properties of this labour, and thus
confirm the point, that they are engaged in a wearisome labour.

1. It is hard labour, and sore toil. Jer. ix. 5.
' They weary themselves to commit iniquity.' None
win the devil's wages for nought, they eat no idle
bread where he is task-master, and they must needs
run, whom he drives. The devil's yoke is of all
yokes the heaviest. To clear this point, consider,

(1.) What the scriptures compare this labour in
lusts unto ; whereby it will appear hard labour. It
compares it,

[1.] To the labour of a man going to a city, and
not knowing the way. Eccles. x. 15. ' The labour
of the foolish wearieth every one of them, because
he knoweth not how to go to the city.' That is
hard labour, as many know by experience. Many
a weary foot such must go, many a hardship they
must endure, and so must these in pursuit of happiness. It compares it,

[2.] To a labouring in the fire. Hab. ii. 13. ' Behold, is it not of the Lord of hosts, that the people
shall labour in the very fire, and the people shall
weary themselves for very vanity ?' How hard is
their labour that lieth about a fire ! what sweat !
what toil ! Jer. vi. 29. The bellows are burned, the

lead is consumed of the fire, the founder melteth in
vain, for the wicked are not plucked away.' But
how much more hard in the fire! As when a house
is on fire, and men in it, labouring to preserve that
which the fire consumes even among their hands.
These labour, 1*st*, In the fire of lusts, that inflames
the heart, and scorches the very soul. Prov. vi.
27, 28. ' For, by means of a whorish woman, a man
is brought to a piece of bread, and the adulteress
will hunt for the precious life. Can a man take fire
in his bosom, and his clothes not be burned?' 2*dly*,
In the fire of divine wrath that is kindled by the former. Isa. ix. 18. ' For wickedness burneth as the
fire, it shall devour the briars and thorns, and shall
kindle in the thickets of the forest, and they shall
mount up like the lifting up of smoke.' This con-
sumeth what they are working for in the other; so
that when, like the spider, they have spun out their
own bowels for a covering, yet it is by far too narrow, and they have but wearied themselves for very
vanity. It is compared,

[3.] To labouring under a burden, as in the text
itself, which will not let the man get up his back.
They are the devil's drudges, labouring under that
load that will crush them at last, if they do not, as
in Psal. lv. 22. cast their burden on the Lord, that
he may sustain them. They are laden with divers
lusts, which lie on them as a burden on the weary
beast, which weary them indeed, but they are bound
on as with bands of iron and brass. It is compared,

[4.] To the labour of a soldier in war; they watch
for iniquity as a centry at his post, Isa. xxix. 20.
The natural man himself is the very field of battle.
Jam. iv. 1. ' From whence come wars and fightings
among you? come they not hence, even of your lusts
which war in your members?' The war itself you
may see described in the three following verses.
Who cannot but be well laboured with the feet of
men and horse in that confusion? Though there be

not grace and corruption to war in them, there are
lusts, and lusts opposed to one another, lusts and
light also. It is compared,

[5.] To the labour of the husbandman in ploughing,
Hos. x. 13. ' Ye have ploughed wickedness, ye have
reaped iniquity.' They devise wickedness, which
the Hebrew calls ploughing it. ' Devise not evil
against thy neighbour,' Prov. iii. 29. ' An ungodly
man diggeth up evil, and in his lips there is a burning fire,' Prov. xvi. 27. It is compared,

[6.] Not to insist on more, to the labour of a woman in child-birth. Psal. vii. 4. ' Behold, he travail-
eth with iniquity, and hath conceived mischief, and
brought forth falsehood.' What pangs do raging
lusts create to the soul? What cords of death does
it straiten with? No small toil at conceiving of sin,
and bearing it in the heart, and bringing it forth ;
but nothing in the abominable brat to satisfy the
soul after all.

(2.) It is hard labour, if you consider that eminent
emblem of our natural state, the Egyptian bondage
Their deliverance out of Egypt was typical of their
spiritual deliverance by Christ, and so that must
needs signify man's natural state ; concerning which
it may be remarked, 1st, that as the children of Israel went down to Egypt in the loins of their parents,
so we in Adam. 2d, As the deliverance was wrought
by the angel of the covenant, by the hands of Moses
the lawgiver, and Aaron the priest, so this by the
law and the gospel. 3d, As Pharaoh opposed the
children of Israel to the utmost, so the devil opposeth here. Pharaoh was ' the great dragon which
lieth in the midst of his rivers, which said, My river
is mine own, and I have made it for myself,' Ezek.
xxix. 3. and was a type of that great red dragon,
mentioned Rev. xii. 3. &c. But for that which concerns this point, see Exod. v. There you will find
persons labouring, and heavy-laden, ver. 4, 5. It is
hard labour to satisfy lusts, the devil's task-masters.

Ephes. ii. 2, 3. ' He worketh in the children of disobedience : Among whom also we had our conversation in times past, in the lusts of our flesh, fulfilling
the desires of the flesh, and of the mind.' The Israelites had their tasks doubled, to put religion out
of their heads and hearts, Exod. v. 10. Lusts also
must be satisfied, but wherewith to do it is with-
held, as straw was from the Israelites, ver. 11.
They are scattered up and down among the creatures
for it, but can never squeeze out a sufficiency for
them, even as the Israelites could not find stubble
enough to prepare their bricks, ver. 12, 13, 14. If
any appearance of deliverance, the labour is made
the harder. Says Paul, Rom. vii. 9. ' I was alive
without the law once ; but when the commandment
came, sin revived, and I died.' It is hard labour,

(3.) If ye consider the effects this labour hath, 1*st*,
On the souls of men. The minds of men have a toilsome task, where sin is on the throne. Isa. v. 20.
' Woe unto them that call evil good, and good evil,
that put darkness for light, and light for darkness,
that put bitter for sweet, and sweet for bitter.' That
soul must needs be in a continual fever, while inordinate affections are in their strength, as in all out of
Christ. A fermentation of lusts cannot but make a
tossed mind. Anxiety and cares of the world stretch
the mind, as on tenter-hooks. A conceived slight,
like that of Ahab, 1 Kings xxi. 4. sets the proud
man's heart in a fire of wrath and revenge, and
squeezes the sap out of all their enjoyments, as in
the instance of Haman, Esther v. 9. 13. Envy slays
the silly one, lust strikes as a dart through the liver ;
anger, malice, discontent, and the like, make a man
his own executioner ; they are tossed between hopes,
fears, and vanity, tumbled hither and thither with
every wind of temptation, as a ship without either
pilot or ballast. 2*dly*, Even the body is oft-times
hard put to it in this labour. The covetous rises
early, eats the bread of sorrow for what is not ; the

drunkard uses his body worse than his beast. More
bodies have fallen sacrifices to lusts, one way or another, than ever fell by all the hardships either in or
about religion.

2. It is base, mean, and abject labour. See Jer.
ii. 21. compared with ver. 23. and 24. Were we to
die like beasts, we might live like beasts, with our
souls grovelling still downward on the earth. If the
soul had been so narrow, as to be satisfied with less
than an infinite good, he had not spoke like a fool,
who said to his soul, Luke xii. 19. ' Soul, take thine
ease, eat, drink, and be merry,' when his barns were
full ; in that case, the swine and his soul might have
fed together. But we have immortal souls, capable
of enjoying an infinite good, and such working in the
earth must needs be a base labour for an heaven-born
soul, which God breathed into the formed dust, but
gave not to be drowned in a mass of flesh and blood,
nor to be only as salt, to keep the body a while from
rotting.

3. It is a constant labour. The sea rests sometimes, the carnal heart never. Isa. lvii. 20. ' But
the wicked are like the troubled sea, when it cannot
rest, whose waters cast up mire and dirt.' Lusts
are ever craving, never say they have enough ; they
are rolling the stone to the top of the hill, which still
comes down on them again and again, and creates
new labour ; see Psal. lxxviii. 18. 20. 29, 30 ' And
they tempted God in their heart, by asking meat for
their lust. Behold, he smote the rock, that the waters gushed out, and the streams overflowed ; can he
give bread also ? can he provide flesh for his people ?
So they did eat, and were well filled : for he gave
them their own desire ; they were not estranged from
their lust.' Two things make it a continual labour.
1st, Continual disappointments. These they cannot
miss, seeing there is no satisfaction to be had in the
creatures ; yet their soul still craves, hence no rest,
but are urged on to work again. Isa. lvii. 10.

' Thou art weary in the greatness of thy way, yet saidst thou not, There is no hope.' Men are like the silly doves without heart, who still go to the same nest where they have been herried never so often before, and will even big there, where they have got a thousand nay-says. 2*dly*, What is got in them enlarges the desire, instead of satisfying it ; the more that lusts are fed, the more they require to maintain them. Sin is an insatiable tyrant ; to labour in its service, is but to cast oil into the flame. The dropsy-thirst can never be quenched.

4. It is vain labour, they can never reach the end of it. Isa. lv. 2. ' Wherefore do you spend money for that which is not bread, and your labour for that which satisfieth not ? ' They shall as soon fill a triangle with a circle, as the heart with such things ; the grave shall sooner give back its dead, than the lusts of the heart say, It is enough. It is impossible to find satisfaction in these things, for they are not suitable to the soul, more than stones for the nourishment of the body. The body gets its nourishment from the earth, because it is of the earth ; the soul is from heaven, and so its satisfaction must come from thence. The things of the world cannot satisfy the soul, because they have no word of divine appointment, to be the staff of that bread which nourishes it ; without this, grass could no more satisfy the beasts, nor bread the hunger of man, than sand. Matt. iv. 24. ' Man liveth not by bread alone, but by every word that proceedeth out of the mouth of God.' God has kept this as his own prerogative, to satisfy the soul, incommunicable to the creatures conjunctly or separately.

Lastly, It is notwithstanding costly labour ; for time that is precious is spent on it, which men should husband well, Eph. v. 16. ' Redeeming the time, because the days are evil.' By time well improved, we might attain true happiness ; time once gone can never be recalled. But, ah ! what preci-

ous hours are cast away on these things, which might
be improved in trading for heaven. It is costly, because the gifts of the mind are thrown away on it.
Reason makes us differ from the beasts, but by the
abuse of it men make themselves worse than the
beasts. Jer. viii. 7. ' Yea, the stork in the heaven
knoweth her appointed times : and the turtle, and
the crane, and the swallow, observe the time of their
coming ; but my people know not the judgment of
the Lord.' Men's minds are employed not to know
God, but other things ; their choice also is not fixed
upon him, their affections are bestowed on other
things. Finally, It is costly, because the outward
good things of the body, and estate in the world, are
bestowed upon it. Health and strength go in the
pursuit of vanity, and in the service of their lusts,
yea, are sacrificed many times on the altar of intem-
perance and sensuality. Riches, power, honours, as
the feeding of the horse does, make people kick against
him who lays these things to their hands. Yea,
to crown all, the soul itself is thrown away upon it :
Matt. xvi. 26. ' For what is a man profited, if he gain
the whole world, and lose his own soul ? or what
shall a man give in exchange for his soul ?' Men
seeking vanity, lose what is most excellent ; and it
is dear-bought that is purchased at that rate. I
shall now consider what is meant by,

2*d*, A labouring in the law.

1. It is most hard labour, for it requires the most
exact obedience, under pain of the curse. Gal.
iii. 10. ' Cursed is every one that continueth not in
all things written in the book of the law, to do them.'
Nothing but perfect obedience is accepted, according to the law ; and for the least failure, it dooms
the sinner to death. Now, no man can perform this ;
and yet, so foolish are men, that they think to please
God with their works. Again, it is hard, because
the law neither promiseth nor giveth strength. God
gave Adam strength to perform ; he lost it, the

law does not restore it ; so that in this case they must make the brick, but no straw is laid to their hands. This makes hard work, and so, by the Spirit, it at length breaks the heart of the elect, and makes them die to the law, as a wife to a rigorous husband, Gal. ii. 19.

2. It is a vain and useless labour. There are much pains, and yet no gain, in this labour. It is vain, in respect of the soul thriving ; they that labour in the law do but sow their seed in the sand ; all they reap is wind, which may puff them up, but cannot nourish. Why so many barren dry professors ? but because they are not trading with Christ, but with the law. Men go to duties, and rest in them ; the pipe is laid short of the fountain. It is vain, in respect of acceptance with God. It is thankless work, for it supersedes the commandment to believe. John vi. 29. ' This is the work of God, that ye believe on him whom he hath sent.' It is a sad word. Rom. ix. 31, 32. ' Israel, which followed after the law of righteousness, hath not attained to the law of righteousness. Wherefore ? Because they sought it not by faith, but as it were, by the works of the law.' Turtles were accepted on the altar at Jerusalem, when bullocks were rejected on these at Dan and Bethel.

Farther, it is vain, in respect of answering the demands of the law, Gal. iii. 10. Our curtailed obedience will not answer the measuring reed of the law ; it demands satisfaction for what is past, and perfect obedience for what is to come. Finally, it is vain, in respect of salvation. The way to heaven by the first covenant is blocked up ; the angel with the flaming sword guards it, Gal. iii. 10. O Sirs ! duties are a sandy foundation, and great will be the fall of legal professors.

Why sinners labour for Happiness, yet come not to Christ for it.

1. Because they have lost God, the fountain of happiness, and therefore they seek to squeeze it out of the creatures. Eph. ii. 12. ' Having no hope, and without God in the world.' For, says God, Jer. ii. 13. ' They have forsaken me, the fountain of living waters.' The sun is gone down upon them, and therefore they light their candles, and compass themselves with their own sparks ; for the empty soul must have something to feed on. The prodigal wanted bread, and therefore fed on husks. Doves' dung is precious, when there is no bread in Samaria. Sinners labour in these things,

2. Because, by the power of a strong delusion, they still expect satisfaction from them ; they are represented in a magnifying glass, as the forbidden fruit was to our first parents, Gen. iii. 5, 6. That delusion took with them, is conveyed to their posterity, and will never be cured till grace do it. Hence men, though they meet with a thousand disappointments in these things, yet still from new hopes they renew the attempt. Sinners labour thus,

3. Because these things are most suitable to the corrupt nature. Rom. viii. 5. ' For they that are after the flesh, do mind the things of the flesh.' Fishes swim in the river, and care not for the most pleasant meadow ; swine prefer the dunghill to a palace ; because every thing seeks its like. Lusts must be nourished with these ; even the way of the law, though just and good in itself, is the way that agrees best with self. Rom. iii. 27. ' Where is boasting then ? It is excluded. By what law ? Of works ?

Nay, but by the law of faith.' Sinners are engaged
in this labour,

4. Because they know no better. Christ is a hidden Christ to men in their natural estate ; they see
not his glory, fulness, and excellency ; they say, as
in Song, v. 9. ' What is thy Beloved more than another beloved ?' The fowl scrapes by the jewels,
and takes up a corn beside them, because it knows
not their worth. 1 Pet. ii. 7. ' Unto you, therefore,
which believe, he is precious, but unto them which
be disobedient, the stone which the builders disallow-
ed, the same is made the head of the corner, and a
stone of stumbling, and a rock of offence, even to
them that stumble at the word, being disobedient.'—
Sinners continue this labour,

Lastly, Because men naturally are enemies to the
way of salvation by Jesus Christ.

The sinner earnestly expostulated with.

Why do you spend your labour for that which satisfieth not ? I would beseech you, in the most earnest manner, not only to cease from, to give up with,
your present unpleasant and unprofitable labour,
but also to change your labour ; I would have you,
not only to depart from evil, but even to do good ; I
would call upon you to engage in the service of a
new Master, and run in the way of his commandments. You are labouring, you must be labouring,
one way or other ; will you not then engage in the
labour of true religion, real godliness ? If we must
serve, surely it is better to serve Christ than the devil. The labour that there is in religion affrights
the world at it ; but why should it, seeing their labour is so great while out of Christ ? Consider,

1. We are not calling you from idleness to work-

ing, but from labour to labour. And even if we were still to be slaves, better be so to God than to the devil. What will men say to Christ at the last day, who will be at pains in their lusts, but be at none in holiness, that will bear a yoke, but not Christ's yoke ?

2. We call you, not from one base labour to another, but from a base to an honourable work. Should one be called from the stone-barrow to be a king's cup-bearer, it were not comparable to what is proposed. 1st, They will have a more honourable Master. 2d, More honourable fellow-labourers, for the angels serve him. 3d, More honourable work, God himself is glorious in holiness. 4th, A more honourable office ; from being slaves to the devil, they are made kings and priests unto God.

3. We call upon you from vain labour, to that which shall be prosperous and successful ; you are labouring for happiness there, where you will never get it, but here are full breasts ; you are in vain striking at the flinty rock for water, here is an open fountain, where none ever went away disappointed.

4. We call you from a barren labour, where you will get nothing but sorrow to take away with you, to a labour which, when you have finished your works, will follow you, Rev. xiv. 13. Ah! miserable is your present labour, Isa. lix. 5, 6. The spider wastes its bowels to spin its web, and when all is done, one stroke of the besom sweeps all away ; it is either killed in its web, or drawn by it as a rope unto death ; so that it doth but spin its winding-sheet, or plait the rope for itself. Consider,

5. That the worst which can be made of it is, that religion is hard labour. But this should be no prejudice against it with you, seeing, as has been said, the labour out of Christ is also hard labour. But to cast the balance, observe,

(1.) If it is hard labour, it is worth the pains ; the other is not so ; for, Prov. ii. 4, 5. ' If thou seekest her as silver, and searchest for her as hid treasures, then shalt thou understand the fear of the Lord, and find the knowledge of God.' There is hard labour in digging stones, as well as in digging for gold ; nay, it is hard labour digging disappointments, that which is not ; whereas the gain of the other is precious and certain. 1*st*, The promise, Prov. viii. 21. ' That I may cause those that love me to inherit substance, and I will fill their treasures.' 2*d*, The experience of all the labourers confirm the certainty of it : ' I, God, said not unto the seed of Jacob, seek ye my face in vain.'

(2.) If it is hard labour, it is short ; if the work be sore, yet it is not longsome. You shall soon rest from your labours. Rev. xiv. 13. ' And I heard a voice from heaven saying unto me, Write, Blessed are the dead which die in the Lord from henceforth : Yea, saith the Spirit, that they may rest from their labours ; and their works do follow them.' He that is tired with his journey, his spirits will revive when near the end. The shadow of the evening makes the labourer work heartily, for loosing-time is at hand. The trials, afflictions, weeping, &c. of the saints, endure but for a moment. On the other hand, the labour of other persons knows no end ; no rest abides them, but an everlasting toil under wrath that never ends.

6. We call you from a hard to an easy labour. ' My yoke is easy,' Christ has said it, we must believe it. But to clear it, consider for this time, only these two things.

(1.) All the difficulties in religion arise from that active corruption which is in men, putting them to labour in their lusts and in the law. Matthew, xi. 12. ' The kingdom of heaven suffereth violence, and the violent take it by force.' Violence and force, not with God, he opposeth us not, but with our own corruptions. And in this sense only the scripture holds out the labour of religion to be hard. But men do not state the matter fairly : Lay a ton-weight upon a rolling-stone, certainly it is harder to roll both together than the stone alone ; but is the stone therefore lighter than the ton-weight? Take them separately, and absolutely the labour in religion is easy, the other hard. Men cannot bear Christ's burden. Why? because they still keep on the devil's burden, and they cannot bear the one above the other ; that is not fair. Lay off the one, take up the other ; see which is lightest. A meek and a passionate man, which of them has the hardest task in bearing an affront? the sober man, or the drunkard? the worldly man, or he that lives above the world? The more power grace has, the more easy ; the more power lusts have, the more hard is the labour.

(2.) There is true help in the one, not in the other. The labour in religion has outward helps ; the labourers are not helpless, they have a cloud of witnesses gone before them, whom they may see with their crowns upon their heads, Heb. xii. 1. Ye are not the forlorn in hope. Armies of saints have stormed heaven before you, and have left it behind them ; that the work is possible, and the reward certain. The other have not this ; if they get satisfaction in their lusts, they are the first. They see thousands before them, who have laboured as hard as they, disappointed, and are lain down in sorrow. This labour has inward helps. Christ bears the heaviest part of his own yoke ; he gives strength, he works the will for the work ; and the work for us, when we have the will. Phil. ii. 13. ' For it is God that worketh in us, both to will and to do of his good pleasure.' Isa. xxvi. 12. ' Thou also hast wrought all our works in us.' The others have not. True, they have that within them which puts them on to this labour, but the more of the one, the harder is the other, as the wearied beast is goaded by the spur, and worn out by their being beaten when no straw is allowed them. But where is the help to work satisfaction and happiness out of the creatures, or from the law ?

7. We call you from a wearisome to a lightsome pleasant labour. I have proved the first ; for the last, see Prov. iii. 17. ' Her ways are ways of pleasantness, and all her paths are peace.' But let us hear what can be said for both.

(1.) Is there much pleasure in sin ? *Ans.* In some there is none. What pleasure has the passionate man, that kindles a fire in his own bosom ? What pleasure has the envious, that gnaws himself like a serpent for the good that others enjoy ? What pleasure has the discontented, that is his own executioner. Consider the calm of spirit that the contrary graces bring, and judge who has the better part. As for those sins in which pleasure is found,

[1.] It is common to them with these creatures with whom they will not desire to be ranked. For these things that gratify men's sensual appetite are common to them with beasts, as gluttony, drunkenness, filthiness, &c. A sow can drink, and be as drunk as the greatest drunkard, and so on. And they have the better of them, as being under no law, and therefore, they can go the full length of their appetite. 1*st*, They do it without remorse. 2*d*, They find satisfaction in these things, seeing they are not capable of desiring greater things. Now, put these together, where is the pleasure ? Is it not surpassed by the pain ? As to the desires of the mind, these are common to them with devils. The greatest swearer, liar, and proud opposer of religion, have the trade but from the second hand. The devil can satisfy his curiosity better than the most curious, reason more closely against religion than any atheist. Only obstinate despisers of reproof and mockers surpass the devil, for the devils believe and tremble ; whereas for a time they do not.

[2.] The pleasure is but momentary, the pain follows hard at the heels, and is eternal. What plea-

sure can be devised, for which a man would hold his
finger over a burning candle for a quarter of an
hour ? how much more dreadful to endure eternal
burnings !

[3.] The struggle that conscience makes against
corruption, brings more torment than that which
corruption makes against grace. Conscience is more
dreadfully armed than corruption ; there is here as
much difference as there is betwixt the hand of God
and the hand of the devil. See now what becomes
of the pleasure !

(2.) The labour in religion is truly pleasant.   It
is truly holy labour ; for of that we speak, and scrip-
ture-testimony proves its pleasantness ; see Prov.
iii. 17. ' Her ways are ways of pleasantness, and all
her paths are peace.' Ask David, and he will tell
you, in Psal. lxxxiv. Paul, in 2 Cor. xii. 10.

[1.] It is a labour suited to the nature of the soul,
the better part, their divine supernatural nature,
2 Pet. i. 4.   Believers are partakers of a divine nature.   This must needs create ease and delight ; the
stream easily flows from the fountain ; birds with
pleasure fly in the air. The reason of the difficulty
in religion to many is, they are out of their element
when engaged in it.

[2.] Therein the soul carries on a trade with heaven ; entertains communion with God, through the
Spirit of Christ, by a mutual intercourse of grace
and duty, the soul receiving influences, and returning them again in duties ; as the rain falls on the
earth freely, so the waters run freely toward the sea
again.

[3.] Great peace of conscience usually attends
this ; and the more labour, the more peace. Psal.
cxix. 165. ' Great peace have they who love thy law.'
Here is a feast which nothing but sin mars.   2 Cor.
i. 12. ' For our rejoicing is this, the testimony of our
conscience, that in simplicity and godly sincerity,
not with fleshly wisdom, but by the grace of God, we

have had our conversation in the world.' Men cannot take it from us, John, xiv. 27.

[4.] Sometimes they have great manifestations of Christ, evidences of the Lord's love raising a high spring-tide of joy in their souls, greater than that which the whole congregation of the world enjoys, Psal. iv. 6, 7. It is joy unspeakable, and full of glory, 1 Pet. i. 8.

[5.] It is a lightsome way they walk in, whereas the other is darksome ; the light of the Lord's word shines in it. The Mahometans have a tradition, that Moses' law and Christ's gospel were written first with ink made of pure light. Sure the scripture points out duty, as if it were written with a sun-beam.

8. We call you from a labour against yourselves, to a labour for your advantage. Ye must either do the work of God or the devil. Every sin is a new impediment in your way to heaven, a new stone laid on the wall of separation. What a mad thing is it to be working out our damnation, instead of our own salvation!

9. We call you not to more, but to other labour. We are all laborious creatures ; the greatest idler is in some sort busy. Paul calls even them that work not at all, *busy bodies*, 2 Thess. iii. 11. Our life is nothing but a continual succession of actions, even as the fire is ever burning, and the rivers running. It is in some respect impossible to do more than we do ; the watch runs as fast when wrong as when right. Why may we not then keep the highway while we are travelling.—Consider,

10. That the same pains that men are at to ruin themselves, might possibly serve to save them. There are difficulties in the way of sin as well as of religion. Does not sin oftentimes bereave men of their nights' rest? Are they more disturbed when communing with their own souls, and with God? Do not men draw sin as with cart-ropes? Isa. v. 18.

Why might not labour be employed in drawing the heart to God ? If men would but change, and suck as greedily and incessantly at the breasts of God's consolations, as they do of the creature's, how happy would they be !

Lastly, Consider that the labour in religion is not greater, nay, it is less than in sin, for religion contracts our work to one thing. Luke, x. 41, 42. ' Martha, Martha, thou art careful and troubled about many things, but one thing is needful.' Sinners have many lusts to please, the saints have but one God to please ; the work of religion is all of a piece, sin not so. There is a sweet harmony betwixt all the graces and all the duties of religion. But lusts are quite contrary ; and as they war against grace, so against one another. James iv. 1. ' From whence come wars and fightings among you ? come they not from hence, even of your lusts that war in your members ? ' So that the sinner is dragged by one lust one way, by another, another. And how hard is it to serve contrary masters !

....

Christless sinners under a heavy burden.

1. Observe, that Satan has a load on all out of Christ ; it is a load of sin. Isa. i. 4. ' Ah, sinful nation, a people laden with iniquity.' This load is twofold

1st, A load of guilt, Gen. iv. 13. ' And Cain said unto the Lord, My punishment is greater than I can bear,' (Heb. *sin.*) Guilt is the heaviest load ever was on the shoulders of men or angels. The scriptures hold it forth,

(1.) As debt. He that is in debt is under a burden. It is the worst of debts, we cannot pay it, nor escape the hands of our creditor ; yea, we deny the

debt, care not for count and reckoning, we wave our
creditor as much as we can ; so it stands uncan-
celled.   But it is a debt that must be paid.   2 Thess.
i. 9. ' Who shall be punished with everlasting destruction from the presence of the Lord, and from the
glory of his power.'   They shall pay what justice
demands.   It is represented,

(2.) As a yoke tied fast on the sinner's neck ; hence
pardon is called a loosing of it, guilt being, as it were,
cords of wrath, whereby the sinner is bound over to
God's wrath.   Pardon is also called remission or
relaxation.   Rom. iii. 25. ' To declare his righteousness for the remission of sins that are past, through
the forbearance of God.'—It is pointed out,

(3.) As a burden.   Hos. xiv. 2. ' Take away all
iniquity.'   Take away, namely, as a burden off a
man's back.   Hence Christ is said to have borne our
sins, the burden of the elect's guilt being laid on his
back.   What a heavy load is it! 1st, It makes the
whole creation groan, Rom. viii. 22.   It caused them
take their pains five thousand years since, and they are
not yet delivered of their burden.   All the groans that
ever men gave on earth and in hell were under this
burden ; it sunk the whole world into ruin : ' Christ
took our nature,' to prevent us going down to the
pit.   Heb. ii. 16. (Greek, *caught hold*), as of a drowning man, not of the whole seed of Adam, for great
part of it fell to the ground, but of the seed of Abraham, the elect.   2d, This load sunk the fallen angels, made them fall as stars from heaven to the bottomless pit.   And what a load was it to Christ, that
made him sweat as it were great drops of blood, that
made him groan and die! It is,

2dly, A load of servitude to lusts, which of themselves are heavy burdens ; the very remainder of
which made the apostle groan.   Rom. vii. 24. ' O
wretched man that I am ! who shall deliver me from
the body of this death ?'   What greater burden can
be, than for a man to have a swarm of unmortified

corruptions hanging about him, whose cravings he is still obliged to answer. This is that which creates that weary labour, of which we have already spoken ; better a man were burdened with serpents sticking in his flesh, than with these. I observe,

2. The law has a load on the Christless sinner ; and that,

(1.) A load of duties, as great and numerous as the commandment, which is exceeding broad, can lay on. Though they perform them not, yet they are bound upon them by the commandment ; and they shall sooner dissolve the whole fabric of the world, than make void this commandment. This is a heavy load. True, they that are in Christ have a yoke of duties laid on them, but not by the law, but by Christ. The difference is great ; the law exacts perfect obedience, but gives no strength ; Christ, when claiming obedience to his law, gives strength for the performance, which makes it an easy obedience. There is,

(2.) A load of curses. Gal. iii. 10. ' Cursed is every one that continueth not in all things written in the book of the law, to do them.' Every commandment of the law is fenced with a curse, denounced against the breakers of it. How great must be the load, then, where every action is a sin, and every sin brings a curse ! This is a heavy load, that makes the earth reel to and fro, like a drunkard, under the weight of it. I observe,

3. That God has a load on the Christless sinner, that is, of wrath. Eph. ii. 3. ' And were by nature children of wrath.' This is an abiding load. John iii. 36. ' He that believeth not the Son, shall not see life, but the wrath of God abideth on him.' This load is far heavier than mountains of brass ; it is weightier then can be expressed.

****

The nature of coming to Christ explained.

To come to Christ is to believe on him : John, vi. 35. ' And Jesus said unto them, I am the bread of life ; he that cometh to me shall never hunger, and he that believeth on me shall never thirst.' Unbelief is the soul's departing, not from a living law, but from the living God, Heb. iii. 12. Christ is the Lord, God is in him, he calls sinners to come to him ; faith answers the call, and so brings back the soul to God in Christ. Now, the scripture holds forth Christ many ways answering to this notion of coming to him by faith. And that you may see your privilege and call, I shall hold forth some of these to you,

1. The devil's drudges and burden-bearers are welcome to Christ, as the great gift of the Father to sinners, to come and take it. John iii. 16. ' God so loved the world, that he gave his only-begotten Son, that whosoever believeth on him might not perish, but have everlasting life.' The world was broken by Adam ; God sends Christ as an up-making gift, and the worst of you are welcome to him, yea, he bodes (urges) himself upon you. Come to him, then, ye broken impoverished souls, that have nothing left you but poverty, wants, and debt.—Such are to come to him,

2. As the great Physician of souls. Matt. ix. 12. ' They that be whole need not a physician, but they that are sick.' Christ in the gospel comes into the world as to an hospital of sin-sick souls, ready to administer a cure to those that will come to him for it. Our diseases are many, all of them deadly, but he is willing and able to cure them all. He is lifted up on the pole of the gospel, and says, ' Look unto me, and be ye saved, all the ends of the earth ; for I

am God, and there is none else,' Isa. xlv. 22.—Such should come to him,

3. As the satisfying food of the soul. Isa. lv. 1—3. ' Ho, every one that thirsteth, come ye to the waters ; and he that hath no money, come ye, buy and eat, yea, come, buy wine and milk, without money, and without price. Wherefore do ye spend money for that which is not bread? and your labour for that which satisfieth not? hearken diligently unto me, and eat that which is good, and let your soul delight itself in fatness. Incline your ear, and come unto me ; hear, and your soul shall live ; and I will make an everlasting covenant with you, even the sure mercies of David.' The soul is an empty thing, and has hungry and thirsty desires to be satisfied ; the creatures cannot satisfy ; Christ can. John vi. 35. ' My flesh, says he, is meat indeed, and my blood is drink indeed.' God has made a feast of fat things in Christ, in him all the cravings of the soul may be satisfied ; there are no angels to guard the tree of life ; no seal on this fountain. Zech. xiii. 1. ' In that day, there shall be a fountain opened to the house of David, and to the inhabitants of Jerusalem, for sin and for uncleanness.' There is no enclosure about this flower of glory, Cant. ii. 1. Here is the carcase ; where are the eagles that should gather together? Such come to Christ,

4. As one on whom they may rest. Song viii. 5. ' Who is this that cometh up from the wilderness, leaning on her Beloved?' We are not able to do our own turn, but on him we should rely. 2 Chron. xvi. 8. ' Because thou didst rely on the Lord, he delivered thine enemies into thine hand.' Guilt makes the mind to be in a fluctuating condition. By coming to Jesus we are stayed, as is a ship at anchor. In, or from ourselves, we have nothing for justification and sanctification. God has laid help upon one that is mighty ; the weary soul is welcome to rest in him. —Such come to him,

Q q

5. As one on whom they may cast their burdens. Psal. lv. 22. ' Cast thy burden on the Lord, and he shall sustain thee.' The soul is heavy-laden while out of Christ; Jesus holds forth the everlasting arms, Deut. xxxiii. 27. faith settles down on them, casting the soul's burden upon them ; ' Come, says he, with all your misery, debts, beggary, and wants, I have shoulders to bear them all ; I will take on the burden, ye shall get rest.' He is content to marry the poor widow. Such come to him,

6. As one in whom they may find refuge. Heb. vi. 18. ' Who have fled for refuge, to lay hold on the hope set before us.' The law, as the avenger of blood, pursues the soul. Christ is that city of refuge, where none can have power against them. The gates are never shut ; here is a refuge from the law, from justice, and from the revenging wrath of God. Here is shelter under the wings of Christ : how willing is he to gather his people, as a hen gathereth her chickens under her wings ! Such come to him,

7. As one in whom the soul may at length find rest. Psal. xxxvii. 7. ' Rest in the Lord, and wait patiently for him.' The soul out of Christ is in a restless state, still shifting from one creature to another, not finding content in any. But by coming to Christ, the soul takes up its eternal rest in him, and he becomes a covering of the eyes to it. We are like men in a fever, still changing beds ; like the dove out of the ark, we have no rest, till we come to Christ. Such come to Christ,

8. As a husband. Matt. xxii. 4. ' All things are ready, come unto the marriage.' Your maker is content to be your husband, Psal. xlv. 10. Ministers are sent, as Abraham's servant, to seek a spouse for Christ. He is willing to match with the worst, the meanest of you ; he seeks no dowry ; he is the richest, the most honourable, the most tender and loving husband. Such come to Christ,

Lastly, As a powerful deliverer. Christ stands

at our prison-doors, as in Isa. lxi. 1. ' proclaiming
liberty to the captive, and the opening of the prison
to them that are bound.' All who come to him, as
in 2. Cor. viii. 5. first give their own selves unto the
Lord. Whosoever will come to Jesus, must give up
themselves to him. It is the work of faith to give
up the soul to Christ, that he may save it, that he
may open the prison-doors, take the prey from the
mighty, and deliver the lawful captive.

****

*Several things imported in our Lord's kind
Invitation to Sinners,* Matt. xi. 28.

1. It imports that sinners are welcome to come to
Christ, that they may unite with God by him ; Christ
is ready to receive you on your coming.—As to this,
consider,

(1.) Christ has made a long journey to meet with
sinners. What brought him out of the Father's bosom into the world, but to bring sinners to himself,
and so back to God again ? What was the errand
of the great shepherd, but to seek them, even them
that were straying on the mountains of vanity ?
Luke, xix. 10. ' For the son of man is come to seek
and to save that which was lost.' Consider,

(2.) How dear it cost him to purchase your union
with God by him. 2 Cor. v. 21. ' For he hath made
Him, who knew no sin, to be sin for us, that we
might be made the righteousness of God in him.'
Though ye should little value his blood, he will not
undervalue it himself ; for sinners it was shed, and
will he not welcome the reward of it, the fruit of the
travail of his soul ? Why were his arms stretched on
a cross, and his side pierced through, but that he
might open up our way to God ? Consider,

(3.) How near lost sinners lay to Christ's heart,

that he would refuse no hardship, in order that he might see the travail of his soul. His love was ancient love ; from eternity, ' his delights were with the sons of men,' Prov. viii. 31. ; see his choice, Heb. xii. 2. ; and therefore, when he was to suffer, his heart was upon the work. Luke, xii. 50. ' I have a baptism to be baptised with, and how am I straitened till it be accomplished!' Jacob's love to Rachel showed itself by his long service for her, which seemed to him but a few days. Consider,

(4.) Why has he set up a ministry in the world, but to bring sinners to himself? Matt. xxii. 3. ' And he sent forth his servants to call them that were bidden to the wedding.' He would not have left ambassadors to treat with sinners in his name, if he were not willing to receive them, nay, were he not anxious that they should come to him. Consider,

(5.) He heartily invites you to come to him ; as in the text ; in Isa. lv. 1. ' Ho! every one that thirsteth, come ye to the waters, and he that hath no money, come ye, buy and eat, yea, come, buy wine and milk, without money and without price ;' and in Rev. iii. 2. ' Behold I stand at the door and knock, if any man hear my voice, and open the door, I will come in to him, and will sup with him, and he with me.' These invitations look not like one who cares not whether sinners come or not, far less like one who is not willing to receive them. Consider,

(6.) The earnestness of the invitations ; he deals with sinners as one that will not take a nay-say. Luke, xiv. 23. ' Compel them to come in, that my house may be filled.' He not only knocks, but stands and knocks : strives with sinners by his word, his providences, and the motions of his Spirit ; answers their objections, Isa. lv. 1. and downwards ; while none can refuse, but those that rush wilfully on in their ruin ; as in Ezek. xxxiii. 11. ' As I live, saith the Lord God, I have no pleasure in the death of the wicked, but that the wicked turn from his way and live ; turn ye, turn ye, from your wicked ways, for why will ye die, O house of Israel?' Consider,

(7.) How he complains of these that will not come, John, v. 40. ' And ye will not come to me that ye might have life.' He speaks as one that has been working in vain. Isa. xlix. 4. ' I have laboured in vain, I have spent my strength for nought and in vain.' He complains of Jerusalem, Matt. xxiii. 37. ; yea, he weeps over obstinate incorrigible sinners, Luke, xix. 41, 42. ' And when he came near, he beheld the city, and wept over it, saying, If thou hadst known, even thou at least in this thy day, the things which belong unto thy peace ; but now they are hid from thine eyes.' Sure he has lost no bowels of compassion by going to heaven ; they flow out as freely and tenderly as ever. Consider,

(8.) He commands sinners to come to him. The invitations are all commands ; they are most peremptory. 1 John, iii. 23. ' This is his commandment, that we should believe on the name of his Son, Jesus Christ.' If you do it not, you can do nothing that will please him. John, vi. 29. ' Jesus answered and said unto them, This is the work of God, that ye believe on him whom he hath sent.' And he leaves it on us with the most dreadful certification. Mark, xvi. 16. ' He that believeth not shall be damned.' And hence it follows, that the hearers of the gospel who perish, are inexcusable ; the door was open, but they would not enter in.—The invitation imports,

2. That the worst of sinners are welcome to Christ. However great their burden of sin and misery be, it is no hinderance in their way to come to Christ. Where all are invited, none are excluded. But upon this I do not enlarge here. All that I shall just now observe is, that this consideration should shame you out of your slighting of Christ, and strike at the root of that bitter despair which lodges in the breasts of many, who are yet far enough from absolute despair of their case. The invitation imports,

3. That Christ allows sinners to come to him, rather on account of the desperateness of their case, than otherwise : *Come unto me, all ye that labour, and are heavy-laden.* As if he had said, ' Ye have been labouring, and yet can get no rest ; let that engage you to come to me. Sit down, and consider your case, if nothing else will prevail with you, let the desperateness of your disease bring you to the great Physician.' You are cordially welcome to do so. For, consider,

(1.) That it is for this very end God discovers the worst of a man's case to himself, drives him to his wit's end, in order that he may begin to be wise. Hos. ii. 6. ' Therefore, behold, I will hedge up thy way with thorns, and make a wall, that she shall not find her paths.' Ver. 7. ' Then shall she say, I will go and return to my first husband, for then was it better with me than now. Consider,

(2.) That Christ has made offers of himself to those in the worst of cases. Isa. i. 18. ' Come now, and let us reason together, saith the Lord ; though your sins be as scarlet, they shall be white as snow ; though they be red like crimson, they shall be as wool.' And he holds out himself as a Saviour in particular for these, Rev. iii. 17, 18. Isa. lv. 7. Consider,

(3.) Such have been made welcome, who have employed such arguments with him. Psal. xxv. 11. ' For thy name's sake, pardon mine iniquity, for it is very great ; ' and also in the case of the Canaanitish woman with Jesus, Matt. xv. 26—28. ' But he answered and said, It is not meet to take the children's bread, and to cast it to dogs. And she said, Truth, Lord : yet the dogs eat of the crumbs which fall from their master's table. Then Jesus answered and said unto her, O woman, great is thy faith : be it unto thee even as thou wilt. And her daughter was made whole from that very hour.' Consider,

(4.) He has the more glory, the more desperate

that the case is ; none see the stars so well as from the bottom of a deep pit. His power is the greater to pardon, his grace to overcome, when there is most occasion for these being displayed ; it is the worst of diseases that do best proclaim the physician's skill, when a cure is effected.

From what has been just now observed, we may see and admire the divine condescension, that Christ is so willing to take the sinner in, when he sees himself cast out at all doors, can get rest nowhere else ; that he will give him rest, and embrace the sinner, when he sees he can do no better, when he can make no other shift. Hence also learn, how to make an excellent use of the badness of your case, even to take up these stumbling-blocks, and break up heaven's door with them ; to make a virtue of necessity, and the more that the burden presseth, the more readily to go to Christ with it. True, it is never right coming to Christ, which sense of misery alone produceth ; but love may thus crown a work, which terror begins, and which when from the Holy Spirit it leads to. In a word, you are absolutely inexcusable that come not to Christ, be your case what it will.

The nature of that rest which Christ graciously promises, and actually gives, to weary and heavy-laden sinners.

Here it must be observed, that there is a rest which they may have in Christ ; a rest here, and a rest hereafter. In this life there is a fourfold rest to be had in Christ. A rest,

1. In respect of sin. The rest Christ gives from sin is twofold.

(1.) A rest from the guilt of sin. Guilt is a poison infecting the conscience, which makes it so to smart that it can get no rest, as in the case of Cain and Judas, and also with those, Acts ii. 37. ' They were pricked in their hearts.' This, when it festers and becomes immoveable, is the gnawing worm in hell. Christ gives rest from it, Heb. ix. 4. ; his blood purges the conscience from dead works. The conscience, when like the raging sea, is stilled by him. Isa. lvii. 18, 19. ' I have seen his ways, and will heal him ; I will lead him also, and restore comforts unto him and to his mourners. I create the fruit of the lips ; Peace, peace to him that is far off, and to him that is near, saith the Lord ; and I will heal him.' The soul finds this rest in the wounds of Christ, for, ' by his stripes we are healed,' Isa. liii. 5. The blood of Jesus Christ, God's own Son, cleanses from all sin. The soul dipped in this fountain is washed from this poison, and is delivered from this sting of guilt. There is rest,

(2.) From the reigning power of sin. Rom. vi. 14. ' For sin shall not have dominion over you.' Sin on the throne makes a confused restless soul, like the raging sea, continually casting out mire and dirt. Christ, by his Spirit's efficacy, turns sin off the throne, and restores rest to the soul. He casts down these Egyptian task-masters, and thus the soul enters into his rest. Heb. iv. 10. ' For he that is entered into his rest, he also hath ceased from his own works, as God did from his.' In the day of the soul's coming to Christ, he acts like a king, setting all in order in the kingdom, that was a mere heap of confusion before his accession to the throne. There is in Christ,

2. Rest from the law ; not that he makes them lawless, but that he takes off from them the insupportable yoke of the law, and gives them ease. He does so,

(1.) From the burden of law-duties, which are exacted in all perfection, under the pain of the curse, while no strength is furnished wherewith to fulfil them. Rom. vii. 4. ' Wherefore, my brethren, ye

also are become dead to the law by the body of Christ.'
This is the yoke on all men's necks naturally; Christ
put his neck in this yoke, and bare it, satisfying the
law's demands completely, and so frees all that come
to him from this service. Christ carries his people
without the dominions of the law. He does so,

(2.) From the curse of the law. Gal. iii. 13.
' Christ hath redeemed us from the curse of the law,
having been made a curse for us.' Rom. viii. 1.
' There is, therefore, now no condemnation to them
that are in Christ Jesus.' These that come to him,
he takes from off them that curse which they are under, and gives them his blessing, which he hath merited ; carries them from mount Sinai to mount Zion,
where they hear the blood of Jesus speaking peace,
silencing the demands of vengeance, and affording a
refuge for the oppressed. There is in Christ,

3. Rest from that weary labour in which persons
are engaged when in quest of happiness, leading the
soul to the enjoyment of God. Psal. cxvi. 7. ' Return
unto thy rest, O my soul! for the Lord hath dealt
bountifully with thee.' The soul, restless in seeking
happiness among the creatures, he leads to God, the
fountain of all perfection, opening their eyes, as he
did Hagar's, to see the well, and bringing them into
the enjoyment of all good in him, uniting the soul
with himself; where,

(1.) The soul finds a rest of satisfaction from Christ,
which it can find in no other quarter whatever, for
the soul finds a rest of satisfaction from him, when
by faith it is set on the breasts of his consolations.
In these there is an object adequate to all the desires
of the soul, answering all its needs ; thus, Prov.
xiv. 14. ' A good man shall be satisfied from himself.'
There is the triumph of faith in the enjoyment of
God. Phil. iv. 18. ' But I have all and abound.'
The soul finds,

(2.) A rest in him of settled abode, insomuch that
the soul goes not abroad, as it was wont, among the

creatures for satisfaction. John iv. 14. ' But whosoever drinketh of the water that I shall give him, shall
never thirst ; but the water that I shall give him,
shall be in him a well of water springing up to everlasting life.' Christ becomes precious to the soul.
Like the released lady, that did not so much as look
on or take notice of Cyrus, notwithstanding of the
noble part he acted, but on him (her husband) who
said, he would redeem her with his own life. ' The
kingdom of heaven is like unto a treasure hid in a
field, the which when a man hath found, he hideth,
and for joy thereof, goeth and selleth all that he hath,
and buyeth that field.' There is in Christ,

4. Rest in respect of troubles. Christ gives rest,

(1.) From troubles in the world, now and then,
when he sees meet. Psal. xxxiv. 19. ' Many are the
afflictions of the righteous. but the Lord delivereth
them out of them all.' Zion's God reigneth, be on
the throne who will ; and when he speaks peace,
neither devils nor men can create his people trouble ;
for, Lam. iii. 37. ' Who is he that saith, and it cometh to pass, when the Lord commandeth it not ? '
There is no such security from trouble as the godly
have, but that is from heaven, and not from earth.
Therefore,

(2.) Christ gives rest in trouble. John xvi. 33.
' These things I have spoken unto you, that in me
ye might have peace. In the world ye shall have
tribulation ; but be of good cheer, I have overcome
the world.' You may, nay, you shall meet with troubles, but he can make you get sweet rest in your
souls ; even when you are on a bed of thorns as to
the outward man, he can give his people a sweet rest
even in troubles. How can these things be ? may
some say. In answer,

[1.] Christ gives his people in trouble an inward
rest, that is, an inward tranquillity of mind in midst
of trouble. Psal. iii. 1—5. ' Lord ! how are they
increased that trouble me ? many are they that rise

against me. Many there be which say of my soul,
There is no help for him in God. Selah. But thou,
O Lord, art a shield for me ; my glory, and the lifter up of my head. I cried unto the Lord with my
voice, and he heard me out of his holy hill. Selah.
I laid me down and slept ; I awaked, for the Lord
sustained me.' Christ can make the believer as a
vessel of water tossed here and there, yet not jum-
bled. There was a greater calm with the three children in the furnace, than with the king in the palace,
Dan. iii. 24. Fear may be on every side where there
is none in the centre, because Christ makes a blessed calm in their hearts. Christ gives in trouble,

[2.] A rest of contentment. ' I have learned, (says
Paul, Phil. iv. 11.), in whatsoever state I am, therewith to be content.' This is not only the duty, but
the privilege of believers. If the lot of the godly be
not brought up to their spirit, Christ will bring their
spirit down to their lot ; and there must needs be
rest there, where the spirit of the man and his lot
meet in one. Psal. xxxvii. 19. ' They shall not be
ashamed in the evil time, and in the days of famine
they shall be satisfied.' Then follows,

[3.] A rest of satisfaction in the enjoyment of better things. What though the world hath a bitter
taste in their mouths ? Christ can hold a cup of con-
solation to them in that very instant, the sweetness
of which will master the bitterness of the other.
' Your sorrow, (says he, John xvi. 20.) shall be turned into joy.' Our rejoicing (says Paul, 2 Cor. i. 12.)
is this, the testimony of our conscience, that in simplicity and godly sincerity, not with fleshly wisdom,
but by the grace of God, we have had our conversation in the world.' They are not indeed stocks, to
be unmoved with troubles, but their sorrow is so
drowned in spiritual joy, that it is *but as sorrow*,
2 Cor. vi. 10. ' As sorrowful, yet always rejoicing ; '
even as the joy of the wicked is *but as joy*. Troubles
may raise a mutiny of lusts within, but the peace of

God quells them : ' It keeps their hearts and minds through Jesus Christ.' Christ gives,

[4.] A rest in confidence of a blessed issue. 2 Tim. i. 12. ' For the which cause I also suffer these things; nevertheless, I am not ashamed, for I know whom I have believed, and I am persuaded, that he is able to keep that which I have committed unto him against that day.' The soul in Christ has the promise to rest on ; and however dark a side the cloud may have, faith will see through it; though they may sink deep, they will never drown, who have a promise to bear them up. Thus, you see, they rest in Christ in trouble ; and this rest is a most secure rest, where people may rest confidently. Isa. xxvi. 3. ' Thou wilt keep him in perfect peace, whose mind is stayed on thee, because he trusteth in thee.' The wicked may have rest, but not with God's good will ; therefore the more rest, the more dangerous is their case. 1 Thess. v. 3. ' For when they shall say peace and safety, then sudden destruction cometh upon them, as a woman in travail, and they shall not escape.' But there is perfect security in Christ, and that in the worst of times, Song, iii. 7, 8. Again, it is a rest so rooted, that the soul can never be deprived of it. Isa. xxxii. 17. ' And the work of righteousness shall be peace, and the effect of righteousness, quietness, and assurance for ever.' How soon is the rest of the wicked broken, their candle put out! But this, although it may meet with some disturbance by temptations, as the clouds may go over the sun, yet it shall be as sure as the sun fixed in the firmament ; it will be proof against the disturbances of the world, against the temptations and accusations of the devil ; yea, against the demands of justice, and the threatnings of the law. Then in the life to come, he will give them all complete rest who come to him. Heb. iv. 9. ' There remaineth, therefore, a rest for the people of God.' He will give their bodies rest in the grave, Isa. lvii. 2. and both soul and body rest in heaven hereafter ; and that is a rest beyond expression.

If it should be enquired, Who is it that gives this rest ? this is answered in our text ; Christ says to such labouring and heavy-laden sinners, and he is able to make good his word, *I will give you rest.* The gift of this rest is his prerogative ; they that obtain it must get it out of his hands. For illustrating and confirming this, consider,

1. That all creatures cannot give rest to a restless soul. Not any thing in them, or the whole of what can be afforded from them, can give it. Eccles. i. 2. ' Vanity of vanities, saith the preacher, vanity of vanities, all is vanity.' Men, the best of men, cannot do it. Ministers may be directed to speak a word in season, but the Lord himself can only make that word effectual, 2 Sam. xii. 13. compared with Psal. li. Nay, angels cannot do it, Exod. xxxiii. 2. compare ver. 15. It requires a creating power. Isa. lvii. 18. ' I have seen his ways, and I will heal him.' Consider,

2. There can be no rest to the soul without returning to a reconciled God, for it is impossible the soul can find true rest elsewhere ; and there is no returning to God but by Christ. John, xiv. 6. ' I am the way, the truth, and the life ; no man cometh unto the Father, but by me.' He is the only ladder by which the soul can ascend to heaven.

3. Christ is the great Lord Treasurer of heaven. The fulness of power is lodged in him. Matthew, xxviii. 18. ' All power is given unto me in heaven and in earth.' There is nothing that any can get from heaven but what comes through his hands : John v. 22. ' The Father judgeth no man, but hath committed all judgment unto the Son.' Jesus also hath the keys of hell and death, Rev. i. 18.

4. He is the store-house, where the treasure is laid up, and out of which all needful supplies come : John

i. **16.** 'And of his fulness have all we received, and grace for grace.' Consider,

5. The glorious types illustrating this : Joseph, Gen. xli. 40—44. ; Joshua that brought the people to the rest in Canaan. Consider,

6. That high character which he sustains : Heb. xii. **2.** 'He is the author and finisher of our faith.' Consider,

Lastly, It is reasonable it should be so, he hath purchased this rest with his blood ; and therefore there is an high propriety that he should be the giver, the dispenser of this glorious blessing. *

* " Ho, every thirsty soul, and all
    That poor and needy are,
Here's water of salvation's well
    For you to come and share.

Here's freedom from sin and wo,
    And blessings all divine,
Here streams of love and mercy flow,
    Like floods of milk and wine.

Approach the fountain head of bliss,
    That's open like the sea,
The buyers that are moneyless,
    To poorest beggars free.

Why spend you all your wealth and pains,
    For that which is not bread,
And for unsatisfying gains,
    On which no soul can feed ?

While vain ye seek with earthly toys,
    To fill an empty mind,
You lose immortal solid joys,
    And feed upon the wind.

Incline your ear, and come to me ;
    Hear and your soul shall live :
For mercies sure as well as free,
    I bind myself to give."

                    Ralph Erskine's Scripture Songs.

••••••••••••••

Consideration of the preserving and governing acts of God's Providence.

1. God by his providence preserves all the creatures. This preservation of the creatures is an act of providence, whereby they are preserved in their being and power of acting, Heb. i. 3. ' Upholding all things by the word of his power.' In this God sometimes makes use of means, and sometimes acts without means. We have both described, Hos. ii. 21, 22. ' I will hear, saith the Lord, I will hear the heavens, and they shall hear the earth, and the earth shall hear the corn, and the wine, and the oil, and they shall hear Jezreel.' He preserves the heavens immediately, the earth, the corn, the wine, and the oil, &c. mediately. And thus by his providence he provides all things necessary for the preservation of all things : Psal. cxlv. 15, 16. ' The eyes of all wait upon thee, and thou givest them their meat in due season. Thou openest thine hand, and satisfiest the desire of every living thing.' This act of providence is so necessary, that nothing could subsist one moment without it. For there is no necessary connexion betwixt the being of the creatures this moment and their being the next : and as they could not give themselves a being, so they cannot continue it, but must be upheld by God as a ball in the air, Heb. i. 3. There is a continual efflux of providence necessary for preserving and upholding the creatures in their being, otherwise they would be independent, and could preserve themselves, which is grossly absurd.

2. God does not only preserve the creatures, but governs and manages them, which is the second act of providence ; whereby he disposes of all things, persons, and actions, according to his will, **Prov.**

xxi. 1. ' The king's heart is in the hand of the Lord,
as the rivers of water : he turneth it whithersoever
he will, Prov. xvi. 33. ' The lot is cast into the lap :
but the whole disposing thereof is of the Lord.' Chap.
xvi. 9. ' A man's heart deviseth his way ; but the
Lord directeth his steps.' And this act of providence
is also necessary : for, as the creature cannot be or
exist without God, so neither can it act without him :
Acts xvii. 28. ' For in him we live, and move, and
have our being.' God does not make man as the car-
penter doth the ship, which afterwards sails without
him ; but he rules and guides him, sitting at the helm,
to direct and order all his motions : so that whatever
men do, they do nothing without him ; not only in
their good actions, where he gives grace, and excites
it, working in them both to will and to do of his good
pleasure ; but also in their evil actions, wherein they
are under the hand of Providence, but in a very different manner.

For understanding this point, how the providence
of God reacheth to and is concerned in sinful actions,
we are to consider, that God neither puts evil into the
hearts of men, nor stirs them up to it : for, says the
apostle, Jam. i. 13. God cannot be tempted with evil ;
neither tempteth he any man.' And therefore he is
not the author of sin. But,

1. God permits sin, when he does not hinder it,
which he is not obliged to do. Not that it falls out
so as he cannot hinder it, for he is omnipotent, and
can do all things ; nor yet as if he cared not what
fell out in the world ; but he does wisely, for his holy
ends, efficaciously will not to hinder it ; hence we
read, Acts xiv. 16. that ' God in times past suffered
all nations to walk in their own ways.' He does not
permit sin, for that he will not violate or force the
creature's free will ; for God's providence offers no
violence to the will of the creature ; and if so, he
should never hinder sin at all, for the same reason.
But certainly he has holy ends in the permission of

sin : for thereby his justice, mercy, wisdom, and love, in sending his Son to save sinners, do conspicuously appear, which otherwise would have been under an eternal cloud, hid from the view of men and angels.

For the further illustration of this doctrine relating to the concern of providence in sinful actions, we are to consider them in a twofold respect, as simple actions, or natural actions of the creature, abstract from any obliquity or deformity cleaving to them; and as actions having irregularity and pravity in them. Considered as natural actions of the creature, they are all effected by the providence of God, which co-operates with, and enables the creature to produce them, in such a manner that without the efflux of providence the creature could not move a hand or foot, or perform any action whatever; ' for in him we move;' and no action of the creature simply considered, or as a natural action, can be sinful, but has a goodness of being in it, and is effected by the influence of providence. As to the pravity or sin that is in actions, as God decreed the futurition of sin, or permitted it to take place, and did not hinder it ; so all the sin or vitiosity that is in actions, proceeds entirely from the creature, and the evil lusts and passions that are in his heart.

Thus a man's taking up a stone, and throwing it, is a natural action, which the providence of God enables him to perform ; but his throwing it at another man with an intention to kill him, is permitted by God, otherwise it could not take place ; for if a hair cannot fall from our head without the providence of God, much less can a man be murdered without it ; and the killing of the man by the throwing of the stone, proceeds entirely from the malice and wickedness that was in the heart of the murderer, the operation of which God did not hinder, which he is nowise obliged to do.

2. God leaves the sinner so far as he sees meet, to the swing of his own lusts, and denies him restrain-

s s

ing grace. Thus, it is said of Hezekiah, a godly king, that, ' in the business of the ambassadors of the princes of Babylon, who sent unto him to enquire of the wonder that was done in the land, God left him, to try him, that he might know all that was in his heart,' 2 Chron. xxxii. 31. And when the restraint is taken off the sinner, he runs furiously to evil.

3. God bounds sin, and restrains men in their sins, as he does the raging sea, allowing it to go so far, but no further. He has such a power and command over wicked men, that they are not masters of their own affections and dispositions, but many times act quite contrary to what they had firmly resolved and proposed ; as in the case of Laban. He pursued Jacob, when he left Padan-aram, in order to return into his own country, with a wicked intention to do him hurt, by robbing him of his wives, children, and cattle ; but the Lord restrained him, and influenced him to enter into a covenant of friendship with the good patriarch, Gen. xxxii. Thus Esau had resolved on Jacob's death, and went out to meet him with a purpose to destroy him ; but when providence brought them together, it is said, ' Esau embraced Jacob, and fell on his neck, and kissed him.' Thus Balaam came with an express intention to curse Israel, and yet he fell a blessing them. Thus he bent the hearts of the Egyptians to favour the Israelites, so that they sent them away with great riches, by lending them jewels of silver, and jewels of gold, and costly garments. Thus, by a secret instinct, he turned Jehoshaphat's enemies away from him, when they came with a purpose to destroy him, 2 Chron. xviii. 31. ; and at another time he turned his enemies against themselves, so that they sheathed their swords in one another's bowels, 2 Chron. xx. Thus also he restrained the soldiers that broke the legs of the two thieves that were crucified with Christ, from touching his, in order to accomplish his word, that a bone of the paschal lamb, which was a type of Christ, the

Lamb of God, should not be broken. So true is that saying of the Psalmist, Psal. lxxvi. 10. ' Surely the wrath of man shall praise thee ; the remainder of wrath shalt thou restrain.' God has a bridle in the mouths of wicked men, when they are under the most impetuous fury of their lusts, to turn them as he will, restraining and curbing in respect of some, and giving swing to others.

Lastly, God over-rules all to a good end. God has one end in wicked actions, and the sinner another. The sinner minds and intends evil, but God means and designs good by them all. So Joseph's brethren, in their cruelly selling him for a slave, meant evil to the poor youth ; but God, in that dispensation meant it for good, and brought much good out of it to Joseph, and his father, and his brethren. Thus the Jews crucified Christ out of malice against him ; but God by that crucifixion intended satisfaction to his justice for the sins of men, and the redemption and salvation of an elect world. Thus God brings good, the greatest good out of the worst of evils. What greater evil or more atrocious wickedness can be imagined, than the violent death of the innocent Son of God, who went about doing good, and was holy, harmless, undefiled, separate from sinners ? and yet what a rich and astonishing good resulted therefrom, even glory to God, and peace and good-will towards men !

Properties of God's Providence.

1. God's providence is most holy, Psal. cxlv. 17. ' The Lord is righteous in all his ways, and holy in all his works.' Even though providence reach to and be conversant in sinful actions, yet it is pure ; as the sun contracts no defilement, though it shine on a

dunghill. For God is neither the physical nor moral cause of the evil of any action, more than he who rides on a lame horse is the cause of his halting. All the evil that is in sinful actions proceeds and flows from the wicked agent, as the stench of the dunghill does not proceed from the heat of the sun, but from the corrupt matter contained in the dunghill.

2. It is most wise, Isa. xxviii. 29. 'This cometh forth from the Lord of hosts, who is wonderful in counsel, and excellent in working.' Infinite wisdom always proposes the most excellent ends in all its operations, and uses the best methods for accomplishing its ends. However perplexed, confused, and void of wisdom providential administrations may appear to us poor mortals of narrow, shallow capacities, yet they are the result of the highest wisdom and the deepest counsel, as proceeding from and directed by him whose name is *the only wise God*, and cannot but manage all things with the greatest understanding. And the day will at last come when it shall be said by the united voice of the whole assembly and church of the first-born, that God hath done all things well : and then the plan of providence will appear in every respect to have been most wise, harmonious and consistent.

3. Providence is most powerful. Hence the Lord says to Sennacherib, the king of Assyria, 'I will put my hook in thy nose, and my bridle in thy lips, and I will turn thee back by the way by which thou camest,' 2 Kings, xix. 28. 'The king's heart is in the hand of the Lord, as the rivers of water ; he turneth it whithersoever he will.' Who can resist his will which is almighty ? He can never fail of his end, but all things fall out according to his decree, which is efficacious and irresistible.

****

Directions to be observed in considering the Providence of God.

1. Beware of drawing an excuse for your sin from the providence of God ; for it is most holy, and has not the least efficiency in any sin you commit. Every sin is an act of rebellion against God ; a breach of his holy law, and deserves his wrath and curse ; and therefore cannot be authorised by an infinitely-holy God, who is of purer eyes than to behold iniquity without detestation and abhorrence. Though he has by a permissive decree allowed moral evil to be in the world, yet that has no influence on the sinner to commit it. For it is not the fulfilling of God's decree, which is an absolute secret to every mortal, but the gratification of their own lusts and perverse inclinations, that men intend and mind in the commission of sin.

2. Beware of murmuring and fretting under any dispensations of providence that ye meet with ; remembering that nothing falls out without a wise and holy providence, which knows best what is fit and proper for you. And in all cases, even amidst the most afflicting incidents that befal you, learn submission to the will of God, as Job did, when he said upon the back of a train of the heaviest calamities that happened to him, ' The Lord gave, and the Lord hath taken away, blessed be the name of the Lord,' Job, i. 21. In the most distressing case, say with the disciples, ' The will of the Lord be done,' Acts, xxi. 14.

3. Beware of anxious cares and diffidence about your through-bearing in the world. This our Lord has cautioned his followers against, Matt. vi. 31. ' Take no thought, (that is, anxious and perplexing

thought,) saying, What shall we eat? or, What shall
we drink? or, Wherewithal shall we be clothed?'
Never let the fear of man stop you from duty, Matt.
x. 28, 29.; but let your souls learn to trust in God,
who guides and superintends all the events and administrations of providence, by whatever hands they
are performed.

4. Do not slight means, seeing God worketh by
them; and he that hath appointed the end, orders
the means necessary for gaining the end. Do not
rely upon means, for they can do nothing without
God, Matt. iv. 4. Do not despond if there be no
means, for God can work without them, as well as
with them; Hosea, i. 7. ' I will save them by the
Lord their God, and will not save them by bow, nor
by sword, nor by battle, by horses, nor by horsemen.'
If the means be unlikely, he can work above them,
Rom. iv. 19. ' He considered not his own body now
dead, neither yet the deadness of Sarah's womb.' If
the means be contrary, he can work by contrary
means, as he saved Jonah by the whale that devour-
ed him. That fish swallowed up the prophet, but
by the direction of providence, it vomited him out
upon dry land.

Lastly, Happy is the people whose God the
Lord is: for all things shall work together for their
good. They may sit secure in exercising faith upon
God, come what will. They have ground for prayer;
for God is a prayer-hearing God, and will be enquired of by his people as to all their concerns in the
world. And they have ground for the greatest encouragement and comfort amidst all the events of
providence, seeing they are managed by their covenant God and gracious friend, who will never neglect or overlook his dear people, and whatever concerns them. For he hath said, ' I will never leave
thee, nor forsake thee,' Heb. xiii. 5.

Practical observation of the dispensations of Providence.

FIRST, Providences may be considered with respect to their objects, which are all the creatures and all their actions. And here let us,

FIRST, Look into the invisible world, and trace providence a little there. It becomes Christians to cause their eye to follow there where God's hand is before them at work. David tells us, Psal. cxxxix. 8. ' If I ascend up into heaven, thou art there ; If I make my bed in hell, behold thou art there.' God is there with his hand of providence, ver. 10. ' Even there shall thy hand lead me, and thy right hand shall hold me.' And the apostle gives the Christian that character, 2 Cor. iv. 18. that ' he looks not at the things which are seen, but at the things which are not seen.'

First, Look to the lower part of that world, the kingdom of darkness, and there you see devils and damned spirits of men, with the providence of God about them in an awful manner. A fearful web of providence encompasses them.

1. Concerning devils, view the awful providences they are under, and observe,

(1.) How these once glorious creatures are now irrecoverably lost, and reserved to a certain and dreadful judgment, 2 Pet. ii. 4. ' For if God spared not the angels that sinned, but cast them down to hell, and delivered them into chains of darkness, to be reserved unto judgment.' Jude, 6. ' And the angels which kept not their first estate, but left their own habitation, he hath reserved in everlasting chains, under darkness, unto the judgment of the great day.' Behold and learn the severity of God's justice from

this his work ; how no natural excellency will preserve the creature from wrath when once defiled with
sin.   They were the first that ventured to break over
the hedge of the holy law, and God set them up for
dreadful examples to the whole creation.   Behold the
power of God, whose hands devils themselves cannot
rid themselves out of.   And understand the loving-
kindness of the Lord, in providing a Saviour for man,
and not for them, Heb. ii. 16.

(2.) How, notwithstanding, these malicious creatures are not so pent up in their prison, but they
are permitted to go about through the world ; yet
this world is generally inhabited without molestation
from them.   Only now and then, in some very rare
cases, they are suffered to molest men, by a particular providential permission as in the case of Job,
chap. ii.   This general case of the world is a continued wonder of providence.   How is it that ever
we get any rest from them in house or field ?   It is
not for want of will or natural power, but from the
restraint of providence upon them, continued upon
them, notwithstanding of the world's wickedness.
Observe this thankfully, and understand the loving-
kindness of the Lord.

2. Concerning damned spirits, who are in hell
under the wrath of God, see the awful providences
about them, and observe how miserable they are,
Luke, xvi. 23. ' And in hell he lifted up his eyes,
being in torments, and seeth Abraham afar off, and
Lazarus in his bosom ;' being ' punished from the
presence of the Lord,' 2 Thess. i. 9. all hopes of recovery being now lost for ever.   And learn how precious time is, that what we have to do, ye may do
quickly : how deceitful sin and the world are ; and
how severely God punishes at length, though he may
long bear with sinners.   And understand the loving-
kindness of the Lord, that ye are yet in the land of
the living, under means of grace, and hopes of glory.

Secondly, Look to the upper part of the invisible

world, the regions of bliss ; and there you will see
angels and the spirits of just men made perfect wrapt
up in a glorious web of providence, sparkling with
goodness and mercy.   See the Larger Catechism on
Providence.

Concerning the blessed angels, observe,

1. How they are established in holiness and happiness. 1 Tim. v. 21.   They were of the same
changeable nature with those that fell ; but God
held them up, and has confirmed them, that they
cannot fall now.   And learn the power of sovereign
grace, which can establish one tottering creature
when another falls ; and how happy they are who
cheerfully do the will of God, for so the angels do in
heaven.   Though proud shining hypocrites fall away
and perish, yet trembling saints shall be made to
stand.

2. How they are employed in the administration
of his power, mercy, and justice, 2 Kings xix. 35.
In one night the angel of the Lord smote in the
camp of the Assyrians an hundred fourscore and
five thousand, Heb. i. 14. ' Are they not all ministering spirits, sent forth to minister for them who shall
be heirs of salvation ?' God sends them to take care
of his children, who no doubt receive many benefits
off their hands, which they are not sensible of.   Understand the loving-kindness of the Lord in sending
them, and their love to God and man in taking such
employment.   The living creatures have the wheels
going by them.

Concerning the souls of the blessed, observe how
blessed and happy they are in the enjoyment of God,
where no clouds interpose betwixt them and the light
of his countenance, Heb. xii. 23. Luke xvi. 22.   And
learn here what a vain thing this world is, and how
we may be happy without it, yea cannot be completely happy till we be beyond it.   What a rich harvest
the seed of grace in the soul brings in, and how holiness leads the way to complete happiness.   Won-

T t

derful is the loving-kindness of the Lord, that takes those who serve him here, to be his attendants in his palace and brings them to the full enjoyment of himself in glory.

Let this suffice for a sample of providence in the invisible world.

SECONDLY, Look to the visible world, and trace providence there. See how the hand of the Lord is constantly at work about these his creatures which he has made, John v. 17. ' My Father worketh hitherto, and I work.'

1. Consider the inanimate or lifeless creatures, which are the objects of providence as well as other things. They are not capable of self-governing, but he that made them, guides them to their ends.

The heavenly bodies, sun, moon and stars, are under the government of wise providence. They got their orders at first, Gen. i. 16. ' God made two great lights ; the greater light to rule the day, and the lesser light to rule the night : he made the stars also.' And they have still observed these orders since, Psal. civ. 19. ' He appointeth the moon for seasons : the sun knoweth his going down.' Sometimes indeed, by a particular commission, they have altered their ordinary course, as in Joshua's time, chap. x. 12, 13. when the sun stood still upon Gibeon, and the moon in the valley of Ajalon, for a whole day ; but they returned to their course again. The sun keeps his course allotted him by the divine decree ; for should he go at random, our earth would either be burnt or quite frozen up, that we could not live on it. O the loving-kindness of the Lord, that makes the very heavenly bodies punctually to keep pace with our necessities, and has not avenged himself on men's disorders, by suffering these to go into disorder and confusion !

The raging sea is under the management of providence. God manages it as easily as the nurse does the infant, whom she swaddles and lays in its cradle, from whence it cannot get out, while she will have it to stay there. Job xxxviii. 11. ' Hitherto shalt thou come (says Providence to this unruly element), but no farther ; and here shall thy proud waves be stayed.' O look to his work, and learn his loving-kindness, Psal. civ. 24, 25, 26. O Lord, how manifold are thy works ! in wisdom hast thou made them all : the earth is full of thy riches. So is this great and wide sea, wherein are things creeping innumerable, both small and great beasts. There go the ships ; there is that leviathan, whom thou hast made to play therein.' Behold his greatness, and adore him, Matt. viii. 27. ' What manner of man is this, that even the winds and the sea obey him ?' Fear before such a mighty One, Isa. xxviii. 2. And let it quiet your hearts under all the tossings ye meet with in the world ; for it will cost him but to say, ' Peace and be still ; ' Psal. xciii. 4. ' The Lord on high is mightier than the noise of many waters, yea, than the mighty waves of the sea.'

The air and wind, which no man can lay hold of, are entirely under the conduct of Providence, John iii. 8. ' The wind bloweth where it listeth,' in respect of man ; but in respect of God, where he listeth, Matt. viii. 27. forecited. What a wonder is it, (not to speak of tempests, hail, rain, snow, &c. Psal. cxlvii. 15—18.), that such a thin, invisible body should bear up all the fowls of the air, the heavy clouds also, and carry them from place to place, so that we may say, as Psal. xviii. 10. ' He rode upon a cherub, and did fly ; yea, he did fly upon the wings of the wind ! How then can our God be at a loss for means to support us ? he has filled the world with it ; it is about us, in us, in our nostrils, in our bowels, nay in every pore of our bodies, yea, without it we could not breathe, yet we see it not, Shall we then think it strange, that the God who made it is every where present ? Nay, he is without and within us, though we see him not. If he mix pesti-

lential vapours with it, we are dead men, as if poison
were mixed with our drink : for at every breathing
we draw it in ; so entirely do we depend on the Lord.
O then understand the loving-kindness of the Lord
in this respect.

The earth is under the care and government of the
same wise Providence.   He made it, and that was a
great work ; he preserves it and governs it, and that
is another.   He supports it, Heb. i. 3.   The earth
bears us, but what bears the earth ?   You cannot
think it is infinite or boundless, and therefore that it
must have another side opposite to that we are on.
Yes, and by the powerful providence of God it hangs
like a ball in the air, Job xxvi. 7. ' He hangeth the
earth upon nothing.'   O then, is there any thing too
hard for our God to do ?   He fills it with his riches,
the surface of it, and the bowels of it, Psal. civ. 24.
But what is most necessary for men's use is on the
surface of it, easiest to be come at, Job, xxviii.   He
feeds it, that it may feed us, Deut. xi. 11. Hos. ii.
21, 22.   When the strength thereof is weakened,
with new influences from the heavens, he renews it,
Psal. civ. 30.   And since the flood, the promise then
given, Gen. viii. 22. that ' while the earth remaineth,
seed-time and harvest, and cold and heat, and sum-
mer and winter, and day and night shall not cease,'
has been punctually performed. O understand the
loving-kindness of the Lord in these things, what a
gracious and bountiful God he is! And learn how
surely all his promises to his people shall be accomplished.

2. Consider the vegetative part of the world,
things that have life, but not sense, such as trees,
plants. &c. how Providence cares for and manages
them.   Our Lord calls us to observe these things,
and thereby understand the loving-kindness of the
Lord, Matt. vi. 28. ' Consider the lilies of the field,
how they grow: they toil not, neither do they spin.'
Lilies of the field have not the care of man about

them, as those of the garden, but Providence cares
for them.   This teaches us to lay by anxiety, and
trust God, ver. 30.   See how the earth is kindly furnished with vegetables by providence, not only for
men's necessity, but their conveniency and delight,
Psal. civ. 14—17. ' He causeth the grass to grow for
the cattle, and herb for the service of man : that he
may bring forth food out of the earth, and wine
that maketh glad the heart of man, and oil to make
his face to shine, and bread which strengtheneth
man's heart.   The trees of the Lord are full of sap ;
the cedars of Lebanon, which he hath planted ;
where the birds make their nests : as for the stork,
the fir-trees are her house.'   And shall not this good
God be loved and cheerfully served by us ? Every
pile of grass is a preacher of the loving-kindness of
the Lord.

3. Consider the sensitive part of the world, such
as have life and sense, but not reason, as birds, beasts,
and fishes.   And observe what a vast family are
maintained on the Creator's cost.   And though we
cannot trust Providence, yet what an innumerable
company there is of dependants on mere providence !
Psal. civ. 27. ' These all wait upon thee ; that thou
mayest give them their meat in due season.'   Observe this provision, and thence learn to believe
even where ye cannot see.   Matt. vi. 26. ' Behold
the fowls of the air : for they sow not, neither do
they reap, nor gather into barns ; yet your heavenly
father feedeth them.   Are ye not much better than
they.'   For Providence does for them that have none
to do for them.   Psal. cxlvii. 9. ' He giveth to the
beast his food, and to the young ravens that cry.'
Observe how Providence has subjected them to man
as servants that could easily be his masters in respect of strength, as the horse, ox, &c. yet the face
of man strikes a damp upon them, which is the more
remarkable, that man by sin did forfeit his dominion
over the creatures.   But this must be resolved into

the virtue of that word, executed daily by providence,. Gen. ix. 2. ' The fear of you, and the dread of you, shall be upon every beast of the earth, and upon every fowl of the air, upon all that moveth upon the earth, and upon all the fishes of the sea.' O what a power is in a word of divine appointment !

4. Consider the rational part of the world, men having life, sense, and reason. In these providence shows itself most brightly. Man is the compend of the creation, having a spirit as angels are spirits, and a body with the rest. And he is the peculiar care of Heaven. This is the main object of our observation.

1*st*, We should observe the dispensations of providence towards societies ; and the nearer our relation to them be, we should observe them the more narrowly.

(1.) Towards societies of men in the world, kingdoms, churches, congregations, families, &c.

[1.] Much of the power, wisdom, goodness, justice, &c. of God, might be learned from the revolutions and changes in states and kingdoms, which should make us inquisitive for the knowledge of public affairs. And O what a glorious scene of providence has been opened of late in Britain, shining with illustrious mercy to the church and nation, in delivering us when at the brink of ruin ; depth of wisdom, in baffling in a moment the cunning projects of enemies ; almighty power, in so easily crushing their towering hopes ; radiant justice, in making the stone tumble down on the heads of those that rolled it, and making enquiry for the blood of the saints shed many years ago.

[2.] Providences toward the church of God are mainly to be observed, 1 Sam. iv. 13. The angels themselves notice these, to learn something from them, Eph. iii. 10. What concerns the church is the greatest work on the wheel of providence ; and in most, if not all the great works of God through the world, he has in them an eye to his church. As she is for God, so other things are for her.

Particularly we should observe the way of providence towards the church of Scotland, whereof we are members; which has been as admirable a mixture of mercy and judgment, as perhaps any church since the apostles' days has met with. How high has she been raised in peace and purity, and how low laid at other times! How often has she been at the brink of ruin, and wonderfully preserved? How have her faithful friends been signally owned of God, and her enemies often borne the evident marks of God's displeasure! &c. And yet, more particularly,

We should observe the way and aspect of providence towards the congregation, how the Lord has been and is dealing with us, that we may accommodate ourselves to his dispensations, and answer the call of them.

[3.] Towards families. Sometimes the Lord causes a warm sunshine of prosperity on families, and sometimes the heavens are louring above them; they have their risings and fallings, as all other societies in this changeable world, as is beautifully described by the Psalmist, Psal. cvii. 38, 39. 41. ' He blesseth them also, so that they are multiplied greatly, and suffereth not their cattle to decrease. Again they are diminished and brought low through oppression, affliction and sorrow. Yet setteth he the poor on high from affliction, and maketh him families like a flock.' How does Job mournfully observe the way of providence with his family, chap. xxix. 2—5. and David on his death-bed the humbling circumstances of his! 2 Sam. xxiii. 5.

There are few of our families but God has of late one way or other visited them; his voice has cried to our houses, as well as to the land. It is our duty to observe the same, read the language of it, and comply with the design thereof.

2dly, Towards particular persons; for we may

learn something from God's way with every one.
And,

(1.) Towards others, whether godly or wicked.
This was the Psalmist's practice to have his eyes in
his head, and to look about him in the world, and
learn something for his own establishment, both from
the harms and happiness of others, Psal. xxxvii.
35—37. ' I have seen the wicked in great power ;
and spreading himself like a green bay-tree. Yet
he passed away, and lo, he was not ; yea, I sought
him, but he could not be found. Mark the perfect
man, and behold the upright : for the end of that
man is peace.' It is observable, that the holy scripture is not written as a system of precepts, with the
reasons of them ; but the body of it is a cluster of
examples, wherein we may see, as in a glass, what we
are to follow, if we would be happy, and what we are
to shun. Rom. xv. 4. ' For whatsoever things were
written aforetime were written for our learning.' A
plain evidence, that whoso would please God, must
observe those things that are set before his eyes in
providence.

(2.) Towards ourselves in particular. These providences come nearest us, and therefore should be
most narrowly observed. In these we are the parties to whom God directs his speech immediately ;
but, alas ! often it is not observed. Job xxxiii. 14.
' For God speaketh once, yea twice, but man perceiveth it not.' There is none of us that are not the
objects of wonderful providences, but especially true
Christians, who may well say, as Psal. xl. 5. ' Many,
O Lord my God, are thy wonderful works which
thou hast done, and thy thoughts which are to us-
ward : they cannot be reckoned up in order unto thee :
if I would declare and speak of them, they are more
than can be numbered.' We might each of us fill a
volume with accounts of the wonderful works of God,
and yet confine ourselves to what has happened to
ourselves, if we had but the wisdom to observe the

same. Every moment we would be a wonder to ourselves, if we could but discern the beautiful mixture
of that web of providence wherein every moment we
are wrapt up.

(1.) Let us observe how we are powerfully preserved by Providence, Heb. i. 3. Ps. xxxvi. 6. Lord,
thou preservest man and beast.' When we consider
how unlike our souls are to our bodies, we may more
wonder at the continuance than the breach of that
union. When we think how death has as many
gates to come in by, as our body has pores, how the
seeds of a thousand diseases are in our bodies, what
a train of perishing principles they are made up of,
how easily, while we walk amidst the creatures of
God here, fire may be set to the train, and the house
of clay quickly blown up, we may say there is something more astonishing in our life than in our death.
And it must be a powerful providence that preserves
this life of ours, as a spark of fire in the midst of an
ocean of water, or as a bag of powder amidst sparks
of fire flying on every hand.

Besides, how few of us are there, but sometimes
there has been but as a hair-breadth betwixt death
and us, by reason either of diseases or unforeseen accidents, which we could not therefore ward off. So
that we might say of our preservation, This is the
finger of God.

What remarkable deliverances has the Lord
wrought for some by unordinary means, as Jonah
preserved by a whale, and Elijah fed by the ravens!

(2.) How we are holily, wisely, and powerfully governed by Providence, our persons and actions disposed of according to his will, either in mercy or in
wrath, Dan. iv. 35. ' All the inhabitants of the earth
are reputed as nothing : and he doth according to
his will in the army of heaven, and among the inhabitants of the earth : and none can stay his hand, or
say unto him, What dost thou ?' Psal. cxxxv. 6.
' Whatsoever the Lord pleased, that did he in heaven,

and in earth, in the seas, and all deep places.'
While we sail the sea of this world, we may well
perceive, that it is not we ourselves, but holy providence that guides the ship. Jer. x. 23. ' O Lord,
(says the prophet,) I know that the way of man is
not in himself; it is not in man that walketh to direct his steps.' And while men will not see this, to
engage them to a life of holiness, faith, and dependance on God, they are often made to feel it, by their
dashing on rocks, to the bruising, if not to the split-
ting of them : Isa. xxvi. 11. ' Lord, when thy hand
is lifted up, they will not see ; but they shall see, and
be ashamed.' Let me instance here but in two things,
to show that God sits king, and rules among men.

(1.) Man proposeth, but God disposeth : Lam.
iii. 37. ' Who is he that saith, and it cometh to pass,
when the Lord commandeth it not ?' How often are
men's towering hopes levelled with the ground in a
moment? Their projects are laid with all the wit
and industry they are capable of, managed with all
diligence and circumspection, so that they cannot see
how they can misgive, but must take effect according to their wish. But he that sits in heaven, in a
moment looses a pin, and all the fabric falls to the
ground, their projects are baffled, their measures dis-
concerted, some stroke of providence, which ungodly
men call an unlucky accident, mars all. This was
evident in Haman's case. Sometimes it is done by
an invisible hand, whereby the wheels are taken off,
that they can drive no farther : Job xx. 26. ' All
darkness shall be hid in his secret places : a fire not
blown shall consume him ; it shall go ill with him
that is left in his tabernacle.' How often do men
find their greatest cross where they looked for their
greatest comfort! and things turn about quite the
contrary way to what was their design.

(2.) Man's extremity is God's opportunity, Gen.
xxii. 14. How often does the Lord begin his work
where man ends his, and can do no more? When

men know not what to do, God opens a door ; and
when they have no firm ground of their own left to
stand upon, he sets their foot on a rock : Psal cvii.
27, 28. ' They reel to and fro, and stagger like a
drunken man, and are at their wits' end. Then they
cry unto the Lord in their trouble, and he bringeth
them out of their distresses.' Their hopes are disappointed, but their fears and desperate conclusions
are prevented. Something threatens them a stroke,
which they see not how to escape ; but an invisible
arm wards off the blow ; and what they look for their
ruin in, there they find, by an over-ruling providence,
healing and upmaking, Est. ix. i. What is most unlikely is brought about, while the fairest hopes are
made like the blossom that goes up as dust. Thus
God baffles men's hopes on the one hand, and their
fears on the other, that they may see, there is a wheel
within a wheel that moves and guides all.

SECONDLY, We may consider providences with
respect to their kinds, Psal. xl. 5. forecited. The
wisdom of God is manifold wisdom, and produces
works accordingly, Psal. civ. 24. And each of them
is to be observed. I will instance in these three dis-
tinctions of providence.

First, Providences are either cross, or smiling and
favourable. Both ought to be observed, and may be
so profitably.

1. We should observe cross providences that we
or others meet with. They come not by chance, but
under the guidance of a holy sovereign God : Job
v. 6. ' Affliction cometh not forth of the dust, neither
doth trouble spring out of the ground.' Amos iii. 6.
' Shall there be evil in a city, and the Lord hath
not done it ? ' God makes himself known by them,
his justice, truth, holiness, wisdom, and power : Psal.
ix. 16. ' The Lord is known by the judgment which
he executeth.' And he requires us to observe them :
Micah vi. 9. ' Hear ye the rod, and who hath appointed it.' And it is a horrible provocation not to observe

them, Isa. xxvi. 11. forecited, and not to comply with
the design of them ; to murmur, but not kindly mourn
under them, Job xxxv. 9, 10. and xxxvi. 13. Sometimes men meet with crosses in the way of their duty,
Gal. vi. 17. and sometimes in the way of sin, as Jonah.
The design of both is to purge away sin, Isa. xxvii. 9.
But, without observations, the plaister is not applied
to the sore.

2. Smiling and favourable providences towards
ourselves or others, Psal. xl. 5.   Many, in their observations of providence, are like the flies that pass
over the sound places, and swarm about the sores.
They are still complaining of their crosses and sorrows, and will nicely reckon them up : but as to their
mercies, they will not go the length of the unjust
steward, of a hundred to set down fifty, Luke xvi. 6.
They have their language, but it cannot be understood without observation, Rom. ii. 4.   Dependance
on God, and humility of heart, would teach us carefully to observe our mercies ; Lam. iii. 22. ' It is of
the Lord's mercies that we are not consumed, because his compassions fail not.'   Gen. xxxii. 10. ' I
am not worthy of the least of all the mercies, and of
all the truth, which thou hast showed unto thy servant ; for with my staff I passed over this Jordan,
and now I am become two bands.'   Even when we
are meeting with heavy crosses : Job i. 21. ' Naked
came I out of my mother's womb, and naked shall I
return thither : the Lord gave, and the Lord hath
taken away ; blessed be the name of the Lord.'

Secondly, There are great lines and small lines
of providence.   And,

1. We should observe the great lines of providence
in signal events.   Some dispensations bear such a
signature of a divine hand, and so flash like lightning on men's faces, that one can hardly miss to observe, but must say, as in Exod. viii. 19. ' This is the
finger of God.'   2 Chron. xvi. 19, 20. ' Then Uzziah
was wroth, and had a censer in his hand, to burn in-

cense : and while he was wroth with the priests, the
leprosy even rose up in his forehead before the priests
in the house of the Lord, from beside the incense altar.   And Azariah the chief priest, and all the priests
looked upon him, and behold, he was leprous in his
forehead, and they thrust him out from thence, yea,
himself hasted also to go out, because the Lord had
smitten him.' It is rare that God leaves himself
without a witness, by some such signal providences ;
yet such is the perverseness of the heart of man, that
as the blind cannot observe the flash of lightning,
even these are lightly looked at, 1 Sam. vi. 9.

2. The small lines of providence.   The most minute things are guided by the all-ruling hand, Matt.
x. 29, 30.   And if God do manage them, it becomes
us to notice them.   All the king's coin, from the mas-
siest piece of gold to the smallest penny, bears the
king's image and superscription, and therefore the
least as well as the greatest is current in trade.   So
the smallest lines of providence pass current with
those that keep a trade with heaven.   Gideon notices his hearing a fellow tell a dream, Judges vii. 13,
&c. Heman, the removing of an acquaintance, Psal.
lxxxviii. 8. and Jacob, a kind word, the show of his
brother's countenance. Gen. xxxiii. 10.

Thirdly, There are common and uncommon providences.

1. We should observe common and ordinary dispensations, such as fall out every day in the common
road of providence.   These, because they are common, lie neglected : yet the 104th Psalm is penned
on that subject.   I have observed to you already,
how providence appears in the constant revolutions
of seasons, day and night ; by the one the weary
earth is refreshed, and by the other weary man, the
night being fit for rest.   The subjection of the beast
to man, by virtue of that divine word, Gen. ix. 2.
forecited, without which man could not have his necessary designs served.   I add, that wonderful diver-

sity of faces and features, without which the man could not know his wife, nor the parents their own children, nor the judge the criminal ; so that without this there could be no orderly society, no government, commerce, &c. These are a sample of common providences, which, studied, might be of great use.

2. Uncommon and unordinary providences, as miracles, which are beyond the power of nature ; extraordinary deliverances, judgments, discoveries of secret crimes; which are bright spots here and there interspersed in the web of providence, and challenge a peculiar regard.

THIRDLY, We may consider providences with respect to the time of their falling out. The works of providence run parallel with the line of time, and the continuance of the world, John v. 17.

1. We should observe the past dispensations of providence: Psalm lxxvii. 5. ' I have considered the days of old,' says Asaph, ' the years of ancient times.' An observer of providence must look off unto others, look into himself, and, with respect to himself and others, look back also.

(1.) Past providences towards others afford a large field for observation, reaching from the creation till now : Psal. cxliii. 5. ' I remember the days of old,' says David. He remembered how the Lord dealt with Nimrod, Abimelech, Pharaoh, &c. What a chain of wise providences has encompassed the world in the several generations thereof ! What a beautiful mixture of providences has always appeared towards the church, while the mystery of God, not yet finished, has been a carrying on ! What very remarkable things have fallen out in the life and death of particular persons ! From all the particulars of these we might draw something for our spiritual advantage, as the bee from every flower extracts her honey.

(2.) Past providences towards ourselves in particular afford also a large field, reaching from our first being till now. Look back and consider that wonderful providence that framed thee in the womb, Job x. 10, 11. The Psalmist finds himself in a transport of wonder upon this reflection, Psal. cxxxix. 14, &c. Consider how the same kind providence brought thee safe out of the womb, that the womb was not made thy grave, or that thou wast not stifled in the birth, Psal. xxii. 9. How thou wast provided for and preserved from the dangers in infancy, by the same kind providence, whilst thou couldst do nothing for thyself, Psal. xxii. 9, 10. Observe the providences of God towards thee in thy childhood, youth, middle age, and forward to the present time ; and thou must say, as old Jacob, Gen. xlviii. 15. ' God fed me all my life long unto this day ; ' and with the Psalmist, Psal. lxxi. 17. ' O God, thou hast taught me from my youth.' Observe how God gave thee such and such education, ordered thy lot in such and such a place in his earth, and in such sort as he has done, how he brought thee into such and such company, saved thee from such and such dangers, &c.

2. We should observe the present dispensations of providence towards ourselves and others, Zech. vi. 1, 2. It is a stream that still runs by us, like those rivers that bring down the golden ore, Psal. lxv. 11. By day nor night it ceaseth not, Psal. xix. 2. Providence with the one hand bids us stoop and take on the day's load of benefits, Psal. lxviii. 19. and with the other hand lays on the day's burden of evils, Matt. vi. ult. And therefore that is our duty : Psal. iv. 4. ' Commune with your own hearts upon your bed, and be still ; ' that having made our observations through the day, we may cast up our accounts against night.

••••••••••••••

A fourfold harmony to be observed in the dispensations of Providence.

1*st*, Their harmony with the word, which they a-
gree with as the copy with the original. The sealed
book of God's decrees is opened in providences.
Hence that of the opening the seals, in the Revelation. And the book of the scripture is written over
again in providence, so that as in water face answereth to face, so do God's works to his word, Psal
xlviii. 8. Providence is a most regular building, and
the word is the draught of that building Providence is a curious piece of embroidery, and the word
is the pattern. So that in providence the word has
been a-fulfilling ever since it was given, and still it is
a-fulfilling, and the pattern will be wrought out when
the mystery of God is finished, and not till then :
Matt. v. 18. ' For verily I say unto you, Till heaven
and earth pass, one jot or one tittle shall in no wise
pass from the law, till all be fulfilled.' And thus it
is a-fulfilling, not only by the extraordinary but ordinary providences. If a man quarrel any thing in
a building or embroidery, there must be a comparing
it with the draught or pattern of the house or embroidery, and he will be satisfied. Psal. lxxiii. 16, 17.

Ye will never observe providences aright, if ye do
not observe their harmony with the word ; for the
word is the instituted means of the conveyance of influences, Isa. lix. ult. By neglecting of this, some
dispensations prove stumbling-blocks, over which
some break their necks, Mal. iii. 15. Many draw
harsh and ungodly conclusions against others, whereby they only discover their own ignorance of the
scriptures, and of the method of providence : Luke,
xiii. 1—5. ' There were present at that season some

that told him of the Galileans, whose blood Pilate had mingled with their sacrifices. And Jesus answering, said unto them, Suppose ye that these Galileans were sinners above all the Galileans, because they suffered such things? I tell you, Nay: but, except ye repent, ye shall all likewise perish. Or those eighteen upon whom the tower in Siloam fell, and slew them, think ye that they were sinners above all men that dwelt in Jerusalem? I tell you, Nay: but, except ye repent, ye shall all likewise perish.' John ix. 2, 3. ' And his disciples asked him, saying, Master, who did sin, this man, or his parents, that he was born blind? Jesus answered, Neither hath this man sinned, nor his parents: but that the works of God should be made manifest in him;' like Job's censorious uncharitable friends, Job v. i.

O Sirs, learn this lesson, that all providences which you, or I, or any person or society in the world meet with, are accomplishments of the scripture. And they may be reduced to and explained by one of these five things. Either they are accomplishments of,

(1.) Scripture-doctrines: Psal. xlviii. 8. ' As we have heard, so have we seen in the city of the Lord of hosts, in the city of our God.' May not every one see, that few great men are good men? Do not stumble at it; it is but a-fulfilling of the scripture: 1 Cor. i. 26. ' Not many wise men after the flesh, not many mighty, not many noble are called.' That the safest condition for the soul, is the medium between great wealth and pinching poverty, according to Augur's prayer, Prov. xxx. 8, 9. ' Give me neither poverty, nor riches, feed me with food convenient for me: lest I be full, and deny thee, and say, Who is the Lord? or lest I be poor, and steal, and take the name of my God in vain.'—That Satan and the corruptions of the heart are sometimes most busy, when people are setting themselves to serve the Lord, agreeable to Paul's experience, Rom. vii. 21. ' I find a law,

that when I would do good, evil is present with me.'
—That the generality of the hearers of the gospel
are not savingly wrought on by it, according to these
scripture-passages : Isa. liii. i. ' Who hath believed
our report ? and to whom is the arm of the Lord revealed ?' Matt. xxii. 14. ' Many are called, but few
are chosen.' And so in other cases. Or of,

(2.) Scripture-prophecies ; 1 Tim. i. 18. ' This I
commit unto thee, O Timothy, according to the prophecies which went before on thee.' What astonishing providences were the deliverance of Israel out of
Egypt, the expulsion of the Canaanites, Cyrus' over-
turning the Babylonian empire, and loosing the captivity, and the destruction of Jerusalem by the Romans ? But all these were but a-fulfilling of scripture-prophecies. What an astonishing providence
was the rise, reign, and continuance of the Anti-
christian kingdom, and the reformation of religion in
many nations, after they had lain many hundreds of
years under Popish darkness. These are the fulfilling of the apocalyptic prophecies. And what an astonishing providence was the introduction of the gospel into Britain, and the preservation of it hitherto,
amidst so many attempts to destroy it ? It is an accomplishment of that prophecy, Isa. xlii. 4. ' The
isles shall wait for his law.' Or of,

(3.) Scripture-promises : Josh. xxi. 45. ' There
failed not out of any good thing which the Lord had
spoken unto the house of Israel : all came to pass.'
Psal. cxix. 65. ' Thou hast dealt well with thy servant, O Lord, according unto thy word.' You see
the orderly revolutions of the year, and seasons thereof ; that is the fulfilling of the scripture, Gen. viii. 22.
—That those who have suffered loss in the cause of
Christ, have been bountifully treated with so much
in hand, that they have had more content and inward satisfaction in that, than any other time of their
life, is a fulfilling of scripture : Mark x. 29, 30. ' There
is no man that hath left house, or brethren, or sisters,

or father, or mother, or wife, or children, or lands,
for my sake and the gospel's, but he shall receive
an hundred-fold now in this time, houses, and brethren, and sisters, and mothers, and children, and
lands, with persecutions ; and in the world to come
eternal life.'—That the way of duty has been not only the most honourable but the safest way, is an accomplishment of scripture-promises : Prov. x. 9.
' He that walketh uprightly, walketh surely.' Chap.
xvi. 7. ' When a man's ways please the Lord, he
maketh even his enemies to be at peace with him.'
—That communion with God is to be had in ordinances, is conformable to promise : Exod. xx. 24.
' In all places where I record my name, I will come
unto thee, and I will bless thee.' Or of,

(4.) Scripture-threatenings : Lev. x. 3. ' This is
that the Lord spake, saying, I will be sanctified in
them that come nigh me, and before all the congregation I will be glorified.' Hos. vii. 12. ' I will chastise them, as their congregation hath heard.'—You
may observe how dangerous it is to meddle for the
ruin of the work and people of God, from that passage : Micah iv. 11, 12. ' Now also many nations are
gathered against thee, that say, Let her be defiled,
and let our eye look upon Zion. But they know
not the thoughts of the Lord, neither understand
they his counsel : for he shall gather them as the
sheaves into the floor.'—How their faces are covered
with shame that despise the Lord, from 1 Sam. ii. 30.
' The Lord God of Israel saith, I said indeed, that
thy house, and the house of thy father, should walk
before me for ever : but now the Lord saith, Be it
far from me ; for them that honour me, I will honour, and they that despise me shall be lightly esteemed.'—How the faster people clave to their temporal
comforts, they have the looser hold, from Ezek.
xxiv. 25. ' I will take from them their strength, the
joy of their glory, the desire of their eyes, and that
whereupon they set their minds, their sons and their

daughters.'—How people may run long in an evil
way, but their foot will slip at length, from Deut.
xxxii. 35. ' Their foot shall slide in due time : for
the day of their calamity is at hand, and the things
that shall come upon them make haste.'

(5.) Or they are the parallels of scripture-examples.
Psal. cxliii. 5. ' I remember the days of old.'   The
serióus observer will find a surprising fulness here,
as in the other parts of scripture.   I will instance in
three very astonishing pieces of providence, which
often put good men to their wits' end, to know how
to account for them ; yet being brought to the glass
of scripture-examples, such a harmony appears betwixt the one and the other, as cannot but be extremely satisfying.

(1.) Sometimes we see men walking contrary to
God, and yet providence smiling on them, and cares-
sing them, as if they were the darlings of heaven.
This has puzzled the best of men.   It put Jeremiah
sore to it, chap. xii. 1, 2. ' Righteous art thou, O
Lord, when I plead with thee : yet let me talk with
thee of thy judgments : wherefore doth the way of
the wicked prosper ? wherefore are all they happy
that deal very treacherously ?   Thou hast planted
them, yea, they have taken root : they grow, yea,
they bring forth fruit ; thou art near in their mouth,
and far from their reins.'   It was near carrying Asaph quite off his feet : Psal. lxxiii. 13. ' Verily, I
have cleansed my heart in vain, and washed my
hands in innocency.'   But O ! is there not a beautiful harmony in this with scripture-examples ?   How
did all Israel as one man back Absalom in his rebellion ?   How did Haman rise till he could come no
higher, unless he had got the throne ?   And the tyrant Nebuchadnezzar carries all before him according to his wish, &c.   And scripture-doctrine unrid-
dles the mystery : Psal. xcii. 5, 6, 7. ' O Lord, how
great are thy works ! and thy thoughts are very
deep.   A brutish man knoweth not : neither doth a

fool understand this. When the wicked spring as the grass, and when all the workers of iniquity do flourish : it is that they shall be destroyed for ever.'

(2.) How often do astonishing strokes light on those that are dear to God, as if God selected them from among the rest of the world, to show his hatred of them ? Eccl. viii. 14. ' There is a vanity which is done upon the earth, that there be just men unto whom it happeneth according to the work of the wicked : again, there be wicked men to whom it happeneth according to the work of the righteous.' O Sirs, this has been very puzzling to those that have met with it. But, behold the harmony with scripture-examples ; as in Job's case. Eli loses his two sons at one blow, his daughter-in-law dies, and himself breaks his neck. Aaron, the saint of God, has two sons slain by fire from heaven. The apostles were set forth as appointed for death, &c. 1 Cor. iv. 9. Babylon is at ease when Zion lies in ruins. See Lam. ii. 20. But further,

(3.) How often has it been the lot of some of God's people to meet with heavy strokes from the hands of the Lord, when they have been going in the way which God himself bade them take ? That will try people to purpose that observe these things. But, blessed be God for the bible, that lets us see this is no untrodden path. Jacob has an express command to return to Canaan, Gen. xxxi. 13. But O what a train of heavy trials attend him ! Laban pursues him as a thief, Esau meets him with four hundred men to slay him, the angel puts the knuckle of his thigh out of joint, his daughter is ravished by the Shechemites, his sons murder the Shechemites, Deborah dies, and his beloved wife Rachel dies, and Reuben defiles Bilhah. It was no wonder he said, ' Few and evil have the days of the years of my life been,' Gen. xlvii. 9.

••••••••••••••

Useful lessons from the doctrine of the wise observation of Providence.

I. It may serve for lamentation. Ah! may we not say, Who is wise to observe these things? Wise observers of providence are thin sown in the world ; because there are few exercised to godliness. God has given us enough to observe in the public and in our private case. He is speaking by his providence to the land, he is speaking loudly at this day to the parish, to you and to me, and to every one in particular. But, alas! it is not observed to purpose. Graceless people are presumptuous, and will not observe ; and even many godly are heedless, and do not observe. There are these six evidences that this wise observation of providence is very rare.

1. How many are there who see God no more in their mercies and crosses than if they were a parcel of atheists, that did not think there were a God, or that believed no providence at all? If they get a mercy, God is not owned in it ; they sacrifice to their own net. If they get a cross, they cry out by reason of the arm of the Almighty. But none saith, Where is God my Maker? In all the turns of their life and lot, they never seriously look to the wheel within the wheel.

2. How many are there to whom God in his providence is speaking plain language, that he who runs may read it, yet they will not understand it? Psal. lxxxii. 5. ' They know not, neither will they understand ; they walk on in darkness : all the foundations of the earth are out of course.' . God plagues the Philistines for the ark most visibly, yet they are at a loss, saying, It may be it is a chance. Balaam's ass refuses to carry him forward on the way, but he

is in a rage against her.   God meets sinners in their
way with speaking providences ; but on they go ;
they do not hear, they will not be stopped.   Like the
dog, they snarl at the stone, but look not to the hand
that threw it.

3. How few are exercised to know the design of
providences that they meet with ? Many signal mercies they meet with, but put not the question, What
is God saying to me by these things ? Many a heavy
dispensation they meet with, partly by the rod's hanging over their heads, partly by its lying on them ;
yet they never seriously take up Job's exercise, chap.
x. 2. ' I will say unto God, Do not condemn me ;
show me wherefore thou contendest with me.'   These
things let them come and go, with as little concern
to know the design of them, as if they had none.

4. How few are exercised to comply with the design of providences, to accommodate themselves to
the divine dispensations ? Job xxxiii. 13, 14. ' Why
dost thou strive against him ? for he giveth not account of any of his matters.   For God speaketh once,
yea twice, yet man perceiveth it not.'   If men were
wise observers of providence, it would be their constant practice to be answering the several calls thereof, still facing about towards it, as the shadow on the
dial to the body of the sun : Psal. xxvii. 8. ' When
thou saidst, Seek ye my face ; my heart said unto
thee, Thy face, Lord, will I seek.'   But, alas ! men
meet with humbling providences, but they are not
exercised to mortify their pride : they meet with
awakening providences, yet they are not exercised
to rouse up themselves to their duty : they meet with
afflicting providences in worldly things, yet they are
not exercised to get their hearts weaned from the
world : they meet with reproving providences, yet
they are not exercised to repent and mourn over the
sins thereby pointed out.   But they really strive with
their Maker, and, while he draws by his providence,
they hold fast, and will not let it go, Jer. vi. 29.

5. The little skill that people have in judging of providences. A man will readily have skill in his own trade ; but it is no wonder to see people unacquainted with things in which their business does not lie. O what commentaries on providence are in the world, that destroy the text! How miserably is the doctrine of particular dispensations perverted! Despisers of God and his ordinances are very easy ; and therefore the world concludes, ' it is vain to serve God, and that there is no profit in keeping his ordinances,' Mal. iii. 14. ' The proud are called happy,' ver. 15. They are best that have least to do with them. Good men meet with signal strokes : the world concludes that they are hypocrites, and they must be guilty of some heinous wickedness beyond other people, Job v. 1. Luke xiii. 1, 2. And a thousand such blunders there are.

6. They rank poverty in respect of Christian experience found among professors. What a learned Egyptian said to a Greek, may be said to many in whom there is some good thing towards the God of Israel. Ye professors are ever children, 2 Cor. iii. 1. Heb. v. 12. And what is the reason, but that we have never yet fallen close to the study of observing of providences ? See the text. There is a daily market in providence, but ye do not trade in it ; and therefore ye are always poor. There is perhaps a lesson put in your hands this day, that ye had several years since, but ye did not learn it ; and so it is now as great a mystery to you as then.

Important instructions concerning Providence.

1. The design of Providence may sometimes lie very hid ; and therefore it is good to wait, and not be rash, Psal. lxxvii. 19.

2. Sometimes Providence seems to forget the promise ; but it is not so, but only the time of the promise is not then come, Gen. xv. 4. with xvi. 2.

3. Sometimes Providence seems to go quite cross to the promise, and his work to go contrary to his word. But wait ye, they will assuredly meet, Gen. xxii.

4. Ofttimes Providence favours a design, which yet will be blasted in the end, for that it was not the purpose of God, Jonah i. 3.

5. Ofttimes Providence will run counter in appearance to the real design, and, by a tract of dispensations, will seem to cross it more and more, till the grave-stone appear to be laid on it. And yet ' at evening-time it shall be light,' Zech. xiv. 7.

6. Providence many times lays aside the most likely means, and brings about his work by that which nothing is expected of, 2 Kings v. 11, 12.

Lastly, Sometimes Providence works by contraries, as the blind man was cured with laying clay on his eyes.

Learn to live by faith, and be frequent in meditation and self-examination, and be much in prayer.*

* " To suppose that events fall out by chance, without any particular care or superintendency exercised over them by the great Creator, is to reject the doctrine of a Divine providence. The belief of a God infers the doctrine of a providence. The Almighty cannot be an indifferent spectator of the affairs of that world to which he has given being. His goodness must as certainly engage him to manage and direct them, as his wisdom and power must enable him to do it, in the most effectual manner possible. That supreme intelligence and love which are present to all things, must govern all. A God without a providence, doubtless implies a contradiction. It is foolish to imagine that mean and insignificant creatures are beneath the attention of the Most High. If it was not unworthy of him to bring them on the stage of existence, it cannot be unworthy of him to preside over them, and take care of their concerns. That adorable Being who formed the universe at first, is every where present in it ; to it he is most nearly, and with it, in all its parts, he has the most constant and active concern."

Jones' Biblical Cyclopædia.

Eph. i. 3, 4, 5, *Explained.*

" Blessed be the God and Father of our Lord Jesus Christ, who hath blessed us with all spiritual blessings in heavenly places in Christ ; According as he hath chosen us in him before the foundation of the world, that we should be holy and without blame before him in love : Having predestinated us unto the adoption of children by Jesus Christ to himself, according to the good pleasure of his will."

In these verses we have—

1. A party brought out of their natural state into a state of salvation, ver 3.—*Who hath blessed us with all spiritual blessings in heavenly places.* For whereas by nature they were under the curse, now they are blessed, and that plentifully, with all blessings, not temporal only, but spiritual and heavenly, coming from heaven, and to be consummated there.

2. The person by whom they are brought into this state. It is by the Redeemer, as the purchaser. God the Father bestows them, as the Father of Christ, viz. for his sake. And they are blessed *in Christ,* upon the account of his merit, and coming from him as their Head.

3. Who those are whom God brings out of their natural state into a state of grace ; the elect, ver. 4, 5. *According as he hath chosen us in him,* &c. Where consider,

(1.) Election itself, *he hath chosen us,* separated us from others in his purpose and decree, selected us from among the rest of mankind, whom he passed by and left to perish in their natural state.

(2.) That to which they are elected : that is, to salvation, and the means leading thereto. The means are, sanctification, *that we should be holy, and without blame before him in love ;* and adoption, ver. 5.

that whereas they are by nature children of the devil, they should be children of God. The end is everlasting life in heaven ; for that is imported in adoption, Rom. viii. 23. as the inheritance of the children of God.

(3.) Through whom this decree is to be executed, *in him ;* that is, Christ, whom the Father chose to be the head of the elect, through whom he would save them.

(4.) When God elected them, *before the foundation of the world,* ere they were created ; that is, from eternity ; as appears from what our Lord says to his Father, John xvii. 24. ' Thou lovedst me before the foundation of the world ;' which can denote nothing else than from eternity.

(5.) That which moved him to elect them, *according to the mere good pleasure of his will ;* that is, his mere good pleasure, so he would do it ; and there was nothing without himself to move him thereto.

What sinners of mankind are chosen to.

1. They are chosen to be partakers of everlasting life. Hence the scripture speaks of some being ' ordained to eternal life,' Acts xiii. 48. and of ' appointing them to obtain salvation,' 1 Thess. v. 9. God appoints some to be rich, great, and honourable, some to be low and mean in the world ; and others to be in a middle station, objects neither of envy nor contempt ; but electing love appoints those on whom it falls to be saved from sin, and all the ruins of the fall ; its great view is to eternal glory in heaven. To this they were appointed before they had a being.

2. They are chosen also to grace as the mean, as well as to glory as the end. God's predestinating of them to eternal blessedness, includes both, as in the

text ; ánd it further appears from 2 Thess. ii. 13.
' God hath from the beginning chosen you to salvation through sanctification of the Spirit and belief of
the truth.' Hence faith is held out as a certain consequent of election, Acts xiii. 48. ' As many as weie
ordained unto eternal life believed.' The man who
intends to dwell in a house yet unbuilt, intends also
the means by which it may be made a fit habitation.
So God having from eternity pitched on a select
number of the ruined race of mankind as objects of
his love, and having predestinated them to everlasting life, intended also the means necessary and proper
for obtaining that glorious end. And therefore there
is no ground from the decree of election to slight the
means of salvation. God has so joined the end and
the means, that none can put them asunder.

****

The glorious properties of God's election of sinners.

1. It is altogether free, without any moving cause,
but God's mere good pleasure. No reason can be
found for this but only in the bosom of God. There
is nothing before, or above, or without his purpose,
that can be pitched upon as the cause of all that
grace and goodness that he bestows upon his chosen
ones. There was no merit or motive in them, as
Christ told his disciples, John xv. 16. ' Ye have not
chosen me, but I have chosen you.' His choice is
antecedent to ours. The persons who are singled
out to be the objects of his special grace, were a part
of lost mankind, the same by nature with others who
were passed by, and left to perish in their sin. When
God had all Adam's numerous progeny under the
view of his all-seeing eye, he chose some, and passed
by others. He found nothing in the creature to cast
the balance of his choice, or to determine it to one

more than another. Those that were rejected, were
as eligible as those that were chosen. They were
all his creatures, and all alike obnoxious to his wrath
by sin. It was grace alone that made the difference.
So the prophet argues, Mal. i. 2, 3. ' I have loved
you, saith the Lord : yet ye say, wherein hast thou
loved us ? was not Esau Jacob's brother ? saith the
Lord : yet I loved Jacob, and I hated Esau.' And
this is abundantly clear in the text. Why doth God
write some men's names in the book of life, and
leave out others ? why doth he enrol some whom he
intends to make citizens of Zion, and heirs of immortal glory, and refuse to put others in his register?
The text tells us, it is the *good pleasure of his will*.

You may, says an eminent divine, render a reason
for many of God's actions, till you come to this, which
is the top and foundation of all ; and this act can be
reduced to no other head of reason, but that of his
royal prerogative. If you inquire, why doth God
save some, and condemn others at last ? the reason
is, because of the faith of the one, and the unbelief
of the other. But why do some men believe ? It is
because God hath not only given them the means of
grace, but accompanied these means with the power
and efficacy of the Spirit. But why did God accompany these means with the efficacy of his Spirit
in some, and not in others ? It is because he decreed by his grace to prepare them for glory. But
why did he decree and choose some to glory, and not
others ? Into what can you resolve this, but only
into his sovereign pleasure ? Salvation and damnation at the last upshot are acts of God as the righteous Judge and Governor of the world, giving life
and eternal happiness to believers, and inflicting
death and eternal misery upon unbelievers, conformable to his own law. Men may render a reason for
these proceedings. But the choice of some, and the
preterition of others, is an act of God as he is a sovereign monarch, before any law was actually trans-

gressed, because not actually given. What reason can be given for his advancing one part of matter to the noble dignity of a star, and leaving another part to make up the dark body of the earth ? to compact one part into a glorious sun, and another part into a hard rock, but his royal prerogative ? What is the reason that a prince subjects one malefactor to condign punishment, and lifts up another to a place of profit and trust ? It is merely because he will, Rom. ix. 18. ' Therefore hath he mercy on whom he will have mercy, and whom he will he hardeneth.' Hence we may infer,

(1.) That God did not choose men to everlasting life and happiness for any moral perfection that he saw in them ; because he converts those, and changes them by his grace, who are most sinful and profligate, as the Gentiles, who were soaked in idolatry and superstition. He found more faith among the Romans, who were Pagan idolaters, than among the Jews, who were the peculiar people of God, and to whom his heavenly oracles were committed. He planted a saintship at Corinth, a place notorious for the infamous worship of Venus, a superstition attended with the grossest uncleanness ; and at Ephesus, that presented the world with a cup of fornication in the temple of Diana. And what character had the Cretians from one of their own poets, mentioned by the apostle in his epistle to Titus, whom he had placed among them to further the progress of the gospel, but the vilest and most abominable ? liars, and not to be credited ; evil beasts, not to be associated with ; slow bellies, fit for no service. Now, what merit and attractive was here ? What invitements could he have from lying, beastliness, and gluttony, but only from his own sovereignty ? By this he plucked firebrands out of the burning, while he left straiter and more comely sticks to consume to ashes.

(2.) God doth not choose men to grace and glory for any civil perfection that is in them ; because he

calls and renews the most despicable. He doth not
elevate nature to grace on account of wealth or honour, or any civil stations and dignities in the world,
1 Cor. i. 26. ' For ye see your calling, brethren, how
that not many wise men after the flesh, not many
mighty, not many noble, are called.' A purple robe
is very seldom decked and adorned with the jewel of
grace. He takes more of the mouldy clay, than of
refined dust, to cast into his image, and lodges his
treasures more in the earthly vessels, than in the
world's golden ones. Should God impart his grace
most to those who abound in wealth and honour, it
had laid a foundation for men to think, that he had
been moved by those vulgarly esteemed excellencies,
and to indulge them more than others. But such a
conceit languisheth, and falls to the ground, when we
behold the subjects of divine grace as void originally
of any allurements as they are full of provocations.

(3.) Their foreseen faith and good works, or perseverance in either of them, are not the cause of e-
lection ; because these are the fruits and effects, and
therefore cannot be the causes of election, Rom.
viii. 29. ' For whom he did foreknow, he also did predestinate to be conformed to the image of his Son.'
Acts xiii. 48. ' And when the Gentiles heard this,
they were glad, and glorified the word of the
Lord : and as many as were ordained to eternal
life believed.' It is clear also from this text, where
it is said, they are chosen to be holy, and to adoption, and therefore to faith, by which we obtain
it, John i. 12. God did not choose and eiect men
to grace and glory because they were holy, or because he did foresee that they would be so, but that
he might purify and make them holy. And let it be
observed, that the scripture attributes election only
to God's good pleasure, Rom. ix. 11. 13. 16. ' (For
the children being not yet born, neither having done
any good or evil, that the purpose of God according
to election might stand, not of works, but of him that

calleth.) As it is written, Jacob have I loved, but
Esau have I hated. So then it is not of him that
willeth, nor of him that runneth, but of God that
sheweth mercy.' Matt. xi. 25. ' At that time Jesus
answered and said, I thank thee, O Father, Lord of
heaven and earth, because thou hast hid these things
from the wise and prudent, and hast revealed them
unto babes.' And indeed, if it depended on foreseen
faith or good works, we should rather be said to
choose God than he to choose us.

(4.) God did not choose some to life and happiness, because he was under any obligation to do so.
He is indebted to none, and he is disobliged by all.
He was under no tie to pity man's misery, and repair the ruins of the fall. He owes no more debt to
fallen man than to fallen angels, to restore them to
their first station by a superlative grace. God as a
sovereign gave laws to man, and strength sufficient
to observe them. Now, what obligation is upon God
to repair that strength which man hath wilfully lost,
and to pull him out of that miserable pit into which
he had voluntarily plunged himself? None at all. So
then there was nothing in the elect more than others
to move God to choose them either to grace or glory.
It was, and must be, the gracious issue and result
of his sovereign will and mere good pleasure.

2. Election is eternal. They are elected from all
eternity, Eph. i. 4. *chosen before the foundation of
the world,* 2 Tim. i 9. ' He hath saved us, and called us with an holy calling, not according to our
works, but according to his own purpose and grace
which was given us in Christ Jesus before the world
began.' All God's decrees are eternal, Eph. i. 11.
' We are predestinated according to the purpose of
him who worketh all things after the counsel of his
own will. God takes no new counsels, to do which
would be inconsistent with his infinite perfection.
Because God is eternal, his purposes must be of equal
duration with his existence. And to imagine that an

infinitely wise and sovereign Being existed from eternity, without any forethought, or resolution what to do, would be to suppose him to be undetermined or unresolved, at the time of his giving being to all things. And to suppose that the divine will is capable of new determinations, is to argue him to be imperfect; which would be as much an instance of mutability in him, as for him to alter his purpose. Election to everlasting life must therefore be eternal.

3. It is particular and definite. God has chosen a certain number of the children of men to life, whom he knows by name, so as they can neither be more nor fewer. Hence their names are said to be written in the book of life, Luke x. 20. ' Notwithstanding, in this rejoice not that the spirits are subject unto you ; but rather rejoice, because your names are written in heaven.' Phil. iv. 3. ' And I entreat thee also, true yokefellow, help those women which laboured with me in the gospel, with Clement also, and with other my fellow-labourers, whose names are in the book of life;' and others are said not to be written there, Rev. xvii. 8. Though they are known to none, yet God knows them all, 2 Tim. ii. 19. ' Nevertheless the foundation of God standeth sure, having this seal, The Lord knoweth them that are his. And, Let every one that nameth the name of Christ depart from iniquity.' And they are given to Christ, John xvii. 9. ' I pray for them : I pray not for the world, but for them which thou hast given me ; for they are thine.' Therefore God's decree of election is not a general decree only to save all who shall believe and persevere in the faith ; for that way it might happen that none at all might be saved.

4. It is secret, or cannot be known, till God be pleased to discover it. Hence it is called ' the mystery of his will,' Eph. i. 9. as being hid in God from before the foundation of the world, and would for

ever have been so, had he not discovered it in his word.

It is unchangeable.   Mutability is an imperfection peculiar to creatures.   As the least change in God's understanding, so as to know more or less than that hid from eternity, would be an instance of imperfection ; the same must be said with respect to his holy will, which cannot be susceptible of new determinations.   Though there are many changes in the external dispensations of his providence, which are the result of his will, as well as the effects of his power ; yet there is no shadow of change in his purpose. No unforeseen occurrence can render it expedient for God to change his mind, nor can any higher power oblige him to do it ; nor can any defect of power to accomplish his designs, induce him to alter his purpose.   Those who are once elected can never be reprobated.   All that are elected shall most certainly be saved.   None of them can be left to perish.   For all the divine purposes are unchangeable, and must be fulfilled, Isa. xlvi. 10. ; and this in particular, 2 Tim. ii. 19.   Election is the foundation of God's house, laid by his own hand, which cannot be shaken, but stands sure ; and a sealed foundation, as men seal what they will have ; a seal of two parts securing it ; on God's part, God loves and keeps them that are his, that they fall not away ; on our part, the same God takes care that his elect depart from iniquity.   It is not possible they can be totally and finally deceived, Matt. xxiv. 24. and whom God has chosen he glorifies, Rom. viii. 29, 30. When we are bid make our election sure, it is meant of certainty and assurance as to our knowledge of it, and by no means of God's purpose.

....

By whom God's chosen are redeemed and saved.

It is by Christ. He is the Redeemer of God's
elect. Hence the apostle says, Tit. iii. 4, 5, 6. ' After that the kindness and love of God our Saviour
toward man appeared, not by works of righteousness
which we have done, but according to his mercy he
saved us, by the washing of regeneration, and renewing of the Holy Ghost ; which he shed on us abundantly, through Jesus Christ our Saviour.' There is
no other way of salvation but by him, Acts iv. 12.
' Neither is there salvation in any other : for there
is none other name under heaven given among men
whereby we must be saved,' By him is all grace and
glory purchased, and by his satisfaction there is a
way opened for the venting of mercy with the good
leave of justice. More particularly,

1. Before the elect could be delivered from that
state of sin and misery into which they had brought
themselves, a valuable satisfaction behoved to be
given to the justice of God for the injury done by
sin. It is evident from scripture, that God stood
upon full satisfaction, and would not remit one sin
without it. Several things plead strongly for this :
As,

(1.) The infinite purity and holiness of God. There
is a contrariety in sin to the holiness of his nature,
which is his peculiar glory ; and from thence his
hatred of it doth arise, which is as essential to him
as his love to himself. The infinite purity and rectitude of his nature infers the most perfect abhorrence
of whatever is opposite to it. Hence says the Psalmist, Psal. v. 4, 5. ' Thou art not a God that hath
pleasure in wickedness : neither shall evil dwell with
thee. The foolish shall not stand in thy sight : thou

hatest all workers of iniquity.' God cannot but hate all the workers of iniquity, and he cannot but punish them. His holiness is not only voluntary, but by necessity of nature. He is of purer eyes than to behold evil, and cannot look on iniquity.

(2.) The justice of God pleads for a valuable satisfaction for sin. And here we are not to consider God as a private person wronged, but as the righteous Judge and Governor of the world, and the sovereign Protector of those sacred laws by which the reasonable creature is to be directed. Now, as it was most reasonable and convenient, that at the first giving of the law he should lay the strongest restraint upon man for preventing sin by the threatening of death ; so it was most just and congruous, when the law was broken by man's rebellion, that the penalty should be inflicted either upon the person of the offender, according to the immediate intent of the law, or that satisfaction equivalent to the offence should be made, that the majesty and purity of God might appear in his justice. He is the Judge of all the earth, and cannot but do right.

(3.) The wisdom of God, by which he governs the rational world, admits not of a dispensation or relaxation of the threatening without a valuable satisfaction. For it is as good to have no king as no laws for government, and as good to have no law as no penalty, and as good that no penalty be annexed to the law as no execution of it. Hence, says a learned divine, It is altogether indecent, especially to the wisdom and righteousness of God, that that which provoketh the execution of the law, should procure the abrogation of it as that should supplant and undermine the law, for the alone prevention of which the law was made. How could it be expected, that men should fear and tremble before God, when they should find themselves more scared than hurt by his threatenings against sin ?

(4.) The truth and veracity of God required a satisfaction for sin. The word had gone out of God's mouth, ' In the day that thou eatest thereof, thou shalt surely die ; ' and again it is said, ' Cursed is every one that continueth not in all things which are written in the book of the law to do them.' Now, this sentence was immutable, and the word that had gone out of his mouth must stand. Had God violated his truth by dispensing with the punishment threatened, he had rendered himself an unfit object of trust ; he had exposed all the promises or threatenings which he should have made after man's impunity, to the mockery and contempt of the offender, and excluded his word from any credit with man for the future. And therefore God's word could not fall to the ground without an accomplishment. Heaven and earth shall pass away, but his word shall stand firm. He will be true to his threatenings, though thousands and millions should perish.

2. As satisfaction to justice was necessary, and that which God insisted upon, so the elect could not give it themselves, neither was there any creature in heaven or earth that could do it for them. Heaven and earth were at an infinite loss to find out a ransom for their souls. We may apply to this purpose what we have, Isa. lxiii. 5. ' I looked, and there was none to help ; and I wondered that there was none to uphold.' This is the desperate and forlorn condition of the elect by nature as well as others.

3. God pitched upon Christ in his infinite grace and wisdom as the fittest person for managing this grand design. Hence it is said, ' I have laid help upon one that is mighty.' And the apostle saith, he ' hath set him forth to be a propitiation for sin.' On this account he is called ' his servant whom he hath chosen, and his elect in whom his soul delighteth.' God speaks to them, as Job xxxiii. 24. ' Deliver him from going down to the pit ; I have found a ransom.'

4. Christ accepted the office of a Redeemer, and engaged to make his soul an offering for sin. He

cheerfully undertook this work in that eternal transaction that was between the Father and him. He
was content to stand in the elect's room, and to submit himself to the terrible strokes of vindictive justice.   He is brought in by the Psalmist offering himself as a Surety in their stead, Psal. xl. 6, 7. ' Sacrifice and offering thou didst not desire, &c.   Then
said I, Lo, I come,' &c.   He willingly yielded to all
the conditions requisite for the accomplishment of
our redemption.   He was content to take a body,
that he might be capable to suffer.   The debt could
not be paid, nor the articles of the covenant performed, but in the human nature.   He was therefore to
have a nature capable of and prepared for sufferings.
Hence it is said, Heb. x. 5. ' Sacrifice and offering
thou wouldst not ; but a body hast thou prepared
me.'   It behoved him to have a body to suffer that
which was represented by these legal sacrifices wherein God took no pleasure.   And he took a body of
flesh, surrounded with the infirmities of our fallen
nature, sin only excepted.   He condescended to lay
aside the robes of his glory, to make himself of no
reputation, to take upon him the form of a servant,
and be found in the likeness of men.

    5. Christ satisfied offended justice in the room of
the elect, and purchased eternal redemption for them.
' He became obedient unto death, even the death of
the cross,' Phil. ii. 8.   This was the prime article in
the covenant of grace, ' When he shall make his
soul an offering for sin, he shall see his seed,' Isa.
liii. 10.   God required this sacrifice exclusive of all
others in the first treaty.   ' Sacrifice and burnt-offerings thou wouldst not; in them thou hadst no pleasure : then said I, Lo, I come,' &c.   These sacrifices
were entirely useless for the satisfaction of justice,
though fit to prefigure the grand sacrifice that God intended.   It was by the death of Christ alone that redemption was purchased for men : Rom. v. 10. ' For if,
when we were enemies, we were reconciled to God by

the death of his son ; much more, being reconciled, we shall be saved by his life.' Eph. ii. 13. ' But now, in Christ Jesus, ye who sometimes were far off are made nigh by the blood of Christ.' Col. i. 21. ' And you, that were sometime alienated, and enemies in your mind by wicked works, yet now hath he reconciled.' And when he was upon the cross, he cried, ' It is finished ; ' that is, the work of redemption is accomplished ; I have done all that was appointed for me to do ; the articles on my part are now fulfilled ; there remain no more deaths for me to suffer.

Thus the elect are saved by the Lord Jesus Christ.

****

Useful lessons from the doctrine of God's election.

1. Behold here the freedom and glory of sovereign grace, which is the sole cause why God did not leave all mankind to perish in the state of sin and misery, as he did the fallen angels. He was no more obliged to the one than the other. Why did he choose any of the fallen race of men to grace and glory? It was his mere good pleasure to pitch on some, and pass by others. He could have been without them all, without any spot either on his happiness or justice ; but out of his mere good pleasure he pitched his love on a select number, in whom he will display the invincible efficacy of his sovereign grace, and thereby bring them to the fruition of glory. This proceeds from his absolute sovereignty. Justice or injustice comes not into consideration here. If he had pleased, he might have made all the objects of his love ; and if he had pleased, he might have chosen none, but have suffered Adam and all his numerous offspring to sink eternally into the pit of perdition. It was in his supreme power to have left all mankind under the rack of his justice ; and, by the same right of

dominion, he may pick out some men from the common mass, and lay aside others to bear the punishment of their crimes. There is no cause in the creature, but all in God. It must be resolved into his sovereign will. So it is said, Rom. ix. 15, 16. He saith to Moses, ' I will have mercy on whom I will have mercy, and I will have compassion on whom I will have compassion.' So then, it is not of him that willeth, nor of him that runneth, but of God that showeth mercy.' And yet, God did not will without wisdom. He did not choose hand over head, and act by mere will without reason and understanding. An infinite wisdom is far from such a kind of procedure. But the reason of God's proceedings is inscrutable to us, unless we could understand God as well as he understands himself. The rays of his infinite wisdom are too bright and dazzling for our weak and shallow capacities. The apostle acknowledges not only a wisdom in his proceeding, but riches and a treasure of wisdom ; and not only that, but a depth and vastness of these riches of wisdom ; but was wholly incapable to give a scheme and inventory of it. Hence he cries out, Rom. xi. 33. ' O the depth of the riches both of the wisdom and knowledge of God ! how unsearchable are his judgments, and his ways past finding out ! ' Let us humbly adore the divine sovereignty. We should cast ourselves down at God's feet, with a full resignation of ourselves to his sovereign pleasure. This is a more becoming carriage in a Christian, than contentious endeavours to measure God by our line.

2. This doctrine should stop men's murmurings, and silence all their pleadings with or against God. O what strivings are there sometimes in the hearts of men about God's absolute sovereignty in electing some and rejecting others ? The apostle insists much upon this in Rom. ix. where, having represented the Lord speaking thus by Moses, ver. 15. ' I will have mercy on whom I will have mercy, and I will have

compassion on whom I will have compassion ; ' he presently prevents an objection, or the strife of man with God about that saying, ver. 19. ' Thou wilt say then unto me, Why doth he yet find fault, for who hath resisted his will ? ' This is man's plea against the sovereign will of God. But what saith the Lord by the apostle to such a pleader ? We have his reproof of him for an answer in ver. 20. ' Nay, but, O man, who art thou that repliest against God ? shall the thing formed say unto him that formed it, ' Why hast thou made me thus ? ' The apostle brings in this argument as to man's eternal state, He must not strive with God about that. He must not say, Why doth God find fault with man ? His absolute power is his reason why he disposeth thus or thus of thee, or any other man. He will give thee no account why it is so ; but his own will to have it so. He may choose some for the glory of his rich, free, and sovereign grace, and leave others to perish in their sins, for the glory of his power and justice. This should stop men's mouths, and make them sit down quietly under all God's dealings.

3. This is ground of humility and admiration to the elect of God, and lets them see to what they owe the difference that is between them and others, even to free grace. Those who are passed by were as eligible as those that were chosen. Though God hath dignified them, and raised them to be heirs of glory, yet they were heirs of wrath, and no better than others by nature, Eph. ii. 3. Well may they say with David in another case, ' Lord, what am I, or what is my father's house, that thou hast brought me hitherto ? ' All were in the same corrupt mass, and nothing but free grace made the difference between the elected and the non-elected.

4. Then the elect shall not persist in their infidelity and natural state, but shall all be effectually called and brought in to Christ. Whatever good things God hath purposed for them shall surely be

3 A

conferred upon, and wrought in them, by the irresistible efficacy of his powerful grace. God's counsel shall stand, and he will do all his pleasure.

5. Then people may know that they are elected. Hence is that exhortation, 2 Pet. i. 10. ' Give diligence to make your calling and election sure.' Though we cannot break in at the first hand upon the secrets of God, yet if we do believe in the Lord Jesus Christ, receive him as our only Saviour, and submit to him as our Lord and Sovereign, we may know that we are elected, seeing the elect and they only are brought to believe. Others may be elected, but they cannot know it till they actually believe.

6. The Lord will never cast off his elect people. He that chose them from eternity, while he saw no good in them, will not afterwards cast them off. God's decree of election is the best security they can have for life and salvation, and a foundation that standeth absolutely sure. Whatever faults and follies they may be guilty of, yet the Lord will never cast them off. They shall be kept by the power of God through faith unto salvation.

Lastly, This doctrine may teach us to form our judgment aright concerning the success of the gospel. The gospel and the ministrations thereof are designed for the bringing in of God's chosen ones. All never did nor ever will believe : but one thing is sure, that all who are ordained to eternal life shall believe and obey the gospel, Rom. xi. 7. ' What then ? Israel hath not obtained that which he seeketh for ; but the election hath obtained it, and the rest were blinded.'

GENESIS ii. 17. *Explained.*

" But of the tree of the knowledge of good and evil, thou shalt
not eat of it : for in the day that thou eatest thereof thou shalt
surely die."

In which words we have account of the original
transaction between God and our first father Adam,
in paradise, while yet in the state of primitive integrity. In which the following things are to be remarked, being partly expressed and partly implied.

1. The Lord's making over to him a benefit by
way of a conditional promise, which made the benefit a debt upon the performing of the condition. This
promise is a promise of life, and is included in the
threatening of death, thus : If thou eat not of the tree
of the knowledge, &c. thou shalt live ; even as in the
sixth commandment, ' Thou shalt not kill,' is plainly implied, Thou shalt preserve thy own life, and the
life of others. And thus it is explained by Moses,
Rom. x. 5. ' The man which doth those things shall
live by them.' Besides, the licence given him to eat
of all the other trees, and so of the tree of life, which
had a sacramental use, imports this promise.

2. The condition required to entitle him to this
benefit ; namely, obedience. It is expressed in a prohibition of one particular, ' Of the tree of the knowledge of good and evil, thou shalt not eat of it.' There
was a twofold law given to Adam ; the natural law,
which was concreated with him, engraven on his
heart in his creation. For it is said, Gen. i. 27.
' That God created man in his own image ;' compared with Eph. iv. 24. ' That ye put on the new man,
which after God is created in righteousness and true
holiness.' This law was afterwards promulgated on
mount Sinai, being much obliterated by sin. An-

other law was the symbolical law, mentioned in the text, which, not being known by nature's light, was revealed to Adam, probably by an audible voice. By this God chose to try, and by an external action exemplify his obedience to the natural law concreated with him. And this being a thing in its own nature altogether indifferent, the binding of it upon him by the mere will of the divine Lawgiver, did clearly import the more strong tie of the natural law upon him in all the parts of him. Thus perfect obedience was the condition of this covenant.

3. The sanction, or penalty in case of the breach of the covenant : ' In the day that thou eatest thereof, thou shalt surely die.' For if death was entailed on a doing of that which was only evil, because it was forbidden ; much more might Adam understand it to be entailed on his doing of any thing forbidden, because evil, or contrary to the nature or will of God, the knowledge of which was impressed on his mind in his creation. The sanction is plainly expressed, not the promise ; because the last was plainly enough signified to him in the tree of life, and he had ample discoveries of God's goodness and bounty, but none of his justice, at least to himself. And it does not appear that the angels were yet fallen ; or if they were, that Adam knew of it.

4. Adam's going into the proposal, and acceptance of those terms, is sufficiently intimated to us by his objecting nothing against it. Thus the Spirit of God teaches us Jonah's repentance, and yielding at length to the Lord, after a long struggle, ch. iv. 11. ; as also Adam's own going into the covenant of grace, Gen. iii. 15. Besides, his knowledge could not but represent to him how beneficial a treaty this was ; his upright will could not but comply with what a bountiful God laid on him ; and he, by virtue of that treaty, claimed the privilege of eating of the other trees, and so of the tree of life, as appears from Eve's words, Gen. iii. 3. ' But of the fruit of the tree which

is in the midst of the garden, God hath said, Ye shall not eat of it, neither shall ye touch it, lest ye die.

Now, it is true, we have not here the word *covenant ;* yet we must not hence infer, that there is no covenant in this passage, more than we may deny the doctrine of the Trinity and sacraments, because those words do not occur where these things are treated of in scripture, nay, are not to be found in the scripture at all. But as in those cases, so here we have the thing ; for the making over of a benefit to one, upon a condition, with a penalty, gone into by the party it is proposed to, is a covenant, a proper covenant, call it as you will.*

Evidences of a Covenant of Works between God and the first man Adam.

1. Here is a concurrence of all that is necessary to constitute a true and proper covenant of works : The parties contracting, God and man ; God requiring obedience as the condition of life ; a penalty fixed in case of breaking ; and man acquiescing in the proposal. The force of this cannot be evaded, by comparing it with the consent of subjects to the laws of an absolute prince. For such a law proposed by a

---

* " The very conscience of man dictates, that this covenant is in all its parts highly equitable. For what can be conceived, even by thought, more reasonable than that man esteeming God as his chief good, should seek to be delighted in him, and rejoice at the offer of that good ? That he should readily receive the law, which is a transcript or copy of the divine holiness, as the rule of his nature and actions ? In fine, that he should submit his guilty head to the most just vengeance of the Deity, if he should happen to make light of this promise, and violate the law ? From which it follows that man was not at liberty to reject God's covenant."

Witsius' Œcon. of the Covenants.

prince, promising a reward upon obedience to it, is indeed the promising of a covenant, the which the subject consenting to for himself and his, and taking on him to obey, does indeed enter into a covenant with the prince, and having obeyed the law, may claim the reward by virtue of paction. And so the covenant of works is ordinarily in scripture called *the law*, being in its own nature a pactional law.

2. It is expressly called a covenant in scripture, Gal. iv. 24. 'For these are the two covenants, the one from the mount Sinai,' &c. This covenant from mount Sinai was the covenant of works, as being opposed to the covenant of grace, namely, the law of the ten commandments, with promise and sanction, as before expressed. At Sinai it was renewed indeed, but that was not its first appearance in the world. For there being but two ways of life to be found in scripture, one by works, the other by grace ; the latter hath no place, but where the first is rendered ineffectual : therefore the covenant of works was before the covenant of grace in the world ; yet the covenant of grace was promulgated quickly after Adam's fall ; therefore the covenant of works behoved to have been made with him before. And how can one imagine a covenant of works set before poor impotent sinners, if there had not been such a covenant with man in his state of integrity ? Hos. vi. 7. ' But as for them ; like Adam, they have transgressed the covenant.' Our translators set the word *Adam* on the margin. But in Job xxxi. 33. they translate the very same word, *as Adam*. This word occurs but three times in scripture, and still in the same sense, Job xxxi. 33. ' If I covered my transgressions, as Adam.' Psal. lxxxii. 7. ' But ye shall die like Adam.' Compare ver. 6. ' I have said, Ye are gods ; and all of you are children of the Most High ;' compared with Luke iii. 38. ' Adam, which was the son of God.' And also here, Hos. vi. 7. While Adam's hiding his sin, and his death are

made an example, how natural is it that his transgression, that led the way to all, be made so too?
This is the proper and literal sense of the words : it
is so read by several, and is certainly the meaning
of it.

3. We find a law of works opposed to the law of
faith, Rom. iii. 27. ' Where is boasting then? It is
excluded. By what law? of works? Nay; but by
the law of faith.' This law of works is the covenant
of works, requiring works, or obedience, as the condition pleadable for life; for otherwise the law as a
rule of life requires works too. Again, it is a law
that does not exclude boasting, which is the very nature of the covenant of works, that makes the reward to be of debt. And further, the law of faith is
the covenant of grace; therefore the law of works is
the covenant of works. So Rom. vi. 14. ' Ye are
not under the law, but under grace.' And this was
the way of life, without question, which was given
to Adam at first.

4. There were sacramental signs and seals of this
transaction in paradise. As it has pleased the Lord
still to deal with man in the way of a covenant, so
to append seals to these covenants. God's covenant
with Noah, that he would not destroy the earth again
with water, had the rainbow as a sign of it to confirm it, Gen. ix. 12, 13. ' And God said, This is the
token of the covenant which I make between me and
you, and every living creature that is with you, for
perpetual generations : I do set my bow in the cloud,
and it shall be for a token of a covenant between me
and the earth.' The covenant with Abraham had
circumcision ; that with the Israelites, circumcision
and the passover ; and the new covenant with the
New Testament church, baptism and the Lord's
supper. So to the covenant of works God appended
the two trees ; the tree of life, Gen. iii. 22. ' And now
lest he put forth his hand, and take also of the tree
of life, and eat, and live for ever ;' and the tree of the

knowledge of good and evil, mentioned in the words of the text. When we find, then, confirming seals of this transaction, we must own it to be a covenant.

Lastly, All mankind are by nature under the guilt of Adam's first sin, Rom. v. 12. ' As by one man sin entered into the world, and death by sin, and so death passed upon all men, for that all have sinned.' And they are under the curse of the law before they have committed actual sin : hence they are said to be ' by nature children of wrath,' Eph. ii. 3. which they must needs owe to Adam's sin, as imputed to them. This must be owing to a particular relation betwixt them and him : which must either be, that he is their natural head simply, from whence they derive their natural being ; but then the sins of our immediate parents, and all other mediate ones too, behoved to be imputed rather than Adam's, because our relation to them is nearer : or because he is our federal head also, representing us in the first covenant. And that is the truth, and evidences the covenant of works made with Adam, to have been a proper covenant.*

In the Covenant of Works, Adam was constituted a public person, and the representative of all his posterity.

Adam, in the covenant of works, is to be consi-

* " And this is called a covenant of life ; as the man was thereby to be entitled to eternal life, upon a determined condition. But it is more commonly called a covenant of works ; as the man's right or title to eternal life, according to that covenant, was to lie in his works of obedience, or to depend upon this condition : Not from any natural merit of these works, but from the gracious constitution which God then made concerning them."

Gibb's Sacred Contemplations.

dered as the first man, 1 Cor. xv. 47. in whom all mankind were included. And he was,

1*st*, The natural root of mankind, from which all the generations of men on the face of the earth spring.

This is evident from Acts xvii. 26. ' God hath made of one blood all nations of men for to dwell on all the face of the earth ; ' which determines all men to be of one stock, one original, or common parentage. And this also appears from Gen. iii. 20. ' Adam called his wife's name Eve ; because she was the mother of all living ; ' which determines that to be only Adam's family. And of him was also Eve, who was not only formed for him, but of him : Gen. ii. 21, 22, 23. ' And the Lord God caused a deep sleep to fall upon Adam, and he slept : and he took one of his ribs, and closed up the flesh instead thereof. And the rib, which the Lord God had taken from man, made he a woman, and brought her unto the man. And Adam said, This is now bone of my bones, and flesh of my flesh : she shall be called Woman, because she was taken out of man.' Thus Adam was the compend of the whole world.

2*d*, The moral root, a public person, and representative of mankind. And as such, the covenant of works was made with him. As to this representation by Adam, we may note,

(1.) That the man Christ was not included in it : Adam did not represent him, as he stood covenanting with God. This is manifest, in that Christ is opposed to Adam, as the last and second Adam to the first Adam : 1 Cor. xv. 45. ' And so it is written, The first man Adam was made a living soul, the last Adam was made a quickening spirit.' One representative to another : ver. 48. ' As is the earthy, such are they also that are earthy : and as is the heavenly, such are they also that are heavenly. And if that covenant had been kept, Christ had not come, whose work it is to repair the loss by the breach of the first covenant, by establishing another

3 B

covenant for that end. Besides, Christ was not born, as all others are, by virtue of that blessing of fruitfulness, given before the fall, under the covenant of works, while it yet remained unbroken ; but by virtue of a special promise, given after the fall, which promise was the erecting of another covenant, namely, the covenant of grace, whereof Christ was the head, Gen. iii. 15.

(2.) Whether Eve was included in this representation, is not so clear. I find she is excepted by some. It is plain, that Adam was the original whence she came, as he and she together are of all their posterity. He was her head, Eph. v. 23. ' For the husband is the head of the wife.' The thread of the history, Gen. ii. gives us the making of the covenant of works with Adam, before the formation of Eve. The covenant itself runs in terms as delivered to one person, ver. 16, 17. ' Thou mayest—Thou shalt' From whence it seems to me that she was included. It is true, she fell by her own transgression : and so might any of Adam's posterity have fallen to themselves, as she did to herself, during the time of probation in this covenant ; but the ruin of mankind was not completed till he did eat. And therefore Adam is first convicted, though Eve was first in the transgression, Gen. iii. 9.

(3.) Without question, all his posterity by ordinary generation were included in it. He stood for them all in that covenant, and was their federal head, that covenant being made with him as a public person representing them all. For,

[1.] The relation which the scripture teaches betwixt Adam and Christ, evinces this. The one is called the *first Adam*, the other the *last Adam*, 1 Cor. xv. 45. ; the one the *first man*, the other the *second man*, ver. 47. Now, Christ is not the second man, but as he is a public person representing all his elect seed in the covenant of grace, being their federal head : therefore Adam was a public person representing all his natural seed in the covenant of works, being their federal head ; for if there be a second man, there must be a first man ; if a second representative, there must be a first. Again, Christ is not the last Adam, but as the federal head of the elect, bringing salvation to them by his covenant-keeping ; therefore the first Adam was the federal head of those whom he brought death upon by his covenant-breaking, and these are all, ver. 22. ' For as in Adam all die, even so in Christ shall all be made alive.' And therefore the apostle, Rom. v. 14. calls Adam a figure or type of Christ. Accordingly each of these representatives are held forth with their respective parties represented by them, being made like unto them : 1 Cor. xv. 48. ' As is the earthy, such are they also that are earthy ; and as is the heavenly, such are they also that are heavenly.'

[2.] Adam's breaking of the covenant is in law their breaking of it : it is imputed to them by a holy God, whose judgment is according to truth, and therefore can never impute to men the sin of which they are not guilty : Rom. v. 12. ' All have sinned.' Now, if we enquire what is the particular sin here meant, the apostle makes it evident, that it is Adam's first sin, ver. 15. 19. ' If through the offence of one many be dead. As by the offence of one judgment came upon all men.' And that sin was the breaking of the covenant. Now, we could never be reckoned breakers of the covenant in him, if we were not reckoned first makers of it in him ; that is, that Adam was our federal head in that covenant, so that it was made with us in him.

[3.] The ruins by the breach of that covenant fall on all mankind, not excepting those who are not guilty of actual sin. Hence believers are said 'to have been ' the children of wrath, even as others,' Eph. ii. 3. and that ' death hath reigned over them that had not sinned after the similitude of Adam's transgression,' Rom. v. 14. All were excluded from paradise, and from the tree of life, in the loins of Adam ; the ground was cursed to them, as well as to him.   Yea, all die spiritually, and that in him, 1 Cor. xv. 22. forecited.   Yet it is only, ' the soul that sinneth, shall die,' Ezek. xviii. 4.   They thus die who are not chargeable with personal sins, Rom. v. 14. also above cited.   It must be by virtue of that original threatening then : Gen. iii. 17. ' Dust thou art, and unto dust shalt thou return.'   And if they die by virtue of that threatening, they were under that law to which it was annexed : but they could no other way be under it, than as in Adam their federal head and representative.

Lastly, The sin and death we come under by Adam is still restrained unto that sin of his by which he brake the covenant of works : Rom. v. 15 —19. ' Through the offence of one many be dead. The judgment was by one to condemnation.   By one man's offence death reigned by one.   By the offence of one judgment came upon all men to condemnation.   By one man's disobedience many were made sinners.'   As for Adam's after sins, the scripture takes no notice of them that way.   If our communion with him in sin and death did depend merely on his natural relation to us, the conveyance of guilt from him unto us could not have ceased, till his whole guilt contracted all his life over had disburdened itself upon us : because the natural relation ceased not, but was still the same.   It depended then upon some supervenient relation, the which could be no other but that he was constituted a public person, representing us in the first covenant : the which ceased, when he went in for himself into the second covenant.   The ship whereof he was made steersman being split, the covenant of grace, as another ship, came up, of which Christ was the steersman ; and this covenant was let out as a rope to hale the passengers to land.   This Adam laid hold on, and

so quitted his first post, that his after mismanagement could no more harm as formerly.*

•••••••••••••••

The justice and equity of Adam's representation in the Covenant of Works.

1. God made the choice ; he pitched on Adam as
a fit person to represent all mankind ; and there is
no mending of God's work, which is perfect, Eccl.
iii. 14. ' I know that whatsoever God doeth, it shall
be for ever : nothing can be put to it, nor any thing
taken from it ; and God doeth it, that men should
fear before him.'   There was infinite wisdom at
making of it, and sovereign authority to establish it.
The covenant proposed to Adam, could not but in
duty be consented to by him ; and there is the same
obligation to his posterity.   If judges on earth may
name and give tutors to minors, might not the Judge
of all the earth do the same to his own creatures ?
2. Adam was undoubtedly the most fit choice.
He was the common father of us all : so being our
natural head, he was fittest to be our federal head.
He was in case for managing the bargain to the

---

* " The whole history of the first man evinces, that he was
not looked upon as an individual person, but that the whole human nature was considered in him."
Witsius' Œconomy of the Covenants.

" That God's dealing with the first man was of a covenant
nature, and that he was so dealt with, as not only the root, but
likewise the public summary of mankind, doth generally appear
from the account given of this matter by Moses, Gen. ii.   But
the same thing was more particularly revealed afterwards in the
holy scriptures.   The principle evidence on this subject arises
from the New Testament, in the glorious character of Jesus
Christ, with the parallel betwixt him and the first man, as
therein most expressly revealed."
Gibb's Sacred Contemplations.

common advantage, Eccl. vii. 29. being ' made ·up-
right,' and furnished with sufficient abilities.   And
his own interest was on the same bottom with that
of his posterity.   Thus his abilities, and natural affection concurring with his own interest, spoke him
to be a fit person for that office.

Lastly, The choice was of a piece with the covenant.   The covenant, in its own nature most advan-
tageous for man, though it could not be profitable to
God, Job xxxv. 7. was a free benefit and gift on
God's part ; for as much as man had not a claim to
the life promised, but by the covenant.   So that as
the covenant owed its being, not to nature, but a positive constitution of God ; so did the choice owe its
being to the same.   God joined the covenant and representation together ; and so the consent of Adam
or his posterity to the one, was a consenting to the
other.*

---

* " That God was righteous in this constitntion, is not to be
disputed.   For it does not become us to question the right of
God, or to enquire too curiously into it, much less to measure it
by the standard of any right established amongst us despicable
mortals ; when the fact is evident, we are previously to judge of
God, ' Thou art righteous in what Thou speakest, and pure in
thy judgments.'

" What if we consider the matter thus ? If Adam had, in his
own and our name, stood to the conditions of the covenant ; if,
having finished the course of his probation, he had been confirmed
in happiness, and we his posterity in him ; if, fully satisfied with
the delights of animal life, we had together with him, been
translated to the joys of heaven ; no body would have complained that he was included in the head of mankind : every one
would have commended both the wisdom and goodness of God ;
not the least suspicion of injustice would have arisen in any one
on account of God's putting the first man into a state of probation in the room of all, and not every individual for himself."

                              Witsius' Œcon. of the Covenant.

*The nature of the obedience to which man is obliged
by the Covenant of Works.*

1. Perfect obedience. Imperfect obedience could
not have been accepted under this covenant ; neither
for justification, for it would have condemned man,
Gal. iii. 10. formerly cited ; nor under the covenant
of grace, could it be accepted for that end neither,
Matt. iii. 15. ' as it became' the second Adam ' to
fulfil all righteousness : ' nor yet could it be accepted
in point of justification under that covenant, though
under the covenant of grace it is. The reason is,
because under the first covenant the work must be
accepted for its conformity to the law, and then the
person for the work's sake ; but imperfect obedience
could never be accepted of God for its own sake ;
for God ' is of purer eyes than to behold evil, and
cannot look on iniquity,' Hab. i. 13. But under the
second covenant the persons of believers are first accepted for Christ's sake : Eph. i. 6. ' To the praise
of the glory of his grace, wherein he hath made us
accepted in the beloved.' And then their works for
the same Christ's sake : Heb. xi. 4. ' By faith Abel
offered unto God a more excellent sacrifice than Cain,
by which he obtained witness that he was righteous,
God testifying of his gifts ; and by it, he being dead,
yet speaketh.' So then the condition of this covenant
was perfect obedience, and that,

(1.) Perfect in respect of the principle of it. His
nature, soul, and heart behoved always to be kept
pure and untainted, as the principle of action. So
the law is explained, Luke x. 25—28. ' And behold
a certain lawyer stood up, and tempted him, saying,
Master, what shall I do to inherit eternal life ? He
said unto him, What is written in the law ? how

readest thou ? and he answering, said, Thou shalt love the Lord thy God with all thy heart, and with all thy soul, and with all thy strength, and with all thy mind : and thy neighbour as thyself. And he said unto him, Thou hast answered right : this do, and thou shalt live.' Where the least blemish is in the soul, mind, will, or affections, it must needs make the actions sinful : ' Who can bring a clean thing out of an unclean ? ' Job xiv. 4. ' A corrupt tree cannot bring forth good fruit,' Matt. vii. 18. Where there is any indisposition for, or reluctancy to duty, there is a blemish in the frame of the soul. Therefore of necessity man behoved to retain a perfect purity in his soul, as the condition of that covenant. God gave man a heart perfectly pure, and commanded him to keep it from being in the least tainted ; put on him a fair white garment of habitual inherent righteousness, and commanded it to be kept free from the least spot, under the pain of death.

(2.) Perfect in parts, nowise defective or lame, wanting any part necessary to its integrity, James i. 4. And it behoved to be thus perfect, *1st*, In respect of the parts of the law : Gal. iii. 10. ' For as many as are of the works of the law are under the curse : for it is written, Cursed is every one that continueth not in all things which are written in the book of the law to do them.' His obedience behoved to be as broad as the whole law, natural and positive ; extending to all the commands thereof laid on him : nothing committed that the law forbade, nothing omitted that the law required. One link of this chain being broken, all was broke together ; ' for whosoever shall keep the whole law, and yet offend in one point, he is guilty of all,' James ii. 10. *2d,* In respect of the parts of the man, Luke x. 27, 28. forecited. His mind, will, and affections, his soul and his body, all of them behoved to be employed in obedience to the law ; and it behoved to be the obedience, as of the whole law, so of the whole man. Thus was he bound to internal and external obedience in the whole compass of both, according to the law. 3*d*, In respect of the parts of every human action, Gal. iii. 10. The law requires in every such action, a goodness of the matter, manner, and end : a failure in any of these in any one action broke this covenant. So in every action what he did behoved to be good, well done ; and all to the glory of God, as the chief end. The least mismanagement in any of these, the least squint look, would have marred all.

(3.) Perfect in degrees, Luke x. 27, 28. above cited. His obedience, as the condition of the covenant, was to be not only of equal breadth with the law, but of equal height with it, in every point. Every part of every action behoved to be screwed up to that pitch determined by the law : all that was lower than it was to be rejected as sinful.

2. Adam was obliged to perpetual obedience, Gal. iii. 10. Not that he was for ever to have been upon his trial ; for that would have rendered the promise of life vain and fruitless, since he could never at that rate have attained the reward of his obedience. But it behoved to be perpetual, as a condition of the covenant, during the time set by God himself for the trial ; which time God has not discovered in his word. The time of this life is now the time of trial. Our Lord Jesus Christ, in the room of the elect, obeyed the law about the space of thirty-three years ; for so long he lived. Whatever was the time appointed for man's trial, according to the covenant ; his obedience behoved to be perpetual during that time, without interruption of the course of it, without defection and apostacy from it : Till that time had expired in a course of continued obedience, he could not have claimed the final reward of his work. But that time being so expired, he would have been confirmed in goodness, so that he could no more fall away, as a part of the life promised. And the cove-

3 c

nant of works would have for ever remained as man's
eternal security for, and ground of his eternal life ;
but no longer as a rule of his obedience, for that
would have been to reduce him to the state of trial
he was in before, and to have set him a-new to work
as a title to what he already possessed, by virtue of
his supposed keeping of that covenant. Yet man
could be in no state, wherein he should not owe obedience to his Creator, no not in the state of glory :
And if he owed obedience still, he behoved still to
have a rule: and for that effect, the law of nature,
which is perpetual, would have returned to its primitive constitution, the form of the covenant of works
being done away from it : and so have been man's
rule in the state of confirmation. Hence it follows,

(1.) That forasmuch as the Lord Jesus Christ has
mended and perfected that work, which Adam marred ; believers being united to him, are so confirmed
in a state of grace, that they cannot but persevere,
and that for ever. Hence it is observable, that the
just by faith are declared to be entitled to that very
benefit which Adam was by his obedience to have
been entitled to: Hab. ii. 4. ' The just shall live by
his faith ;' namely, a life which shall persevere and
endure for ever. And therefore the apostle useth
that scripture to prove the perseverance of believers,
and the certainty of their eternal salvation: Heb. x.
38, 39. ' Now the just shall live by faith : but if any
man draw back, my soul shall have no pleasure in
him. But we are not of them who draw back unto
perdition ; but of them that believe to the saving of
the soul.' And believers are declared actually to
have eternal life, though that life is not yet come unto its full vigour, which is reserved for heaven : John
xvii. 3. ' This is life eternal, that they might know
thee the only true God, and Jesus Christ whom thou
hast sent.' 1 John v. 13. ' These things have I
written unto you, that believe on the name of the

Son of God ; that ye may know that ye have eternal life.'

(2.) As it is in vain for Christless sinners, utterly impotent for any good, to pretend to work that they may procure themselves life ; so believers ought not to work for life, or that they may, by their holiness and obedience, gain life. For believers in Christ have life already in him, by virtue of his working perfectly and perpetually in their room and stead ; and for them to pretend so to work for it, is to cast dishonour on Christ's perfect and perpetual obedience. The truth is, holiness is a main part of that life and salvation we have by Jesus Christ. ' Of him [i. e. God] are ye in Christ Jesus, who of God is made unto us—sanctification,' 1 Cor. i. 30. ' Not by works of righteousness, which we have done, but according to his mercy he saved us by the washing of regeneration, and renewing of the holy Ghost,' Tit. iii. 5. ' Who gave himself for us, that he might redeem us from all iniquity, and purify unto himself a peculiar people, zealous of good works,' Tit. ii. 14. And were there more pressing of faith to obtain holiness, and less dividing of holiness from life and salvation, making the former the means to procure to ourselves the latter, there would be more true holiness in these dregs of time.

(3.) They that are not holy have no saving interest in Jesus Christ ; and while they continue so, shall never see the face of God in peace : Heb xii. 14. ' Follow—holiness,' says the apostle, ' without which no man shall see the Lord.' Where is the man that pretends to be in Christ, and to have faith, and yet makes no conscience of a holy life, of the duties of piety towards God, righteousness and mercy towards his neighbour ; but tramples on any of the ten commandments ; I say to him with confidence, as the apostle Peter said to Simon Magus, Acts viii. 21. ' Thou hast neither part nor lot in this matter ; for thy heart is not right in the sight of God.' Has

Christ fulfilled the covenant, which Adam broke ;
and are not all that are united to him made thereupon partakers of life ? How can it be otherwise according to the faithfulness of God ? Surely then thou
who art living in sin, and so art dead while thou
livest, hast no saving interest in him.

(4.) Though the believer is under the law of the
ten commandments as a rule of life, he is not under
the law as a covenant of works in any sense : neither
does the law he is under adjudge him to eternal life
upon his obedience, nor lay him under the curse, and
adjudge him to eternal death, for his sins.   But the
law as to him is stripped of its promise of eternal
life to obedience, and of its threatening of eternal
death to his sins.   This is the apostle Paul's doctrine : ' Ye are become dead to the law by the body
of Christ,' Rom. vii. 4.   ' Ye are not under the law,
but under grace,' chap. vi. 14.   ' There is no condemnation to them that are in Christ Jesus,' Rom.
viii. 1.   ' That no man is justified by the law in the
sight of God, it is evident ; for the just shall live by
faith.   And the law is not of faith ; but the man
that doeth them, shall live in them.   Christ hath redeemed us from the curse of the law, being made a
curse for us,' Gal. iii. 11, 12, 13.   And how can it
be otherwise, unless one will say, that Christ, by his
perfect and perpetual obedience, has not set his
people beyond the reach of the curse, nor secured
their life ?

3. Adam was obliged to personal obedience. Hence
says the Lord, ' Ye shall keep my statutes and my
judgments ; which if a man do, he shall live in them,
Lev. xviii. 5. which words the apostle Paul quotes,
Rom. x. 5. ' Moses describeth the righteousness
which is of the law, That the man which doeth these
things shall live by them.'   It behoved to be personal
obedience.   Not that every person of Adam's race,
according to the original constitution, behoved to
yield this obedience for himself, in order to obtain

the life promised. It is true indeed that all Adam's children, who should have been born and grown up, before the time of his trial was expired, would have been obliged, it would seem, to that obedience for that end, in their own persons; and, if they had failed in it, the loss would have been to themselves, and to themselves only. This may be learned from the case of Eve, noticed before. But that, in case Adam had stood out the whole time of his trial, every one of his posterity after that should yet have been obliged to yield obedience for life in their own persons is what I cannot comprehend. For then, to what purpose was the representation of mankind by Adam? for what end was he constituted their federal head? It is plain, that by Adam's breaking of the covenant, death has come on them, who had no being in the world in Adam's time: and how this can be consistent with the goodness of God, and the equity of his proceedings, unless they were to have had the promised life upon running the set course of his obedience, I see not: and therefore must conclude, that after Adam's standing out the set time, all mankind then standing with him, would have been confirmed; and those who should afterwards have come into the world, would not only have had original righteousness conveyed to them from him, but have been confirmed too in holiness and happiness, so that they could not have fallen.

It is true, the covenant of works now proposes the same condition to every man under it, that it did to Adam, to be performed in his own person for himself, if he will have life by it. The reason is plain, Adam sinning is no more the representative in that covenant, to act for them; so they must take the same way every one for themselves, that he was to have taken for himself and all his posterity. While the pilot manages the ship carefully and skilfully, so as she makes her way towards the port, the passengers have nothing to do for their own safety, all is

safe by his management : but if he run the ship on
a rock, and split it, and make his escape, every one
of the passengers must be pilot for himself, and work
for his own life and safety.

But this obedience behoved to be personal in the
following respects.   It behoved to be performed,

(1.) By man himself and not another for him, Lev.
xviii. 15. forecited.   The covenant of works knew
nothing of a surety or mediator.   ' In the day thou
eatest thou shalt die,' plainly imports, that man, the
moment he sinned, broke the covenant, and was a
dead man in law.   If he could have provided a surety
who should have obeyed, when he disobeyed, that
would not have fulfilled that covenant, or kept it.
If a surety was to have place, it behoved to be by a
new bargain, wherein a new representation was settled.

(2.) By one person, and not by more : that is, the
righteousness of the covenant behoved to be of one
piece, and not one part wrought by one, and another
part by another.   The sinning soul behoved to die ;
and imperfect righteousness could not be accepted
in part, more than it could be in whole, because such
righteousness is not righteousness indeed, but sinful
want of conformity to the law.   Hence it follows,

[1.] That God's accepting of a surety, as well as
his providing one for lost sinners in the second covenant, was purely of free grace.   For ' in him,' says
the apostle, ' we have redemption through his blood,
the forgiveness of sins, according to the riches of his
grace,' Eph. i. 7.   He might have held man to the
first bargain, and made all mankind utterly miserable without remedy, having once broke the first covenant.   But the riches of sovereign free love and
grace brought forth a new bargain, wherein a surety
was admitted, when that benefit to us might have
been refused ; yea, and was provided by him too,
when we could never have procured one to take that
burden on him for us.

[2.] That the purchase of our salvation by the precious blood of Christ, which was a full price for it, is so far from lowering the riches of free grace in it, that it exceedingly heightens the same. When you hear of free pardon and salvation to sinners, through the satisfaction of Christ, beware of imagining, that satisfaction spoils the freedom of it ; but remember, that God, the Father, Son, and Holy Ghost, might have in justice insisted on our own personal, perfect satisfying of the demands of the covenant of works ; and yet such was their love and grace to poor sinners, that the Father parts with his Son to die for us, the Son lays down his life in our stead, and the Holy Spirit freely applies his purchase to sinners. So that all is of free grace to us. If it had been consistent with the nature of God, to have forgiven sin without satisfaction, such remission would have been of free grace : but when there behoved to be a satisfaction made, and God admitted a surety, and provided the same himself, this speaks unspeakable riches of grace : as if a king should give his own son to satisfy the law for a traitor : John iii. 16. ' For God so loved the world, that he gave his only begotten Son, that whosoever believeth in him should not perish, but have everlasting life.'

[3.] That there can be no mixing of our own righteousness, in greater or lesser measure, with the righteousness of Christ, in our justification, by the second covenant: Gal. iii. 12. ' For the law is not of faith : but, the man that doeth them shall live in them.' We must betake ourselves wholly to the one or to the other. For the demands of the first covenant must be answered, by that righteousnes on which we can be justified ; and unless we have of our own a perfect righteousness to produce for that end, nothing we have can be accepted in that point, since there is no admitting of a pieced righteousness. And evident it is, that we cannot pretend to a perfect righteous-

ness of our own, and therefore must go wholly to
Christ for one

*********••••

The difference between Adam's and the Believer's heaven.

There are four things that would have been wanting, if we may so speak, in innocent Adam's heaven,
that will be found in the believer's heaven.   As,
1. The additional sweetness of the enjoyment that
arises from the experience of want and misery.   Two
men are set down at a feast ; the one never knew
what hunger and want meant ; the other never got
a full meal all his days, but want and hunger were
his daily companions.   Which of the two would the
feast be sweetest to ?   The case is plain.   Sin is the
worst of things, there is no good in it ; the effects of
sin, sorrow, misery, and trouble, are bitter : but God
permitted the one, and has brought the other on, in
depth of wisdom ;   for out of these is a sauce drawn
that will give an additional sweetness to the supper
of the Lamb in the upper house.   While the saints
walk in their white robes, and remember the filthy,
ragged, black garments they went in some time a
day, it will raise their praises a note higher, than innocent Adam's, while he should have looked on his,
which there was never a spot upon.   When after
many tossings on the sea of this world, and the numerous floods of difficulties and dangers from sin and
Satan which have beset them, the saints happily arrive on the shore of the heavenly Canaan, their relish
of the pleasures to be enjoyed there will be the greater and the more delightful.
2. The fairest flower in heaven to be seen by bodily eyes, would have been wanting in innocent
Adam's heaven, namely, the man Christ.   It is a

groundless antiscriptural notion, that the Son of God would have been incarnate, though man had never sinned : John iii. 16. ' For God so loved the world, that he gave his only begotten Son, that whosoever believeth in him should not perish, but have everlasting life.' 1 Tim. i. 15. ' This is a faithful saying, and worthy of all acceptation, that Christ Jesus came into the world to save sinners.' It was for sinners the Saviour was sent. The ruin of man's nature in the first Adam, was the occasion sovereign love took to raise it up to the highest possible pitch of glory and dignity, in the person of the Son of God. There our nature is personally united to the divine nature, even in the person of the Son : and the man Christ is in heaven more glorious than a thousand suns. It is true, Adam would have had the sight and enjoyment of God, Father, Son, and Holy Ghost; but he could not have said, as they, Behold God in our nature, our elder brother, &c.

(3.) The charter, written with blood, securing the enjoyment of heaven's happiness. Adam would have had good security indeed for it, by the fulfilled covenant of works ; but behold a more glorious charter, the covenant of grace, written with the blood of the Son of God, Heb. xiii. 20. Every draught of the well of the water of life, innocent Adam would have had in his heaven, he might have cried out with wonder concerning it, O the gracious reward of my obedience! But the saints shall say of theirs, The glorious purchase of my Redeemer's blood ; this is the purchase of the Son of God : Rev. vii. 9, 10. ' After this, I beheld, and lo, a great multitude which no man could number, of all nations, and kindreds, and people, and tongues, stood before the throne, and before the Lamb, clothed with white robes, and palms in their hands ; and cried with a loud voice, saying, Salvation to our God which sitteth upon the throne, and unto the Lamb.'

Lastly, The manner of living, as members of the

3 D

mystical body of Christ. Innocent Adam would have lived for ever in heaven as the friend of God : but the saints shall live there as members of Christ : John vi. 57. ' As the living Father hath sent me, and I live by the Father ; so he that eateth me, even he shall live by me ;' and xiv. 19. ' Yet a little while and the world seeth me no more ; but ye see me : because I live, ye shall live also.' They shall be more nearly allied to the Son of God than Adam would have been : Eph. v. 30. ' For we are members of his body, of his flesh, and of his bones.' He will be their husband in an everlasting marriage-covenant, their elder brother, the head, of which they are members, and through whom they will derive their glory, as they do their grace, from the Godhead, as united to Christ, the prime receptacle of grace and glory : Rev. vii. *ult.* ' For the Lamb which is in the midst of the throne, shall feed them, and shall lead them unto living fountains of waters : and God shall wipe away all tears from their eyes.' Rev. xxi. 23. ' And the city had no need of the sun, neither of the moon to shine in it : for the glory of God did lighten it. and the Lamb is the light thereof.'

How Man's nature is wholly corrupted, and how Man in his first sin transgressed the whole law.

The heathens perceived that man's nature was corrupted ; but how sin had entered they could not tell. But the scripture is very plain in that point, Rom. v. 12. ' By one man sin entered into the world,' ver. 19. ' By one man's disobedience many were made sinners.' Adam's sin corrupted man's nature, and leavened the whole lump of mankind, We putrified in Adam, as our root. The root was poisoned, and so the branches were envenomed ; the vine turned the vine of Sodom, and so the grapes became grapes of gall. Adam, by his sin, became not only guilty, but corrupt; and so transmits guilt and corruption to his posterity, Gen. v. 3. Job xiv. 4. By his sin he stript himself of his original righteousness, and corrupted himself; we were in him representatively, being represented by him, as our moral head, in the covenant of works; we were in him seminally, as our natural head; hence we fell in him, and by his disobedience were made sinners, as Levi, in the loins of Abraham, paid tithes, Heb. vii. 9, 10. His first sin is imputed to us; therefore justly are we left under the want of his original righteousness, which, being given to him as a common person, he cast off, by his sin; and this is necessarily followed, in him and us, by the corruption of the whole nature; righteousness and corruption being two contraries, one of which must needs always be in man, as a subject capable thereof. And Adam our common father being corrupt, we are so too; for who can bring a clean thing out of an unclean?

Although it is sufficient to evince the righteousness of this dispensation, that it was from the Lord, who doth all things well; yet to silence the murmurings of proud nature, let these few things further be considered. (1.) In the covenant wherein Adam represented us, eternal happiness was promised to him and his posterity, upon condition of his, that is, Adam's perfect obedience, as the representative for all mankind: whereas, if there had been no covenant, they could not have pleaded eternal life, upon their most perfect obedience, but might have been, after all, reduced to nothing, notwithstanding, by natural justice, they would have been liable to God's eternal wrath, in case of sin. Who in that case would not have consented to that representation? (2.) Adam had a power to stand given him, being made upright. He was as capable to stand for himself, and all his posterity, as any after him could be for themselves. This trial of mankind in their head, would soon have been

over, and the crown won to them all, had he stood;
whereas, had his posterity been independent of him,
and every one left to act for himself, the trial would
have been continually a carrying on, as men came
into the world. (3.) He had natural affections the
strongest to engage him, being our common father.
(4.) His own stock was in the ship, his all lay at
stake as well as ours. He had no separate interest
from ours; but if he forgot ours, he behoved to have
forgot his own. (5.) If he had stood, we should have
had the light of his mind, the righteousness of his
will, and holiness of his affections, with entire purity
transmitted unto us; we could not have fallen: the
crown of glory, by his obedience, would have been
for ever secured to him and his. This is evident from
the nature of a federal representation; and no reason
can be given why, seeing we are lost by Adam's sin,
we should not have been saved by his obedience. On
the other hand, it is reasonable, that he falling, we
should with him bear the loss. Lastly, such as quarrel this dispensation, must renounce their part in
Christ, for we are no otherwise made sinners by
Adam, than we are made righteous by Christ; from
whom we have both imputed and inherent righteousness. We no more made choice of the second Adam,
for our head and representative in the second covenant, than we did of the first Adam in the first covenant.

Let none wonder that such a horrible change would
be brought on by one sin of our first parents, for
thereby they turned away from God as their chief
end, which necessarily infers an universal depravation. Their sin was a complication of evils, a total
apostacy from God, a violation of the whole law. By
it they broke all the ten commands at once. (1.)
They chose new gods. They made their belly their
god, by their sensuality; self their God, by their ambition; yea, and the devil their God, believing him,
and disbelieving their Maker. (2.) Though they

received, yet they observed not that ordinance of God, about the forbidden fruit. They contemned that ordinance so plainly enjoined them, and would needs carve out to themselves, how to serve the Lord. (3.) They took the name of the Lord their God in vain; despising his attributes, his justice, truth, power, &c. They grossly profaned that sacramental tree; abused his word, by not giving credit to it; a-bused that creature of his, which they should not have touched, and violently misconstrued his provi-dence, as if God, by forbidding them that tree, had been standing in the way of their happiness: and therefore he suffered them not to escape his righteous judgment. (4.) They remembered not the Sabbath to keep it holy, but put themselves out of a condition to serve God aright on his own day. Neither kept they that state of holy rest wherein God had put them. (5.) They cast off their relative duties: Eve forgets herself, and acts without advice of her hus-band, to the ruin of both. Adam, instead of admo-nishing her to repent, yields to the temptation, and confirms her in her wickedness. They forgot all duty to their posterity. The honoured not their Fa-ther in heaven; and therefore their days were not long in the land which the Lord their God gave them. (6.) They ruined themselves and all their posterity. (7.) Gave up themselves to luxury and sensuality. (8.) Took away what was not their own, against the express will of the great Owner. (9.) They bore false witness, and lied against the Lord, before angels, devils, and one another; in effect giv-ing out that they were hardly dealt by, and that heaven grudged their happiness. (10.) They were discontented with their lot, and coveted an evil co-vetousness to their house; which ruined both them and theirs. Thus was the image of God on man defaced all at once.

Man's natural state, matter of deep lamentation.

Well may we lament thy case, O natural man, for it is the saddest case one can be in out of hell. It is time to lament for thee; for thou art dead already, dead while thou livest; thou carriest about with thee a dead soul in a living body: and because thou art dead thou canst not lament thy own case. Thou art loathsome in the sight of God; for thou art altogether corrupt. Thou 'hast no good' in thee; thy soul is a mass of darkness, rebellion, and vileness before the Lord. Thou thinkest, perhaps, that thou hast a good heart to God, good inclinations, and good desires; but God knows there is nothing good in thee, but 'every imagination of thine heart is only evil.' Thou 'canst do no good'; thou canst do nothing but sin. For,

1. Thou art 'the servant of sin,' Rom. vi. 17. and therefore 'free from righteousness,' ver. 20. Whatever righteousness be, (poor soul) thou art free of it; thou dost not, thou canst not meddle with it. Thou art under the dominion of sin, a dominion where righteousness can have no place. Thou art a child and servant of the devil, though thou be neither wizard nor witch, seeing thou art yet in the state of nature: John viii. 44. 'Ye are of your father the devil.' And to prevent any mistake, consider, that sin and Satan have two sorts of servants. (1.) There are some employed, as it were, in coarser work: those bear the devil's mark in their foreheads, having no form of godliness; but are profane, grossly ignorant, mere moralists, not so much as performing the external duties of religion; but living to the view of the world, as sons of earth, only 'minding earthly things,' Phil. iii. 19. (2.) There are some employ-

ed in a more refined sort of service to sin, who carry
the devil's mark in their right hand ; which they can
and do hide from the view of the world. These are
close hypocrites, who sacrifice as much to the corrupt mind, as the other to the flesh, Eph. ii. 3.
These are ruined by a more undiscernable trade of
sin : pride, unbelief, self-seeking, and the like swarm
in, and prey upon their corrupted, wholly corrupted
souls. Both are servants of the same house ; the latter as far as the former from righteousness.

2. How is it possible that thou shouldst be able to
do any good, thou whose nature is wholly corrupt ?
Can fruit grow where there is no root ? Or can
there be an effect without a cause ? ' Can the fig-
tree bear olive berries ? Either a vine figs ? ' If thy
nature be wholly corrupt, as indeed it is, all thou
dost is certainly so too ; for no effect can exceed the
virtue of its cause. ' Can a corrupt tree bring forth
good fruit ? ' Matt. vii. 18.

Ah ! what a miserable spectacle is he that can do
nothing but sin ? Thou art the man, whosoever thou
art, that art yet in thy natural state. Hear, O sinner, what is thy case !

1st, Innumerable sins compass thee about. Mountains of guilt are lying upon thee. Floods of impurities overwhelm thee. Living lusts of all sorts
roll up and down in the dead sea of thy soul, where
no good can breathe, because of the corruption there.
Thy lips are unclean : the opening of thy mouth is
as the opening of an unripe grave, full of stench and
rottenness : Rom. iii. 13. ' Their throat is an open
sepulchre.' Thy natural actions are sin, for ' when
ye did eat, and when ye did drink, did not ye eat
for yourselves, and drink for yourselves ? ' Zech. vii. 6.
Thy civil actions are sin : Prov. xxi. 4. ' The plow-
ing of the wicked is sin.' Thy religious actions are
sin : Prov. xv. 8. ' The sacrifice of the wicked is an
abomination to the Lord.' The thoughts and imaginations of thy heart are only evil. A deed may be

soon done, a word soon spoken, a thought swiftly passed through the heart : but each of these is an *item* in thy accounts. O sad reckoning! as many thoughts, words, actions ; as many sins. The longer thou livest, thy accounts swell the more. Should a tear be dropt for every sin, thine head behoved to be waters, and thine ' eyes a fountain of tears :' for nothing but sin comes from thee. Thy heart frames nothing but ' evil imaginations ;' there is nothing in thy life, but what is framed by thine heart ; and therefore there is nothing in thy heart or life but evil.

2*d*, All thy religion, if thou hast any, is lost labour; as to acceptance with God, or any saving effect to thyself. Art thou yet in thy natural state? Truly then thy duties are sins, as was just now hinted. Would not the best wine be loathsome in a vessel wherein there is no pleasure? So is the religion of an unregenerate man. Under the law, the garment which the flesh of the sacrifice was carried in, though it touched other things did not make them holy; but he that was unclean touching any thing, whether common or sacred, made it unclean. Even so thy duties cannot make thy corrupt soul holy, though they in themselves be good ; but thy corrupt heart defiles them, and makes them unclean, Hag. ii. 12, 13, 14. Thou wast wont to divide thy works into two sorts, some good, some evil; but thou must count again and put them all under one head ; for God writes on them all, only evil. This is lamentable : It will be no wonder to see those beg in harvest, who fold their hands to sleep in seed time : but to be labouring with others in the spring, and yet have nothing to reap when the harvest comes, is a very sad case; and will be the case of all professors living and dying in their natural state.

Lastly, Thou canst not help thyself. What canst thou do to take away thy sin, who art wholly corrupt? Nothing truly but sin. If a natural man begin to relent, drop a tear for his sin and reform, pre-

sently the corrupt heart apprehends, at least a merit
of congruity : he has done much himself (he thinks,)
and God cannot but do more for him on that account.
In the meantime he does nothing but sin : so that
the congruous merit is that the leper be put out of
the camp, the dead soul buried out of sight, and the
corrupt lump cast into the pit. How canst thou
think to recover thyself by any thing thou canst do ?
Will mud and filth wash out filthiness ? and wilt
thou purge out sin by sinning ? Job took a potsherd
to scrape himself, because his hands were as full of
boils as his body. This is the case of thy corrupt
soul ; not to be recovered but by Jesus Christ, whose
strength was dried up like a potsherd, Psal. xxii. 15.
Thou art poor indeed, extremely miserable and poor,
Rev. iii. 17. Thou hast no shelter but a refuge of
lies ; no garment for thy soul, but filthy rags ; nothing to nourish it, but husks that cannot satisfy.
More than that, thou hast got such a bruise in the
loins of Adam, which is not as yet cured, that thou
art without strength, Rom. v. 6. unable to do or work
for thyself ; nay, more than all this, thou canst not
so much as seek aright, but liest helpless, as an infant exposed in the open field, Ezek. xvi. 5.

*The necessity of having a special eye upon the
corruption and sin of our nature.*

God sees it : O that we saw it too, and that sin
were ever before us ! What avails it to notice other
sins, while this mother sin is not noticed ? Turn
your eyes inward to the sin of your nature. It is to
be feared, many have this work to begin yet ; that
they have shut the door, while the grand thief is yet
in the house undiscovered. This is a weighty point ;
and in the handling of it,

3 E

1. I shall, for conviction, point at some evidences of men's overlooking the sin of their nature, which yet the Lord takes particular notice of. 1*st*, Men's looking on themselves with such confidence, as if they were in no hazard of gross sins. Many would take it very heinously to get such a caution, as Christ gave his apostles: Luke xxi. 34. ' Take heed of surfeiting and drunkenness.' If any should suppose them to break out in gross abominations, they would be ready to say, ' Am I a dog ?' It would raise the pride of their hearts, but not their fear and trembling ; because they know not the corruption of their nature. 2*d*, Untenderness towards those that fall. Many in that case cast off all bowels of Christian compassion ; for they do not ' consider themselves, lest they also be tempted,' Gal. vi. 1. Men's passions are often highest against the faults of others, when sin sleeps soundly in their own breasts. Even good David, when he was at his worst, was most violent against the faults of others. While his conscience was asleep under his guilt, in the matter of Uriah, the Spirit of the Lord takes notice, that his ' anger was greatly kindled against the man,' in the parable, 2 Sam. xii. 5. And, on good grounds, it is thought, it was at the same time that he treated the Ammonites so cruelly, as is related, ver. 31. ' Putting them under saws, and under harrows of iron, and under axes of iron, and making them pass through the brick kiln.' Grace makes men zealous against sin in others, as well as in themselves : but eyes turned inward to the corruption of nature, clothe them with pity and compassion, and fill them with thankfulness to the Lord, that they themselves were not the persons left to be such spectacles of human frailty. 3*d*, There are not a few, who, if they be kept from affliction in worldly things, and from gross out-breakings in their conversation, know not what it is to have a sad heart. If they meet with a cross, which their proud hearts cannot stoop to bear, they

will be ready to say, O to be gone : but the corruption of their nature never makes them long for heaven. Lusts scandalously breaking out at a time, will mar their peace ; but the sin of their nature never makes them a heavy heart. 4*th*, Delaying of repentance, in hopes to set about it afterwards. Many have their own appointed time for repentance and reformation : as if they were such complete masters over their lusts, that they can allow them to gather more strength, and yet overcome them. They take up resolutions to amend, without an eye to Jesus Christ, union with him, and strength from him : a plain evidence they are strangers to themselves ; and so they are left to themselves, and their flourishing resolutions wither : for as they see not the necessity, so they get not the benefit of the dew from heaven to water them. 5*th*, Men's venturing frankly on temptations, and promising liberally on their own heads. They cast themselves fearlessly into temptation, in confidence of their coming off fairly : but were they sensible of the corruption of their nature, they would beware of entering on the devil's ground ; as one girt about with bags of gunpowder would be loth to walk where sparks of fire are flying, lest he should be blown up. Self jealousy well becomes Christians. ' Lord, is it I ? ' They that know the deceit of their bow, will not be very confident that they shall hit the mark. 6*th*, Unacquaintedness with heart plagues. The knowledge of the plagues of the heart, is a rare qualification. Others are indeed some of them written in such great characters, that he who runs may read them ; but there are others more subtile, which few do discern. How few are there to whom the bias of the heart to unbelief is a burden ? Nay, they perceive it not. Many have had sharp convictions of other sins, that were never to this day convinced of their unbelief ; though that is the sin specially aimed at in a thorough conviction : John xvi. 8, 9. ' —He will reprove the world of sin,—because they believe not on me.' A disposition to establish our own righteousness is a weed that naturally grows in every man's heart ; but few sweat at the plucking of it up, it lurks undiscovered. The bias of the heart to the way of the covenant of works, is a hidden plague of the heart to many. All the difficulty they find is, in getting up their hearts to duties ; they find no difficulty in getting their hearts off them, and over them to Jesus Christ. How hard is it to stave men off from their own righteousness ? Yet it is very hard to convince them of their leaning to it at all. *Lastly*, Pride and self conceit. A view of the corruption of nature would be very humbling ; and oblige him that has it, to reckon himself the chief of sinners. Under the greatest attainments and enlargements, it will be ballast to his heart, and hide pride from his eyes. The want of thorough humiliation, piercing to the sin of one's nature, is the ruin of many professors : for digging deep makes great diffeience betwixt wise and foolish builders, Luke vi. 48, 49.

2. I will lay before you a few things, in which ye should have a special eye to the sin of your nature. 1*st*, Have a special eye to it in your application to Jesus Christ. Do you find any need of Christ, which sends you to him, as the Physician of souls ? O forget not this disease when you are with the Physician. They never yet knew well their errand to Christ, that went not to him for the sin of their nature ; for his blood to take away the guilt of it, and his Spirit to break the power of it. Though in the bitterness of your souls, ye should lay before him a catalogue of your sins of omission and commission, which might reach from earth to heaven ; yet if the sin of your nature were wanting in it, assure yourselves, you have forgot the best part of the errand a poor sinner has to the Physician of souls. What would it have availed the people of Jericho, to have set before Elisha all the vessels in the city full of ' the water that was naught,' if they had not led him forth

to the spring, to cast in the salt there ? 2 Kings ii.
19, 20, 21. The application is easy. 2*d*, Have a
special eye to it in your repentance, whether initial
or progressive ; in your first repentance, and in the
renewing of your repentance afterwards. Though a
man be sick, there is no fear of death, if the sickness
strike not his heart ; and there is as little fear of the
death of sin, as long as the sin of our nature is not
touched. But if ye would repent indeed, let the
streams lead you up to the fountain ; and mourn
over your corrupt nature, as the cause of all sin, in
heart, lip, and life ; Psal. li. 4, 5. ' Against thee,
thee only have I sinned, and done this evil in thy
sight.—Behold, I was shapen in iniquity, and in sin
did my mother conceive me.' 3*d*, Have a special
eye upon it, in your mortification : Gal. v. 24. ' And
they that are Christ's, have crucified the flesh.' It
is the root of bitterness, that must be struck at, which
the axe of mortification must be laid to, else we labour in vain. In vain do men go about to purge the
streams, while they are at no pains about the muddy
fountain. It is vain religion to attempt to make the
life truly good, while the corruption of nature retains
its ancient vigour, and the power of it is not broken.
Lastly, Ye are to eye it in your daily walk. He
that would walk aright, must have one eye upward
to Jesus Christ, and another inward to the corruption of his own nature. It is not enough that we
look about us, we must also look within us. There
the wall is weakest ; there our greatest enemy lies ;
and there are grounds for daily watching and mourning.

3. I shall offer some reasons, why we should
especially notice the sin of our nature.

(1.) Because of all sins it is the most extensive
and diffusive. It goes through the whole man, and
spoils all. Other sins mar particular parts of the
image of God ; but this doth at once deface the
whole. A disease affecting any particular member

of the body is ill ; but that which affects the whole
is worse. The corruption of nature is the poison of
the old serpent, cast into the fountain of action ; and
so infects every action, every breathing of the soul.

(2.) It is the cause of all particular lusts, and
actual sins, in our hearts and lives. It is the spawn
which the great Leviathan has left in the souls of
men ; from whence comes all the fry of actual sins
and abominations : Mark vii. 21. ' Out of the heart
of men proceed evil thoughts, adulteries,' &c. It is
the bitter fountain : particular lusts are but rivulets
running from it ; which bring forth into the life a
part only, and not the whole of what is within. Now
the fountain is still above the streams ; so where the
water is good, it is best in the fountain ; where it is ill,
it is worst there. The corruption of nature being
that which defiles all, itself must needs be the most
abominable thing.

(3.) It is virtually all sin ; for it is the seed of all
sins, which want but the occasion to set up their
heads ; being in the corruption of nature, as the effect in the virtue of its cause. Hence it is called ' a
body of death,' (Rom. vii. 24.) as consisting of the
several members, belonging to such ' a body of sins,'
(Col. ii. 11.) whose life lies in spiritual death. It is
the cursed ground, fit to bring forth all manner of
noxious weeds. As the whole nest of venomous
creatures must needs be more dreadful, than any
few of them that come creeping forth : so the sin of
thy nature, that mother of abominations must be
worse than any particular lusts, that appear stirring
in thy heart and life. Never did every sin appear in
the conversation of the vilest wretch that ever lived ;
but look thou into thy corrupt nature, and there thou
mayest see all and every sin in the seed and root
thereof. There is a fulness of all unrighteousness
there, Rom. i. 29. There is atheism, idolatry, blasphemy, murder, adultery, and whatsoever is vile.
Possibly none of these appear to thee in thy heart ;

but there is more in that unfathomable depth of wickedness, than thou knowest. Thy corrupt heart is like an ant's nest, on which, while the stone lieth, none of them appear ; but take of the stone, stir them up but with the point of a straw, you will see what a swarm is there, and how lively they be. Just such a sight would thy heart afford thee, did the Lord but withdraw the restraint he has upon it, and suffer Satan to stir it up by temptation.

(4.) The sin of our nature is, of all sins, the most fixed and abiding. Sinful actions, though the guilt and stain of them may remain, yet in themselves they are passing. The drunkard is not always at his cup, nor the unclean person always acting lewdness. But the corruption of nature is an abiding sin ; it remains with men in its full power by night and by day, at all times, fixed as bands of iron and brass, till their nature be changed by converting grace : and the remains of it continue with the godly, until the death of the body. Pride, envy, covetousness, and the like, are not always stirring in thee; but the proud, envious, carnal nature is still with thee : even as the clock that is wrong, is not always striking wrong ; but the wrong set continues with it, without great intermission.

(5.) It is the great reigning sin : Rom. vi. 12. ' Let not sin therefore reign in your mortal body, that ye should obey it in the lusts thereof.' There are three things you may observe in the corrupt heart. 1*st*, There is the corrupt nature ; the corrupt set of the heart, whereby men are unapt for all good, and fitted for all evil. This the apostle here calls sin, which reigns. 2*d*, There are particular lusts, or dispositions of that corrupt nature, which the apostle calls the lusts thereof ; such as pride, covetousness, &c. 3*d*, There is one among these, which is (like Saul amongst the people) higher by far than the rest, namely, ' sin which doth so easily beset us,' Heb. xii. 1. This we usually call the predominant sin, be-

cause it doth, as it were, reign over other particular
lusts ; so that other lusts must yield to it.   These
three are like a river which divides itself into many
streams, whereof one is greater than the rest.   The
corruption of nature is the river head, which has
many particular lusts, in which it runs ; but it mainly disburdens itself into what is commonly called
one's predominant sin.   Now all of these being fed
by the sin of our nature, it is evident, that sin is the
great reigning sin which never loseth its superiority
over particular lusts, that live and die with it, and
by it.   But as in some rivers, the main stream runs
not always in one and the same channel ; so particular predominants may be changed, as lust in youth
may be succeeded by covetousness in old age.   Now
what doth it avail, to reform in other things, while
the great reigning sin remains in its full power ?
What though some particular lust be broken ?   If
that sin, the sin of our nature, keep the throne, it
will set up another in its stead : as when a water-
course is stopt in one place, while the fountain is not
dammed up, it will stream forth another way.   And
thus some cast off their prodigality, but covetousness
comes up in its stead ; some cast away their profanity, and the corruption of nature sends not its main
stream that way as before ; but it runs in another
channel, namely, in that of a legal disposition, self-
righteousness, or the like.   So that people are ruined by their not eyeing the sin of their nature.

   Lastly, It is an hereditary evil : Psal. li. 5. ' In
sin did my mother conceive me.'   Particular lusts
are not so, but in the virtue of their cause.   A prodigal father may have a frugal son ; but this disease
is necessarily propagated in nature, and therefore
hardest to cure.   Surely then the word should be
given out against this sin, as against the king of Israel : 1 Kings xxii. 31. ' Fight neither with small,
nor great, save only with this, for this sin being

broke, all other sins are broken with it ; and while it stands entire, there is no victory.

4. That ye may get a view of the corruption of your nature, I would recommend to you three things. 1*st*, Study to know the spirituality and extent of the law of God, for that is the glass wherein ye may see yourselves. 2*d*, Observe your hearts at all times, but especially under temptation. Temptation is a fire that brings up the scum of the vile heart : do ye carefully mark the first risings of corruption. *Lastly*, Go to God through Jesus Christ for illumination by his Spirit. Lay out your soul before the Lord, as willing to know the vileness of your nature ; say unto him, ' That which I know not teach thou me,' and be willing to take in light from the word. Believe, and you shall see ; it is by the word the Spirit teacheth, but without the Spirit's teaching, all other teaching will be to little purpose. Though the gospel should shine about you like the sun at noon-day, and this great truth be ever so plainly preached, you will never see yourselves aright, until the Spirit of the Lord light his candle within your breast. The fulness and glory of Christ, the corruption and vileness of our nature, are never rightly learned but where the Spirit of Christ is the teacher.

And now to shut up this weighty point, let the consideration of what is said commend Christ to you all. Ye that are brought out of your natural state of corruption unto Christ, be humble ; still coming to Christ, and improving your union with him, to the further weakening of the remains of this natural corruption. Is your nature changed ? It is but in part so. The day was ye could not stir, now ye are cured ; but remember the cure is not yet perfected, ye still go halting. And though it were better with you than it is, the remembrance of what you were by nature should keep you low. Ye that are yet in your natural state, take with it ; believe the corruption of

3 F

your nature, and let Christ and his grace be precious in your eyes. O that ye would at length be serious about the state of your souls ! What mean ye to do ? Ye must die ; ye must appear before the judgment seat of God. Will ye lie down, and sleep another night at ease, in this case ? Do it not, for before another day you may be sisted before God's dreadful tribunal in the grave clothes of your corrupt state, and your vile souls cast into the pit of destruction, as a corrupt lump, to be for ever buried out of God's sight : for I testify unto you all, there is no peace with God, no pardon, no heaven for you in this state ; there is but a step betwixt you and eternal destruction from the presence of the Lord : if the brittle thread of your life, which may be broke with a touch, ere you are aware, be indeed broken while you are in this state, you are ruined for ever, and without remedy : but come speedily to Jesus Christ ; he has cleansed as vile souls as yours, and he will yet ' cleanse the blood that he hath cleansed,' Joel iii. 21.

The reason why God was pleased to deal with man in the way of a Covenant.

I know no reason can be given for this, but what must be resolved into the glory of the grace and goodness of God. It was certainly an act of grace and admirable condescension in God, to enter into a covenant with his own creature. Man was not at his own but God's disposal ; nor had he any thing to work with but what he had from God ; so that there was no proportion betwixt the work enjoined and the reward promised. Man before that covenant was bound, but God was free : for man was under the law of nature before he was under the covenant ; for the law was created with him, that is, he was no

sooner a rational creature than he was under the
law ; but this covenant was not made with him till
after he was brought into the garden to dress it. Before that covenant, God was free to dispose of man
as he saw fit, however perfectly he kept the law ;
but when in the covenant, he made the promise of
conferring life upon Adam in case of continued obedience, during the time set for his trial, then he was
debtor to his own faithfulness, which is necessarily
engaged to perform whatever it hath promised.   A-
gain, death was the natural wages of sin, though
there had been no covenant, and that by the rule of
justice, which plainly requires that man should be
dealt with as he has done.   But man having given
consent, however tacit, and not expressed in so many
words, which yet is equivalent to a formal consent to
the covenant, implying the threatening, the Lord proceeds not by simple justice, but by express formal
covenant, in punishing for the breach of it.   But we
may consider the reason of God the Almighty Creator and Lawgiver's entering into a covenant with
man a little more particularly, and that to the end
our hearts may be impressed with a just sense of the
glorious perfections of the great God, and the great
goodness shown to man in that whole transaction.
I say, then, that God was pleased to deal with man
by way of covenant, for two very important ends,
the manifestation of his own glory, and man's greater good.

1. For his own glory, which is the supreme end
of all his actions.   More particularly,

(1.) To display the lustre of his manifold or varie-
gated wisdom : Eph. iii. 10. ' To the intent that now,
unto the principalities and powers in heavenly places,
might be known by the church the manifold wisdom
of God.'   This way of dealing was the most effectual method for securing man's obedience ; for the covenant being a mutual engagement between God and
his creature, as it gave him infallible assurance to

strengthen his faith, so it was the sweetest bond to preserve his felicity. Divine wisdom shines clearly, in suiting the method of dealing to the nature of the reasonable creature, which was to be led with its own consent. It is true, the precept alone is binding upon man by virtue of the authority of the imposer; but man's own consent increases the obligation, twisting the cords of the law, and binding them more strongly to obedience. Thus Adam was God's servant by the condition of his nature, and also by his own choice, accepting the covenant, from which he could not recede, without the guilt and infamy of the worst perfidy. The terms of the covenant were such as became the parties concerned, God and man: it established an inseparable connexion between duty and happiness; as is plain from the sanction, *In the day that thou eatest thereof, thou shalt surely die.*

(2.) To show his wonderful moderation. For though he be Sovereign Monarch of the world, and has absolute power over all creatures to dispose of them as he pleases; yet, in covenanting with man, he sweetly tempered his supremacy and sovereign power, seeking as it were to reign with man's consent. And when, by virtue of his sovereign authority and absolute right, he might have enjoined harder terms to man, and those too altogether just and righteous, he chose to use so much moderation, that he would require nothing of man, but that which man himself should judge, and behoved in reason to be a just and easy yoke; and which, in accepting the terms, he acknowledged to be such.

(3.) For the praise of the glory of his grace. It was free condescension on God's part to make such a promise to man's obedience. He might have required obedience from him by virtue of his sovereignty, as his Lord and Maker, without binding himself by any promise to reward his service. All that he was capable to do was but mere duty to his Creator; and when he had done all that was commanded him, it was no

more than what he was bound to do as God's creature. It was simply impossible for man to merit any
thing at God's hand. It must be owned, there was
much grace in this transaction, in that God entered
into terms of agreement with man, not his equal, but
his own creature, and the work of his hands; and in
promising him a reward for his service, which was
certainly due to God by the law of creation previous to that federal deed, and so great a reward, even
eternal life, between which and the work there was
no proportion.

(4.) For venting his boundless love, in the communications of his goodness to man. For God did
not create man or angels because he needed them,
but that there might be proper objects for receiving
the displays of his goodness. Nor did he enter into
a covenant with man from any natural necessity, but
on design of communicating his bounty to him, Deut.
vii. 7, 8. 'The Lord did not set his love upon you,
nor choose you, because ye were more in number than
any people; (for ye were the fewest of all people;)
but because the Lord loved you, and because he
would keep the oath which he had sworn unto your
fathers, hath the Lord brought you out with a mighty
hand, and redeemed you out of the house of bond-
men, from the hand of Pharaoh king of Egypt.'
Ezek. xvi. 8 'Now, when I passed by thee, and
looked upon thee, behold, thy time was the time of
love; and I spread my skirt over thee, and covered
thy nakedness: yea, I sware unto thee, and entered
into a covenant with thee, saith the Lord God, and
thou becamest mine.' Though the Lord might have
exacted all that obedience and service from man,
which possibly he could yield, and reduced him into
his first nothing by annihilation at last, or at least
not have bestowed everlasting happiness upon him,
not bound himself by covenant whereby he might
expect it; yet, to show the greatness of his goodness and love, he chose a way to reward that service

in a most bountiful manner, which otherwise was due to him.

(5.) For the manifestation of his truth and faithfulness in keeping covenant with his creature, which could not otherwise have been so gloriously discovered. God had made illustrious displays of his wisdom, power, and goodness, in the creation of all things, and in that excellent piece of workmanship, man, the chief of his works in this world ; but his faithfulness and veracity could not have been known, at least in its effects, without some such transaction.

(6.) That he might be the more cleared and justified in resenting the injuries done him by the disobedience of his creature, with whom he had condescended to deal so graciously. For the more condescension and goodness there is on God's part, the greater ingratitude appears on man's part in trampling on the divine goodness. But,

2. God condescended to enter into covenant with man for man's greater good.

(1.) That thereby he might put the higher honour upon him. It was indeed a very distinguishing respect put upon man to be an ally of heaven, and the confederate friend of God. If it be an honour for a mean country peasant to be joined in a formal bond of friendship with a prince or potentate on earth, how much greater honour and dignity was it unto man to be joined in a bond of love and friendship with God, the Supreme Monarch of the whole world ?

(2.) To bind him the faster to his duty. The Lord knew man's mutable state, and how slippery and inconstant the heart of man is, where confirming grace is not vouchsafed ; therefore, to prevent this inconstancy incident to man, a finite creature, and to establish him in his obedience, he laid him under a covenant-obligation to his service. Man was bound to obey God by virtue of his creation ; but his making a covenant with man, which he willingly consented to, was a superadded tie to bind him the faster to his duty. By the covenant that was made with Adam, he had a kind of help to make him the more careful to observe the law which was written on his heart, and a prop to make him stand the more fixed and steady. For, on the one hand, he was warned of his danger in case of disobedience, that so he might beware of offending God ; and, on the other, he was encouraged to serve his Maker with the greater alacrity, from the greatness of the reward set before him, and the greatness of the punishment threatened in case he should disobey : both which tended notably to incline him to constancy in his duty.

(3.) That his obedience might be more cheerful, being that unto which he had willingly tied himself. God chose to rule man by his own consent, rather than by force. An absolute law might have extorted obedience from man, but a covenant made it appear more free and willing. It made man's obedience look as if it were the result of his own choice, rather than of any obligation lying upon him. This tended much to the honour of God ; for one volunteer that goeth to the war, doth honour the service more than ten soldiers pressed by force.

(4.) For his greater comfort and encouragement. By this he might clearly see what he might expect from God as a reward of his diligence and activity in his service.

(5.) That he might manifest himself to him, and deal with him the more familiarly. The dealing by way of covenant is the way of dealing betwixt man and man that hath least of distance in it, and most of familiarity, wherein parties come near to each other with greatest freedom. There is more nearness and familiarity in this than in any other way whereby God hath expressed his will. It is a more familiar way than that of commands and precepts, which imports nothing but authority and sovereignty. Yea, it is more familiar than the way of absolute promises, which might indeed set forth God's abundant goodness, but not so much God's familiar condescension, as the way of a covenant, when so great and so glorious a Majesty stoops to treat and deal by reciprocal engagements with so mean a creature as man, who is sprung of dust.

Consideration of what our first parents fell from, and of what they fell into.

1. They fell from a holy into a sinful state. They lost the image of God. Observe the opposition betwixt the image of God and that of Adam, Gen. v. 1. 3. There we are told, ' that God made man in his own likeness,' or image ; and that Adam begat a son ' in his own likeness,' even Seth, from whom the whole human race is sprung. Sin was a turning from God as their chief end, and making themselves their chief end ; whereby all their uprightness behoved to be lost. It broke the whole law of God at one touch, and violently struck against God and man's neighbour, that is, his posterity ; and so could not but waste and defile the conscience. This was the sense of the threatening, ' In the day that thou eatest thereof, thou shalt surely die.' And in this unholy state are all born of the first man.

(1.) They lost their knowledge, and fell under horrible blindness. Witness their fig-leaf cover for shrouding their nakedness, and their hiding themselves from the presence of the Lord, Gen. iii. 7, 8. A plain indication of their falling into dreadful ignorance of the Divine Being, the opposite of that great knowledge they had of him in their primitive state of integrity.

(2.) They lost the righteousness of their will, Eccl. vii. 29. And they fell under an aversion to God. Witness their running away from him, ver. 8. their excusing their sin, transferring the guilt every one off themselves, till it landed at length on God himself, ver. 12. ' And the man said, The woman whom thou gavest to be with me, she gave me of the tree, and I did eat.'

(3.) They lost the holiness of their affections, which immediately fell into confusion and disorder. Witness their covering their nakedness. While they were innocent, though naked, they were not ashamed; but that jewel being gone, the irregularity of their affections began to appear in discovering themselves to be naked, by the evil operation of concupiscence in their minds.

2. They fell from a happy state into a miserable one. O what a fearful overturn was made by their sin!

(1.) Horror of conscience seizes them, appearing in flying from the divine presence; which nothing but guilt, clasping as a serpent about them, could have induced them to do, ver. 8. ' And they heard the voice of the Lord God walking in the garden in the cool of the day : and Adam and his wife hid themselves from the presence of the Lord God amongst the trees of the garden.' Death was threatened in case of transgression, Gen. ii. 17. They both die spiritually, and are bound with the cords of temporal and eternal death.

(2.) They are driven out of paradise, excommunicated and declared incapable of communion with God in the tree of life in the garden, Gen. iii. 23. ' The Lord God sent him forth from the garden of Eden,' as a divorced woman out of the house of her husband, as the word signifies. Nay, God drove out the man, expelling him from that pleasant and delightful place, which he had forfeited by his transgression, ver. 24.

(3.) The woman, the first transgressor, is condemned to sorrow and pain in breeding, bearing, and bring-

ing forth children, ver. 16. which, as some observe, is
greater in women than other creatures. And frequently women lose their lives in the case.

(4.) She is put under a yoke of subjection to her
husband, ver. 16. Not but that the woman was subject to him before, but it was to a gentle and loving
guide : but now all her desires are subjected to her
husband, to grant them or deny them as he sees fit,
because she eat of the forbidden fruit without asking
his advice ; which now, because of his and her corruption, becomes a heavy yoke.

(5.) The ground is cursed for man's sake ; under
the influence of which curse it is barren of wholesome
fruits, which it does not yield without heavy labour
and diligent cultivation, but fruitful in noxious plants,
as thorns and thistles, ver. 17.

(6.) Man is condemned to singular anxiety, to
weary, toilsome, and ofttimes fruitless labour, whether it be the labour of the hands or of the mind,
ver. 17. 19. ; for this last is to be taken into the account too, as appears from Eccl. i. 13. 18. ' I gave
my heart,' says the preacher, ' to seek and search
out by wisdom concerning all things that are done
under heaven : this sore travel hath God given to
the sons of man to be exercised therewith. For in
much wisdom is much grief : and he that increaseth
knowledge increaseth sorrow.'

*A full explanation of the way by which the lament-
able fall of our first parents happened.*

For understanding this, consider,
1. That our first parents had a freedom of will.
Freedom of will is a liberty in the will, whereby of
its own accord, freely and spontaneously, without
any force upon it, it chooses or refuses what is pro-

posed to it by the understanding. And this freedom
of will man hath in whatever state he be. But there
is a great difference of the freedom of will in the different states of man. In the natural corrupt state,
man has a free will only to evil, Gen. vi. 5. ' Every
imagination of the thoughts of his heart is only evil
continually. Eph. ii. 1. ' He is dead in trespasses
and sins.' He freely chooseth evil without any force
on his will ; and he cannot do otherwise, being under the bondage of sin. In the state of grace, man
has a free-will, partly to good and partly to evil.
Hence the apostle says, Rom. vii. 22. 24. ' I delight
in the law of God after the inward man. But I see
another law in my members, warring against the law
of my mind, and bringing me into captivity to the
law of sin, which is in my members.' In this state the
will sometimes chooses that which is good, and sometimes that which is evil. This freedom of will is in all
regenerate persons who have in some measure recovered the image of God. They choose good freely by virtue of a principle of grace wrought in them by the
sanctifying operations of the Divine Spirit ; yet
through the remainders of corruption that abides in
them, their wills are sometimes inclined to that which
is evil. In the state of glory, man has a free-will to good
only. In this state the blessed choose good freely ;
and, being confirmed in a holy state, they cannot sin.

The freedom of will that man had in the state of
innocence was different from all these. In that state
he had a freedom of will both to good and evil ; and
so had a power wholly to choose good, or wholly to
choose evil ; which differences it from the freedom
of will in the state of grace. He had a free-will to
good, yea, the natural set of his will was to good only,
Eccl. vii. 29. being ' made upright ; ' but it was liable
to change through the power of temptation, and so
free to evil also, as mournful experience has evidenced. Man was created holy and righteous, and
received a power from God constantly to persevere

in goodness, if he would ; yet the act of perseverance was left to the choice and liberty of his own will. To illustrate this a little, we may observe some resemblance of it in nature. God creates the eye, says one, and puts into it the faculty of seeing, and withal he adds to the eye necessary helps by the light of the sun. As for the act of seeing, it is left to man's liberty ; for he may see if he will, and if he will he may shut his eyes. The physician, again, by his art procures an appetite, and provides convenient food for the patient : but the act of eating is in the pleasure of the patient; for he may eat, or abstain from it if he will. Thus God gave Adam strength and power to persevere in righteousness, but the will he left to himself.

Let no man quarrel, that God made Adam liable to change in his goodness ; for if he had been unchangeably holy, he behoved to be so, either by nature or by free grace ; if by nature, that were to make him God ; if of free grace, then there was no wrong done him in with-holding what was not due. And he would have got the grace of confirmation, if he had stood the time of his trial.

Secondly, God left our first parents to the freedom of their own will ; and was in no respect the cause of their falling.

1. The Lord did not withdraw any of that strength and ability which he had bestowed upon them in their creation. There was no subtraction of any grace that was requisite for their standing. God is not like man to give and recal again ; for his gifts are without repentance. Adam left God before he was forsaken by him.

2. The Lord did not infuse any vicious inclinations into man. There was no internal impulsion from God, exciting him to eat the forbidden fruit. He neither moved him to sin, nor approved of it, but forbade it under the severest penalty. It is altogether inconsistent with the divine purity to incline the

creature to sin. As God cannot be tempted to evil, neither tempteth he any man. It is extremely injurious to his infinite wisdom to think, that he would deface and spoil that admirable work which he had composed with so much design and counsel. And it is highly dishonourable to his immense goodness. He loved his creature, the masterpiece of his works; and love is an inclination to do good. It was impossible, therefore, that God should induce man to sin, or withdraw that power from him which was necessary to resist the temptation, when the consequence must be his inevitable ruin.

But by their being left to the freedom of their own will, we are to understand God's withholding of that further grace (which he was nowise bound to give them) that would have infallibly prevented their falling into sin. God only permitted this fall. No doubt he could have hindered either Satan to tempt, or man to have yielded; but in his holy wise providence, without which a sparrow cannot fall, far less all mankind, he permitted Satan to tempt, that is, he did not hinder him, which he was not obliged to do. It was in man's power to continue in his obedience or not. God was not obliged to hinder his fall. As he brings light out of darkness, order out of confusion, and life out of death, so he knew how to bring good out of evil, and glory to himself out of man's fall. Adam's fall was perfectly voluntary; his own will was the sole cause of it, as will plainly appear, if you consider,

(1.) That while he continued innocent, he had a sufficient power to persevere in his holy state. God created him with a perfection of grace. If he had pleased, he might have effectually resisted the temptation, and continued stedfast in his duty to God; and God was under no obligation to give him that further actual grace which would have effectually kept him up. And this grace he was bound neither to give nor continue with him.

(2.) That the devil did only allure, he could not ravish his consent. Though his malice be infinite, yet his power is restrained and limited by the omnipotent hand of Jehovah, that he cannot fasten an immediate, much less an irresistible, impression on the will. He therefore made use of an external object to invite man to sin. Now, objects have no constraining force ; they are but partial agents, and derive all their efficacy from the faculty into which they are agreeable. And although now, in our fallen state, sin hath so disordered the flesh, that there is great difficulty in resisting those objects that pleasantly insinuate themselves ; yet, in the state of innocence, there was such an universal rectitude in Adam, and so entire a subjection of the sensual appetite to the superior power of reason, that he might have obtained an easy conquest. A resolute negative had made him victorious ; by a strong denial, he had baffled that proud spirit.

(3.) That Adam's disobedience was the effect of his own choice. For a specious object was conveyed through the unguarded sense to his fancy, and from that to his understanding, which, by a vicious careless neglecting to consider the danger, commended it to the will, and that resolved to embrace it. Now, it is plain and undeniable, that the action which resulted from the direction of the mind, and the choice of the will, was absolutely free. Besides, as the regret that is mixed with an action is a certain character that the person is under restraint ; so the delight that attends it is a clear evidence that he is free. When the appetite is drawn by the lure of pleasure, the more violent, the more voluntary is its motion. Now, the representation of the forbidden fruit was under the notion of pleasure : *The woman saw that the fruit was good for food*, (that is, pleasureable to the palate) *pleasant to the eye, and to be desired to make one wise*, that is, to increase knowledge, which is the pleasure of the mind ; and these allectives drew

her into the snare. Man was under no necessity to
sin. Force and co-action are inconsistent with the
nature of the will, and entirely destroys it. Adam
might have continued in his obedience if he had
pleased. The devil had no power over him to disturb his felicity. He prevailed against him by a
simple suasion.

Thirdly, The devil tempted our first parents to
sin. The devil in the serpent set on man while he
stood. Where observe,

1. It was a true serpent which the devil appeared
in. What sort of a serpent it was, is not determined :
but it seems to have been a beautiful creature of a
shining colour : for in Deut. viii. 15. there are serpents spoken of that are in the Hebrew called *Seraphim,* the very name given to angels, which were
wont to appear in a splendid form, it may be like
these seraphim ; and so Eve might take the serpent
for one of these good angels. But Moses' plain historical narrative leaves no room to doubt that it was
a real serpent, representing it to be more subtile than
any beast of the field, and as cursed above all cattle,
and above every beast of the field, after the transgression, when it was condemned to go upon its belly,
and to eat dust all the days of its life, Gen. iii. 1. 14.
And it is known that the Egyptians, by the devil's
instigation, worshipped serpents. And in the old
Greek mysteries they used to carry about a serpent,
and cry *Evah :* a sign of the extraordinary service
it had done to the devil.

2. Though Moses makes no mention of the devil
in this affair, yet surely he was the prime instrument
in this fatal seduction. For seeing serpents cannot
speak, and far less reason, we may easily conclude
it was the devil, who therefore is called ' the old serpent, and a liar and murderer from the beginning,'
John viii. 44. See Gen. iii. 15. Compare Heb. ii. 14.
The devil then, one, perhaps the chief, of those rebellious spirits, who by a furious ambition had raised

a war in heaven, and were fallen from their obedience
and glorious state, designing to corrupt man, and
make him a companion with them in their revolt,
set about this work, urged by two strong and powerful passions, hatred and envy.

(1.) The devil was prompted to this action by an
implacable hatred against God. For being fallen
under a final and irrevocable doom, he looked upon
God as an irreconcileable enemy ; and not being able
to injure his essence, he struck at his image ; as the
fury of some beast discharges itself at the picture of
a man. He singled out Adam as the mark of his
malice, that, by seducing him from his duty, he might
defeat God's design, which was to be honoured by
man's free and cheerful obedience ; and so to eclipse
the lustre of his excellencies, as though he had made
man in vain.

(2) He was solicited by envy, the first native of
hell. For having lost the friendship and favour of
God, and being cast out of heaven, the happy region
of blessedness and joy, the sight of Adam's felicity
highly exasperated and accented his grief, that man,
who by the condition of his nature was inferior to
him, should be the prince of the world, and the special friend and favourite of heaven, whilst he himself
was a miserable prisoner, under those fatal chains
which restrained and tormented him, the power and
the wrath of God. This made his state and condition more intolerable. His torment was incapable
of any allay, but by rendering man as miserable as
himself. And as hatred excited his envy, so envy inflamed his hatred, and both joined together in mischief. And being thus pushed on, his subtility being
equal to his malice, he contrives a temptation which
might be most taking and dangerous to man in his
raised and happy state. As soon as Adam was invested with all his glory, the devil, as it were, would
dethrone him on the day of his coronation, and bring
both him and all his posterity under a curse. Here

I shall consider the temptation which was the occasion of man's fall, and the devil's subtility in managing it.

1. As to the temptation itself, it was very suitable and promising. The devil attempted to seduce him by art, in his propounding the lure of knowledge and pleasure, to inveigle the spiritual and sensitive appetites at once. There were three things in which the desirableness of this fruit was represented, which sets forth the great art and sagacity of Satan.

(1.) Its agreeableness to the palate. It is said, *The woman saw the fruit that it was good for food.* Satan told her that it was of a most sweet and delicious taste, and would highly gratify her sensual appetite.

(2.) It *was pleasant to the eye ;* a charming and beautiful fruit, which had an inviting aspect.

(3.) There was a desirableness in it to the rational appetite. It was *a tree to be desired to make one wise.* And the serpent told her, ver. 5. that, upon eating it, *their eyes should be opened, and they should be as gods, knowing good and evil.* He made Eve believe, that, upon her eating the fruit of that tree, she would be raised and elevated from the human to a kind of divine nature and condition. This was the temptation with which the devil assaulted our first parents in paradise, and prevailed against them.

2. I shall take notice of Satan's subtility in managing this temptation. We read of his wiles in scripture ; and indeed they are worse than his darts.

(1.) That he might the better succeed in his hellish design, he addressed himself to the woman, the weakest person, and most liable to seduction. He reckoned, and that justly enough, that his attempt would be most successful here, and that she was less able to resist him. He broke over the hedge where it was weakest. He knew very well that he could more easily insinuate and wind himself into her by a

temptation. An old experienced soldier, when he is
to storm and enter a castle, observes carefully where
there is a breach, or how he may enter with most fa-
cility : so did Satan here when he assaulted Eve, the
weaker vessel. And he tempted the woman first, because he knew, if once he could prevail with her, she
would easily entice and draw on her husband. Satan
knew very well, that a temptation coming to Adam
from Eve, his wife, in this the infancy of their married state, would be more prevailing and less sus-
pected. Sometimes near relations prove strong temptations. A wife may be a snare, when she dissuades
her husband from his duty, or entices him to sin. It
is said of Ahab, 1 Kings xxi. 25. that ' there was
none like unto him, which did sell himself to work
wickedness in the sight of the Lord, whom Jezebel
his wife stirred up.' She blew the coals, and made
his sin flame out with the greater violence. Satan
discovered his great subtility in tempting Adam by
his wife ; for he with complacency received the temptation, and, by the enticement of this old serpent,
committed adultery with the creature, from whence
the cursed race of sin and all miseries proceed.

(2.) He assaulted her when alone, in the absence
of her husband, and so did the more easily prevail.
For ' two are better than one ; ' and, as Solomon observes, ' a threefold cord is not easily broken.' Had
Adam been present at this fatal congress, it is like
the attempt had not been so easily successful.

(3.) The devil's subtility may be seen here in hiding himself in the body of a serpent, which, before
sin entered into the world, was not terrible to Eve.
Satan crept into a serpent, and spake in it, as the
angel did afterwards in Balaam's ass. She was not
afraid of this apparition ; for she knew no guilt, and
therefore was not subject to any fear. She might
look upon this as one of the angels or blessed spirits,
which, as they used after this to appear in the shape
of men, why might not one of them appear now, and

converse with her in the shape of a beautiful serpent; why might not she freely discourse with this, which she reckoned one of those good angels, to whose care and tuition both she and her husband were committed? For we may suppose the fall of the angels was not yet revealed to her, and she thought this to be a good spirit, otherwise she would certainly have declined all conversation with an apostate angel. Some have supposed, and that not very improbably, that more discourse passed between the serpent and Eve than is recorded, Gen. iii. and represent the matter thus: The serpent, catching the opportunity of the woman's being at a distance from her husband, makes his address to her with a short speech, saluting her as empress of the world, and giving her a great many encomiums and dignifying titles. She wonders, and inquires what this meant? and whether he was not a brute creature? and how he came to be endowed with understanding and speech? The serpent replies, that he was nobler than a brute, and did indeed once want both these gifts; but, by eating a certain fruit in this garden, he had got both. She immediately asks what fruit and tree that was which had such a surprising influence and virtue. Which when he had showed her, she replied, This no doubt is an excellent fruit, but God hath strictly forbidden us the use of it. To which the serpent presently replies, as in the close of ver. 1. ' Yea, hath God said, Ye shall not eat of every tree of the garden?' The way how these words are introduced plainly shows that something had passed previous thereto. And some suppose that the serpent, to confirm the truth of his assertion, pulled off some of the fruits of the tree, ate one in her presence, and presented another to Eve, who, before eating it, had the discourse with the serpent recorded in the subsequent verses.

(4.) The devil's subtility appears in accosting our first parents so early, before they were confirmed in their course of obedience. The holy angels in heaven are fully confirmed in righteousness and holiness ; they are called *morning stars,* Job xxxviii. 7. and are all fixed, not wandering stars. But our first parents were not confirmed in their obedience, they were not yet fixed in their orb of holiness. Though they had a possibility of standing, yet they had not an impossibility of falling. They were holy but mutable. It was possible for them to change their state. Now, Satan's subtility was eminently manifested here.

(5.) He first allures with the hopes of impunity, and then he promises an universal knowledge of good and evil.

[1.] He persuades Eve, that though she did eat of the forbidden tree, yet she should not die, ver. 4. ' Ye shall not surely die.' ' God indeed did say so, for your terror, to keep you in awe. But do not entertain such hard and unworthy thoughts of that God, who is infinitely good and gracious. Do not think that, for such a trifle as the eating of a little fruit, he will undo you and all your posterity for ever, and so suddenly destroy the most excellent piece of his own workmanship, wherein his image shines in a most resplendent manner.

[2.] He promiseth them an universal knowledge, as the effect of eating this fruit, ver. 5. ' For God doth know, that in the day ye eat thereof, then your eyes shall be opened : and ye shall be as gods, knowing good and evil.' ' God's design in that prohibition is only this : He knows that you shall be so far from dying, that thereby you shall certainly be entered into a new and more noble and excellent kind of life. The eyes of your understandings, which are now shut in a great measure as to the knowledge of many things, shall then be wide opened, and ye shall see more clearly and distinctly than now you do. You shall be as God, and shall attain to a kind of omniscience.'

(6.) Satan's subtility was manifested here, in assaulting Eve's faith. He would persuade her, that

God had not spoken truth in that threatening. He managed the whole business with a lie ; yea, he adds one lie to another. ' Ye shall not surely die,' says he ; and then he represents God as envying our first parents that great honour and happiness that was attainable by them, ver. 5. and himself as one that wished their happiness, and would tell her how to arrive at it ; and alleges they might easily understand, by the very name of the tree, the truth of what he says to her. ' It is,' says he, ' because God envies your felicity, that he hath forbidden you the use of this tree. But know ye, if ye eat of it, ye shall be as gods.' Here was subtility indeed. The devil was first a liar, and then a murderer. This was Satan's master-piece to weaken her faith ; for when he had shaken that, and brought her once to distrust, then she was easily overcome : and presently put forth her hand to pluck the forbidden fruit. By these pretences he ruined innocence itself : for the woman being deceived by these allectives, swallowed down the poison of the serpent ; and, having tasted death herself, she betook herself to her husband, and persuaded him by the same means to despise the law of their Creator.

Thus sin made its entrance into the world, and brought an universal confusion into it. For the moral harmony of the world consisting in the just subordination of the several ranks of beings to one another, and of all to God, when man, who was placed next to him, broke the union, his fall brought a desperate disorder into God's government. And though the matter of the offence may seem small, yet the disobedience was infinitely great ; it being the transgression of that command which was given to be the real proof of man's subjection to God. The honour and majesty of the whole law was violated in the breach of that symbolical precept.

Fourthly, Man being thus left to the freedom of his own will, abused his liberty in complying with

the temptation, and freely apostatized from God.
And so man himself, and he only, was the true and
proper cause of his own sinning. Not God, for he
is unchangeably holy ; not the devil, for he could
only tempt, not force : therefore man himself only is
to blame, Eccl. vii. 29. ' God made man upright, but
they have sought out many inventions.'

****

Useful lessons from the doctrine of the Fall.

1. Hence see the great weakness, yea, the nothing-
ness of the creature, when left to itself. When Adam
was in the state of integrity, he quickly made a defection from God, he soon lost the robe of his primitive
innocence, and all the blessedness of paradise. If our
nature was so weak when at the best, then how miserably weak is it now when it is at its worst? If
Adam did not stand when he was perfectly holy and
righteous, how unable are we to stand, when sin has
entirely disabled us? If purified nature could not resist the temptation, but was quite overturned at the
first blast, how shall corrupt nature stand, when besieged and stormed with a long succession of strong
and violent assaults ? If Adam in a few hours sinned
himself out of paradise, O! how quickly would even
those who are regenerated sin themselves into hell,
if they were not preserved by a greater power than
their own ; nay, ' kept by the power of God through
faith unto salvation ?' God left some of the angels to
themselves, and they turned devils ; and he left innocent Adam, and he fell into a gulph of misery. May
we not then much more now say, ' Let him that
standeth take heed lest he fall;' especially seeing
we have a violent bent and strong propensity of heart
and will to go away from God, which Adam had not.

2. There is no reason to blame God for the misery of the fall. He gave man sufficient power and ability to stand if he would, promised a large reward to excite his obedience, and severely threatened disobedience : but man would needs try experiments to make his case better than God made it ; and so fell by his own inventions. The fault then was his own, he alone was culpable, and he was the author of his own ruin.

3. Watch and pray that ye enter not into temptation. You see that you have to do with an impudent devil, who is still going about seeking whom he may devour. No state, while ye are in this world, can secure you from his temptations. Though ye be in a state of reconciliation and friendship with God, ye are not secure from his assaults. No place, though it were a paradise, can protect you. He has malice enough to push you on to the most atrocious sins ; subtility and experience, acquired by hellish art in the course of some thousand years, to suit his baits so as they may best take with you. Do not parley with the tempter : listening to him may bring on doubting, and doubting may bring on the denial of God's truths, and so end in full compliance with his horrid temptations, as it did with our first mother.

4. If Adam fell so soon after he was created, and could not be his own keeper, then certainly he can much less be his own saviour. If he could not preserve himself from falling into the gulph, much less can he pull himself out of it again. We are by nature without strength, and have no inclination to that which is good ; and therefore God must work powerfully and efficaciously in us. We cannot break the chains and knock off the fetters of sin and Satan by which we are held. We can make no reparation to the honour of God for the wrongs and indignities we have done him. To Christ alone we must be indebted for all this. We have destroyed ourselves, but in him is our help.

5. There is no justification by the works of the
law. Adam broke the covenant of works, and so
rendered it impracticable for him or his posterity to
attain to life and happiness by it. For it is written,
' Cursed is every one that continueth not in all things
which are written in the book of the law to do them,'
Gal. iii. 10. ' As many as are of the works of the
law are under the curse.' The law requires a perfect
spotless righteousness, but the best righteousness of
fallen man is but filthy rags. It is not only torn and
ragged, but polluted and defiled. We have all sinned
and come short of the glory of God : and there is no
possibility of obtaining justification by the works of
the law now ; ' for by the works of the law,' says
Paul, ' shall no flesh be justified.'

Lastly, See your absolute need of Christ ; for there
is no other name under heaven given among men,
whereby ye can be saved. Go not about to establish
a righteousness of your own, or seek to get to heaven
by any works of your own. That is indeed still the
thing man aims at. First he sins, and then, like
Adam, sets to work to cover himself with a cover of
his own making, to procure a title to eternal life by
his own works. But is it easier to recover yourselves
from the ruins of the fall, than to stand while yet in
an innocent and upright state ? Have ye gathered
strength by sinning, and are ye able to walk to heaven
on your own legs ? Come then to Christ, who by his
obedience and death hath procured a righteousness
which alone can stand you in stead, and by which
alone you can obtain a right to eternal life. Ye must
then either come to Christ, or perish for ever.

****

An affecting view of that in which the evil of sin doth lie.

The evil of sin doth lie,

1. And principally, in the wrong done to God, and its contrariety. 1*st*, To his nature, which is altogether holy. Hence the Psalmist says, Psal. li. 4. ' Against thee, thee only have I sinned, and done this evil in thy sight.' David had exceedingly wronged Uriah in defiling his wife, and procuring the death of himself ; yet he considers his great sin in that matter as chiefly against God, and contrary to his holy nature. 2*d*, In its contrariety to God's will and law, which is a sort of a copy of his nature. And God being all good, and the chief good, sin must needs be a sort of infinite evil.

2. In the wrong it doth to ourselves. ' He that sinneth against me,' says the personal Wisdom of God, ' wrongeth his own soul, Prov. viii. 36. For, 1*st*, It leaves a stain and spiritual pollution on the soul, whereby it becomes filthy and vile ; and therefore sin is called filthiness, and is said to defile the soul, whereupon follows God's loathing the sinner, Isa. i. 15. and shame and confusion on the sinner himself, Gen. iii. 7. 2*d*, It brings on guilt, whereby the sinner is bound over to punishment, according to the state in which he is, until his sin be pardoned. This ariseth from the justice of God, and the threatening of his law, which brings on all miseries whatsoever.

But more particularly upon this head, when men pass the bounds and limits which God hath set them in his law, then they transgress it. All the violations of negative precepts are transgressions of God's law. The design of the moral law is to keep men within

3 I

the bounds of their duty ; and when they sin they go beyond them.   Sin is indeed the greatest of evils ; it is directly opposite to God the supreme good.   The definition that is given of sin expresses its essential evil.   It is the transgression of the divine law, and consequently it opposes the rights of God's throne, and obscures the glory of his attributes, which are exercised in the moral government of the world. God is our King, our Lawgiver, and our Judge. From his right and property in us as his creatures, his title to, and sovereign power and dominion over us doth arise and flow.   Man is endued with the powers of understanding and election, to conceive and choose what is good, and to reject what is evil ; is governed by a law, even the declared will of his Maker.   Now, sin being a transgression of this law, contains many evils in it.   As,

1. It is high rebellion against the sovereign Majesty of God, that gives the life of authority to the law.   Therefore divine precepts are enforced with the most proper and binding motive to obedience, *I am the Lord.*   He that commits sin, especially with pleasure and design, implicitly denies his dependance upon God as his Maker and Governor, and arrogates to himself an irresponsible liberty to do his own will. This is clearly expressed by those atheistical designers who said, ' Our lips are our own ; who is Lord over us ? ' Psal. xii. 4.   The language of men's actions, which is more convincing than their words, plainly declares, that they despise his commandments, and contemn his authority, as if they were not his creatures and subjects.

2. It is an extreme aggravation of this evil, that sin, as it is a disclaiming our homage to God, so it is in true account a yielding subjection to the devil ; for sin is in the strictest propriety his work.   The original rebellion in paradise was by his temptation ; and all the actual and habitual sins of men, since the fall, are by his efficacious influence.   He darkens

the carnal mind ; he sways and rules the stubborn
will ; he excites and inflames the vicious affections,
and imperiously rules in the children of disobedience.
He is therefore styled the prince and god of this
world.   And what more contumelious indignity can
there be, than to prefer to the glorious Creator of
heaven and earth, a damned spirit, the most cursed
part of the whole creation ? More particularly, sin
strikes at the root of all the divine attributes.

(1.) It is contrary to the unspotted holiness of God,
which is the peculiar glory of the Deity.   Of all the
glorious and benign constellations of the divine attributes which shine in the law of God, his holiness
hath the brightest lustre.   God is righteous in all his
ways, and holy in all his works : but the most precious and venerable monument of his holiness is the
law.   This is a true draught of his image, and a
clear copy of his nature and will.   It is the perspi-
cuous rule of our duty, without any blemish or imperfection.   See what a high encomium the apostle
gives it, ' The commandment is holy, just, and good,'
Rom. vii. 12.   It enjoins nothing but what is absolutely good, without the least mixture and tincture
of evil.   It is a full and complete rule, in nothing
defective, and in nothing superfluous, but comprehends the whole duty of man.   The sum of it is set
down by the apostle, Tit. ii. 11.   We are *to live soberly, i. e.* we are to abstain from every thing that
may blemish and stain the excellency of our reasonable nature.   We are to live *righteously.*   This respects the state and situation wherein God hath placed
us in the world for the advancing of his glory.   It includes and comprehends in it all the respective duties
we owe to others, to whom we are united by the bands
of nature, of civil society, or of spiritual communion.
And we are to live *godly,* which takes in all the internal and outward duties which we owe to God,
who is the Sovereign of our spirits, whose will must
be the rule, and his glory the end of all our actions.

In short, the law is so contrived and framed, that, abstracting from the authority of the Lawgiver, its holiness and goodness lays an eternal obligation upon us to obey its dictates. Now, sin is directly and formally a contrariety to the infinite sanctity and purity of God ; consisting in a not doing what the law commands, or in doing that which it expressly forbids ; and God cannot look upon it, but with infinite detestation : Hab. i. 13. ' Thou art of purer eyes than to behold evil, and canst not look on iniquity : wherefore lookest thou upon them that deal treacherously, and holdest thy tongue when the wicked devoureth the man that is more righteous than he ?' He cannot but hate that which is opposite to the glory of his nature, and to the lustre of all his perfections.

(2.) Sin vilifies the wisdom of God, which prescribed the law to men as the rule of their duty. The divine wisdom shines resplendently in his laws. They are all framed with an exact congruity to the nature of God, and his relation to us, and to the faculties of man before he was corrupted. And thus the divine law being a bright transcript both of God's will and his wisdom, binds the understanding and will, which are the leading faculties in man, to esteem and approve, to consent to and choose, all his precepts as best. Now, sin vilifies the infinite wisdom of God, both as to the precepts of the law, the rule of our duty, and the sanction annexed to it for confirming its obligation. It taxes the precepts as an unequal yoke, and as too severe and rigid a confinement to our wills and actions. Thus the impious rebels complained of old, ' The ways of the Lord are not equal :' they are injurious to our liberties, they restrain and infringe them, and are not worthy of our study and observation. And it accounts the rewards and punishments which God has annexed as the sanction of the law to secure our obedience to its precepts, weak and ineffectual motives to serve that purpose. And thus it reflects upon the wisdom

of the Lawgiver as lame and defective, in not binding his subjects more firmly to their duty.

(3.) Sin is a high contempt and horrid abuse of
the divine goodness, which should have a powerful
influence in binding man to his duty. His creating
goodness is hereby contemned, which raised us out
of the dust of the earth unto an excellent and glorious being. Our parents were indeed instrumental
in the production of our bodies ; but the variety and
union, the beauty and usefulness of the several parts,
was the high design of his wisdom, and the excellent work of his hands. Man's body is composed
of as many miracles as members, and is full of wonders. The lively idea and perfect exemplar of that
regular fabric was modelled in the divine mind. This
affected David with a holy admiration : Psal. cxxxix.
14, 15, 16. ' I will praise thee ; for I am fearfully and
wonderfully made : marvellous are thy works ; and
that my soul knoweth right well. My substance was
not hid from thee, when I was made in secret, and
curiously wrought in the lowest parts of the earth.
Thine eyes did see my substance, yet being unper-
fect ; and in thy book all my members were written,
which in continuance were fashioned, when as yet
there was none of them.' The soul, or principal part,
is of a celestial origin, inspired by the Father of Lights.
The faculties of understanding and election are the indelible characters of our honour and dignity above
the brutes, and make us capable to please God and
enjoy our Maker. Now, God's design in giving us
our being was to communicate of his own fulness to,
and to be actively glorified by, intelligent creatures :
Rev. iv. 11. ' Thou art worthy, O Lord, to receive
glory, and honour, and power : for thou hast created
all things, and for thy pleasure they are and were
created.' None are so void of rational sentiments,
as not to own, that it is our indispensable duty and
reasonable service to offer up ourselves an entire living sacrifice to the glory of God. What is more na-

tural, according to the laws of uncorrupted reason,
than that love should correspond with love ? As the
one descends in benefits, the other should ascend in
praise and thankfulness.   Now, sin breaks all these
sacred bonds of grace and gratitude, which engage
us to love and obey our Maker.   He is the just Lord
of all our faculties, intellectual and sensitive ; and
the sinner employs them all as weapons of unrighteousness to fight against God.   Again, it is he that
upholds and preserves us by the powerful influence
of his providence, which is a renewed creation every
moment, daily surrounding us with many mercies.
All the goodness which God thus bestows upon men,
the sinner abuses against him.   This is the most unworthy, shameful, and monstrous ingratitude imagin-
able.   This makes forgetful and unthankful men
more brutish than the dull ox or stupid ass, who
serve and obey those that feed and keep them.   Yea
it sinks them below the insensible part of the creation, which invariably observes the law and order
prescribed by the Creator.   This is astonishing de-
generacy.   It was the complaint of God himself:
Isa. i. 2. ' Hear, O heavens, and give ear, O earth :
I have nourished and brought up children, and they
have rebelled against me.'

(4.) The sinner disparages the divine justice, in
promising himself peace and safety, notwithstanding of the wrath and vengeance that is denounced
against him by the Lord.   He labours to dissolve
the inseparable connexion that God hath placed betwixt sin and punishment, which is not a mere arbi-
trary constitution, but founded upon the desert of
sin, and the infinite rectitude of the divine nature,
which unchangeably hates it.   The sinner sets the
divine attributes a contending as it were with one
another, presuming that mercy will disarm justice,
and suspend its power by restraining it from taking
vengeance upon impenitent sinners.   And thus sinners become bold and resolute in their impious

courses, like him mentioned, Deut. xxix. 19. who
said, ' I shall have peace though I walk in the imagination of my heart, to add drunkenness to thirst.'
This casts such an aspersion on the justice of God,
that he solemnly threatens the severest vengeance
for it; as you may see in ver. 20. ' The Lord will
not spare him, but the anger of the Lord, and his
jealousy shall smoke against that man, and all the
curses that are written in this book shall lie upon
him, and the Lord shall blot out his name from under heaven.'

(5.) Sin strikes against the omniscience of God,
and at least denies it implicitly. There is such a
turpitude adhering to sin, that it cannot endure the
light of the sun, nor the light of conscience, but seeks
to be concealed under a mask of virtue or a vail of
darkness. What is said of the adulterer and the
thief, is true in proportion of every sinner, ' If a man
sees them, they are in the terrors of the shadow of
death.' And hence it is, that many who would blush
and tremble if they were surprised in their sinful actings by a child or a stranger, are not at all afraid of
the eye of God, though he narrowly notices all their
sins, in order to judge them, and will judge them in
order to punish them.

(6.) *Lastly*, Sin bids a defiance to the divine power.
This is one of the essential attributes of God that
makes him so terrible to devils and wicked men.
He hath both a right to punish and power enough
to revenge every transgression of his law that sinners
are guilty of. Now his judicial power is supreme
and his executive power is irresistible. He can with
one stroke dispatch the body to the grave, and the
soul to the pit of hell, and make men as miserable as
they are sinful: and yet sinners as boldly provoke
him as if there were no danger. We read of the in-
fatuated Syrians, how they foolishly thought that
God the protector of Israel had only power on the
hills but not in the valleys, and therefore renewed

the war to their own destruction.   Thus proud sinners enter the lists with God, and range an army of
lusts against the armies of heaven, and being blindly
bold, run on headlong upon their own ruin.   They
neither believe God's all-seeing eye, nor fear his almighty hand.   You see then what an evil sin is in
its nature.   It is high rebellion against God, and
strikes at the root of all his attributes.

*How Adam's first sin comes to be imputed to all his
posterity.*

   The great reason of this is, because we are all included in Adam's covenant.   The covenant was
made with him, not only for himself, but for all his
posterity.   Consider here,
   1. It was the covenant of works that was made
with Adam, the condition whereof was perfect obedience.   This was the first covenant.   As for the
covenant of grace, it was made with the second
Adam.
   2. It was made with him for himself.   That was
the way he himself was to attain perfect happiness ;
his own stock was in that ship.
   3. It was made not only for himself, but for all
his posterity descending from him by ordinary generation.   So that he was not here as a mere private
person, but as a public person, the moral head and
representative of all mankind.   Hence the scripture
holds forth Adam and Christ, as if there never had
been any but these two men in the world, 1 Cor. xv.
47. 'The first man is of the earth, earthy, (says he) :
the second man is the Lord from heaven.'   And this
he does, because they were two public persons, each
of them having under them persons represented by
them, Rom. v. 14, 18. ' Death reigned from Adam

to Moses, even over them that had not sinned after the similitude of Adam's transgression, who is the figure of him that was to come. As by the offence of one, judgment came upon all men to condemnation; even so by the righteousness of one, the free gift came upon all men unto justification of life.' This is plain from the imputation of Adam's sin, which necessarily requires this as the foundation of it. We being thus included and represented in that covenant, what he did he did as our head, and therefore it is justly imputed to us.

But some may be ready to say, we made not choice of Adam for that purpose. *Ans.* (1.) God made the choice, who was as meet to make it for us as we for ourselves. And 'who art thou that repliest against God.' (2.) Adam was our natural head, the common father of us all, Acts xvii. 26. and who was so meet to be trusted with the concerns of all mankind as he? But to clear further the reasonableness of this imputation, and to still the murmurings of proud nature against the dispensation of God, consider,

(1.) Adam's sin is imputed to us, because it is ours. For God doth not reckon a thing ours, which is not so, Rom. ii. 2.—'The judgment of God is according to truth.' For God's justice doth not punish men for a sin which is no way theirs. And it is our sin upon the account aforesaid. Even as Christ's righteousness is ours by virtue of our union with him. As if a person that has the plague infects others, and they die, they die, by their own plague, and not by that of another.

(2.) It was free for God, antecedently to the covenant made with man, either to have annihilated all mankind, or if he had preserved them, to have given them no promise of eternal life in heaven, notwithstanding by natural justice they would have been liable to his wrath in case of sin. Was it not then an act of grace in God to make such a rich covenant

3 K

as this ? and would not men have consented to this
representation gladly in this case ?

(3.) Adam had a power to stand if he would, being
made after the image of God, Gen. i. 26.   He was
set down with a stock capable to be improved to the
eternal upmaking of all his posterity.   So that he
was as capable to stand as any afterwards could be
for themselves : and this was a trial that would have
soon been over, while the other would have been continually a-doing, had men been created independent
on him as their representative.

4. He had natural affection the strongest to engage him.   He was our father, and all we the children that were in his loins, to whom we had as good
ground to trust as to any other creature.

5. His own stock was in the ship ; his all lay at
stake as well as ours.   Forgetting our interest, he
behoved to disregard his own, for he had no separate
interest from ours.

6. If he had stood, we could never have fallen ; he
had gained for us eternal happiness ; the image of
God, and the crown of glory, would have descended
from him to us by a sure conveyance.

And is it not reasonable, on the other hand, that if
he fell, we should fall, and bear the loss ? No man
quarrels, that when a master sets his land in tack to
a man and his heirs upon conditions, if the first pos-
sessor break the bargain, the heirs be denuded of it.

Lastly, All that quarrel this dispensation must
renounce their part in Christ : for we are made righteous by him, as sinners are made guilty by Adam.
If we fall in with the one, why not with the other ?
We chose Christ for our head in the second covenant,
no more than we did Adam in the first covenant.

....

Psalm li. 5. *Explained.*

" Behold, I was shapen in iniquity, and in sin did my mother
conceive me."

Man that was holy and happy is now fallen ; and
his fall should never be forgotten, but lamented,
though it were with tears of blood. Man's first sin
was the spring of all our woes, the poisonous fountain from whence all our misery flowed. It brought
mankind into an estate of sin and misery ; a state
wherein man can do nothing but sin, wherein every
thought, every word, and every action is tainted with
sin, wherein enmity to God and his holy nature, and
rebellion against, and opposition to his righteous law
universally reign and prevail. In this dismal state to
which mankind are reduced by the fall, no true holiness is attainable, for it is a state of sin ; and no salvation from wrath can be had, for it is a state of
misery. The state we must be brought into, out of
our sinful and miserable state under the breach of
the covenant of works, if we would attain unto salvation, is the state of grace under the new covenant.
Those that are delivered from their natural state,
under the broken covenant, are persons effectually
called by grace, and are ' in Christ Jesus,' Rom.
viii. 1. Those that are still under the bondage of
the old covenant, are out of Christ, and ' have no
hope,' Eph. ii. 12. This state is a very sinful and
miserable state. For the power that the covenant of
works has over them, is a commanding, cursing, and
condemning power : it commands them to yield perfect obedience, under pain of the curse, but affords
no strength for performing it ; and it curses and
condemns them for every the least failure. The

source of all is the total corruption and depravity of
human nature, which we derive from our first father,
in whom we all sinned, and with whom we fell, in his
first transgression.   In the text we have,

1. A plain confession of the being of original sin.
Here is *sin* and *iniquity*, which the Psalmist owns
he had while yet in the womb, *sin* in which he was
shapen, and *iniquity* in which he was *conceived*.
This was not peculiar to the Psalmist, but is common to all mankind sprung in an ordinary way from
the first transgressor Adam.

2. The way of the conveyance of this original sin,
viz. by natural generation.   In this way every son
and daughter of Adam are infected with this leprosy.

3. The malignant efficacy it hath on men's lives :
Behold, says David, *I was shapen in iniquity*, &c.
He points out original sin as the fountain of all his
actual transgressions.   For how can a corrupt fountain send out wholesome streams ?

*Original sin proved, in what this sin consists, and
how far it extends.*

1. Consider scripture testimonies.   In the text we
have David, a man after God's own heart, yet confessing he was *shapen in iniquity, and conceived in
sin*.   Adam begets Seth, from whom the whole race of
mankind derive their origin, after ' his own image,'
Gen. v. 1. opposed to ' the image of God,' after which
he was made, Gen. i. 26. consisting in knowledge,
righteousness, and true holiness.   Job says, chap.
xiv. 4. ' Who can bring a clean thing out of an unclean ? not one.'   This is God's verdict on all mankind : Gen. vi. 5. ' Every imagination of the thoughts
of his heart is only evil continually.'

2. This is plain from the case of infants, which

we all once were. We may plainly read in their faces, that we are covered over with sin and guilt before any other covering come on us. For, 1*st*, What else mean scripture ordinances about them ? If there were not in them a superfluity of naughtiness, why were they circumcised ? If they are not unclean, why are they baptised ? This corruption of human nature was also shadowed forth by the law, concerning purifying of women. 2*d*, Consider the sad effects of sin upon them, which meet them as soon as they come into the world, yea in the womb, such as sickness, pains, death, &c. ; which says, that ' by nature we are the children of wrath,' Eph. ii. 3. 3*d*, Consider the early appearances of Adam's image in them, before ever they come to the use of reason. What a deal of pride, ambition, curiosity, vanity, wilfulness, and averseness to good, appears in them ; and when they creep out of infancy, what obstinacy and incorrigibleness appears in them ; so that there is a necessity of using the rod of correction to drive away the foolishness that is bound in their heart, Prov. xxii. 15.

3. The universal necessity of regeneration plainly proves the corruption of our nature : John iii. 3. ' Except a man be born again, he cannot see the kingdom of God.' Were we not disjointed by nature, what need would there be for us to be taken down, and put up again ? If the first birth were right, what need would there be for a second ?

I come now to show wherein original sin consists. It consists in these three things : the guilt of Adam's first sin, the want of original righteousness, and the corruption of the whole nature.

First, Original sin consists in the guilt of Adam's first sin. Guilt is an obligation to punishment. For this sin, which is ours by imputation, we are liable to punishment. This guilt lies on all men by nature : Rom. v. 18. ' Therefore, as by the offence of one, judgment came upon all men to condemnation; even

THE BEAUTIES OF

so by the righteousness of one, the free gift came upon all men unto justification of life." And this guilt of Adam's first sin is original sin imputed ; of which I spoke in the former discourse. The only remedy for it is in Jesus Christ : 1 Cor. xv. 22. ' For as in Adam all die, even so in Christ shall all be made alive.' Eph. 1. 7. ' In whom we have redemption through his blood, the forgiveness of sins, according to the riches of his grace.' Rom. iii. 24. ' Being justified freely by his grace, through the redemption that is in Christ Jesus.'

Secondly, It consists in the want of original righteousness. Original righteousness is that righteousness and entire rectitude of all the faculties of the soul wherein man was created. Man's soul was so adorned with it, that it resembled its great Maker.

But now, man is stript of these ornaments, he is left quite naked.

1. There is a want of that knowledge in the mind wherewith man was created. That light that was set up in the soul of man is now gone ; though the candlestick is not removed, the candle is, Job xi. 12. ' For vain man would be wise, though man be born like a wild ass's colt.' The mind is like the ostrich, whom God hath deprived of understanding. ' The understanding is darkened, being alienated from the life of God through the ignorance that is in men, because of the blindness of their heart, Eph. iv. 18. ' The natural man receiveth not the things of the Spirit of God ; for they are foolishness unto him : neither can he know them, because they are spiritually discerned,' 1 Cor. ii. 14.

2. That righteousness which was in the will of man, that bent and inclination to good, is now removed, Eccl. vii. 29. ' I know [says the apostle] that in me (that is, in my flesh) dwelleth no good thing : for to will is present with me, but how to perform that which is good, I find not,' Rom. vii. 18.

3. The holiness of the affections is gone. Spiritual

affections have taken the wing, and left the soul as a bird without wings, which hath nothing whereby it can mount, Rom. vii. 18. forecited.

This want of original righteousness is a sin, being a want of conformity to the law of God, which requires all moral perfection. It is also a punishment of sin, and so is justly inflicted by God. And though the want of this righteousness be sin, yet God's depriving man of it, or rather not giving it him, is a most just act; seeing Adam, having got it for himself and his posterity, threw it away, and God is not obliged to restore it. And it can be no other sin but the first sin, whereof this withholding of original righteousness is the punishment. So true it is, that if the imputation of Adam's first sin be denied, original sin is quite razed, there is no foundation left for it.

Thirdly, It consists in the corruption of the whole nature. Concerning which two things are to be considered.

1. That the nature of man is indeed corrupted, We must not think that original sin lies only in the want of original righteousness. No, man is not only void of good qualities naturally, but he is filled with evil ones.

(1.) The scripture holds it forth so, while it calls this sin ' the flesh which lusteth against the Spirit, the old man, the body of death, the law of the members warring against the law of the mind,' &c.

(2.) The soul of man cannot be otherwise. It must needs be morally right or wrong; either it is habitually conformable to the law of God, or not; if it be not, its inclinations are against it. The soul has either God's image or that of the devil upon it. If there is not light in the mind, there must be darkness there.

2. Consider the nature and extent of this corruption. As to its extent,

1*st.* All men are corrupted. There is no excep-

440

tion of any one of Adam's posterity descending from
him by ordinary generation : Gen. vi. 5. 'God saw
that the wickedness of man was great in the earth,
and that every imagination of the thoughts of his
heart was only evil continually.' Job xiv. 4. ' Who
can bring a clean thing out of an unclean? not one.'
The virgin Mary, of the substance of whose body the
holy human nature of Christ was formed by the operation of the Holy Spirit, is included among the rest.
Even the children of holy parents are corrupted; for
generation is by nature, not by grace. The circumcised father begets an uncircumcised child, as
the purest corn that is sown produceth chaff.

2d, All of every man is corrupted ; it is a leprosy
that has overspread universally ; a leaven that hath
leavened the whole lump. It has overspread,

1. The soul in all its faculties, Tit. i. 15. ' Unto
them that are defiled and unbelieving, is nothing
pure; but even their mind and conscience is defiled.'

1st, If we look to the understanding there we will
see,

(1.) Darkness over all that region. It is the land
of darkness and shadow of death, where the very
light is darkness ; darkness in the abstract, Eph. v.
8. We are born blind, and cannot be restored without a miracle. There is a dreadful stupidity in spiritual things ; the natural man cannot take them up,
1 Cor. ii. 14.; but he is a fool, and a madman, because
in these things he is a mere natural.

(2.) A bitter root of unbelief naturally grows there,
which overspreads the whole life. Men, by nature,
are ' children of disobedience,' Eph. ii. 2. Or, ' of
impersuasibleness.' How like Adam do we look!
how universally is that article embraced, ' Ye shall
not surely die!' and how does it spread itself through
the lives of men, as if they were resolved to fall after
the same example of unbelief!

2d, As for the will, call it no more will, but lust.
It is free to evil, but not to good. ' God made man

upright,' his will straight with his own, with a power
in the will to do good, and an inclination and bent
thereto. But now behold in it,

(1.) A pitiful weakness. Man naturally cannot
will what is good and acceptable to God. He cannot produce one holy act until grace change the heart,
more than a stone can feel, or a beast reason. Hence
the apostle says, Phil. ii. 13. ' It is God which worketh in you both to will and to do of his good pleasure.'
Rom. v. 6. ' We are without strength.' 2 Cor. iii. 5.
' We are not sufficient of ourselves to think any thing
as of ourselves : but our sufficiency is of God.' Men
by nature are dead, spiritually ' dead in trespasses
and sins,' Eph. ii. 1. If they will what is good, it
is in a carnal manner.

(2.) An aversion to good. We are backward to
it, and therefore must be drawn, as a bullock unaccustomed to the yoke. Sin is the natural man's element ; and as the fish is averse to come out of the
water, so is the sinner from the puddle of sin, in
which he delights to lie. Hence, says our Lord,
John v. 40. ' Ye will not come unto me, that ye might
have life.' They were not only naturally unable to
come, but they had no inclination to the duty. Their
stomachs are full, and, like the soul that loathes the
honey-comb, they nauseate the heavenly food in their
offer.

(3.) There is a proneness to evil, a bent and inclination to it : Hos. xi. 7. ' My people are bent to back-
sliding from me.' Hence natural men are mad on
idols. Set sin and duty, death and life, cursing and
blessing, before the natural man, and leave the will
to itself, it will naturally run to sin, to death, and
the curse, as the waters run down a steep place.

(4.) There is a crossness and contrariety in the
will to God and goodness : Rom. viii. 7. ' The carnal
mind is enmity against God : for it is not subject to
the law of God, neither indeed can be.' That God
forbids a thing is a motive to the will to like it. No

3 L

fruit is so sweet to the corrupt appetite as the forbidden fruit. Strip sin naked of all its ornaments
and allurements, and the natural man will court it
for itself. The will naturally lies cross to God.

[1.] It is cross to his nature. He is holiness itself; and the will rejects holiness for itself. Hence
men say to God, ' Depart from us, for we desire not
the knowledge of thy ways,' Job xxi. 14. The will
is an enemy to the scripture God, and hence they
do what they can for the change, Psal. l. 21. It was
most agreeable to nature, that the Pagans made their
gods profane. The proud man desires to have none
above him to control him, or call him to account,
and the natural man wants to have no God, Psalm
xiv. 1.

[2.] It is cross to his will. 1st, To his law, which
binds to conformity to God, which the natural man
hates, Rom. viii. 7. Corrupt nature rises against
this yoke : they would have the law brought down
to their corruptions. Hence that is a distinguishing
mark of the godly man, ' His delight is in the law of
the Lord, and in his law doth he meditate day and
night,' Psal. i. 2. 2d, To his gospel. The will of
man naturally is quite opposite to the grand device
of salvation through the Lord Jesus ; and natural
men, like Judas, would rather hang themselves than
go to Christ, submitting themselves unto the righteousness of God, Rom. x. 3. They say, ' We will
not have this man to reign over us,' Luke xix. 14.
The gospel is designed for humbling the pride and
selfishness of men ; but they are for exalting self,
and placing it on the throne.

Useful lessons from the doctrine of original sin.

1. No wonder then that we are born to trouble as the sparks fly upward ; that we are attacked and made prisoners as soon as we come into the world. This says that the straight way in the course of justice would be, that we go from the womb to the grave, and that the cradle be turned into a coffin. For, in a spiritual sense we are all dead born ; and no wonder that natural death should seize those that are spiritually dead ; and that all sorts of miseries should pursue those that are destitute of every thing that is good.

2. There is no ground for parents to be lifted up on the account of children, however numerous and fair. For though they may have fair faces, they have foul and deformed souls by nature ; and natural beauty is far outbalanced by spiritual ugliness. Parents had much need to carry them by faith and prayer to the fountain of Christ's blood, to get them washed and purified from their spiritual uncleanness.

3. This doctrine lets us see the absolute necessity of Christ as a Saviour, who alone is able to save us from the guilt of sin by his blood, and from the filth and pollution of it by the washing of regeneration and renewing of the Holy Ghost, and from the dominion of it by the power of divine grace. ' Except a man be born again, he cannot see the kingdom of God,' John iii. 3.

Lastly, See the absolute necessity of mortification, of crucifying the flesh ; for from it all actual sins proceed. A form of godliness will not do. No ; we must strike at the root, otherwise the branches will never die. The consideration of the total corruption and depravation of our nature should make us all lie low in the dust before a holy God, watchful against every motion and temptation to sin, restless till we be delivered from it, and indefatigable in the course of the Christian warfare. And it calls every one to mourning and lamenting over the ruins of our nature, and to supplicating the God of all grace, that he may cleanse our polluted souls, and wash us from our sins in the blood of Jesus.

The dreadful misery into which all mankind are brought by Adam's fall.

First, Let us view man's loss by the fall. He has lost communion with God. He enjoyed it before that fatal period ; but now it is gone. It implies two things. *1st,* A saving interest in God as his God. Man could then call God his own God, his Maker, his Husband, his Friend, his Portion, being in covenant with him. *2d,* Sweet and comfortable society and fellowship with God : and all this without a mediator, God and man not having been enemies or at variance. This sweet and agreeable communion he lost, as appears from Gen. iii. 8. where it is said, ' They (our first parents) heard the voice of the Lord God walking in the garden in the cool of the day : and Adam and his wife hid themselves from the presence of the Lord God amongst the trees of the garden.' When God spoke to him before, it was refreshing and comfortable to him ; but now it was a terror to him ; evidently showing that all correspondence was broke up.

Thus man lost God, the greatest, and the fountain of all other losses : Eph. ii. 12. ' That at that time ye were without Christ, being aliens from the commonwealth of Israel, and strangers from the covenants of promise, having no hope, and without God in the world.' He is no more the God of fallen men, till by a new covenant they get a new interest in him. This is the greatest of all losses and miseries. Had the sun been for ever darkened in the heavens, it had been no such loss as this. God is the cause and fountain of all good ; and the loss of him must be the loss of every thing that is good and excellent. Man is a mere nothing without God ; a nothing in nature without his common presence, and a nothing in happiness without his gracious presence : Psal. xxx. 5. ' In his favour is life.' Psal. lxiii. 3. ' Thy loving-kindness is better than life.' That day man fell, the foundation of the earth was drawn away, and all fell down together ; the soul and the life departed from all men, and left them all dead, having lost God, the fountain of life and joy. Hence we may infer,

1. Man is a slave to the devil, 2 Tim. ii. 26. When the soul is gone, men may do with the body what they will ; and when God is gone, the devil may do with the soul what he will. Man without God is like Samson without his hair, quite weak and unable to resist his spiritual enemies, as Samson to oppose the Philistines. Satan has over men in nature the power of a master, so that when he bids them go, they go ; and when to come, they come : Rom. vi. 16. ' Know ye not, that to whom ye yield yourselves servants to obey, his servants ye are to whom ye obey ; whether of sin unto death, or of obedience unto righteousness ? '—that of a conqueror, and so he makes them his slaves and vassals ;—and that of a jailor, keeping them fast bound in chains, so that they cannot escape from his clutches, Isa. lxi. 1.

2. Man has lost his covenant-right to the creatures which he had when in favour with his Maker ; and therefore Adam was driven out of paradise. Men have no right to the creatures or their service now, but that of common providence, until it be otherwise

restored by their coming into the bond of the new covenant.

3. Hence man is in a fruitless search after happiness in the creatures, set, as a poor infant that hath lost the breasts, to suck at the dry breasts of the creatures, where nothing is to be met with but continued disappointments.

4. Man cannot help himself: John xv. 5. ' I am the vine, ye are the branches : he that abideth in me, and I in him, the same bringeth forth much fruit : for without me ye can do nothing.' His help is alone in God in Christ, without whom one can do nothing. He is like a poor infant exposed, that cannot help itself, Ezek. xvi. He is like one grievously wounded, who can neither make a plaister for his wounds, nor apply it. Ah! how miserable is the case of man under the fall!

SECONDLY, Let us consider what man is brought under by the fall.

1. He is brought under God's wrath. Hence sinners are said to be ' the children of wrath :' Eph. ii. 3. ' Among whom also we all had our conversation in times past in the lusts of our flesh, fulfilling the desires of the flesh and of the mind ; and were by nature the children of wrath, even as others.' Wrath in God is mixed with no perturbation, but is pure from all discomposure. It imports,

(1.) That sinners are under the displeasure of God. He can take no delight in them, but his soul loathes them. There is a holy fire of anger burning in his breast against them. Should the sun be continually under a cloud, and the heavens ever covered with blackness, what a miserable place would the world be ! But that is nothing to the divine anger : ' Who knows the power of thine anger ?' says the Psalmist, Psal. xc. 11.

(2.) God deals with them as with enemies, Nah. i. 2. ' God is jealous, and the Lord revengeth, the Lord revengeth and is furious, the Lord will take vengeance on his adversaries; and he reserveth wrath for his enemies,' Isa. i. 24. ' Ah, I will ease me of mine adversaries, and avenge me of mine enemies.' To have men in power enemies to us, is sad; but to have God an enemy, is beyond expression dreadful : seeing we can neither fight nor flee from him, and he can pursue the quarrel through all eternity.

2. They are under his curse : Gal. iii. 10. ' Cursed is every one that continueth not in all things which are written in the book of the law to do them.' Now, God's curse is the binding over the sinner to all the direful effects of his wrath. This is the dreadful yoke which the broken law wreaths about the neck of every sinner as in a natural state. God's curse is the tying of a sinner to the stake, that the law and justice of God may disburden all their arrows into his soul, and that in him may meet all the miseries and plagues that flow from the avenging wrath of God.

Thus every sinner, while in a natural state, is under the wrath and curse of God ; a burden on him, that if not removed by him who was made under the law, and bore the curse thereof, will sink sinners into the lowest pit of hell.

THIRDLY, Let us next consider what man is liable to, both in this world and that which is to come.

First, In this world, he is liable,

1. To all the miseries of this life. Now these are twofold.

1*st*, Outward miseries. There is a flood of these that man is subject to ; as,

(1.) God's curse upon the creature for our sake : Gen. iii. 17. ' Cursed is the ground for thy sake.' Under the weight of this curse the whole creation groans and travails in pain, longing for deliverance. It is not the groan of a wearied beast desiring to be disburdened of its load, but a groan the effect of the fall of man. The treason and rebellion of man against his rightful Lord and Sovereign, brought distress

and misery upon all that was formed for his use ; as
when the majesty of a prince is violated by the rebellion of his subjects, all that belongs to them, and was
before the free gift of the prince, is forfeited and takes
from them.   Their land, palaces, cattle, even all that
pertains to them, bear the marks of his sovereign
fury.   Consult Deut. xxviii. 15, &c.

(2.) Outward miseries, such as sword, famine, and
pestilence.   Many times the curse of the Lord makes
the heavens as brass, and the earth as iron, binds up
the clouds, and restrains their necessary influences,
so that the fruits of the earth are dried up.   It raises
divisions, wars, and mutinies in a kingdom.   All the
confusions and disorders which are to be seen among
men, are the woful fruits and native results of sin.
It kindles and blows up the fire of discord in families, cities, and nations.   This is that fury that brings
a smoking firebrand from hell, and sets the whole
world in a combustion.   Pride and ambition, covetousness and desire of revenge, have made the world
a stage of the most bloody tragedies.   We have some
terrible threatenings with respect to these judgments,
Deut. xxviii. Lev. xxvi.   And they are all summed
up in one verse, Ezek. v. 17. ' I will send upon you
famine, and evil beasts, and they shall bereave thee ;
and pestilence and blood shall pass through thee,
and I will bring the sword upon thee : I the Lord
have spoken it.'

(3.) Miseries on men's bodies, sickness and bodily
pains, as burning fevers, languishing consumptions,
distorting convulsions, ugly deformities, gout and
gravel, and all the dismal train of wasting diseases
and acute pains.   Sin hath made man's body a se-
minary of diseases, and planted in it the fatal seeds
and principles of corruption and dissolution, and
made him liable to attacks from all distempers, from
the torturing stone to the wasting consumption.

(4.) On our estates, as losses, crosses, wrongs, and
oppressions.   How often do those in trade suffer

heavy losses by the bankruptcies of their debtors, by unfair practices, and sinistrous dealings, by cheating and tricking, by extortion, rapine, &c. ?

(5.) On our names, by reproach, disgrace, &c. Many estates are blasted, and families reduced to poverty and contempt, which sometime have made a good figure in the world. People are made to groan under pinching straits and wants, and yet they seldom consider the bitter root from which all this springs. It is sin that makes men poor, mean, low, and contemptible in the world, and that brings reproach and disgrace upon their names, Deut. xxviii. 37.

(6.) On our employments and callings. These are many times full of pain, labour, and disappointments. Men earn wages, and put it into a bag with holes, and they disquiet and vex themselves in vain. Whence are our cares and fears, but from sin? Fear is the ague of the soul that sets it a shaking. Some fear want, and others alarms. Whence come all the disappointments of our hopes and expectations but from sin ? When we look for comfort, there is a cross ; where we expect honey and sweetness, there we find wormwood and gall.

(7.) On our relations, unequal uncomfortable marriages, false and treacherous friends, harsh and cruel masters, undutiful and unfaithful servants. It is sin that makes children ungrateful and undutiful to parents ; they that should be as the staff of their parents' old age, are as a sword many times to pierce their hearts. It is sin that makes wives disobedient to their husbands, and to defile their beds.

2dly, Inward spiritual miseries: As (1.) 'Blindness of mind,' Eph. iv. 18. ' Having the understanding darkened, being alienated from the life of God through the ignorance that is in them, because of the blindness of their heart;' the devil putting out the eyes that would not receive the light of the gospel, 1 Cor. iv. 4. (2.) ' A reprobate sense,' Rom. i. 28. whereby men are left of God, so as to have no sense of discerning betwixt good and evil, but take bitter for sweet, and sweet for bitter. (3.) 'Strong delusions,' 2 Thess. ii. 11. 'And for this cause God shall send them strong delusion, that they should believe a lie,' whereby men, forsaking the truth, dote on the fancies and imaginations of their own hearts, and embrace lies for solid truths. (4.) 'Hardness of heart,' Rom. ii. 5. whereby men's hearts are hardened from the fear of the Lord, and proof against conviction, and means used for awakening them. (5.) 'Vile affections,' Rom. i. 26. eagerly desiring sin and vanity, and all manner of filthiness, without regard to the dictates of reason and a natural conscience. *Lastly*, Fear, sorrow, and horror of conscience, which torment men, embitter life, and often bring death in their train, Isaiah xxxiii. 14. 'The sinners in Zion are afraid; fearfulness hath surprised the hypocrites: who among us shall dwell with the devouring fire? who among us shall dwell with everlasting burnings?'

2. At the end of this life, man is liable to death, Rom. vi. 23. 'The wages of sin is death.' The soul must be separated from the body; the man falls into the hands of the king of terrors, and goes down to the house appointed for all living.

Object. But if these things be the effects of the fall, how comes it that those who are delivered from the curse of the law and the wrath of God by Jesus Christ, sustain these outward miseries, and die as well as others? *Ans.* Because the delivery is but imperfect; but when they shall be free from sin, they shall be free from all these. In the mean time there is a great difference betwixt them: for the sting of God's wrath as a judge is taken out of them to the godly, and they are not accomplishments of the threatenings of the covenant of works, Rom. vi. 14 but of those of the covenant of grace, Psal. lxxxix. 31, 32, 33. and why may not the Lord take some of those things threatened under the covenant of works and give them a gospel-dye, and inflect them according to the second covenant, as well as he does with the commands, which they are still obliged to obey?

Secondly, Let us consider what man is liable to in the world to come. He is liable to the pains of hell for ever. There the Jordan of wrath will overflow all its banks, and that throughout eternal ages. These pains of hell consist of two things, the punishment of loss, and the punishment of sense.

1. In the punishment of loss. This is unspeakably great, and cannot be sufficiently set forth by the tongue of man. I shall only glance at it a little, without enlarging on particulars. (1.) They will lose all the good things which they enjoyed here in the world, their wealth, their riches, their profits, and pleasures, and whatever things they set their heart on while here. (2.) The favourable presence and enjoyment of God and Christ. They will be for ever banished from the beatific vision of God in glory. For he will say to them at the last day, 'Depart from me, ye cursed, into everlasting fire, prepared for the devil and his angels,' Matt. xxv. 41. (3.) The blessed company and society of the holy angels and glorified saints in heaven. (4.) All the glory and blessedness above. (5.) All pity and compassion, having none to commiserate their condition, or regard their pain. (6.) All hope and expectation of deliverance and outgate from their misery. (7.) All possibility of deliverance from their torments. The door of the pit shall be shut upon them for ever, and their fetters shall never be loosed. Thus sinners in hell shall lose every thing that is good and agreeable, even God the chief good, and all the happiness he has prepared for them that love him.

2. In the punishment of sense. They shall suffer the most grievous torments both in soul and body, and that without intermission, for evermore. These torments are beyond expression, and our most fearful thoughts cannot equal the horror of them. 'Who

knows the power of thine anger?' says the Psalmist. No man can tell what those plagues and woes are which infinite justice and almighty power hath prepared for obstinate sinners. O that we may be prevailed upon to flee from this wrath that is to come, that so we may not fall into the hands of the living God, and may not be made the dreadful objects of everlasting vengeance.

****

Useful Lessons from the awful doctrine of Man's misery in his fallen state.

1. See here the great evil of sin. Many reckon it but a small matter to transgress God's holy and righteous law. They can curse and swear, lie and steal, and commit many enormous crimes, and yet have no trouble or remorse about it. But if they would consider the dreadful effects of sin, they would be of another mind. Sin is the worst of evils, and big with all kinds of evils whatsoever. It has brought a flood of miseries into the world, which has overflowed the whole creation, under the weight of which the earth and all its inhabitants are groaning. It is the great makebate between God and sinners ; it has shut the door of access to God upon us, and exposed us to his wrath and curse in this life and that which is to come.

2. Woful is the case of all who are in a state of nature. They are far from God; they have no interest in or fellowship with him ; they are under his wrath and curse, liable to all the miseries of this life, and to the vengeance of eternal fire in the world to come. They are fallen under the power and tyranny of the devil, and if mercy prevent not, shall dwell with him in the lake that burneth with fire and brimstone for ever. Whatever your situation and

circumstances in the world may be, O ye that are in your natural state, ye are in a miserable condition ; for ye are without God, the fountain of all good. Ye may read, pray, and communicate, but ye can have no communion with God. Men may be pleased with and bless you, but ye are under God's wrath and curse, and will continue so till ye by faith embrace God in Christ as your God.

Lastly, Arise, O ye sinners who are yet in your natural state, and depart ; for this is not your rest. Come to the Lord Jesus, who alone can open the door of access to God, whose blood quenches the fire of wrath, and who can deliver from the curse of the law. Who would stay in a house ready to fall? who can sleep sound in a case where God is an enemy? Lay these things seriously to heart, and flee from the wrath ye lie under, for the plague is begun already ; and speedily flee from the wrath to come ; for it is a fearful thing to fall into the hands of the living God.

A full answer to the question: Who among men are still under the broken covenant of works, or still under the curse of the broken law?

To make this the more clear, I premise these four things,

1. Men may be under the covenant of works, and yet living under the external dispensation of the covenant of grace. There is a great difference betwixt one's visible church-state, and the state of their souls before the Lord. The covenant of grace was preached to Adam in paradise, Gen. iii. 15. yet was he in hazard of running back to the covenant of works, ver. 22. The Jews had the dispensation of the covenant of grace among them, and the ceremo-

nial law clearly held out the way of salvation by the
Messiah, yet most of them were under the covenant
of works, being sons of the bond-woman. So under
the gospel dispensation to this day, many to whom
the covenant of grace is offered, continue under the
covenant of works. It is one thing to hear the new
covenant proclaimed, another thing to accept of it
by faith.

2. Men may receive the seals of the covenant of
grace, and yet be under the covenant of works.
Circumcision was a seal of the covenant of grace,
yet many who received it, were still sons of the
bond-woman, to be cast out from inheriting with the
children, Gal. iv. 24, 25. 30. And so will many
who are baptized in the name of Christ, and have
partook of the Lord's Supper, yet be disowned at the
last day, by the Head of the second covenant, as
none of his, Luke xiii. 26. forasmuch as they never
truly came into the bond of that covenant.

3. Men may be convinced in their consciences of
the impossibility of obtaining salvation by Adam's
covenant of works, and yet remain under it still.
Where are they who are so very stupid, as to think
that they can obtain salvation by perfect obedience
to the law ?   The Pharisees of old, and the Papists
to this day, will not venture their salvation on the
absolute perfection of their own obedience ; yet the
former lived, and the latter do live, under that covenant.   Let no man deceive himself here ; such a
conviction as hardly any man can shun, is not sufficient to divorce a man from the law or covenant of
works.

Lastly, Men, upon the offer of the covenant of
grace made to them, may aim at accepting of it, and
so enter into a personal covenant with God, and yet
remain under the covenant of works.   Many miss
their mark in their covenanting with God, and, instead of accepting God's covenant of grace, make a
covenant of works with God, upon other terms than

Adam's covenant was, for which there is no warrant in the word. The Galatians did not cast off Christ's righteousness altogether, but only mixed their own works with his: and thus do many still, looking on their faith, repentance, and obedience, such as they are, to be the fulfilling of a law, upon which they are to be accepted of God.

But more particularly, and directly,

(1.) All unregenerate persons are under the covenant of works. Where is the unconverted man or woman, living in the state of irregeneracy, strangers to a saving change on their souls? That man or woman is yet a branch of the old Adam, growing on the old stock, a stranger to the new covenant, because not in Christ, the head of the covenant. For 'if any man be in Christ, he is a new creature: old things are passed away; behold, all things are become new,' 2 Cor. v. 27. Such an unregenerate person is still under the covenant of works. This is evident, in that the death contained in the threatening of that covenant has full sway over them, so that they are 'dead in trespasses and sins,' Eph. iii. 1. 5. They lie yet without spiritual life, as the first Adam left them. They have no communion with the second Adam, else they had been quickened: for he is a quickening head, as the other was a killing one.

(2.) All that have not the Spirit of Christ dwelling in them are under the covenant of works: For 'if any man have not the Spirit of Christ, he is none of his,' Rom. viii. 9. And says the same apostle, Gal. v. 8. 'But if ye are led by the Spirit, ye are not under the law.' It is one of the first promises of the covenant of grace, the giving of the Spirit, Ezek. xxxvii. 27. '—A new spirit will I put within you.' And the Spirit of Christ once entering into a man never changes his habitation. For, saith Christ himself, John xiv. 16. ' I will pray the Father, and he shall give you another Comforter; that he may

abide with you for ever.' Wo to those then that
have not the Spirit of grace, they are under the curse.
And such are all prayerless persons, Zech. xii. 10.
' And I will pour upon the house of David, and upon
the inhabitants of Jerusalem, the spirit of grace and
of supplication ; and they shall look upon me whom
they have pierced, and they shall mourn for him, as
one mourneth for his only son, and shall be in bitter-
nes for him, as one that is in bitterness for his first-
born ;' ignorant, unconvinced sinners, who have not
yet seen their lost and ruined state, John xvi. 8.
' And when he is come, he will reprove the world of
sin, and of righteousness, and of judgment;' refractory and rebellious ones, who will not be hedged in
within the Lord's way, Ezek. xxxvi. 27. 'And I will
put my Spirit within you, and cause you to walk in
my statutes, and ye shall keep my judgments and
do them;' carnal men, who are under the government of their own lusts and unruly passions, Gal.
v. 16.

(3.) All unbelievers : John iii. 18. ' He that believeth on him is not condemned : but he that believeth not is condemned already, because he hath
not believed in the name of the only-begotten Son of
God.' Whosoever is destitute of saving faith is under the covenant of works : for it is by faith that
one is brought within the bond of the covenant of
grace, is married unto Christ, being dead to the law.
Every soul of man is under one of the two husbands,
Christ or the law. All believers have their Maker
for their husband ; and all unbelievers have the law
as a covenant of works for theirs, a rigorous husband, a weak one, who can do nothing for their life
and salvation, but for their ruin and destruction.
Faith unites the soul to Christ; Eph. iii. 17. ' That
Christ may dwell in your hearts by faith.' The unbeliever, what though he go about the duties of religion, walk soberly and strictly, he is not joined to

Christ, therefore he remains under the covenant of works, under the curse.

(4.) All unsanctified, unholy persons : Rom. vi. 14. ' For sin shall not have dominion over you : for ye are not under the law, but under grace.' The doctrinal staking sinners down under, and wreathing about their necks the yoke of the law as a covenant of works, is so far from being a proper method to bring them to holiness and good works, that contrariwise they shall never be holy, never do one good work, till such time as they are fairly rid of that yoke, and sit down under the jurisdiction of grace. So that true holiness is an infallible mark of one delivered from the law; and unholiness, of one that is yet hard and fast under it, Gal. v. 18. Legalism is rank enmity to true holiness, is but a devil transformed into an angel of light, and never prevails so in the church as in a time of apostacy, growing unholiness, untenderness, regardlessness of the commands of God, when all flesh have corrupted their ways. Take for an example, Popery, the grand apostacy. What set of men that call themselves Christians, set up for the law and good works in their doctrine, more than they do? and among whom is there less of these to be found? How can they be but unholy, who are under the covenant of works? for there is no communion with God in the way of that covenant now; so sanctifying influences are stopt, and they must wither and pine away in their iniquity. Whereas, when once the soul is brought out from that covenant into the covenant of grace, the course of sanctifying influences is opened, the clean and cleansing water flows into their souls : the Head of the covenant is a holy head, conveying holiness to his members ; the Spirit of the covenant is a sanctifying Spirit ; the promises of the covenant are promises of holiness ; the blood of the covenant is purifying blood : and, in a word, every thing in the covenant tends to sanctifying and making holy the convenanters.

3 N

(5.) All profane, loose, and licentious men, are under the covenant of works, Rom. vii. 5. ' For when we were in the flesh, the motions of sins, which were by the law, did work in our members, to bring forth fruit unto death.' and viii. 2. ' For the law of the Spirit of life in Christ Jesus hath made me free from the law of sin and death.' These men of Belial are under that heavy yoke. For under that covenant, being broken, sin and death have the force of a law upon the subjects, as the worms, stench, and rottenness domineer in the grave without control. When one sees so many profane lives, unclean, drunkards, swearers, liars, thieves, cheaters, oppressors, and others, walking after their own lusts ; he may conclude all these to be evidences and consequents of the curse of the broken covenant on them : even as when ye go through a field full of briers, thorns, thistles, nettles, &c. ye may sigh and say, These are the product of the curse laid on the earth. These people think they walk at liberty ; but what liberty is it ? Even such as that madman enjoyed, Mark v. 4. who had been often bound with fetters and chains, and the chains had been plucked asunder by him, and the fetters broken in pieces ; neither could any man tame him. The truth is, they are the arrantest slaves on earth who are slaves to their own domineering lusts and passions : 2 Peter, ii. 19. ' While they promise them liberty, they themselves are the servants of corruption : for of whom a man is overcome, of the same is he brought in bondage.' Such kindly slaves are they of the worst of masters, that they have lost all just notion and sense of true liberty, Psal. cxix. 45.

6. All mere moralists, such as satisfy themselves with common honesty and sobriety, living in the meantime strangers to religious exercises, and without a form of godliness. These are under the covenant of works, as seeking justification and acceptance with God, by their conformity (such as it is) to the letter of the law : Gal. v. 4. ' Christ is become of no

effect unto you, whosoever of you are justified by the
law: ye are fallen from grace.' These are they who
please themselves, in their wronging no man, doing
justly betwixt man and man, and in their pretended
keeping of a good heart towards God ; while, in the
meantime, the rottenness of their hearts appears in
their ignorance of God and Christ, and the way of
salvation by him, their estrangedness from the duty
of prayer and other holy exercises. Some of these
have that scripture much in their mouth, Mic. vi. 8.
' What doth the Lord require of thee, but to do justly
and to love mercy, and to walk humbly with thy God?'
little considering that the last clause thereof writes
death on their foreheads. They are under the covenant of works with a witness, having betaken themselves to their shreds of moral honesty, as so many
broken boards of that split ship.

Lastly, All formal hypocrites, or legal professors,
these sons and daughters of the bond-woman, Gal.
iv. 24, 25. ' Which things are an allegory : for these
are the two covenants ; the one from the mount Sinai,
which gendereth to bondage, which is Agar. For
this Agar is Mount Sinai in Arabia, and answereth
to Jerusalem which now is, and is in bondage with
her children.' These are they who have been convinced, but never were converted ; who have been
awakened by the law, but were never laid to rest by
the gospel ; who are brought to duties, but have never
been brought out of them to Jesus Christ; who pretend to be married to Christ, but were never yet divorced from nor dead to the law; and so are still
joined to the first husband, the law, as a covenant of
works. Though they be strict and zealous professors, and therein go beyond many, they are as really
enemies to Christ as the profane are, Rom. x. 3. ' For
they, being ignorant of God's righteousness, and going about to establish their own righteousness, have
not submitted themselves to the righteousness of God.'
Though they will not let an opportunity of duty slip,

but take heed to their ways, and dare not walk at
random as many do ; all that they do is under the
influence of the covenant of works, and therefore God
regards it not, but they remain under the curse.

....

Reasons why many in a Christian land still remain under the broken covenant of works.

1. It is natural to men ; this covenant being made
with Adam, and with us in his loins : it is ingrained
in the hearts of all men naturally. ' Tell me,' says
the apostle, Gal. ii. 21. ' ye that desire to be under
the law, do ye not hear the law ? ' And there are
impressions of it to be found in the hearts of all,
among the ruins of the fall. The law as a covenant
of works was the first husband that human nature
was wedded to ; and so it is still natural to men to
cleave to it. And we have a clear proof of it,

(1.) In men left to the swing of their own nature ;
they all go this way in their dealing with God for
life and favour. Look abroad into the world, and
behold the vast multitudes embracing Paganism,
Judaism, Mahometism, and Popery. All these agree
in this, that it is by doing man must live, though
they hugely differ in the things that are to be done
for life. Look into the Protestant churches, and you
shall see readily, that the more corrupt any of them
is, the more they incline to the way of this covenant.
Consider persons among us ignorant of the principles of true religion, who, not having received instruction, speak of the way of life and salvation as
nature prompts them, and you shall find them also
of the same mind. Finally, consider all unrenewed
men whatsoever, having the knowledge and making
profession of the expectation of life and salvation in

the way of the covenant of grace; yet they in practice stumble at this stumbling-stone, Matt. v. 3.

(2.) In men awakened and convinced, and in moral seriousness seeking to know what course they shall take to be saved, and plying their work for that end. They all take this principle for granted, that it is by doing they must obtain life and salvation: Matt. xix. 16. ' What good thing shall I do that I may have eternal life?' Luke x. 25. ' What shall I do to inherit eternal life?' And this obtains when they are pricked to the very heart, and the law as the covenant of works has wounded them to the very soul. They never think of a divorce from the law, that they may be married to Christ; but how they shall do to please the old husband, and so be saved from wrath; as is plain in the case of Peter's hearers, Acts ii. 27. when being pricked in their hearts, they said, ' Men and brethren, what shall we do?' and in the case of the Philippian jailor, Acts xvi. 30. who, being awakened by a train of very alarming incidents, and trembling through terror, cried out, ' What must I do to be saved?'

(3.) In the saints, who are truly married to Jesus Christ, O what hankering after the first husband, how great the remains of a legal spirit, how hard is it for them to forget their father's house? Psal. xlv. 10. Adam having embraced the promise of the Messiah, yet was in hazard of running back to this covenant. There is a disposition to deal with God, in the way of giving so much duty for so much grace and favour with God, in the best, that they have continually to strive with. Self-denial is one of the most difficult duties in Christianity.

2. The way of that covenant is most agreeable to the pride of man's heart. A proud heart will rather serve itself with the less, than stoop to live upon free grace; Rom. x. 3. ' For they being ignorant of God's righteousness, and going about to establish their own righteousness, have not submitted them-

selves unto the righteousness of God.' Man must be broken, bruised, and humbled, and laid very low, before he will embrace the covenant of grace. While a broken board of the first covenant will do men any service, they will hold by it, rather than come to Christ; like men who will rather live in a cottage of their own, than in another man's castle. To renounce all our own wisdom, works, and righteousness, and to cast away all those garments as filthy rags, which we have been at so much pains to patch up, is quite against the grain with corrupt nature, Rom. vii. 4. ' Wherefore, my brethren, ye also are become dead to the law by the body of Christ ; that ye should be married to another, even to him who is raised from the dead, that we should bring forth fruit unto God.

3. It is most agreeable to man's reason, in its corrupt state. If one should have asked the opinion of the philosophers, concerning that religion which taught salvation by a crucified Christ, and through the righteousness of another ; they would have said, it was unreasonable and foolish, and that the only way to true happiness was the way of moral virtue. The Jewish Rabbis would have declared it scandalous, 1 Cor. i. 23. where the preaching of Christ crucified is said to be to the Jews *a stumbling-block*, in the Greek, *a scandal ;* and would have maintained the only way to eternal life to be by the law of Moses. To this day, many learned men cannot see the reasonableness of the gospel-method of salvation, in opposition to the way of the covenant of works : and therefore our godly forefathers, who reformed from Popery, and maintained the reformed truth against Popery by their heroic zealous wrestlings even unto blood, while they showed that acquaintance with practical godliness and real holiness, whereof there is little in our day, are in effect looked upon as a parcel of well-meaning simple men, whose doctrine must be reformed over again, and rendered

more agreeable to reason. A rational religion is like to be the plague of this day. But assure ye yourselves, that wherever the gospel comes in power, it will make the reason of the wisest sit down at its feet, and learn, and give over its questions formed by Hows and Whys: 2 Cor. x. v. It 'casts down imaginations, and every high thing that exalteth itself against the knowledge of God, and bringeth into captivity every thought to the obedience of Christ.'

Even unlearned and simple men, in whom this appears less, because they do not enter deep into the thought, will be found sick of the same disease, when once they are thoroughly awakened, and take these matters to heart. How will they dispute against the gospel-method of salvation, against the promise, against their believing their welcome to Christ, who are so sinful and unworthy! The matter appears so great as indeed it is, that they look on the gospel-method as a dream, and they cannot believe it.

4. Ignorance and insensibleness of the true state of that matter, as it now is. There is a thick darkness about mount Sinai, through the whole dominion of the law; so that they who live under the covenant of works, see little but what they see by the lightnings now and then flashing out. Hence they little know where they are, nor what they are.

(1.) They do not understand the nature of that covenant to purpose, Gal. iv. 21. Any notion they have of it is lame and weak, without efficacy. They see not how forcibly it binds to perfect obedience and satisfaction, how rigorous it is in its demands, and will abate nothing, though a man should do to the utmost of his power, and with cries and tears of blood, seek forgiveness for the rest. They are not acquainted with the spirituality of the law, and the vast compass of the holy commandment, but stick too much in the letter of it. Hence 'they are alive without the law,' Rom. vii. 9. They narrow the demands of it, that so they may be the more likely to fulfil them.

(2.) They are not duly sensible of their own utter inability for that way of salvation : ' There is one that accuseth them, even Moses,' or the law, ' in whom they trust,' John v. 45. They know they are off the way, and that they have wandered from God ; but they hope they will get back to him again by repentance ; while, in the mean time, their heart is a heart of stone, and they cannot change it ; and ' the Ethiopian shall be able as soon to change his skin, the leopard his spots, as they may do good, that are accustomed to do evil, Jer. xiii. 23. ; and there is no coming to God but by Christ, John iv. 6. They know they have sinned, and provoked justice against them : but they hope to be sorry for their sin, to pray to God for forgiveness, and bear any thing patiently that God lays on them ; while in the mean time they see not that none of those things will satisfy God's justice, which yet will have full satisfaction for every the least sin of theirs, ere they see heaven. They know they must be holy : but they hope to serve God better than ever they have done ; while in the mean time they consider not that their work-arm is broken, and they can work none to purpose till they be saved by grace.

An affecting view of the awful consequences of a sinner's dying under the curse of the broken law.

1. It is the ruining stroke from the hand of an absolute God, proceeding according to the covenant of works against the sinner in full measure : ' He shall be driven from light into darkness, and chased out of the world,' Job xviii. 18. It is the fatal wound, the wound of an enemy, for the sinner's utter de-

struction. To a saint, death is a friend's wound, a stroke from the hand of a father, proceeding against his children in the way of the covenant of grace, for their complete happiness. But the ungodly in death fall into the hands of the living God, who then is, and ever will be, to them, a consuming fire. Having led their life under that covenant, they are then crushed in pieces by the curse for the breaking of it.

2. It is the breaking up of the peace betwixt God and them for ever: it is God setting his seal to the proclamation of an everlasting war between them; after which no message of peace is to go betwixt them any more for ever. It fixeth an impassable gulf, cutting off all comfortable communication with heaven, for the ages of eternity: Luke xvi. 26. 'And besides all this, between us and you there is a great gulf fixed: so that they which would pass from hence to you cannot; neither can they pass to us that would come from thence.' Now, the sinner under the curse, living within the visible church, has the privilege of offers of life and salvation: but then, there is no more gospel, nor are there any more good tidings of peace, when once death has done its work. The curse which in life might have been got removed, by the sinner's embracing of Christ, is then fastened for ever on him without remedy. The door is shut, and that for ever.

3. It puts an end to all their comfort of whatsoever nature: Luke xvi. 25. 'But Abraham said, Son, remember that thou in thy life-time receivedst thy good things, and likewise Lazarus evil things: but now he is comforted, and thou art tormented.' Lazarus is then comforted, but the wicked tormented. It utterly quenches their coal, and puts out all their light: Job xviii. 18. 'He shall be driven from light into darkness, and chased out of the world.' To the godly, death puts an end to their worldly comforts, but then it lets them into the full enjoyment of their

3 o

Lord in heaven : but as for the ungodly, at death
they leave all their worldly comforts behind them,
and they have no comfort before them in the place
whither they go.   The curse then draws a bar
betwixt them and every thing that is pleasant and
easy.

4. It is death armed with its sting, and all the
strength it has from sin, and a holy just broken law.
The sting of death, whereby it pierces like a stinged
serpent, is sin. 1 Cor. xv. 56. and the strength of sin
is the law.   Now, when death comes on the ungodly man, all his sins are unpardoned ; the guilt of
them all binding him, as with innumerable cords,
over to eternal wrath, lies upon him.   And these
cords of guilt cannot be broken ; for the law is their
strength, which threatens sin with eternal wrath ;
and God's truth and faithfulness therein plighted,
cannot fail.   Thus is death armed against the unbeliever, and herein lies the truly-killing nature of it.
Where that sting is away, as it is to all in Christ, it
can do them no real harm, whatever way they die,
whether a lingering or sudden death, a violent or natural one, under a cloud or in the light of comfort :
1 Cor. xv. 55—57. ' O death, where is thy sting ? O
grave, where is thy victory ?   The sting of death is
sin ; and the strength of sin is the law.   But thanks
be to God, which giveth us the victory through our
Lord Jesus Christ.

Lastly, It is the fearful passage out of this world,
into everlasting misery: Luke xvi. 22, 23. ' And it
came to pass that the beggar died, and was carried
by the angels into Abraham's bosom : the rich man
also died, and was buried ; and in hell he lifted up
his eyes, being in torments, and seeth Abraham afar
off, and Lazarus in his bosom.'   It is a dark valley
at best, but the Lord is with his people while they
go through it, Psal. xxiii. 4.   It is a deep water at
best ; but where the curse is removed, the Lord Jesus
will be the lifter up of the head, that the passenger

shall not sink.   But who can conceive the horror of
the passage the sinner under the curse has, upon
whom that frightful weight lies ?   It leads him as
an ox to the slaughter; it opens like a trap-door un-
derneath him, by which he falls into the pit, and like
a whirlpool swallows him up in a moment, and he is
staked down in an unalterable state of unspeakable
misery.

Secondly, He is immediately after death haled before the tribunal of that God, under whose curse he
lies : Eccl. xii. 7. ' The spirit shall return unto God
who gave it.'   Compare Heb. ix. 27. ' It is appointed unto men once to die, but after this the judgment.'
There the soul is judged according to its state, and
the deeds done in the body : and there it must receive its particular sentence.   And what can it be,
but ' Depart ye cursed ' ?   Where can such a soul
expect to find its own place, but in the place of torment ? Luke xvi. 23.   The cause is already judged,
the sinner is under the curse, bound over to hell by
the sentence of the holy law.   And those whom the
law has power to curse and does curse while they
are in this world, God will never bless in the other
world.   Consider the sinner under the curse before
this tribunal ; and,

1. All his sins, of all kinds, in all the periods of
his life, from the first to the last breathing on earth
are upon him.   The curse seals them up as in a bag,
that not one of them can be missing : Hos. xiii. 12.
' The iniquity of Ephraim is bound up.'   Where a
pardon takes place, the curse is removed, and being
once removed, it never returns : so where the curse
is, their neither is, nor has been a pardon ; for these
are inconsistent, the one being a binding over of the
sinner to wrath, the other a dissolution of that band,
so that God will remember their iniquities no more.
But where no pardon is, God has sworn he will not
forget any of that sinner's works, Amos viii. 7.   How
fearful then must the case be, while the sinner stands

before this tribunal, with all his sins whatsoever upon him?

2. As the man's sins were multiplied, so the curses
of the law were multiplied upon him; for it is the
constant voice of the law, upon every transgression
of those under the covenant of works, ' Cursed is
every one that continueth not in all things which are
written in the book of the law to do them,' Gal.
iii. 10. How then can such a one escape, while innumerable cords of death are upon him, before a just
Judge, with their united force binding him over to
destruction? His misery is thereby insured without
all peradventure; and the more of these cords there
are upon him, the greater must his punishment be.

3. There is no removing of the curse then: Luke
xiii. 25. ' When once the Master of the house is
risen up, and hath shut to the door, and ye begin to
stand without, and to knock at the door, saying,
Lord, Lord, open unto us; and he shall answer and
say unto you, I know you not whence ye are.' The
time of trial is over, and judgment is to be passed
according to what was done in the flesh. When a
court is erected within a sinner's own breast in this
world, and conscience convicts him as a transgressor
of the law, a covenant-breaker, and therefore pronounces him cursed; there is a Surety for the sinner
to fly to, an Advocate into whose hands he may commit his cause, a Mediator to trust in and roll his burden on by faith. But before that tribunal there is
none for the sinner who comes thither under the
curse. As the tree fell, it must lie; that throne is a
throne of pure justice to him, without any mixture
of the grace he despised. By the law of works,
which he chose to live under, despising the law of
grace, he must be judged.

4. Wherefore he must there inevitably sink under
the weight of the curse for ever: Psal. i. 5. ' Therefore the ungodly shall not stand in the judgment, nor
sinners in the congregation of the righteous.' He

must fall a sacrifice for his own sin, who now slights
the only atoning sacrifice, even Christ our passover
sacrificed for us. In the course of justice sin must
be satisfied for, and without shedding of blood there
is no remission. The satisfaction must be proportioned to the injury done to the honour of an infinite
God by it. In the gospel, Christ is set before the
sinner as the scape-goat before Aaron : he is called
to lay his hand on the head thereof, by faith transferring the guilt on the Surety. Since the sinner
did not so, but lived and died under the curse, his
iniquity must fall and lie for ever on his own head.

Thirdly, The soul is shut up in hell, by virtue of
the curse : Luke xvi. 22, 23. '—And in hell he lifted up his eyes.' Thus, by the sentence of the broken
covenant, the sinner is cut asunder by the sword of
death, and his soul receives its portion, where shall
be weeping and gnashing of teeth, being haled from
the tribunal into the pit. Then falls the great rain
of God's wrath on the men of his curse, the sinner
being to his own conviction, entered in payment of
the debt which he can never discharge, and which
can never be forgiven. The state of the separate
soul under the curse, after its particular judgment,
who can sufficiently express the horror of? Consider
these things following on that head,

1. Separate souls under the curse, after their particular judgment, are lodged in the place of the damned, called *Hell* in the scriptures. Then the godly
and the wicked change places, who lived together in
this world as a mixed company : the soul, which
through faith received the blessing, is carried to heaven ; and the soul which parted with the body under
the curse, is carried to hell. This is evident from
the parable of Dives and Lazarus, Luke xvi. 22, 23.
In hell the souls of the wicked are lodged as in a
prison, reserved to a further judgment against the
great day : 1 Pet. iii. 19. ' By which also he went
and preached unto the spirits in prison.' And who

can imagine what thoughts of horror must, at its entrance thither, seize the soul, which a little before was in the body in this world, but then goes into an unalterable state of misery, and hath the bars of the pit shut upon it, without hope of relief? O the fearful sudden change it will be to them who lived in wealth and ease, and to them who lived in poverty and distress here! Who can say to which of them it shall be the most frightful change?

2. The dregs of the curse shall there be wrung out to them, and they made to drink them, in the fearful punishment inflicted upon them for the satisfaction of offended justice, for all their sins, original and actual. Then shall be, more remarkably than ever before, accomplished that passage, Psal. lxxv. 8. ' In the hand of the Lord there is a cup, and the wine is red ; it is full of mixture, and he poureth out of the same : but the dregs thereof all the wicked of the earth shall wring them out, and drink them.' The separate soul doth not sleep, nor is void of feeling, nor is it extinguished till the resurrection, as some have dreamed: no, no ; it lives, but lives in misery ; it feels, but feels nothing but anguish. It is laid under the punishment of loss, being at once deprived of all those things wherein it sought its satisfaction in this world, and of all the happiness of the other world : and it is punished also with the punishment of sense, the wrath of an angry God being poured into it, Luke xvi. 23, 24. which is expressed under the notion of being *tormented in a flame*. Then all the joys of the cursed soul are killed, plucked up by the root ; and a flood of sorrows surrounds it, having neither brim nor bottom.

3. They are sensible of their lost happiness, Luke xvi. 23. They see it to their unspeakble anguish. Whatever they heard of heaven, and the happiness of those who die in the Lord, while they were on earth they will get a more affecting discovery of it then, which will cause them rage against themselves, that

ever they should have preferred the pleasures of sin and a vain world to such a blessed state. And how must it pierce the wretched soul, to think that not only all is lost, but lost without possibility of recovery! Luke xvi. 26. O that men would be wise in time, and believe that the state of trial will end with them ere long, and so bend their cares and endeavours, that, amidst the throng of the world's business, cares, vanities, and temptations, they lose not their souls.

4. Their consciences are then awakened, never to fall asleep any more for ever. They will scorch them then like a fire that cannot be quenched, and gnaw them like a worm that never dieth. Without question, separate souls are capable of calling things past to remembrance, as is evident in the case of the rich man, when in the separate state, Luke xvi. 25. where Abraham bids him remember what a portion he had in this life : the rich man remembers his five brethren, and what a life he and they led, verse 28. The conscience that was seared till it was past feeling, will then be fully sensible. The evil of sin will then be clearly seen, because felt ; the threatenings of the holy law will then no more be accounted scarecrows, nor will there be any such fools there as to make a mock at sin. The soul there will be under continual remorse and regret for ever the ill-spent life, where there is no place for repentance. The soul that would never search and try its ways, while there was occasion to mend what was amiss, will there go through the several steps of life and conversation here ; and every new sin that casts up to it as done in the body, will pierce the soul like an envenomed arrow.

5. They will be filled with torturing passions, which will keep the soul ever on the rack. Their sinful nature remains with them under the curse, and they will sin against God still, as well as they did in this life ; but with this difference, that whereas they had

pleasure in their sins here, they shall have none in their sins there ; they shall be for ever precluded from acting that wickedness that may give pleasure, and the restraint upon them that way in their prison may contribute to their torment : for, no doubt, the seeds of all sin remain still in them there under the curse : but their sins there shall be their felt misery too. The scripture holds out those torturing passions which they will be filled with, by ' weeping, and wailing, and gnashing of teeth ;' which intimates to us, that souls there are overwhelmed with sorrow, anguish, and anxiety, with wrath, grudge, murmuring, envy, rage, and despair.

6. In this state they must continue till the last day, that they be reunited to their respective bodies, and so the whole man get his sentence at the general judgment, adjudging both soul and body to everlasting fire, Matt. xxv. For after they are gone out of this world, their wickedness may be living behind them, and the stream of it may be running when their bodies are consumed in the grave, and their souls have been long in the pit of destruction, like the sin of Jeroboam, who made Israel to sin ; all which must be accounted for. And hence it appears, that the expectation of reuniting with their bodies can be no comfortable thought to them, but a thought of horror, a fearful expectation.

A view of the wicked rising from the grave under the curse.

They shall rise again out of their graves, at the last day, under the curse: John v. 29. ' They that have done evil shall come forth unto the resurrection of damnation.' Compare Matt. xxv. 41.' Depart from me, ye cursed, into everlasting fire, prepared for the devil and his angels.' Our Lord Jesus Christ, who became a curse for all his people, was carried from the cross to the grave : but there the debt was fully paid, and the curse was exhausted ; the cursing law and justice had no more to exact of him : So he was brought forth out of the prison of the grave, as one free person who had completely discharged the debt which he was laid in prison for. And hence believers in Christ, though they fall down into the grave, as well as others, yet they do not fall down into it under the curse, far less do they rise again at the last day under the curse. But the natural man having lived and died under the covenant of works, goes to the grave under the curse : and forasmuch as 'all that comes on him in the state of the dead, cannot satisfy completely for his debt, therefore as the curse remains on him all along while he is there, so he rises again under it. And in this doleful event three things may be considered.

1. They shall rise again out of their graves by virtue of the curse. This is implied in that forecited, John v. 29. When the end of time is come, the last trumpet shall sound, and all that are in the graves shall come forth, godly and ungodly ; but the godly shall rise by virtue of their blessed union with Christ, Rom. viii. 11. ; the ungodly by virtue of the curse of the broken covenant on them. As the malefactor is, in virtue of sentence of death passed on him, shut up in close prison till the time of execution ; and in virtue of the same sentence brought out of prison at the time appointed for his execution : even so the unbeliever is, in virtue of the curse of the law adjudging him to eternal death in hell, laid up in the grave till the last day ; and, in virtue of the same curse, brought out of the grave at that day. Hence, by the by, one may see, that there is no force in that arguing, viz. The separation of the soul and body was not the sanction of the law ; else why should the wicked be clothed with their bodies at the resurrection ? It is true, that

separation was not the whole of the sanction, but it was a remarkable part of it; and there is no inconsistency in the separation and reuniting of soul and body, being both comprehended in the sanction, more than in the laying up of the malefactor for, and bringing him forth to execution, being both comprehended in the sentence of death. The same curse that separated soul and body at death, and separated each part of the body from another in the grave, shall at the time appointed, have another kind of effect in bringing together the scattered pieces of dust, and joining them together in one body, and joining it again to the soul.

2. All their sin and guilt shall rise again with them; the body that was laid in the grave, a vile body; a foul instrument of the soul in divers lusts; an unclean vessel, stained, polluted, and defiled, with divers kinds of filthy impure lusts; shall rise again with all its impurities cleaving to it, Isa. lxvi. 24. ' They shall be an abhorring unto all flesh.' It is the peculiar privilege of believers to have their vile bodies changed, Phil. iii. 21. If the bodies of sinners be not cleansed by the washing with that pure water, Heb. x. 22. viz. the blood and Spirit of Jesus Christ: though they be strained in never so minute parts, through the earth in a grave, they will lose nothing of their vileness and pollution, it will still cleave to every part of their dust, and appear again therewith at the resurrection. Then shall they get a new and horrible sight of the use they made of their tongues in profane swearing, cursing, mocking at religion, lying, reproaching, cruel and unjust threatenings, &c. in undue silence, when God's honour, their own souls' interest, and their neighbours' good, required them to speak; of the use they made of their bellies, in gluttony, and drunkenness, and pampering of the flesh; of their bodies, in uncleanness, lasciviousness, and wantonness; of their hands, in pilfering, stealing, unjust beating and abusing their fellow-creatures, immo-

derately busying them in the things of this life, to
the neglect of their souls ; in a word, of the use they
made of their whole body, and every member thereof;
with the qualities and endowments thereof, its youth,
beauty, comeliness, health, and strength ; together
with the memorials of dying put into their hands, as
hurts, wounds, weakness, sickness, old age ; all of
them to have been improved for God, the good of
mankind, and their own eternal welfare. O, if men
could look upon these things now, as then they will
appear, the sweet morsel of sin would be accounted
as the poison of asps.

3. Their appearance will be frightful and horrible
beyond expression, when they come forth of their
graves under the curse, and set their feet on the earth
again. When, at the sound of the trumpet, the dead
shall arise out of their graves, and the wicked are
cast forth as abominable branches, what a fearful a-
wakening will they have out of their long sleep!
When they get another sight of this earth, upon
which they led their ungodly lives ; see their godly
neighbours taken out from among them in the same
spot of ground where they all lay, and carried away
with joy to meet the Lord in the air ; and when they
see the Judge come to the judgment of the great day,
in awful state ; and they are going forward to appear
before his tribunal : no appearance of malefactors
going, under a guard, to the place of execution ; no
case of a besieged city taken, and soldiers burning
and slaying, and the inhabitants running and crying
for fear of the sword ; can sufficiently represent the
frightful appearance, which men risen again at the
last day, under the curse, will make. What ghastly
visages will they then have! How will the now fairest
ungodly faces be black as a coal, through extreme
terror, anguish, and perplexity! How will they shiver,
tremble, their knees smite one against another, and
their hearts be pierced as with arrows, while they see
the doleful day they would not believe! what roarings

and yellings, and hideous noise will then be amongst the innumerable crowd of the ungodly, driven forward to the tribunal as beasts to the slaughter? What ' crying to the rocks and the mountains to fall on them, and hide them from the face of the Lamb,' but all in vain! Rev. vi. 16, 17. Then will the weight of the curse be felt to purpose, how lightly soever men now walk under it.

The wicked, under the curse, appearing at the judgment-seat of Christ.

They shall appear before the tribunal of Christ under the curse, like a malefactor in chains before his judge, Matt. xxv. 41. ' Then shall he say also unto them on the left hand, Depart from me, ye cursed, into everlasting fire, prepared for the devil and his angels.' All must appear there, great and small, good and bad ; none shall be amissing; Rom. xiv. 10. ' We shall all stand before the judgment-seat of Christ.' But they who now receive the blessing through faith, shall be in no hazard of the curse then or there. But it is not possible, that those who lived and died under the curse, should not have it upon them before that tribunal ; for after death there is no removing of it. The fearful state of those under the curse before that judgment-seat may be viewed in these particulars.

1. In virtue of the curse they shall be set on the left hand, Matt. xxv. 33. ' And he shall set the sheep on his right hand, but the goats on the left.' No honour is designed for them, but shame and everlasting contempt ; no sentence, but what will fix them in an unalterable state of misery : so no access for them to the right hand amongst the blessed ; but they must be ranged together on the left hand as a company of cursed ones.

2. The face of the judge must needs be terrible to them, as being under the curse of him who sits upon the throne, Rev. vi. 16, 17. When they see him, they shall know him to be he, who with his Father and the Holy Spirit gave that law which they transgressed, made that covenant which they broke, whose voice the curse of the law against transgressors was and is; the which must needs take effect in their everlasting ruin, by reason of his justice, holiness, and truth. And he will be in a special manner terrible to such as had the gospel-offer made to them, and the more terrible, the more plainly, affectionately, and powerfully it was pressed on them to accept it. O how will it strike them as a dart, when they look towards the throne, thinking with themselves, Lo there he sits to judge me now, and destroy me, who so often made offer of life and salvation to me by his messengers, which I slighted! I might through him have obtained the blessing, but now I stand trembling under the weight of the curse. The despised Lamb of God is turned into a lion against me. Consider this, O sinners, while God is on a throne of grace for you; least it be taken down, and a tribunal of pure justice be set up for you.

3. To clear the equity of the curse, and the execution thereof upon them, their works shall be brought into judgment, Eccl. xii. 14. Their whole life shall be searched into, and laid to the rule of the holy law, and the enormity and sinfulness thereof be discovered. Their corrupt nature, with all the malignity and venom against the rule of righteousness, shall be laid open. Their sins shall be set in the light of God's countenance, in such full tale, that they shall see God is true to his word and oath, that he would not forget any of their works. The mask will then be entirely taken off their faces, and all their pretences to piety solemnly rejected, and declared to have been but hypocrisy. Their secret wickedness, which they rejoiced to have got hid, and which they

so artfully managed, that there was no discovering of it while they might have confessed and found mercy, shall then be set in broad day light before God and the world, when there is no remedy. Conscience shall then be no more blind nor dumb ; but shall witness against them and for God ; and shall never be silent any more. The sin and misery brought upon others, by their ungodly courses, taking effect when they themselves were gone out of the world, shall then be pursued in all their breadth and length, laid to their charge, and proved against them. And so the account of their debt to the divine justice shall be fully stated at that day.

4. Their doom shall be pronounced, Matt. xxv. 41. Depart from me, ye cursed, into everlasting fire, prepared for the devil and his angels.' Thus shall they receive their final sentence, never to hear more from the mouth of him that sits upon the throne. This determines the full execution of the curse on the whole man, soul and body together. The godly shall get their final sentence too ; but O the vast difference betwixt Come ye blessed, and Depart ye cursed. The unspeakable happiness of the saints in heaven, and the unspeakable misery of the damned in hell, will shew the difference. But the weight of both lies, you see, in the state of the parties, as under the blessing, or under the curse. There is the turning point in respect of one's eternal state.

An affecting view of sinners lying for ever in hell, under the curse of the broken law.

They shall lie for ever, under the weight of the curse, in hell, on soul and body together, Matt. xxv. 41. ' Depart from me, ye cursed, into everlasting fire.' Here is there misery completed ; here is the full execution of the curse. The curse was big with wrath, indignation, and fury of a holy, jealous just God, against sin and sinners for sin, ever since it first entered, upon the breach of the covenant: and it has since that time still been bringing forth; yet there has likewise still been some allay in it, and the storm of wrath has not yet come to the height. While men, even the men of the lord's curse, live in this world, much patience is exercised towards them; and partly through the slenderness of the strokes laid on them, partly through their insensibleness, and partly through the mixture of mercy in their cup, they make a shift to live at some ease; and if there ease be at any time disturbed, yet they ordinarily, though not always, find some means to recover it: and even while their souls are in hell, during the time betwixt their death and the last judgment, their bodies lie at ease in the grave; so but the one half of the man is in torment, and a part of him is easy, without any sense or feeling of the least annoyance. But when once the dead are raised again, and the men of the curse have got their last sentence, and time is absolutely at an end, the mystery of God finished, and a quite new state of the creation brought in, to wit, the eternal state; then shall the curse bring forth the threatened death in its full strength and force on the undischarged covenant-breakers; and as Christ, standing surety for the elect, knew by his experience, so shall the men of the curse know by their experience, what was within the compass of the threatening of the covenant of works, Gen. ii. 17. '—In the day that thou eatest thereof thou shalt surely die.' Many a commentary has heaven wrote upon it unto men, in flaming fire, in blood and gore, in sighs, groans, and swooning of the whole creation: but never a full one yet, excepting in the sufferings of the Son of God on the cross. The elect of God get their eyes opened to read that, and so they make haste and escape out of the dominion of that covenant to which the curse belongs : but the rest are blinded, they cannot read it there. But God will write another full commentary on it, after the last judgment, whence all the men of the Lord's curse shall, in their horrible experience, learn what was in it, namely, in the threatening of the covenant of works. The dregs of the cup of the curse shall then be brought above, and they shall drink them.

1. In virtue of the curse, the pit, having received them, shall close its mouth on them. A fearful emblem of this we have, Numb. xvi. 32, 33. in the case of Korah and his company : ' And the earth opened her mouth, and swallowed them up, and their houses, and all the men that appertained unto Korah, and all their goods. They, and all that appertained to them, went down alive into the pit, and the earth closed upon them.' Compare that threatening, Psal. xxi. 9. ' Thou shalt make them as a fiery oven in the time of thine anger ; the Lord shall swallow them up in his wrath, and the fire shall devour them.' They shall be cast into the lake of fire, as death and hell are, to be shut up there without coming forth again any more Rev. xx. 14, 15. By the force of the curse upon them, they shall be confined in the place allotted for damned men and devils. It shall so draw the bars of the pit about them, that sooner shall they remove mountains of brass, than remove them. It shall be stronger than chains of iron to bind them hand and foot, that they make no escape, Matt. xxii. 1. ; yea and to bind them in bundles for the fire of God's wrath, that companions in sin may be companions in punishment : Matt. xiii. 30. ' Let both grow together until the harvest : and in the time of harvest I will say to the reapers, Gather ye together first the tares, and bind them in bundles to burn them ; but gather the wheat into my barn.'

2. The curse shall then be like a partition-wall of adamant, to separate them quite from God, and any the least comfortable intercourse with him, Matt. xxv.

41. ' Then shall he say also unto them on the left hand,
Depart from me, ye cursed, into everlasting fire, prepared for the devil and his angels.' While on the
other side of the wall the light of glory shines, more
bright than a thousand suns, filling the saints with joy
unspeakable, and which we cannot comprehend, and
causing the arch of heaven to ring with their songs
of praise; on their side is nothing but utter darkness,
without the least gleam of light; and there shall be
weeping, wailing, and gnashing of teeth. For why,
God himself is the only true happiness of the creature, and Christ the only way to the Father; but
then there is a total and final separation betwixt God
and Christ, and them. The day of the Lamb's
wrath is come, all possibility of reconciliation is removed, and patience towards them is quite ended,
and the curse hath its full stroke: So God, the fountain of all good, departs quite from them, abandons
them, casts them off utterly; and that moment all
the streams of goodness towards them dry up, and
their candle is quite extinguished. Then shall be
known what is in that word: Hos. ix. 12. ' Woe to
them when I depart from them.' And then there is
no getting over the wall, no passing of the great gulf
for ever: Luke xvi. 26. ' And besides all this, between us and you there is a great gulf fixed: so that
they which would pass from hence to you cannot;
neither can they pass to us that would come from
thence.

3. It shall hence be a final stop to all sanctifying
influences towards them. While they are in this
world, there is a possibility of removing the curse,
and that the worst of men may be made holy: but
when there is a total and final separation from God
in hell, surely there are no sanctifying influences
there. The corrupt nature they carried with them
thither, must then abide with them there; and they
must needs act there, since their being is continued;
and a corrupt nature will ever act corruptly, while

3 Q

it acts at all: Matt. vii. 17. 'Even so every good tree bringeth forth good fruit; but a corrupt tree bringeth forth evil fruit.' And therefore there will be sin in hell after the last judgment, unless one will suppose that they will be under no law there; which is absurd, seeing a creature, as a creature owes obedience to God, in what state soever it be. Yea, they will sin there at a horrible rate, in blasphemies against God, and other sins a-kin thereto, as men absolutely void of all goodness, in a desperate state of misery: Rev. xiv. *ult.* 'And the wine-press was trodden without the city, and blood came out of the wine-press, even unto the horse-bridles, by the space of a thousand and six hundred furlongs;' Matt. xxii. 13. 'Then said the king to the servants, Bind him hand and foot, and take him away, and cast him into outer darkness; there shall be weeping and gnashing of teeth.' The curse will be a dry wind, not to fan nor to cleanse, but to wither, blast, and kill their souls.

4. It shall be the breath that shall blow the fire continually, and keep it burning, for their exquisite torment in soul and body: Isa. xxx. 33. 'For Tophet is ordained of old: yea, for the king it is prepared: he hath made it deep and large: the pile thereof is fire and much wood: the breath of the Lord, like a stream of brimstone, doth kindle it.' There the worm which shall gnaw them, shall never die; for the curse will keep it in life: the fire that shall burn them, shall never be quenched; for the curse shall nourish it, and be as bellows blowing it, to cause it flame without intermission. The curse shall enter into their souls, and melt them like wax before the fire; it shall sink into their flesh and bones, like boiling lead, and torment them in every part. It will stake them down there as marks for the arrows of God, which, dipt in the poison of the curse, shall be continually piercing and burning them up. No pity, no compassion to be shown any more, but the fire-

balls of the curse will be flying against them incessantly: Rev. xiv. 11. 'The smoke of their torment ascendeth up for ever and ever: and they have no rest day nor night.

5. The curse shall lengthen out their misery to all eternity: Matt. xxv. 41. 'Depart ye cursed, into everlasting fire.' It binds the sinner to make complete and full satisfaction, for all the wrongs he has done to the honour of an infinite God; it binds him to pay, till there be a sufficient compensation made for them all. Now, there being no proportion betwixt finite and infinite, the finite creature can never, by its sufferings, expiate its crimes against an infinite God. Hence, when the sinner has suffered millions of ages in hell, the curse still binds him down to suffer more, because he has not yet fully satisfied: and since he can never fully satisfy, it will bind him down for ever and ever, Rev. xiv. 11. and will bring new floods of wrath over his head; and renew its demands of satisfaction through the ages of eternity, but never, never say, It is enough.

The covenant of grace, the grand foundation of all saving mercy to lost sinners of Adam's race.

1. It is the foundation of the first saving mercy that a poor sinner meets with; and that is the first grace given to the dead soul, viz. spiritual life, the new heart, the first resurrection, by which the soul is enabled to believe and embrace Jesus Christ: Ezek. xxxvi. 26. 'A new heart will I give you, and a new spirit will I put within you.' This is saving mercy: Tit. iii. 5. 'According to his mercy he saved us by the washing of regeneration, and renewing of the Holy Ghost.' Upon what bottom can this stone in the building be laid, but on the covenant betwixt

the Father and Christ? No doing of the sinner can be pretended here, for life and salvation, since the sinner is really dead spiritually, and can do nothing; but it is a performing of the promise of the covenant to Christ: Eph. ii. 5. 'Even when we were dead in sins, he hath quickened us together with Christ.'

2. It is the foundation of the middle saving mercies. Look to the soul's actual believing; it is the budding of a promise, a branch of that covenant; Psal. xxii. 29. 31. 'None can keep alive his own soul. They shall come and shall declare his righteousness.' Compare John vi. 37. 'All that the Father giveth me shall come to me.' Justification is the fruit that grows upon it, Isa. liii. 11. 'By his knowledge shall my righteous servant justify many.' So is sanctification; they are sanctified in Christ Jesus, in virtue of that covenant, as they were corrupted and defiled in Adam by virtue of the breach of the first covenant, 1 Cor. i. 2. compare Ezek. xxxvi. 25. 'I will sprinkle clean water upon you, and ye shall be clean: from all your filthiness, and from all your idols will I cleanse you.' This is an absolute promise with respect to the sinner. All their obedience itself, and persevering in holy obedience, are fruits of the covenant, ver. 27. 'I will put my spirit within you, and cause you to walk in my statutes, and ye shall keep my judgments, and do them;' Jer. xxxii. 40. 'I will put my fear in their hearts, and they shall not depart from me'; and so belong to the promise of it, and are no part of the proper condition of it, which must go before partaking of the fruits of it.

3. It is the foundation of the crowning mercy, eternal life in heaven: Tit. i. 2. 'In hope of eternal life, which God that cannot lie, promised before the world began.' To whom could this be promised before the world began, but to the Son of God in the eternal compact? So that the sinner comes to be partaker of it in him, as he is of death in Adam:

John xvii. 2. ' Thou hast given him power over all
flesh, that he should give eternal life to as many as
thou hast given him.' Hence, notwithstanding of
all the good works of the saints, wrought all their
life long, they receive eternal life as freely, and as
much a gift, as if they had done nothing : Rom.
vi. 21. ' The gift of God is eternal life through Jesus
Christ our Lord.' Hence they who have done most
for God, are as deep in the debt of free grace for
their crown, as the thief on the cross, who believed
in Christ, and then expired. For all is made over
to the several persons of the seed, upon one bottom
of the covenant, the proper condition of which was
fulfilled by Jesus Christ.

To confirm it, consider,

(1.) The justice of God could not admit of mercy
to lost sinners, but upon the ground of this covenant ;
whereby the repairing of the honour of the law by
obedience and suffering was sufficiently provided
for, Psal. xl. 6, 7. The first covenant being broken,
the breakers must ' die without mercy,' Heb. x. 28.
unless salvation to them be brought about by another
covenant, that shall repair the breach ; which could
be no other but that made with the chosen One.

(2.) All saving relation betwixt Christ and us is
founded on that covenant. Christ obeyed and died ;
but what benefit have the fallen angels thereby ?
They are left hopeless for all that, and must encounter with unatoned justice. Why ? Not that Christ's
doing and dying was not able to save them ; the
blood of infinite value can have no bounds set to its
sufficiency : but because their names were not in
that covenant, it had no relation to them, but to lost
sinners of Adam's race : Heb. ii. 16. ' For verily he
took not on him the nature of angels ; but he took
on him the seed of Abraham.'

(3.) The very design of making that covenant was,
that it might be the channel of saving mercy, in
which the whole rich flood of it might run, for the

quickening, purifying, blessing, fructifying, and perfecting of an elect world, lying under the bands of
death and the curse by the breach of the first covenant; Psal. lxxxix. 2. ' Mercy shall be built up for
ever;' compared with the text, *I have made a covenant with my chosen.* It was the Father's design ;
and it was the Son's design, Cant. iii. 10. Men are
apt to devise unto themselves other channels of mercy: but this being the only channel designed by infinite wisdom, here the sinful creature will find saving mercy flowing freely, but all other channels he
will find quite dry.

(4.) It has been the ground of all the saints' expectations and hopes of mercy, in all ages. It was
first published in the promise made to Adam, Gen.
iii. 15. ' The seed of the woman shall bruise the
head of the serpent;' and that was the stay of the
souls of the faithful till Abraham's time : then it was
more clearly discovered in the promise given to him,
Gen. xxii. 18. ' In thy seed shall all the nations of
the earth be blessed.' The ceremonial law, and the
prophecies of Christ, pointed out very fully. And
thus believers under the Old Testament built their
faith of mercy on it. And since that time it has
been most clearly and full discovered in the gospel;
and so the New Testament church have raised their
faith of mercy on it.

*Instructions deduced from the consideration of
saving mercy exhibited in the covenant of grace.*

1. Behold here the freeness of saving mercy.
There is a fountain of mercy opened to sinful creatures ; and it was not only provided for them without
any merit of theirs, but without so much as any application made by them for it. Rom. xi. 34. A cov-

enant of grace is made betwixt the Father and his
own Son as party-contractor on man's side, who did
this for their salvation while they knew nothing about
the matter.   Here is rich and free grace.

2. It is a vain thing to remain about the ruins of the
old building, which stood on the covenant of works,
and to expect mercy, life, or salvation there, Gal.
ii. 16. ' Man is not justified by the works of the law.'
It is evident, that man must have mercy now, else he
is ruined for ever, without any possible outgate from
his misery.   If the building of mercy could have been
without a new foundation, why was it laid, and laid
so deep ? But a new foundation was not laid in vain,
but because it was necessary that it should be.   Therefore expect no mercy in the way of the first covenant.
Mount Sinai shows only thunders and lightnings,
the voice of the trumpet waxing louder and louder,
and the voice of words, which sinners are not able to
bear.   There is no voice of mercy and grace but from
mount Zion.

3. What a wretched disposition in man's nature is
it, to be so much addicted to the way of the covenant
of works? God saw that there was no hope for fallen man that way ; therefore he made a new covenant
to build mercy upon.   But fallen man will not see it,
but still aims to make a shift for himself that way.
Our father Adam was well housed indeed in the first
building, if he had managed well : but it was by his
sin laid in ruins.   Yet his sinful children still abide
about these ruins, building cottages to themselves of
the ruins, seeking righteousness as it were by the
works of the law, Rom. ix. 32. and pretending to repair it for themselves.   The Jews were never more
addicted to the temple, than mankind naturally is to
that building on the first covenant.   The Jews, after
their temple had been laid in ruins, never to be rebuilt,
did notwithstanding, in the days of Julian the apostate, attempt to rebuild it ; and ceased not, till by an
earthquake which shook the old foundation, and tur-

ned all down to the ground, and by fire from heaven which burnt all their tools, they were forced to forbear. Thus it fares with men with respect to the building on the old covenant; they will never give it over, nor cry for a Mediator in earnest, till mount Sinai, where they work, be all on fire about them. O the mischief of this practice! They thereby affront the wisdom of God, who found out this new way; they despise the grace, free love, and mercy of it; they trample upon the great salvation brought about by it, Heb. ii. 3. And withal they fight against their own interest; will not enter by the door that is opened for them, but hang about the door that is closed, and shall never be opened to them, and so perish. Thus they 'forsake their own mercy,' Jonah ii. 8.

Lastly, Quit the old covenant, then, and take hold of the new, that you may be personally entered into it. This you may do by taking hold of Christ, in the way of believing; for he is given for a covenant of the people, Isa. xlii. 6. So the proposal of the covenant is made to you, Isa. lv. 3. ' Incline your ear, and come unto me, hear, and your soul shall live; and I will make an everlasting covenant with you, even the sure mercies of David.' And thus shall ye be lodged in the building of saving mercy; and mercy shall be built up to you for ever. But if you do not take hold of this covenant, ye are off the foundation of mercy, and can look for none of it.

How Christ the Son of God became the second Adam, and how the covenant of grace was made with him as the second Adam.

First, How Christ, the Son of God, became second Adam? This we may take up in two things.

1. The Father willed and designed, that his own

Son, the eternal Word, should, for the purpose of mercy towards mankind lost, take on their nature, and become man. He saw that sacrifice and offering would not answer the case; the debt was greater than to be paid at that rate; the redemption of souls could not be managed but by a person of infinite dignity: wherefore, having purposed that the darling attribute of mercy should be illustrated in the case of lost mankind, he willed the human nature to be united in time to the divine nature, in the person of the Son.

And hereunto the Son, as the eternal word, the second person of the glorious Trinity, having no nearer relation to man, than as his Sovereign Lord Creator, readily agreed: Heb. x. 5. 'Sacrifice and offering thou wouldst not, but a body hast thou prepared me,' —ver. 7. 'Then said I, Lo I come (in the volume of of the book it is written of me) to do thy will, O God.' The eternal Word consented to be made flesh, that all flesh might not perish: he consented to become man, to take into a personal union with himself, a human nature, to wit, a true body and a reasonable soul, according to the eternal destination of his Father. This was an instance of amazing condescension The highest monarch's consent to lay aside his robes of majesty, to clothe himself with rags, and become a beggar, is not to be compared with it. Nay, the highest angel's consent to become a worm, is not to be named in one day, with the eternal *Son of God the Father's equal*, his consenting to become man: for the distance between the divine nature and the human is infinite; whereas the distance between the angelic nature, and the nature of worms of the earth, is but finite.

Now, the *effect* of this was, that hereby the Son of God was constituted substantial *Mediator*, or Mediator in respect of nature, between God and man. Being from eternity God equal with the Father, he so stood related to heaven; and having from eternity consented to become man, he so stood related to earth:

3 R

for though he did not actually take on him the nature of man, until the fulness of time appointed by the Father; yet forasmuch as he had from eternity consented to take it on, and it was impossible that his consent should miss to take effect, he was reckoned in law, to all intents and purposes thereof, as if he had actually been incarnate. A type of this his substantial mediation was Jacob's ladder, which was set upon the earth, and the top of it reached to heaven, Gen. xxviii. 12. A clear emblem of the divine and human nature in Christ, through whom, as substantial Mediator, there was a way opened, towards a communication for peace, between heaven and earth. Accordingly our Lord Jesus applies it to himself, John i. 51. ' Hereafter you shall see heaven open, and the angels of God ascending and descending upon the Son of man ;' to wit, as on Jacob's ladder, Gen. xxviii. 12.

2. The Father chose him to be head of the election ; to be the last Adam, federal head and representative of such as sovereign pleasure should pitch upon, to be vessels of mercy, and enrolled in the book of life ; a head and representative, with whom he might make the new covenant, for life and salvation to them.

And to this also he readily agreed, consenting to be the last or second Adam, head and representative of the election ; to sustain their persons and transact in their name : Isa. xlii. 1. ' Behold—mine elect in whom my soul delighteth.' Psal. lxxxix. 19. ' I have exalted one chosen out of the people.' 1 Cor. xv. 47. ' The second man is the Lord from heaven.' The breach between God and man was greater than to be done away by a mere intermessenger, who, travelling between parties at variance, reconciles them with bare words. There could be no covenant of peace betwixt God and sinners, without reparation of damages done to the honour of God through sin ; and without honouring of the holy law, by an exact obedience : but these things being quite beyond their

reach, Christ the Son of God saith, ' Lo, I come ; I
am content to take their place, and put myself in
their room, as a second Adam.'

Now, the *effect* of this was, that hereby he was
constituted last Adam, or the second Man, 1 Cor.
xv. 47. and official Mediator, or Mediator in respect
of office, between God and man : 1 Tim. ii. 5, 6.
' There is one God, and one Mediator between God
and man, the man Christ Jesus ; who gave himself
a ransom for all.'   Being called of his Father unto
that office, and having embraced the call thereto, he
was invested with the office, and treated with as such,
before the world began, Tit. i. 2.   And indeed, he,
and he only, was fit for it.   The two families of heaven and earth being at war, there could be no peace
between them, but through a mediator.   But where
could a mediator be found, to interpose between such
parties, who would not either have been too high, or
else too low, in respect of one of the parties at variance ?   Man or angel would have been too low, in
respect of God ; and an unveiled God would have
been too high, in respect of sinful men, unable to
bear intercourse with such heavenly majesty.   Wherefore, the Son of God, that he might be fit to mediate,
as he, being God equal with the Father, was high
enough, in respect of the party offended, so he consented to become low enough, in respect of the party
offending, by his becoming man.

Secondly, It is to be inquired, How the covenant
was made with Christ, as second Adam ?   And this
also may be taken up in two things.

1. The Father designed a certain number of lost
mankind, as it were by name, to be the constituent
members of that body chosen to life, of which body
Christ was the designed head ; and he gave them to
him for that end : Phil. iv. 3. ' My fellow-labourers,
whose names are in the book of life.'   John xvii. 6.
' Thine they were, and thou gavest them me.'   These
were a chosen company, whom sovereign free grace

picked out from among the rest of mankind, on a purpose of love, and gave to the second Adam for a seed ; on which account they are said to have been chosen in him, Eph. i. 4. being in the decree of election laid upon him as the foundation-stone, to be built upon him, and obtain salvation by him, 1 Thess. v. 9. ; which decree, as it relates to the members-elect, is therefore called the book of life, being, as it were, the roll which the Father gave to the second Adam, the head-elect, containing the names of those designed to be his seed, to receive life by him.

Now, our Lord standing as second Adam, head of the election, to wit, such as sovereign pleasure should pitch upon to be vessels of mercy, did accept of the gift of the particular persons elected or chosen by his Father : John xvii. 6. ' Thine they were, and thou gavest them me.' Ver. 10. ' And thine are mine.' Like as the first Adam, in the making of the first covenant, stood alone without actual issue, yet had destinated for him a numerous issue, to be comprehended with him in that covenant, to wit, all mankind ; the which Adam did at least virtually accept : so, a certain number of lost mankind being elected to life, God, as their original proprietor, gave them to Christ, the appointed head, to be his members, and comprehended with him in the second covenant, though as yet none of them were in being ; and he accepted of the gift of them, being well pleased to take them in particular, for his body mystical, for which he should covenant with his Father. And, in token thereof, he, as it were, received and kept as his own, the book of life containing their names, which is therefore called the Lamb's book of life, Rev. xxi. 27.

2. The Father proposed to him as second Adam, the new covenant for life and salvation to them, in the full tenor, promises, and condition thereof; treating in him, with all these particular persons of lost mankind, elected unto life, and given to him, even

as he treated with all mankind, in Adam, in the first
covenant. The promises therein proposed, were indeed great and glorious; but withal the condition
or terms, on which they were proposed, were exceeding high.

Howbeit, as the first Adam, standing as head and
representative of all his natural seed, entered into
the first covenant with God, accepting the promise
thereof, upon the terms and condition therein proposed, which he engaged to fulfil: so our Lord Jesus, standing as second Adam, head and representative of the particular persons of lost mankind, by
name elected to life, and given to him as his spiritual
seed, entered into the second covenant with his Father; accepting the promises thereof, upon the terms
and condition therein proposed; consenting and engaging to fulfil the same, for them. And thus the
covenant of grace was made, and concluded, betwixt
the Father, and Christ the second Adam, from all
eternity; being the second covenant, in respect of
order and manifestation to the world, though it was
first in being: 1 Cor. xv. 47. ' The second man is
the Lord from heaven.' Isa. liii. 10. ' When thou
shalt make his soul an offering for sin, he shall see
his seed.' Tit. i. 2. ' In hope of eternal life, which
God that cannot lie, promised before the world began.' Psal. xl. 6. ' Sacrifice and offering thou didst
not desire, mine ears hast thou opened,'—7. ' Then
said I, Lo, I come,'—8. ' I delight to do thy will, O
my God: yea, thy law is within my heart.' *

* " The covenant of grace has no parallel, or any other transaction that may be properly brought into a comparison with
it; but the covenant of works which was made with the first
man. This parallel is proper; as it is expressly stated in several
passages of Scripture. The first man was a covenant-head, or
representative of all his natural seed: who were to stand or fall
in and with him; as he should fulfil or break the condition of
that covenant which was made with him for them, and with
them in him. Accordingly Jesus Christ is a covenant-head or
representative of all his spiritual seed: who have a standing in

*For what, Christ, in the covenant of grace, became
surety to God, for his people.*

1. He became surety for their debt of punishment,
which they as sinners, were liable in payment of, as
the original phraseth it, 2 Thess. i. 9. That was
the debt owing to the divine justice, for all and every
one of their sins, original or actual. The demerit of
their sins, as offences against an infinite God, was
an infinite punishment. They were liable to bear
the pains of death, in the full latitude thereof; to
suffer the force of revenging wrath, to the complete
satisfaction of infinite justice, and full reparation of
God's injured honour. This was their debt of
punishment: a debt which they themselves could
never have cleared, though paying to the utmost of
their power, through ages of eternity. But this their
debt Christ became surety for, obliging himself to
lay down his life for theirs, which was lost in law:
Psal. xl. 6, 7. 'Sacrifice and offering thou didst not
desire, mine ears hast thou opened.—Then said I,
Lo, I come.' John x. 15. 'I lay down my life for
the sheep;' ver. 18. 'I lay it down of myself: I have
power to lay it down, and I have power to take it a-
gain. This commandment have I received of my
Father.' Here is a suretiship that never had a
match! David, in a transport of grief for the death
of his son Absalom, wishes he had died for him,
2 Sam. xviii. 33.; Reuben will venture the life of
his two sons for Benjamin, Gen. xlii. 37.; and Judah
will venture his own for him, chap. xliii. 9. while yet

a state of acceptance with God, and a title to eternal life; wholly upon his fulfilled condition of that covenant which is made
with him for them, and with them in him."

Gibb's Sacred Contemplations.

there was hope that all would be safe : But our Lord
Jesus deliberately pledgeth his own life for sinners,
when it was beyond all peradventure, the precious
pledge would be lost in the cause, and that the death
he would suffer, would be a thousand deaths in one.
Some have offered themselves sureties in capital
causes, and embraced death, for their country, or
friends : and 'peradventure for a good man some
would even dare to die. But God commendeth his
love towards us, in that while we were yet sinners,
(and enemies), Christ died for us,' Rom. v. 7, 8. 10.

Now, in the second Adam's suretiship for the criminal debt of his spiritual seed, there was not an en-
suring of the payment thereof one way or other,
only ; as in simple cautionary : but there was an exchange of persons in law ; Christ substituting himself in their room, and taking the whole obligation
on himself. This the free grace of God the creditor
did admit, when he might have insisted, that the soul
that sinned should die : and a delay being withal
granted as to the time of the payment, God thus manifested his forbearance, celebrated by the apostle,
Rom. iii. 25. And in virtue of that substitution,
Christ became debtor in law, bound to pay that debt
which he contracted not ; to restore that which he
took not away, Psal. lxix. 4. For, becoming surety
for them, to the end there might be laid a foundation, in law and justice for exacting their debt of
punishment from him, their guilt was transferred on
him : Isa. liii. 6. ' The Lord laid on him the iniquity
of us all.' This was pointed at, in the laying of the
hand on the head of the sacrifices under the law,
especially on the head of the scape-goat : Lev. xvi.
21. ' And Aaron shall lay both his hands upon the
head of the live-goat, and confess over him all the
iniquities of the children of Israel, and all their
transgressions in all their sins, putting them upon
the head of the goat.' All the sins of all the elect
were at once imputed to the Surety, and so became

his, as his righteousness becomes ours, namely, in
law-reckoning : 2 Cor. v. 21. ' For he hath made him
to be sin for us, who knew no sin ; that we might
be made the righteousness of God in him.'   And he
himself speaks so of them : Psal. xl. 12. ' Mine iniquities have taken hold upon me ; ' as several valuable interpreters do understand it, according as the
apostle gives us direction, determining Christ himself to be the speaker in this psalm, Heb. x. 5, 6, 7.
He was indeed without sin inherent in him ; but not
without sin imputed to him, till in his resurrection
he got up his discharge, having cleared the debt by
his death and sufferings.   Then was he ' justified in
the Spirit,' 1 Tim. iii. 16. and so ' shall appear the
second time, without sin, Heb. ix. 28. ; the sin which
was upon him, by imputation, the first time he appeared, being done away at his resurrection.   This
relation of our sin to Christ, is necessary from the
nature of suretiship for debt ; in which case, nobody
doubts but the debt becomes the surety's, when once
he hath stricken hands for it.   And how else could
the law have justly proceeded against Christ ? How
could our punishment have been, in justice, inflicted
upon him, if he had not had such a relation to our
sin ?   If the law could not charge our sin on him, in
virtue of his own voluntary undertaking, it could
have no ground in justice to inflict our punishment
on him.

2. He became surety for their debt of duty or obedience : the which also is a debt according to the
style of the holy scripture, Gal. v. 3. ' A debtor to
do the whole law.' The law as a covenant of works,
though it was broken by them, and they had incur-
red the penalty thereof, yet had neither lost its right,
nor ceased to exact of them the obedience which at
first it required of man, as the condition of life.
They were still bound to perfect obedience, and on
no lower terms could have eternal life, as our Lord
taught the lawyer for his humiliation : Luke x. 28.

'Thou hast answered right: this do, and thou shalt live.' The paying of the debt of punishment, might satisfy as to the penalty of the bond: but there is yet more behind, for him who will meddle in the affairs of the broken company. How shall the principal sum therein contained, be paid: namely, the debt of obedience to the law, for life and salvation? The honour of God could not allow the quitting of it: and they were absolutely unable to pay one mite of it, that would have been current in heaven; forasmuch as they were 'without strength,' Rom. v. 6. and 'dead in trespasses and sins,' Eph. ii. 1. quite as unfit for the doing part, as for the suffering part. But Christ became surety for this debt of theirs too, namely, the debt of obedience to the law as a covenant, which was, and is the only obedience to it for life; obliging himself to clear it, by obeying in their room and stead, and fulfilling what the law could demand of them in this kind: Psal. xl. 7, 8. 'Then said I, Lo, I come—I delight to do thy will, O my God: yea, thy law is within my heart.' Matt. iii. 15. 'Thus it becometh us to fulfil all righteousness.' Chap. v. 17. 'Think not that I am come to destroy the law—I am not come to destroy, but to fulfil.'

And here also there was an exchange of persons in law, Christ substituting himself in their room, and taking their obligation on himself: in virtue of which, he became the law's debtor for that obedience owing by them; and this he himself solemnly owned, by his being circumcised, Luke ii. 21. according to that of the apostle, Gal. v. 3. 'I testify again to every man that is circumcised, that he is a debtor to do the whole law.' For, becoming surety for them in this point also, he transferred on himself their state of servitude, whereby the law had a right to exact that debt of him, which they, upon the breach of the covenant of works, were liable in payment of.

For clearing of this, it is to be considered, that all mankind was by the first covenant, the covenant of

3 s

works, constituted God's hired servants : and actually entered to that their service, in their head the first
Adam.   And in token hereof, we are all naturally
inclined in that character to deal with God; though
by the fall we are rendered incapable to perform the
duty of it, Luke xv. 19. 'Make me as one of thy
hired servants.' The work they were to work, was
perfect obedience to the holy law; the hire they
were to have for their work, was life, Rom. x. 5.
'The man that doth those things, shall live by them.'
The penalty of breaking away from their Master,
was bondage under the curse, Gal. iii. 10. 'Cursed
is every one that continueth not in all things which
are written in the book of the law to do them.' But
violating that covenant of hired service, they brake
away from their Lord and Master : so they not only
lost all plea for the hire, but they became bond-men
under the curse; still obliged to make out their service, and that, furthermore, in the misery of a state
of servitude or bondage : Gal. iv. 24. ' These are the
two covenants ; the one from the mount Sinai, which
gendereth to bondage.' Their falling under the curse,
inferred the loss of their liberty, and constituted them
bond-men ; as appears from the nature of the thing,
and instances of the cursed in other cases, as Gen.
ix. 25. 'Cursed be Canaan; a servant of servants
shall he be.' Josh. ix. 23. ' Now therefore ye, (namely, the Gibeonites) are cursed, and there shall none
of you be freed from being bond-men.' The very
ground being cursed, (Gen. iii. 17.) falls under bondage, according to the scripture, Rom. viii. 21.

Now, Christ saw all his spiritual seed in this state
of servitude ; but unable to bear the misery of it, or
to fulfil the service : and he put himself in their
room, as they were bond-men ; transferring their
state of servitude on himself, and so sisting himself
a bond-servant for them.

The holy scripture sets this matter in a clear light.
That is a plain testimony unto it, Phil. ii. 6, 7, 8.

'Who being in the form of God—took upon him the form of a servant—and became obedient unto death, even the death of the cross.' The form of a servant, which he took upon him, was the form of a bond-servant. For so the word in the original properly signifies; being the same word that is constantly used in the New Testament phrase, which we read *bond or free*, or *bond and free*, 1 Cor. xii. 13. Gal. iii. 28. Eph. vi. 8. Col. iii. 11. Rev. xiii. 16. and xix. 18. And the apostle leads us to understand it so here, telling us, that this great Surety servant 'became obedient unto death, even the death of the cross.' The which kind of death was a Roman punishment, called by them, the servile punishment, or punishment of bond-servants: because it was the death that bond-men malefactors were ordinarily doomed unto; free-men seldom, if ever, according to the law. And forasmuch as his being in the form of God, denotes his being *very* God, having the very nature and essence of God; for the form is that which essentially distinguisheth things, and makes a thing to be precisely what it is; and this form is, according to the apostle, the foundation of his equality with God his Father, which nothing really different from the divine essence, can be: Therefore his taking upon him the form of a bond-servant, must necessarily denote his becoming really a bond-servant, as really as ever man did, who was brought into bondage, or a state of servitude.

The Father solemnly declares the transferring of our state of servitude on Christ, speaking to him under the name of Israel, as was cleared before: Isa. xlix. 3. 'Thou art my servant, O Israel, in whom I will be glorified.' As if the Father had said to him, 'Son, be it known, it is agreed that I take thee in the room and place of Israel, the spiritual seed, to perform the service due in virtue of the broken original contract: Thou in their stead art my servant; my bond-servant, (as the word is rendered, Lev.

xxv. 39. and elsewhere): it is from thy hand I will look for that service.' Agreeable hereunto is the account we have of our redemption from the curse, Gal. iii. 13. namely, that it was by Jesus Christ ' being made a curse *for* us : for it is written, Cursed is every one that hangeth on a tree ; ' the which Christ did, dying on a cross, the capital punishment of bond-men.

Behold the solemnity of the translation : Psal xl. 6. ' Sacrifice and offering thou didst not desire, mine ears hast thou opened.' The word here rendered *opened*, properly signifies *digged*, as may be seen in the margin of our Bibles : and so the words are, ' Mine ears thou *diggedst* through ; ' that is *boredst*, as it is expressed in our paraphrase of the Psalms in metre, ' Mine ears thou bor'd.' This has a manifest view to that law concerning the bond-servant : Exod. xxi. 6. ' Then his master shall bring him unto the judges ; he shall also bring him to the door, or unto the door-post : and his *master* shall *bore* his *ear* through with an awl ; and he shall *serve* him for ever ; ' that is, in the language of the law, till death. This is confirmed from Hos. iii. 2. ' So I bought her to me for fifteen pieces of silver ; ' which was the half of the stated price of a bond-woman, Exod. xxi. 32. In the original it is, ' So I digged her through to me ; ' the same word being here used by the Holy Ghost, as Psal. xl. 6. It is a pregnant word, which is virtually two in signification : and the sense is, I bought her, and bored her ear to my door-post, to be my bond-woman ; according to the law : Deut. xv. 17. ' Thou shalt take an awl, and thrust it through his ear unto the door, and he shall be thy servant for ever : and also unto thy maid-servant thou shalt do likewise.' That the boring of her ear as a bond-woman, was no ways inconsistent with the prophet's betrothing of her to himself, Hos. iii. 3. appears from Exod. xxi. 8.

Joseph was an eminent type of Christ as the Fa-

ther's servant. And it is observable, that he was
first a bond-servant, and then an honorary servant.
In the former state, being sold for a servant, Psal.
cv. 17, he was a type of Christ, a bond-servant in
his state of humiliation ; whose most precious life
was accordingly sold by Judas for thirty pieces of
silver, the stated price of the life of a bond-servant :
Exod. xxi. 32. ' If the ox shall push a man-servant
or maid-servant, he shall give unto their master thirty
shekels of silver, and the ox shall be stoned.' In the
latter state, being made ruler over all the land of
Egypt, Psal. cv. 21, 22. Gen. xli. 40. he was a type
of Christ, in that most honourable and glorious office
or ministry, which was conferred on him in his state
of exaltation, wherein he was constituted a servant,
for whose law the isles shall wait, Isa. xlii. 4. ; God
having ' given him a name which is above every
name, that at the name of Jesus, every knee should
bow, Phil. ii. 9, 10. This latter service of Christ
belongs to the promise of the covenant ; but the former, to wit, the bond-service, being his surety-service,
belongs to the condition of the covenant. Wherefore,
rising from the dead, having fulfilled the condition of
the covenant, paid the debt for which he became
surety, and got up the discharge, he put off for ever
the form and character of ' a bond-servant, and rose
and revived, that he might be Lord both of the dead
and living,' Rom. xiv. 9.

And hence it clearly appears, how the obedience
of the man Christ comes, in virtue of the covenant,
to be imputed to believers for righteousness, as well
as his satisfaction by suffering : for that kind of o-
bedience which he performed as our surety, was no
more due by him, antecedently to his contract of suretiship, than his satisfaction by suffering. It is true,
the human nature of Christ, being a creature, owed
obedience to God in virtue of its creation ; and must
owe it for ever, forasmuch as the creature, as a creature, is subject to the natural law, the eternal rule of

righteousness : but Christ's putting himself in a state of servitute, taking on him the form of a bond-servant, and in the capacity of a bond-servant, performing obedience to the law, as it was stated in the covenant, for life and salvation, was entirely voluntary. Obedience to the natural law was due by the man Christ, by a natural tie ; but obedience to the positive law, binding to be circumcised, baptized, and the like, which supposed guilt on the party subjected thereto, was not due but by his own voluntary engagement. And the obedience of a son to the natural law, he owed naturally ; but obedience to that or any other law, in the character of a bond-servant, and thereby to gain eternal life and salvation, he owed not but by compact. The human nature of Christ had a complete right to eternal life, and was actually possessed thereof, in virtue of its union with the divine nature ; so that there was no occasion for him to gain life to himself by his obedience. Wherefore, Christ's taking on him the form of a bond-servant, and in that character obeying the law for life and salvation, were a mere voluntary work of his, as surety for sinners ; wherein he did that which he was no otherwise bound to, than by his own voluntary undertaking. Now, forasmuch as the obedience of Christ imputed to believers for righteousness, is his obedience of this kind only ; there is a clear ground for its imputation to them, according to the covenant.

The absolute necessity of Christ's priesthood.

1. Those whom he represented were sinners ; and there could not be a new covenant without provision made for removing of their sin ; and that required a priest. The first covenant was made without a priest, because then there was no sin to take away ; the

parties therein represented, as well as the representative, were considered as innocent persons. But the second covenant was a covenant of peace and reconciliation between an offended God and sinners, not to be made but by the mediation of a priest, who should be able to remove sin, and repair the injured honour of God : Zech. vi. 13. ' He shall be a Priest upon his throne, and the counsel of peace shall be between them both.' And there was none fit to bear that character but Christ himself. No man was fit to bear it ; because all men were sinners themselves, and ' such an high priest became us, as was undefiled, separated from sinners,' Heb. vii. 26. It is true, the elect angels were indeed undefiled ; but yet none of them could be priest of the covenant ; because,

2. Sin could not be removed without a sacrifice of sufficient value, which they were not able to afford. The new covenant behoved to be a covenant by sacrifice, a covenant written in blood : and without shedding of blood there was no remission, Heb. ix. 22. Therefore the typical covenant with Abraham was not made without the solemnity of sacrifice, Gen. xv. 9. ; that he might know the covenant to be a covenant of reconciliation, in which a just God did not show his mercy but in a way consistent with the honour of his justice. Now, the sacrifices of beasts, yea, and whatsoever the creatures could afford for sacrifice in this case, were infinitely below the value. But Jesus Christ becoming a priest, gave *himself* a sacrifice to God, for establishing the covenant ; and that sacrifice was for a sweet-smelling savour, Eph. v. 2. or, as the Old Testament phrase is, a savour of rest, Gen. viii. 21. marg. The represented, being sinners, were corrupt and abominable before God ; and he, as it were, smelled a savour of disquiet from them, they being a smoke in his nose, Isa. lxv. 5. ; their sin set his revenging justice and wrath astir. But the sacrifice of Christ himself, was fit to send forth such a sweet-smelling savour unto God, as

should quite overcome the abominable savour rising from them, and lay his avenging justice and wrath to the most calm and the profoundest rest.

The necessity of a sacrifice in the second covenant, arose from the justice of God requiring the execution of the curse of the broken first covenant ; whereby the sinner should fall a sacrifice for his sin, according to that, Psal. xciv. 23. ' He shall bring upon them their own iniquity, and shall cut them off in their own wickedness.' It was an ancient custom, in making of covenants, to cut a beast in twain, and to pass between the parts of it : and that passing between the parts, respected the falling of the curse of the covenant upon the breaker : Jer. xxxiv. 18. ' And I will give the men that have transgressed my covenant, which have not performed the words of the covenant which they had made before me, when they cut the calf in twain, and passed between the parts thereof ;' or rather, more agreeably to the original, ' I will make the men that have transgressed my covenant—the calf which they cut in twain, and passed between the parts thereof :' that is, I will make them as that calf which they cut in twain ; I will execute the curse on them, cutting them asunder as covenant-breakers, Matt. xxiv. 51. Now, the covenant of works being broken, justice required this execution of the curse of it, in order to the establishing of a new covenant, the covenant of grace and peace. But had it been execute on the sinners themselves, the fire of wrath would have burnt continually on them ; but never would such a sacrifice have sent forth a savour smelling so sweet, as to be a savour of rest to revenging justice ; forasmuch as they were not only mere creatures, whose most exquisite sufferings could not be a sufficient compensation for the injured honour of an infinite God ; but they were sinful creatures too, who would still have remained sinful under their sufferings. Wherefore Jesus Christ, being both separate from sinners, and equal with God, consented in the covenant to be the sacrifice, on which the curse of the first covenant might be executed, in their room and stead.

This is lively represented in the covenant made with Abraham, in which he was a type of Christ, Gen. xv. In that covenant, God promised the deliverance of Abraham's seed out of the Egyptian bondage, and to give them the land of Canaan ; a type of the deliverance of Christ's spiritual seed from the bondage of sin and Satan, and of putting them in possession of heaven, ver. 13, 14. 16. 18. Awful was the solemnity used at the making of this covenant. There were taken a heifer, a she-goat, and a ram, each of them of three years old : typifying Christ, who was about three years in his public ministry, ver. 9. These were, each of them, divided in the midst, hacked asunder by the middle ; which typified the execution of the curse of the broken first covenant, on Christ, our surety and sacrifice for us, ver. 10. Abram's driving away the fowls that came down upon the carcases, typified Christ's victory over the devils, all along during the state of his humiliation, and especially his triumphing over them on the cross, ver. 11. And, finally, there was a smoking furnace, and a burning lamp that passed between the pieces ; which signified the revenging wrath of God seizing on Christ the sacrifice, and justice therewith satisfied, ver. 17.

3. No sacrifice could be accepted, but on such an altar as should sanctify the gift to its necessary value and designed effect, Matt. xxiii. 19. And who could furnish that but Christ himself, whose divine nature was the altar, from whence the sacrifice of his human nature derived its value and efficacy as infinite ? Heb. ix. 14. ' How much more shall the blood of Christ, who, through the eternal Spirit, offered himself without spot to God, purge your conscience from dead works ?' His blessed body suffering and bleed-

3 T

ing to death on the cross, and his holy soul scorched
and melted within him with the fire of the divine
wrath, both in the mean time united to his divine
nature, were the sacrifice burning on the altar, from
the which God smelled a sweet savour, to the appeasing of his wrath, and satisfying of his justice fully.
Not that Christ was a sacrifice only while on the
cross : but that his offering of himself a sacrifice,
which was begun from his incarnation in the womb,
the sacrifice being laid on the altar in the first moment thereof ; and was continued through his whole
life ; was completed on the cross, and in the grave :
Heb. x. 5. ' Wherefore, when he cometh into the
world, he saith, Sacrifice and offering thou wouldst
not, but a body hast thou prepared me :'—ver. 7.
' Then said I, Lo, I come.' Isa. liii. 2. ' When we
shall see him, there is no beauty that we should desire him.' Ver. 3. ' He is—a man of sorrows, and
acquainted with grief.' 2 Cor. v. 21. ' He hath made
him to be sin for us.'

Lastly, There behoved to be a priest to offer this
sacrifice, this valuable sacrifice, unto God upon that
altar ; else there could have been no sacrifice to be
accepted, and so no removal of sin, and consequently
no new covenant. And since Christ himself was the
sacrifice, and the altar too, he himself alone could be
the priest. And forasmuch as the weight of the salvation of sinners, lay upon his call to that office, he
was made priest of the covenant by the oath of God,
Heb. vii. 20, 21. As he had full power over his own
life, to make himself a sacrifice for others ; so his
Father's solemn investing of him with this office by
an oath, gave him access to offer himself effectually ;
even in such sort as thereby to fulfil the condition of
the covenant, and to purchase eternal life for them.*

* " Arise, my soul ; with wonder see
  What love divine for thee hath done !
  Behold, thy sorrows, sin, and grief,
  Are laid on God's eternal Son.

*Christ's fulfilling all righteousness, as the Surety
and Representative of his people, is the grand
and only condition of the Covenant of Grace.*

To evince this, consider,

1. Christ's fulfilling all righteousness, as second
Adam, is what the Father proposed unto him, as the
terms on which his seed should be saved, and upon
which he founded his promise of eternal life to be
given them ; and not any work or deed of theirs :
Isa. liii. 10. ' When thou shalt make his soul an offering for sin, he shall see his seed.' Ver. 11. ' He
shall see of the travel of his soul, and shall be satisfied : by his knowledge shall my righteous servant
justify many : for he shall bear their iniquities.'
Luke xxii. 20. ' This cup is the New Testament in
my blood, which is shed for you.' And the same is
that which Christ, as the second Adam, did from
eternity consent unto, undertake, and bind himself
for ; and which he did in time, according to agreement, perform. Thus he himself represents it, Matt.
iii. 15. ' Thus it becometh us to fulfil all righteousness ;' namely, as it becometh a person of honour and
credit to fulfil his bargain. Luke xxiv. 26. ' Ought
not Christ to have suffered these things ? ' to wit, as
one ought to perform the condition of a covenant or
bargain he has agreed to.

> " See ! from his head, his hands, his feet,
>   Sorrow and love flow mingling down !
> Did e'er such love—such sorrow meet,
>   Or thorns compose so bright a crown !
>
> " Were the whole realm of nature mine,
>   That were a present far too small :
> Love so amazing, so divine,
>   Demands my soul, my life, my all."
>
> Toplady's Hymns.

2. This is the only ground of a sinner's right and title to eternal life ; and upon nothing else can he safely found his plea before the Lord, for life and salvation : Eph. i. 7. ' In whom we have redemption through his blood, the forgiveness of sins, according to the riches of his grace.' Phil. iii. 8, 9. ' That I may win Christ, and be found in him, not having mine own righteousness—but—the righteousness which is of God by faith.' Surely, upon the condition of the covenant fulfilled, one may found his plea before the Lord, for the benefits promised in the covenant : but no man may found his plea before the Lord, for these, on any work or deed of his own whatsoever, no not on faith itself ; but only on Christ's fulfilling all righteousness : therefore no work nor deed of ours whatsoever, no not faith itself, can be the condition of the covenant of grace properly so called ; but only Christ's fulfilling all righteousness. The sinner standing in the court of conscience, trembling before the Lord, flees in under the covert of that righteousness fulfilled by the Mediator, and dare oppose nothing but it to the condemning sentence of the law, giving up with all other pleas for life and salvation. Believing in Christ is the pleading upon that ground, not the ground of the sinner's plea : it saith, My Lord and my God in the promise, upon the ground of Christ's fulfilling all righteousness allenarly, as the condition of the covenant. If any will make it the ground of their plea, they must needs produce it as a work of a law, that is, as a deed done by them, whereby they have fulfilled and answered a law, and whereupon they crave the benefit promised : the which will, according to the scripture, be found a dangerous adventure, Rom. iii. 20. ; Gal. ii. 16. ; and v. 4.

3. It is by this, and this alone, the salvation of sinners becomes a debt : therefore this alone is the condition of the covenant. For the reward is of debt to him, and him only, who fulfils the condition

of a covenant; to him that worketh, not to him that
worketh not, but believeth, Rom. iv. 4, 5. And so
it is of debt to Christ alone, not to us: and therefore
it was he that fulfilled the condition of the covenant;
we fulfil no part of it. This is confirmed from the
primitive situation of mankind with reference to eternal life, in the first Adam's covenant, duly considered. The condition thereof was perfect active obedience. And, according to the nature of that covenant, if this obedience had been fulfilled by Adam,
eternal life to him and his, would thereupon have become a debt to him. And the plea of his posterity
for life, in that case, would not have been founded
on their personal obedience coming after that fulfil-
ment; since it would not have been the performance
of the condition, but the fruit of the promise of the
covenant: but it would have been founded on that
performance of Adam their representative; forasmuch as, in the case supposed, it would have been
the only obedience whereby the condition of that covenant was fulfilled: and so they would have obtained life, not for any personal work or deed of theirs,
but for the obedience of the first Adam their representative, to which God did graciously make the promise of life, in the first covenant.

4. Faith and obedience are benefits promised in
the covenant, upon the condition of it, as hath been
already evinced; and, in virtue of the promises of the
covenant, they are produced in the elect: therefore
they cannot be the condition of the covenant. And
elect infants are saved, though they are neither capable of believing or obeying; howbeit, the condition
of the covenant must needs be performed, either by
themselves who are saved, or else by another in their
stead. Therefore Christ's fulfilling all righteousness,
which is the only obedience performed in their stead,
must be the alone proper condition of the covenant.

Lastly, The covenant of grace doth so exclude our
boasting, as the covenant of works did not. This is

clear from Rom. iii. 27. 'Where is boasting then ?
It is excluded. By what law ? of works ? Nay : but
by the law of faith.' But if any deed or work of ours
be the condition of the covenant of grace, in whole
or in part, our boasting is not excluded, but hath
place therein, as in the covenant of works ; the difference being at most but in point of degrees : for,
according to the scripture, it is working, or fulfilling
the condition of a covenant, that gives the ground of
boasting ; forasmuch as to him that worketh, the reward is reckoned of debt : and life being of or by
works in the covenant of works, though not in the
way of proper merit, but in way of paction or compact only, this gave men the ground of boasting in
that covenant, according to the scripture. Therefore, so far as life and salvation are of or by any
work or deed of ours, as fulfilling the condition of
the covenant of grace, our boasting is not excluded,
but hath place therein as in the covenant of works.
Wherefore, since the covenant of grace is so framed,
as to leave no ground for our boasting, no work nor
deed of ours, but Christ's fulfilling all righteousness,
even that alone, is the condition of the covenant of
grace : and our life and salvation are neither of works,
nor by works, as fulfilling the condition of the covenant : Tit. iii. 5. 'Not by works of righteousness,
which we have done, but according to his mercy he
saved us.' Eph. ii. 9. 'Not of works, lest any man
should boast.'

God forbid we should go about to justle faith and
obedience out of the covenant of grace ! Those who
do so in principle or practice, will thereby justle
themselves out of the kingdom of heaven, Matt. v. 19.
' Whosoever shall break one of these least commandments, and shall teach men so, he shall be called the
least in the kingdom of heaven :' that is, he shall be
treated as he treated that one of these commandments, he shall be judged unworthy of the fellowship of that kingdom. Faith is necessary savingly

to interest us in Jesus Christ, the head of the covenant : and none can attain to eternal happiness, without actual believing, who are subjects capable of it ;
nor can any attain it without the spirit of faith indwelling in them. Obedience is necessary, as the
chief subordinate end of the covenant, being that
whereby God hath his glory he designed therein :
and without obedience begun here, none who are subjects capable of it, can see heaven. But withal it is
necessary, that they be kept in the place and station
assigned them in the covenant, by the Father and
the Son, from eternity. By faith we personally embrace the covenant, consent to, and rest in the condition of the covenant, fulfilled by Christ ; and so
are justified and brought into a state of salvation :
John x. 9. ' I am the door : by me if any man enter
in, he shall be saved.' Compare John i. 12. and iii.
16. and xiv. 6. By evangelical repentance and gospel obedience, we testify our thankfulness to God,
and evidence the truth of our faith, and our being
within the covenant : 1 Pet. ii. 9. ' Ye are a chosen
generation, a royal priesthood, an holy nation, a peculiar people ; that ye should shew forth the praises
of him who hath called you out of darkness into his
marvellous light ;' ver. 10. ' Which in time past were
not a people, but are now the people of God : which
had not obtained mercy, but now have obtained mercy.' Compare Rom. vi. 13. and xii. 1, 2. ; 1 Cor.
vi. 20.

This the prophet taught the Jewish church of old,
Mic. vi. 8. ' He hath shewed thee, O man, what is
good, and what doth the Lord require of thee, but to
do justly, and to love mercy, and to walk humbly
with thy God ?' In the 6th verse, a most important
question is put, concerning the acceptance of a sinner with God, how it may be obtained, Wherewith
shall I come before the Lord ? and several costly ex-
pedients for that purpose are proposed by the sinner,
even to the ' giving of the fruit of his body for the

sin of his soul,' ver. 6, 7.   But the prophet answers
that-question in a word, tacitly upbraiding them with
gross stupidity, in their groping for the wall in broad
day-light, even as in the night ;   He hath shewed thee,
O man, what is good ; that is, what is goodly, valuable, and acceptable, in the sight of God, for that
purpose, even for a sinner's obtaining pardon and
acceptance with God ; namely, the Messias, Jesus
Christ, sacrificed for sinners.   This was what God
had all along, by his prophets, and by the whole ceremonial law, pointed out to them, and set before
them, as the good for that purpose, that they might,
by faith, ' look thereunto, and be saved,' Isa. xlv. 22.
And in the style of the Holy Ghost, Christ crucified
is elsewhere spoken of under the same notion : 2
Chron. xxx. 18. ' The good Lord pardon every one
that prepareth his heart to seek God.'   Orig. ' Jehovah the good make atonement for,' &c.   Psalm
lxxxv. 12. ' The Lord shall give that which is good ;
or, shall give the good.'   Compare John iv. 10. ' If
thou knewest the gift of God, and who it is.'   Isa.
lv. 2. ' Eat ye that which is good.'   Compare John
vi. 55. ' My flesh is meat indeed.'   Job xxxiv. 4.
' Let us know among ourselves what is good.'   Ver. 5.
' For Job hath said, I am righteous.'   Now, being
thus accepted of God, what doth he require of thee,
in point of gratitude, but to do justly, as one accepted not without a righteousness answering the demands of justice and judgment ; and to love mercy,
as one who hath obtained mercy ; and to walk humbly with thy God, as one who is free grace's debtor ?
In the same manner of expression doth Moses address himself to the people secured of the possession
of Canaan by the oath of God, and being just to enter upon it, Deut. x. 11, 12. ' And now, Israel, what
doth the Lord thy God require of thee, but to fear
the Lord thy God,' &c. : namely, in point of gratitude, for his giving thee that good land.

Several things of awful import, agreed to between the Father and the Son in the Covenant of Grace.

It was agreed to,

1. That the curse might be executed on the blessed body of Christ, in the room of his people; forasmuch as their bodies were liable to it, as being instruments of sin and dishonour to God : that it should be hanged on a tree, that all the world might therein read the anger of God against the breaking of the first covenant, by eating of the forbidden tree ; and his being made a curse for us, since it is written, ' Cursed is every one that hangeth on a tree:' that the curse should go over, and death pass through, every part of that blessed body : that his head should be disgracefully wounded with a crown of thorns put upon it; his visage marred more than any man ; his back given to the smiters; his cheeks to them that plucked off the hairs ; his face not hid from shame and spitting ; his tongue made to cleave to his jaws; his hands and feet pierced, nailed to a cross ; all his bones drawn out of joint; his heart melted like wax in the midst of his bowels; his blood shed; his strength dried up : and that in end it should expire and die, be separate from his soul, pierced with a spear, and laid in the dust of death.

2. That it should be executed on his holy soul in a special manner; forasmuch as their souls were the principal actors in sin : that he should undergo the wrath of God in it, being all along his life a man of sorrows, and acquainted with grief: and that towards the latter end, there should be an hour and power of darkness, wherein the malice of men, the power and rage of devils, should be jointly engaged against him, making their utmost efforts on him ; and then

3 U

the full floods of heaven's revenging wrath should
come rolling in upon his soul: that they should so
overflow it, as to strike him with sore amazement,
fill him with trouble, load him with heaviness, and
overwhelm him with exceeding sorrow: that there
should be such a pressure of divine wrath on his
holy soul, as should put him into an agony, even to
his sweating great drops of blood ; and should bring
over it a total eclipse of comfort, and as it were melt
it within him ; that so, while he was dying a bodily
death on the cross, he might die also a spiritual
death, such as a most pure and holy soul was capable of.

Here was the death determined in the covenant,
for the second Adam our representative ; a death in
virtue of the curse transferred on him, long, lasting,
and exquisite, for the full satisfaction of revenging
justice. 1st, It was long-lasting death. He was a-
dying, in the style of the covenant of works, not only
upon the cross, but all along the time of his life ; the
death that was the penalty of that covenant, working in him from the womb, till it laid him in the
grave. Wherefore, he behoved to be conceived of a
woman of low estate; and born in the stable of an
inn, no room for him in the inn itself; laid in a man-
ger, no cradle to receive him ; his infant blood shed
in his circumcision, as if he had been a sinner; yea,
his infant life sought by a cruel persecutor, and his
mother obliged to run her country with him, and go
to Egypt. Returning, he behoved to live an obscure
life, in an obscure place, from which nothing great
nor good was expected, John i. 46. ; and, coming
out of his obscurity, to be set up as the object of the
world's ill will and spite, obloquy and maltreatment,
till by the hands of Jew and Gentile he was put to
death on the cross. 2d, It was an exquisite death.
No pity, no sparing in it: but the curse carried it to
the highest pitch. No sparing from an angry God,
Rom. viii. 32. No sparing from wicked men let

loose on him, pushing him like bulls, roaring on him and devouring him like lions, and renting him like dogs, when once their hour and power of darkness was come, Psal. xxii. 12, 13. 16. Not a good word spoken to him in the midst of his torments, by those that stood by; but he cruelly mocked and insulted in them. Much less a good deed done him. Not a drink of water allowed him, but vinegar offered him, in his thirst caused through the fire of divine wrath drinking up his spirits and moisture. Nay the very face of the heavens was lowring on him : the sun must not give him its light, but wrap up itself from him in darkness; because light is sweet, and it is a pleasant thing to behold the sun.

Lastly, In this article it was established, That he should suffer all this voluntarily, submissively, and resignedly, out of regard to the wronged honour of God. Accordingly, speaking of this life, he saith, ' No man taketh it from me, but I lay it down of myself, John x. 18. compare Psal. xl. 6, 7, 8. This the law demanded of them whom he suffered for, condemning all murmuring and impatience, and binding them to obedience and suffering conjunctly. But how could they have so borne the load of revenging wrath, who cannot bear a sharp fit of the gout or gravel, without some degree of impatience in the eye of the holy law? Wherefore, it was provided, That Christ, as their representative, should bear their punishment voluntarily, and with perfect patience and resignation : that he should go as a lamb to the slaughter, quietly resigning his human will to the divine will; and make his obedience in his sufferings, as conspicuous as his sufferings themselves : that in midst of the extremity of his torments, he should not entertain the least unbecoming thought of God, but acknowledge him holy in them all, Psal. xxii. 3. : nor yet the least grudge against his murderers ; in token of which, he prayed for them while he was on the cross, saying, ' Father, forgive them ; for they know not what they do,' Luke xxiii. 34.

Instructive Lessons from the consideration of the singular condition of the Covenant of Grace.

1. The redemption of the soul is precious. Is it not? Look to the price of the purchase, the ransom of souls, as stated in the covenant; the holy birth, righteous life, and satisfactory death of the Son of God; and ye must conclude it to be a costly redemption. Turn hither your eyes, *1st,* Ye who value not your own souls. See here the worth of those souls ye sell for a thing of nought, for satisfying a corrupt passion, a pang of lust of one sort or another. Costly was the gathering of what ye thus throw away. Ye let them go at a very low price; but Christ could not have one of them at the hand of justice, but at the price of his precious blood. Ye cannot forego the vanities of a present world for them, nor spend a serious day or hour about them; but he, after a lifetime of sorrows, underwent a most bitter death for them. What think ye? was he inconsiderate and too liberal in his making such a bargain for the redemption of souls? He was infinitely just, who proposed the condition; and he was infinitely wise, who went in to it. He was a Father that exacted this ransom for souls; and he was his own Son that paid it. Be ashamed and blush to make so low an estimate of those souls which heaven set such a high price on. *2d,* Ye who have cheap thoughts of the pardon of sin, and of salvation, correct your mistake here. You fearlessly run on in sin, thinking all may soon be set to rights again, with a 'God forgive me! have mercy on my soul!' so as you may leap out of Delilah's lap into Abraham's bosom. O fearful infatuation! Is the mean and low birth, the sorrowful life, and the bitter death of Jesus the Son of God, not sufficient to give

men a just and honourable notion of the pardon of sin? Look into the condition of the covenant for pardon, written in the blood of Lamb of God, and learn the value a just God puts upon his pardons and salvation. See, O sinner, that it is not words, but deeds; not promises and resolves to do better, but perfection of holiness and obedience; not drawing of sighs and shedding of tears, but shedding of blood; and not thy blood neither, but blood of infinite value, that could procure the pardon of sin, and salvation. And if thou have not upon thee, by faith, all that righteousness Christ fulfilled, to be presented unto God for a pardon, thou shalt never obtain it. Particularly, ye are apt to think light of the sin ye were born in, and the corruption cleaving to your nature; but know that God does not think light of these. It behoved to be an article of the covenant, that Christ should be born holy, and retain the holiness of human nature in him to the end; else the unholy birth and corrupt nature we derived from Adam, would have staked us all down eternally under the curse. 3d, Ye that have mean thoughts of the holy law, rectify your dangerous mistake by the help of this glass. Ye make no bones of transgressing its commands; ye neglect and despise its curse: as it is a law, ye show not so much regard to it as to the laws of men; and as it is a covenant, ye look upon it as out of date, being in no concern how it may be satisfied for you. And shall the honour of the holy law lie in the dust in your case? Rather than it should so lie in the case of Sodom and Gomorrah, God would have them laid in ashes with fire and brimstone. Yea, for vindicating the honour of the law, this whole world shall be burnt to ashes, and all the unholy cast out from the presence of the Lord for ever. And in the case of them that are saved, God will have the curse of the law executed upon his own Son as their surety, and the commands of it perfectly obeyed, in all points, by him in their name. Sure, if you are possessed of any share herein, it will be great and honourable in your sight, as it is in the sight of God.

2. The law is no loser, in that life and salvation are bestowed on believers in Christ. It is so far from being made void through faith, that it is established thereby, as the apostle witnesseth, Rom. iii. 31. God would never dispense his pardons at the expense of the honour of his law; nor declare one righteous, without the righteousness of the law being fulfilled, either by him, or in him by another, Rom. viii. 4. Wherefore, life and salvation being designed for the elect, the law's whole accounts of all it had to charge on them for life were taken in; and an infallible method was laid down for clearing them, the burden of the payment being transferred on Christ their surety. By this exchange of persons the law had no loss. Nay, it was more for the honour of the law, that he was made under it, and satisfied it, in virtue of the claim it had upon him by the second covenant, than if they, being mere creatures, had satisfied it in all points. But the truth is, they being sinners, could never by any means have fully satisfied it; though it had eternally pursued them and exacted of them, it would never have had enough from them; whereas now, by Christ's taking their debt on him, it was paid to the utmost farthing.

3. Faith hath a broad and firm bottom to stand on before the Lord. The believer hath a strong plea for life and salvation, which cannot miscarry; namely, the condition of the covenant fulfilled by Jesus Christ, even all righteousness: 'Having therefore, brethren, boldness to enter into the holiest by the blood of Jesus—let us draw near with a true heart, in full assurance of faith,' Heb. x. 19—22. The broken boards of uncovenanted mercy, and men's own works, which presumption fixeth upon, cannot but fail, since the law admits no life for a sinner on these grounds. But forasmuch as there is a gift of Christ and his righteousness proclaimed in the gospel, by the authority of

THE REV. THOMAS BOSTON.

heaven, he who by faith receiveth that gift, and makes
the same his only plea before the Lord, cannot miss
of salvation : Rom. v. 17. ' They which *receive* (Gr.
the) abundance of grace, and of the *gift* of righteousness, shall reign in life by one Jesus Christ ;' where
the abundance mentioned relates not to different degrees of the grace or gift, but to the offence, as appears from ver. 20: As if he had said, ' Who receive
the grace and gift of righteousness, which abound
beyond Adam's offence, saving them out of the gulf
of ruin it plunged them into.' Faith uniting a sinner to Christ the head of the second covenant, makes
him a partaker of Christ's righteousness, as really as
ever his covenant relation to Adam made him partaker of his guilt. So, having all that Christ was,
did, or suffered, for fulfilling the condition of the second covenant, to plead for life and salvation ; it is
not possible the claim can miscarry, justice as well
as mercy befriending the plea of faith, as a righteous
thing with God, 2 Thess. i. 6, 7.

4. All who are in Christ the head of the covenant
of grace, and so brought into it personally, are inherently righteous, or holy. For likeas though Adam
alone did personally break the first covenant by the
all ruining-offence ; yet they to whom his guilt is imputed do thereupon become inherently sinful, through
the corruption of nature conveyed to them from him :
so, howbeit Christ alone did perform the conditions
of the second covenant, yet those to whom his righteousness is imputed, do thereupon become inherently righteous, through inherent grace communicated
to them, from him, by the Spirit. So teacheth the
apostle in the forecited passage, Rom. v. 17. ' For if
by one man's offence, death reigned by one ; much
more they which receive the abundance of grace, and
of the gift of righteousness, shall reign in life by one
Jesus Christ.' How did death reign by Adam's offence ? Not only in point of guilt, whereby his posterity were bound over to destruction, but also in

point of their being dead to all good, dead in trespasses and sins ; therefore the receivers of the gift of
righteousness must thereby be brought to reign in
life, not only legally in justification, but also morally
in sanctification begun here and perfected hereafter.

****

*The true character of those who are personally and
savingly interested by faith in the Covenant of
Grace.*

1. They are all born again, and so made partakers of a new and holy nature : 2 Cor. v. 17. ' Therefore, (namely, since he died for all, ver. 15.) if any
man be in Christ, he is a new creature.' Christ's
being born holy, secured a holy new birth to them
in him ; so they are all new creatures, created *in*
Christ Jesus unto good works, Eph. ii. 10. ; new-
made in Christ, as sure as they were marred in
Adam. And how can it be otherwise ? Can a man
be ingrafted in the true vine, and not partake of the
sap and juice of the stock, that is, the Spirit and
grace of Christ ? No sure : ' If any man have not
the Spirit of Christ, he is none of his,' Rom. viii. 9.
Or, can the Spirit and grace of Christ be in any, and
yet no change made on their nature, but it still remain unrenewed ? No, indeed. ' If Christ be in you,
the body is dead, because of sin : but the Spirit is
life, because of righteousness,' ver. 10. Consider this,
ye who pretend to rely on the righteousness of Christ,
but are very easy in this point, whether ye are born
again, or not ; whether there is a holy nature derived
from Christ to you, or not. Believe it, Sirs, if it be
not so, ye have no saving interest, part, nor lot, in
Christ's righteousness. Ye may on as good grounds
pretend, that howbeit the guilt of Adam's sin was

imputed to you, yet there was no corrupt nature derived from him to you ; as pretend that Christ's righteousness is imputed to you, while yet ye are not born
again, your nature is not changed, by the communication of sanctifying grace from Christ unto you.
Deceive not yourselves ; ye must be regenerate, else
ye will perish ; for ' except a man be born again, he
cannot see the kingdom of God,' John iii. 3.

2. They are all righteous and holy in their lives :
Isa. lx. 21. ' Thy people also shall be all righteous.'
Chap. lxii. 12. ' And they shall call them the holy
people.' How did ungodliness, unrighteousness, and
profanity, enter the world, the which are now over-
flowing all banks ? was it not by one man, by Adam's
sin, which is imputed to all mankind ? Rom. v. 12.
Then be sure, if the second Adam's righteousness
be imputed to you, holiness of life will come along
with it : 1 Cor. vi. 11. ' But ye are washed, but ye
are sanctified, but ye are justified.' Does sanctification then go before justification ? No ; but it hath a
necessary dependence on justification, and evidenceth
it to the world, and to one's own conscience. Unjustified, unsanctified ; and unsanctified, unjustified.
Did our blessed Saviour come into the world, and in
our nature lead a holy righteous life, that men might
live as they list ? Nay, quite the contrary ; even ' that
we, being delivered out of the hands of our enemies,
might serve him without fear, in holiness and righteousness before him, all the days of our life,' Luke
i. 74, 75. If then Christ lived for you, assuredly ye
shall live for him. Consider this, ye who are far
from righteousness of life, living in the neglect of
the duties either of the first or second table, or both.
Your ungodly and unrighteous life declares you to
be yet in your sins, under the curse, and far from
righteousness imputed. There is indeed a righteousness of Christ ; but alas ! it is not upon you : ye are
naked for all it, and stand exposed to revenging
wrath.

3 x

3. The old man is crucified in them all : Gal. v. 24.
' They that are Christ's have crucified the flesh, with
the affections and lusts.'   Therefore I say to you, in
the words of the apostle, Rom. viii. 13. ' If ye live
after the flesh, ye shall die ; but if ye through the
Spirit do mortify the deeds of the body, ye shall live.'
When our Saviour hung on the cross, he hung there
as representative of all that are his, with all their
sins on him by imputation, that the body of sin might
be destroyed, in his sufferings for it, Rom. vi. 6. He
hung there as the efficient meritorious cause of their
mortification, that by his death he might destroy the
power of death in them ; which appears not in any
thing more, than in living lusts preying on their
souls : Hos. xiii. 14. ' I will redeem them from death :
O death, I will be thy plagues.' See Tit. ii. 14. Rom.
vi. 6, 7. Eph. v. 25, 26.   And he hung there as the
exemplary cause of their mortification ; so that all
who are his, and have sinned after the similitude of
Adam's transgression, are likewise crucified, and die
to sin, after the similitude of his crucifixion and
death ; being crucified with him, Gal. ii. 20. ; planted
together with him in the likeness of his death, Rom.
vi. 5. ; the fellowship of his sufferings making them
conformable unto his death, Phil. iii. 10.   Will you
then live after the flesh, not wrestling against, but
fulfilling the lusts thereof ; living in sin, and to sin,
instead of being mortified to it ; and yet pretend that
the satisfaction of Christ is imputed to you for righteousness ?   Truly you may on as good grounds say,
that the blood of Christ shed for you, hath proven
ineffectual ; and that he hath so far missed of his
aim and design, in suffering for you ; or that he died
for you, that you might live in your sin, without danger.   These would make a blasphemous profession.
Accordingly, your presumptuous sinful life and practice, is a course of practical blasphemy against the
Son of God, making him the minister of sin ; and
evidenceth your pretensions to the imputation of his

satisfaction to be altogether vain. Nay, of a truth,
if ye have any saving interest in the death of Christ,
your old man is crucified with him, Rom. vi. 6. ; and
ye are dead with him, ver. 8 ; dead with him to sin,
to the world, and to the law.

(1.) If ye have a saving interest in Christ's death,
ye are dead with him to sin : Rom. vi. 10. ' In that
he died, he died unto sin once. Ver. 11. ' Likewise
reckon ye also yourselves to be dead indeed unto sin.'
While our Lord Jesus lived in the world, the sins of
all the elect, as to the guilt of them, hung about him,
and made him a man of sorrows all along : when he
was upon the cross, they wrought upon him most
furiously, stinging him to the very soul, till they killed
him, and got him laid in the grave. Then they had
done their utmost against him, they could do no more.
So dying for sin, he died unto it, he was delivered
from it : and in his resurrection he shook them all
off, as Paul shook the viper off his hand into the fire,
and felt no harm ; rising out of the grave, even as he
will appear the second time, without sin. Wherefore,
if you do indeed know the fellowship of his sufferings,
if you really have fellowship with him in them, death
will have made its way from Christ the head unto
you as his members ; his death unto sin cannot miss
to work your death unto it also. If you are dead
indeed with Christ, as ingrafted into him, sin hath
got its death wounds in you ; the bond that knit
your hearts and your lusts together, is loosed ; and
ye will be shaking off the viperous brood of them
into the fire, in the daily practice of mortification.
But if ye are not dead, but still living unto sin, it is
an infallible evidence ye are none of the members of
Christ : Rom. vi. 2. ' How shall we that are dead to
sin, live any longer therein ?' Ver. 3. ' Know ye not,
that so many of us as were baptized into Jesus Christ,
were baptized into his death ?'

(2.) If ye have a saving interest in Christ's death,
ye are dead with him to the world : Col. iii. 1. ' If

ye then be risen with Christ, seek those things which are above.' Ver. 3. ' For ye are dead, and your life is hid with Christ in God.' The world hated him, and used him very unkindly while he was in it ; and when he died, he parted with it for good and all : John xvii. 11. ' Now I am no more in the world—I come to thee.' The quietest lodging that ever the world allowed him in it, was a grave : and coming out from thence, he never slept another night in it. He tarried indeed forty days in it after that ; as many days as the Israelites' years in the wilderness ; the former an exemplar, the latter a type of the Christian life, from conversion till the removal into the other world : nevertheless he was dead to the world still ; he conversed now and then with his own, but no more with the world. Now, if ye are his, ye are dead with him unto the world too, in virtue of his death ; being crucified unto it, Gal. vi. 14. Union with Christ by faith lays sinners down in death, in Christ's grave ; and so separates between them and the world for ever : and withal, it raiseth them up again with Christ unto a quite new manner of life ; no more that manner of life which they lived before their union with him, than that which Christ lived after his re-surrection, was the manner of life he lived before his death : Rom. vi. 4. ' We are buried with him by bap-tism into death : that like as Christ was raised up from the dead by the glory of the Father, even so *we also* should walk in *newness* of life.' If your title to heaven is indeed settled, by your receiving the atonement, now is your forty days before your ascen-sion into it ; now are ye no more of the world, although ye be in it : your treasure and heart are no more there. Ye are no more indwellers in it, as natives ; but travelling through it, as ' strangers, coming up from the wilderness, leaning on the Beloved,' Cant. viii. 5.

Lastly, If ye have a saving interest in Christ's death, ye are dead with him to the law also: Gal.

ii. 19. ' I through the law am dead to the law.'
Ver. 20. ' I am crucified with Christ.' Our Lord
Jesus took on our nature to satisfy the law therein ;
the whole course of his life was a course of obedience
to it, for life and salvation to us ; and he suffered,
to satisfy it in what of that kind it had to demand,
for that effect. In a word, he was born to the law,
he lived to the law, and he died to the law ; namely,
for to clear accounts with it, to satisfy it fully, and
get life and salvation for us with its good leave. He
was ' made under the law, to redeem them that were
under the law, Gal. iv. 4, 5. And when once it fell
upon him, it never left exacting of him, till it had
got the utmost farthing, and he was quite free with
it, as dead to it, Rom. vii. 4. In token whereof, he
got up the bond, blotted it out, yea, rent it in pieces,
nailing it to his cross, Col. ii. 14. Now, Christ became dead to it, dying to it in his death on the cross :
so that the holiness and righteousness of the man
Christ did thereafter no more run in the channel in
which it had run before, namely, from the womb to
his grave ; that is to say, it was no more, and shall
be no more for ever, obedience performed to the law
for life and salvation ; these having been completely
gained and secured, by the obedience he gave it
from the womb to the grave. ' Wherefore, my brethren,' if ye are his, ' ye also are become dead to the
law by the body of Christ,' which became dead to it
on the cross, Rom. vii. 4. As ye will not be liber-
tines in your life and practice, being dead to sin,
and the world, with Christ ; so ye will not be legal-
ists in your life and practice neither, being also dead
with him to the law as a covenant of works. Your
obedience will run in another channel than it did
before your union with Christ, even in the channel
of the gospel. Ye will serve in newness of spirit,
in faith and love. The frowns of a merciful Father
will be a terror to you, to fright you from sin ; love
and gratitude will prompt you to obedience. The

grieving of the Spirit of a Saviour, will be a spring
of sorrow to you ; and his atoning blood and perfect
righteousness will be the spring-head of all your
comfort before the Lord ; your good works but
streams thereof, as they evidence your saving interest
in these, are accepted through them, and glorify God
your Saviour. Ye will not continue to serve in the
oldness of the letter, as before ; at what time the
law was the spring of all the obedience ye performed ; fear of the punishment of hell for your sins, and
hope of the reward of heaven's happiness for your
duties, being the weights that made you go, though
for all them you often stopped ; your sorrows springing from your ill works, under the influence of the
law allenarly ; and your comforts from your good
works, under the same influence ; ye being alive to
the law, and dead to Christ. Rom. vii. 6. ' But now
we are delivered from the *law*, that being dead
wherein we were held ; that we should serve in *newness* of spirit, and not in the *oldness* of the letter.'
If by faith you wholly rely on Christ's righteousness,
the holiness of his nature, the righteousness of his
life, and his satisfaction for sin, how is it possible
but ye must be dead to the law ? for the law is not
of faith, Gal. iii. 12. But if you perform your obedience for life and salvation, looking for acceptance
with God on the account of your works, you go in a
way directly opposite to the way of faith, and either
altogether reject Christ's satisfying of the law, or
else impute imperfection unto his payment of the
bond. And ' Christ is become of no effect unto you,
whosoever of you are justified by the law ; ye are
fallen from grace,' Gal. v. 4.

****

Promises peculiar to Christ made in the Covenant of Grace.

First, Our Lord Jesus had a promise of *assistance* in his work : Psal. lxxxix. 21. 'Mine arm shall strengthen him.' Having undertaken the work of our redemption, he had his Father's promise, that when it came to the setting to, he would strengthen and uphold him in going through with it, Isa. xlii. 1—4. And in the faith of this covenanted assist- ance, he went through the hardest pieces thereof : chap. l. 6. 'I gave my back to the smiters, and my cheeks to them that plucked off the hair : I hid not my face from shame and spitting ;' ver. 7. 'For the Lord God will help me.' Accordingly, in his heavi- ness in the garden, 'there appeared an angel unto him from heaven strengthening him,' Luke xxii. 42. And this promised assistance was the token of his Father's good pleasure in, and liking of the work, while it was a-doing.

Secondly, He had a promise of the *acceptance* of his work, when once done ; of the acceptance there- of, as a full discharge and performance of the con- dition of the covenant, entitling him to the promised reward. Hence, in view of the sure performance of his work, the acceptance thereof was, at his baptism, proclaimed by ' a voice from heaven, saying, This is my beloved Son, in whom I am well pleased, Matt. iii. 17. And it was renewed at his transfiguration, a little before his passion, chap. xvii. 5. Unto this promise of acceptance, belongs the promise of his re- surrection, and of his justification.

1. The promise of his resurrection from the dead : Psal. xvi 10. 'Thou wilt not leave my soul in hell ; neither wilt thou suffer thine holy One to see corrup-

tion ; ' which is expounded of the resurrection of
Christ, Acts ii. 31. God, by raising Christ from the
dead, did in effect declare his acceptance of the work
by him performed. It evidenced the debt to be fully cleared, that he who laid him up in the prison of
the grave, did bring him out of it again ; sending
his angel to roll away the stone from the door of it,
and so to dismiss him legally. For thus it was a-
greed in the covenant, that as Christ should give
himself to the death, for the satisfaction of justice ;
so the Father should bring him again from the dead,
in respect of that satisfaction made by his blood,
Heb. xiii. 20.

2. The promise of his justification : Isa. l. 8. ' He
is near that justifieth me.' The accomplishment of
which is observed by the apostle, 1 Tim. iii. 16.
' God was manifest in the flesh, justified in the Spirit.' Our Lord Jesus Christ having no personal
sins to be pardoned, needed no personal justification ;
but as he was the surety of the elect, and had the
iniquities of them all laid on him, it was provided in
the covenant as just, that, the work he had undertaken being performed, he should have an official
justification. Having paid the debt, he had by promise a full and ample discharge thereof, under the
hand and seal of heaven. And here lies the great
security of his people against the law's demand of
satisfaction from them.

Lastly, He had a promise of a glorious *reward* to
be conferred on him, as the proper merit of his work
done. There was a joy set before him in the promise, for which he ' endured the cross, despising the
shame, Heb. xii. 2. Never was there such a work
wrought ; and never was there such a reward promised. Unto it there belongs a fivefold promise.

1. The promise of a new kind of interest in GOD,
as his God and Father : Psal. lxxxix. 26. ' He shall
cry unto me, Thou art my Father, my God.' Our
Lord Jesus had God to his Father, by eternal birth-

right : but there was a new relation constituted between God and Christ as the second Adam head of
the covenant, founded upon his undertaking and fulfilling the covenant-condition ; whereby he became
heir of God as his heritage, according to that of the
apostle, Rom. viii. 17. ' Heirs of God, and joint-heirs
with Christ ; ' namely, with Christ as the primary
heir. For by his obedience unto death, he purchased the enjoyment of God, as a God and Father. I
do not say, he purchased it for himself ; the man
Christ needed not to do that, forasmuch as he had it,
in virtue of the personal union of the two natures :
but he purchased it for sinners, who had lost all
saving interest in God, but could not be happy without it.

2. The promise of a glorious exaltation, to be the
Father's honorary Servant, prime Minister of heaven,
as great Administrator of the covenant : Isa. lii. 13.
' Behold, my servant shall deal prudently, he shall
be exalted and extolled, and be very high.' Chap.
xlix. 8. ' I will—give thee for a covenant of the people.' In fulfilling the condition of the covenant, he
took upon him the form of a bond-servant, and humbled himself, even unto the death of the cross : wherefore God also, according to the promise of the covenant, hath highly exalted him to the prime ministry
of heaven, and given him a name as great Administrator of the covenant, which is above every name ;
that at the name of Jesus every knee should bow,
Phil. ii. 7, 8, 9, 10. The nature, vast extent, and
importance of this promise, will afterwards be unfolded, when we come to treat of the administration
of the covenant, in virtue thereof put in the Mediator's hand.

3. The promise of a seed and offspring, numerous
as the stars of heaven : Isa. liii. 10. ' He shall see
his seed.' Gen. xv. 5. ' So shall thy seed be ; ' namely, ' as the stars of the sky in multitude,' Heb. xi.
12. : even the whole multitude of the elect, all of

3 y

them to live by his death, and to bear his image, as a child doth that of his father. He consented to suffer the pangs of death; but they were travailing pains, to issue in a numerous birth. He was as a corn of wheat to fall into the ground, and die; but the promise secured to him, on that condition, his bringing forth much fruit, John xii. 24. It is in pursuance of the accomplishment of this promise, the gospel continues to be preached from age to age; forasmuch as, in virtue thereof, as many as are ordained to eternal life, shall believe.

4. The promise of his inheriting all things, as primary heir: Psal. lxxxix. 27. 'I will make him my first-born.' So the apostle says, 'God hath appointed him heir of all things,' Heb. i. 2. and Christ himself declares his being put in possession accordingly, Matt. xi. 27. 'All things are delivered unto me of my Father.' Thus he hath by promise, suitable treasures for the supporting of the dignity conferred on him. But of this also more afterwards.

5. The promise of victory and dominion over all his and his people's enemies: Psal. lxxxix. 23. 'I will beat down his foes before his face.' He was to encounter with Satan, sin, and death, in the quarrel of the designed heirs of glory; and no sooner was he engaged against them, but the wicked world of men began a war with him too: but he had his Father's promise, for victory and dominion over them all; that, howbeit he should get the first fall, and die in the battle, yet his death should be the destruction of Satan's dominion, sin's power, and death's bands over his people; and that whosoever should go about to support that tottering interest, should fall under him: Psal. cx. 2. 'The Lord said unto my Lord, Sit thou at my right hand, until I make thine enemies thy footstool.'

....

*Promises of the Covenant of Grace to God's elect
while yet in their state of rebellion against him.*

I. *The promise of* PRESERVATION.

The promise of eternal life to the elect in the covenant, comprehends a promise of their *preservation,*
till the happy moment of their spiritual marriage
with Jesus Christ, wherein they shall be settled in
a state of grace: Ezek. xvi. 6. 'And when I passed
by thee, and saw thee polluted in thine own blood,
I said unto thee when thou wast in thy blood, Live.'
Heb. ' I said to thee, Live in thy blood ; ' as several
approven versions do read it. In this illustrious passage of scripture is showed, under the similitude of
an exposed or out-cast infant, the natural state and
wretched condition in which God found Israel, and
finds all the elect ; the former being a type of the
latter. There is a twofold passing by this wretched
out-cast, and these at two very distant times, intimated by the Holy Ghost. The first, on the day
she was born and cast out, ver. 4, 5, 6. The second,
after she was grown, and become marriageable ; at
what time she was actually married, ver. 7, 8. The
former refers to the time of the elect's coming into
the world in their natural state, not only as born into it, but as beginning to act in it as rational creatures ; the latter, to the time prefixed in the eternal
purpose, when by means of the law in the hands of
the spirit of bondage, their breasts as it were, are
fashioned in the work of conviction ; upon which
ensues their spiritual marriage with Christ. But
how is the out-cast preserved in the interval, that
she perisheth not in her wretched condition ? Why ;
though no hand was upon her, yet a word was spoken,
which secured her life in a case naturally deadly.

At the *first* passing by her, in the day she was born
and cast out, God said to her, ' Live in thy blood :'
that is, ' Notwithstanding that thou art lying in the
open field, in thy blood, thy navel not dressed, so that
according to the course of nature, thy blood and spirits must quickly fail, and this thy birth-day must
be thy dying day : yet 1 say unto thee, *Live :* thou
shalt not die in that condition, but grow up in it,
being preserved till the happy moment of the designed marriage.' And this is the promise of the elect's
preservation in their natural state. And it hath two
great branches ; one respecting their natural life, another respecting their spiritual death. The

First is a promise of the continuation of their natural life, till such time as they be made partakers
of life in Christ Jesus. God has said it ; they shall
live, though in the blood of their natural state. So
it is not possible they should die before that time,
whatever dangers they are brought into ; even though
a thousand should fall at their side, and ten thousand
at their right hand ; for by the promise of the covenant, there is an unseen guard about them, to defend
them. It is in virtue hereof, that all along during
the time they are in that state, they are preserved,
whether in the womb, or coming out of it, or in all
the dangers of infancy, childhood, youth, or whatsoever age they arrive at therein. This is it that, so
long as they are unconverted, doth so often bring
them back from the gates of death ; returning them
in safety, when either by diseases, or other accidents,
they are past hope in their own eyes, and in the eyes
of friends and physicians. Though the elect thief
was in his natural state, nailed to the cross ; yet
death had no power to come at him, so as to separate
his soul from his body, till such time as he was once
united to Christ by faith, and made partaker of a
new life in him. The

Second is a promise of keeping the grave-stone
from off them in their spiritual death. The grave-

stone is the sin against the Holy Ghost, the unpardonable sin ; which, on whomsoever it is laid, makes their case, from that moment, irrecoverable, that thenceforth they can never rise from spiritual death to life : Mark iii. 29. ' He that shall blaspheme against the Holy Ghost, hath *never* forgiveness.' But although the elect in their natural state, being dead in sin as well as others, may, through the activity of reigning and raging lusts, so rot in their graves, as to be most abominable in the eyes of God and all good men ; yet, because of the promise of the covenant, it is not possible that that grave-stone should be laid on them. There is an invisible guard set on their souls, as well as on their bodies : and so it is infallibly prevented, as may be learned from that expression of our Saviour, Matt. xxiv. 24. ' Insomuch that, if it were possible, they shall deceive the very elect. While they are Satan's captives, he may drive them to a prodigious pitch of wickedness. So did he with Manasseh and Paul : but as far as he had carried them, he could not carry them forward that step.

This promise of the elect's preservation, as it is, with the rest, founded on the obedience and death of Christ ; whereby eternal life was purchased for them, and consequently these benefits in particular, failing which they would be ruined for ever : so it is a-kin to, and seems to be grafted upon the promise of assistance made to Christ in the covenant ; by which a divine support was insured to him, during all the time the sins of the elect, and the wrath of God for them, should lie upon him. And at this rate, the case of the head, and of the members, was jointly provided for in the covenant.

II. *The promise of the* SPIRIT.

The promise of eternal life to the elect, comprehends also a promise of the Spirit of life to be communicated to them, and each one of them, at the nick of time prefixed in their cases respectively, in

the eternal council ; that is, the time appointed to be
the time of love, the dawning of the day of grace to
them, however long and dark their night may be.
This promise is found, Isa. xliv. 3. ' I will pour my
Spirit upon thy seed.'   Ezek. xxxvi. 27. ' I will put
my Spirit within you.' The elect of God being, even
as the rest of mankind, dead in sin, through the
breach of the first covenant, could not be recovered,
but through a communication of the Spirit of life to
them : but that Spirit they could not have from an
unatoned God.   Wherefore, in the covenant, Christ
undertook to fulfil all righteousness in their name,
thereby to purchase the Spirit for them ; upon which
was made the promise of the Spirit, the leading fruit
of Christ's purchase ; called therefore the Father's
promise by way of eminency, Luke xxiv. 49.   In
token hereof, the great outpouring of the Spirit was
at Christ's ascension ; when he, as our great High
Priest, carried in the blood of his sacrifice into the
most holy place not made with hands, Acts ii.   For,
as the fire which was set to the incense on the gold-
en altar, the altar of incense, was brought from off
the brazen altar, the altar of burnt-offering in the
court of the temple ; so the Spirit, which causeth
dead sinners to live, issueth from the cross of Christ,
who suffered without the gate.

Now, of the promise of the Spirit there are two
chief branches ; namely, the promise of spiritual
moral life, and the promise of faith.

1. The promise of spiritual *moral* life, in virtue
whereof the soul morally dead in sin, is raised to life
again, through the Spirit of life communicated unto
it from heaven. This is the beginning, the very first
of the eternal life itself promised in the covenant.
It is the lightning of the sacred lamp of spiritual life
in the soul, which can never be extinguished again,
but burns for evermore thereafter. This promise we
have, Isa. xxvi. 19. ' Thy dead men shall live.' And
it belongs to the promise of the Spirit ; as appears

from Ezek. xxxvii. 14. ' And shall put my Spirit in you, and ye shall live.'

The effect of it is, the quickening of the dead soul, by the Spirit of Christ passively received : Eph. ii. 5. ' When we were dead in sins (God, ver. 4.) hath quickened us.' This is the same with the *renewing* in effectual calling, whereby we are enabled to embrace Jesus Christ, mentioned in our Shorter Catechism on that question. And it is fitly called by some divines, the first regeneration, agreeable to the style of the holy scripture : John i. 12. ' But as many as *received* him, to them gave he power to become the sons of God, even to them that *believe* on his name : ' ver. 13. ' Which *were born*, not of blood, nor of the will of the flesh, nor of the will of man, but *of God*.' Sinners in their natural state lie dead, lifeless, and moveless ; they can no more believe in Christ, nor repent, than a dead man can speak or walk : but, in virtue of the promise, the Spirit of life from Christ Jesus, at the time appointed, enters into the dead soul, and quickens it ; so that it is no more morally dead, but alive, having new spiritual powers put into it, that were lost by Adam's fall.

2. The other chief branch of the promise of the Spirit, is the promise of *faith ;* to wit, that Christ's spiritual seed shall believe in him, come unto him, and receive him, by faith : Psal. cx. 3. ' Thy people shall be willing in the day of thy power :' and Psal. xxii. 31. ' They shall come.' God hath promised, that, upon the shedding of the blood of his Son, for the satisfaction of justice, there shall spring up in the earth, after that costly watering, a plentiful seed, to the satisfying of his soul, Isa. liii. 10. And therefore, whoever they be that believe not, all those who were represented in the covenant, shall infallibly be brought to believe, as our Lord himself, upon the credit of this promise doth declare, John vi. 37. ' All that the Father giveth me, shall come to me.' Now, this also belongs to the promise of the *Spirit ;* who

is therefore called the Spirit of faith, 2 Cor. iv. **13**.
as being the principal efficient cause thereof, Zech.
xii. **10**.

The effect of this promise is actual believing, produced by the quickening Spirit in the soul, immediately out of the spiritual life given to it by the
communication of himself thereto : John v. **25**. ' The
dead shall hear the voice of the Son of God ; ' compared with chap. i. **12, 13**. ; 2 Cor. iv. **13**.   As receiving Christ passively, the sinner that was spiritually
dead, is quickened ; so being quickened, he receives
Christ actively.   Christ comes into the dead soul by
his Spirit : and so he is passively received ; even as
one, having a power to raise the dead, coming into
a house, where there is none but a dead man ; none
to open the door to him, none to desire him to come
in, nor to welcome him.   But Christ being thus received, or come in, the dead soul is quickened, and
by faith embraceth him ; even as the restorer of the
dead man to life, would immediately be embraced by
him, and receive a thousand welcomes from him, who
had heard his voice and lived.   When Christ in the
womb of his mother, entered into the house of Zacha-
rias, and she saluted Elizabeth, the mother of John
the Baptist, he, the babe, in Elizabeth's womb, leaped
as at the entrance of life : so doth the soul, in actual
believing, at Christ's coming into it by his Spirit.
As God breathed into the first man the breath of life,
and he became a living soul, who was before but a
lifeless piece of fair earth ; that is, God put a spirit,
a soul, into his body, which immediately showed itself in the man's breathing at his nostrils : so Jesus
Christ, in the time of loves, puts his Spirit into the
dead soul, which immediately shows itself alive, by
believing, receiving, and embracing him, known and
discerned in his transcendent glory.   And thus the
union betwixt Christ and the soul is completed ;
Christ first apprehending the soul by his Spirit ; and
then the soul thus apprehended and quickened, ap-

prehending him again in the promise of the gospel by faith.

Now, the promise of the Spirit, in both branches thereof, is grafted upon the promise of a resurrection from the dead, made to Christ; and it is so interwoven therewith, that there is no separating of them. The promise of his resurrection, like the oil on Aaron's head, runs down to the skirts of his garments, in the promise of quickening his members too. Herein the scripture is very plain, Isa. xxvi. 19. ' Thy dead men shall live, together with my dead body shall they arise.' Eph. ii. 5. ' Even when we were dead in sins, hath quickened us together with Christ.' Our Lord Jesus, in the eternal covenant, became the head of a dead body, to wit, of the body of elect sinners dead in sin; and that to the end he might restore it to life. And being legally united with that body, that so death might have access to spread itself from it unto him in due time, he had the promise of a resurrection, both for himself and his members, made unto him. The appointed time being come, death drew together its whole forces, and made an attack upon the head of the body, which alone remained alive. It stung him to the heart upon the cross, and laid him too in the dust of death : and so it had them all dead together, head and members. Thus the condition of the covenant was fulfilled. Now, the promise comes next, in its turn, to be fulfilled; particularly, the promise of a resurrection : namely, that death having exhausted all its force and vigour on the head, he should be raised again from the dead; and that as death had spread itself from the members into the head, so life, in its turn, should spread itself from the head into the members, they, together with his dead body, arising. It was in virtue hereof, that the spirit or soul that animated Christ's body, and which he yielded up upon the cross, Matt. xxvii. 50. showed by his breathing out his last there, Luke xxiii. 46. *Gr.* was returned again into his blessed body ; whereupon he came forth out of the grave. And it is in virtue of the same, that the Spirit of life returns into the dead souls of the elect again ; upon which they live and believe. The time of the return of the Spirit, both into the head, and into the members, was prefixed in the covenant, respectively : so that as it was not possible Christ should be held in the grave after three days ; even so it is not possible, that his elect should be held in the bonds of spiritual death, after the time prefixed for their delivery : Hos. vi. 2. ' After two days will he revive us, in the third day he will raise us up, and we shall live in his sight.'

And thus the promise of eternal life to the elect, works in this dark period of their days ; which dark period ends here. It appears now, and runs above ground ever after.

***

Promises of the Covenant of Grace to God's elect, from the time of actually embracing Christ till death.

I. *The promise of* JUSTIFICATION.

The promise of eternal life to the elect, comprehends the promise of justification, to be conferred on them, and each one of them, being united to Christ through the Spirit. This is found, Isa. liii. 11. ' By his knowledge shall my righteous servant justify many.' Chap. xlv. 25. ' In the Lord shall all the seed of Israel be justified.' It is the leading promise of this period : and the effect of the accomplishment thereof is, that the soul legally dead under the sentence of the law, or curse of the broken covenant of works, is caused to live again accordingly ; as it is written, ' The just shall live by faith,' Rom. i. 17. And this is the beginning of that life, which is re-

ceived from Christ by faith, and is mentioned John
v. 40. ' Ye will not come to me, that ye might have
life by me.' Chap. vi. 57. ' He that eateth me, even
he shall live by me.' There is a life received from
Christ before faith, whereby one is enabled to believe ;
of which we have already spoken : and there is a
life received from Christ through faith, according to
John xx. 31. ' That believing ye might have life
through his name.' And this last is, according to
the scripture, eternal life too : chap. v. 24. ' He that
heareth my word, and believeth on him that sent me,
hath everlasting life, and shall not come into condemnation ; but is passed from death unto life.'

The elect of God, lying under the breach of the
first covenant, were dead in law, as being under the
curse. They could not be restored to life in the eye
of the law, but upon the fulfilling of the righteousness of the law ; the which they not being able to
do for themselves, Christ in the covenant undertook
to do it for them : and thereupon was made the promise of their justification. This promise taking effect
upon their believing, the curse is removed, and they
are actually and personally justified. Thus they are
restored to life in the eye of the law ; which kind of
life, received by faith, is everlasting ; forasmuch as,
according to the covenant, the curse can never return
upon them, for shorter or longer time : Isa. liv. 19.
' As I have sworn that the waters of Noah should
no more go over the earth ; so have I sworn· that I
would not be wroth with thee.'

Of the promise of justification there are two branches ; namely, the promise of pardon, and of acceptance.

1. The promise of pardon of sin, whereby the guilt
of eternal wrath is done away : Heb. viii. 12. ' Their
sins and their iniquities will I remember no more.'
The sins of the elect being, in the eternal covenant,
imputed to, and laid on Christ ; who becoming legally one with them, transferred their debt on himself,
and undertook to pay the same ; a promise was there-

upon made of pardon to them, and each one of them. Now, as soon as they are mystically and really united to him by faith, by means of that union, they have communion with him in his righteousness : whereupon his perfect satisfaction is imputed to them ; and upon the account of it alone, and not any deed of theirs whatsoever, the free promise is accomplished, and the pardon actually bestowed on them, according to the eternal agreement : Eph. i. **7**. ' In whom we have redemption through his blood, the forgiveness of sins, according to the riches of his grace.'

Here is life from the dead ; a pardon put into the hand of the condemned man, disarming the law of its condemning power, and death of its sting, as to him ; causing him to lift up his head from off the block, and go away with acclamations of praise of the King's mercy, and his Son's merit. And it is eternal life ; for all his sins past, present, and to come, are pardoned, as to the guilt of eternal wrath ; a formal remission of these of the two former kinds being granted, and a not-imputing of these of the latter sort, as to that guilt, being secured ; as the apostle teacheth, Rom. iv. **7**. ' Blessed are they whose iniquities *are forgiven*, and whose sins *are covered.*' Ver. **8**. ' Blessed is the man to whom the Lord *will not impute* sin.' And God will never revoke his pardons : chap. xi. **29**. ' For the gifts and calling of God are without repentance.'

2. The other branch of the promise of justification, is the promise of acceptance of their persons as righteous in the sight of God ; according to that, Isa. xlii. **21**. ' The Lord is well pleased for his righteousness' sake.' Compared with Matt. iii. **17**. ' This is my beloved Son, in whom I am well pleased ;' and Eph. i. **6**. ' He hath made us accepted in the Beloved.' A holy righteous God, whose judgment is according to truth, cannot accept sinners as righteous, without a righteousness, even a perfect righteousness. They that are not truly righteous in law, can never pass for righteous, but for unrighteous ones, in the view of his piercing eye : ' For in thy sight,' says the psalmist, Psal. cxliii. 2. ' shall no man living be justified ;' to wit, by the deeds of the law, or inherent righteousness, which is imperfect, as the apostle expounds it, Rom. iii. 20. But our Lord Jesus having in the covenant undertaken to fulfil all righteousness for them, who of themselves could fulfil no righteousness ; a promise was thereupon made, to accept them as righteous upon the account of his surety-righteousness, which becomes truly theirs through faith, and that by a double right. 1st, By right of free gift received : inasmuch as Christ's righteousness being made over, in the gospel, as Heaven's free gift to sinners, the gift is by faith actually claimed and received ; whence it is called the *gift* of righteousness, Rom. v. 17. revealed unto faith, chap. i. 17. ; namely, to be believed on, and so received. 2d, By right of communion with Christ ; inasmuch as sinners being united with him by faith, have thereby communion, or a common interest with him in his righteousness : Phil. iii. 9. ' And be found in him, not having mine own righteousness, which is of the law, but that which is through the faith of Christ.' Upon these grounds, the holiness of Christ's nature, the righteousness of his life, and the satisfaction made by his death and sufferings, being the constituent parts of that righteousness, are, according to truth, imputed to the believer, or legally reckoned his : and, upon the account thereof precisely, he is accepted of God as righteous, being ' made the righteousness of God *in him*,' 2 Cor. v. 21. ; ' the righteousness of God being *upon* all that believe,' Rom. iii. 22.

II. *The promise of a NEW and SAVING COVENANT-RELATION to God.*

The promise of eternal life to the elect, doth also comprehend the promise of a new and saving covenant-relation to God, which they, and each one of

them, being justified, shall be brought into : Hos.
ii. 23. ' I will say to them which were not my people, Thou art my people ; and they shall say, Thou
art my God.' Dying both morally and legally, through
the breach of the first covenant, they fell under a
relative death too ; whereby the blessed relation between God and them was dissolved : and it could
not be constituted again, while they lay under the
condemnatory sentence of the law. But upon Christ's
undertaking, in the covenant, to bring in an everlasting righteousness, the price of the redemption of
all saving benefits, this promise was made. Wherefore they being come to Christ by faith, united with
him, and justified through his righteousness, which
they partake of in him ; God meets them there, even
in Christ the appointed meeting-place : and there,
with the safety of his honour, he takes them by the
hand, and joins them again in a saving relation.
Thus they have a relative life, according to that,
Psal. xxx. 5. ' In his favour is life.' The which life
is eternal : forasmuch as the relation is for ever in-
dissoluble ; the bond of the second covenant being
so much surer than the bond of the first, as the
second Adam's undertaking was surer than the first
Adam's.

Now, of this promise there are three chief branches ;
namely, the promise of reconciliation, of adoption,
and of God's being their God.

1. The promise of reconciliation between God and
them : Ezek. xxxvii. 26. ' I will make a covenant of
peace with them, it shall be an everlasting covenant.'
They were by sin in a state of enmity with God :
on their part, there was a real enmity against God ;
on God's part, a legal enmity against them, such as
a judge hath against a malefactor, whom notwithstanding he may dearly love. But Jesus Christ having undertaken, in the covenant, to expiate their
guilt, by the sacrifice of himself, the Father made a
promise of peace and reconciliation with them there-

upon. Hence we are said to be reconciled to God
by the death of his Son, Rom. v. 10.; inasmuch as
by his death and sufferings he purchased our reconciliation, which was promised on these terms.

Now, this promise is accomplished to the justified
sinner: being pardoned, he is brought into a state
of peace with God, as saith the apostle, Rom. v. 1.
' Being justified by faith, we have peace with God.'
God lays down his legal enmity against him, never
to be taken up again. And more than that, he takes
him into a bond of friendship: so that he is not
only at peace with God, but is the friend of God:
James ii. 23. ' Abraham believed God, and it was
imputed unto him for righteousness: and he was
called the friend of God.'

This promise is grafted upon the promise of acceptance and justification made to Christ. For his
sacrifice being accepted as well pleasing to God, and
he discharged of the debt he became surety for; the
reconciliation, as well as the pardon, of those united
to him by faith, natively follows thereupon: 2 Cor.
v. 19. ' God was in Christ reconciling the world unto himself, not imputing their trespasses unto them.'
Eph. i. 6. ' He hath made us accepted in the Beloved.' Ver. 7. ' In whom we have redemption through
his blood, the forgiveness of sins.'

2. Another branch of this promise, is the promise
of their adoption into the family of God: Hos. i. 10.
' It shall be said unto them, Ye are the sons of the
living God.' And this is more than the former; as
it is more to be one's son, than to be his friend. We
have before declared, how all mankind was, by the
first covenant, constituted God's hired servants; and
by the breach of that covenant, bond-servants under
the curse: and how Christ transferred that state of
servitude of his spiritual seed on himself. Now, upon consideration of his taking on him the form of a
bond-servant for them, the promise of their adoption
into the family of God was made. He was ' made

under the law, to redeem them that were under the law, that we might receive the adoption of sons, Gal. iv. 4, 5.

And being justified by faith, and reconciled to God, it is accomplished to them : forasmuch as then Christ's service is imputed to them, and a way is opened withal for their admission into the family of God, through their actual reconciliation to him : Rom. v. 1. ' Being justified by faith, we have peace with God, through our Lord Jesus Christ.' Ver. 2. ' By whom also we have access by faith into this grace wherein we stand.' John i. 12. ' As many as received him, to them gave he power to become the sons of God.' Then are they taken as children into the family of heaven : God becomes their Father in Christ ; and they his sons and daughters, to abide for ever in his house, John viii. 35. And so they have a right to all the privileges of that high relation.

Now, this promise is grafted upon the promise made to Christ of a new kind of interest in God as his Father ; according to that, John xx. 17. ' I ascend unto my Father and your Father.' For by the Spirit of adoption, we call God our Father, in the right of Jesus Christ our elder brother, spiritual husband and head.

3. The last branch is the promise of God's being their God : Heb. viii. 10. ' I will be their God.' This is more than reconciliation, and adoption : it is the height of the relation to God, which a sinful creature could be advanced unto. They were by nature ' without God,' Eph. ii. 12. : but forasmuch as the Son of God did, in the covenant, undertake to give himself for them, in their nature perfectly to satisfy the law, in his holy birth, righteous life, and exquisite death ; a ransom of infinite value, quite beyond all created things whatsoever, graces, pardons, heavens ; there was made, upon that consideration, a promise of God's giving himself to them, as the

adequate reward of that service ; which being performed by the Mediator, this reward was purchased
for them. Hence God saith to Abraham, Gen. xv. 1.
' I am thy exceeding great reward.'

III. *The promise of* SANCTIFICATION.

In the promise of eternal life to the elect, is comprehended in like manner the promise of their sanctification : Ezek. xi. 19. ' I will take the stony heart
out of their flesh, and will give them an heart of
flesh : ' ver 20. ' That they may walk in my statutes.'
See Joel iii. 17. 21. ; Heb. viii. 10. Through the
breach of the first covenant, they lost the image of
God : their whole faculties were so depraved, that
they could neither do, speak, nor think any thing
truly good and acceptable to God : they were by
nature altogether unholy ; unclean, loathsome, and
abominable, in their nature, heart, and life. And it
was quite beyond their power to make themselves
holy again : for mending of their nature could not
effect it ; it behoved to be renewed, Eph. iv. 23.
And the curse of the law lying upon them, extinguished all saving relation between God and them ;
and so blocked up all saving communication with
heaven : for it barred, in point of justice, all sanctifying influences from thence ; these being the greatest benefit they were capable of, as assimilating the
creature unto God himself, or rendering it like him.
The curse fixed a gulf betwixt God and them, so
that sanctifying influences could not pass from him
unto them ; more than their unholy desires and prayers could pass from them unto him. So the fallen
angels always were, and the damned now are, beyond all possibility of sanctification, or of receiving
sanctifying influences from heaven ; there being no
remedy to remove the curse, neither from the one,
nor from the other. And in this case, all Adam's
posterity had lain for ever, had not Jesus Christ, as
the head of the elect, undertaken in the second cove-

nant to remove that bar, to fill up that gulph, and
to found a new saving relation between God and
them, through his own obedience and death. But
upon that undertaking of the Mediator, the Father
did by promise ensure their sanctification; that
Christ's people should be willing in the day of his
power, in the beauties of holiness, Psal. cx. 3.; and
that a seed should serve him, Psal. xxii. 30.

And this promise, the promise of sanctification, is
indeed the chief promise of the covenant made to
Christ for them: among the rest of that kind, it
shines like the moon among the lesser stars. Sanctification is the very chief subordinate end of the covenant of grace, standing therein next to the glory
of God, which is the chief and ultimate end thereof.
The promise of it, is the centre of all the rest of these
promises. All the foregoing promises, the promise
of preservation, the Spirit, the first regeneration or
quickening of the dead soul, faith, justification, the
new saving relation to God, reconciliation, adoption,
and enjoyment of God as our God, do tend unto it
as their common centre, and stand related to it as
means to their end. They are all accomplished to
sinners, on design to make them holy. And all the
subsequent promises, even the promise of glorifica-
tion itself, are but the same promise of sanctification enlarged and extended; they are but as so many
rays and beams of light, shooting forth from it as
the centre of them all.

This appears from the scriptural descriptions of
the covenant, in the promissory part thereof respecting the elect: Luke i. 73. 'The oath which he
sware to our father Abraham,' ver. 74. 'That he
would grant unto us, that we being delivered out of
the hands of our enemies, might serve him without
fear,' ver. 75. 'In holiness and righteousness before
him, all the days of our life.' Here is the oath, or
covenant sworn to Abraham as a type of Christ:
wherein his seed's serving the Lord in holiness, is

held forth as the chief thing sworn unto the Mediator by the Father ; and their deliverance from their enemies, as the means for that end. See Heb. viii. 10, 11, 12. ; where God's writing his law in their hearts, is set on the front, as the first thing in the divine intention, though the last in execution, as appears by comparing the 10th and 12th verses. This matter is also evident from the nature of the thing. For the great thing Satan aimed at in seducing our first parents, was the ruin of the image of God in them, that so mankind might be no more like God, but like himself : and the mystery of God, for the recovery of sinners, is then finished, when holiness is brought in them to perfection in heaven, and not till then.

From all which, one may plainly perceive, that the sanctification of all that shall see heaven, is secured in the covenant, upon infallible grounds, beyond all possibility of failure : and that the unholy have no saving part nor lot in the covenant ; and that the less holy any man is, the less is the covenant-promise accomplished to him. For the sanctification of sinners is the great design of that contrivance : it is that which the Father and the Son, looking therein to them, had chiefly in their view : and the promise thereof is the capital promise of the covenant respecting them ; being as it were written in great letters.

Now, at the time appointed for every one in the eternal council, this promise is accomplished. The sinner being justified by faith, and taken into a saving relation to God, being reconciled, adopted, and made an heir of God through Christ, is sanctified. The bar being removed, the gulph filled up as to him, his saving interest in, and relation to a holy God being established ; the communication between Heaven and the sinner is opened, and sanctifying influences flow amain, to the sanctifying of him throughout.

This is by some divines called the second regenera-

tion, agreeable to the scripture : Tit. iii. 5. ' He
saved us by the washing of regeneration, and renewing of the Holy Ghost;' compared with Eph.
v. 26. ' That he might sanctify and cleanse it with
the washing of water;' 2 Cor. v. 17. ' If any man
be in Christ, he is a new creature;' namely, being
' created in Christ Jesus unto good works,' as the
apostle himself explains it, Eph. ii. 10. And as in
regeneration taken strictly for the quickening of the
dead soul, and called the first regeneration, new vital
powers are given ; so in regeneration taken largely
for the forming of the new creature in all its parts
and distinct members, which is called the second regeneration, there are new qualities and habits of
grace infused ; and it is the same with the second
renewing, mentioned in our *Shorter Catechism*, on
the head of sanctification, ' whereby we are renewed
in the whole man, after the image of God.'

The matter lies here. The sinner being by faith
united to Christ, through the communication of the
quickening Spirit from Christ unto him, and thereupon justified, reconciled, adopted, and made an heir
of God ; there is a measure of every grace, even the
seeds of all saving graces, derived from, and communicated out of the all-fulness of grace in the man
Christ the head, unto the sinner as a member of his,
by the same Spirit dwelling in the head and members. Hereby the man is not only a spiritually living creature, but an all-new creature, sanctified wholly or throughout, renewed in the whole man, after
the image of God. For the immediate effect of that
communication of grace from Christ, must be the
sealing of the person with the image of Christ; forasmuch as he receives grace for grace in Christ, as
the wax doth point for point in the seal. So that
the restored image of God is expressed on us immediately from Christ the second Adam, who is the
image of the invisible God : even as Eve was made
after God's image, being made after Adam's, accord-

ing to Gen. ii. 18. ' I will make him an help-meet for him ; ' marg. as before him, that is, in his own likeness, as if he sat for the picture. Compare 1 Cor. xi. 7. ' He (to wit, the man) is the image and glory of God ; but the woman is the glory of the man ; ' ver. 8. ' For the man is not of the woman ; but the woman of the man ; ' and 2 Cor. viii. 23. ' Our brethren are the messengers of the churches, and the glory of Christ.' And thus our uniting with Christ, through the Spirit, by faith, issues in our becoming one spirit, that is, of the same spiritual holy nature with him ; as really as Eve was one flesh with Adam, being formed of him, of his flesh and of his bones, Gen. ii. 23. ; to which the apostle alludes, in the matter of the mystical union between Christ and believers : Eph. v. 30. ' For we are members of his body, of his flesh, and of his bones.'

IV. *The promise of* PERSEVERANCE *in Grace.*

The promise of eternal life doth, in like manner, comprehend the promise of perseverance in grace, to be conferred on all the covenant-people, being justified, new-related to God, and sanctified ; so that, being once brought into the state of grace, they shall never fall away from it totally nor finally. This promise we have, Jer. xxxii. 40. ' And I will make an everlasting covenant with them, that I will not turn away from them, to do them good ; but I will put my fear in their hearts, that they shall not depart from me.' Here they are secured on both sides ; that God will never cast them off, and that they shall never desert him. And that this benefit is included in the promise of eternal life, is clear from the apostle's adducing this last to prove it : Heb. x. 38. ' Now the just shall live by faith.' Such is the malice of Satan, and the advantage he hath against the saints in this life ; so manifold are the snares for them in the present evil world ; such a tender bud of heaven is the implanted grace of God in them ; and so corrupt, fickle, and inconstant are the hearts of the best, while here ; that if their perseverance had not been secured by promise in the covenant, but made the condition of the covenant, and left to the management of their own free will, they would have had but a sorry restoration of it into the state of grace ; much as if they had got a spark of fire to keep alive in the midst of an ocean. At that rate they might all have perished ; and Jesus Christ, notwithstanding of the shedding of his blood for them, might have eternally remained a head without members, a king without subjects. But the glory of Christ, and the salvation of his redeemed, were not left at such uncertainty. That perseverance which the first Adam failed of, and was made the condition of the second covenant, the second Adam did undertake in their name : and thereupon was made the promise of their perseverance. And he having accordingly persevered unto the end, in obedience to the law for them, being obedient even to the death, it was purchased for them. Thus Christ's perseverance in obedience to the law, till the condition of the covenant was perfectly fulfilled, is the ground in law upon which the perseverance of the saints is infallibly secured, in virtue of the faithfulness of God in the promise.

Now, this promise begins to be performed to them, as soon as they are united unto Christ ; and it goes on all along, until their death, that they enter into glory : yea, strictly speaking, death is not the last, but a middle term of their perseverance ; after which it proceeds far more illustriously than before. Upon their union with the second Adam, being savingly interested in his obedience which he persevered in unto the end, they are confirmed, that they can no more fall away : even as the first Adam's natural seed would have been confirmed, upon his having completed the course of his probationary obedience, and fulfilling the condition of the covenant of works. The mystical members of Christ do then obtain the

former, as the reward of his continued obedience ;
as in the other supposed event, Adam's natural seed
would have obtained the latter, as the reward of his
continued obedience.

The promise of the perseverance of the saints,
seems to be grafted upon the promise of assistance
made to Christ in his work. The Father promised
to him, that he would uphold him, so as he should
not fail, Isa. xlii. 1. 4. The which promise being
made to him as a public person, carries along with
it the preservation and support of his members, in
all their temptations, trials, and dangers of perishing ; insuring the safe conduct, as of the head, so of
the mystical members, through this world, till they
be out of the reach of danger.

Now, of the promise of perseverance there are
two chief branches.

1. A promise of continued influences of grace, to
be from time to time conferred on them, being once
brought into a state of grace : Isa. xxvii. 3. ' I will
water it every moment.' Their stock of inherent
grace would soon fail, if they were left to live upon
it, without supply coming in from another hand ; of
itself it would wither away and die out, if it were
not fed, Luke xxii. 32. ; John xv. 6. Innocent Adam
had a larger stock of inherent grace than any of the
saints in this life, and yet he lost it. But the grace
of God in believers cannot be so lost : for, in virtue
of the promise, there are continued influences secured for them ; namely, preserving influences, whereby grace given, is kept from dying out, that as they
are sanctified by God the Father, so they are preserved in Jesus Christ, Jude 1. ; exciting influences,
whereby the grace preserved beginning to languish,
or being brought low by the prevailing of corruption
and temptation, is stirred up and put in exercise
again ; and strengthening influences, whereby the
grace excited, is increased, and gathers more strength,
to the overtopping of corruption, and repelling of

temptation : Hos. xiv. 7. ' They shall revive as the
corn, and grow as the vine.' Accordingly, their
faith is never suffered to fail totally, but is preserved,
excited, and strengthened ; and all the other graces
with it, and by it. And this is brought to pass,
through the communication of new supplies of grace
to them, by the Spirit, from Christ their head, from
which all the body having nourishment ministered,
(namely, through the supply of the Spirit, Phil. i. 19.)
increaseth with the increase of God, Col. ii. 19.

2. The other chief branch of this promise, is a promise of pardon, continued pardon for the sins of
their daily walk ; whereby emergent differences betwixt God and them, come to be done away from
time to time, so that a total rupture is prevented :
Jer. xxxiii. 1. ' I will pardon all their iniquities.'
Howbeit the justified have, as to their state, no need
of a new formal pardon, but only of a manifestation
of their former pardon ; since the pardon given in
justification is never revoked, though by means of
their after sins they may lose sight of it : yet as to
their daily walk, they have great need of a formal
pardon ; forasmuch as they are daily contracting
new guilt : John xiii. 10. ' He that is washed, needeth not, save to wash his feet.' For howbeit no sins
of the justified can bring them any more under the
guilt of eternal wrath ; nevertheless they do bring
them under the guilt of fatherly anger, Psal. lxxxix.
30, 31, 32. And therefore they need to pray every
day, *Our Father, forgive us our debts.*

V. *The promise of* TEMPORAL BENEFITS.

In the fifth and last place, the promise of eternal
life to the elect, considered in this period, comprehends a promise of temporal benefits to be conferred
on them, and every one of them, being united to
Christ ; and that in such measure, as God sees meet
for his own glory and their good. This promise
stands embodied with the spiritual promises in the

covenant : Ezek. xxxvi. **29.** ' I will also save you from all your uncleannesses ; and I will call for the corn, and will increase it.' Hos. ii. **22.** ' The earth shall hear the corn, and the wine, and the oil, and they shall hear Jezreel.' Indeed, this is not the principal thing contained in the promissory part of the covenant : but it is a necessary addition thereto ; as the present state of the saints, while in this world, doth require, Matt. vi. **33.** And thus godliness, as the apostle observes, 1 Tim. iv. **8.** ' hath promise of the life that now is, and of that which is to come.'

When God took man into the first covenant, he made provision in it for his temporal, as well as for his spiritual and eternal welfare. He gave him a right to, and dominion over the creatures in the earth, sea, and air ; giving and granting unto him full power, soberly to use them, and to dispose of them, for God's glory and his own comfort : and this lordship to be holden of him as Sovereign Lord of all, firm and irreversible, by the tenor of that covenant, as long as he should continue in his obedience ; but to be forfeited to all intents and purposes, in case he should by transgression break the covenant, Gen. i. **28.** and ii. **16, 17.** But man continued not in this honour : he brake God's covenant, and so fell from that his right to, and dominion over the creatures. By his transgression he forfeited life itself ; and consequently lost his covenant-right to all the means and comforts of life. And in this condition are all natural men, with respect to these things. They have no covenant-right to the means and comforts of life, whatever portion of them they are possessed of. All the right that they have to them, is a mere providential, precarious right ; such as a condemned man hath to his food, during the time his execution is delayed at the pleasure of the prince. This is a most uncertain and uncomfortable holding : nevertheless it so far avails, that they are not, properly speaking, violent possessors of temporal benefits ; having just the same right to them, as to their forfeited life, while it is left them by the disposal of providence. Wherefore the worst of men may lawfully eat and drink, and take the benefit of other necessaries of life, whatever Satan may suggest to the contrary in the hour of tempta- tion ; yea, they ought to do it, and they sin against God egregiously if they do it not ; because he hath said, *Thou* shalt not kill.

But the second Adam having undertaken to bear the curse, and to give perfect obedience to the law, in the name of his spiritual seed ; there was thereupon made a promise of restoring to them the forfeited life, with all the means thereof ; and parti- cularly, a promise of the good things requisite for the support and comfort of their temporal life in this world, till at death they be carried home to heaven. And the performance of this promise to them, is be- gun immediately upon their uniting with Christ : then their covenant-relation to the first Adam is found to be lawfully dissolved ; the forfeiture is taken off ; and a new covenant-right to the creatures is given them ; 1 Cor. iii. 22, 23. ' All are yours ; and ye are Christ's.' And it goes on, all along till death ; so much of this their stock being from time to time put into their hands, as the great Administrator sees needful for them. And whether that be little or much, they do from that moment possess it by a new title : it is theirs by covenant.

Now this promise is grafted upon the promise made to Christ, of his inheriting all things. For they that are his, are joint-heirs with him, Rom. viii. 17. to inherit all things too, through him, Rev. xxi. 7. The estate and honour which the first Adam lost for him- self and family, by his disobedience in breaking of the first covenant, was, in the second covenant, made over by promise to Christ the second Adam for him and his, upon the condition of his obedience. The which obedience being performed, the whole ancient estate of the family was recovered, together with the honours thereunto belonging. The ancient dominion was restored, in the person of *Christ* as second Adam : and all his mystical members partake thereof in him. This the Psalmist teacheth : Psal. viii. 4. ' What is man, that thou art mindful of him ? and the son of man, that thou visitest him ?' ver. 5. ' For thou hast made him a little lower than the angels, and hast crowned him with glory and honour.' Ver. 6. 'Thou madest him to have dominion over the works of thy hands : thou hast put all things under his feet:' ver. 7. ' All sheep and oxen, yea, and the beasts of the field :' ver. 8. ' The fowl of the air, and the fish of the sea, and whatsoever passeth through the paths of the seas.' Though there is here a manifest view to the first Adam and all mankind in him, as they were happily and honourably stated at their creation ; yet we are infallibly assured by the apostle, that this passage is meant of *Christ* the second Adam, Heb. ii. 6—9. and his mystical members in him, ver. 6. Accordingly, Abraham had the promise, that he should be the heir of the world : and he had it through the righteousness of faith, *i. e.* the righteousness which faith apprehends, Rom. iv. 13. Now, Abraham was a type of Christ, and the father of the faithful, who are all blessed as he was. Therefore this promise was primarily to *Christ*, through the righteousness by him wrought ; secondarily to his members, through the same righteousness apprehended by faith.

This promise of temporal benefits, carries believers' possession of the same, as far as their need in that kind doth go, Phil. iv. 19. Of which need, not they themselves, but their Father is the fit judge, Matt. vi. 32. Accordingly, there are two chief branches of the promise, namely, a promise of provision, and a promise of protection.

1. A promise of provision of good things necessary for this life ; upon which they may confidently trust God for them, whatever straits they are at any

time reduced to : Psal. xxxiv. 10. ' The young lions
do lack, and suffer hunger : but they that seek the
Lord, shall not want any good thing.'   Their meat
and drink are secured for them in the covenant : the
which being perceived by faith, cannot miss to give
them a peculiar relish ; however mean their fare be,
as to quantity or quality : Isa. xxxiii. 16. ' Bread
shall be given him, his waters shall be sure.'   They
shall be fed, though they be not feasted : Psal.
xxxvii. 3. ' Verily thou shalt be fed.'   They shall
have enough, they shall be satisfied, Joel ii. 26. And
even days of famine shall not mar that their satisfaction : Psal. xxxvii. 19. ' In the days of famine
they shall be satisfied.'   And as sleep for their refreshment is necessary too, the promise bears it also :
Prov. iii. 24. ' Thou shalt lie down, and thy sleep
shall be sweet.'   They need clothing, and provision
is made as to it : Matt. vi. 30. ' If God so clothe the
grass of the field,—shall he not much more clothe
you, O ye of little faith ? '   Having made them, by
covenant, a new grant of life and of a body, which
are more than meat and clothing, he will not refuse
them these lesser things necessary for the support
of the greater : ver. 25. ' Is not the life more than
meat, and the body than raiment ? '   Thus our fallen first parents, having believed and embraced the
promise of life, had, with the new grant of life, food
and raiment provided for them, as is particularly
taken notice of, Gen. iii. 15. 18. 21.   A blessing also
on their labours is promised, and success in their
lawful callings and affairs, Isa. lxv. 21—23.   In a
word, the covenant bears, that God will withhold no
good thing from them that live uprightly, Psal.
lxxxiv. 11.

2. There is also a promise of protection from the
evil things that concern this life : Psal. xci. 10.
' There shall no evil befall thee ; ' ver. 11. ' For he
shall give his angels charge over thee, to keep thee
in all thy ways.'   Together with the bread and the

water provided by the covenant for them to live on,
the munitions of rocks are secured to them for a place
of defence, where they may safely enjoy them, Isa.
xxxiii. 16. The same Lord who is a sun to nourish
them, will be a shield to protect them, Psal. lxxxiv.
11. He will be a wall of fire round about them, to
cherish them, and to keep off, scare, and fright away
their enemies, Zech. ii. 5. The covenant yields a
broad covert for the safety of believers : Psal. xci. 4.
' He shall cover thee with his feathers.' The covert
of the covenant is stretched out over their bodies ;
over their health to preserve it, while it is necessary
for God's honour and their own good : Prov. iii. 7.
' Fear the Lord, and depart from evil ; ' ver. 8. ' It
shall be health to thy navel, and marrow to thy
bones ; ' over their lives, as long as God has any
service for them in this world : so in sickness they
are carefully seen to : Psal. xli. 3. ' Thou wilt make
all his bed in his sickness ; ' their diseases healed,
and they recovered, Psal. ciii. 3, 4. And they are
delivered from enemies that seek their life, Psal xli.
2. Yea, when death rides in triumph, having made
havoc on all sides of them, as by sword or pestilence, they are found safe under the covert of the covenant, Psal. xci. 6, 7. This covert is stretched over
their names, credit, and reputation : Job v. 21.
' Thou shalt be hid from the scourge of the tongue : '
either the tongues of virulent men shall not reach
them ; or they shall not be able to make the dirt to
stick on them ; or else if they shall be permitted to
make it stick for a while, the covert of the covenant
shall wipe all off at length, and their righteousness
shall be brought forth as the light, and their judgment as the noon-day, Psal. xxxvii. 6. It is stretched over their houses and dwelling-places : Psal. xci.
10. ' Neither shall any plague come nigh thy dwelling.' It goes round about their substance, making
a hedge about all that they have, Job i. 10. Yea,
and there is a lap of it to cast over their widows and

children, when they are dead and gone : Jer. xlix. 11.
'Leave thy fatherless children, I will preserve them
alive, and let thy widows trust in me.'

****

*Promises of the Covenant of Grace to God's elect,
from the period of their death, through the ages
of eternity.*

I. *The promise of VICTORY over death.*

The promise of eternal life comprehends a promise
of victory over death, to be conferred on all and every
one of the spiritual seed, in the encounter with that
last enemy : Isa. xxv. 8. 'He will swallow up death
in victory, and the Lord God will wipe away tears
from off all faces.' After the wearisome march, and
the reiterated fights of faith, they have in their passage through the wilderness of this world, they have
to pass the Jordan of death, and to fight the last
battle with that enemy. But the victory is secured
on their side by promise ; of which there are two
chief branches, to wit, a promise of disarming death,
and a promise of destroying it.

1. There is a promise of disarming death to the
dying believer ; so that it shall at no rate be able to
reach him a ruinating stroke : Hos. xiii. 14. 'O death,
I will be thy plagues ;' namely, by taking the sting
quite away, 1 Cor. xv. 55. When sin entered the
world, death followed ; and sin furnished death with
an envenomed sting, wherewith to kill the sinner,
both soul and body at once : the holy law, with its
curse, fixed this sting in death's hand ; having first
so pointed it, that it could not miss of doing execution. But Christ, the second Adam, having undertaken to bear the curse, and to die in the room and

stead of his people ; there was thereupon made a
promise of disarming death to them : since the Surety
suffering the pains of death armed with its sting, the
principal behoved to be liberated from suffering the
same over again.   And thus the covenant secures
believers from death's harm.   Yea, it so alters the
nature thereof, that it makes it a quite new thing to
them from what it was originally.   Hence death is
found in the inventory of the saint's treasure : 1 Cor.
iii. 22. ' Whether life, or death, or things present, or
things to come ; all are yours.'   Not only is life theirs
by the covenant, but death is theirs too by the same
tenor.   And indeed as it is new framed by the covenant, it is of excellent use to them, bringing them
unto a state of perfection, and everlasting rest, Heb.
xii. 23. ; Rev. xiv. 13.

This promise is granted upon the promise of victory made to Christ, as appears from the forecited
Isa. xxv. 8.   He encountered death armed with its
sting, on purpose to disarm it to his people : he received the sting thereof into his own soul and body,
that they might be delivered from it.   Wherefore the
promise of victory over death made to him, secures
the disarming of it to them.   And as the promise
makes them safe, in the encounter with that last
enemy ; so the lively faith of it may deliver from fear
in the case.

2. There is a promise of destroying death to the
dead believer, by a glorious resurrection at the last
day : Hos. xiii. 14. ' O grave, I will be thy destruction.'   When death entered into the world by sin,
then came the grave, as death's attendant, to keep
fast his prisoners for him, till the general judgment :
and thus the grave serves death, in the case of all
who die in a state of enmity with God.   But Christ,
the second Adam, having in the second covenant
engaged to go, in the room and stead of his people,
death's prisoner, into the grave, and there to lie till
their debt should be fully paid ; there was made

thereupon a promise of a glorious resurrection to his members, whereby they shall be put out of the reach of death for good and all, at the last day : for ' then shall be brought to pass the saying that is written, Death is swallowed up in victory,' 1 Cor. xv. 54 ; and then shall they triumphantly sing, ' O death, where is thy sting ? O grave, where is thy victory ?' ver. 55. And thus the covenant secures the forming anew of their dissolved bodies, the return of their departed souls into them, and their coming forth of their graves glorious, immortal, and incorruptible. In the faith of which, the saints may with comfort consider the grave as but a retiring place, from whence after a while they shall come forth with unspeakable joy.

This promise is grafted upon the promise of a resurrection made to Christ : Isa. xxvi. 19. ' Thy dead men shall live, together with my dead body shall they arise.' The promise of a resurrection being made to him as a public person, it must take place also in his mystical members, whose federal head he was. Hence the Psalmist says, his flesh should rest in hope, namely, in the grave, in hope of a glorious resurrection, because the holy one Jesus was not to see corruption, Psal. xvi. 9, 10. with Acts xiii. 35. ; thereby teaching, that Christ's resurrection would ensure his glorious resurrection, as a member of the mystical body by faith. And indeed there is such a connexion between Christ's resurrection and the happy resurrection of the saints, that they stand and fall together : 1 Cor. xv. 16. ' For if the dead rise not, then is not Christ raised.'

II. *The promise of everlasting Life in Heaven.*

The promise of eternal life doth, in the last place, comprehend a promise of everlasting life in heaven, to be conferred on all and every one of the spiritual seed after death : Dan. xii. 2. ' And many of them that sleep in the dust of the earth shall

awake, some to everlasting life.' This was more
sparingly revealed under the Old Testament than
under the New, 2 Tim. i. 10. Yet was it, even then,
so clearly revealed, that all the holy patriarchs lived
and died in the faith of it, Heb. xi. 13—16. The
fathers before Abraham saw it in the promise of the
seed of the woman, which was to bruise the serpent's
head : and from Abraham, they saw it in the promise of Canaan. But now by the gospel this life
and immortality are set in a full light. By the breach
of the first covenant, that life was forfeited, the heavenly paradise lost to Adam and all mankind ; in
token whereof he was turned out of the earthly paradise. But the second Adam having, in the second
covenant, undertaken the redemption of the forfeited
inheritance, there was a new promise of it made in
favour of his seed : and they are invested with an
indefeasible right thereto, in the first moment of their
union with Christ by faith : howbeit they are not
instantly put in possession thereof. And when they
do come to the possession, it is not given them all at
once, but at two different periods, in different measures ; according to the two chief branches of the
promise thereof, namely, a promise of transporting
their souls into heaven at death, and a promise of
transporting them, soul and body, thither at the last
day.

1. There is a promise of transporting their souls,
separate from their bodies, into heaven, there to behold and enjoy the face of God. And it is accomplished to them immediately after their death. It
was most plainly declared and applied by our Saviour to the penitent thief on the cross : Luke xxiii. 43.
' To-day shalt thou be with me in paradise.' But it
was in the faith of it, that the covenant was to David,
even in the face of death, all his salvation and all his
desire, 2 Sam. xxiii. 5. ; and that Paul had a desire
to depart, knowing that he was to be with Christ
upon his departure, Phil. i. 23. And it is in the

faith of the same, that the whole church militant
doth groan earnestly, desiring to be clothed upon
with the house which is from heaven, that is, the
heavenly glory, 2 Cor. v. 2. Indeed the curse of
the first covenant did, upon the breaking of that
covenant, fall to their lot, as well as to the rest of
mankind : and that curse would natively have issued
in cutting them asunder as covenant-breakers, and
appointing them their portion with the hypocrites ;
but that being executed to the full on Christ their
head, to the parting asunder of his holy soul and
body, it can operate no more on them. Wherefore,
howbeit others die in virtue of the curse, separating
their souls and bodies, the one to the place of torment, the other to the grave, till the last day ; yet
they do not so die. Being redeemed from the curse,
Gal. iii. 13. they shall never see such death, John
viii. 51. But they die in conformity to Christ their
head, being ' predestinate to be conformed to his
image,' Rom. viii. 29. who is ' the first-born from the
dead,' Col. i. 18. and the first fruits of them that
sleep, which every man is to follow in his own order,
1 Cor. xv. 20. 23. That, as in the case of the head,
so in the case of the members, as death came on by
sin, sin may go off by death. In virtue of their communion with Christ in his death, the union betwixt
their souls and mortal bodies is dissolved ; their souls
dismissed in peace into the heavenly glory, there to
remain till such time as their bodies, laid down in
the grave, come, in virtue of their communion with
Christ in his resurrection, to put on incorruption and
immortality.

This promise is grafted upon the promise of acceptance made to Christ, when he should make his
soul an offering for sin. In confidence of which
acceptance, dying on the cross, he commended his
spirit, or soul, into the hands of his Father, Luke
xxiii. 46. ; and told the penitent thief, he was to be
that very day in paradise, though then it was towards

the evening of it, ver. 43. The words in which he commended his soul to his Father, were David's : Psal. xxxi. 5. ' Into thine hand I commit my spirit :' thereby intimating, that the reception of the souls of his dying people into the hands of his Father, depends on the reception of his soul into them. For his soul was, in virtue of the covenant, so received, as a public soul, representing the souls of the whole seed ; whence David, speaking of *Christ*, saith, ' Thou wilt not leave my soul in hell,' Psal. xvi. 10. with Acts ii. 31. Wherefore in the promise of receiving Christ's soul, was comprehended a promise of receiving the souls of all his mystical members.

2. There is a promise of transporting them, soul and body, into heaven, there to be ever with the Lord ; which is to be accomplished unto them at the last day : Dan. xii. 2. ' And many of them that sleep in the dust of the earth shall awake, some to everlasting life, and some to shame and everlasting contempt.' Ver. 3. ' And they that be wise, shall shine as the brightness of the firmament ; and they that turn many to righteousness, (or rather, they that do righteously, of the many), as the stars for ever and ever.' Whereas the many mentioned, ver. 2. and comprehending all, are there divided into two sorts, in respect of their future state in the event of the resurrection : the happy part, being the first sort of them, is designed, ver. 3. from their present state in this life, the wise, and they that do righteously ; that is, in New-testament language, the righteous, Matt. xiii. 43. and they that have done good, John v. 29. in opposition to the foolish, and they that have done evil. Those having come forth, unto the resurrection of life, John v. 29. shall shine as the brightness of the firmament, and as the stars for ever and ever : yea, they shall shine forth as the sun, in the kingdom of their Father, Matt. xiii. 43. This is the highest pinnacle of the saints' hopes ; wherein they, in their whole man, shall have the whole of eternal life in its

perfection. Man had a conditional promise hereof, in the covenant of works ; but the condition being broken, the benefit promised was lost ; heaven's gates were shut against Adam and all his natural seed. Howbeit, Christ, the second Adam, having undertaken to fulfil the condition of the second covenant, which was stated from an exact consideration of the demands that the broken first covenant had on his spiritual seed ; there was a new promise of it made in their favour ; and it absolute. And to his fulfilling of that condition, both the making and performing of this promise are owing allenarly. None other's works but his could ever have availed to reduce the forfeiture, and purchase a new right : and his works do it so effectually, that they secure the putting all his seed in actual possession of the purchased inheritance ; so that they shall reign in life, by one Jesus Christ, Rom. v. 17.

This is the promise of the covenant, which is the last of all in performing ; as being the consummation of all the rest, not to be accomplished, until the mystery of God be finished. The Old Testament saints died in the faith of it ; and it is not as yet performed to them : nay, the New Testament saints have died, and still must die, in the faith of it ; not having it performed to them neither, till it be at once accomplished to the whole seed together, at the end of the world. Thus this promise remains to be an unseen object of faith to the church militant ; and to the church triumphant too, whose flesh must rest in hope till that day, Psal. xvi. 9. But because the term prefixed for performing thereof, is, in the depth of sovereign wisdom, for reasons becoming the divine perfections, set at such a distance ; there have been some signal pledges given of it, to confirm the church's faith in the case. Such was the translating of Enoch, soul and body, into heaven, in the patriarchal period ; Elias, in the time of the law ; and our blessed Saviour, in the time of the gospel.

This promise is grafted upon the promise of a glorious exaltation made to Christ ; by which was secured to him his ascension, in soul and body, into heaven, and entering into his glory : Luke xxiv. 26. ' Ought not Christ to have suffered these things, and to enter into his glory ?' Both these were necessary in respect of the covenant : his suffering was necessary, in respect of the condition thereof, which behoved to be fulfilled by him ; and his entering into his glory was necessary, in respect of the promise thereof, which behoved to be fulfilled unto him. Now, Christ ascended and entered into glory as a public person, as a forerunner entering for us, Heb. vi. 20. And therefore the promise, in virtue of which he ascended and entered into it, comprehends the ascension and glory of all his mystical members, who are therefore said to ' sit together in heavenly places in Christ Jesus,' Eph. ii. 6. And then, and not till then, will the promise be perfectly fulfilled to him, when all the mystical members are personally there, together with their head ; when the whole seed, perfectly recovered from death, shall reign there, together with him, in life, for evermore.

Sinners of mankind the object of the Administration of the Covenant of Grace.

The object of the administration of the covenant, is sinners of mankind indefinitely : that is to say, Christ is impowered by commission from his Father, to administrate the covenant of grace to any of all mankind, the sinners of the family of Adam without exception : he is authorised to receive them into the covenant, and to confer on them all the benefits thereof, to their eternal salvation ; according to the settled order of the covenant. The election of particular persons is a secret, not to be discovered in the administration of the covenant, according to the established order thereof, till such time as the sinner have received the covenant, by coming personally into it.

For confirming of this truth, let the following things be considered :—

1. The grant which the Father hath made of Christ crucified, as his ordinance for the salvation of lost sinners of mankind. In the case of the Israelites in the wilderness, bitten by fiery serpents, God instituted an ordinance for their cure, namely, a brazen serpent lifted up on a pole; and made a grant thereof to whosoever would use it for that purpose, by looking to it. No body whosoever that needed healing was excepted : the grant was conceived in the most ample terms : Num. xxi. 8. ' It shall come to pass, that *every one* that is bitten, when he looketh upon it shall live. So all mankind being bitten by the old serpent, the devil, and sin as his deadly poison, left in them ; God hath appointed *Jesus Christ* the ordinance of heaven for their salvation. There is a word of divine appointment passed upon a crucified Christ, making and constituting him the ordinance of God for salvation of sinners ; and God hath made a grant of him as such, to whosoever of Adam's lost race will make use of him for that purpose, by believing on him ; in the which grant, none of the world of mankind is excepted. All this is clear from John iii. 14, 15, 16. ' And as Moses lifted up the serpent in the wilderness, even so must the Son of man be *lifted up :* that *whosoever* believeth in *him,* should not perish, but have eternal life. For God so loved the *world,* that he *gave* his only begotten Son, that *whosoever* believeth in him, should not perish, but have everlasting life.' Now, the administration of the covenant being settled in pursuance of this grant, therein made for a reward of the Mediator's obedience ; the object

of the former, can be no less extensive than that of the latter.

2. The Mediator's commission for the administration, is conceived in the most ample terms ; and he is clothed with most ample powers, with relation to that business. It carries his administrating the covenant, not only to the meek, the poor, the broken-hearted ; but to the captives, blind, bruised, prisoners, bond-men and broken men, who have sold their inheritance and themselves, and can have no hope of relief but by a jubilee, Luke iv. 18, 19. with Is. lxi. 1, 2. What sort of sinners of mankind can one imagine, that will not fall in under some of these denominations ? Christ is indeed given for a covenant of people ; not of this or that people, but of people indefinitely. ' All power is given him in heaven and in earth,' Matt. xxviii. 18. So there none on earth excepted from his administering the covenant to them. He is impowered to save the guilty law-condemned world, by administering it to them : ' For God sent not his Son into the world to condemn the world ; but that the world through him might be saved,' John iii. 17. ; forasmuch as he is the ordinance of God for taking away the sin of the world, chap. i. 29. ; though many to whom he offers the covenant, do refuse it, and so are not saved eventually. Accordingly, from this fulness of power, he issues forth the general offer of the gospel ; wherein all without exception are declared welcome to come and suck of the full breasts of the divine consolations in the covenant : Matt. xi. 27. ' All things are delivered unto me of my Father.' Ver. 28. ' Come unto me, all ye that labour, and are heavy laden, and I will give you rest.' Chap. xxviii. 18. ' All power is given unto me in heaven and in earth.' Ver. 19. ' Go ye therefore and teach all nations.' Mark xvi. 15. ' Preach the gospel to every creature.'

3. He executes his commission in an unhampered manner, administering the covenant to any sinner of

mankind : Prov. viii. 4. ' Unto you, O *men*, I call, and my voice is to the sons of *men*.' The object of his administration is not this or that party of mankind, under this or the other denomination ; but men, any men, sons of men indefinitely. So the gospel, in which he administers the covenant, is good tidings to all people, Luke ii. 10. a feast made unto all people, Isa. xxv. 6. though many, not relishing the tidings, never taste of the feast. Accordingly, he commissioned his apostles for that effect, in terms than which none can imagine more extensive, Mark xvi. 15. ' Go ye into *all* the *world*, and preach the gospel to *every creature*.' The Jews called man the creature, as being God's creature by way of eminence : so by every creature is meant every man. There are in the world some men, who, by reason of their monstrous wickedness, are like devils ; there are other men, who, by reason of their savageness, seem to differ but little from brutes : but our Lord saith here in effect, ' Be what they will, if ye can but know them to be men, ask no questions about them on this head, what sort of men they are : being men, preach the gospel to them, offer them the covenant ; and if they receive it, give them the seals thereof : my Father made them, I will save them.' *

* " God giveth us sufficient ground in scripture to come to Christ with confident faith, at the very first, trusting assuredly, that Christ and his salvation shall be given to us, without any failing and delay, however vile and sinful our condition hath been hitherto. The scripture speaketh to the vilest sinners in such a manner as if it were framed on purpose to beget assurance of salvation in them immediately. This promise is universal, that whosoever believeth on Christ shall not be ashamed, without making a difference between Jew and Greek. Christ's invitation is free to any, If any man thirst, let him come unto me and drink : and this drink is promised to every one that believeth."

Marshall on Sanct.

Christ as a Prophet administers the Covenant of Grace.

This may be taken up in three things,

1. His intimating and offering the covenant to sinners, by his word, for bringing them personally into it. This he did from the time of Adam's fall, is now doing, and will do even unto the end of time, that the mystery of God shall be finished. He began the Old Testament dispensation thereof, in person. Appearing in human shape, with his own mouth he gave the first notice of the covenant that ever there was in the world, and made the first offer of it in paradise, Gen. iii. 8. 15. He carried it on by prophets and ordinary teachers, whom he commissioned for that effect, and furnished with gifts for the work. The former of these he employed to write in his name, as well as to speak therein, in that matter: and by both he spoke to sinners, intimating and offering the covenant unto them, by their means; whether through the word written or spoken. And thus he managed that work, to the salvation of those who believed, in the patriarchal ages before and after the flood; and all along the time of the Jewish church, from Moses to the end of that dispensation. Then he also began the New Testament dispensation in his own person. Having by his incarnation become man, he applied himself to this work. Though he was born king of the Jews, Matt. ii. 2. and many of them would have had him to have mounted their throne, John vi. 15.; yet he choosed rather to appear in the character of a prophet, and betake himself, unto the work of the ministry, for to preach the gospel, and intimate and offer the covenant to perishing sinners; and so he was a minister of the cir-

4 D

cumcision, Rom. xv. 8. Of him in this capacity
particularly, Solomon, that king-preacher, was a
type, Eccl. i. 1. And this also he did, and still doth,
carry on mediately and by proxy, especially after his
ascension into heaven ; and that, partly by his a-
postles and other extraordinary officers, whom he
employed to write, as well as to speak, in his name ;
and partly by ordinary ministers of the gospel, to be
continued in the church, to the end of the world, Eph.
iv. 11, 12, 13. Thus he is now administering the
covenant unto us, by putting his written word of the
Old and New Testaments in our hands, and sending
men in his name to preach the gospel unto us. By
these means he speaks to sinners, intimating, and
offering them the covenant : and so he carries on the
work, to the salvation of those that believe, and rendering unbelievers inexcusable, 2 Cor. v. 20. ; Rev.
iii. 22. ; Luke x. 16. Wherefore the offer of the covenant, made to us in the gospel, is his offer : and
though the word is sent to us by men, they are but
his voice in the matter, he is the speaker. Then
' see that ye refuse not him that speaketh,' Heb.
xii. 25.

2. His making the intimation and offer of the covenant effectual to the elect, by the Spirit : 1 Pet.
i. 12. ' By them that have preached the gospel unto
you, with the Holy Ghost sent down from heaven.'
The great Prophet of the covenant can effectually
teach the most unteachable sinners of mankind ;
causing light not only to break forth in a dark world,
by his word, but in dark hearts, by his Spirit : for
the fulness of the Spirit of light is in him, and he hath
eye-salve for the spiritually blind, Rev. iii. 18. He
knoweth who are his, in whose name he contracted
with the Father, and received the promise of the
Spirit : and sooner or later, he so enlightens them,
that he rescues them from under the power of their
spiritual darkness, and renders the administration of
the covenant effectual to them, however ineffectual

it be to others, Col. i. 13. And this he doth, by
bringing his word to them with power; through the
efficacy of his Spirit opening their eyes. In the first
place, by his Spirit acting upon them, as a Spirit of
bondage, he sets home on their consciences, the holy
law in the commands and curse thereof, as of divine
authority, and binding on them in particular. Hereby they are convinced of their sin and misery, seeing
their sin as heinous in the sight of God, and his
wrath due to them for their sin : they are filled with
remorse, terror, and anxiety ; are made to pant for
relief, feel an absolute need of *Christ* and his righteousness, and despair of relief by any other way,
Acts ii. 37. and xvi. 29, 30. And then, by the same
Spirit acting within them, as a Spirit of life, and
communicated unto them from himself, in the word
of the gospel, he sets home on their hearts and consciences, the glorious gospel in its free promise of
life and salvation to sinners through Jesus Christ,
as it stands in the holy scriptures ; clearing and de-
monstrating the same unto them, to be the infallible
word of the eternal God, and his word to them in
particular : 1 Thess. ii. 13. ' Ye received it not as
the word of men, but (as it is in truth) the word of
God.' Chap. i. 5. ' For our gospel came not unto
you in word only, but also in power, and in the
Holy Ghost, and in much assurance.' This demonstration of the Spirit is that which immediately clear-
eth to them the ground of their believing in particular; as saith the apostle, 1 Cor. ii. 4, 5. ' My preaching was in demonstration of the Spirit, and of power :
that your faith should not stand in the wisdom
of men, but in the power of God.' And it is an internal attestation of the word of the gospel unto them,
distinct from the clearest external or ministerial attestation of it ; according to the saying of our Saviour, John xv. 26. ' The Spirit of truth, which proceedeth from the Father, he shall testify of me ;' ver.
27. ' And ye also shall bear witness.' By the power

hereof, getting, by way of spiritual sight, John vi.
40. a knowledge of *Christ* in his transcendent glory
and excellency, exhibited to them in the free promise
of the gospel, they are infallibly brought to believe.
The Spirit thus applying the word of the gospel to
them, they greedily embrace it, and apply it to themselves by faith ; as may be seen in these converts,
Acts ii. 38. ' Then Peter said unto them, Repent,
and be baptized every one of you in the name of
Jesus Christ, for the remission of sins ; ' ver. 39.
' For the promise is unto you ; ' ver. 41. ' Then they
that gladly received his word, were baptized.'

Lastly, His teaching and instructing them by his
word and Spirit, from thenceforth, as children of the
covenant, his own disciples. The whole plan of salvation is laid down in the covenant, being a mystery
of the manifold wisdom of God, whereof there is still
more and more to be learned : and Christ is the
great Prophet to teach it.   And ' the secret of the
Lord is with them that fear him ; and he will shew
them his covenant,' Psal. xxv. 14.   The saints, by
reason of the remains of darkness in their minds
while here, are apt to lose sight of the parties in the
covenant : but the great Prophet is to shew them
the Father, and to manifest himself unto them, by
the Spirit.   The condition of the covenant, the Mediator's own righteousness, the sole ground of all
their hopes, cannot be kept in view, but by means
of the light of life from himself.   And in his light
only can they have a believing view of the promises
and privileges of the covenant.   The duties of the
covenant, whereof the exceeding broad law of the
ten commandments is the rule, are many ; and though
they be clear in themselves, yet are they often so
dark and perplexed to us, that we cannot distinguish
between sin and duty : but the children of the covenant have an infallible Teacher, whom they may consult in all cases, and of whom they may learn how
to steer their course in every point ; and ' the meek

will he guide in judgment, the meek will he teach
his way,' Psal. xxv. 9.

The darkness brought on mankind by sin, nothing
but the grace of the new covenant can effectually
dispel.   The true light is a benefit of that covenant,
purchased by the blood of Christ, and lodged with
him among the rest of the benefits of his great trust :
and he hath the dispensing of it, as the great Prophet of the covenant.   To him then must we have
our recourse for light in all cases, whether we be under the midnight-darkness of a natural state, or under the twilight-darkness of the present imperfection
of a state of grace ; yea, in the mid-day light of glory,
the Lamb is the light of the heavenly city, Rev. xxi. 23.

*The chief acts of Christ administering the Covenant
of Grace as a King.*

1. His appointing ordinances of his kingdom, both
for bringing of sinners personally into the covenant,
and for confirming and strengthening the covenanted ;
as also officers of his kingdom, to administer these
ordinances in his name and authority.   Both the one
and the other were different, under the Old Testament, and under the New ; which hath made two
different forms of external administration of the covenant ;   the old, which is passed away, and the new,
that will continue to the end of the world :   but both
were from the same authority, and for compassing
the same great designs of the covenant, agreeable to
the different times for which they were appointed ;
and are all of them to be found in the scriptures of
the Old and New Testament, the book of the manner
of the kingdom.   It was the same Lord Jesus, the
Angel of the covenant, which spake to Moses in the
mount Sinai, Acts vii. 38. who instituted the New-

testament church and ordinances, and ' gave some
apostles, and some prophets, and some evangelists,
and some pastors and teachers, for the perfecting of
the saints, for the work of the ministry,' Eph. iv. 11, 12.
The Saviour, King, and Lawgiver of the church, are
one : Isa. xxxiii. 22. ' The Lord is our Lawgiver, the
Lord is our King, he will save us.'

2. Emitting his royal proclamations into the world
by the hand of his messengers, in the gospel ; bearing, that whosoever will come unto him, and unite
with him as the head of the covenant, by faith, shall
be readily received into it, and have a right to all the
privileges thereof, in him : Mark xvi. 15. ' Go ye
into all the world, and preach the gospel to every
creature.' Ver. 16. ' He that believeth and is baptized, shall be saved.' Therein the covenant is published, and offered in his name to every sinner of
mankind unto whose ears this voice reacheth : and
they are called, commanded, and charged to come
into it, and submit to his royal sceptre. His call
and offer is their warrant to come : his command
obligeth them, that they cannot refuse, but in rebellion and disobedience against his royal authority.
The promises are set before them indefinitely, that
whosoever will, may, by believing, apply them to
themselves. The King's proclamation meddles not
with the secrets of the eternal election, to reveal them.
But the promises of the covenant, infallibly to be
accomplished in some, are, in Christ's testament, as
indorsed to sinners of mankind indefinitely, to be fulfilled unto all and every one who shall by faith embrace them : and the proclamation makes lawful
intimation of the testament. This intimation is the
appointed means of begetting faith, and of bringing
sinners into the covenant thereby : for ' faith cometh
by hearing,' Rom. x. 17. And it is made effectual
to some by the Spirit, through the grace of the covenant secured by promise for them.

And hence it is, that, the covenant being thus ad-

ministered to all promiscuously, there is an use of
conditional phrases in the administration thereof;
though in the covenant itself, there are no conditions,
properly so called, but what were fulfilled by Jesus
Christ in his own person. The word of the covenant
coming with alike warrant to the elect and the non-
elect; to them who certainly will believe, and to
them who will continue in their unbelief; the administering of it equally to both in the gospel-proclama-
tion, must needs be by proposing the promises indefinitely as to persons; the which must at length be
resolved into conditional phrases. So it is proclaimed
in the ears of all, I will betroth thee unto me, and I
will be to them a God. And one believes and applies the same; and he is thereupon united to Christ,
and instated in the covenant to all saving purposes:
another, who hath as good a revealed warrant to
believe as the former, yet believes not; and so comes
short of the promise. Now, to speak alike to these
who will thus differently entertain the words of the
covenant, it follows of course to resolve them into
such expressions as these, ' Believe on the Lord
Jesus Christ, and thou shalt be saved;' and, ' He
that believeth shall be saved, he that believeth not
shall be damned.' Mean while the covenant itself
is a different thing from the form of the external administration of it.

3. Effectually subduing the elect to himself, through
the power of his Spirit so managing the word, that it
operates on them like a sword, piercing their souls,
conquering their natural aversion and obstinacy, and
making them willing to yield, and embrace the covenant. Rev. i. 16. ' Out of his mouth went a sharp
two-edged sword.' What that sword is, and by what
a strong arm it is wielded, in this case, may be learned
from the apostle calling it ' the sword of the Spirit,
which is the word of God,' Eph. vi. 17.; and what
the effect of it is, being managed by that arm of the
Lord revealed, is declared by the Psalmist, Psal.

cx. 3. ' Thy people shall be willing in the day of thy power ;' and by the prophet, Isa. xliv. 3. ' I will pour my Spirit upon thy seed :'—ver. 4. ' And they shall spring up—ver. 5. ' One shall say, I am the Lord's.' Christ communicates to them, and every one of them, at the time appointed in the eternal council, the Spirit and grace of the covenant, therein secured for them by promise : and thereby they are quickened, enabled, and determined to believe. And whereas he finds them prisoners, though prisoners of hope, he opens the house of their bondage, breaking the yoke of sin, death, and the devil, from off their necks, by his Spirit applying to them his satisfaction. The which has that mighty effect, inasmuch as then the law hath full satisfaction as to them ; and the law being satisfied, the strength of sin is broken ; and the strength of sin being broken, the sting of death is taken away ; and the sting of death being taken away, the devil loseth his power over them ; and Satan's power over them being lost, the present evil world, which is his kingdom, can hold them no longer. Thus are they separated from the world lying in wickedness, and constituted members of the kingdom of Christ ; delivered from the power of darkness, and translated into the kingdom of God's dear Son, Col. i. 13. And from thenceforth, though they be in the world, yet they are no more of it ; but strangers and pilgrims in it, true and lively members of the invisible kingdom of Christ ; a society to which the world is an implacable enemy : John xv. 19. ' Ye are not of the world, but I have chosen you out of the world, therefore the world hateth you.' And herein Christ doth, in a special manner, show himself a King mighty in battle, by the power of his grace overcoming the most perverse and rebellious, to a cordial submission, and rescuing them from the bondage and dominion of their enemies.

4. Gathering them and others with them together, into a visible church state : Gen. xlix. 10. ' Unto

him shall the gathering of the people be.' Thus is erected the visible church or kingdom of Christ in the world ; a society separate from the visible kingdom of the devil, and professing faith in, and obedience to Christ, outwardly bearing his badge, and the signs of his covenant. Among them is the ordinary seat of the administration of the covenant, the ordinary means of salvation, and offers of grace. In their land the voice of the turtle is heard, and the singing of birds, in the preaching of the glorious gospel ; while there is a lasting winter over all the world besides. They have the bible, and sabbaths, the ministry of the word, and the holy sacraments. Among them is to be found the communion of saints, and a church-government, instituted for controlling the unruly, suppressing of sin and wickedness, and encouraging an orderly walk. And they have the privilege of heaven's protection ; insomuch that the church shall be defended, and her enemies so restrained and conquered by her King, that she shall continue while the world stands, maugre all opposition that hell can make against her: Matt. xxviii. 20. ' Lo, I am with you alway, even unto the end of the world.'

Lastly, Ruling and governing his true and kindly subjects, agreeably unto the covenant, by which his royal prerogative is stated, and their privileges are secured : Isa. ix. 6. ' The government shall be upon his shoulder.' Of this his government there are several acts, the chief of which are these following :—

1st, He gives them the laws of the covenant ; not only intimating the same unto them externally, by his word ; but teaching them internally, by his Spirit, writing them upon the tables of their hearts, and leaving an indelible copy of them affixed there : Heb. viii. 10. ' I will put my laws into their mind, and write them in their hearts.' These laws of the covenant are no other but the laws of the ten commandments, originally given to Adam in his creation,

4 E

and at his transportation into Paradise and settlemen t
there, vested with the form of the covenant of works ;
and now, unto believers in Christ, standing without
that form, in the covenant of grace, as the eternal
rule of righteousness, whereunto they are to be conformed by the grace of the covenant ; the effectuating
of which is committed by the Father to Jesus Christ
as Administrator thereof. And accordingly he carries
it on, by his word and Spirit, in a suitableness to their
nature as rational agents, and to their state ; making
these laws known to them, as the rule of life, unto
which they stand bound by the sovereign authority
and matchless love of God, their Creator and Redeemer ; and withal inclining their hearts unto the
obedience of the same.

    2dly, He gives them the rewards of the covenant,
in the course of their obedience : Psal. xix. 11. ' In
keeping of them there is great reward.' He puts his
people indeed to work and labour ; but not to labour
in the fire, and for vanity, as the servants of sin do :
they are to work and labour, like the ox treading out
the corn, which was not to be muzzled, but to have
access at once to work and to eat. The service now
done to Zion's King, hath a reward in this life, as
well as a reward in the life to come. By the order
of the covenant, there is privilege established to follow duty, as the reward thereof ; the which order is
observed by the King in his administration. Accordingly, he proposeth the privilege of comfort, to
excite to the duty of mourning : Matt. v. 4. ' Blessed
are they that mourn ; for they shall be comforted :'
the special tokens of heaven's favour, to excite unto
a holy tender walk : John xiv. 21. ' He that hath
my commandments, and keepeth them,—shall be
loved of my Father, and I will love him, and will manifest myself to him.' In like manner, to excite to
the same holy obedience, he proposeth the full reward in the life to come : 1 Cor. ix. 24. ' So run that
ye may obtain.' Rev. iii. 21. ' To him that over-

cometh, will I grant to sit with me in my throne.'
And so certainly doth he accomplish the promise of
the reward of both kinds, that his people may be
assured, ' their labour is not in vain in the Lord,'
1 Cor. xv. 58. : for faithfulness is the girdle of his
loins ; and, in dispensing of the privileges to his people, upon the back of their duty, he doth but observe
the stated order of the covenant. Not that the order
of the covenant is, in every particular, first duty, then
privilege : nay, it is, first, privilege ; next, duty ;
then, privilege again ; and so forward, till privilege
and duty come both to perfection in heaven, not to
be distinguished more. Wo to us, if it were otherwise ! Truly, if it were otherwise, we could neither
be brought into the covenant, nor kept within it in
life : for how shall one at first believe, till once he is
privileged with the quickening Spirit? and how shall
a fallen saint renew his faith and repentance, till once
he is privileged with new influences of grace ? John
xv. 5. ' Without me ye can do nothing.' But here
lies the matter, the leading privilege bringing in duty,
there follows further privilege on the back of duty,
according to the order of the covenant : and these
further privileges are the rewards we speak of. And
the scripture calls them rewards, even in respect of
the saints ; because they are given to a working saint,
on the back of his work. Howbeit, they are as far
from the nature of a reward, strictly and properly so
called, the which on the account of one's work, is of
debt to him, as the leading privileges are, that produce the working : but both the one and the other
are equally the reward of Christ's work, in the most
strict and proper notion of reward.

3dly, He ministers unto them the discipline of the
covenant, in case of their disobedience. The discipline of the covenant is fatherly chastisement, which
their state of imperfection in this life makes necessary
to their welfare ; and therefore it is secured for them
in the covenant : Psal. lxxxix. 30. ' If his children

forsake my law :'—ver. 32. ' Then will I visit their transgression with the rod'—ver. 33. ' Nevertheless' —ver. 34. ' My covenant will I not break, nor alter the thing that is gone out of my lips.' It belongs to the promissory part of the covenant, and particularly to the promise of sanctification : forasmuch as it is not vindictive, but medicinal ; being an appointed means of advancing holiness in them. He chastens for our profit, that we might be partakers of his holiness, Heb. xii. 10. And thus it serves to purge iniquity, and to take away sin, Isa. xxvii. 9. ; namely, in that as a fire melting down the paint and varnish of the defiling objects in the world, in our sight, and as a looking-glass showing us our pollution, it occasions and excites us unto washing in the only laver of the blood of Christ, by faith. Now, the administering of the discipline of the covenant is committed unto Zion's King : John v. 22. ' The Father hath committed all judgment unto the Son.' Rev. iii. 19. ' As many as I love, I rebuke and chasten.' And, as to the nature of it, it comprehends all manner of strokes upon their worldly substance, name, employments, and relations ; all manner of bodily afflictions, diseases, and pains, incident to sinful flesh ; even natural death itself, 1 Cor. xi. 30. 32. ; and generally, all outward strokes which any of the children of men are liable to : Eccl. ix. 2. ' All things come alike to all.' Moreover, it comprehends spiritual strokes, such as desertion, God's hiding his face from them, withdrawing the light of his countenance, their losing some measure of their graces and comforts, woundings of spirit, horrors of conscience, whereby they may be brought to the very brink of despair : so that, howbeit the casting them into hell is not within the compass of the discipline of the covenant, yet the casting a kind of hell into them, making them to roar by reason of disquietness of heart, Psal. xxxviii. 8. is within the compass of it. And, what is worse than any of all these, it comprehends their being harassed with horrid temptations, and set up as marks for Satan's fiery darts, Eph. vi. 16. the hardening of their hearts, Isa. lxiii. 17. and their being suffered to fall into one sin, and that a gross sin too, for the punishment of another, as in the case of David and Peter. All these things are within the compass of the discipline of the covenant ; and believers are particularly and directly threatened with them, in case of their disobedience, to move them to beware of it : yea, and they are often inflicted by Zion's King on his beloved subjects, that, by these marks of his displeasure against their sin, he may correct them, make sin bitter to them, and stir them up to repentance and watchfulness. And the worst of them all, even the very hardening of their hearts, and the punishing of one sin with another, are, by the sovereign grace of the covenant, made effectual for these holy ends : the which grace opening the heart in renewed repentance, godly sorrow for sin breaks forth the more forcibly, as waters do which have been long dammed up. Thus these bitter waters, running in the channel of the covenant, become healing waters : these sharp swords are, by the covenant, beaten into ploughshares ; and these piercing spears, into pruninghooks. Of this discipline of the covenant, all the subjects of Christ in this world do partake ; and they must be under it, till they arrive at perfection in the other world, Heb. xii. 6, 7, 8.

4thly, He gives them the pardons of the covenant ; the pardoning of crimes committed against the laws of God, being one of the royal prerogatives of Zion's King, whom ' God hath exalted to be a Prince and a Saviour, for to give repentance to Israel, and forgiveness of sins,' Acts v. 31. He gives them the first pardon, removing the guilt of revenging wrath, in their justification ; and he gives them also the subsequent pardons, removing the guilt of fatherly anger, upon their renewing the actings of faith and repentance, as was observed before. The Father having committed all judgment unto the Son, he hath the dispensing of heaven's favours, according to the method and order of the covenant ; and they are not only conferred for his sake, but by his hand.

5thly, He affords them the defence of the covenant, while in this life they are amongst their enemies : Psal. lxxxix. 18. ' For the Lord is our defence : and the holy One of Israel is our King.' Satan is their enemy, a malicious, subtile, and powerful enemy : but Christ is their friend, and takes them under his protection. He loves them dearly, as the purchase of his own blood, the members of his own mystical body, and bearing his Father's image : he is infinitely wise, and can outshoot the devil in his own bow : and he is the stronger man, who can bind the strong man. The world joins issue with Satan in opposing them ; but shall not prevail to ruin them, neither by force nor fraud : for greater is he, than the God of this world and all his dominion : 1 John iv. 4. ' Ye are of God, and have overcome them : because greater is he that is in you, than he that is in the world.' Their worst enemies are within them, namely, the remains of corruption, which, in the depth of sovereign wisdom, are not expelled during this life ; but left for their exercise and trial, and for the discovery of the power of the grace of their King. And he manifests his power, in keeping alive in them the spunk of holy fire, in the midst of an ocean of corruption ; and causing it to make head against the same, until it quite dry it up : Rom. vii. 24. ' O wretched man that I am, who shall deliver me from the body of this death !' Ver. 25. ' I thank God, through Jesus Christ our Lord.' He has all their enemies in chains, that they can act no further against them, than he sees meet to permit : and at his pleasure he restrains them, bounding them by his power, as to the kind, degree, and continuance of their attacks : Psal. lxxvi. 10. ' The remainder of wrath shalt thou restrain.'

Lastly, He authoritatively completes the happiness of the covenant in them. He purchased it for them as a Priest; he reveals it to them as a Prophet: but as a King, he doth, in the way of authority, put them in full possession thereof: Matt. xxv. 34. ' Then shall the King say unto them on his right hand, Come ye blessed of my Father, inherit the kingdom prepared for you from the foundation of the world.' And by the same authority he will pass sentence against his and their enemies, having fully conquered them, ver. 41. And so he will complete for ever the peace of his covenant-subjects.

Discovery of the means by which Sinners embrace the Covenant of Grace.

And this, in one word, is by faith, or believing on Jesus Christ: Acts xvi. 31. ' Believe on the Lord Jesus Christ, and thou shalt be saved.' The covenant of grace is held forth in the gospel unto you : God saith to every one of you, ' I will make an everlasting covenant with you, even the sure mercies of David : ' and to close the bargain with you, and state you personally in it, to all the intents and purposes of salvation, all that is required of you is to hear, that is, to believe ; ' Hear, and your soul shall live,' Isa. lv. 3. He that believeth, is within the covenant of grace personally and savingly : he that believeth not, is still under the covenant of works, where the first Adam left him. Faith is the hand whereby one taketh hold of the covenant, signs it for himself, and closeth the bargain for his own salvation. It is the mouth whereby sinners consent to the covenant, that God becomes their God, and they his people. Although, while ye are without the covenant, the working of perfect obedience under the

pain of the curse, is required of you ; and more than
that, suffering also, even to the satisfaction of justice ; and both these, in virtue of the broken first covenant : and, when ye are once brought within the
covenant, obedience to all the ten commandments,
and suffering of the discipline of the covenant in
case of your failures, are required of you, in virtue
of the new covenant ye are entered into : yet to enter
you into the covenant, and instate you in it unto salvation, nothing is required of you, but that ye believe
on Christ. Only believe, Mark v. 36. is the constant
doctrine of the gospel, in this point. Do what you
will, and believe not, you remain in a state of damnation : whatever is done, or not done by you, believe, and you are in a state of salvation. If you
should say it with your lips, a thousand times over,
that you accept of the covenant ; if you should come
under the most solemn and awful bond and engagement to be the Lord's, expressly taking the same
upon you, in prayer, or otherwise ; if you should
write your covenant, and subscribe it with your
hand ; and should take the sacrament of Christ's
body and blood upon it, to confirm all : yet if you
do not with the heart believe on Jesus Christ, you
embrace not the covenant, you miss the saving hold
of it, and remain without the saving bond of it.
And if you should this moment with the heart believe on Christ, having no access to speak, pray,
write, or communicate : yet the moment you believe,
you are personally and savingly instated in the covenant, never to fall out of it, through the ages of
eternity ; God is your God, and all the promises of
the covenant are yours : though you had missed the
grip of the covenant ten thousand times before ; in
that case, you have it firm and sure : Mark xvi. 16.
' He that believeth and is baptized, shall be saved :
he that believeth not, shall be damned.'

And, that believing on Christ should be the appointed means of entering sinners into the covenant

of grace, is very agreeable to the nature and end of that great transaction. The which appears by these two considerations following :—

1. Hereby the grace of the covenant is preserved entire in the dispensation of the covenant ; and, by that means, the promise is made sure to all the seed, Rom. iv. 16. Faith is contradistinguished to works, as grace is to debt, chap. iv. 4, 5. If any work or doing of ours, were that upon which we were instated in the covenant, and got the right in the promises ; then the covenant and benefit thereof would be of debt to us, contrary to the declared end and design of that method of salvation, which is to exalt the free grace of God, and to cut off all boasting from us, Eph. ii. 8, 9. But the nature of faith's efficacy in the business, is adapted to that end and design of the covenant: inasmuch as it is a grace, not giving, but purely receiving ; taking all freely from Christ, without money, and without price, laying the stress of the soul's acceptance with God, wholly on what Christ hath done and suffered ; and entirely renouncing all doings and sufferings of our own, in that point. And thus the promise is sure to us: for whereas the plea of any work of ours, would be a very uncertain one ; faith's plea is ever sure and stedfast, as grounded allenarly on what Christ hath wrought.

2. Hereby the sinner's entering into the covenant, is by uniting with Christ the representative, with whom it was made, as party-contractor ; which is the scripture account of the matter: John x. 9. ' I am the door: by me if any man enter in, he shall be saved:' and so the unity of the covenant, and the representation in it, are preserved. If men entered into the covenant some other way, as by their accepting, properly called, terms to them proposed, and promising for themselves the performance of them : in that case, the representation in the covenant is marred ; and there would be, in effect, as many co-

4 F

venants of grace, as there are persons embracing it
at different times ; at least, Christ's covenant would
be one, and ours another distinct therefrom ; the
contrary of which is before evinced from the scripture.   But the covenant of grace being made with
Christ as second Adam, in the name of all such as
should be his ; it plainly follows, that the only way
of one's entering personally into it, must be by becoming his, standing related to the Head of the covenant as our Head : and it is by faith, and no work,
nor consent of ours differing from faith, that we are
united to him, and become members of his body,
Eph. iii. 17.   How do we all enter personally into
the covenant of works, so as to partake of the curse
in it ?   Is it not, through our becoming, by natural
generation, branches of the first Adam the representative in that covenant ?   Hereby every one of us is
personally entered and instated in that covenant, before we are capable to approve or disapprove of the
same, to consent to it, or dissent from it.   Even so,
we enter personally into the covenant of grace, so
as to partake of the benefits in it, by our becoming
branches of the second Adam the representative
therein : and that is through faith, in subjects capable of actual believing.   It is by being ingrafted
into Christ, we come to partake of the covenant and
benefits thereof.   And hence it is, that infants not
capable of actual believing, nor of knowing what the
covenant is, yet having the Spirit of faith, are personally entered into it, and instated in it; forasmuch
as that Spirit of faith is effectual in them, to a real
uniting them with Christ.   Hereunto agrees God's
giving Christ for a covenant ; that in him people
may have the covenant, and all the benefits thereof.
As God, in making of the covenant, took Christ for
all, for the condition, and for the parties to receive
the promises ; he being a second Adam : so sinners,
in accepting and embracing of the covenant, are to
take him for all ; the whole of the covenant, the par-

ties and parts of it too, being in him, forasmuch as he is God, as well as man, second Adam.

And thus it appears, that uniting with Christ the head of the covenant, is a sinner's formal entering into the covenant : the which uniting with him, being by faith on him, it is evident, that it is by believing on Christ, a sinner embraceth, enters into, and is instated in the covenant, unto salvation. Wherefore, reach Christ by faith, and ye reach the covenant : if ye miss him, ye miss the covenant, in point of life and salvation. But here ariseth a weighty question, to wit,

QUEST. What is that believing, by which one unites with Jesus Christ, and so enters into the covenant of grace ?

ANS. The clearing of this point being so necessary to direct sinners in their way into the covenant, for their eternal salvation ; we shall, for what now remains, address ourselves to the consideration thereof only.

And to begin with the word, by which the Holy Ghost expresseth what we call believing, whether in the Old or New Testament ; whosoever shall duly consider the import of it, in the scripture use thereof, will find that it is just trusting, trusting a word. person, or thing. And hence the scripture phrases of believing to, and believing in, that is, trusting to, and trusting in ; the former phrases, however unusual with us in conversation, yet ordinary, both in the Old and New Testaments, according to the originals. It is the trusting a word, as to a report, Isa. liii. 1. In his words, Psal. cvi. 12. It is the trusting a person : so, in the style of the Holy Ghost, the Israelites believed in the Lord, and in Moses his servant, Exod. xiv. 31. ' He believed not in his servants,' Job iv. 18. that is, as we read it, He put no trust in them. And it is the trusting a thing too : so, in the same style, Job xxxix. 12. ' Wilt thou believe in him (to wit, the unicorn) that he will bring home thy seed?' that is, Wilt thou trust in him, that he will do it? Deut. xxviii. 66. 'Thou shalt not believe in thy life;' that is, as we read it, 'Thou shalt have none assurance of thy life;' no trust in it, because no certainty about it. The phraseology is the same in the New Testament, as being brought into it from the Old, only in a different language. And taking the meaning of the Holy Ghost in this matter, from the words which he teacheth, as we are directed, 1 Cor. ii. 13. we conclude, That faith or believing, so expressed by him in the scripture, is, in the general, *trusting*, the trusting of a word, and of a person, and thing, held forth in that word.

The Faith of the Law necessary to our entering into the Covenant of Grace.

Whosoever then would enter into the covenant of grace, must, in the first place, have a faith of the law: for which cause, it is necessary, that the law, as well as the gospel, be preached unto sinners. And that faith of the law consists in a belief of these three things:—

1. By it a man believes that he is a sinner. The holy law pronounceth him guilty: and he believes the report of the law concerning himself in particular; his heavy and sorrowful heart, by this faith, echoing to the voice of the law, guilty, guilty! Rom. iii. 19. The which faith rests not on the testimony of man, whether spoken or written; but is a divine faith, founded upon the testimony of *God*, in his holy law, demonstrated by the spirit of bondage, to be the voice of the eternal God, and the voice of that God to him in particular. And thus he believes, 1*st*, That his life and conversation is sinful, displeasing, and hateful in the sight of a holy God, according to the

divine testimony : ' They are all gone out of the way, they are together become unprofitable, there is none that doeth good, no not one.' He is convinced, that he is gone out of the way of God, and walking in the way of destruction ; that the number of his errors of omission and commission he cannot understand ; and that all his righteousnesses, as well as his unright-eousnesses, are as filthy rags before the Lord. 2d, That his heart is full of mischief and iniquity, accor-ding to the divine testimony : Jer. xvii. 9. ' The heart is deceitful above all things, and desperately wicked.' The law shining into the heart, discovers divers lusts there, which he little noticed before ; and pressing the unholy heart, irritates them : and thus such a mystery of iniquity within his breast opens to his view, as he could never before believe to have been there : Rom. vii. 9. ' I was alive without the law once : but when the commandment came, sin revived, and I died.' 3d, That his nature is quite corrupted, as one dead in trespasses and sins, according to the divine testimony, Eph. ii. 1. To the verdict of the law, ' Who can bring a clean thing out of an unclean ?' Job xiv. 4. his soul, by this faith, echoes back, Un-clean, unclean ! ' I was shapen in iniquity, and in sin did my mother conceive me.' He is convinced, his disease is hereditary and natural ; and that there-fore his nature must be renewed : that otherwise, he not only does no good, but can do no good. In all these respects, he believes himself to be an object loathsome in the sight of God, loathsome in his na-ture, heart, and life.

2. By it a man believes, that he is a lost and un-done sinner, under the curse of the law ; liable to vengeance, according to the divine testimony, Gal. iii. 10. ' Cursed is every one that continueth not in all things written in the book of the law to do them.' He can no more look upon the curse as some strange thing, belonging only to some monsters of wickedness, and not to him ; for the Spirit of the Lord, as a spi-

rit of bondage, applies it closely to him ; as if he said, ' Thou art the man.' And, like one under sentence of death pronounced against him, he groans out his belief of it, under the pressure thereof, Luke xv. **17**. ' I perish.'

Lastly, By it a man believes his utter inability to recover himself. He believes, that he cannot, by any doings or sufferings of his, remove the curse of the law from off him, according to the divine testimony of our being without strength in that point, Rom. v. **6**. ; nor change his own nature, heart, and life, so as to render them acceptable to God ; according to the infallible testimony, Jer. xiii. **23**. ' Can the Ethiopian change his skin, or the leopard his spots ? then may ye also do good, that are accustomed to do evil.' He is, in his own eyes, as in the sight of God, a spiritually dead man ; legally dead, and morally dead, as the apostle testifies of himself in that case, Rom. vii. **9**.

This is the faith of the law. And the effect of it is a legal repentance, whereby a sinner is broken and bruised with fear and terror of the wrath of God ; grieves and sorroweth for sin, as a ruining and destructive evil ; and therefore really desires to be freed from it ; despairs of salvation by himself; and seriously looks out for relief another way, Acts ii. **37**. and xvi. **29, 30**. Thus the law is our schoolmaster to bring us unto Christ ; and the faith of the law, makes way for the faith of the gospel. Not that either this legal faith, or legal repentance, is the condition of our welcome to Christ and the covenant of grace : our access to Christ and the covenant is proclaimed free, without any conditions or qualifications required in us, to warrant us sinners of mankind to believe on Jesus Christ, as was shown before. But they are necessary-to move and excite us, to make use of our privilege of free access to Christ and the covenant ; insomuch that none will come to Christ, nor embrace the covenant, without them in greater or lesser measure. Even as if a physician should cause proclaim, that he will freely cure all the sick of such a place, that will employ him : in which case, it is plain, none will employ him, but such as are sensible of some malady they labour under ; yet that sense of a malady is not the condition of their welcome to that physician ; nor is it requisite for his curing them, but for their employing him.

Now, in calling you to embrace the covenant, ye are called indirectly, and by consequence, to this faith of the law, namely, to believe that ye are sinners in life, heart, and nature ; lost and undone, under the curse ; and utterly unable to recover yourselves. Yet it is not saving faith, nor doth it instate one in the covenant of grace ; that is peculiar to another kind of believing ; of which in the next place.

The Faith of the Gospel necessary to our entering into the Covenant of Grace.—This Faith fully explained, and objections satisfactorily answered.

Saving faith, which unites to Christ, is the faith of the gospel. For the gospel only is the ministration of righteousness, 2 Cor. iii. 9. It is in it that the righteousness of faith is revealed unto faith, revealed to be believed on, Rom. i. 17. It is the alone word, which gives sinners the notice of a Saviour, of the atoning blood, and the new covenant in that blood ; and therefore is the only word, by which saving faith is begotten in the heart of a lost sinner. In the word of the gospel, the Lord and Saviour Christ, with all his benefits and covenant, is ; and that to be believed on, as appears from Rom. x. 6—9. So that the word of the gospel being received by believing, we have Christ and his covenant, with all

the benefits thereof : saving faith being indeed the
echo of the quickened soul, to the word of grace that
bringeth salvation ; a trusting of the word of the
gospel, and the person, to wit, the Saviour, and the
thing therein held forth to us, to be believed on for
salvation. Mark i. 15. ' Believe the gospel ; ' Isa.
liii. 1. ' Who hath believed our report ? ' Gal. iii. 2.
' The hearing of faith.' This is that believing, by
which we are united to Christ, entered into the covenant of grace, and instated therein unto salvation.
The which believing may be explained in four particulars. 1*st*, The faith of Christ's sufficiency ; 2*d*,
The faith of the gospel-offer ; 3*d*, The faith of our
right to Christ ; and, 4*th*, The faith of particular
trust for salvation. So putting the

QUESTION, What is that believing, by which I, a
lost sinner, under the curse of the law, may unite
with Jesus Christ, and so enter into, and be instated
in the covenant of grace, to my eternal salvation.

We answer thereto directly in these four particulars, by way of direction in this momentous point,
whereon salvation depends.

I. *The faith of Christ's* SUFFICIENCY.

In the first place, you are to believe, that there is
a fulness of salvation in Christ for poor sinners. This
is the constant report of the gospel concerning him :
Eph iii. 8. ' That I should preach among the Gentiles the unsearchable riches of Christ.' Heb. vii.
25. ' He is able to save them to the uttermost, that
come unto God by him.' In the word of the gospel,
Christ is held forth as an able Saviour ; able to save
men from their sins, and from the wrath of God.
His merit is a sufficient sconce against the tempest
of fiery wrath, which incensed justice is ready to
cause to fly forth against transgressors : Isa. xxxii.
2. ' A man shall be a covert from the tempest.' His
Spirit is sufficient to sanctify the most unholy :
1 Cor. vi. 11. ' And such were some of you : but ye

are washed, but ye are sanctified, but ye are justified
in the name of the Lord Jesus, and by the Spirit of
our God.' The righteousness he fulfilled as the condition of the covenant, is so valuable in itself, and in
the eyes of his Father, that it is sufficient to procure
justification, santification, and all other saving benefits to sinners, who in themselves deserve death and
damnation : so that they are happy who are in him ;
they shall never perish, but have everlasting life,
being eternally secure under the covert of his righteousness, as a sufficient defence. Believest thou this ?

This is the general faith of the gospel, which being
without particular application, doth not unite the sinner to Christ, nor enter him into the covenant ; and
may be found in reprobates and fallen angels, being
only an assent in general to the truth of the doctrine
of the gospel, Matt. xiii. 20, 21. and viii. 29. But,
by the nature of the thing, it is necessarily prerequi-
site to a faith of particular application : for I must
first believe a saying to be true in itself, before I can
trust to it for my part ; I must first believe a thing
to be good in itself, before I can believe that it is
good for me.

But where the faith of the gospel is carried forward to uniting with Christ, the effect of this general
faith is very valuable, as well as necessary. And
that is, an high esteem of Christ and his covenant,
an ardent desire of union and communion with him,
a longing for his righteousness, as a hungry man
longs for meat, or a thirsty man for drink The man
sees indeed, that he has no special interest in Christ
and his righteousness ; but he would fain have it :
all is sapless to him without it ; his soul within him
cries, ' Give me Christ, or else I die :' and he is content to part with all for him, and to take him for all.
This is taught us in the parables of the treasure hid
in the field, and of the pearl of great price, the finding out of which moves to sell all, and to buy them,
Matt. xiii. 44, 45, 46.

4 G

Howbeit this esteem and desire of Christ is different from that which follows upon the soul's union
with Christ, when once faith hath taken possession
of him and his benefits, and hath got a view of his
intrinsic supereminent worth and value ; the which
is mentioned, 1 Pet. ii. 7. Psal. lxxiii. 25. The true
spring of all this esteem and desire, is the principle
of self-preservation, and the view of Christ, as suited
to that end. The merchant-man is seeking goodly
pearls for his own enriching ; and seeing that the one
pearl will answer that design, he is restless till he
have it. The poor sinner is hotly pursued with the
law's curse, which is still ringing death and damnation in his ears. In the mean time, he gets a distant
view of the city of refuge ; and therefore he makes
forward to it with all speed : but what makes him
run, but life, life, precious life, that he may not perish ? Verily, he cannot be expected to act from a
more generous principle, before he is united to Christ;
John xv. 5. ' Without me ye can do nothing.'

II. *The Faith of the Gospel OFFER.*

In the next place, you must believe, That *Jesus
Christ*, with his righteousness and all his salvation,
is by *himself* offered to sinners, and to you in particular. This is the plain voice of the gospel to all
unto whom it comes, Isa. lv. 1. ' Ho, every one that
thirsteth, come ye to the waters, and he that hath no
money ; come ye, buy and eat, yea, come, buy wine
and milk without money, and without price.' Rev.
xxii. 17. ' Whosoever will, let him take the water of
life freely.' Prov. viii. 4. ' Unto you, O men, I call,
and my voice is to the sons of men.' But alas! few
believe it : yea, none will believe it to purpose, till
the Spirit of the Lord make it plain to them, and
persuade them by an inward illumination. Many
secure sinners hear the gospel, and are glad of the
offer : but they discern not *Christ's* voice in it. They

hear it not, as the word of the *Lord* Christ himself,
to them ; but as the word of men : hence it hath no
due authority upon their consciences ; so they pass
it over lightly.   Thus were his offers of himself entertained, when made by his own mouth, but he not
discerned as the eternal *Son of God*, and Saviour of
the world.   So, in the congregation of Nazareth, all
bare him witness, and wondered at the gracious
words which proceeded out of his mouth.   But ' they
said, Is not this Joseph's son ?' Luke iv. 22.   And
in a little, they ' rose up, and thrust him out of the
city,' ver. 29.   Again, when the voice of *Christ* is
discerned in the offer, by the convinced sinner ; then
the sinner is ready to conclude, that it is to others,
but not to him.   Unbelief saith, but ' our bones are
dried, and our hope is lost, we are cut off for our
parts,' Ezek. xxxvii. 11.   They cannot believe, that
so good news from heaven concerns them, or that
such a good word is directed unto them.   And thus
men not believing God, in the record given of his
Son, that he is with all his salvation offered to them,
do make him a liar, 1 John v. 10.

   But where saving faith is a-working, the word of
the gospel-offer is, by the Holy Spirit, applied to the
soul in particular, with power, as the word of the
Lord himself, and not of men ; whereby the man is
assured, that it is the voice of *Christ*, and to him in
particular : whereupon he applies it to himself, by
believing : 1 Thess. i. 5. ' For our gospel came not
unto you in word only, but also in power, and in the
Holy Ghost, and in much assurance.'   Chap. ii. 13.
' The word of God which ye heard of us, ye received
it not as the word of men, but (as it is in truth) the
word of God, which effectually worketh also in you
that believe.'   This is altogether necessary ; insomuch that without it there can be no receiving of
Christ, forasmuch as otherwise the soul can see no
solid ground and foundation of faith for itself : for it
is evident, there can be no receiving aright, where

the sinner doth not believe the offer to be to him in particular.

But here it is necessary to remove the following objections :—

OBJECT. 1. But Christ is now in heaven, and I hear no voice from thence : how then can I believe, that he himself is offering himself to me ?

ANS. Though Christ is in heaven, yet he is speaking from heaven to us ; howbeit, not by a voice sounding through the clouds, yet by a voice sounding in the gospel : Heb. xii. 25. 'See that ye refuse not him that speaketh—that speaketh from heaven.' And not only is his voice in the word of the gospel, but he himself by his Spirit is in it, as the apostle teacheth, Rom. x. 6, 7, 8.   Thence it is, that it is a quickening word to dead souls : John vi. 63. 'The words that I speak unto you, they are spirit, and they are life.'   It is the lively seed, whereof the new creature is formed, 1 Pet. i. 23.   Jesus Christ did once, by a voice sounding through the clouds, speak a word of conviction, Acts ix. 4, 5.   But even in that case, the word of the offer of himself, was remitted to the preaching of the gospel by a messenger thereto appointed, ver. 6.   And the voice of Christ sounding in his written word, is more sure than a voice sounding through the clouds, 2 Pet. i. 18, 19. This voice in the word is the stated ground of faith, with which faith must close for salvation : Rom. i. 16. 'The gospel of Christ, it is the power of God unto salvation, to every one that believeth.' Ver. 17. 'For therein is the righteousness of God revealed from faith to faith.'   And there is no true saving faith, where it is not received as the very voice of the *Lord* himself, 1 Thess. ii. 13.   Therefore you must receive the word of the gospel, as the word of *Christ* himself, as in very deed it is.

OBJECT. 2. But Christ, in the word of the gospel, doth not name me: how then can I believe, that he of-

fereth himself, his righteousness and salvation, to me
in particular?

Ans. Neither doth he name you in the word of
the law, whether in the commands thereof, or in
the curse thereof. How do you come to believe that
you are a sinner? Is it not, that the commands of
the law being directed to all men, you conclude and
believe, that you being of the number of mankind,
they are therefore directed to you in particular, as
well as to others? And how come you to believe,
that you in particular are under the curse of the broken law? Is it not, that since the law denounceth
its curse against every one, that being under it,
breaks it, Gal. iii. 10. Rom. iii. 19. you do conclude
and believe, that it curseth you, forasmuch as you
are one of these breakers thereof? Now, you have
as sufficient ground to believe, that the offer of the
gospel is to you in particular; forasmuch as it is
made to all, without exception, unto whom the gospel comes, Rev. xxii. 17. Isa. lv. 1. It is ordered to
be made to every creature under heaven, Mark xvi.
15.: and how sinful soever you are, you are one of
these creatures. Christ's voice is unto men, sons of
men: and be what you will, you are one of man-
kind-sinners: and therefore the offer is to you in
particular, Prov. viii. 4. Accordingly, we are warranted to apply the general offer to every one in particular; and every one is warranted to apply it to
himself: Acts xvi. 31. 'Believe on the Lord Jesus
Christ, and *thou* shalt be saved.'

Object. 3. But alas! I fear I want the qualifications determinative of those to whom the gospel-offer
is particularly directed. I dread, that I have not as
yet got a due sense of sin: and our Lord says expressly, 'They that be whole need not a physician,
but they that are sick. I am not come to call the
righteous, but sinners to repentance,' Matt. ix. 12, 13.
The gospel-offer runs in these terms, ' Ho, every one
that thirsteth, come,' Isa. lv. 1. ' Come unto me, all

ye that labour, and are heavy laden,' Matt. xi. 28.
' Whosoever will, let him take the water of life freely,' Rev. xxii. 17. But when I view my own condition, I very much fear I have not as yet reached
that thirst after Christ, and that willingness to take
him, which these texts speak of ; and that I cannot
be accounted one truly labouring and heavy laden :
how then can I believe, that Christ offers himself to
me in particular ?

ANS. It is most certain truth, that unless you have
a due sense of sin, unless you thirst after Christ and
his righteousness, unless you be heavy laden with
the felt burden of sin, and willing to take Christ on
any terms ; you will never take him by a true faith.
Nevertheless, whatever qualifications you have, or
have not, yet if you are a sinner of Adam's race,
(and I hope you doubt not that), Christ is offered to
you, together with his righteousness, and all his salvation, Prov. viii. 4. John iii. 16. Mark xvi. 15. For
howbeit there are indeed certain qualifications necessary to move you to take Christ ; yet there are none
at all to hamper the gospel-offer ; but Christ is really offered to you, be in what case you will ; so really, that if you do not believe it, and thereupon receive an offered Saviour, you will be damned for not
believing, Mark xvi. 16.

It is undeniable, the less that sinners are sensible
of their sins, they are the farther from righteousness ;
they do the more need Christ, and are the more to
be called to repentance. This is evident from the
whole tenor of the holy scripture, and from the very
nature of the thing. And therefore it is sinners in
the general, and not sensible sinners only, who are
meant, Matt. ix. 12, 13. Even as it is sick people
in general, comprehending even those of them, who
are so delirious, as to think nothing ails them, that
need a physician ; and not those sick only, who are
sensible of their state and hazard. This is the plain
literal sense of that passage, from which there is no

necessity to depart : and the departing from it is attended with a manifest inconvenience.

Neither is the thirst, mentioned Isa. lv. 1. to be
restricted to a gracious thirst, a thirst after *Christ*
and his righteousness.   For some at least of the
thirsting ones, to whom the offer is there made, are
' spending money for that which is not bread, and
their labour for that which satisfieth not,' ver. 1, 2.
But it is evident, that sinners duly sensible, who are
thirsting after Christ and his righteousness, are not
spending their money and labour at that rate ; but,
on the contrary, for that which alone is bread, and
satisfieth, namely, Jesus Christ, the true bread which
came down from heaven.   Wherefore, the thirst there
meant, must needs comprehend, yea, and principally
aim at, that thirst after happiness and satisfaction,
which, being natural, is common to all mankind.
Men pained with this thirst do naturally run, for
quenching thereof, to the empty creation, and their
fulsome lusts : and so they ' spend money for that
which is not bread, and their labour for that which
satisfieth not ;' finding nothing there, that can satisfy that, their appetite or thirst.   Now, to men in this
wretched case, is the gospel-offer of the waters of life
made : *Christ* is offered to them, as bread, fatness,
what is good, and will satisfy that, their painful thirst,
which otherwise will never be quenched, ibid.

And as little is the solemn gospel offer, Matt. xi.
28. restricted to a certain set of men, endued with
some laudable qualifications, going under the name
of labouring and being heavy laden ; the which do
indeed denote the restlessness natural to the sinful
soul of man, ' spending *its* labour for that which satisfieth not,' Isa. lv. 2.   Our father Adam left his
whole family with a conscience full of guilt, and a
heart full of unsatisfied desires.   Thus, we naturally
having a restless conscience, and a restless heart, the
soul as naturally falls a labouring for rest to them.
And it labours in the barren region of the fiery law,

for a rest to the conscience ; and in the empty creation, for a rest to the heart.   But after all, the conscience is still heavy laden with guilt, whether it has
any lively feeling thereof, or not ; and the heart is
still under a load of unsatisfied desires.   So neither
the one, nor the other, can find rest indeed.   This is
the natural case of all men.   And to souls thus labouring and laden, Jesus Christ calls, that they may
come to him, and he will give them rest ; namely, a
rest for their consciences, under the covert of his
blood ; and a rest to their hearts, in the enjoyment
of *God* through him.   To this interpretation we are
led by the style of the scripture, the phraseology of
the Holy Ghost, both in the Old and New Testament ; the which may be viewed in the following
texts compared, to wit, Eccles. x. 15. Hab. ii. 13.
Isa. lv. 2. and i. 3, 4. 2 Tim. iii. 6, 7.

Finally, as for the willingness which you are afraid
you are defective in, surely, in all other cases, he that
saith, Whosoever will, let him take such a thing,
will, according to the common sense and understanding of such words amongst mankind, be reckoned to
offer that thing unto all, and to exclude none from it ;
however it may bear an intimation, that it is not to
be forced on any.   Why then should this manner of
speech, Rev. xxii. 17. be thought to limit the gospel-
offer to a certain set of men ?

III. *The faith of our* RIGHT *to* CHRIST.

Furthermore, you must believe, That *Jesus Christ*
is the Saviour of sinners, and your Saviour in particular, by his Father's appointment, and his own offer ; and that, by the same appointment and offer,
his righteousness, the condition of the covenant, and
eternal life, the promises of the covenant, are yours ;
yours (I mean not, in possession, but) in right thereto ; so far as that you may lawfully and warrantably
take possession of the same, and use them as your
own to all intents and purposes of salvation : John

iv. 42. 'We know that this is indeed the Christ, the *Saviour* of the *world ;*' 2 Sam. xxii. 3. and Luke i. 47. my Saviour. Do not think this too much for you ; it is no more than what is necessary to saving faith in Christ. If you believe only, in the general, that Christ is the Saviour of the world, but believe not that he is your Saviour in particular ; what do you believe more than devils do ? They believe him to be Jesus a Saviour, Mark i. 24. If you would go beyond them, you must believe he is your Saviour ; and consequently, that his righteousness and salvation are yours, in the sense before opened : for where Christ is given, with him are freely given all things. And pray consider, how can ye take him or receive him as your Saviour, if he is not yours indeed ? A man may fraudulently take possession of what he doth not believe to be his by right : but no man can fairly and honestly claim and take possession of what he doth not believe to be his own. Certainly God must first give Christ to us, before we can receive him : for ' a man can *receive* nothing, except it be *given* him from heaven,' John iii. 27. Giving on God's part, and receiving on ours, here, are correlates : and the former is the foundation of the latter. Now, God's gift is sufficient to make a thing ours. Therefore believe firmly, that Christ is your Saviour in particular ; that his righteousness is yours, and eternal life yours.

QUEST. But how can I, a poor sinner, by nature under the curse, believe that Christ is my Saviour, that his righteousness, and eternal life, are mine ?

ANS. You may firmly believe it, because you have the word and testimony of the eternal God upon it, in his holy gospel. What is the gospel, which the apostles were sent, in the name of God, to testify ? The apostle John declares it, 1 John iv. 14. 'We *testify*, that the Father sent the Son to be the Saviour of the world.' Why then will ye not believe it ? God set the sun in the heavens to be a light to the

4 H

world ; and do not you therefore judge, that you have a right to the light of that sun, as well as the rest of mankind ; and accordingly use it freely, to work or read by it, as your own by God's free gift? Jesus Christ also is the light of the world, John viii. 12. ; given for a light to the gentiles, Isa. xlix. 6. : and faith appropriates him, saying, 'The Lord is *my* light, and *my* salvation, Psal. xxvii. 1. Now, you are a member of these societies, to wit, the world, and the Gentiles ; therefore he is your light, that is, given for a light to you. Will you take Christ's own word upon it? You have it John vi. 32. 'My Father *giveth* you the true bread from heaven.' If your neighbour give you bread, you will reckon his gift thereof sufficient to make it yours ; and so eat of it freely as your own. If your prince shall give you a house or land, which he hath an unquestionable right to dispose of, you would reckon them truly yours by his gift ; and would freely go and dwell in that house, and possess that land as your own. How is it then, that when the Father gives you his Christ, yet you will not believe that he is yours, nor take possession of him as your own? Why, the truth of the matter lies here : you believe your neighbour, you believe your prince ; but you believe not your God, in his holy gospel, but 'make him a liar, not believing the record that God gave of his Son,' 1 John v. 10. But whether you will believe it or not, it is a truth, that Christ is your Saviour : and if you will not believe it now, to your salvation, you will undoubtedly see your mistake hereafter ; when perishing, you will be convinced that you perish, not because you had no Saviour offered, but because you neglected to make use of him.

In like manner, the righteousness of Christ is yours, namely, that which he fulfilled as the condition of the covenant. It is yours by Heaven's gift, being given you with himself ; and therefore it is called the gift of righteousness, Rom. v. 17. It is a testamentary gift, made over to you in Christ's testament,

wherein sinners of mankind, without exception, are
the legatees, as hath been already cleared. Eternal life is another such gift or legacy : so it is yours
too. And you have the record, testimony, or witness
of God himself upon it, that it is given you, 1 John
v. 11. ' And this is the record, that God hath given
to us eternal life : and this life is in his Son.' Is not
God's own record a sufficient ground for believing ?
will you venture to disbelieve it, on any pretence
whatsoever ? Here you have that record, namely,
that God hath *given* to us eternal life. It may be,
you will imagine, that it relates only to actual believers in Christ, or at most to the elect; and use that
for a defence of your unbelief. But, I pray you consider it is the ground and warrant for all to believe
on Christ, and to lay hold of eternal life in him ; being the witness of God, which he hath testified of
his Son, to be received by all to whom the gospel
comes, ver. 9. : but that God hath given eternal life
to a certain select set of men, can never, in reason,
be deemed to be a warrant for all men to believe.
Moreover, the great sin of unbelief lies in not believing this record : but it doth not lie in not believing,
that God hath given eternal life to actual believers,
or to the elect ; for the most desperate unbelievers
believe that, insomuch that their belief of it adds to
their torment : but it lies in their not believing, that
to mankind sinners, and to themselves in particular,
God hath given eternal life. This is what flies in
the face of the gospel of God, which is the proclaimed deed of the gift and grant of Christ and all his
benefits, to sinners of mankind, declaring the grant
thereof to be made them, and calling them to take
possession of the same as their own : Isa. ix. 6.
' Unto us a child is born,' (the word signifies presented born, as to his relations having a particular
interest in him ; as Machir's children were presented
to Joseph, and laid on his knees, Gen. l. 23. and
Ruth's son to Naomi, Ruth. iv. 17.) ' unto us a Son

is *given.*' John iii. 16. 'God so loved the world,
that he *gave* his only-begotten Son, that whosoever
believeth in him, should not perish, but have everlasting life.' 1 Cor. i. 30. 'Christ Jesus, who of
God is made unto us (namely, by legal destination,)
wisdom, righteousness, sanctification, and redemption.'

And thus you see you have an infallible ground
for this act of faith, namely, the testimony of God
that cannot lie. Wherefore, as ever you would be
united to Christ, and so instated in the covenant, believe firmly, that *Christ* is yours, his righteousness
yours, and eternal life in him yours.

This is a more close application of faith than the
former, and ariseth from it ; for thus one believeth
the efficacy of the divine appointment, and of the
gospel-offer. If God appoints Christ a Saviour to
you, with his righteousness and eternal life ; and
Christ offers himself to you accordingly : surely, the
effect of that appointment and offer must be, that
they are indeed yours, to be used by you, as your
own, for your salvation. If you believe that appointment of the Father, and the Son's offer, you must
needs believe this : for if they be real, and not ludi-
crous deeds, they certainly convey to you a right to
Christ, his righteousness and salvation ; so that, in
virtue of them, these must be yours, to be warrantably claimed and used by you as your own for the
purposes of salvation.

OBJECT. 1. If it be true, that *Christ* is my Saviour,
that his righteousness, and eternal life in him, are
mine ; then I may be easy, I will certainly be saved
without any more ado.

ANS. That is but a cavil, best suiting those, who,
being indifferent about Christ and salvation, think it
not worth their pains seriously to consider such
things. One truly weighed with the matter, and
duly considering, being once brought to believe this,
would rather say, 'Then, since *Christ* is really my

Saviour, his righteousness and eternal life mine ; I
will take him to me, I will receive and rest on him
as my Saviour, I will rely on his righteousness, and
look for eternal life in him : why should I be lost for
ever, since I have a full Saviour ? why should I go
naked, since I have a complete righteousness made
over to me by heaven's gift? why should I die, when
I have eternal life in Christ ?' Put the case, you did
see a man at the point of starving for want of bread ;
and, out of kindness and pity to him, you should ap-
point and ordain meat for him, out of your own store,
for preservation of his life ; and withal should carry
it to him, and set it before him, saying, Ha, there is
meat I and my father have ordained for you ; eat, and
welcome. If that man should say, O! I may not
take it, for it is not mine own ; would you not tell
him, that your gift, appointment, and offer of it to
him, makes it his, so that, with a good conscience,
he may freely eat it as his own bread ? But should
he then reply, and say, Why then, if it is mine, without any more ado I am secured from starving, I need
not at all be at pains to take and eat it ; would you
not reckon him either mad, or but jesting with you,
not sensible of his hazard of starving ? The application is obvious. It is not meat's being one's own,
so that he may use it freely as such, that will keep
him from starving : he must take and eat it, and so
use it as his own, if he would have that benefit by it.
Even so it is not Christ's being yours, with his righteousness and salvation, that will save you : you must
take possession of him, and make use of him as your
own, for salvation, if you would be actually saved by
him. There is a wide difference betwixt a thing's
being ours in simple right thereto, and its being ours
in possession. It is in the former way only, that
Christ is yours, before uniting with him : and if you
do not improve that, by receiving him, and taking
possession, you will perish eternally : Heb. iv. 1.
' Let us therefore fear, lest a promise being left us

THE BEAUTIES OF

to come short of it.' Luke xvi. 12. ' If ye have
not been faithful in that which is another man's, who
shall give you that which is your own ?'

OBJECT. 2. But *Christ* a Saviour, his perfect righteousness, and eternal life, are things so exceeding
great and precious, and I am so very sinful and unworthy, that it is mighty hard for me to believe they
are mine.

ANS. Yea, here indeed lies a great difficulty of believing ; when once a sinner's eyes are opened, to see
the transcendent excellency of Christ, the exceeding
sinfulness of sin, and his own utter unworthiness : a
difficulty not to be surmounted, but by the effectual
operation of the Spirit of faith, causing one to ' believe, according to the working of his mighty power,'
Eph. i. 19. But for your help, consider, they are
yours by mere free gift ; which is so far from requiring any worth in the creature, that it excludes all
respect thereto, *Christ* himself is the Father's gift
to you, John iv. 10. and iv. 32. His righteousness
is a gift too, Rom. v. 17. And so is eternal life in
him, 1 John v. 11. Now, what is freer than a gift ?
And then, howbeit they are indeed a gift far beyond
whatever you could have expected ; yet they are not
too great for an infinite *God* to give. In making of
this gift, he acted not according to the dignity of the
party in whose favour it was made ; but according
to *himself*, his own greatness and majesty. Mean-
while, though the gift is quite above your dignity ;
yet it is no more than what your need required. If
less could have answered your necessity, there is no
ground to think, a crucified Christ, the Son of God,
would have been prepared for you. If you do but
suppose it, you mar that expression of matchless
love, John iii. 16. ' God so loved the world, that he
gave his only-begotten Son.' Wherefore, argue with
yourself in this manner : ' The gift is indeed unspeakable, but no less can serve my need ; if Christ

be not mine, I must perish : since therefore God
hath said it, that he hath given me *Christ ;* and the
gift is not above him to give, and no less can serve
my turn ; I must and will believe that he is mine,
with his righteousness and salvation.'

IV. *The Faith of particular* TRUST *for* SALVATION.

Finally, You must wholly trust on him as your
Saviour, and in his righteousness as made over to
you ; and that for his whole salvation to you in particular, upon the ground of God's faithfulness in his
word.   And this is that saving faith, or believing on
Christ Jesus, by which a sinner is united to him, and
personally entered within the covenant of grace unto
salvation : Acts xvi. 31. 'Believe on the Lord Jesus
Christ, and thou shalt be saved.' Psal. ii. 12. 'Kiss
the Son lest he be angry, and ye perish : blessed are
all they that put their trust in him.'   And Psal.
xxxvii. 40. 'He shall save them, because they trust
in him.'   Rom. xv. 12. 'In him shall the Gentiles
trust.'   Compare Isa. xi. 10. Rom. i. 17. 'Therein
is the righteousness of God revealed from faith to
faith ;' or, 'Therein is the righteousness of God by
faith, revealed unto faith,' to wit, to be believed or
trusted on.   See Phil. iii. 9. Gal. ii. 16. 'We have
believed in Jesus Christ, that we might be justified.'
Acts xv. 11. 'We believe, that, through the grace
of the Lord Jesus Christ, we shall be saved.' 1 Thess.
ii. 13. 'Ye received it not as the word of men, but,
as it is in truth, the word of God.' 1 Cor. ii. 5. 'That
your faith should not stand in the wisdom of men,
but in the power of God.'   This, according to the
scripture, is a sinner's receiving and resting upon
Christ for salvation, as saving faith is defined in our
Catechism : and this is indeed believing, and nothing
but believing, according to the scriptural use of that
word.

1. I say, This is the scriptural receiving and resting on Christ.   It is the receiving of him in the sense

of the holy scripture ; John i. **12.** ' As many as *re-ceived* him, to them gave he power to become the sons of God, even to them that *believe on* his name : ' where the receiving of Christ is explained by be-lieving on his name. God hath appointed Christ Sa-viour of sinners. You hear the same published in the gospel ; and you accordingly believe, that he is your Saviour by his Father's appointment, and his own offer : hereupon you trust on him, and on him alone, for salvation, and all that you need for your sal-vation. Is not this a receiving of him for your part, in the character of a Saviour, wherein his Father sent him forth to you ? is it not a taking of him to yourself, as offered to you ? Our Lord complains of the Jews, John v 43. that whereas he came in his Father's name, they received him not, to wit, in the character wherein he was sent, namely, as the Messias, their Saviour, trusting in him that he would save them. This plainly appears to be the meaning, if one compares herewith the words there immediately following ; ' If another shall come in his own name, him ye will receive ; ' q. d. Ye will believe him to be the Messias, and your Saviour, and trust on him ac-cordingly, that he will save you ; the which has been often verified in that unbelieving people. Moreover, this is resting on Christ in the scripture sense of that manner of expression : Isa. xxvi. 3. ' Thou wilt keep him in perfect peace, whose mind is stayed on thee : because he trusteth in thee.' And indeed one cannot devise what way a person can rest on a word, or a soul or spirit can rest upon a person, but by trusting them, or trusting in or on them.

2. This is believing, in the scriptural use of that word, which, in our entry on the question under con-sideration, we established from the scripture itself. For it is a trusting of, or trusting in a person, name-ly, Jesus Christ, and God in him, the personal object of saving faith, Acts xvi. 31. ; a trusting in a thing, namely, the righteousness of Christ, the ultimate real

object of faith, Rom. i. 17. ; and a trusting in a word, namely, the record and testimony of God, the word of the promise of the gospel, the proximate or near-est real object of faith, *ibid. ;* and all this for the great purpose of salvation. And then, it is nothing but such believing : for thus faith is not explained away into, but is a thing quite distinct from the na-ture of a work, as the scripture contradistinguisheth works to faith.

Wherefore, we conclude, that this *trust* is that be-lieving on Christ, by which the soul is united to him, and savingly instated in the covenant. And for opening of it, we shall take notice of these five things plainly imported in it.

1. This trust imports not only a willingness, but a sincere and honest desire to be delivered from sin and wrath ; a desire to be sanctified, as well as to be justified ; to be delivered from the reigning power, pollution, practice, and inbeing of sin, as well as from the guilt of it ; according to that of the apos-tle, Rom. vii. 24, 25. ' Who shall deliver me from the body of this death! I thank God, through Jesus Christ our Lord.' For it is a trusting on Christ, not for the half of his salvation, to wit, salvation from wrath only, which is all the trust of many, be-ing by no means desirous to part with sin ; but for the whole of it, namely, salvation from wrath, and salvation from sin too, which is the principal part thereof, Matt. i. 21. Now, a man may indeed fear that from one, which he doth not desire ; but nobody trusts in one, for what he desires not. Faith is a be-lieving with the heart, Rom. x. 10. The whole sal-vation of Christ is the believer's choice ; it is the end he desires to compass : and the trust of faith is ex-erted as the means to compass that end.

2. A renouncing of all confidence in all that is not Christ, or in Christ, as to the matter of salvation particularly. In this trust is overturned self-confi-dence, law-confidence, creature-confidence ; and the

4 i

soul builds on a quite new ground : Phil. iii. 3. ' We rejoice in Christ Jesus, and have no confidence in the flesh.' Jer. xvi. 19. ' The Gentiles shall come unto thee,—and shall say, Surely our fathers have inherited lies, vanity, and things wherein there is no profit.' For it is a trusting wholly on Christ and his righteousness, a trusting or a believing, with all the heart, Prov. iii. 5. Acts viii. 37. At this rate, the believer is carried off from the works of the law, to the blood of Jesus, for his justification ; and carried out of himself too, unto the Spirit of holiness in Christ, for his sanctification : being persuaded, that no doing nor suffering of his own, can procure him the pardon of, or atone for, the least piece of guilt ; and that he is not able truly to mortify one lust, more as to purge away the guilt of one sin, Matt. v. 3. Isa. xlv. 24.

3. A hearty approbation of the plan or device of salvation according to the covenant, manifested in the gospel, as suited to the divine perfections, and to the case of sinners, and their own in particular : 1 Cor. i. 23. ' We preach Christ crucified, unto the Jews a stumbling-block, and unto the Greeks foolishness ; ' ver. 24. ' But unto them which are called, both Jews and Greeks, Christ the power of God, and the wisdom of God.' Without this, no man knowing what God is, what sin is, and what is the work of his own soul, will ever venture his salvation upon it: but one's trusting his salvation to Christ and his righteousness, speaks him to be well pleased therewith, as what one may safely trust to, even in the sight of a holy God. And this is that rejoicing in Christ Jesus, which makes an illustrious piece of the believer's character, Phil. iii. 3.

Withal it bears three things : 1*st*, An eyeing of Christ in this matter, as a crucified Saviour, who hath fulfilled all righteousness, according to the stated condition of the covenant, 1 Cor. ii. 2. It is not Christ in the eternal glory he had with his Father

before the world was, that faith fixeth its view on,
while the soul in this case stands trembling before a
holy God ; but Christ the Son of God made man,
come in the flesh, being born holy, leading a life perfectly righteous, and at last dying on the cross, to
satisfy the demands which the law had on poor sinners.   It looks unto him lifted up on the cross, as
those who were bitten by the serpents in the wilderness, looked unto the brazen serpent lifted up on the
pole, Isa. xlv. 22. Numb. xxi. 8. John iii. 14, 15.
Therefore it is called faith in his blood, Rom. iii. 25.
his righteousness, whereof the shedding of his blood
was the completing part, being the spring of the believer's hope.   2*d*, A real persuasion of the sufficiency of Christ's righteousness to save sinners, and
us in particular, from sin and wrath ; to answer for
us before a holy just God, in the eye of his holy law ;
and to procure for us eternal holiness and happiness.
There is no saving faith without this : Christ's ability to save must be believed, and that with application to your own case in particular, Matt. ix. 28.
' Believe ye that I am able to do this ? '   And in order hereunto, faith eyes Christ's righteousness as the
righteousness of God, and therefore of infinite value
and efficacy, Phil. iii. 9. 1 John i. 7.   The reason
why the gospel, and no other doctrine whatsoever,
is the power of God unto salvation of sinners, is, because therein is revealed the righteousness of God
unto faith, Rom. i. 16, 17. and that is the only righteousness, suited at once to the divine perfections and
our case.   3*d*, An acquiescing to that way of salvation, for ourselves in particular.   The believer hath
a cordial liking of it, for the way of his salvation, as
perfectly safe, being the power of God, and the wisdom of God, 1 Cor. i. 24.   His soul pronounceth
them safe and happy that are in it ; he desires for
his own part to be found in it ; and is persuaded he
would be saved if he were in it.   Thus faith acted
in the woman diseased with an issue of blood, Matt.

ix. 21. 'She said within herself, If I may but touch his garment, I shall be whole.' And thus it acteth in all believers, determining them to that way, and to that way alone, for their case in particular.

4. A betaking one's self unto Christ and his righteousness alone, for salvation from sin and wrath. This is done by this trusting. For the sinner believing that Christ is his Saviour, and that his righteousness is made over to him by free gift; and withal, that this his Saviour, with his righteousness, is sufficient to save him from sin and wrath; doth accordingly trust on Christ and his righteousness for his own salvation, and so betake himself thereto : even as a beggar, once having, and withal believing himself to have, riches and wealth made over to him, by a friend, leaves off to beg, and for his maintenance trusts to that wealth allenarly ; and thereupon betakes himself to it. It is true, that wealth being a corporal thing, to which there is a bodily motion, the betaking one's self thereto is not the same thing with the trusting to it ; howbeit the former is a native consequent of the latter : but Christ and his righteousness, as revealed unto faith, being things purely spiritual, to which there is no bodily motion requisite, that we may betake ourselves to them ; the trusting and betaking one's self thereto, are one and the same. So by this trust, the soul takes possession of Christ and his righteousness ; and useth the same as its own, to the purpose of salvation. By it, the sinner betakes himself, as a condemned man, unto Jesus Christ as the propitiatory mercy-seat through his blood, affording safety to thë guilty, before a holy God : and by it, the sinner betakes himself, as a sick man, unto the same Jesus as the physician of souls, having the fulness of the Spirit of sanctification in him, to be communicate. Accordingly, faith is called a coming to Christ, John vi. 35. ; a fleeing for refuge, as one in hazard of his life by a pursuer, Heb. vi. 18. ; and is often expressed, as Psal. ii. 12. by a

word, which properly signifies to retire, as into a shadow, Judg. ix. 15. or as the chickens do under the wings of the hen, Ruth ii. 12. ' The Lord God of Israel, under whose wings thou art come to trust ; ' properly, to retire. Compare Matt. xxiii. 37. ' How often would I have gathered thy children together, even as a hen gathereth her chickens under her wings.'

Lastly, This trust of faith imports an affiance, confidence, or trust on Christ and his righteousness, that he will save us from sin and wrath, according to his promise set before us in the gospel, ' Whosoever believeth in him, shall not perish, but have everlasting life.' Isa. xxv. 9. ' We have waited for him, and he will save us.' Heb. iii. 6. ' Whose house are we, if we hold fast the confidence.' Isa. l. 10. ' Let him trust in the name of the Lord, and stay upon his God.' And that this trust of faith is thus particular, is evident also from the nature of the thing. For whosoever trusts in a person for any thing, hath a persuasion, of the same degree of firmness with the trust, that that person will do that thing for him. And for a sure token of this, where the party trusted fails, the party trusting is ashamed and confounded ; as being disappointed in that which he trusted he would do for him. Wherefore, since the trust of faith is never disappointed, the scripture doth therefore assure us, that ' he that believeth on him shall not be confounded,' 1 Pet. ii. 6. nor ashamed, Rom. x. 11. The which doth sufficiently intimate, that he that believeth on Jesus Christ for salvation, doth trust that he will save him : otherwise there could be no place for his being confounded or ashamed, whatever should be the event of his trust. Accordingly, the trust of faith doth, in proportion to the firmness thereof, establish and fix the heart, Psal. cxii. 7. ' His heart is fixed, trusting in the Lord :' and hereof we have a plain instance in Paul's case, 2 Tim. i. 12. ' I am not ashamed ; for I know whom I have believed,' marg. or trusted. Agreeable here-

unto, faith is called in effect a building on Christ, as
upon a foundation that will bear our weight, Isa.
xxviii. 16. with 1 Pet. ii. 6.   It is called a leaning
upon him, Cant. viii. 5. ; a staying on him, Isa. xxvi.
3. ; a resting or relying on him, 2 Chron. xiv. 11.
and xvi. 8. as upon one that will bear us up ; a looking unto him, Isa. xlv. 22. having our eyes upon him,
2 Chron. xx. 12. as one from whom we look for help
and salvation ; and, finally, believing *on* him, 1 Pet.
ii. 6. as one by whom we shall be saved, Acts xv. 11.

OBJECT. 1. Since it is not true of all who hear the
gospel, that they shall be saved ; there cannot be,
in the case of every one of them, a ground on which
this particular trust may be warrantably founded.

ANS. All and every one of them, notwithstanding
that, have a solid ground for it, even for trusting on
Christ and his righteousness for their own salvation
in particular.   And that is the record and testimony
of God in his gospel, that ' whosoever believeth in
him, should not perish, but have everlasting life,'
John iii. 16.   The true sense of which, as appears
from what is said, is, that whosoever shall have this
trust and confidence in Christ, shall not be disappointed, but shall certainly be saved.   Here then is
the faithfulness of God in his word, for the foundation of this faith of particular trust : and true faith
is always built on that foundation.   It is certain, indeed, that in the event, many to whom the gospel
comes will not be saved : but then, it is as certain,
that those who will not be saved, will not believe
neither ; that is, they will not come up to this particular trust and confidence we have described from
the word, Isa. liii. 1. ' Who hath believed our report ?
and to whom is the arm of the Lord revealed ? '
Howbeit, at this rate, they have a firm ground of
particular confidence.   If they will not believe for
all it, their ruin is of themselves, they will perish
without excuse, and their unbelief will be the great
ground of their condemnation.   Jesus Christ, with

his righteousness and salvation, is so far made theirs
by the Father's appointment, and his own offer, that
they may lawfully and warrantably trust on him as
their Saviour, each one for his own salvation. If
they will not believe it, or not trust on him accordingly; they do, by their unbelief and distrust, dishonour the Father and his Son, and most justly perish.

OBJECT. 2. Many trust in Christ as their Saviour,
with a particular confidence, that he will save them;
and yet are grossly ignorant, profane, or formal hypocrites : and therefore not true believers, nor united to Christ.

ANS. The apostle speaking of faith unfeigned,
1 Tim. i. 5. doth suppose that there is a feigned faith.
And indeed such trusters in Christ have it : but as
for this trust, which we have described from the
word, it is as certain they have it not, as it is certain
that true faith purifies the heart, Acts xv. 9. and
truly sanctifies, chap. xxvi. 18. As such trusters
say, that they receive Christ, and rest on him alone
for salvation, embrace, accept, and consent to him
in the gospel-offer ; even so they say, that they trust
on him. But this trust on him they really have not.
For, *first*, They trust not on him for his whole salvation ; nay, as for the chief part thereof, to wit, salvation from sin, they are by no means reconciled
thereto : wherefore it may well be an object of their
fears and aversion ; but it cannot be an object of
their trust. *Secondly*, They trust not on him alone,
for the salvation they really desire : they do not trust
on him with all their heart ; but partly to him, and
partly to their own doings and sufferings, betwixt
which and the Saviour, their heart is divided. This
is clear from Matt. v. 3. ' Blessed are the poor in
spirit : for theirs is the kingdom of heaven.' *Lastly*,
Their trust is not grounded on the faithfulness of
God in the free promise of the gospel ; but reared up
on some one or other sandy foundation : Isa. liii. 1.

'Who hath believed our report?' Matt. vii. 26.
'Every one that heareth these sayings of mine, and doeth them not, shall be likened unto a foolish man which built his house upon the sand.'

And thus have we shown, what is that faith or believing, by which a sinner unites with Jesus Christ, and so enters savingly into the covenant of grace.

THE END.